# Bilingual Education

BILINGUAL EDUCATION AND BILINGUALISM
**Series Editors:** Professor Nancy H. Hornberger, *University of Pennsylvania, Philadelphia, USA* and Professor Colin Baker, *University of Wales, Bangor, Wales, Great Britain*

**Recent Books in the Series**
Continua of Biliteracy: An Ecological Framework for Educational Policy, Research, and Practice in Multilingual Settings
  *Nancy H. Hornberger (ed.)*
Languages in America: A Pluralist View (2nd edn)
  *Susan J. Dicker*
Trilingualism in Family, School and Community
  *Charlotte Hoffmann and Jehannes Ytsma (eds)*
Multilingual Classroom Ecologies
  *Angela Creese and Peter Martin (eds)*
Negotiation of Identities in Multilingual Contexts
  *Aneta Pavlenko and Adrian Blackledge (eds)*
Beyond the Beginnings: Literacy Interventions for Upper Elementary English Language Learners
  *Angela Carrasquillo, Stephen B. Kucer and Ruth Abrams*
Bilingualism and Language Pedagogy
  *Janina Brutt-Griffler and Manka Varghese (eds)*
Language Learning and Teacher Education: A Sociocultural Approach
  *Margaret R. Hawkins (ed.)*
The English Vernacular Divide: Postcolonial Language Politics and Practice
  *Vaidehi Ramanathan*
Bilingual Education in South America
  *Anne-Marie de Mejía (ed.)*
Teacher Collaboration and Talk in Multilingual Classrooms
  *Angela Creese*
Words and Worlds: World Languages Review
  *F. Martí, P. Ortega, I. Idiazabal, A. Barreña, P. Juaristi, C. Junyent, B. Uranga and E. Amorrortu*
Language and Aging in Multilingual Contexts
  *Kees de Bot and Sinfree Makoni*
Foundations of Bilingual Education and Bilingualism (4th edn)
  *Colin Baker*
Bilingual Minds: Emotional Experience, Expression, and Representation
  *Aneta Pavlenko (ed.)*
Raising Bilingual-Biliterate Children in Monolingual Cultures
  *Stephen J. Caldas*
Language, Space and Power: A Critical Look at Bilingual Education
  *Samina Hadi-Tabassum*
Developing Minority Language Resources
  *Guadalupe Valdés, Joshua A. Fishman, Rebecca Chávez and William Pérez*
Language Loyalty, Language Planning and Language Revitalization: Recent Writings and Reflections from Joshua A. Fishman
  *Nancy H. Hornberger and Martin Pütz (eds)*
Language Loyalty, Continuity and Change: Joshua A. Fishman's Contributions to International Sociolinguistics
  *Ofelia Garcia, Rakhmiel Peltz and Harold Schiffman*

For more details of these or any other of our publications, please contact:
Multilingual Matters, Frankfurt Lodge, Clevedon Hall,
Victoria Road, Clevedon, BS21 7HH, England
http://www.multilingual-matters.com

**BILINGUAL EDUCATION AND BILINGUALISM 61**
Series Editors: Nancy H. Hornberger and Colin Baker

# Bilingual Education

## An Introductory Reader

**Edited by**
# Ofelia García and Colin Baker

**MULTILINGUAL MATTERS LTD**
Clevedon • Buffalo • Toronto

**Library of Congress Cataloging in Publication Data**
Bilingual Education: An Introductory Reader/Edited by Ofelia García and Colin Baker.
Bilingual Education and Bilingualism: 61
Includes bibliographical references and index.
1. Education, Bilingual. I. García, Ofelia. II. Baker, Colin
LC3715.B575 2006
370.117–dc22        2006018042

**British Library Cataloguing in Publication Data**
A catalogue entry for this book is available from the British Library.

ISBN-13: 978-1-85359-908-8 (hbk)
ISBN-13: 978-1-85359-907-1 (pbk)

**Multilingual Matters Ltd**
*UK*: Frankfurt Lodge, Clevedon Hall, Victoria Road, Clevedon BS21 7HH.
*USA*: UTP, 2250 Military Road, Tonawanda, NY 14150, USA.
*Canada*: UTP, 5201 Dufferin Street, North York, Ontario M3H 5T8, Canada.

Typeset by Archetype-IT Ltd (http://www.archetype-it.com).
Printed and bound in the United States of America.

# Contents

## Part 3: Languages and Literacies in Bilingual Education

## Part 4: Issues in Teaching, Learning and Assessment in Bilingual Education

# Introduction

## The Contents of the Reader

This Reader contains a comprehensive and contemporary selection of important contributions on bilingual education. The Reader provides an instant introduction to fundamental and formative ideas on Bilingualism and Bilingual Education in four parts:

1. Varieties of Bilingual Education.
2. History, Policy and Politics of Bilingual Education.
3. Languages and Literacies in Bilingual Education.
4. Issues in Teaching, Learning and Assessment in Bilingual Education.

## Use of the Reader by Instructors and Students

The Reader can be used as a comprehensive introduction for instructors, researchers and students in a variety of courses. It is also designed for 'interactive' use by students. After each article, there is a set of **student questions**. Such questions invite students to review some of the essential themes of each article. Following the questions, there is a set of **student activities**. Each activity aims to extend reading by generalization to the student's locality or experience. Some activities require research or a project, others require a group discussion or a presentation. Such activities are designed to make the reading more relevant to a student, to widen an understanding of the topic, and to stimulate a process of introspection, generalization and personalization.

We have designed the Reader so that the instructor can structure the course in differing ways to suit their own pedagogical styles. For example, most questions and activities can be performed in cooperative learning groups and are meant to engage students in a process of inquiry and discovery. Many of the activities extend beyond the classroom, involving students in a process of discovery, experiential learning, collaboration with the community, creating familiarization with, and incorporation of their cultural and linguistic resources. Sometimes the products of these activities are important; other times learning comes from the process, with a product less important.

Students working through the questions and activities will be helped to become **critical thinkers** and allow them to take on an advocacy-oriented role. This is accomplished by giving students practice in 'critical pedagogy', involving them not only in reading and reflection, but also in actual practice which becomes the source for further reflection and action. Thus, students can themselves experience some of these practices and their relationship to their own learning, while reflecting on how to use such practices in their teaching.

Thus many of the activities involve students in **structured self reflection, reflection within a small group** and **direct observation** of classrooms and students. When the student is already a teacher, her classroom may become the laboratory for her study. Those who are training to become teachers can visit classrooms and engage administrators, educators, parents and students for their answers.

The student questions and activities are designed to give instructors and students ample **choice**. Some questions and activities will be more relevant to some classes and contexts than others. All questions and activities can easily be **adapted** by instructors to fit a particular class in a particular educational and geographic context. Where United States contexts are cited, instructors in other countries will be able to adapt questions and activities to ensure local relevance.

Although the totality of the questions form an integrated review of the reading, the activities are independent of each other. The **instructor** will need to decide whether to give the students the option to choose how many activities to complete, and will need to select those activities that are most relevant to their students and community. Questions may be completed in small groups, but the activities are the real source for cooperative learning. The instructor will usually need to give students further direction and advice to structure these cooperative tasks.

Because teachers need to be researchers and inquirers, the activities give teachers practice in some of the most common methods of research: ethnographic observation, interviews, surveys and content analysis. Many of the activities involve teachers in humanistic forms of research, enabling them to express themselves in writing, creating WWW pages, acting and drawing. **Further reading** is listed under each article so that students can extend their professionalism by reading deeper and wider. Such a multiple 'process' approach to student learning reflects the best of contemporary educational practice.

The Reader relates to the experience of both **language minority** and **language majority** students, to those directly involved in any form of bilingual education, and those that have, or will have students of different language backgrounds in their classrooms. All students will learn about the importance of bilingualism and biliteracy for all, and the value of cultural and linguistic pluralism in society. In addition, they will gain understandings about the education of language minority students – immigrants, as well as indigenous and autochtonous peoples. **Bilingual teachers** will have better understanding of present policy and practices, and how these could be structured to develop the bilingualism and biliteracy of all students. All teachers can benefit from a perspective of how to incorporate languages and cultures in their classroom.

While the Reader is designed to be a 'stand alone', it links with the fourth edition of *Foundations of Bilingual Education and Bilingualism* (published by Multilingual Matters, 2006). By concentrating on policies and practices in Bilingual Education, students who have first read that introduction will find this Reader deliberately extends and enlarges that book. Many instructors using the 'Foundations' book also require students to read individual articles. This book is designed to fulfill that need.

## Rationale of the Reader

In the process of compiling this Reader, we started with a 'long list' of potential articles to include. We then consulted some instructors and experts in the areas of bilingual education and bilingualism. The final selection represents a balanced, comprehensive and challenging set of articles. Each article has been chosen because it does one, and usually many of the following:

- summarizes well an important topic;
- provides fresh and original thinking;
- challenges through its ideas and beliefs;
- authoritatively analyzes a topic;
- is historically important in the development of a major issue;
- provides a seminal and creative research study.

Together, the articles, followed by questions, activities and further readings, construct a comprehensive and thorough study of recent bilingual education policies and practices particularly within the context of the United States but also wherever bilingual education exists throughout the world.

## WWW Links for Study Activities

**Note**: Internet pages on bilingual education can be problematic as addresses frequently change, even disappear. The stability of such WWW sources is variable. Therefore, we have not included WWW references with each activity. Instead, there is a list of **major links** below that will provide access to important resource materials and to further links.

1. Bilingualism database
   http://www.edu.bham.ac.uk/bilingualism/database/dbase.htm
2. National Clearinghouse for English Language Acquisition & Language Instruction Educational Programs (US)
   http://www.ncela.gwu.edu/
3. The Office of English Language Acquisition, Language Enhancement, and Academic Achievement for Limited English Proficient Students (US)
   http://www.ed.gov/about/offices/list/oela/index.html
4. Center for Applied Linguistics (US)
   http://www.cal.org/
5. Center for Research on Education, Diversity & Excellence (CREDE) (US)
   http://www.crede.ucsc.edu/
6. USC Center for Multilingual, Multicultural Research (US)
   http://www-bcf.usc.edu/~cmmr/
7. Center for Language Minority Education (US)
   http://www.clmer.csulb.edu/
8. James Crawford's Language Policy Web Site and Emporium (US)
   http://ourworld.compuserve.com/homepages/JWCRAWFORD/
9. National Association for Bilingual Education (US)
   http://www.nabe.org/
10. California Association for Bilingual Education
    http://www.bilingualeducation.org/
11. New York State Association for Bilingual Education (NYSABE)
    http://www.nysabe.org/
12. Language Policy Research Unit (US)
    http://www.asu.edu/educ/epsl/lpru.htm
13. OISE, University of Toronto, Second Language Education on the Web (Canada)
    http://www.oise.utoronto.ca/~aweinrib/sle/

14.   CILT (Centre for Information of Language Teaching and Research) (UK)
      http://www.cilt.org.uk/
15.   Language Policy Research Center (Israel)
      http://www.biu.ac.il:80/HU/lprc/
16.   Research Centre on Multilingualism (Belgium)
      http://www.kubrussel.ac.be/onderwijs/onderzoekscentra/ovm/ovm.htm
17.   Research Unit for Multilingualism and Cross-Cultural Communication (Australia)
      http://www.rumaccc.unimelb.edu.au/
18.   Centre for Language Immersion and Multilingualism (Finland)
      http://www.uwasa.fi/hut/svenska/ImmLing.html
19.   Centre for Research on Bilingualism (Sweden)
      http://www.biling.su.se/
20.   Multilingual Matters
      http://www.multilingual-matters.com/

# Part 1: Varieties of Bilingual Education

# Reviewing the Research on Language Education Programs

## Rebecca Freeman

This chapter presents an overview of the research on language education programs that we find in the United States and it is intended to serve a range of purposes. First, educators can use this review to guide their analysis of their own language education programs and practices so that they can determine whether and how their program is realizing its goals for its target populations. Second, language planners can use this review to determine the type of program that is appropriate for a particular school context, given an assessment of student needs and school requirements. [Third, readers can use this review as a foundation for understanding my discussion of language education programs and practices throughout this book.] This review is thus intended to provide a basis for working in the field of language education, broadly defined.

Language education in the United States is not generally discussed as one coherent field. Instead, we have seen language education professionals segregated in the fields of bilingual education, English as a second language (ESL), and world language education, and researchers and practitioners in each of these areas have focused on specific parts of the larger language education field. However, the United States is experiencing tremendous changes in demographics and language learning needs, and these changes are challenging traditional disciplinary distinctions. Language educators today in the subfields of bilingual education, ESL, and world languages are beginning to look to each other to develop programs and practices that can meet the language education needs of all language learners in the United States. We also see increasing interest in the needs of heritage language speakers and we see growing numbers of heritage language programs in secondary schools and universities.

My discussion of language education in this chapter is intended to bring together important developments in bilingual education, ESL, and world language education so that school districts and schools can make informed decisions about how to address the varied and changing language learning needs of all of their students. I use the following questions to structure my discussion of prototypical bilingual, ESL, and world language education programs:

1. Who is the target population?
2. What are the goals of the program for the target population?
3. How is the program structured?
4. How long do students spend in the program?
5. Is the program effective? That is, does the program enable its target populations to reach the stated goals in the allocated time?

Throughout this discussion, I consider research on second language acquisition, biliteracy development, standards-driven instruction, performance-based assessments, and program effectiveness. This review is intended to help educators make decisions about which types of language education programs are appropriate for their schools based on a solid research base, and to determine whether a program is well-implemented on the local school level.

## Bilingual Education

Bilingual education is a controversial and frequently misunderstood field in the United States. There is considerable confusion and conflict about what bilingual education means, who is served by bilingual programs, what the goals of a bilingual program are for its target populations, and whether bilingual education

3

is or can be effective. General bilingual education policies are often made, amended, and/or abandoned without an understanding of how actual programs function on the local level. California's Proposition 227 and the ensuing local and national debates about bilingual education and English language development highlight some of this confusion and controversy.

Rather than legislate against bilingual education based on anecdotal evidence about particular programs, we need to consider what research tells us about bilingual education. We need to begin by clearly defining what we mean by bilingual education, and we need to look closely at what the research says about how English language learners (ELLs) develop expertise in academic English and/or in their primary language over time in different kinds of bilingual and English as a second language (ESL) programs. Perhaps most importantly, we need to be clear about our goals. Some argue that one of the reasons that Proposition 227 passed in California was that people simply did not understand that a primary goal of bilingual education is English language development.

This point should not be underemphasized. All well-implemented bilingual education programs should be aligned with the TESOL (Teachers of English to Speakers of Other Languages) standards, which are discussed later in this chapter. Moreover, all bilingual programs must now address all federal and state accountability requirements for ELLs' English language development and academic achievement in English, which means that all bilingual programs must be aligned with all state content-area and English language proficiency standards. Title III of the No Child Left Behind Act of 2001 grants states flexibility to develop programs that research demonstrates are effective for ELLs. To comply with federal accountability requirements, states are now required to do the following:

- Articulate concrete, standards-based, observable, and measurable, targets for ELLs' English language development and academic achievement over time.
- Identify and use state-approved standardized assessment tools to measure students' performance relative to those targets.
- Articulate annual yearly progress (AYP)

objectives for English language development and academic achievement. These objectives must reflect the annual rate of growth of cohorts of ELLs from one year to the next in learning the English language, attaining English language proficiency, and achieving academically in the content areas according to the state's AYP measures.
- Demonstrate that all students have reached their performance targets in reading, language arts, and mathematics by the 2013–2014 school year (TESOL, 2003).

With this understanding of the current accountability criteria that are mandated for all bilingual and ESL programs in mind, I turn to a discussion of the kinds of bilingual education programs that we find in research and practice, and I review the research on program effectiveness.

Part of the confusion about bilingual education is that the same term is actually used to refer to a wide range of programs that may have different ideological orientations toward linguistic and cultural diversity, different target populations, and different goals for those target populations (Hornberger, 1991). My review of bilingual education models and program types in this section is organized around a major ideological distinction between the transitional bilingual model on the one hand and the dual language model on the other. As I discuss in more detail below, although transitional bilingual programs use ELLs' first language in the early years of their education, the goal of transitional bilingual education is English language development and academic achievement in English for ELLs. Dual language programs, in contrast, aim for bilingualism, biliteracy, and academic achievement in two languages for their target populations. Transitional bilingual programs tend to lead to subtractive bilingualism, and dual language programs generally lead to additive bilingualism. As I stress throughout, the choice between these program orientations has serious implications for individual students, for schools, and for society overall.

### Transitional bilingual education

The majority of bilingual programs that have been funded in the United States are transitional, and they encourage students who have traditionally been defined as 'limited English proficient' (LEP) to transition to the all-English academic mainstream as quickly as possible.

The prototypical transitional bilingual education (TBE) program provides one to three years of content-area instruction through the students' primary language while the ELLs are enrolled in ESL classes. According to Thomas and Collier's (2002) national review of programs for ELLs, some TBE programs may provide as many as five years of bilingual instruction, and some may emphasize first language literacy development as a foundation for literacy development in English.

According to Ruiz (1984), TBE programs are characterized by a 'language-as-problem' orientation because the primary language is viewed as a problem to be overcome. The primary language is only used until the student has acquired sufficient English to transition to the mainstream English-only classroom (but see below for research about how long it takes to develop expertise in academic English). Once the 'limited English proficient' (LEP) student is deemed 'fully English proficient', he/she is exited to the English-only academic mainstream and, in most cases, not eligible for continued ESL instruction. Because TBE programs provide no continued support for the native language at school, and because they pressure ELLs to acquire English as quickly as possible, ELLs who attend TBE programs tend to assimilate to monolingualism in English.

Although transitional bilingual programs are the most common bilingual programs in the United States, research demonstrates that they are less effective than dual language programs for ELLs (Thomas & Collier, 2002; Lindholm-Leary, 2001). Cummins' (1987) distinction between 'basic interpersonal communication skills', or 'BICS', and 'cognitive academic language proficiency', or 'CALP' is generally forwarded to explain this difference, although Cummins (2001) now uses the terms 'conversational fluency' and 'academic language proficiency' to refer to these notions. He defines conversational fluency as the ability to carry on a conversation in familiar face-to-face situations, and he defines academic language proficiency as the ability to comprehend and produce the increasingly complex oral and written language used in the content areas (e.g. literature, social studies, science, mathematics). Cummins and others argue that while it only takes second language learners one to two years of exposure to the second language at school and/or in other contexts to develop conversational fluency, it takes ELLs at least five years

of exposure to academic English to catch up to native speaker norms. Since prototypical TBE programs only last one to three years, they do not allow sufficient time for ELLs to develop the academic English they need to participate and achieve as equals in the academic mainstream. As Thomas and Collier's (2002) longitudinal research on program effectiveness for ELLs demonstrates, most ELLs who go through early-exit transitional bilingual programs are not able to reach parity with their English-speaking counterparts by the time they complete the program, or throughout their academic career in US public schools (see also Ramirez *et al.*, 1991).

### Dual language education

Dual-language education is another model of bilingual education, and it stands in stark ideological contrast to transitional bilingual education. According to Ruiz (1984), dual language programs are characterized by a 'language as resource' orientation that sees languages other than English as resources to be developed rather than as problems to be overcome. Three types of dual language education programs are found in the United States: second or foreign language immersion programs for English speakers; one-way developmental bilingual education programs for ELLs; and two-way immersion programs for English speakers and speakers of another language. Before I discuss these program types, I consider how my use of the term 'dual language education' in this book relates to other uses of this term in the field.

The term 'dual language education' is currently used in two different ways in the field. Consistent with the Center for Applied Linguistics and Cloud *et al.* (2000), I adopt a broad view of dual language education that includes the following three types of programs:

- Second or foreign language immersion programs for English speakers.
- One-way developmental bilingual education programs for ELL.
- Two-way immersion (TWI) programs for English speakers and speakers of another language.

Cloud *et al.* (2000) use the term 'enriched education' to refer collectively to these types of programs because they all use the minority language (e.g. Spanish in the US) for at least 50 percent of the students' content area instruction and they all lead to bilingualism, biliteracy development, and academic achievement in two languages for their target populations. Lindholm-Leary (2001), in contrast, uses the term 'dual language education' in a narrower sense to refer exclusively to two-way immersion programs that target English speakers and speakers of another language. With this broader notion of dual language education in mind, let's look more closely at each of the types of programs.

## Second/Foreign Language Immersion Programs

Dual-language programs that exclusively target speakers of the dominant language in society (e.g. English speakers in the United States and Canada) are called second or foreign language immersion programs. Immersion programs use a second/foreign language (e.g. French, Chinese) to teach at least 50 percent of the curriculum, and they last at least five to seven years. Immersion programs can vary in terms of the grade level at which the immersion experience begins and the amount of curriculum taught through the second/foreign language. According to Cloud *et al.* (2000), *early immersion education* begins in kindergarten and continues through the elementary grades. *Delayed immersion* typically does not begin until the middle elementary grades (around 4th grade). *Early total immersion* teaches 100 percent of the curriculum through the second or foreign language in kindergarten and 1st grade and begins to add English around 2nd or 3rd grade. *Early partial immersion* teaches between 50 and 90 percent of the curriculum through the second or foreign language and the remainder of the curriculum through English.

Extensive research on French immersion programs in Canada clearly demonstrates that second or foreign language immersion programs enable English speakers to become bilingual and biliterate and to achieve academically through two languages with no negative impact on English language and literacy development. English speakers are also reported to develop more positive attitudes toward French and French speakers through their participation in the immersion programs (see Cloud *et al.* (2000) and Lindholm-Leary (2001) for further discussions and references). Although considerable research evidence demonstrates the effectiveness of second/foreign language immersion education for English speakers, there are only a few such programs in the United States today (see www.cal.org for more information on immersion programs in the United States).

At first glance, many see a parallel between (a) French immersion programs for English speakers in Canada and (b) the all-English academic mainstream in the United States for Spanish-speaking ELLs. Consideration of the larger sociolinguistic contexts in Canada and in the United States, however, makes it clear why these two cases are in fact radically different. In the case of the province of Quebec, both French and English have official status and both have considerable symbolic capitol in the linguistic marketplace (Bourdieu, 1991; Heller, 1994). Because English has such prestige in Canada and in the world, English-speaking children do not resist speaking English while they acquire French. Moreover, because English is the language of wider communication outside of school, English speakers have considerable support for their native language development. English speakers continue to develop expertise in English even as they are immersed in French, and this environment is conducive to additive bilingualism.

In the United States, in contrast, English is the language of power and Spanish does not have nearly as much symbolic capital. As a result, Spanish speakers, especially low-income Spanish speakers, tend to resist speaking Spanish in favor of English. This encourages subtractive bilingualism, and we see that Spanish speakers in the United States, like speakers of other languages in this country, tend to assimilate to English. Although we hear the term 'immersion' used (incorrectly) to refer to the educational experience of ELLs who are placed in the all-English academic mainstream, 'submersion' is a more appropriate term. English language learners who are submersed in the all-English academic mainstream with no support for their English language development are expected to 'sink or swim'. Immersion and submersion are very different experiences, and they have very different outcomes.

## One-way Developmental Bilingual Education (DBE) Programs

Dual language programs that exclusively target speakers of another language (e.g. Spanish speakers in the United States) are called 'developmental' or 'maintenance' bilingual programs. These programs are often referred to as 'one-way developmental bilingual education (DBE) programs' because they only target one population (see below for discussion of two-way bilingual programs). While DBE programs are more common than immersion programs in the United States, they are not nearly as common as TBE programs.

The majority of the DBE programs in the United States target Spanish speakers. They provide content-area instruction through the native language as well as ESL instruction, and they last for at least five to seven years. The primary distinctions between DBE programs and the TBE programs discussed previously are that DBE programs continue to support the development of the student's primary language once the student has begun to use English for academic purposes, and DBE programs expect students to achieve academically through two languages. Because these programs last for at least five to seven years, ELLs have the time necessary to acquire the academic language and literacies they need in English while they continue to develop expertise in their primary language. And according to Thomas and Collier's (1998, 2002) research, ELLs who graduate from well-implemented DBE programs achieve educational parity with their English-speaking counterparts over time. The key here is implementation. Unfortunately not all programs are well-implemented.

## Two-way Immersion (TWI) Programs

Two-way immersion programs (TWI) are dual language programs that target balanced numbers of English speakers and speakers of a language other than English, and they provide content-area instruction through both languages to all students in integrated classes. These programs are sometimes referred to as *bilingual immersion, dual-language immersion, two-way immersion,* or *two-way bilingual programs,* and they combine the best features of immersion education for English speakers and of one-way developmental bilingual programs for ELLs (Lindholm, 1990; Lindholm-Leary, 2001). The goals of TWI programs are for all students, English speakers and ELLs, to become bilingual and biliterate, achieve academically through both languages, and develop positive intergroup understanding and relations (Christian, 1994; Cloud *et al.*, 2000; Lindholm-Leary, 2001).

We find two major variants in TWI programs in the United States, which are referred to as the 90:10 and the 50:50 models. The 90:10 model provides 90 percent of the content-area instruc-tion in the non-English language (e.g. Spanish) and 10 percent in English in the early elementary grades. As students progress through the grade levels the amount of instruction in English increases to 50 percent in Spanish and 50 percent in English in the upper grades. The 50:50 model provides 50 percent of students' content-area in instruction in Spanish and 50 percent in English across all grades. According to Thomas and Collier (2002) and Lindholm-Leary (2001), well-implemented TWI programs enable all students to develop oral and written expertise in two languages. But again, the key is implementation.

TWI programs have attracted considerable attention and funding in the United States since the mid-1990s. Prior to 1990, the Department of Education's Title VII Program primarily funded transitional bilingual programs. However, the Bilingual Education Act (Title VII) was reauthorized in 1994, and the new guidelines specified that up to 25 percent of the grant money could be used for alternative forms of bilingual education. Furthermore, Rita Esquivel, the Director of the Office of Bilingual Education and Minority Language Affairs in 1994, was a strong supporter of dual language education and federal funds began to be available for dual language programs at that time. Over the past three decades, we have seen the numbers of TWI programs grow from fewer than five to 261 programs in 24 states. While Spanish is by far the most common language used in TWI programs, we also see TWI programs that use other languages. At the time of this writing six programs use Cantonese, four use Korean, four use French, two use Navajo, two use Japanese, one uses Arabic, one uses Portuguese, and one uses Russian for instructional purposes (Lindholm-Leary, 2001: 35; see also the TWI Directory at www.cal.org for updated information).

In March 2000, Richard W. Riley, then Secretary of Education delivered an address entitled 'The Progress of Hispanic Education and the Challenges of the New Century' in which he lauded the two-way immersion model and challenged the United States to increase the number of these programs to at least 1,000 over the next five years. Riley said,

> Right now we have about 260 dual-immersion schools and that is only a start. We need to invest in these kinds of programs and make sure they are in communities

that can most benefit from them. In an international economy, knowledge – and knowledge of language – is power.

Title VII continued to aggressively fund two-way immersion programs, and at the time of this writing, more and more schools were designing and implementing TWI programs that would ideally meet the language and education needs of their target populations.

In 2003, The Center for Applied Linguistics convened a national dual language standards panel that is developing national standards for dual language programs. According to Hamayan (2003), a member of the national panel, the national dual language standards are inspired by the dual language standards developed in New Mexico, and they are organized around seven strands; program structure, assessment and accountability, staff quality, family and community involvement, curriculum, instructional practices, and resources/support. Each strand includes a number of specific standards that are intended to guide dual language program and professional development efforts. The national standards are to be made public during the fall of 2003.

Valdés (1997) makes a strong cautionary note about TWI programs. She argues that educators need to consider power relations between the target populations at schools, especially between white middle-class standard-English speakers and low-income Spanish speakers. Since white middle-class students tend to outperform their low-income Spanish-speaking counterparts academically in most US schools today, Valdés urges educators to ensure that their TWI programs provide Spanish speakers with the opportunities they need to reach equally high standards in their content-area classes. Otherwise, Valdés argues, Spanish speakers may be exploited for the Spanish resource that they offer to English-speaking students. If teachers do not ensure that their low-income Latinos are getting equal access to educational opportunities in their TWI programs, middle-class English speakers may continue to outperform Spanish speakers AND they will have developed expertise in two languages. In this case, TWI programs would have the unintended outcome of taking jobs that require bilingual proficiencies from bilingual Latinos because bilingual whites would now be more prepared to fill those jobs. Valdés maintains that this does not have to be the case if TWI teachers attend to the power

relations between languages and speakers of those languages on the local level and provide a high quality content-based program in Spanish as well as English. Again, the key is implementation, and the national dual language standards are intended to support the development of pedagogically sound, well-implemented dual language programs nationally.

## International Research on Bilingual Education

There is a solid international research base that supports findings from the research on the effectiveness of different types of bilingual education in the United States. For example, Dutcher (1995) carried out a comprehensive review of research for the World Bank on the use of first and second languages in education. This review examined three different types of countries: (1) those with no (or few) mother-tongue speakers of the language of wider communication (e.g. Haiti, Nigeria, the Philippines); (2) those with some mother-tongue speakers of the language of wider communication (e.g. Guatemala); and (3) those with many mother-tongue speakers of the language of wider communication (e.g. Canada, New Zealand, the United States). Tucker (1999) draws the following conclusions from this review of the research:

1. Success in school depends upon the child's mastery of cognitive/academic language, which is very different from the social language used at home.
2. The development of cognitive/academic language requires time (4 to 7 years of formal instruction).
3. Individuals most easily develop literacy skills in a familiar language.
4. Individuals most easily develop cognitive skills and master content material when they are taught in a familiar language.
5. Cognitive/academic language skills, once developed, and content-subject material, once acquired, transfer readily from one language to another.
6. The best predictor of cognitive/academic language development in a second language is the level of development of cognitive/academic language proficiency in the first language.
7. Children learn a second language in different ways depending upon their culture and their individual personality.

8.  If the goal is to help the student ultimately develop the highest possible degree of content mastery and second language proficiency, time spent instructing the child in a familiar language is a wise investment.

The cumulative evidence from research conducted over the last three decades at sites around the world demonstrates conclusively that cognitive, social, personal, and economic benefits accrue to the individual who has an opportunity to develop their bilingual repertoire when compared with a monolingual counterpart. Dual language programs that promote bilingualism, biliteracy development, and academic achievement through two languages for their target population(s), when well-implemented, show real promise in our efforts to address our national language needs.

This section has discussed the types of bilingual education program that we find in US schools today. All well-implemented bilingual programs hold students to the same high academic standards as the all-English academic mainstream. Furthermore, all well-implemented bilingual programs provide ESL services to their students that are aligned with the TESOL standards. The next section looks more closely at the kinds of ESL programs and practices that we can find in the US today.

## English as a Second Language

We can find a wide range of English as a second language (ESL) programs and practices in US schools today. For example, we may see pull-out ESL programs that take ELLs out of the all-English academic mainstream for ESL instruction. We may see push-in ESL programs in which the ESL teacher enters the all-English classroom and works to support the ESL students' needs within the context of that classroom. In schools that have large numbers of ELLs, we may see sheltered ESL programs that segregate ELLs for content-area instruction (see below for further discussion). The organization of the actual ESL program depends on the local context, including the number of ELLs that the school serves, and on the relationship between the ESL teachers and content-area teachers at the school.

Regardless of the program structure, all ESL programs are to use a communicative approach to language teaching and learning (Canale & Swain, 1980), and all ESL programs are to address the

goals and standards that the professional organization for Teachers of English to Speakers of Other Languages has defined for pre-K–12 students (TESOL, 1997). The No Child Left Behind Act now requires each state to develop English language proficiency (ELP) standards that are aligned with state content-area standards, and we see variation across states in the ways that they develop ELP standards that are aligned with the national TESOL standards, their state (English/Spanish) language arts standards, and standards in other content areas. This section begins with a brief discussion of the theoretical notion of communicative competence used in the language teaching and learning field. Then I introduce the TESOL goals and standards and review the range of ESL program types we find in US schools. Future research is necessary to document the range of ELP standards that are developed and how they are translated into programs and practices for ELLs across contexts.

Hymes' (1966) notion of communicative competence is fundamental to most contemporary approaches to language teaching and learning, and it informed the development of the TESOL standards discussed in this section and the ACTFL (American Council for Teachers of Foreign Languages) world language standards discussed later in this chapter. Communicative competence can be broadly defined as what a speaker needs to know to be able to communicate correctly and appropriately within a particular speech community (Saville-Troike, 1996). Canale and Swain (1980) extend this notion to the field of language teaching and learning and identify and define the following four aspects of communicative competence:

1.  Linguistic competence means that the forms, inflections, and sequences used to express the message are grammatically correct.
2.  Sociolinguistic competence means that the expression of the message is appropriate in terms of the person being addressed and the overall circumstances and purpose of communication.
3.  Discourse competence means that the selection, sequence and arrangement of words and structures are clear and effective means of expressing the intended message.
4.  Strategic competence means that the strategies used to compensate for any weaknesses in the above areas are effective and unobtrusive.

A language learner is considered 'communicatively competent' relative to the target speech community when he/she demonstrates competence in each of these areas. Communicative language teaching in US schools is intended to facilitate the learners' acquisition of the spoken and written language they need in order to use language correctly and appropriately in social settings and in all academic content areas.

The three goals that TESOL established for ELLs in pre-K–12 schools reflect this fundamental notion of communicative competence. Each goal is associated with three distinct standards, and ELLs are to meet the standards as a result of the instruction they receive. As they meet the specific standards, ELLs realize the more general social, academic, and personal goals. The ESL goals and standards are as follows (TESOL, 1997: 9–10):

*Goal 1: To use English to communicate in social settings.*

Standards for Goal 1

Students will:

1.  Use English to participate in social interaction.
2.  Interact in, through, and with spoken and written English for personal expression and enjoyment.
3.  Use learning strategies to extend their communicative competence.

*Goal 2: To use English to achieve academically in all content areas.*

Standards for Goal 2

Students will:

1.  Use English to interact in the classroom.
2.  Use English to obtain, process, construct, and provide subject matter information in spoken and written form.
3.  Use appropriate learning strategies to construct and apply academic knowledge.

*Goal 3: To use English in socially and culturally appropriate ways.*

Standards for Goal 3

Students will:

1.  Use the appropriate language variety, register, and genre according to audience, purpose, and setting.
2.  Use nonverbal communication appropriate to audience, purpose, and setting.
3.  Use appropriate learning strategies to extend their sociolinguistic and sociocultural competence.

A framework for ESL language planning and for making use of the standards is also outlined (TESOL, 1997). The TESOL standards describe the kinds of English that ELLs need to acquire so that they can attain the same high-level standards within and across content areas, including English language arts, as fully proficient English-speaking students.

Research on effective ESL programs demonstrates that the most effective way to enable students to develop the academic language and literacies that they need in English to reach the standards across all content areas is through a content-based second language instruction approach (Brinton *et al.*, 1989). Brinton *et al.* define content-based second language instruction as

> the integration of particular content with language teaching aims. More specifically . . . it refers to the concurrent teaching of academic subject matter and second language skills. The language curriculum is based directly on the academic needs of the students and generally follows the sequence determined by particular subject matter in dealing with the language problems which students encounter. The focus for students is on acquiring information via the second language and, in the process, developing their academic language skills (1989: 2).

Brinton *et al.* identify three models of content-based second/foreign language programs that are appropriate for use in different instructional contexts. These are (1) the sheltered model, (2) the adjunct model, and (3) the theme-based model.

Sheltered courses are content-area courses (e.g. math, science, social studies) that are taught by a content-area specialist to a segregated group of language learners, and the primary goal of these courses is content-area mastery. Sheltered ESL courses follow the tradition of second or foreign language immersion education for elementary and secondary school students. Because the content-area teacher employs strategies that make complex content comprehensible to second language learners, language tends to be learned incidentally. Adjunct courses are paired content and language courses that language learners enroll in concurrently. Two teachers are necessary for adjunct courses. The content-area teacher teaches the content area (e.g. math, science, social studies), and the language teacher teaches the content-obligatory and content-compatible language that students need to participate and achieve in the content-area class (Snow *et al.*, 1992). Theme-based classes are taught by language teachers who structure the language course around particular topics or themes. The common feature of all of these types of courses and/or programs is that content material is used as the basis for language learning (see Brinton *et al.*, 1989, for further discussion).

Research on second language teaching and learning highlights several important reasons for integrating language and content for instructional purposes. First, content provides a motivational basis for language learning. When students are interested in the content they are learning about, they tend to learn the language forms and functions they need because those language forms and functions provide access to that content. Content also provides a meaningful context within which learners can connect language forms and functions. Furthermore, students learn language most effectively when they need to use that language in meaningful, purposeful social and academic contexts (see Brinton *et al.*, 1989; Chamot & O'Malley, 1994; Cloud *et al.*, 2000; Snow *et al.*, 1992).

The key to an effective ESL program is implementation. The educators who work with ELLs (i.e. ESL teachers, bilingual teachers, mainstream classroom teachers who have ELLs in their classes) must clearly understand their students' content and language strengths and needs, and their programs need to be aligned with the TESOL standards and with state content-area standards. The No Child Left Behind Act holds mainstream teachers accountable for ELLs' academic achievement, and holds ELS teachers accountable for ELLs' English language development. Mainstream classroom teachers and ESL teachers should work together to provide a coherent program that enables all ELLs to acquire the academic language and literacies that they need for access

to equal educational opportunities in the all-English academic mainstream. These programs should have clearly articulated objectives for their ELLs' English language development and academic performance, and educators should use multiple forms of assessment to determine how well ELLs are performing relative to those objectives. Educators at these schools must understand that it takes at least five to seven years for ELLs to develop expertise in academic English and to close the gap between their performance and the performance of their English-speaking counterparts across content areas, and exit criteria and promotion and graduation requirements should reflect this understanding (see also Echevarria *et al.*, 2001; NSSE, 2002).

## World Language Education in the United States

As national recognition of the need for languages other than English grows in the United States, we see exciting new developments in a field that was traditionally called 'foreign' language education. In this book, I use the term 'world language' to refer to the teaching of a language as a subject area to a student who does not speak that language (e.g. Spanish to English speakers in the United States). This section considers how the changes in language learning goals and changes in students' language learning strengths and needs have influenced the ways that we are beginning to think about world language education in the United States today. First, I review the American Council on the Teaching of Foreign Languages (ACTFL) *Standards for Foreign Language* (1999) and the *ACTFL Performance Guidelines for K–12 Learners* (1999) to determine realistic and attainable goals and expectations for world language learning at school. Then I describe the prototypical FLES (Foreign Language in the Elementary School) program structure that is recommended for elementary school world language programs, and discuss the increase in elementary and secondary school world language programs that we see nationally. I conclude this section by considering the impact that heritage language speakers have had on a field that traditionally targeted only monolingual English speakers.

In 1995, the ACTFL standards were released to the world language profession at their annual meeting, and they were endorsed by 46 state, regional, and national language organizations. Like the standards-based projects in other disciplines, the world language standards attempt to outline the focus of instruction with specific reference to 4th, 8th, and 12th grades. The goal of the standards is to clearly articulate what students need to know and what they need to be able to do as a result of their study of world languages.

The standards are arranged into five major goal areas: communication, cultures, connection, comparisons, and communities. Like the TESOL standards, each goal area includes specific standards. These standards do not describe specific course content, they do not provide a recommended scope and sequence, and they do not prescribe an instructional approach or teaching methodology. Instead, the goal areas are intended to be seen as interconnected, and they emphasize using language for communication with other peoples, gaining understanding of other cultures, and accessing information in a wide range of disciplines (Omaggio Hadley, 2000). Educators who are familiar with their students' language learning needs and preferences are encouraged to select the content, sequence, and method that are appropriate for their context.

The *Standards for Foreign Language Learning* (1999) outline *what* students need to know, and the *ACTFL Performance Guidelines for K–12 Learners* (1999) provide a framework for assessing *how well* novice, intermediate, and pre-advanced learners can use the world language for communicative purposes. The performance guidelines do not focus on the traditional skills areas of reading, writing, listening, and speaking in isolation. Instead, they define how well students at different levels can use language in what the guidelines refer to as three different communicative modes: the interpersonal, interpretive, and presentational. The interpersonal mode is characterized by active negotiation of meaning among individuals (e.g. in face-to-face communication). The interpretive mode is focused on the appropriate cultural interpretation of meanings that occur in written and spoken form where there is no active negotiation of meaning with another interlocutor (e.g. reading a novel, listening to the radio, watching a film). The presentational mode refers to the creation of spoken and/or written messages in a manner that facilitates interpretation by members of the other culture where no direct opportunity for the active negotiation of meaning between members of the two cultures exists (e.g. writing a report, presenting a speech).

Both the standards and the performance guidelines are designed to reflect second language learning that begins in kindergarten and that continues in an uninterrupted sequence through 12th grade. These guidelines suggest that English speakers who have been enrolled in a well-articulated, long-sequence foreign language program can demonstrate intermediate to advanced levels of proficiency in the western languages that are most commonly taught in American schools. The authors of the performance guidelines explain why we can expect different kinds of performances by English speakers studying western languages on the one hand and by English speakers studying less commonly taught languages on the other. They write,

> Students whose native language is English find many similarities between English and the languages of the western world, both in oral and written forms, which aid students in their acquisition of the new language. Conversely, when students encounter the less commonly taught languages such as Arabic, Chinese, Japanese, Korean, and Russian, new hurdles await them: unfamiliar sounds, different writing systems and new grammars. These linguistic features, which oftentimes cannot be linked to anything the students know in their native language, present challenges and generally tend to extend the language acquisition process. It cannot be expected, therefore, that students learning the less commonly taught languages should reach the same levels of performance as those who study the western languages more frequently offered in American schools (p. 3).

Because it may take longer for English speakers to develop expertise in the less commonly taught languages, it is even more important to begin study of these languages earlier. However, since an uninterrupted 13-year sequence of world language study is not commonly found in the United States today, the ACTFL K–12 performance guidelines also account for various entry points that reflect most major language sequences (see American Council of Teachers of Foreign Languages [1999] for further discussion and for performance indicators).

What does a 'well-articulated, long-sequence' world language program look like in practice? *Lessons Learned: Model Early Foreign Language Programs* (Gilzow & Branaman, 2000) describes seven foreign language programs in the United States that they identified through a selection process informed by the national standards for foreign language education and by research on effective language instruction for elementary and middle school students (Curtain & Pesola, 1994; National Standards for Foreign Language Education Project, 1996). Each of the programs selected met the following criteria (Gilzow & Branaman 2000: 2):

- Curricula based on the 'five Cs' of the national foreign language standards – communication, cultures, connections, comparisons, and communities
- Regular program evaluation
- Outcomes that meet program goals
- Accessibility for all students
- Communication and coordination across content areas
- A student population that reflects the ethnic and socioeconomic diversity of the local population
- Articulation from elementary to middle school and from middle school to high school
- Professional development for teachers
- Support from the community

The seven programs included five content-enriched FLES programs, one partial immersion program, and one middle school immersion continuation program. Because we reviewed the characteristics of second/foreign language immersion programs in our discussion of dual language education earlier in the chapter, the focus here will be on the prototypical FLES program structure.

While secondary world language programs teach the language as a separate subject area, FLES programs integrate language instruction into the students' regular classroom schedule. According to Curtain and Pesola (1994) and Gilzow and Branaman (2000), elementary school students should have a 30- to 45-minute language class three to five times per week for a minimum of 90 minutes total per week. Of course, when schools allocate more time to target language instruction, students can be expected to develop a broader range of expertise in that language. What is important to emphasize is that the language program be treated as an integral part of the whole school program. Students need to have regular opportunities to participate in language class each week throughout the years of the program if they are to realize the annual and long-term objectives and goals of the program.

Prototypical FLES programs assume that the language teacher and the classroom teacher are two different people, and FLES teachers either travel to the mainstream classroom or the students travel to a separate language classroom for FLES class. Like any pedagogical choice, there are pros and cons to each teaching arrangement. For example, having the FLES teacher travel to the regular classroom can present a wide range of challenges for that teacher (e.g. physical wear and tear, difficulty transporting materials, time to get from one class to the next), but the traveling teacher can help make the target language an integral part of the regular classroom and school. Having a separate classroom for the FLES class can be much easier for the FLES teacher (e.g. to develop libraries full of authentic texts in the target language, display teacher-made materials and student work), but this arrangement could contribute to the marginalization of the world language class in the school.

What is the content of a FLES program? Each of the FLES programs described in Gilzow and Branaman (2000) focused on content, although the ways that they focused on content varied across programs and grade levels. Following Curtain and Pesola (1994), I differentiate between a content-based second language program (like those implemented in English as a second language and foreign/second language immersion programs discussed earlier in the chapter) and a content-related second language program. According to Curtain and Pesola (1994),

> In the typical FLES classroom, in which twenty to thirty minutes per day is devoted to foreign language instruction, it is not realistic to base the curriculum on concepts taken from grade-level curriculum of other content areas, nor is it probable that the foreign language program can take full responsibility for teaching grade-appropriate concepts from the general curriculum in the target language. While many hands-on activities related to content may still be successful, language skills in a second language simply do not develop quickly enough in a FLES setting to permit the effective initial teaching of increasingly sophisticated and abstract ideas. Through theme-based, integrative teaching, however, the foreign language class can reenter and reinforce important concepts from mathematics, social studies,

and other areas, drawing from earlier grade levels as well as from grade-level-appropriate curriculum (p. 151).

According to Gilzow and Branaman (2000), some FLES programs align language curricula with curricula in the subject areas at the district level, and the world language curricula are revised as the district curricula are revised. In other programs, the language class content is closely tied to the content of regular classes, but curriculum development and revision are handled informally by the teachers involved.

What is the state of world language education in the United States today? In 1999, the Center for Applied Linguistics (CAL) published *Foreign Language Instruction in the United States: A National Survey of Elementary and Secondary Schools*. This survey was intended to explore current patterns and shifts in enrollment, languages and programs offered, curriculum, teaching methodologies, teacher qualifications and training, and reactions to national reform issues, and it was designed to replicate CAL's 1987 survey in an effort to show trends during the 1987–1997 decade. According to CAL's executive summary, 'foreign language education in the United States is at a unique moment historically'. World languages were recognized as part of the core curriculum in the Goals 2000: Educate America Act, and there was evidence of considerable increases in K–12 world language instruction throughout the country (Center for Applied Linguistics, 1997).

The CAL survey found that in the past decade, world language instruction in the elementary schools increased significantly. In 1997 one in three elementary schools reported offering world language instruction, and this represented a 10 percent increase since 1987. While most programs offer Spanish, there was some increase in Japanese, Russian, and Italian on the elementary level and in Japanese and Russian on the secondary level. However, CAL's executive summary concludes by saying that there is still reason for concern about the limited number of K–12 long-sequence world language programs that enable students to develop communicative competence in languages other than English. The National Foreign Language Center (NFLC) echoes this concern and highlights the need for well-articulated long-sequence language programs in the less commonly taught languages like Chinese and Russian (Brecht & Rivers, 2000).

Both CAL and NFLC emphasize that well-articulated elementary and secondary foreign language programs are still the exception rather than the norm. Unfortunately, the increasing interest in world language programs in the United States today is not accompanied by sufficient numbers of well-implemented programs that could dramatically alter the US ability to meet the kinds of language needs outlined [in Chapter 1].

## Heritage Language Programs

Traditionally, world language classes have targeted monolingual English speakers who generally begin their language study with no expertise in the target language and minimal knowledge about the people who speak it. Until recently, little attention has been paid to developing and coordinating well-designed and carefully articulated language programs for heritage language speakers. However, student populations enrolled in world language programs on the elementary, secondary, and university levels are rapidly changing, and world language teachers see increasing numbers of heritage language speakers in classes with monolingual English-speaking students. These students have a wide range of proficiencies in spoken and / or written languages, and they pose a serious challenge to teachers who are not trained to work with such diversity.

Since the 1990s, we have seen considerable interest in the teaching of heritage Spanish speakers in particular and speakers of other heritage languages more generally. The CAL survey of foreign language programs found a significant increase in Spanish for native speakers (SNS) classes on the elementary and secondary levels. Two major volumes of articles were published that reflected new energy within the Spanish-teaching profession, and we see SNS teachers and researchers looking critically at how they can assess and build on their students' linguistic and cultural strengths (Merino *et al.*, 1993 and Colombi & Alarcón, 1997).

Valdés (2000) encourages SNS teachers to draw on the framework of communicative modes (interpersonal, interpretive, presentational) discussed previously in their efforts to understand and expand the bilingual range of students who have grown up in homes where non-English languages are spoken. She offers a wealth of ideas that can help SNS teachers determine what strengths a particular heritage Spanish speaker brings to class (e.g. strong interpersonal abilities) and what needs that student has relative to the framework (e.g. the need to develop interpretive and presentational modes of communication, including reading and writing authentic texts, understanding films, making formal presentations).

Teachers of Spanish to native speakers, Valdés argues, have much to teach, but they must take a different approach from that traditionally taken by world language educators. They need to see heritage Spanish speakers' linguistic and cultural expertise as resources that they can build on. They must not see their students' expertise in nonstandard varieties of Spanish (e.g. vernacular Puerto Rican Spanish) as deficits that they must overcome. Instead SNS teachers need to organize their programs and practices so that heritage Spanish speakers can add standard Spanish and literacies in Spanish to their linguistic repertoires. In the process, teachers can encourage heritage Spanish speakers to think critically about the sociolinguistic variation in Spanish that is a very real part of their everyday lives.

World language programs in the United States face enormous challenges today. National, state, and local education policies are beginning to emphasize the need for US citizens to develop proficiency in more than one language in order to participate in the global economy and to ensure national security. High schools are increasingly requiring expertise in world languages to meet graduation criteria, which has encouraged many school districts to offer world language education in the elementary grades. At the same time, student populations enrolled in world language programs on the elementary, secondary, and university levels are rapidly changing, and we see heritage language speakers attending the same language classes as monolingual English speakers. Not only is there a serious shortage of world language teachers available to fill an increasing number of positions in the field, but many world language educators have not been trained to meet the diverse and rapidly changing needs of students today. Some university world language programs, in-service professional development programs, and individual world language teachers are working in creative ways to address these challenges, but much work remains (for futher discussion see Peyton, 2001).

## Conclusion

This chapter has reviewed prototypical bilingual education, English as a second language, and world language programs that we find in the United States today, and it has related these kinds of program to research on second language acquisition, biliteracy development, content-based second language instruction, and program effectiveness. As we have seen, there are a number of different kinds of language education programs that educators can draw on to promote additive bilingualism on the local school level.

However, language educators face several important challenges as they work to design and implement context-responsive programs and practices. First, program planners need to have a clear understanding of who their students are and they must be able to clearly articulate their language education goals for their target populations. Program planners also need to have a clear understanding about how language education programs are structured to realize those goals so that they can develop and implement programs that are pedagogically sound. Perhaps most importantly, program planners need to understand the ways that languages are taught, learned, used, and evaluated on the local school and community level in order to build on the linguistic and cultural resources that are available.

## References

American Council of Teachers of Foreign Languages. (1999) *ACTFL K–12 Performance Guidelines.* Yonkers: ACTFL.

Brecht, R.D. and Rivers, W.P. (2000) *Language and National Security in the 21st Century: The Role of Title VI/Fulbright-Hays in Supporting National Language Capacity.* Dubuque: Kendall/Hunt.

Brinton, D.M., Snow, M.A. and Bingham Wesche, M. (1989) *Content-based Second Language Instruction.* Boston: Heinle and Heinle.

Bourdieu, P. (1991) *Language and Symbolic Power.* Cambridge: Polity Press.

Canale, M. and Swain, M. (1980) Theoretical bases of communicative approaches to second-language teaching and testing. *Applied Linguistics* 1, 1–47.

Center for Applied Linguistics (1997) *National Survey of Foreign Language Instruction in Elementary and Secondary Schools in the United States.* Washington, DC: Center for Applied Linguistics.

Chamot, A.U. and O'Malley, J.M. (1994) *The CALLA Handbook: Implementing the Cognitive Academic Language Learning Approach.* Reading: Addison-Wesley.

Christian, D. (1994) Two-way bilingual education: Students learning through two languages. In *The National Center for Research on Cultural Diversity and Second Language Learning: Educational Practice Report 12.* Washington, DC: Center for Applied Linguistics.

Cloud, N. Genesee, F. and Hamayan, E. (2000) *Dual Language Instruction: A Handbook for Enriched Education.* Boston: Heinle and Heinle.

Colombi, M.C. and Alarcón, F.X. (eds) (1997) *La Eseñanza del Español a Hispanohablantes: Praxis y Teoría.* Boston: Houghton Mifflin.

Cummins, J. (1987) Bilingualism, language proficiency, and metalinguistic development. In P. Homel, M. Palij and D. Aaronson (eds) *Childhood Bilingualism: Aspects of Linguistic, Cognitive and Social Development* (pp. 57–73). Hillsdale, NJ: Lawrence Erlbaum.

Cummins, J. (2001) *Negotiating Identities: Education for Empowerment in a Diverse Society.* Los Angeles: California Association for Bilingual Education.

Curtain, H. and Pesola, C.A.B. (1994) *Languages and Children: Making the Match.* New York: Longman.

Dutcher, N. (1995) *Overview of Foreign Language Students in the United States.* National Clearinghouse for Bilingual Education. Resource Collection Series, 6. Washington, DC: Center for Applied Linguistics.

Echeverria, J., Vogt, M. and Short, D.J. (2000) *Making Content Comprehensible for English Language Learners: The SIOP Model.* Boston: Allyn and Bacon.

Gilzow, D.F. and Branaman, L.E. (2000) *Lessons Learned: Model Early Foreign Language Programs.* McHenry: Delta Systems Co., Inc.

Hamayan, E. (2003) National dual language standards. Draft presented at Desplaines, IL: Illinois Resource Center.

Heller, M. (1994) *Crosswords: Language, Education and Ethnicity in French Ontario.* Berlin: Mouton de Gruyter.

Hornberger, N.H. (1991) Extending enrichment bilingual education: Revisiting typologies and redirecting policy. In O. García (ed.) *Bilingual education Focusschrift in honor of Joshua A. Fishman* (Vol. 1) (pp. 215–234). Philadelphia: John Benjamins.

Hymes, D. Paper presented at the Research Planning Conference on Language Development among Disadvantaged Children. New York: Yeshiva University.

Lindholm, K. (1990) Bilingual immersion education: Criteria for program development. In A. Padilla, H.H. Fairchild and C.M. Valdez (eds) *Bilingual Education: Issues and Strategies* (pp. 91–105). Newbury Park: Corwin Press Inc.

Lindholm-Leary, K. (2001) *Dual Language Education.* Clevedon: Multilingual Matters.

Merino, B.J., Trueba, H.T. and Santiago, F.A. (eds) (1993) *Language and Culture in Learning: Teaching Spanish to Native Speakers of Spanish.* London: Falmer Press.

National Study of School Evaluation. (2002) *Program Evaluation: English as a Second Language.* Indicators of Schools of Quality Program Evaluation Series. Schaumburg, IL: NSSE.

Omaggio Hadley, A. (2000) *Teaching Language in Context.* Boston: Heinle and Heinle.

Peyton, J., Reynard, D. and McGinnis, S. (2001) Charting a new course: Heritage language in the United States. In J. Peyton, D. Reynard and S. McGinnis (eds) (pp. 3–26) *Heritage Languages in America: Preserving a National Resource.* McHenry: Delta Systems Co., Inc.

Ramirez, J.D., Yuen, S.D. and Ramey, D.R. (1991) *Executive Summary Final Report: Longitudinal Study of Structures English Immersion Strategy, Early-exit and Late-exit Transitional Bilingual Programs for Language Minority Children.* San Mateo: Aguirre International.

Ruíz, R. (1984) Orientations in language planning. *NABE Journal* 8(2), 15–34.

Saville-Troike, M. (1996) The ethnography of communication. In S. McKay and N. Hornberger (eds) *Sociolinguistics and Language Teaching* (pp. 351–382). New York: Cambridge University Press.

Snow, C.E., Met, M. and Genesee, F. (1992) A conceptual framework for the integration of language and content instruction. In P.A. Richard-Amato and M.A. Snow (eds) *The Multicultural Classroom: Reading for Content-area Teachers.* New York: Longman.

*Standards for Foreign Language Learning: Preparing for the 21st Century.* Yonkers: National Standards in Foreign Language Education Project.

Teachers of English to Speakers of Other Languages. (1997) *ESL Standards for Pre-K–12 Students.* Alexandria: TESOL.

Thomas, W. and Collier, V. (2002) *A National Study of School Effectiveness for Language Minority Students' Long Term Academic Achievement.* Santa Cruz: Center for Research, Education,

Diversity and Excellence, University of California, Santa Cruz.

Tucker, G.R. (1999) A global perspective on bilingualism and bilingual education. *ERIC Digest.* Washington, DC: ERIC Clearinghouse on Languages and Linguistics.

Valdés, G. (1997) Dual-language immersion programs: A cautionary note concerning the education of language minority students. *Harvard Education Review* 67, 391–429.

Valdés, G. (2000) Introduction. *Spanish for Native Speakers. AATSP Professional Development Series Handbook for Teachers K–16* (pp. 1–20). Orlando: Harcourt College.

## Questions

1. What are the main types of bilingual education? How do the following vary in different types of bilingual education: the language background of the students; the language goals and outcomes of programs; the language(s) used in the classroom; languages in assessment/testing; the age range (length) of the program; the desired societal outcomes (e.g. assimilation, integration, pluralism).

2. What is the difference between schools that are bilingual and those that are organized for second language teaching? What are the differences in the students, personnel, instruction, services and philosophy? Are there political differences?

3. Explain the difference between teaching a new language and using a language as a medium of education. Also, indicate what is the way languages are used in any *five* of the following:
   a. transitional bilingual education
   b. maintenance/heritage bilingual education
   c. two-way dual language education
   d. foreign language (FL) classes
   e. second language (SL) classes
   f. immersion classes
   g. structured immersion or sheltered SL classes

   (You may want to refer to 'Foundations of Bilingual Education and Bilingualism' (4th edition, 2006), chapters 10 and 11 in order to expand on this question).

4. What are the main types of English as a second language program? How do they differ in content, aims and outcomes?

5. Using Tucker's (1999) eight conclusions from research on bilingual education listed in Freeman's chapter, explain the meaning of each using local schools and students as examples.

## Activities

1. Using a local school with which you're familiar, interview parents, teachers and administrators. Find out the school's *current* policy with regard to language minority students and the use of minority languages in education.

   Profile the bilingualism of that school in terms of its students, staff, curriculum content (especially biliteracy or multilingual literacies, cultural awareness, anti-racism), use of language assessment/testing, mission and aims, performance and achievements, and its relationship with the local community.

   Also find out whether the school's policy responds to any societal policy or demands. Summarize answers on a chart or in a Powerpoint presentation. Different groups might select schools with different characteristics. For example, an urban school might be compared to a suburban or rural one; a private one to a public one; a large one to a small one. Share your answers.

2. Select a school with which you are familiar. Interview parents, teachers and administrators. Write a *historical* account of the changes that have taken place in the student population of the school, the education of language minority students, and the presence of a minority language(s) in education.

3. Find out whether the city or state or community you live in has a specific policy on the education of second language learners, the use of minority languages in instruction, bilingual education, or English language acquisition. Find relevant documents. Share them with the class. Write a short report in which you summarize the policy, quoting from the documents.

4. Make a chart containing any four types of bilingual education programs. In this chart, for each type of bilingual education:
   a. give a definition
   b. give an example
   c. say whether the type leads to monolingualism, subtractive bilingualism or additive bilingualism
   d. indicate which pedagogic and language factors that make bilingual education programs successful are present or absent in each type.
   e. say whether the type is available in your local school district.

5  Using the WWW, research the way No Child Left Behind (2001) treats: the English language, Native Indian languages in the US, and other older and more recent 'immigrant' languages. What are No Child Left Behind's political ambitions for language minority students? What types of bilingual education are implicitly accepted and disallowed? What can you conclude about the language motivations behind NCLB? Create a poster or a WWW page to summarize your findings.

6. Freeman makes frequent references to California's Proposition 227. In groups of three to six and using the WWW and other bibliographical sources, research the following three aspects of Proposition 227: 1) the process that led to its passage, 2) the outcome of the referendum itself, 3) the educational consequences for California's English language learners. Put the three pieces together and make a presentation to the class or to a local audience.

## Further Reading

Baker, C. (2002) Bilingual education. In R. B. Kaplan (ed.) *The Oxford Handbook of Applied Linguistics*. Oxford: Oxford University Press.

Baker, C. (2003) Education as a site of language contact. *Annual Review of Applied Linguistics 'Language Contact and Change'* 23, 95–112.

Baker, C. (2005) Bilingual education. In K. Brown (ed.) *Encyclopedia of Language and Linguistics* (2nd edition). Oxford: Elsevier.

Baker, C. (2006) *Foundations of Bilingual Education and Bilingualism* (4th edition). Clevedon: Multilingual Matters.

García, O. (1997) Bilingual education. In F. Coulmas (ed.) *The Handbook of Sociolinguistics*. Oxford: Blackwell.

Genesee, F. (ed.) (1999) *Program Alternatives for Linguistically Diverse Students*. Santa Cruz: Center for Research on Education, Diversity & Excellence, University of California.

# Characteristics of Immersion Programmes

## R. Johnstone

### An International Phenomenon

#### Immersion in Canada

Although immersion in a second language has been a feature of education for centuries, it has in recent years become best known through developments in Canada. 'The first immersion programs were designed to provide Canada's majority-group English-speaking learners with opportunities to learn Canada's other official language' (Genesee, 1994a: 1). Since the 1960s Canadian learners mainly from English-speaking homes have had the opportunity to receive most or much of their education through the medium of French from teachers who are native speakers of the language. Immersion programmes are implemented across the whole of Canada, presently involving some 350,000 learners of whom some 155,000 are in Ontario, and have been extensively researched. In Canada immersion differs from 'Core French' which is 'French-as-a-subject' taught across the anglophone provinces of Canada in primary and secondary schools in ways that resemble a foreign language at school in Scotland.

As a result of this extensive and systematic planning, development, experimentation, evaluation and research, it is nowadays possible in Canada to make informed predictions as to what levels of subject attainment, language proficiency and social attitudes will be delivered by Core French and by the different models of immersion education by the time learners reach the end of their primary and secondary education. Information of this sort is useful to parents and educational planners wishing to know in advance what outcomes a particular type of immersion programme is likely to yield.

#### Immersion elsewhere

However, 'immersion' is by no means restricted to Canada. In one form or another, it has been introduced in many other states or regions such as Hungary, Austria, France, Germany, Finland, Australia, Hawai'i, Spain (both Catalonia and the Basque region), Hong Kong, Singapore, South Africa and the USA (where Met and Lorenz, 1997, report 187 immersion programmes in twenty-five states).

Immersion is one of the most extensively researched aspects not only of languages education but of education more generally. In addition to a large number of research reports on particular immersion programmes there have been several reviews of immersion research. The present report draws on these reviews, whether as conventionally published texts, e.g. Johnson and Swain (1997), Branaman and Rennie (1997), Ottawa Board of Education (1996), Carleton Board of Education (1994), Artigal (1993), Swain and Lapkin (1990, 1986, 1982), Willig (1982), Baker (1993a), Gaudart (1987), Snow (1990a), Safty (1989), Harley (1991, 1994), Genesee (1994a), McLaughlin (1984), Doyé (1997), Read (1996), Fortune and Jorsted (1996), or as information put on the web by established research centres (see web-bibliography, e.g. Cummins, 1999).

In Scotland a review of international immersion/bilingual approaches to second language acquisition (Wolfe, 1994) helpfully 'problematises' the issue by arguing that the large number of contextual, cultural and linguistic variables involved can make it difficult to draw valid general conclusions. 'Second language learning and use clearly must be understood within the context of interpersonal and inter-group relations, and wider socio-cultural factors.' (Wolfe, 1994: 6).

#### Immersion in: National–foreign–community–heritage languages

While most immersion in Canada has been in

French as another official language of the same country, there are also examples in Canada and elsewhere of immersion in languages that may be 'foreign' (e.g. English immersion in Austria or Hungary) or 'heritage' (e.g. Gaelic or Welsh immersion in Scotland and Wales respectively) or 'community', reflecting new communities that have settled in particular countries: (e.g. French, Japanese, Indonesian or Mandarin immersion in Australia, or Korean, Japanese or Russian immersion in the USA). Sometimes an immersion programme may involve a combination of the above (e.g. Japanese immersion in Australia could reflect a foreign language for some (e.g. with European family backgrounds) and a community language for others (e.g. with a Japanese family background).

The process is not always called 'immersion'. Sometimes the term 'bilingual education' is used, corresponding to 'partial immersion', whereby learners receive part of their education through one language and part through another (one of the two often but not always being their first language).

## Social Purposes Underlying Immersion

In the UK and in several other countries, immersion may serve a wide range of diverse purposes that go beyond being educational only. To illustrate this, six examples are provided:

*Social background to immersion in Canada*

In Canada, immersion programmes serve not only to educate learners but to fulfil two additional purposes: first, to show the French-speaking population that the English-speaking population is committed to the notion of Canada as a bilingual and multicultural nation, and second to establish a Canadian identity that is different from that of its massive neighbour to the south. As was recently stated in a public talk by a leading Canadian authority on French immersion, the big cities of Canada are strung out in a line across the entire country. None of them are very far from the border with the USA, hence the importance of immersion programmes in establishing a bilingual Canadian identity that differentiates it from that of its neighbour. Harley (1994) suggests that 'immersion is seen ultimately as a means of strengthening national unity' (Harley, 1994: 230).

*Social background to immersion in Australia*

In Australia, 'the main impetus for setting up immersion programmes in schools has been the desire to find a more effective foreign language pedagogy, against a background of strong governmental support for the learning of languages other than English (LOTE) during the 1980s and 1990s' (Read, 1996: 471). According to Read there were two main sources of motivation behind the strong governmental support. First, waves of immigration to Australia had led to large numbers of children whose first language was not English. This had encouraged the growth of Australia as a multicultural nation and the adoption of multilingual policies. Second, Australia's geographical situation on the Pacific rim meant that for economic reasons it would benefit Australians to speak Asian languages.

*Social background to immersion in the United States*

In the United States, according to Genesee (1985), three purposes may be discerned in the introduction of immersion programmes: as linguistic and cultural enrichment, e.g. the Culver City Program; as magnet schools to bring about a more balanced ethnolinguistic mix, e.g. the Cincinnati program; and as a means of promoting two-way bilingualism in communities with large non-English-speaking background populations, e.g. the San Diego Bilingual Immersion Program (Read, 1996: 470).

*Social background to immersion in Catalonia*

In Catalonia, following the Statutes of Autonomy of the Catalan Autonomous Community (1979) and 'in accordance with the Law of Linguistic Normalisation (1982), Catalan, as the rightful language of Catalonia, must also be the rightful language of education. This very law defends the right of infants to receive education in their customary language and establishes the objective that by the end of their basic education period, all children will have to master Catalan and Spanish' (Bel Gaya, 1994: 27). Although immersion is not the only way of achieving this requirement, it does play a key role. The Language Immersion Programme (LIP) aims to enable children from homes where Catalan is not the L1 (many are Spanish-speaking) to acquire the language, beginning during the kindergarten and Initial Cycle stages from three to eight years of age. Some schools continue the LIP programme throughout the entire primary education period. According to

Arenas (1994), the general pedagogical model in Catalonia, entitled the *escola catalana*, 'represents the educational response to the sociopolitical will to recuperate and strengthen Catalan and Catalan culture. The *escola catalana* is a general, obligatory education model for all pre-University education in Catalonia. It is defined as the educational community which, while exercising its prerogatives as a school, and respecting the language rights of all the pupils, integrates the pupils by making Catalan and Catalan culture the language and culture of their education. It is therefore a process of integration, both socially and in the language, avoiding any type of linguistic assimilation . . . ' (Arenas, 1994: 15).

## Social background to immersion in Germany

In Germany, bilingual French-German education in *Gymnasien* (the most academic type of secondary school) arose from the treaty of Co-operation in 1963 between France and Germany. This was based on a desire for post-war reconciliation. Bilingual education aimed 'to arrive via linguistic comprehension at understanding and awareness between neighbours whose roots lay in common western European cultural background. Former sentiments of hereditary enmity which had historically influenced the relationships between France and Germany were to be replaced by the goal of partnership through the conscious fostering of neighbourly goodwill' (Mäsch, 1993: 155).

## Social background to Gaelic immersion in Scotland

In Scotland, Gaelic-medium primary education is certainly intended to provide learners with an education that does not suffer in comparison with English-medium education but in addition it has a fundamental role in helping to preserve and reinvigorate the Gaelic speech community which throughout most of the 20th century witnessed a serious decline in the numbers speaking it. Exactly the same applies in Wales for Welsh and in Ireland for Irish Gaelic.

Two points are worth noting in respect of the above examples. First, what has been given are the justifications for immersion. No claim is made here that all of these ambitious social aims are in fact achieved. Second, if we extrapolate to languages other than Gaelic in Scotland it is worth noting that, diverse and compelling though these reasons are, none of them would necessarily apply completely to (say) French, German, Spanish or Italian immersion in Scottish primary schools. This means that a different justification for foreign language immersion in Scotland would be required. It is not difficult to think of one, e.g. in relation to a new sense of multilingual European and global community and an intention through immersion to prepare pupils for full participation in it. The point is, however, that the justification and driving force have to come not so much from those with a research perspective or a national decision-making role as from those most directly involved: pupils, teachers, school management and parents. Much therefore would rest on a change taking place in public attitudes to languages in Scottish society and the extent to which sufficient numbers of interested persons would wish to commit themselves and their children to making this happen through immersion programmes.

### Immersion and socio-cultural ideology

Not that immersion is universally applauded in Canada. Several commentators have maintained that in French-speaking Quebec, for example, English-immersion programmes do not have the same momentum as French-immersion programmes in anglophone Canada, perhaps because of a fear that by immersing French-speaking children in English, Québecois parents may possibly be compromising their children's francophone identity. Moreover, 'anglophone Canadians disagree about how important it is to know French' (Nagy & Klaiman, 1988: 264). Safty's (1992a) review of the sociocultural implications of French immersion reveals an undercurrent of anglophone reservation. She refers to Allison's (1978) and Andrew's (1977) views that some opposition to French immersion came from those who discerned a Trudeauian 'master plan (Andrew, 1977) to increase the French-culture influence in Canada through the accumulation of *French power*' (Allison, 1978). Indeed, the title of Andrew's paper is '*Bilingual today, French tomorrow: Trudeau's master plan and how it can be stopped*' – all of which suggests that immersion programmes can be about much more than the acquisition of a second language or even the learning of other subject-matter through that language.

### Differing views about immersion attainments

Not only has immersion been criticised in Canada for its alleged underlying socio-political ideology but a minority have also contested its outcomes in terms of learners' attainments in the immersion language. Hammerley (1988) for example claims that many learners after hundreds of hours of immersion may have developed a working vocabulary, some degree of fluency and a capacity to make themselves understood but have formed defective grammatical habits. A more favourable view is taken by Pawley (1985), on the basis of a range of tests of communicative proficiency (involving reading, listening, speaking, writing, grammar) administered to early-entry and late-entry immersion learners. By Grade 11 the early-entry group had received well over 6000 hours of French immersion, compared with the roughly 3000 hours for the late-entry group. She concludes: 'Although the results … have not led us to a magical response to the question (How bilingual are French immersion students?), they have given indications of how profitable, in general, our graduates of immersion programmes are, particularly with respect to external criteria. We have seen that on a reading and grammar based test, although the students did not perform as well as Quebec francophone students, their results were nonetheless quite credible in comparison. It must be recalled again that there are not only students who have gone through immersion programmes and emerged with an excellent proficiency in the language, but also those whose ability seems still to be quite basic. One would suspect that the average student, described by the statistical results, could fairly easily become fluent in the language with greater and more constant exposure to French-speaking milieu' (Pawley, 1985: 874). Most scholars in fact consider that the second-language outcomes of immersion programmes are impressive, provided it is recognised that they cannot turn children into native-speakers of the second language.

### Changing views of bilingual education in Wales

In the UK the most extensive developments in immersion education have taken place in Wales. As in Scotland with Scottish Gaelic, there has been a consistent decline in the numbers of speakers of Welsh over the last century (over 900,000 in the 1911 UK census declining to under 500,000 in the 1991 census). For much of the last century bilingual education in Wales was perceived by some as having negative effects: Baker (1993a) citing an article in the *British Journal of Educational Psychology* 'connecting bilinguals with mental confusion and relatively lower school achievement compared to monolinguals' (Williams, 1960). Over the last four decades of the 20th century however there was a change of view concerning the benefits of bilingualism and a substantial increase in a range of forms of bilingual or Welsh-medium education. These include Designated Bilingual Schools, mainly in English-speaking urban areas and 'natural' Welsh schools in the mainly Welsh-speaking areas where the main medium of instruction is Welsh.

According to Baker, the reasons for the growth of bilingual or Welsh-medium education through what he terms a 'gentle revolution' (reminding us perhaps of *la révolution tranquille* that allowed Québecois cultural identity to assert itself as a reaction to the inroads of anglophone culture in Quebec) go far beyond any educational advantages that Welsh-English bilingualism may offer to individuals. 'The growth of nationalistic political consciousness, a reaction to the authoritarian imposition of the English language and Anglophone culture are similarly important external effects on the development of Welsh bilingual education' (Baker, 1993a: 9). By 1990 one in four children at primary school in Wales were being educated mostly or partly through Welsh; there were 417 Welsh-speaking or bilingual primary schools (24.1% of the national total) and 42 Welsh-speaking or bilingual secondary schools (17.7%). In addition there was a substantial rise in the number of secondary schools offering certain subjects through the medium of Welsh. As a result of the national curriculum Welsh is a core or foundation subject that is compulsory for all learners from 5 to 14 and the national assessments at 7, 11, 14 and 16 are available through Welsh as well as English.

### Immersion as a response to demographic decline

Welsh-medium and bilingual education in Wales are fundamental to the survival of the Welsh speech community. As Baker states: 'Simply stated, without the growth of bilingual education, there is good reason to believe the Welsh language would not survive' (Baker, 1993a: 23). This will of a speech community to survive and retain its cultural identity perhaps explains the commitment and dedication of teachers, as evidenced by a number of researchers from the 1980s onwards: 'One function of the school, to promote the Welsh language and culture, appears to provide teachers with increased motivation, commitment and sense of direction' (Baker, 1993a: 23).

## Core Features of Immersion Programmes

It is possible to establish a number of core features of immersion programmes. The list below owes much to the authoritative account provided by two of the world's leading authorities on immersion (Johnson & Swain, 1997). These are set out in Figure 1.

## Variable Features of Immersion Programmes

Johnson and Swain (1997) argue that immersion programmes also have a number of 'variable' features, e.g. the grade at which a programme is introduced; the amount of time devoted to the immersion language in comparison with the majority language of the school; the status of the immersion language. For example, French enjoys high status in Canada but the same has not applied to Scottish Gaelic in Scotland, though the status of this language is nowadays improving.

## Different Models of Immersion Education

A number of different 'models' of immersion have been developed, most of which contain the core features as described above but which differ from each other according to the 'variable' features. The main models are:

- Early total immersion
- Early partial immersion
- Delayed total immersion
- Delayed partial immersion
- Late total immersion
- Late partial immersion.

The 'early immersion' models usually begin from the start of primary schooling or in pre-primary education; the 'delayed' models usually begin in the middle to late primary school years; the 'late' models usually begin with adolescent learners at secondary school or with adults. 'Late total immersion' for example, is now being used in Scotland in order to bring adults (young and old) rapidly up to a high level of proficiency in Scottish Gaelic.

These six models constitute what Walker and Tedick (2000) call the 'macrocontext' of immersion education. It can be very helpful to parents and the public to know what each model delivers in terms of proficiency in the immersion language and mastery of subject content, so as to make informed choices on which model they might prefer for their children. However, Walker and Tedick rightly offer a word of caution in that these six models are in fact abstractions. They argue that there is also a 'microcontext' for immersion education where each school is different. Their study provides insight into the sorts of variable that affect immersion education at the micro-level.

## Features of Early Total Immersion

In early total immersion, the teacher speaks the immersion language from the start and uses a wide range of verbal and non-verbal techniques in order to help learners understand what is being said. The learners initially tend to go through a 'silent period' in which they develop comprehension skills in the immersion language and use their first language in order to express themselves. At some point (usually in Year 2) a productive competence in the L2 immersion language begins to show itself and by the end of Year 2 they have usually acquired fluency. A working hypothesis behind early total immersion programmes is that initially in respect of learning subject-matter at school the learners will lag behind their counterparts who are being educated through their first language. By the end of their primary schooling however they will have caught up with them, will suffer no disadvantage in respect of their first language and will have the additional advantage of having become highly fluent (though not totally bilingual) in a second language.

The Ottawa Board of Education (1996) identifies three conditions known to facilitate second language learning and has built these into its immersion programmes:

- An early start, during children's 'optimum age' for language learning.
- Intensive exposure to the language over an extended period.
- Use of the language for (non-trivial) communication. (OBE, 1996: 1)

Harley (1994) indicates that when immersion learners go to high school they will tend to select

- **L2 is the main or a major medium of instruction**. That is, learners study the L2 not only in order to learn it and become proficient in it but also in order to learn other subject-matter through it.
- **The immersion L2 curriculum parallels the local L1 curriculum.** This is normally considered necessary, in order to reassure both parents and educational decision-makers that immersion learners will not lose out on anything that is important in mainstream education.
- **Overt psychological and other support exists for the L1, both from parents and the school.** That is, immersion is not intended in any way to devalue or threaten a learner's first language. It is unlikely that this would be the case if a learner's L1 is the majority language of the country, but the situation could be very different if their L1 were an ethnic minority language.
  **The programme aims for additive bilingualism**. That is, it is designed to add to and strengthen a learner's language repertoire and to help them avoid falling between two languages and into a state described as 'semi-lingualism' in which they may have a surface fluency in their two languages but are unable to use either at a deeper, more cognitive level for the learning of serious subject-matter at school.
- **Exposure to the L2 is largely confined to the classroom.** That is, learners taking immersion programmes generally do not live in an area where their immersion L2 is spoken widely as a language of the community, though it may feature in the national media.
- **Learners generally enter with similar (and limited) levels of L2 proficiency.** In Canada, for example, a French immersion class would tend to consist of learners who do not have French as the language of the home.
- **The teachers are bilingual.** Or, if they are native speakers of the majority language, they are highly fluent in the immersion language. This enables primary school immersion teachers to understand what their first-grade learners are saying to them (since by definition at the start of an immersion programme learners will normally not be able to speak the immersion language) and at the same time to respond to them from the start in the 'immersion' language.

**Figure 1** Core features of immersion programmes
Adapted from Johnson & Swain, 1997

on average two subjects in French each year plus a course in French language arts, with the remainder of their schooling in English. Harley's (1994) review indicates a tendency for immersion classes to attract learners from backgrounds that are comparatively favoured socially, though this is not always the case. In some cities there are substantial numbers of immersion learners who come from minority community homes where one or other parent speaks a third language, and where the language of the home is not necessarily English.

## A View of the Conditions for Success

Some of the key conditions for the success of immersion programmes are set out by Branaman and Rennie (1997): 'In kindergarten through grade 6 all academic subjects (mathematics, science, social studies, and French language arts) are taught in French except English language arts (reading and spelling), which is introduced in grade 2. As in all other elementary schools,

the focus is on learning the subject-matter of the regular curriculum; the difference is that it is taught in French, providing an opportunity for learners to learn the regular curriculum while becoming fluent in another language. Important features of the program are co-ordination and communication at the district and school levels … a team of immersion teachers and the foreign language supervisor work together to ensure a strong academic curriculum, translating and adapting the regular curriculum into French … strong teaching skills and a high level of proficiency in the foreign language are extremely important to the success of the program … the total immersion program … enjoys a high degree of support from parents, teachers, staff and administrators' (Branaman & Rennie, 1997: 20).

## Pre-school Immersion

Early immersion does not necessarily begin at the start of primary school education. It may begin before then, as it often does at kindergarten in Canada. Pre-school schemes, often incorporating a mix of second-language immersion and first-language maintenance exist in many other countries or regions. These include Wales, Israel, Catalonia, the Basque region, the Netherlands, Finland, France, Italy, Luxembourg, Denmark, Belgium and Northern Ireland – plus Scotland itself through the Gaelic pre-school activity of *Comhairle nan Sgoiltean Araich* (Council of Nursery Schools). In the Republic of Ireland there has been a substantial growth in the number of *naíonrai* or Irish-medium pre-schools, amounting to over 190 by 1993, located in both the *Gaeltacht* (Irish-speaking) and *Galltacht* (English-speaking) parts. Hickey (1997) provides a comprehensive account of the *naíonrai* in respect of their origins, background, processes and outcomes. Hickey identifies the rationale behind the movement as being based on the belief that:

- pre-school education is beneficial to the child, family and community
- young children acquire a second language naturally in appropriate conditions
- pre-schooling through Irish assists in expanding the use of Irish in the realm of the family, which in turn helps to promote integration in the community. (Hickey, 1997: 4)

### Two-way immersion

In recent years a new variant of L2 immersion has been developed: two-way immersion. This tends to arise when a school draws on two language communities. Christian's (1996) review of the two-way immersion in the USA shows for example, that Hispanic and anglophone learners may share a common programme in which the Hispanic learners have Spanish as L1 and learn English as L2, while the reverse applies in the case of the anglophone learners. As a consequence, each learner experiences a bilingual Spanish-English programme. An advantage of two-way immersion is that learners are exposed not only to bilingual teachers but also to classmates who have the immersion language as their L1. Each language-group of learners therefore has a teaching role (i.e. helping the other language-group) and a learning role (i.e. learning from the other language-group). This can help to establish levels of cultural and linguistic equity that may serve broader educational goals such

as citizenship and respect for diversity. The goals of a two-way immersion programme in San José (USA) are stated as:

- learners will become bilingual and bi-literate (in Spanish and English) by the end of their seven-year program
- learners will experience academic success as demonstrated by achievement at or above grade level in all subject areas
- learners will acquire an appreciation and understanding of other cultures while developing positive attitudes toward themselves and their academic abilities (Branaman & Rennie, 1997: 22).

## Partial Immersion at Secondary School

### Subject-teaching via L2 at secondary school in Germany

Immersion is by no means confined to primary schools. A form of **late partial immersion**, sometimes called **content-teaching** or **content-based instruction**, is achieving increasing uptake across several European states and elsewhere in the world. Initially it tended to be adopted in 'European Schools' with learners from favoured social backgrounds whose professional parents in some cases had important 'European' posts but since the mid-1990s its range has been considerably broadened. Schmidt-Schönbein, Goetz and Hoffknecht (1994) report that by 1991/1992 a large number of initiatives in secondary schools in Germany had been introduced, with important subject matter (history, geography, biology, social studies, economics and technology) being taught by means of one of several languages (English – 118 initiatives, French – 52 initiatives plus others for Spanish, Dutch, Russian and Italian). Although statistical information on content-teaching in France does not seem available, discussion with members of the national inspectorate in France suggests a similar number.

In a highly informative account from an administrator's perspective, Mäsch (1993) outlines two models of bilingual education in German *Gymnasien* (academic secondary schools):

- the **additive model** consisting of French as a foreign language plus three disciplines (geography, politics/civics and history), each shared between two teachers one of whom has French as L1 and the other with German as L1, each teaching via their mother tongue; and

- the **integrative model** in which the teaching is done by teachers with French as L1, with the effect that each discipline is taught in a more integrated way.

*Bilingual Mention in German Abitur*

Mäsch reports that the integrative model has become by far the most common in Germany and has moved from being an experimental model to one that has become highly developed and consolidated. Students taking their Abitur (final examinations at secondary level) aim to obtain the 'Bilingual Mention' which exempts them from language examination upon entry to further studies in France. The next step, according to Mäsch, will be the implementation of arrangements which lead to the simultaneous acquisition of both the German *Abitur* and the French *Baccalauréat*.

*Subject-teaching via L2 at secondary school in Hungary*

Duff (1997) reports on bilingual education initiatives since 1985 in the Hungarian *gimnázium* schools which prepare 14–18 year-olds for university education. The immersion languages are English, German, French, Italian, Spanish or Russian and the subjects tend to be history, mathematics, geography, biology and physics. These are considered particularly suitable for immersion while chemistry, Hungarian, art, music, PE and optional subjects are taught in Hungarian. Both the German and the Hungarian examples show clearly that the immersion languages are not directed to subjects that are intellectually less demanding than the subjects covered by the national language; indeed, one might say 'on the contrary'.

*Subject-teaching via L2 at secondary school in England*

Several other countries in Europe and elsewhere have been piloting schemes based on content-teaching. Fruhauf, Coyle and Christ's (1997) volume on teaching content in a foreign language describes experiments in nine different European countries. This includes a chapter on England in which Coyle (1997) focuses in particular on two state schools. In one of them, a boys' comprehensive, the allocation of time was as set out in Figure 2.

At the other school (state comprehensive for girls) lessons were held during normal class hours. In both cases the provision was for the most able learners only.

*Subject-teaching via L2 at secondary school in Australia*

The Australian model of late immersion differs from most others in that: 'Students start cold with virtually no previous experience of the language, yet study academic subjects such as science, history and mathematics concurrently with acquiring basic language skills' (Read, 1996: 473). As an example in one particular school, over Years 8, 9 and 10 five core subjects are taught in French (maths, science, PE, social science and French), amounting to 1,600 hours of lessons. After Year 10 they resort to the monolingual curriculum but may continue with French in Years 11 and 12. Participation in the immersion programme is by choice, with students selected for aptitude. The reasons for the distinctive late-immersion cold-start approach in Australia are three-fold according to Read (1996): a general lack of articulation in Australia between primary and secondary education (possibly making early immersion a generally less strong option); an optimistic 'Have a go' attitude that Australians possess; and a general freedom of curricular decision-making in Australian schools.

**Immersion in post-school education**

Burger, Wesche and Migneron (1997) report on a form of immersion at university level at the University of Ottawa's Second Language Institute. There it is possible for students to take courses through the medium of their second language, with most take-up being by anglophone students with French as L2. In addition to taking courses in a range of subject disciplines they have available to them a set of 'adjunct' courses of advanced study in their L2 itself. These are tailored to the subject discipline course, e.g. in respect of strategies for understanding lectures, specialised terminology, and practice in researching and writing papers. Both types of course carry credit. A series of formal evaluations found consistent gains in second language proficiency for L2 students taking these courses and students were almost without exception successful in their subject-matter learning. They also generally reported greater self-confidence and lower anxiety in using the second language.

Read (1996) describes the world's first Initial

| Secondary education | Lessons per week (45 minutes) during school hours | Lessons per week outside school hours, e.g. early morning |
|---|---|---|
| Years 1 and 2 (aged 11–13) Compulsory. | 2 x Spanish 2 x geography in English. | |
| Year 3 (aged 13–14) Top ability group only. Compulsory. | 2 x Spanish (intensive) 2 x geography in Spanish. | |
| Year 4 (aged 14–15) Learner choice to continue. | 2 x Spanish (intensive) Take Spanish GCSE exam one year early. | 2 x geography in Spanish. (1 x early morning. 1 x after school.) |
| Year 5 (aged 15–16) As in Year 4. | 2 x geography in Spanish. Take geography GCSE exam in Spanish. | |

**Figure 2** Framework for teaching geography in Spanish: Boys' comprehensive school in England
Adapted from Coyle, 1997

Teacher Education (ITE) programme in Australia offered by means of immersion through Japanese, within LACITEP (Language and Culture Initial Teacher Education Programme). It is available to students who have completed Japanese to Year 12 at high school. Some of the ITE subjects are entirely in Japanese, others are partially so and others are in English. The programme offers a qualification for primary school teaching (general), for methods of teaching Japanese; for immersion education pedagogy; and for Asian Studies. The University of Southern Queensland, a world leader in distance education, has developed a semester-length unit on immersion teaching which is becoming accessible in several countries.

## Language Minorities: Beyond Submersion

There is a wide range of research bearing on subtractive bilingualism as a by-product of 'submersion'. However, it is beyond the scope of the present review to present this research, since the purpose of the review is to present research on additive bilingualism as a by-product of 'immersion'. Nonetheless, since immersion and submersion are often confused, it was considered appropriate to present some key ideas concerning language minorities and the 'submersion' of their first language.

The reader wishing to gain an overview of this issue has a range of excellent books on which to draw, e.g. Tosi and Leung, 1999; García and Baker, 1995; Genesee, 1994b; Baker, 1993b;

Baetens-Beardsmore, 1993; Skutnabb-Kangas and Cummins, 1988.

### Empowering language minority learners

One of the leading authorities on language minorities and second language learning, Cummins (1988) argues that language minority students become empowered through their education to the extent that:

- minority language students' language and culture are incorporated into the school programme;
- minority community participation is encouraged as an integral component of children's education;
- the pedagogy promotes intrinsic motivation on the part of students to use language actively in order to generate their own knowledge; and
- professionals involved in assessment become advocates for minority students by focusing primarily on the ways in which students' academic difficulty is a function of interactions within the school context rather than legitimising the location of the 'problem' with students (Cummins, 1988: 138).

Although he is one of the leading theorists of multilingual education, Cummins' (2001) study of the instructional conditions for trilingual development is intended to offer a practical discussion of how teachers within their weekly teaching approach might have three different sorts of focus as they seek to empower bi- or tri-lingual students, many of whom will be from minority language backgrounds. These are: focus on meaning by making input comprehensible and developing critical literacy; focus on language through awareness of language forms and uses and including critical analysis of language forms and uses; and focus on use, i.e. using language to generate new knowledge, to create literature and art and to act on social realities. Central to the approach is the development of critical literacy and the questioning of assumptions. This will be particularly beneficial to students from historically subordinated groups (many of whom have two or more languages) by enabling them (p. 74) 'to identify and challenge manifestations of coercive relations of power, e.g. the stigmatised status of certain nonstandard varieties of language'.

### Importance of L1 Literacy for Language Minority Learners

Reviewing the research on the relationship between L1 and L2 in the case of language minority (L1) students, Cummins claims:

> the implication of these data is that bilingual programs that strongly promote students' L1 literacy skills are viable means to promote academic development in English. The positive results of programs that continue to promote L1 literacy throughout elementary school can be attributed to the combined effects of reinforcing the students' cultural identity and their conceptual growth as well as to the greater likelihood of parental involvement in such programs (Cummins, 1994: 39).

### Differential time taken by language minority pupils to reach conversational and academic proficiency in English

Referring to his own research (Cummins, 1981) and to that of Collier (1987), Cummins concludes that:

> very different time periods are required for students to attain peer-appropriate levels in conversational skills in English as compared to academic skills. Specifically, while there will be major individual differences (Wong Fillmore, 1991), conversational skills often approach native-like levels within about two years of exposure to English, whereas

a period of four to nine years (Collier, 1987, 1989) or five to seven years (Cummins, 1981) of school exposure has been reported as necessary for second language students to achieve as well as native speakers in academic aspects of English (Cummins, 1994: 39).

This gap between the time it takes language minority students to acquire peer-appropriate levels of conversational fluency and academic skill in English has great significance for teachers. The very fluency with which such pupils speak English may lead in some cases to a false diagnosis in which such pupils are classi-fied as academically less able when in fact what they require is an appropriate amount of devel-opmental time in which to master academic skill in their second language.

### California: Proposition 227

If the research referred to above indicates a key role for a language minority learner's L1 in avoiding the negative effects of submer-sion, an alternative and competing approach has been developed in California, aimed at projecting language minority learners fast into English as L2. The passing of Proposi-tion 227 into California state legislation (1998) has been described as 'California's elimina-tion of bilingual education' (web-reference for Maceri, 1999). Proposition 227 requires all school students who do not have English as L1 to receive an intensive one-year programme of 'structured immersion' in English as a prelude to being transferred into mainstream English language classes. Protests have been raised (web-references for Mora, 1999; Minor, 1999) claiming that this will be disadvanta-geous to the students concerned. It is feared that they will not acquire literacy in their first language and therefore will have greater dif-ficulty in developing academic and literacy skills in English as L2, particularly as their subsequent progress will be evaluated prema-turely alongside that of their majority English L1 classmates. Another fear is that it will undermine two-way immersion programmes which by definition require the participation of students from two different language groups.

What underlies Proposition 227 is not clear. Perhaps it has to be understood in part at least as an attempt to re-assert a dominant role for the English language in a state where there are increasing numbers of Spanish speakers. If so, this would lend support to my earlier argument that in order to understand language education policy developments of this sort it is necessary to ask what socio-cultural issues lie concealed behind them.

# References

Allison, S. (1978) *French Power, the Francisation of Canada*. Richmond Hill, ON: BMG.

Andrew, J.V. (1977) *Bilingual Today, French Tomorrow: Trudeau's Master Plan and How It Can be Stopped*. Richmond Hill, ON: BMG.

Arenas i Sampera, J. (1994) The Catalan immersion programme: assessment and recent results. In C. Laurén (ed.) *Evaluating European Immersion Programmes. From Catalonia to Finland* (pp. 13–26). Vaasa, Finland: University of Vaasa.

Artigal, J.M. (1993) Catalan and Basque immersion programmes. In H. Baetens-Beardsmore (ed.) *Models of European Bilingual Education* (pp. 133–150). Clevedon: Multilingual Matters.

Baker, C. (1993a) *Foundations of Bilingual Education and Bilingualism*. Clevedon: Multilingual Matters.

Baker, C. (1993b) Bilingual education in Wales. In H. Baetens-Beardsmore (ed.) *European Models of Bilingual Education* (pp. 7–29). Bristol: London Press.

Baetens-Beardsmore, H. (ed.) *Models of European Bilingual Education*. Clevedon: Multilingual Matters.

Bel Gaya, A. (1994) Evaluating immersion peogrammes: the Catalan case. In C. Laurén (ed.) *Evaluating European Immersion Programmes. From Catalonia to Finland* (pp. 27–46). Vaasa, Finland: University of Vaasa.

Branaman, L. and Rennie, J. (1997) More ways to learn: Elementary school foreign language programs. In *ERIC Review K–12. Foreign Languages in Education* (pp. 14–23). Educational Resources Center, National Library of Education, Office of Educational Research and Improvement, US Department of Education.

Burger, S., Wesche, M. and Migneron, M. (1997) 'Late, late immersion': discipline-based second language teaching at the University of Ottawa. In K. Johnson and M. Swain (eds) *Immersion Education: International Perspectives* (pp. 85–102). Cambridge: Cambridge University Press.

Carleton Board of Education (1996) *Comparative Outcomes and Impacts of Early, Middle and Late Entry French Immersion Options: Review of Recent Research and Annotated Bibliography*. Ottawa: Carleton Board of Education.

Christian, D. (1996) Two-way immersion education: learners learning through two languages. *The Modern Language Journal* 80, 1, 66–76.

Collier, V.P. (1987) Age and rate of acquisition of second language for academic purposes. *TESOL Quarterly* 23, 509–532.

Collier, V.P. (1989) Future trends and challenges in French immersion. *Canadian Modern Language Review* 45, 3, 561–568.

Coyle, D. (1997) Language medium teaching in Britain. In G. Fruhauf, D. Coyle and I. Christ (eds) *Teaching Content in a Foreign Language: Practice and Perspectives in European Bilingual Education* (pp. 155–176). Alkmaar: Europees Platform.

Cummins, J. (1981) Age on arrival and immigrant second language learning in Canada. A reassessment. *Applied Linguistics* 2, 132–149.

Cummins, J. (1988) From multicultural to anti-racist education: an analysis of programmes and policies in Ontario. In T. Skutnabb-Kangas and J. Cummins (eds) *Minority Education* (pp. 127–160). Clevedon: Multilingual Matters.

Cummins, J. (1994) Knowledge, power and identity in teaching english as a second language. In F. Genesee (ed.) *Educating Second Language Children. The Whole Child, the Whole Curriculum, the Whole Community* (pp. 33–58). Cambridge: Cambridge University Press.

Cummins, J. (2001) Instructional conditions for trilingual development. *International Journal of Bilingual Education and Bilingualism* 4, 1, 61–75.

Doyé, P. (1997) Bilinguale Grundschulen. *Zeitschrift für Fremdsprachenforschung* 8, 2, 161–196.

Duff, P. (1997) Immersion in Hungary. An EFL experiment. In K. Johnson and M. Swain (eds) *Immersion Education: International Perspectives* (pp. 19–43). Cambridge: Cambridge University Press.

Fortune, T. and Jorsted, H.L. (1996) U.S. immersion programs: a national survey. *Foreign Language Annals* 29, 2, 163–190.

Fruhauf, G., Coyle, D. and Christ, I. (1997) *Teaching Content in a Foreign Language: Practice and Perspectives in European Bilingual Education*. Alkmaar: Europees Platform.

García, O. and Baker, C. (eds) (1995) *Policy and Practice in Bilingual Education. Extending the Foundations*. Clevedon: Multilingual Matters.

Gaudart, H. (1987) A typology of bilingual education in Malaysia. *Journal of Multilingual and Multicultural Development* 8, 6, 529–552.

Genesee, F. (1985) Second language learning

immersion: a review of US programs. *Review of Education Research* 55, 4, 541–561.

Genesee, F. (ed.) (1994a) *Integrating Language and Content: Lessons from Immersion.* Practice Report 11. McGill University: National Center on Cultural Diversity and Second Language Learning.

Genesee, F. (ed.) (1994b) *Educating Second Language Children. The Whole Child, the Whole Curriculum, the Whole Community.* Cambridge: Cambridge University Press.

Hammerley, H. (1988) French immersion: Does it work and the 'Development of bilingual proficiency' report. *Canadian Modern Language Review* 45, 3, 567–578.

Harley, B. (1991) Instructional strategies and SLA in early French immersion. *Studies in Second Language Acquisition* 15, 245–249.

Harley, B. (1994) After immersion: maintaining the momentum. *Journal of Multilingual and Multicultural Development* 15, 2&3, 229–244.

Hickey, T. (1997) *Early Immersion Education in Ireland: Na Naíonraí.* Institiúid Teangeloaíochta Eireann.

Johnson, K. and Swain, M. (eds) (1997) *Immersion Education: International Perspectives.* Cambridge: Cambridge University Press.

McLaughlin, B. (1984) Are immersion programs the answer for bilingual education in the United States? *Bilingual Review* 11, 1, 3–11.

Mäsch, N. (1993) The German model of bilingual education: an administrator's perspective. In H. Baetens-Beardsmore (ed.) *Models of European Bilingual Education* (pp. 155–172). Clevedon: Multilingual Matters.

Met, M. and Lorenz, L. (1997) Lessons from US immersion programs: Two decades of experience. In K. Johnson and M. Swain (eds) *Immersion Education: International Perspectives* (pp. 243–265). Cambridge: Cambridge University Press.

Nagy, P. and Klaiman, R. (1988) Attitudes to and impact of French immersion. *Canadian Journal of Education* 13, 2, 263–276.

Ottawa Board of Education (1996) *Comparative Outcomes and Impacts of Early, Middle and Late Entry French Immersion Options: Review of Recent Research and Annotated Bibliography.* OBE, 330 Gilmour Street, Ottawa, Canada K2P 0P9.

Pawley, C. (1985) How bilingual are French immersion learners? *Canadian Modern Language Review* 41, 5, 865–876.

Read, J. (1996) Recent developments in Australian late immersion language education.

*Journal of Multilingual and Multicultural Development* 17, 6, 469–484.

Safty, A. (1989) Some reflections on a decade in the French immersion classroom. *The Canadian Modern Language Review* 45, 3, 549–560.

Safty, A. (1992a) Effectiveness and French immersion: a socio-political analysis. *Canadian Journal of Education* 17, 1, 23–32.

Schmidt-Schönbein, G., Goetz, H. and Hoffknecht, V. (1994) Mehr oder anders? Konzepte, Modelle und Probleme des bilingualen Unterrichts. *Der Fremdsprachliche Unterricht* 1, 94, 6–11.

Skutnabb-Kangas, T. and Cummins, J. (eds) (1988) *Minority Education.* Clevedon: Multilingual Matters.

Snow, M.A. (1990a) Language immersion: an overview and comparison. In A.M. Padilla, H. Halford, D. Fairchild and C.M. Valadez (eds) *Foreign Language Education: Issues and Strategies* (pp. 109–126). London: Sage Publications.

Swain, M. and Lapkin, S. (1982) *Evaluating Bilingual Education: A Canadian Case-study.* Clevedon: Multilingual Matters.

Swain, M. and Lapkin, S. (1986) Immersion French in secondary schools: the 'goods' and the 'bads'. *Contact* 5, 3, 2–9.

Swain, M. and Lapkin, S. (1990) Aspects of the sociolinguistic performance of early and late French immersion learners. In R. Scarcella, E. Andersen and S. Krashen (eds) *Developing Communicative Competence in a Second Language* (pp. 41–54). New York: Newbury House.

Tosi, A. and Leung, C. (eds) (1999) *Rethinking Language Education: From a Monolingual to a Multilingual Perspective.* London: CILT.

Walker, C.L. and Tedick, D.J. (2000) The complexity of immersion education: teachers address the issues. *The Modern Language Journal* 84, 1, 5–27.

Williams, J.L. (1960) Comments on articles by Mr D.G. Lewis and Mr W.R. Jones. *British Journal of Educational Psychology* 30, 271–272.

Willig, A. (1982) The effectiveness of bilingual education: review of a report. *NABE Journal* VI, 2&3, 1–19.

Wolfe, A. (1994) *Immersion/Bilingual Approaches to Second Language Acquisition.* Aberdeen: Northern College, Language Research and Development Unit.

Wong Fillmore, L. (1991) Second language learning in children: A model of language learning in social context. In E. Bialystock (ed.) *Language Processing in Bilingual Children* (pp. 49–69). Cambridge: Cambridge University Press.

## Questions

1. What is 'immersion' in an immersion program? Define the linguistic goals, parental involvement, use of second language, use of first language, approaches to language learning, teacher characteristics and classroom structure of immersion education. How does this differ from the structure of a bilingual school with which you're familiar? How does this differ from mainstreaming/submersion education and structured immersion programs for language minority students in the United States? Why is the term 'immersion' inappropriate for minority language students?

2. What is the difference between early immersion, delayed immersion and late immersion? What is the difference between total immersion and partial immersion? What are the justifications for these different forms of immersion?

3. Describe the findings of early total immersion programs for students with regard to:
    a. students' first language literacy
    b. students' first language oracy
    c. students' second language literacy
    d. students' second language oracy
    e. students' academic achievement in math and science
    f. students' attitudes.

    What can you conclude from these results? If these programs have been so successful for Anglophone students in Quebec, why are they not recommended for Francophone students in Quebec nor for Latino students in the United States?

4. What are the social and political purposes of immersion education? Does this mean that there is immersion in more than language?

5. List the core and variable features of immersion programs. Then indicate which of these may be more connected to successful outcomes and attainments.

6. Is immersion education possible in secondary/high schools either extending elementary school immersion or as late partial immersion? Discuss this in a group and summarize your conclusions.

7. What are some of the differences between immersion bilingual education in Canada and in any one other country of your choosing?

## Activities

1. Role-play an imaginary scenario of activists trying to get an immersion bilingual education program started in your community. Enact different situations; for example, talking to the educational authorities, language specialists, parents, politicians, opposers, and potential students.

2. Survey a school community. Find out which languages are represented and how many children speak those languages. Make a graph showing your results. Then, interview a school administrator or teacher. Find out how languages are used in:
    a. education of language students when they are learners of a language
    b. education of language minority students when they are bilingual
    c. education of all students, including language majority students
    d. testing and assessment, including psychological and learning evaluations
    e. school life, including staffing (all jobs), assemblies, announcements, correspondence, offices

Make a chart with your results.

3.  Write your own Policy Document outlining a language policy that supports linguistic and cultural pluralism in education in your community. Make sure that you take your local community's sociolinguistic profile into account. Read your document to your class. The class may then select the document with the most appropriate language policy for education in that community. Read that language policy to a teacher or school administrator in your area. Write up their reactions and share them with the class.

4.  Write an imaginary story on the school life of Maria, a 2nd grade Spanish speaker who goes to a mainstream elementary school in the U.S. Then write a story on the imaginary school life of Jim, a Canadian 2nd grade student from an English-speaking home who is learning solely through the medium of French in an early total immersion school. Compare their stories.

5.  For a specific grade level, make a poster to celebrate the diversity of the world's languages.

6.  Design lessons on 'The Diversity of the World's Languages' to include details of the activities and materials used. Share the results with the class.

7.  Interview at least three people you know using the following quote taken from Baker's (2007) *Parents' and Teachers' Guide to Bilingualism* (Clevedon: Multilingual Matters). Focus on U.S. language minority children in submersion/mainstreaming and not in bilingual education.

> Children are born ready to become bilinguals and multilinguals. Too many are restricted to becoming monolinguals. No caring parent or teacher denies children the chance to develop physically, socially, educationally or emotionally. Yet we deny many children the chance to develop bilingually and multilingually.

Tape and transcribe your interviews. Share the main themes with the class.

Different groups might select to interview people with different characteristics. For example, the following characteristics might be considered: language majority vs. language minority, racial majority vs. racial minority, professional vs. working class, urban dweller vs. suburban dweller, speakers of international languages vs. speakers of community/heritage languages, bilingual speakers vs. monolingual speakers. Compare differences between groups. Make a summary chart of the class results.

## Further Reading

Baker, C. (2006) *Foundations of Bilingual Education and Bilingualism* (4th edition). Clevedon: Multilingual Matters (chapter 11).

Cenoz, J. and Genesee, F. (eds) (1998) *Beyond Bilingualism: Multilingualism and Multilingual Education.* Clevedon: Multilingual Matters.

Freeman, R. (1998) *Bilingual Education and Social Change.* Clevedon: Multilingual Matters.

Genesee, F. (ed.) (1999) *Program Alternatives for Linguistically Diverse Students.* Santa Cruz: Center for Research on Education, Diversity & Excellence, University of California.

Mejia, A-M. de (2002) *Power, Prestige and Bilingualism: International Perspectives on Elite Bilingual Education.* Clevedon: Multilingual Matters.

Swain, M. (1997) French immersion programs in Canada. In J. Cummins and D. Corson (eds), *Bilingual Education.* Volume 5 of the *Encyclopedia of Language and Education.* Dordrecht: Kluwer.

# Revitalising Indigenous Languages in Homogenising Times

## Teresa L. McCarty

## Introduction

At the dawn of the twenty-first century, the world's linguistic and cultural diversity is under assault by the forces of globalisation – cultural, economic and political forces that work to standardise and homogenise, even as they stratify and marginalise. In the transnational flow of wealth, technology and information, the currency of 'world' languages is enormously inflated, while that of local languages is flattened and devalued. Pattanayak (2000) writes, 'By luring people to opt for globalisation without enabling them to communicate with the local and the proximate, globalisation is an agent of cultural destruction' (p. 47).

These pressures seriously threaten minority linguistic, cultural, and educational rights. In this article, I focus on the struggle for linguistic, cultural, and educational self-determination among Native people in the United States. Of 175 languages indigenous to what is now the USA, only 20 are being naturally acquired by children (Krauss, 1998). 'Our languages are in the penultimate moment of their existence in the world', Northern Cheyenne language activist Richard Littlebear (1996) warns:

> Other American languages are perpetuated by the periodic influx of immigrants . . . Our languages do not have the luxury of this influx . . . They are vulnerable because they exist in the macrocosm of the English language and its awesome ability to displace and eliminate other languages. (p. xiv)

Littlebear is among a small but growing group of committed and informed language educators working to reverse language loss. It is a race against time (Sims, 2001a), for, as Littlebear (1996) observes, Indigenous people have nowhere to turn but their own communities to replenish the pool of heritage language speakers. Increasingly, Native speakers are primarily the elderly. Krauss (1998, pp. 11–12) estimates that for 125 of 175 indigenous languages still spoken in the USA, the speakers represent the 'grandparental generation and up', including 55 languages (31%) spoken only by the very elderly. In a very real sense, Indigenous language loss is terminal (Warner, 1999, p. 72). 'When an indigenous group stops speaking its language, the language disappears from the face of the earth', writes linguist Leanne Hinton (2001, p. 3).

When even one language falls silent, the world loses an irredeemable repository of human knowledge. Nettle and Romaine (2000) observe that

> Every language is a living museum, a monument to every culture it has been a vehicle to. It is a loss to every one of us if a fraction of that diversity disappears when there is something that can have been done to prevent it (p. 14).

More fundamentally, language loss and revitalisation are human rights issues. Through our mother tongue, we come to know, represent, name, and act upon the world. Humans do not naturally or easily relinquish this birthright. Rather, the loss of a language reflects the exercise of power by the dominant over the disenfranchised, and is concretely experienced 'in the concomitant destruction of intimacy, family and community' (Fishman, 1991, p. 4). Thus, efforts to revitalise Indigenous languages cannot be divorced from larger struggles for democracy, social justice, and self-determination (see May, 2001).

The causes of language shift in Native North American communities are as complex as the history of colonisation. Genocide, territorial

usurpation, forced relocation, and transformations of Native economic, cultural and social
systems brought on by contact with Whites,
are all complicit in language attrition. These
causes have been detailed elsewhere and I will
not elaborate on them here (see, for example,
Crawford, 1995a, 1996, 2000; McCarty, 1998,
2001, 2002; Watahomigie & McCarty, 1996). It is
nonetheless important to highlight the singular
role of compulsory English-only schooling in
promoting language loss. For more than two
centuries, schools were the only institutions both
to demand exclusive use of English and prohibit
use of the mother tongue (Kari & Spolsky, 1973,
p. 32). 'There is not an Indian pupil . . . who is
permitted to study any other language than our
own', the US Commissioner of Indian Affairs
wrote in 1887, articulating a federal policy that
would remain in effect for much of the next
century (cited in Crawford, 1992, p. 49). For
many federal boarding school graduates, that
policy left scars of shame and ambivalence about
the Native language, leading them to socialise
their children in English. The words of a young
Hualapai man express the experience of many
adults today:

> I was not taught my language. My mom
> says my dad didn't want us to learn,
> because when he was going through school
> he saw what difficulty *his* peers were having
> because they learned Hualapai first, and
> the schools were all taught in the English
> language. And so we were not taught, my
> brothers and I. (Watahomigie & McCarty,
> 1996, p. 101)

Paradoxically, schools and bilingual education
programmes have become prime arenas for
language reclamation, particularly where those
schools are under at least a modicum of Indigenous community control (Dick & McCarty, 1996;
Greymorning, 1997; Hinton & Hale, 2001; Holm
& Holm, 1990, 1995; McCarty & Watahomigie,
1999; Watahomigie & McCarty, 1996; Wilson,
1998). In this article, I examine these efforts,
focusing on recent developments in heritage
language immersion in the USA. Language
immersion, which provides all or most of children's instruction in the target or heritage
language, is increasingly the pedagogy of
choice among Indigenous communities seeking
to produce a new generation of fluent Native
language speakers.

My analysis is based on 25 years of work
with Indigenous communities as an ethnographer, teacher and collaborator in local, state
and national language education programmes.
I situate this analysis within research on second
language acquisition and bilingual education,
and within a critical theoretical framework that
acknowledges and works to transform coercive
relations of power. Specifically, I address two
questions: How effective have Indigenous
language reclamation efforts been in promoting
children's bi/multilingualism and their success
in school? Here, I define success as equality of
opportunity to achieve, through schooling,
personal, Indigenous community, and larger
societal educative goals. Second, what impacts
have Indigenous language reclamation efforts
had on reversing language shift?

My assumption throughout this analysis is that
local languages are irreplaceable intellectual, social
and cultural resources to their speakers and to
humankind (Ruiz, 1984). I begin with an overview
of the current state of knowledge on bilingual/
bicultural education and second language
acquisition, contextualising that knowledge base
within the USA and Canada. I then present data
on three well-documented Indigenous immersion
programmes and a large-scale comparative
research project currently under way. I conclude
by considering the challenges faced by Indigenous communities in retaining their languages
in the face of globalisation and the concomitant
homogenising and polarising pressures it yields.

## Foundational Research on Bilingual Education and Second Language Acquisition

Research in the fields of education, linguistics, anthropology and cognitive psychology is
unequivocal on one point: students who enter
school with a primary language other than the
national or dominant language perform significantly better on academic tasks when they
receive consistent and cumulative academic
support in the native/heritage language. In a
Congressionally mandated study that followed
over 2000 native Spanish-speaking elementary
students for four years, Ramírez (1992) found
that students who received 40% or more of their
instruction in Spanish throughout their elementary school education performed significantly
better on tests of English reading, oral English,
and mathematics than students in English-
only and early-exit bilingual programmes. A

subsequent investigation by Ramírez of 12,000 students in the San Francisco Unified School District showed that students who received instructional support in their native language for five years before being transitioned to all-English classes outperformed students in all-English classrooms on the Comprehensive Test of Basic Skills.[1] Further, students in long-term or late-exit bilingual education realised a higher overall grade point average and had the highest attendance rates, 'always exceeding the district average' (Ramírez, 1998, p. 1). And in the most extensive longitudinal study of language minority student achievement to date (1982–1996), Thomas and Collier (1997) found that for 700,000 students representing 15 languages in five participating school systems, 'the most powerful predictor of academic success' (p. 39) was schooling for at least four to seven years in the native/heritage language. Here, 'academic success' was defined as 'English learners reaching . . . full parity with native-English speakers in all school content subjects (not just English proficiency) after a period of at least 5–6 years' (Thomas & Collier, 1997, p. 7). What is especially important about the Thomas and Collier study is that these findings held true for children who entered school with no English background, children raised bilingually from birth, and 'children dominant in English who [were] losing their heritage language' (Thomas & Collier, 1997, p. 15). The latter characteristics closely parallel those of Native American learners today.

These studies support earlier research showing that it takes children four to seven years to reach grade-level norms on assessments of cognitively demanding academic tasks in the second language (Cummins, 1981, 1986). This time is necessary to develop cognitive academic language proficiency, the ability to use a second language for context-reduced and intellectually challenging tasks, including literacy (Cummins, 1986, 1989, 1996). As Cummins and others have noted, while second language learners are developing these proficiencies, native speakers – especially those from the privileged social classes – are not 'standing still'. Time and exposure to comprehensible second language input in intellectually challenging and socially significant activity are necessary for second language learners to 'close the gap' (Cummins, 1981; Krashen, 1996; Thomas & Collier, 1997).

The US research is supported by studies of second language learning from around the world (see, for example, Cummins & Corson, 1997; Genesee, 1994; Grosjean, 1982; Hakuta, 1986; Skutnaab-Kangas & Cummins, 1988; Troike, 1978; Tucker, 1980). Of particular note is research on French immersion programmes in Canada, in which monolingual English-speaking children receive all instruction in French for the first several years of school, after which formal English instruction is introduced for a portion of the school day. With each successive year, other content area subjects are taught in English until a 50–50 French-English instructional approach is reached by grade 6. Long-term studies of Canadian immersion show, first, that children's proficiency in French increased without detriment to their English abilities or acquisition of academic content (Genesee, 1987). Moreover, this research indicates that this process is cumulative: the 'ability to function in context-reduced cognitively demanding tasks in the second language is a gradual learning process . . . indicated by the fact that immersion students take up to six to seven years to demonstrate average levels of achievement in the second language relative to speakers of the language' (Cummins & Swain, 1986, p. 56).

Participants in Canadian French immersion programmes have typically been the children of White, middle-class parents who desired an academic enrichment programme for their children. These are children whose mother tongue, far from being threatened, is the language of global power and prestige. As a group, these students have, historically, done well in school. This situation differs markedly from that of Native American learners, whose languages and identities have been the target of explicit school-based eradication campaigns, and whose parents and communities have been economically, politically and socially oppressed. Further, Indigenous students' language backgrounds are more varied and complex: they may enter school speaking the Native language as a primary language, have a passive understanding of the heritage language, or have no heritage language proficiency at all. Their situation is also complicated by the varieties of English spoken within Indigenous communities, which are typically modified by the structures and use patterns of the heritage language (see, for example, Henze & Vanett, 1993; Leap, 1977). Hence, even though more Indigenous students speak English as a first language, they are likely to be stigmatised as 'limited English proficient' and to be 'fore-ordained for failure by being labeled *at risk*' (Ricento & Wiley, 2002, p. 3).

In the next section, I examine the ways in which research on bilingual schooling among non-Indigenous learners applies to the unique characteristics of Indigenous language education. In particular, I consider the ways in which Indigenous bilingual/bicultural education programmes have transformed historically subtractive, deficit-oriented schooling into an additive, enrichment approach – a pedagogy 'associated with superior school achievement around the world' ('Thomas & Collier, 1997, p. 16).

## Foundational Research on Native American Bilingual/Bicultural Education

Although published studies are limited, the positive effects of well-implemented Native American bilingual education programmes are well documented. In the early 1970s, the Navajo community school at Rock Point, Arizona, began one of the first modern Indigenous literacy programmes.[2] Initial data from Rock Point demonstrated that monolingual Navajo-speaking children who learned to read first in Navajo not only outperformed comparable Navajo students in English-only programmes, but also surpassed their own previous annual growth rates and those of comparison-group students in Bureau of Indian Affairs schools (Rosier & Farella, 1976). In a 25-year retrospective analysis of the Rock Point programme, programme cofounders Agnes Holm and Wayne Holm (1990, pp. 182–184) describe the 'four-fold empowerment' engendered through bilingual education there: of the Navajo school board, who 'came to acquire increasing credibility with parents, staff, and students'; of the Navajo staff, whose vision and competence were recognised by outside observers as well as community members; of parents, who for the first time played active roles in their children's schooling; and of students, who 'came to value their Navajo-ness and to see themselves as capable of succeeding because of, not despite that Navajo-ness' (see also Holm & Holm, 1995).

Forty miles south-west of Rock Point is Rough Rock, the site of the first American Indian community-controlled school. I have been active at Rough Rock as a researcher, curriculum writer and consultant to the school's bilingual/bicultural programme for more than 20 years (see,

for example, McCarty, 1989, 1998, 2001, 2002). From 1988 to 1995, Rough Rock teachers and I conducted a long-term study of the development of Rough Rock students' bilingualism and biliteracy using both qualitative and quantitative methods (Begay *et al.*, 1995; Dick & McCarty, 1996; McCarty, 1993, 2002; McCarty & Dick, 2003). Our focus was the K–6 Rough Rock English-Navajo Language Arts Programme (RRENLAP). In this study, we followed a cohort of students who had received consistent, uninterrupted bilingual instruction during their first four years of school, including initial literacy in Navajo, and compared these students' performance on standardised and local assessments with that of Rough Rock students who had not participated in RRENLAP. Although both student cohorts scored below national norms on standardised tests, RRENLAP students consistently outperformed the comparison group on national and local measures of achievement (Begay *et al.*, 1995; McCarty, 1993). On local assessments of English listening comprehension, RRENLAP kindergarteners posted mean scores of 58% at the end of the 1989–90 school year. After four years in the programme, the same students' mean scores rose to 91% (McCarty, 1993). On standardised reading sub-tests, these students' scores initially declined, then rose steadily, in some cases approaching national norms. Further, there was strong evidence of teacher, student and parental empowerment, as Navajo teachers discarded basal readers and scripted skill-and-drill routines and organised instruction around cooperative learning centres and culturally relevant themes. Parents and elders were actively involved in these pedagogical changes, assisting in students' field-based research projects, serving as language models and instructors, and providing cultural demonstrations in Navajo both inside and outside of school.

Our analysis revealed several conditions underlying these outcomes. First and foremost was the presence of a stable core of bilingual educators with shared values and aspirations for their students. Second, teachers received long-term support from the building principal and from outside experts, including educators from the Hawai'i-based Kamehameha Early Education Programme (KEEP). Third, the project received consistent funding over several years, a rare occurrence in American Indian schools, which are the most poorly funded in the USA. These conditions promoted a school culture that valued local expertise and encouraged teachers to reflect critically on their teaching, take risks in enacting instructional reform, and act as agents of positive change. As these conditions became normalised within the elementary school, Native teachers were able to create parallel conditions in their classrooms whereby students could act as critical agents and inquirers in Navajo and English (McCarty & Dick, 2003; see also Begay *et al.*, 1995; Lipka & McCarty, 1994).

Lipka *et al.* (1998) document similar processes of Native teacher, student, and community empowerment for the Yup'ik of southwestern Alaska, where Native teacher-leaders (the *Cuilistet*) worked in apprentice relationships with elders to bring Indigenous knowledge into science and mathematics instruction. Lipka *et al.* report, 'In hindsight, . . . we chose methods that provided insight into the processes that can reverse cultural and linguistic loss' (1998, p. 219; see also Lipka & McCarty, 1994). And among the Hualapai of north-western Arizona, a national bilingual/bicultural demonstration project produced the first practical Hualapai orthography and grammar, an integrated K-8 Hualapai curriculum, and a cadre of certified Native teachers. Long-term studies of the Hualapai programme show significant student gains on standardised and local assessments, as well as improvements in student attendance and graduation rates (Watahomigie & McCarty, 1994, 1996; Watahomigie & Yamamoto, 1987).

In each of these cases, the benefits to students correspond directly to the development and use of curricula grounded in local languages and knowledges, and to the cultivation of a critical mass of Native educational practitioners. These processes can be described as 'bottom-up' language planning: emanating from within Indigenous communities, these initiatives created a means of empowerment for Native teachers, children and communities. Hornberger (1996) notes that such empowerment 'Importantly . . . is one that confirms indigenous identity, language, and culture, while simultaneously promoting development and modernization for the indigenous peoples' (p. 361).

As promising as these achievements are, they have not been sufficient to counter the forces of language displacement and loss. As McLaughlin observes, 'You pave roads, you create access to a wage economy, people's values change, and you get language shift' (cited in Crawford, 1995b, p. 190; see also Lee & McLaughlin, 2001). These realities have led many Native communities to institute full heritage language immersion as a tool for language recovery, cultural survival and academic enrichment. Applying lessons learned from 'superimmersion' models in Canada (Genesee, 1987; Warner, 2001), Māori immersion in New Zealand (May, 1999), and from research such as that reported here, Indigenous language immersion programmes provide all or most instruction in the endangered language. 'There is no doubt that this is the best way to jump-start the production of a new generation of fluent speakers', Hinton (2001, p. 8) states. As the following sections illustrate, Indigenous language immersion programmes are proving to be successful in enhancing Native students' academic achievement as well.

## Hawaiian Immersion

Indigenous immersion in Hawai'i is arguably the most dramatic language revitalisation success story to date, certainly within the US context. From a long and rich tradition in which Hawaiian served as the language of government, religion, business, education, and the media, Hawaiian by the mid-twentieth century had become restricted to a few hundred inhabitants of one island enclave. The European invasion, which began with Captain James Cook's arrival in 1778, had decimated the Native population and disenfranchised survivors from traditional lands. In 1898, following the illegal takeover of the Hawaiian monarchy by the US military, Hawai'i was annexed as a US territory. In 1959, it became the 50th state.

Bans on Hawaiian-medium instruction, and mandates that all government business be conducted in English, further diminished the viability of Hawaiian as a mother tongue. According to Warner (2001, p. 135), between 1900 and 1920, most Hawaiian children began speaking a local variety of English called Hawaiian Creole English. Not until the 1960s, in the context of broader civil rights reforms, did a resistance or 'Hawaiian renaissance' movement take root. 'From this renaissance came a new group of second-language Hawaiian speakers who would become Hawaiian language educators', writes Warner (2001, p. 135).

In a 1978 constitutional convention, Hawaiian and English were designated co-official languages. At the same time, the new constitution mandated the promotion of Hawaiian language, culture and history (Warner, 2001). Encouraged by these developments and the example of the

Te Kōhanga Reo or Māori pre-school immersion 'language nests' in New Zealand, a small group of parents and language educators began to establish a similar programme in Hawai'i (Warner, 2001, p. 136; Wilson, 1998, 1999).

The Hawaiian immersion pre-schools or *Aha Pūnana Leo* ('language nest gathering', Wilson & Kamanā, 2001, p. 149), are designed to strengthen the Hawaiian *mauli* – culture, worldview, spirituality, morality, social relations, 'and other central features of a person's life and the life of a people' (Wilson & Kamanā, 2001, p. 161). The family-run pre-schools, begun in 1983, enable children to interact with fluent speakers entirely in Hawaiian. 'The original concept of the Pūnana Leo,' programme co-founders William H. Wilson and Kauanoe Kamanā write, was not 'academic achievement for its own sake', but rather the re-creation of an environment 'where Hawaiian language and culture were conveyed and developed in much the same way that they were in the home in earlier generations' (2001, p. 151). Wilson and Kamanā (2001) describe a typical 'Pūnana Leo day':

> There is a first circle in the morning, where the children participate in . . . singing and chanting, hearing a story, exercising, learning to introduce themselves and their families . . ., discussing the day, or . . . some cultural activity. This is followed by free time, when children can interact with different materials to learn about textures, colors, sizes, and so on, and to use the appropriate language based on models provided by teachers and other children. Then come more structured lessons [on] pre-reading and pre-math skills, social studies, and the arts . . . Children then have outdoor play, lunch, and a nap, then story time, a snack, a second circle, and outdoor play until their parents come to pick them up again. (pp. 151–152)

As Pūnana Leo students prepared to enter Hawai'i's English-dominant public schools, their parents pressed the state for Hawaiian immersion elementary and secondary schools. Parental boycotts and demonstrations led to the establishment of immersion 'schools-within schools' – streams or tracks within existing school facilities. The exception is one full-immersion school serving children from birth through grade 12 (Warner, 2001). In these schools, children are educated entirely in Hawaiian until fifth grade,

when English language arts is introduced, often in Hawaiian. 'English continues to be taught for one hour a day through high school,' Kamanā and Wilson (1996) state; 'intermediate and high school aged children are also taught a third language' (p. 154).

As of 2001, there were 11 full-day, 11-month immersion pre-schools, and the opportunity for an education in Hawaiian extended from pre-school to graduate school (see Table 1). In 1999–2000, the total pre-K–12 enrolment in Hawaiian immersion schools was 1,760, and approximately 1,800 children had learned to speak Hawaiian through immersion schooling (Warner, 1999, 2001; Wilson, 1999). Wilson and Kamanā (2001) cite two other language revitalisation accomplishments: the development of an interconnected group of young parents who are increasing their proficiency in Hawaiian, and the creation of a more general environment of language support. 'Families speak Hawaiian with their children in supermarkets and find that they are congratulated for doing so by individuals of all ethnic backgrounds', Wilson and Kamanā (2001, p. 153) write.

> Pūnana Leo children are invited to sing in . . . public malls . . . Hawaiian-speaking children are also invited to participate through Hawaiian in the inauguration of [state and community] officials . . . Most importantly, the Pūnana Leo provides a reason for the establishment of official use of Hawaiian in the state's public school system. (Wilson & Kamanā, 2001, pp. 153–154)

Although the programme has emphasised language revitalisation as opposed to academic achievement, Hawaiian immersion schooling has yielded significant academic benefits. Immersion students have garnered prestigious scholarships, enrolled in college courses while still in high school, and passed the state university's English composition assessments, despite receiving the majority of their English, science, and mathematics instruction in Hawaiian. Student achievement on standardised tests has equalled and in some cases surpassed that of Native Hawaiian children enrolled in English-medium schools, even in English language arts (Kamanā & Wilson, 1996; Wilson & Kamanā, 2001). There is also evidence that Hawaiian immersion develops students' critical literacy and cultural pride. 'I understand who I am as a Hawaiian, and where Hawaiians

**Table 1** Hawaiian Immersion Programme, 1999

---

**Pre-K Immersion**

- 11 private, community-based '*Aha Pūnana Leo* pre-schools

**Hawaiian-medium Public Schools**

*Kula Kaiapuni Hawai'i* (Hawaiian Environment Schools), with Hawaiian immersion and English-in-Hawaiian:
- 10 elementary sites
- 3 intermediate sites
- 1 intermediate/high school site
- 1 comprehensive pre-K–12 site

**Institutions of Higher Education**

- Language Centre for teacher preparation, outreach, and curriculum development
- College of Hawaiian language
- Hawaiian Studies departments

---

*Source*: Wilson, 1998, 1999; Wilson & Kamanā, 2001

stood, and where they want to go', a graduate of pre-K–12 immersion schooling states (Infante, 1999, p. E3).

These results have not materialised without substantial struggle or setbacks. For years, the programme fought outdated state laws and regulations that, among other things, prevented Native speakers from obtaining state-required certification to teach in the pre-schools (Warner, 2001). There has also been conflict within the revitalisation movement itself over authority, representation and authenticity of language use norms (Warner, 1999, 2001; Wong, 1999). Finally, Hawaiian is still largely restricted to the domain of schooling, which, as Warner (2001, p. 141) notes, is not in itself sufficient to reverse language shift. Nevertheless, immersion schooling has succeeded in strengthening the Hawaiian *mauli*, awakening consciousness and self-determination within the Native Hawaiian community, and enhancing children's academic success. In the process, the programme has served as a model and a catalyst for Indigenous language reclamation efforts throughout the USA.

## Navajo Immersion

Navajo belongs to the Athabaskan language family, one of the most widespread Indigenous language families in North America. Navajo itself is spoken primarily in the Four Corners region of the US Southwest, where the 25,000-square mile Navajo Nation stretches over parts of Arizona, New Mexico and Utah. With a history of Indigenous literacy spanning back to the nineteenth century (and perhaps the finest Indigenous language dictionary in print),[3] Navajo claims the largest number of speakers – approximately 150,000 – of any Indigenous language group north of Mexico (Hale, 2001; see also Crawford, 1995a).

These characteristics notwithstanding, Navajo is no longer the primary language of a growing number of school-age children. In a 1991 survey of 682 Navajo pre-schoolers, Platero (1992, 2001) found that over half were considered by their teachers to be English monolinguals. In 1993, Holm conducted a study of over 3,300 kindergarteners in 110 Navajo schools and found, similarly, that only half spoke any Navajo and less than a third were considered reasonably fluent speakers of Navajo (Holm & Holm, 1995; Wayne Holm, personal communication, February 14, 2000). My own recent work at Rough Rock suggests that about 50% of Rough Rock elementary students speak Navajo, and that their numbers and Native language proficiencies are declining each year. Some Rough Rock teachers place the numbers of Navajo-proficient primary school students much lower, at 30%. The escalating nature of the language loss crisis is illustrated in the fact that, just 30 years ago, Spolsky found that 95% of Navajo six-year-olds spoke fluent Navajo on entering school (Spolsky, 1976, 2002; Spolsky & Holm, 1977).

Given these statistics, the Navajo Nation has initiated a major language immersion effort in Head Start pre-schools, and a number of K–12 schools have launched language immersion programmes. One of the better documented programmes operates at the public elementary school in Fort Defiance, Arizona, adjacent to the tribal headquarters in Window Rock and very near the reservation border. Fort Defiance is an 'emerging reservation town'; cross-cut by two major highways, it is a small hub of commercial activity with a growing urbanising professional class – individuals who may have ties to the land and traditional pastoral-agricultural life-styles, but who tend to interact primarily in English (Arviso & Holm, 2001). When the Fort Defiance immersion programme began in 1986, less than a tenth of the school's five-year-olds were 'reasonably competent' Navajo speakers (Holm & Holm, 1995, p. 148). Only a third were judged to possess passive knowledge of Navajo (Arviso & Holm, 2001, p. 204). At the same time, 'a relatively high proportion of the English monolinguals had to be considered "limited English proficient"', Holm and Holm report (1995, p. 148). That is, students possessed conversational English proficiency, but were less proficient in more decontextualised uses of English (Arviso & Holm, 2001, p. 205; see Cummins, 1989, pp. 29–32, for a discussion of conversational and academic language proficiencies). In this context, neither conventional maintenance nor transitional bilingual programmes were appropriate. According to the programme cofounders, 'something more like the Maori immersion programmes might be the only type of programme with some chance of success' (Arviso & Holm, 2001, p. 205).

The initial curriculum was kept simple: developmental Navajo, reading and writing first in Navajo, then English, and maths in both languages, with other subjects included as content for speaking or writing (Holm & Holm, 1995, pp. 149–150). The programme placed a heavy emphasis on language and critical thinking, and on process writing and co-operative learning. In the lower grades, all communication occurred in Navajo. By the second and third grades, the programme included a half-day in Navajo and a half-day in English. Fourth graders received at least one hour each day of Navajo instruction. In addition, programme leaders insisted that an adult caretaker or relative 'spend some time talking with the child in Navajo each evening after school' (Arviso & Holm, 2001, p. 210). In fact, the degree of parental involvement has been quite impressive:

> Although the immersion program never constituted more than one-sixth of the total enrollment . . . there were almost always more people at the potluck meetings of the immersion programme than there were at the schoolwide parent–teacher meetings. We began to realize . . . that we had reached a number of those parents who had been 'bucking the tide' in trying to give their child(ren) some appreciation of what it meant to be Navajo in the late 20th century. (Arviso & Holm, 2001, p. 211)

Table 2 summarises findings from the project's first seven years. By the fourth grade, Navajo immersion students performed as well on local tests of English as comparable non-immersion students at the school. Immersion students performed better on local assessments of English writing, and were 'way ahead' on standardised tests of mathematics, discriminatory as these tests are (Holm & Holm, 1995, p. 150). On standardised tests of English reading, students were slightly behind, but closing the gap. In short, immersion students were well on their way to accomplishing what research indicates on bilingual education around the world: they were acquiring Navajo as a heritage language 'without cost', performing as well as or better than their non-immersion peers by the fifth grade (Holm & Holm, 1995, p. 150; Arviso & Holm, 2001, pp. 211–212).

An additional finding from the Fort Defiance study is worthy of special note. By fourth grade, not only did Navajo immersion students outperform comparable non-immersion students on assessments of Navajo, but non-immersion students actually performed *lower* on these assessments than they had in kindergarten (see Table 2). There is much debate about what schools can and cannot do to reverse language shift (see, for example, Fishman, 1991; Krauss, 1998; McCarty, 1998). The Fort Defiance data demonstrate the powerful negative effect of the *absence* of bilingual/immersion schooling and, conversely, its positive effect on the maintenance

**Table 2** Comparison of Fort Defiance Navajo Immersion (NI) and Monolingual English (ME) Student Performance

| Assessment | NI Students | ME Students |
|---|---|---|
| Local evaluations of English | Same as ME students | Same as NI students |
| Local assessment of Navajo | Better than ME students | Worse than NI students and worse than their own kindergarten performance |
| Local assessments of English writing | Better than ME students | Worse than NI students |
| Standardised tests of mathematics | Substantially better than ME students | Worse than NI students |
| Standardised tests of English reading | Slightly behind but catching up with ME students | Slightly ahead of NI students |

*Source*: Arviso & Holm, 2001, pp. 211–212; Holm & Holm, 1995, p. 150

of the heritage language as well as on students' acquisition of English and mathematics.

If Navajo – still the most vital Indigenous language in the USA – is a 'test case' for Indigenous language revitalisation (Slate, 1993), then the Fort Defiance programme is a model for school-based possibilities in reversing language shift. Like the Hawaiian experience, however, data from Fort Defiance clearly show that school-based efforts must be joined by family- and community-based initiatives as well. These data also suggest the ways in which such efforts can be nurtured by schools and their personnel. In the next section, I describe a very different approach – one initiated and undertaken outside schools entirely.

## Keres Immersion

The Pueblos of the US Southwest are among the most ancient and enduring Indigenous communities in North America. Altogether, there are 20 Pueblo tribes, including the Hopis of northern Arizona, with the remaining 19 located along the Rio Grande and Rio Puerco in northern New Mexico. Four language families are represented among the New Mexico Pueblos. In this section, I focus on the Keres-speaking Pueblos of Acoma and Cochiti, both of which are actively involved in language reclamation.

Located 64 miles west of Albuquerque, Acoma Pueblo has a tribal enrolment of 5,000, approximately 3,000 of whom live on the quarter-million acre Acoma reservation (Sims, 2001b). While retaining a traditional matrilineal clan system and a governing system of secular officials appointed annually by religious leaders, Acoma participates vigorously in the wider economy, including tourism, marketing the famed pottery of its artisans, and operating a large tribal casino.

The 58,000-acre Pueblo of Cochiti is located further north, about 30 miles south-west of Santa Fe at the base of the Jemez Mountains along the Rio Grande. There are approximately 600 tribal members, with a median age of 27 (Benjamin *et al.*, 1996). Cochiti, too, retains a traditional religious calendar and a theocratic government that requires fluency in the Native language (Pecos & Blum-Martínez, 2001, p. 75). In both Pueblo communities, however, Native language loss is a growing concern (Romero, 2001; Sims, 2001b).

Cochiti and Acoma share with other New Mexico Pueblos a history of often brutal Spanish colonisation (see, for example, Spicer, 1962, pp. 152–186). The nineteenth century acquisition by the USA of the New Mexico Territory, and the forced incorporation of Pueblo communities into the expanding nation-state 'introduced an even more rapid pace of new foreign influence, . . . especially in the socioeconomic and education domains' (Sims, 2001b, p. 65; see also Minge, 1976, pp. 52–100). Like other Native peoples, the Pueblos were subject to forced assimilation carried out in mission and federal boarding schools. Pueblo communities were also impacted by their proximity to a major east–west railroad and interstate highway (both of which cross Acoma lands), and by the more recent enrolment of their children in nearby public schools. At Cochiti, the construction of a large federal dam destroyed ceremonial sites and family farmlands, precipitating widespread familial and communal displacement and Native language loss (Benjamin *et al.*, 1996, p. 121).

Since the 1990s, both Cochiti and Acoma have been actively involved in community-based language planning. According to Acoma tribal member and language educator Christine Sims (2001b, p. 67), a year-long language planning process revealed that 'there were no children of pre-school or elementary school-age speaking Acoma as a first language'. Mary Eunice Romero, former director of the Cochiti language immersion programme, states that a similar survey at Cochiti showed that two-thirds of the population were not fluent Keres speakers (Romero, 2001). At the same time, both surveys showed a strong interest by adults and young people in revitalising the language (Pecos & Blum-Martínez, 2001; Romero, 2001; Sims, 2001b).

Both tribes began holding community-wide awareness meetings and language forums. 'We had to convince the community, number one, that we were experiencing major language shift, and two, that there is something we can do about it', Romero (2001) reports. In 1996, Cochiti Pueblo launched an immersion programme and in 1997 Acoma held its first summer immersion camp. To model natural dialogue, both programmes paired teams of fluent speakers with small groups of students. At Cochiti, pairing fluent with partially fluent speakers/teachers enabled young people and adult teacher-apprentices to learn Keres together.

Romero (2001) notes that a programme axiom is to 'never, never use English'. Instead, language teachers utilise strategies derived from research on second language acquisition, emphasising communication-based instruction and the use of realia, demonstrations, gestures, and other contextual cues. The focus in both programmes is on strengthening oral skills rather than literacy. Pecos and Blum-Martínez (2001) explain, 'There is widespread support for keeping [the Native language) in its oral form ... The oral tradition ... has been an important element in maintaining [community] values [and the] leaders know that writing the language could bring about unwanted changes in secular and religious traditions' (p. 76). Recently, Cochiti extended its efforts to year-round instruction in the public elementary school, where students receive daily Keres immersion in grades one

to five. The tribe retains fiscal and operational control over the programme.

Preliminary programme data are encouraging. On national assessments of English language arts, students who participated in immersion classes performed significantly better than those in English-only classes (Sims, 2001a). More important to community members are the facts that children have gained conversational ability in Keres and that there is growing evidence of Native language use community-wide. Of Cochiti Pueblo, Pecos and Blum-Martínez (2001) report:

> Across the community and within individual families, one can see closer, more intimate relationships ... as fluent speakers take the time to share their knowledge. In short, the children's success is the community's success, and many people are now aware of the need to speak Keres publicly and consistently. (p. 81)

The Cochiti and Acoma programmes have been recognised as exemplars of community-based language planning. 'It is at the community level that people ... must defend their rights to their own languages and cultures', Wong-Fillmore (1996, p. 439) insists. 'Revitalizing the language is up to us', Romero (2001, oral presentation) observes; 'the true planners and implementers have to be local people'.

## New Developments: the Native Language Shift and Retention Project

The Hawaiian, Navajo and Keres cases highlight the importance of understanding the socio-historical circumstances that have shaped the current status of Indigenous languages, as well as the local dynamics that promote language revitalisation. Documenting these processes and their impacts on Native students' school achievement is the goal of a national research project under way at the University of Arizona.[4] Funded by the US Department of Education Office of Educational Research and Improvement (recently renamed the Institute of Education Sciences), the Native Language Shift/Retention Project is a comparative study of language shift and retention at six representative American Indian school-community sites. Drawing upon anthropological theories of minority student achievement, research on bilingualism, and principles of action research, the project staff are working with research collaborators at each site – Native and non-native educators and community members – to develop in-depth case studies of language education efforts and language proficiencies, ideologies and use patterns among youth and adults, and the relationship of these factors to students' academic success.

The project responds directly to former US President Clinton's 1998 Executive Order, which calls for a comprehensive national research agenda in American Indian education to evaluate the role of Native languages and cultures in the development of educational strategies *(Federal Register*, 63, August 11, 1998, p. 42682). Subsequent to that Order, regional forums identified research priorities; language ability and the quality of educational programmes were key factors named as contributing to student learning. The forums noted that to date, there have been no comparative or multivariate studies of the role of heritage language speaking in Native American student achievement (Boesel, 1999).

Through this project we seek to address this gap in knowledge and to create a national database on the dynamics and implications of language loss and recovery. Equally important, we intend to use this knowledge to assist Native communities in maintaining their languages and advancing Indigenous self-determination.

## Maintaining Linguistic and Cultural Distinctiveness

I began this article with questions concerning the efficacy of Indigenous language reclamation in promoting children's bi/multilingualism and academic success, and in reversing language shift. While research on these questions remains limited, the cases presented here, and early data from the Native Language Shift/Retention Project, suggest that immersion schooling *can* serve the dual roles of promoting students' school success and revitalising endangered Indigenous languages. Indeed, these roles appear to be mutually constitutive. And, given the gravity of the current state of language loss, anything less than full immersion is likely to be too little, too late.

Indigenous language revitalisation confronts not only a colonial legacy of linguicide, genocide, and cultural displacement, but mounting pressures for standardisation. Those pressures are manifest in externally imposed 'accountability' regimes – high-stakes testing, reductionist

reading programmes, and English-only policies such as those recently passed in California and Arizona.[5] These pressures come at a time when the USA is experiencing an unprecedented demographic shift stemming from the 'new immigration' – those who have emigrated to the USA since national origin quotas were abolished in 1965. Unlike earlier waves of immigration, which originated in Europe and were largely White, recent immigrants come primarily from Latin America, Southeast Asia and the Caribbean (Qin-Hilliard *et al.,* 2001). People of colour now comprise 28% *of* the nation's population, with the numbers expected to grow to 38% in 2024, and 47% in 2050 (Banks, 2001, p. ix).

In the context of these demographic transformations and the larger forces of globalisation, we are witnessing increasing intolerance for linguistic and cultural diversity. Nowhere is this more evident than in US schools. In school districts across the country, working-class students, students of colour, and English language learners are simultaneously being deskilled in one-size-fits-all, phonics-based reading programmes, and constructed as deficient for their low performance on English standardised tests (Gutiérrez, 2001). There is nothing neutral about these processes. Masquerading as an instrument of equality – as reflected, for example, in the current US policy of 'leaving no child behind'[6] – the pressures for standardisation are, in fact, creating a new polarisation between those with and without access to opportunity and resources.

Can Indigenous cultural and linguistic distinctiveness be maintained in the face of these homogenising yet stratifying forces? I believe the answer is a qualified but optimistic 'yes'. Achieving this will require sustained community-based consciousness-raising, much like that described for the immersion programmes examined here, and committed efforts by those who, like the Navajo parents at Fort Defiance, are determined to 'buck the tide' of linguistic and cultural repression (Arviso & Holm, 2001, p. 211).

Happily, there is evidence that these instances of community-based resistance are not isolated cases. In the summer of 1988, Native American educators from throughout the USA came together to draft the resolution that would become the 1990/1992 Native American Languages Act, the only federal legislation that explicitly vows to protect and promote Indigenous languages. Although meagrely funded, this legislation has spurred some of the boldest efforts in heritage language recovery to date, as well as having solidified a national network of Indigenous language activists (for examples, see Hinton & Hale, 2001; McCarty *et al.*, 1999).

Language – humankind's indispensable meaning-making tool – *can* be an instrument of cultural and linguistic oppression. But this 'tool of tools' (Gutiérrez, 2001, p. 567) can also be a vehicle for advancing human rights and minority-community empowerment. The programmes discussed here illustrate the ways in which Indigenous communities have been able to protect and promote their distinctive diversity in homogenising times. Their efforts point the way out of the either-or dichotomies of reductionist, English-only pedagogies, toward a vision of democracy in which individuals and communities create and recreate themselves through multiple languages and discourses. Rooted in principles of social justice, this vision holds the promise of creating a more critically democratic, linguistically and culturally rich society for us all.

## Acknowledgements

I thank my colleagues, K. Tsianina Lomawaima, Mary Eunice Romero, and Ofelia Zepeda, for helping me to think through and clarify many of the ideas and data reported here.

## Notes

1. The presentation of these data should not be taken as an endorsement of the validity of standardised tests for evaluating student achievement, and in particular, for such evaluations across cultural contexts. Rather, I want to point out that on these tests, discriminatory and flawed as they are, students in bilingual education programmes outperformed comparable students in English-only programmes.
2. The first documented Indigenous literacy efforts by Indigenous speakers (as opposed to those of missionaries and government officials), was Sequoya's Cherokee syllabary, published in 1821 and reprinted in Holmes and Smith (1976).
3. Young and Morgan's (1987) *The Navajo Language: A Grammar and Colloquial Dictionary* remains a standard-bearer in the field.
4. I serve as co-Principal Investigator on the project with my colleague in the Department of Linguistics, Dr. Ofelia Zepeda. Dr. Mary Eunice Romero of Cochiti Pueblo is Research Assistant Professor and Coordinator for the project.
5. Euphemistically (and deceptively) called 'English for the Children', both the California and the Arizona voter initiatives, financed by California software millionaire Ron Utz, require public schools to replace multi-year bilingual education programmes with one-year English immersion for English language learners. In both states, passage of the proposition was followed by the adoption of an English-only school accountability programme (Gutiérrez *et al.*, 2002).
6. Part of the rhetoric of the 2000 US Presidential campaign, 'Leaving No Child Behind' subsequently became codified in the 2001 No Child Left Behind Act, which calls for 'scientifically-based' (phonics) reading programmes, heightened state surveillance over curricula and instruction, high-stakes testing, and public labelling and state disciplining of 'under-achieving schools'.

## References

Arviso, M. and Holm, W. (2001) Tséhootsooídi Ólta'gi Diné bizaad bíhoo'aah: A Navajo immersion programme at Fort Defiance, Arizona. In L. Hinton and K. Hale (eds) *The Green Book of Language Revitalization in Practice* (San Diego, CA, Academic Press).

Banks, J.A. (2001) Series foreword. In G. Valdés, *Learning and Not Learning English in School: Latino students in American schools* (New York and London, Teachers College Press).

Begay, S., Dick, G.S., Estell, D.W., Estell, J., McCarty, T.L. and Sells, A. (1995) Change from the inside out: a story of transformation in a Navajo community school. *Bilingual Research Journal*, 19 (1), 121–139.

Benjamin, R, Pecos, R. and Romero, M.W. (1996) Language revitalization efforts in the Pueblo de Cochiti: becoming "literate" in an oral society. In N.H. Hornberger (ed.) *Indigenous Literacies in the Americas: language planning from the bottom up* (Berlin and New York, Mouton de Gruyter).

Boesel, D. (1999) *Strategy for the Development of a Research Agenda in Indian Education* (Washington DC, National Library of Education).

Crawford, J. (1992) *Language Loyalties: a source book on the Official English controversy* (Chicago, IL and London, University of Chicago Press).

Crawford, J. (1995a) Endangered Native American languages: what is to be done, and why? *Bilingual Research Journal*, 19 (1), pp. 17–38.

Crawford, J. (1995b) *Bilingual Education: history, politics, theory and practice* (3rd edn) (Los Angeles, CA, Bilingual Education Associates).

Crawford, J. (1996) Seven hypotheses on language loss: causes and cures. In G. Cantoni (ed.) *Stabilizing Indigenous Languages* (Flagstaff, AZ, Northern Arizona University Center for Excellence in Education).

Crawford, J. (2000) *At War with Diversity: US language policy in an age of anxiety* (Clevedon, UK, Multilingual Matters Ltd).

Cummins, J. (1981) *Bilingualism and Minority Language Children* (Toronto, Ontario Institute for Studies in Education).

Cummins, J. (1986) Empowering minority students: a framework for intervention. *Harvard Educational Review*, 56, pp. 18–36.

Cummins, J. (1989) *Empowering Minority Students* (Sacramento, CA, California Association for Bilingual Education).

Cummins, J. (1996) *Negotiating Identities: education for empowerment in a diverse society* (Los Angeles, CA, Association for Bilingual Education).

Cummins, J. and Corson, D. (eds) (1997) *Encyclopedia of Language and Education, Vol. 5: Bilingual Education* (Dordrecht, Netherlands, Kluwer Academic Publishers).

Cummins, J. and Swain, M. (1986) *Bilingualism in Education: aspects of theory, research and practice* (London and New York, Longman).

Dick, G.S. and McCarty, T.L. (1996) Reclaiming Navajo: language renewal in an American Indian community school. In N.H. Hornberger (ed.) *Indigenous Literacies in the Americas: language planning from the bottom up* (Berlin and New York, Mouton de Gruyter).

Fishman, J.A. (1991) *Reversing Language Shift: theoretical and empirical foundations of assistance to threatened languages* (Clevedon, UK, Multilingual Matters Ltd).

Genesee, F. (1987) *Learning through Two Languages: studies of immersion and bilingual education* (New York, Newbury House Publishers, Inc.).

Genesee, F. (ed.) (1994) *Educating Second Language Children: the whole child, the whole curriculum, the whole community* (Cambridge, UK, Cambridge University Press).

Greymorning, S. (1997) Going beyond words: the Arapaho immersion programme. In J. Reyhner (ed.) *Teaching Indigenous Languages* (Flagstaff, AZ, Northern Arizona University Center for Excellence in Education).

Grosjean, F. (1982) *Life with Two Languages: an introduction to bilingualism* (Cambridge, MA and London, Harvard University Press).

Gutiérrez, K.D. (2001) What's new in the English language arts: challenging policies and practices, ¿y qué? *Language Arts*, 78 (6), pp. 564–569.

Gutiérrez, K.D., Asato, J., Moll, L.C., Oson, K., Norng, E.L., Ruiz, R., García, E. and McCarty, T.L (2002) 'Sounding American': the consequences of new reforms on English language learners. *Reading Research Quarterly* 37 (3), pp. 328–343.

Hakuta, K. (1986) *Mirror of Language: the debate on bilingualism* (New York, Basic Books).

Hale, K. (2001) The Navajo language: I. In L. Hinton and K. Hale (eds) *The Green Book of Language Revitalization in Practice* (San Diego, CA, Academic Press).

Henze, R.C. and Vanett, L. (1993) To walk in two worlds – or more? Challenging a common metaphor of Native education. *Anthropology & Education Quarterly*, 24 (2), pp. 116–134.

Hinton, L. (2001) Language revitalization: an overview. In L Hinton and K. Hale (eds) *The Green Book of Language Revitalization in Practice* (San Diego, CA, Academic Press).

Hinton, L. and Hale, K. (eds) (2001) *The Green Book of Language Revitalization in Practice* (San Diego, CA, Academic Press).

Holm, A. and Holm, W. (1990) Rock Point, a Navajo way to go to school: a valediction. *Annals, AASSP*, 508, pp. 170–184.

Holm, A. and Holm, W. (1995) Navajo language education: retrospect and prospects. *Bilingual Research Journal*, 19 (1), pp. 141–167.

Holmes, R.B. and Smith, B.S. (1976) *Beginning Cherokee* (Notman, OK, University of Oklahoma Press).

Hornberger, N.H. (1996) Language planning from the bottom up. In N.H. Hornberger (ed.) *Indigenous Literacies in the Americas: language planning from the bottom up* (Berlin and New York, Mouton de Gruyter).

Infante, E.J. (1999) Living the language: growing up in immersion school taught its own lessons, *The Honolulu Advertiser*, May 30, E1, E3.

Kamanā, K. and Wilson, W.H. (1996) Hawaiian language programs. In G. Cantoni (ed.) *Stabilizing Indigenous Languages* (Flagstaff, AZ, Northern Arizona University Center for Excellence in Education).

Karl, J. and Spolsky, B. (1973) *Trends in the Study*

of Athapaskan Language Maintenance and Bilingualism. Navajo Reading Study progress report no. 21 (Albuquerque, NM, University of New Mexico).

Krashen, S. D. (1996) Under Attack: the case against bilingual education (Culver City, CA, Language Education Associates).

Krauss, M. (1998) The condition of Native North American languages: the need for realistic assessment and action. International Journal of the Sociology of Language, 132, pp. 9–21.

Leap, W. L. (ed.). (1977) Studies in Southwestern Indian English (San Antonio, TX, Trinity University Press).

Lee, T. and McLaughlin, D. (2001) Reversing Navajo language shift, revisited, in: J. A. Fishman (ed.) Can Threatened Languages Be Saved? Reversing language shift, revisited: A 21st century perspective (Clevedon, UK, Multilingual Matters Ltd).

Lipka, J. and McCarty, T.L. (1994) Changing the culture of schooling: Navajo and Yup'ik cases. Anthropology & Education Quarterly, 25 (3), pp. 266–284.

Lipka, J. with Mohatt, G. and the Ciulistet Group (1998) Transforming the Culture of Schooling: Yup'ik examples (Mahwah, NJ, Lawrence Erlbaum Associates).

Littlebear, R. E. (1996) Preface. In G. Cantoni (ed.) Stabilizing Indigenous Languages (Flagstaff, AZ, Northern Arizona University Center for Excellence in Education).

May, S. (1999) Language and education rights for Indigenous peoples. In S. May (ed.) Indigenous Community-based Education (Clevedon, UK, Multilingual Matters Ltd).

May, S. (2001) Language and Minority Rights: ethnicity, nationalism and the politics of language (London, Longman).

McCarty, T.L. (1989) School as community: the Rough Rock demonstration. Harvard Educational Review, 59 (4), pp. 484–503.

McCarty, T.L. (1993) Language, literacy, and the image of the child in American Indian classrooms. Language Arts, 70 (3), pp. 182–192.

McCarty, T.L. (1998) Schooling, resistance, and American Indian languages, International Journal of the Sociology of Language, 132, pp. 27–41.

McCarty, T.L. (2001) Between possibility and constraint: indigenous language education, planning, and policy in the United States. In J. W. Tollefson (ed.) Language Policies in Education: critical issues (Mahwah, NJ, Lawrence Erlbaum Associates).

McCarty, T.L. (2002) A Place to be Navajo: Rough Rock and the struggle for self-determination in Indigenous schooling (Mahwah, NJ, Lawrence Erlbaum Associates).

McCarty, T.L. and Dick, G.S. (2003) Telling the people's stories: literacy practices and processes in a Navajo community school. In A. Willis, G. E. García, R. Barrera and V. J. Harris (eds) Multicultural Issues in Literacy Research and Practice (Mahwah, NJ, Lawrence Erlbaum Associates).

McCarty, T.L. and Watahomigie, L.J. (1999) Indigenous education and grassroots language planning in the USA. Practicing Anthropology, 21 (2), pp. 5–11.

McCarty, T. L., Watahomigie, L. J. and Yamamoto, A. Y. (1999) Reversing Language Shift in Indigenous America: collaborations and views from the field. Special Issue. Practicing Anthropology, 21 (2), pp. 2–47.

Minge, W.A. (1976) Ácoma: pueblo in the sky (Albuquerque, NM, University of New Mexico Press).

Nettle, D. and Romaine, S. (2000) Vanishing Voices: the extinction of the world's languages (New York, Oxford University Press).

Pattanayak, D.P. (2000) Linguistic pluralism: a point of departure. In R. Phillipson (ed.) Rights to Language: equity, power, and education (Mahwah, NJ, Lawrence Erlbaum Associates).

Pecos, R. and Blum-Martínez, R. (2001) The key to cultural survival: language planning and revitalization in the Pueblo de Cochiti. In L. Hinton and K. Hale (eds) The Green Book of Language Revitalization in Practice (San Diego, CA, Academic Press).

Platero, P.R. (1992) Navajo Head Start language study. Manuscript on file, Navajo Division of Education, Navajo Nation, Window Rock, AZ.

Platero, P.R. (2001) Navajo Head Start language study. In L. Hinton and K. Hale (eds) The Green Book of Language Revitalization in Practice (San Diego, CA, Academic Press).

Qin-Hilliard, D.B., Feinauer, E. and Quiroz, B. (2001) Introduction. Harvard Educational Review, 71 (3), pp. v–ix.

Ramírez, J.D. (1992) Executive summary. Bilingual Research Journal, 16 (1 & 2), pp. 1–62.

Ramírez, J.D. (1998) SFUSD Language Academy: 1998 annual evaluation (Long Beach, CA, California State University Long Beach, Center for Language Minority Education and Research).

Ricento, T. and Wiley, T.G. (2002) Editors' Introduction: language, identity, and education and the challenges of multiculturalism and globalisation, *Journal of Language, Identity, and Education*, 1 (1), pp. 1–5.

Romero, M.E. (2001) Indigenous language immersion: the Cochiti experience. Presentation at the 22nd Annual American Indian Language Development Institute, Tucson, Arizona, 9 June.

Rosier, P. and Farella, M. (1976) Bilingual education at Rock Point: some early results, *TESOL Quarterly*, 10, pp. 379–388.

Ruiz, R. (1984) Orientations in language planning. *NABE Journal*, 8, pp. 15–34.

Sims, C. (2001a) Indigenous language immersion. Presentation at the 22nd Annual American Indian Language Development Institute, Tucson, Arizona, 9 June.

Sims, C. (2001b) Native language planning: a pilot process in the Acoma Pueblo community. In L. Hinton and K. Hale (eds) *The Green Book of Language Revitalization in Practice* (San Diego, CA, Academic Press).

Skutnabb-Kangas, T. and Cummins, J. (1988) *Minority Education: from shame to struggle* (Clevedon, UK, and Philadelphia, PA, Multilingual Matters Ltd).

Slate, C. (1993) Finding a place for Navajo. *Tribal College*, 4, pp. 10–14.

Spicer, E.H. (1962) *Cycles of Conquest: the impact of Spain, Mexico, and the United States on the Indians of the Southwest, 1533–1960* (Tucson, AZ, University of Arizona Press).

Spolsky, B. (1976) Linguistics in practice: the Navajo Reading Study. *Theory into Practice*, 24, pp. 347–352.

Spolsky, B. (2002) Prospects for the survival of the Navajo language: a reconsideration. *Anthropology & Education Quarterly*, 33 (2), pp. 139–162.

Spolsky, B. and Holm, W. (1977) Bilingualism in the six-year-old child. In W.F. Mackey and T. Andersson (eds) *Bilingualism in Early Childhood* (Rowley, MA, Newbury House Publishers, Inc.).

Thomas, W.P. and Collier, V. (1997) *School Effectiveness for Language Minority Students* (Washington DC, National Clearinghouse for Bilingual Education).

Troike, R.C. (1978) *Research Evidence for the Effectiveness of Bilingual Education* (Rosslyn, VA, National Clearinghouse for Bilingual Education).

Tucker, G.R. (1980) Implications for US bilingual education: evidence from Canadian research. *Focus*, 2, pp. 1–4.

Warner, S.L.N. (1999) *Kuleana*: The right, respon-

sibility, and authority of indigenous peoples to speak and make decisions for themselves in language and culture revitalization. *Anthropology & Education Quarterly*, 30 (1), pp. 68–93.

Warner, S.L.N. (2001) The movement to revitalize Hawaiian language and culture. In L. Hinton and K. Hale (eds) *The Green Book of Language Revitalization in Practice* (San Diego, CA, Academic Press).

Watahomigie, L.J. and McCarty, T.L. (1994) Bilingual/bicultural education at Peach Springs: a Hualapai way of schooling. *Peabody Journal of Education*, 69 (2), pp. 26–42.

Watahomigie, L.J. and McCarty, T.L. (1996) Literacy for what? Hualapai literacy and language maintenance. In N.H. Hornberger (ed.) *Indigenous Literacies in the Americas: language planning from the bottom up* (Berlin and New York, Mouton de Gruyter).

Watahomigie, L.J. and Yamamoto, A.Y. (1987) Linguistics in action: the Hualapai bilingual/bicultural education programme. In D.D. Stull and J.J. Schensul (eds) *Collaborative Research and Social Change: applied anthropology in action* (Boulder, CO, Westview Press).

Wilson, W.H. (1998) *I ka ʻōlelo Hawaiʻi ke ola*, 'Life is found in the Hawaiian language'. *International Journal of the Sociology of Language*, 132, pp. 123–137.

Wilson, W.H. (1999) The sociopolitical context of establishing Hawaiian-medium education. In S. May (ed.) *Indigenous Community-based Education* (Clevedon, UK, Multilingual Matters Ltd).

Wilson, W.H. and Kamanā, K. (2001) *'Mai loko mai o ka 'i'ni*: Proceeding from a dream.' The 'Aha Pūnana Leo connection in Hawaiian language revitalization. In L. Hinton and K. Hale (eds) *The Green Book of Language Revitalization in Practice* (San Diego, CA, Academic Press).

Wong, L. (1999) Authenticity and the revitalization of Hawaiian. *Anthropology & Education Quarterly*, 30 (1), pp. 94–115.

Wong-Fillmore, L. (1996) What happens when languages are lost? An essay on language assimilation and cultural identity. In D.I. Slobin, J. Gerhardt, A. Kyratzis and J. Guo (eds) *Social Interaction, Social Context, and Language: essays in honor of Susan Ervin-Tripp* (Mahwah, NJ, Lawrence Erlbaum Associates).

Young, R.W. and Morgan, W., Sr. (1987) *The Navajo Language: a grammar and colloquial dictionary* (Albuquerque, NM, University of New Mexico Press).

## Questions

1. What is the current balance sheet of Native American languages? What are the main reasons for decline? What part have schools and education played in the decline?
2. What role can bilingual education play in revitalizing a Native American language? Of the various programs in different geographical areas discussed in this article, what elements appear to be successful?
3. What are the sociohistorical and sociolinguistic differences that distinguish the Hawaiian, Navajo and Keres Immersion programs? Given the review of foundational research on Native American bilingual education provided by McCarty, which community has the best prospect of successfully educating their children and developing their bilingualism and biliteracy?
4. Table 2 compares the performance of students in Navajo Immersion and Monolingual English education. Explain the meaning of each of the five comparisons.

## Activities

1. Make a creative poster that portrays the *history* or *current challenges* or *successes* of Native American bilingual education. Select the best entries and display them in the class.
2. Find out the indigenous languages there are (or were) spoken in at least *five* of the following countries, traditionally seen by some as being monolingual:
    a. United Kingdom
    b. Spain
    c. New Zealand
    d. France
    e. Australia
    f. Japan
    g. Italy
    h. Argentina
    i. Finland
    j. China

    Find out if there are policies that protect minority languages in these countries. Make a table with the languages, the policy and a short quote from the policy.
3. Many countries in Latin America have recently developed bilingual intercultural education programs for their indigenous populations. Using the WWW or other bibliographical sources, research the status of such programs in one of the following countries. Work in groups and make a comparative chart with your findings.
    a. Peru
    b. Mexico
    c. Ecuador
    d. Bolivia
    e. Paraguay
    f. Guatemala
    g. Brazil
4. Interview a student who is bilingual on:
    a. whether they believe their native language competence contributes or detracts from academic achievement.

b. the benefits and any disadvantages of their bilingualism.

Different groups might select students with different characteristics. For example, some may interview language majority students, others may question language minority students (e.g. an indigenous language (e.g. Native American) student); some might include students who are fully bilingual, and others those who are still acquiring the second language. Record their answers and share them with the class. Write an essay with conclusions derived from the class's research.

5. Interview five bilingual parents. Find out their views on bilingualism and whether they want their children to become bilingual. Then ask about their views on bilingual education. Find out whether they think public schools should be teaching non-English languages to language minority students. Record their answers on an answer sheet. Then make a poster to display your conclusions.

6. If you're bilingual, reflect on your own experience. Write an essay about a specific instance in which you have benefited from your ability to speak two languages. If you're not bilingual, write an essay about a specific experience when speaking a second language might have come in handy.

7. In the library, research the sociolinguistic situation of the different Latino groups in the United States and of the different Asian groups. Refer to their migration history, socio-demographic characteristics, geographic concentration, language use and proficiency, and their prospects for language maintenance or language shift. (One importance source for this information is McKay, S.L. & Wong, S-L.C. (eds), 2000, *New Immigrants in the United States*. Cambridge: Cambridge University Press.)

## Further Reading

Baker, C. (2006) *Foundations of Bilingual Education and Bilingualism* (4th edn). Clevedon: Multilingual Matters (chapter 11).

Francis, N. and Reyhner, J. (2002) *Language and Literacy Teaching for Indigenous Education. A Bilingual Approach.* Clevedon: Multilingual Matters.

López, L.E. (2001) Literacies and intercultural education in the Andes. In D. Olson & N. Torrance (eds). *Literacy and Social Development: The Making of Literate Societies.* Oxford: Blackwell.

McCarty, T.L. (2004) Dangerous difference: A critical-historical analysis of language education policies in the United States. In J.W. Tollefson and A.B.M. Tsui (eds) *Medium of Instruction Policies: Which Agenda? Whose Agenda?* Mahwah, NJ: Erlbaum.

McCarty, T.L. and Bia, F. (2002) *A Place To Be Navajo: Rough Rock and the Struggle for Self-Determination in Indigenous Schooling.* Mahwah, NJ: Lawrence Erlbaum.

Special Issue of *International Journal of Bilingual Education and Bilingualism* (2005) volume 8, 2&3 (on Heritage Language Education).

Wiley, T.G. (2001) On defining heritage language education and their speakers. In J.K. Peyton, D.A. Ranard and S. McGinnis (eds.), *Heritage Languages in America: Preserving a National Resource.* McHenry, IL: Delta Systems.

# Dual Language Programs: Key Features and Results

**María E. Torres-Guzmán**

## Introduction

The growth of so-called 'dual language programs' has been swift over the last decade (Loeb, 1999), particularly during the last few years. Despite the apparent growth, however, one must be cautious. What school districts describe as dual language programs is not always clearly aligned with the technical definition – enrichment education programs that foster language equity and are organized with the goals of bilingualism and biliteracy for all children, language minority and mainstream students alike.

Some school districts that report that they have dual language programs have what are essentially second-language enrichment programs (Genesee, 1987), in which language majority children are learning a second language. Educators have also used the dual language label to refer to all bilingual/bicultural education programs (Leslow-Hurley, 2000) because of its literal definition as the 'use of two languages'. Even when dual language programs fall within the technical definition, there is variation in their implementation (Christian *et al.*, 1996; Etxeberria, 1993; Lindholm, 1987).

The intent of this article is twofold: To delineate salient features of dual language programs for educators to keep in mind when making program and policy decisions; and to highlight the educational results ascribed to dual language programs in light of the broader debate surrounding bilingual education.

## Dual Language Programs: A Definition

In this article, dual language refers to an enrichment bilingual/multicultural education program (Hornberger, 1990) in which language equity is structurally defined as equal time exposure to two languages, that is, the 50/50 model (Etxeberria, 1993). These programs are often called developmental because the funding source (Title VII, Improving America's Schools Act, 1994) labels them as such, and because linguistic, psychological, social, and cognitive developmental issues are taken into account in program design. They are sometimes labeled enrichment because a central tenet of such programs is that a language should be added to the one the children already know and that children's academic growth in both languages should be fostered.

> In transitional bilingual education programs, the linguistic goal is to either eradicate a language (mother tongue) or substitute it with English. In the maintenance program, the linguistic goal is to maintain the mother tongue while adding the second. Enrichment programs aim to add a language to that which children already know, and foster children's academic growth in both languages. (Hornberger, 1990) This definition is in contrast to more traditional bilingual education programs, where the educational goal is to be able to function in all-English environments.

Dual language programs are often, but not always, designated as two-way. Two-way programs have existed since the 1960s, with the Coral Way, Florida bilingual alternate day model as the best-known example from this early period. It was two-way because it included mainstream English-dominant students and language minority students. It was bilingual education because it used two languages as the medium of instruction. It was also dual language (although not formerly called so) because its alternate-day structure resulted in the equitable distribution of the two languages involved.

Thomas and Collier (1997), in a study of test performance and program types with a national sample of over 45,000 students, distinguish between two enrichment bilingual education programs: two-way and one-way developmental. The primary distinction is in the student populations the programs serve. Two-way programs include both language minority and language majority children, whereas one-way developmental programs serve the language minority population. Other researchers of two-way programs have referred to this student population distinction in their studies (Christian, 1996; Christian *et al.*, 1996; Christian & Whitcher, 1997; Lindholm, 1988a, 1988b, 1991, 1994).

Another designation for dual language programs is late-exit. This label comes from the Ramirez *et al.* (1991) study, the most comprehensive federally funded study on program types. The study, which included both ESL and bilingual education programs, classified programs according to the degree of native language use. The study's goal was to compare all programs serving students who were not proficient in English rather than just bilingual education programs. The bilingual education programs are described as early-exit or late-exit, depending on the length of time bilingual education was provided. In late-exit programs, students 'receive a minimum of forty percent of their total instruction time in Spanish' and remain in the program for a longer period of time 'regardless of when they are classified as fluent-English-proficient' (Ramirez *et al.*, 1991: 2). Both maintenance and enrichment education programs were included. In other words, the dual language model is included but not used as a distinct category.

Lindholm (1987) uses the broad term bilingual immersion education to refer to enrichment models, and has used the terms bilingual immersion and dual language interchangeably (Lindholm, 1999, 2000). She describes these programs as possessing the following four features:

(1)  ' . . . Instruction through two languages, where the target language is used for a significant portion of the students' instructional day . . . '
(2)  ' . . . periods of instruction during which only one language is used . . . '
(3)  'Both native English speakers and native speakers of the target language are participants.'
(4)  'The students are integrated for most content instruction.' (2000: 13)

Lindholm (1987) includes both the 90/10 and the 50/50 models as bilingual immersion, or two-way programs. The 90/10 model starts in kindergarten with a curriculum that is 90% in the native language and 10% in the second language; there is a gradual increase of English until it reaches 50% at the upper elementary level. There are usually two classes at a grade level (or team teaching) so that the increase in the second language is parallel for each of the populations, the native English and the non-native English. The 50/50 model starts in kindergarten and continues throughout the elementary level, with each language receiving half of the instructional time. Out of the 30 programs Lindholm describes in the *1987 Directory of Bilingual Immersion Programs*, 17 are of the 50/50 model.

Christian and Whitcher (1995), Valdes (1997) and Freeman (1998) similarly use Lindholm's broader definition of bilingual immersion programs when referring to dual language programs, so that this category includes the language majority population and the 90/10 structure.

Researchers have also tended to use a variety of other labels to refer to dual language, including not only two-way bilingual or immersion, but also developmental bilingual, double immersion and other terms. As some scholars point out (Christian & Malone, 1995; Freeman, 1998; Lindholm, 1999), however, not all dual language programs are two-way, i.e. they do not include both language minority and language majority students. Morrison (1995), Foster and Swinney (n.d.), and Marquez-Lopez (1998), for example, define dual language programs as educational programs that foster language equity. A strict separation of languages for instructional purposes is part of the design, with language allocation, at the elementary level, following the 50/50 model. In some programs, a majority of the children are from the same language minority group, but differ in language proficiency.

## Features of Dual Language Programs

However defined, dual language programs foster the goals of academic achievement in English and another language, development of bilingual/

biliterate skills, and positive cross-cultural attitudes. The major theoretical principles that undergird the academic and language goals are embedded in the relationship between language, learning, and cognition. It has been found that:

(1) It takes most individuals from five to seven years to acquire the second language well enough to function academically;
(2) One can transfer the knowledge and skills acquired in one language to the other; and
(3) By continuing to develop the two languages, children's educational and cognitive development is enhanced (Collier, 1992, 1995; Cummins, 1992; Hakuta & Diaz, 1984).

The dual language program design follows consistent and clear linguistic, sociocultural, and educational policies, which include a variety of features:

LINGUISTIC ▶
- Strict language separation
- Equality in language distribution
- Avoidance of simultaneous translation
- Language taught through content
- Whole-language instruction
- Goals of bilingualism and biliteracy
- Heterogeneous language grouping

PEDAGOGICAL ▶
- Appreciation of cultural diversity
- Culturally relevant teaching
- Development of self-esteem
- Mix of language minority with English-speaking and mainstream students
- Cooperative group learning structure
- Parental involvement
- School/community support structure

SOCIOCULTURAL ▶
- Academic achievement for all children
- Math and literature follow distinct linguistic policy
- Developmental level team teaching structures
- Thematic organization of units of study
- Teachers as monolingual models
- Ongoing staff development

Individually, each of these features may appear in other bilingual education models. What is unique about dual language programs is how they come together to ensure equal status of the minority language with English in a structure of commitment (Morrison, 1995). Dual language programming aims at protecting minority languages and cultures, promoting their use among English-speaking students, and focusing on quality education for all.

## Linguistic Features

The guiding aspect of the linguistic component is its clear policy. The dual language program design is such that the languages are kept separate at all times – by alternating days, half days, or teachers. Exactly how the languages are distributed depends on the grade level, instructional goals, and other factors.

If the goal is to achieve equity in language, the time of instruction in each language is distributed on a 50/50 basis. In that case, taking blocks of time, such as a ten-day period, and establishing the language distribution for the period seems to be the norm (Christian, 1994). It may be that the entire ten-day block is organized in one language and the next ten-day block in the other (Bergman *et al.*, 1995). It may be that on a trimester basis, the language distribution is reorganized according to subject. The most common structures are the alternate day or half-day models. In the alternate day model, a student receives instruction in English one day and the next day is in the other language. The third day, the student returns to English. By the end of the ten-day period, the student should have received five days of instruction in English and five in the other language. If this has not occurred, for the many reasons schools must deviate from their schedule, adjustments may be necessary.

The half-day model has at least two variations. One is where the morning is designated for one language for a two-week period; during this period, the second language is the language of instruction in the afternoon. The languages change place during the next time-block. At the end of the semester, each language has received equal time. The second variation is what has been called the roller coaster or serpent model: The morning is organized in one language, while during the afternoon of that same day and the next morning, the children receive instruction in the other language. Teachers report that the roller coaster model offers continuity of work for both the students and the teacher, and permits literacy instruction to occur in both languages during the morning hours.

In some programs and at certain grade levels, depending on the school population, there are a few exceptions to the 50/50 distributions of the languages. In some two-way models, the early grades separate the English dominant from the others, and teach each group literacy in their native language. In these cases, there is usually a gradual increase in the second language until the 50/50 ratio is achieved (Martinez & Moore-O'Brien, 1993). Some programs establish a different language policy for instruction in math and literature, or the language distribution may deviate from the 50/50 rule after elementary school. References to these variations will be made in the pedagogical section.

Whether the language of instruction changes by alternating days, half-days, or teachers, the language is posted outside the door. If a person who doesn't speak the language of instruction for that class enters the room, the teacher is encouraged to direct the person outside the classroom in order to switch the language of communication. At the instructional level, teachers are encouraged to consistently use a distinct color of crayon, marker, or chalk for each language. This is especially important if the individual teacher participates in instruction in both languages (rather than team teaching). Teachers are also encouraged to organize the literature and displays in the classroom to distinguish the languages; and the children are encouraged to have different homework notebooks for each of the languages.

Avoiding simultaneous translation is yet another way in which the dual language policy is maintained. It is natural for a teacher to be tempted to translate, particularly if there is bewilderment on a child's face. Yet in these programs, teachers are encouraged to trust the long-term language-learning process, and to remember that when children know that something will be translated they will devote less effort to figuring out what the second language being spoken means. In addition, it is more tiring for teachers to teach everything twice (Legarreta-Marcaida, 1987) – and they are more likely to translate idiomatic expressions incorrectly when they are doing direct translations. Concurrent translations, unless very systematically organized (Jacobson, 1995), also tend to be less effective educationally. Instead,

when children who are still not producing in the second language speak in their first language on a day that the second language should be spoken, the teacher is encouraged to respond in the second language. Teachers are also encouraged to speak about the process of second-language learning and to offer students 'strategies for getting through the non-dominant language days' (Foster & Swinney, n.d.) through gestures, eye movement, images, and so forth. Students who are dominant in the language being spoken on a given day are encouraged to help the second-language learners.

Instructional approaches are similarly organized to aid both acquisition and learning. In order to include the second-language learners, teachers develop their lessons so that verbal and nonverbal cues, visual aids, and manipulatives serve as support for learning activities. Furthermore, activities that are hands-on, that are organized in small groups, and that require conversation are important for linguistic as well as social development. Language is taught both formally and informally, and instruction is student-centered.

An integrated language philosophy (Goodman, 1986; Goodman *et al.*, 1979; Pérez & Torres-Guzmán, 1996) guides the teaching of language. Teachers are encouraged to approach language learning through the content area, thus creating a context for language use. The skills of listening, speaking, reading, and writing are integrated in authentic and meaningful language activities. Materials and discussion are centered first on the interests and experiences of the students, and then moved beyond to the wider world.

Decoding and encoding are part of the process and the means by which children send and receive messages; they are taught as they become necessary. At the same time, the teacher introduces the world of literature and provides a print-rich environment for the children. Discovery, imagination, creativity, enjoyment, and utility are all part of what teachers aim to accomplish. Again, equity requires that such environments be provided in both languages.

While languages are separated, the students are not. Children are not segregated in different programs, nor isolated instructionally according to their linguistic abilities. Teachers are encouraged to organize instructional groups that are heterogeneous linguistically and academically. In this way, students are allowed to shine on the day that the language of instruction is the one in which they are most proficient. In addition, they hear, and can practice with, native language models consistently.

The goals of the dual language program are bilingualism and biliteracy for all children. When the program is also two-way, and there is a mix of language minority and mainstream/English-speaking populations, even more is accomplished. For the language minority student, the burden of unidirectionality is lifted. Bilingualism is transformed from a deficiency perspective and a compensatory framework to a socially desirable commodity. The goal is to develop competent bilinguals who can manage and manipulate two languages and their complexities in a variety of domains. An important parallel goal is biliteracy, the ability to decode and encode print that conveys messages in a variety of contexts using two linguistic and cultural systems (Pérez & Torres-Guzmán, 1996). As research suggests, the strong foundation in the first language of the child transfers to the second language, and literacy is deemed critical to all academic tasks.

## Sociocultural Features

The structured relationships between the minority language and English help shake the foundations of social stigmas that come from an implicit association between how well individuals express themselves and their intelligence (Hakuta & Diaz, 1984). In two-way, dual language programs, both the language minority and the mainstream/English-speaking students are in situations where they have problems expressing clearly what they know, and they both have opportunities to share and display competence. While social prestige markers may still favor English, the experiences of learning together about each other and in each other's language can help students see each other as human beings developing cognitively, socially, and linguistically (Freeman, 1996; Torres-Guzmán, 1990). Thus, the program is designed to protect the minority culture and to promote cultural and linguistic diversity among all students (Martinez & Moore-O'Brien, 1993).

Culturally relevant teaching is a critical feature. Within this context, the following are important:

(1) Inclusion of original works from the worlds of the language minority groups so that the children see the authors as intellectual role models;

(2) Acknowledgment of what students bring into the classroom – life experiences, cultural ways, and so forth – as legitimate knowledge upon which to build;

(3) Incorporation of homes as knowledge resources for curricular development (Gonzalez, 1994; Mercado & Moll, 1997; Olmedo, 1997); and the

(4) Challenge of social expectations for the language minority children by organizing their classrooms around high expectations (Bergman et al., 1995; Ladson-Billings, 1994; Nieto, 1995).

Furthermore, self-esteem issues are taken into account (Cazabón et al., 1993). Students who see language learning as a natural process that is not threatening to their identity are less likely to resist the learning of the second language. Krashen's (1987) notion of the affective filter, the mechanism the learner uses to resist or open up to learning a second language, is a useful one. Because both language minority and English-speaking students are learning the minority language, the implicit message students receive is that the minority language is of value. The affirmation of students' identity through validation of their language can lower the affective filter of language minority students and favor the learning of English. The mainstream students' attitudes towards the language being learned are important as well. Gardner and Lambert (1972) and others have found that when individuals want to learn a second language as a means to integrating into a new cultural group, they learn the second language better. How language minority and mainstream English-speaking students view themselves and how others view them in this process is important for developing more positive self-images as second-language learners and may ultimately affect their image as academic learners (Griego-Jones, 1994).

Cooperative groups have been shown to be effective academically and socially (Calderon, 1989; Jacob & Mattson, 1995; Kagan, 1986; Slavin, 1990). In order to create instructional structures where children have an opportunity to practice talking (Cazden, 1984), cooperative groups that are engaged in hands-on activities are encouraged. Because the language groups are mixed, there are language role models, there is room for multiple talent, and students receive social support from each other (Crushner *et al.*, 1992). Non-English proficient children will still experience some frustration going through the process of learning in their second language, but no longer will this process be structured in a way that isolates them. English-speaking classmates will understand, emotionally and cognitively, what the process of second-language learning is, since they are also going through it. Understanding the process will predispose students to helping each other and to creating the classroom community.

Parental involvement is a critical component for all children. All parents, mainstream and minority, are asked to trust and support the process (Cazabón *et al.*, 1993). One of the commitments they must make is to keep their children in the program for a certain number of years. Another is to support the minority language actively in a variety of ways. Parents are encouraged to take courses in the second language, to volunteer, to attend monthly meetings, and to meet with teachers on curriculum nights. Ramirez *et al.* (1991) found that these types of programs promote greater involvement of minority parents. Although the ways that language minority parents show support for and participate in schools vary (Marquez-Lopez, 1998), parents are more likely to move from a role of support (Delgado-Gaitán, 1987) to a more active role (Rubio, 1995).

Dual language programs also increase parental involvement because there is an environment in which both languages are encouraged throughout the building (Freeman, 1996; Morrison, 1995). A strategy used to promote the use of minority languages within the school is to physically organize the classrooms into clusters or houses. Usually, a good number of the staff, including the front office, speaks the minority language. Loudspeaker announcements, correspondence to students' homes, and other official school business are in both languages.

## Pedagogical Features

By setting up dual language programs that ask parents for a long-term commitment, schools can design solid academic programs for all children while also attending to the unique needs of language minorities (Collier, 1992, 1995). Dual language programs aim to reach high levels of achievement for all children. As Ramirez *et al.* (1991) found from the late-exit programs they studied, students who had greater opportunities to develop strong foundations in the native language not only began to close the gap between themselves and the norming population, they also performed better than the norming population in the long-run. Moreover, dual language classrooms take into consideration children's developmental learning needs, structuring the language and delivery of instruction appropriately. For example, self-contained classrooms where it is the teacher who switches languages daily is considered the most appropriate approach for K–2 because of this group's developmental attachment issues. Beginning in grade 3, teachers are either in self-contained settings or in team teaching situations where the students are the ones to change classes. Teachers in team teaching situations get to select the subjects and to plan their curriculum with more freedom (Bergman *et al.*, 1995; Foster & Swinney, n.d.; Freeman, 1996). Recent developments such as looping, in which teachers stay with the same children more than one year, enable teams of teachers to deal more effectively with the large number of students.

The thematic organization of units of study and the interdisciplinary curriculum are compatible with the structure of dual language programs because of the team teaching approach. The study of patterns, a mathematically based concept, can be developed in both languages and can go in many directions for varying amounts of time across grade levels. This is also possible in the middle school, where extended instructional periods and trimesters can be organized so that all the subjects are covered in both languages and the language needs of language minorities are met.

To avoid simultaneous translation, teachers try to avoid teaching the same subjects or the same units. For example, a teacher team may decide that for one semester or for one unit, Teacher A may teach social studies in English while Teacher B builds on the concepts in the second language through a different unit or through supplementary readings during literature. In the meantime, Teacher B concentrates on science in the second language, which Teacher A will pick up at a later date. Or, they both choose to teach social studies where one part of the world (e.g. Europe) is studied in English and another part (e.g. Asia) in the other language. There is a lot more flexibility in the curriculum of the latter model, but it requires coordination and collaborative planning between teachers. Some teachers have reported the coordination of chapter books for read-alouds so that the children are able to follow the storyline, whether in the first or the second language. Team teaching also requires discussing the assessment and progress of all children together, sitting down with parents during conferences together, and scheduling periods for joint work (Bergman *et al.*, 1995).

Whatever the structure, teachers are provided ongoing staff development. Staff developers may concentrate on new teachers and serve as mentors; they may organize after-school literature groups where teachers decide what literature they would like to concentrate on, especially in the non-English language; they may videotape and engage teachers in reflection on teaching practices individually and in groups; or they may promote teacher research and study groups.

## The Significance of Dual Language Programs

The growing significance of dual language programs can be examined in light of the claims made about the effectiveness of bilingual education. Studies of dual language programs can help us think through the social and academic issues raised by these debates. In this section, we will look at four claims, using the findings from studies of schools that use the 50/50 model (Cazabón *et al.*, 1993, 1999; Christian *et al.*, 1996; Freeman, 1996, 1998; Howard & Christian, 1997; Mahrer & Christian, 1993).

### Claim: Bilingual education programs by design segregate language minorities

Dual language programs, along with many other two-way programs of different types, are designed to bring language minority and mainstream students together at the program and instructional level (Cazabón *et al.*, 1993). Segregation is avoided at the program level where there is a mix of students. As noted, the unidirectional social burden of bilingualism for the language minority child is also avoided, and language is viewed as a resource. Cazabón *et al.* (1993), for example, report that the majority of students in the Amigos program value both languages; similarly, Lambert and Cazabon (1994) found that students in the program 'enjoy school as it is' (p. 9). Students enjoy the integrated, bilingual environment of dual language programs.

Students also benefit from native-speaker models within language-rich environments; this is true for the language majority and language minority learners. One can argue that English-dominant language minorities can be models for their less fluent peers, but the presence of native English-speaking children from other cultural backgrounds (African American, White, and so on) encourages equity by providing children the experience of cross-cultural living that can lead to greater understanding (Mahrer & Christian, 1993). Academic and social integration is a necessity.

When language majority and language minority populations are not mixed within the program, many dual language programs look for other ways of integration. Populations can be integrated through specialized programs in the arts or in a subject matter; such programs tend to develop when teachers plan curriculum and schedules together (Bergman *et al.*, 1995). Lambert and Cazabón (1994) found that participants in the Amigos program were 'forming close friendships with members of their own cultural group and with members of the other cultural groups involved' (p. 9).

Various researchers have pointed out that even in integrated settings such as the two-way programs, there are societally based power relationships that show up in group work and other instructional settings (Freeman, 1998; de Jong, 1996; Pérez & Torres-Guzmán, in press; Valdes, 1997). It is critical that teachers think about the social interactions they set up through the organization of instruction. All students are likely to benefit from programs that create a social and cognitive space for shared school experiences.

### Claim: Bilingual education programs are designed as compensatory and based on a deficit model

In dual language programs, as in other developmental, two-way, enrichment programs, bilingualism, biliteracy, and academic achievement are goals for all children. All students' growth – education, social, and linguistic – is taken into consideration in a developmentally appropriate fashion, independent of their language and their starting point. Dual language models are the opposite of compensatory, deficit-based models. Their aim is additive with respect to languages rather than subtractive. The languages are positioned socially and structurally so that each has the opportunity to develop fully. Teachers are encouraged to be models of the language, to read original literature for children and adolescents, and to encourage language play.

It is precisely the issue of quality and the perspective of enrichment that make a difference. While language has a primary place because of its relationship to cognition, these programs focus on the quality of education and learning that is taking place. The results of evaluations and studies show this. Thomas and Collier (1997) suggest that developmental (two- and one-way) programs are more effective educationally than either traditional bilingual education or ESL (English as a second language) programs. In a review of evaluations of 27 different programs, Mahrer and Christian (1993) found that 'where comparisons [were] possible, students are on the whole doing as well as or better than their fellow students in other programs' (p. 46). The outcomes of these studies show that for the most part, both language minority and language majority students outperform their norming peers in their first language and, by the upper elementary grades, in the second language.

### Claim: Dual language programs favor language majority children rather than language minority children

Achievement outcome studies of enrichment bilingual education programs have looked at programs using the 90/10 model (Lindholm, 1988a, 1988b, 1991, 1996; Lindholm & Aclan, 1991, 1993; Lindholm & Fairchild, 1988); and the 50/50 model (Cazabón et al., 1993, 1999; Christian et al., 1996; Freeman, 1996, 1998; Howard & Christian, 1997; Mahrer & Christian, 1993). Many of these studies had common findings. Freeman (1988) suggests the following, for example.

> The outcome is that all students do master skills in both languages, but the native Spanish speakers and the native English speakers do not become equally bilingual and biliterate. (p. 190)

In addition, the studies show that both language minority and language majority students outperform their norming peers in their first and second language by the upper elementary grades. Language majority students tend to outperform language minority students in English language and reading tests, and language minority students outperform language majority students in the minority language.

Research by Mahrer and Christian (1993) indicates that both populations may develop 'Spanish language skills far beyond those of other students, either as a first or second language . . .' (p. 46). In their study of a dual language school in Virginia (Key School), Howard and Christian (1997) also found that both native Spanish speakers and native English speakers were 'progressing well, and comparable to native speakers in monolingual English classrooms' (p. 21). Their Spanish language development was 'impressive' (p. 21), although their Spanish speaking and writing skills lagged behind their English language ability; the 'differential [was] wider for native English-speaking students' (p. 21). In Cazabón et al.'s (1993, 2000) studies of reading, Spanish-speaking participants outperformed both 'English Amigos' and Spanish cohorts on tests of Spanish literacy. In English, the scores of the English Amigos were higher than the Spanish Amigos and their English controls in grades K–2, but the gap between the Spanish and the English Amigos lessened by grade 3 (Cazabón et al., 1993).

Work by Christian et al. (1996) and Howard and Christian (1997) found a relationship between student writing and language dominance, with native English speakers tending to commit more errors when writing in Spanish than native Spanish speakers did when writing in English. The results of standardized language and reading tests and writing assessments are as expected: Both populations do well in relation to their control peers, with the Spanish-speakers tending to become more proficient bilinguals, and how well they do in relation to each other depends on language dominance.

Perhaps, looking at the students' achievements in the content area would render a clearer picture. In a review of the Spanish math achievement of 17 programs, Mahrer and Christian (1993) found that only 13 reported on English-speaking and Spanish-speaking participants separately. They found that, overall, students made significant progress. For the Spanish-speaking participants, the statistically significant gains in the Spanish math achievement test were found to be consistent across grade levels in grades 1–8. There were statistically significant declining math scores in grades 2, 3, and 7 in three of the programs. In the English math achievement test, the Spanish-speaking students had a wider range in their scores. Four programs reported significant gains, whereas three reported declines. For the English-speaking participants, statistically significant gains are reported for grades 1, 2, 3, 4, and 6, while one program experienced statistically significant declines in the posttest scores in grade 7. The English-speaking students are also reported to have demonstrated a range in English math achievement, with most students performing at or above average. There was no comparison across groups.

Christian *et al.* (1996) report that 'when comparing native and non-native English speakers on ITBS (Iowa Test of Basic Skills) scores, the native English speakers overall scored higher in all seven academic areas'. The ITBS was given in English and tests vocabulary, reading comprehension, language, work-study skills, mathematics, science, and social studies. The English speakers had been studying many of these subjects – science, social studies, and mathematics – in Spanish. Thus, the results suggest that while the content area concepts are being taught in the second language, the concepts learned are transferred to the native language and that the outcomes of the test are associated with the language of dominance (Cazabón *et al.*, 1993).

Many of these findings confirm that there is a language factor associated with achievement. However, some of the research, such as the reports on achievement test scores in the content area do not have clear comparisons between the English and Spanish-speaking participants.

For programming using the 50/50 model, findings must be interpreted within the context of the power relationships that exist. While language minority students are doing better than the control groups, it is the power relationship of the languages that prevails in judging program effectiveness. The tendency is to look only at the students' achievement in English, without taking into consideration that the availability of resources – structural, policy, instructional, linguistic, human, and financial – are initially asymmetrical (Amrein & Peña, 2000) in favor of the language majority. As Freeman (1998) documents at Oyster School in Washington, DC, the entire school must continually deal with the difference between the ideal and the actual in order to reverse the inequitable experiences that perpetuate the status quo. Some of the individual factors that are central to developing bilingualism, such as positive attitudes, need also to be consistently and consciously developed (Griego-Jones, 1994; McCollum, 1994). Freeman (1998)

shows that even when students have acquired academic skills and crosscultural understandings, are able to position themselves as equal participants, and know effective ways of making claims on society, they still need support beyond the elementary grades in order to develop these skills at higher levels.

Despite the differences in achievement, the studies reviewed show that both groups benefit. They become bilingual and achieve, for the most part, at or above their grade level.

### Claim: Dual language programs are too expensive and they do not have sufficient administrative and financial support

Financial considerations in relation to the objective must always be considered. If two solutions are equally effective, we tend to favor the less expensive. Yet where one solution is more effective for more people or where the solution has a long-term effect, we may consider it as more beneficial, even if more expensive.

The costs of bilingual education programs have been difficult to estimate because their funding is usually integrated with other costs. What we assume is that all special language services cost more because special testing, materials, administrative support, and teaching personnel are needed. Furthermore, we assume that the special costs are associated with the native language component. Yet, indications are that the native language component is not what makes for costly programs: The major factor seems to be the extent to which the programs are supplementary or integrated in the school curriculum. For example, the most popular program implemented in schools, the ESL pullout program, does not rely on native language and is still the most expensive (Chambers & Parrish, 1992). What makes it more costly is that a teacher other than the regular teacher is on payroll working with a small number of children in a concentrated way. While the advantage of the model is that you do not need teachers who know the language of the children, it is the least effective of the language service models (Thomas & Collier, 1997).

The second most costly model is the two-way model. The costs associated with it are related to the quality of the teaching staff, the additional native language resources, the professional development of the teachers, and the time associated with curriculum development. In other words, quality of instruction does have its costs. An advantage of these programs is that they motivate parents, particularly middle- and upper-class parents, to secure greater resources in order to ensure educational excellence.

The reality is that for dual language programs to grow, they need leadership, administrative support, and money. What has made them different from other programs is that administrators and leaders have been more likely to push for educational excellence by creating environments of support for both clients and providers and by securing greater resources. When mainstream parents participate, they are also likely to command power and resources that can be channeled into the operations of the enrichment programs. Thus, financial resources are more likely to be distributed equitably and more likely to benefit all children.

## Summary

In this article, the literature on dual language programs has been examined in an attempt to provide a clearer definition and to describe their salient features. Given that school districts are increasingly using the dual language label, it is imperative that there be guidance as to what they need to develop, and that the parameters are clear as to the variations possible within the model. With respect to the issues raised in the bilingual education effectiveness debate, the findings reviewed here suggest that dual language programs, because they tend to promote greater integration, to treat the languages of both groups as resources, and to use their resources to benefit all children educationally, are a sound choice.

## References

Amerein, A. and Peña, R.A. (2000). Asymmetry in dual language practice: Assessing imbalance in a program promoting equality. *EPAA, 8.* (1997). Retrieved February 5, 2000 from the World Wide Web: http://epaa.asu.edu/epaa/v8n8.html.

Bergman, P., Minicucci C., McLaughlin, B., Nelson B. and Woodworth, K. (1995) *School reform and student diversity: Case studies of exemplary practices for LEP students.* Washington, DC: National Clearinghouse for Bilingual Education.

Calderón, M. (1989) Cooperative learning for LEP students. *Intercultural Development Research Association Newsletter,* 16 (9), 1–7.

Cazabón, M., Lambert, W.E. and Hall, G. (1993) *Two-way bilingual education: A progress report on the Amigos Program* (Research Report 7). Santa Cruz, CA and Washington, DC: National Center for Research on Cultural Diversity and Second Language Learning.

Cazabón, M., Nicoladis, E. and Lambert, W.E. (1999) *Becoming bilingual in the Amigos two-way immersion program* (CREDE Research Report 3). Center for Research on Education, Diversity, and Excellence. Retrieved January 28, 2000 from the World Wide Web: www.cal.org/crede/pubs/research/rr3.htm

Cazden, C.B. (1984) *Effective instructional practices in bilingual education.* (Paper commissioned by the National Institute of Education). Washington, DC: White (E.H.) Co.

Chambers, J. and Parrish, T. (1992) *Meeting the challenge of diversity: An evaluation of programs for pupils with limited proficiency in English (Volume 4). Cost of programs and services for LEP students.* Berkeley, CA: BW Associates.

Christian, D. (1994) *Two-way bilingual education: Students learning through two languages* (Educational Practice Report 12). Santa Cruz, CA and Washington, DC: National Center for Research on Cultural Diversity and Second Language Learning.

Christian, D. (1996) Two-way immersion education: Students learning through two languages. *Modern Language Journal,* 80, 66–76.

Christian, D. and Montone, C. (1994) *Two-way bilingual education programs in the United States: 1993–1994 Supplement.* Washington, DC: Center for Applied Linguistics.

Christian, D., Montone, C., Carranza, I. and Lindholm, K. (1996) Profiles in two-way immersion education. *Language in Education: Theory and Practice: 89.* Washington, DC: Center for Applied Linguistics.

Christian, D. and Whitcher, A. (1995) *Directory of two-way bilingual education programs in the United States.* Revised. Santa Cruz, CA and Washington, DC: National Center for Research on Cultural Diversity and Second Language Learning.

Collier, V.P. (1992) A synthesis of studies examining long-term language minority student data on academic achievement. *Bilingual Research Journal, 16,* 187–222.

Collier, V.P. (1995) A synthesis of studies examining long-term language minority student data on academic achievement. In G. Gonzalez and L. Maez (eds) *Compendium of research on bilingual education* (pp. 231–244).

Washington, DC: National Clearinghouse for Bilingual Education.

Crushner, K., McClelland, A. and Stafford, P. (1992) *Human diversity in education*. New York, NY: McGraw-Hill.

Cummins, J. (1992) Empowerment through biliteracy. In J.V. Tinajero and A.F. Ada (eds) *The power of two languages: Literacy and biliteracy for Spanish-speaking students* (pp. 9–25). New York, NY: Macmillan/McGraw-Hill.

De Jong, E. J. (1996) *Integration: What does it mean for language minority students?* Paper presented at the Annual Meeting of the National Association for Bilingual Education, Orlando, FL.

Delgado-Gaitán, C. (1987) Parent perceptions of school: Supportive environments for children. In H.T. Trueba (ed.) *Success or failure? Learning and language minority students* (pp. 131–155). New York, NY: Newbury House.

Etxeberria, F. (1993) *Descripción y tipología del Modelo 'B' en el sistema educativo del la Comunidad Autónoma Vasca*. San Sebastiftran, España: Universidad del País Vasco.

Foster, J.L. and Swinney, R. (n.d.) *The dual language program of Manhattan's District Three*. Unpublished manuscript.

Freeman, R. (1996) Dual language planning at Oyster bilingual school: It's much more than language. *TESOL Quarterly, 30* (3), 557–582.

Freeman, R. (1998) *Bilingual education and social change*. Philadelphia, PA: Multilingual Matters.

Gardner, R.C. and Lambert, W.E. (1972) *Attitudes and motivation in second-language learning*. Rowley, MA: Newbury House.

Genesee, F. (1987) *Learning in two languages: Studies of immersion in bilingual education*. Cambridge, MA: Newbury House.

Gonzalez, N. (1994) The funds of knowledge for teaching project. *Practicing Anthropology, 17* (3), 3–6.

Goodman, K. (1986) *What's whole in whole language?* Portsmouth, NH: Heinemann.

Goodman, K., Goodman, Y. and Flores, B. (1979) *Reading in the bilingual classroom: Literacy and biliteracy*. Rosslyn, VA: National Clearinghouse for Bilingual Education.

Griego-Jones, T. (1994) Assessing students' perceptions of biliteracy in two-way bilingual classrooms. *Journal of Educational Issues of Language Minority Students, 13*, 79–93.

Hakuta, K. and Diaz, R. (1984) The relationship between bilingualism and cognitive ability: A critical discussion and some new longitudinal data. In K.E. Nelson (ed.) *Children's language* (Vol. 5, pp. 319–344). Hillsdale, NJ: Lawrence Erlbaum.

Hornberger, N.H. (1990) Extending enrichment bilingual education: revisiting typologies and redirecting policy. In O. García (ed.) Festschrift for Joshua A. Fishman; Vol.1. *Focus on bilingual education* (pp. 215–234). Philadelphia, PA: John Benjamin.

Howard, E. and Christian D. (1997) *The development of bilingualism and biliteracy in two-way immersion students*. Paper presented at the meeting of the American Educational Research Association, Chicago.

Jacob, E. and Mattson, B. (1995) Cooperative learning: Instructing limited-English proficient students in heterogeneous classes. In O. García and C. Baker (eds) *Policy and practice in bilingual education: Extending the foundations* (pp. 231–236). Clevedon, UK: Multilingual Matters.

Jacobson, R. (1995) Allocating two languages as a key feature of a bilingual methodology. In O. García and C. Baker (eds) *Policy and practice in bilingual education: Extending the foundations* (pp. 166–175). Clevedon, UK: Multilingual Matters.

Kagan, S. (1986). Cooperative learning and sociocultural factors in schooling. In California State Department of Education, *Beyond language: Social and cultural factors in schooling language minority students* (pp. 231–298). Los Angeles, CA: California State University, Evaluation, Dissemination and Assessment Center.

Krashen, S.D. (1987) Bilingual education and second language acquisition theory. In California State Department of Education, *Schooling and language minority students: A theoretical framework* (pp. 51–79). Los Angeles, CA: California State University, Evaluation, Dissemination and Assessment Center.

Ladson-Billings, G. (1994) *Dreamkeepers: Successful teachers of African-American children*. San Francisco: Jossey-Bass.

Lambert, W. E. and Cazabón, M. (1994) *Students' views of the Amigos Program* (Research Report: 11). Santa Cruz, CA and Washington, DC: National Center for Research on Cultural Diversity and Second Language Learning.

Legarreta-Marcaida, D. (1987) Effective use of primary language in the classroom. In California State Department of Education, *Schooling and language minority students: A theoretical framework* (pp. 83–116). Los Angeles, CA:

California State University, Evaluation, Dissemination and Assessment Center.

Leslow-Hurley, J. (2000) *The foundations of dual language instruction* (3rd edn). White Plains, NY: Longman.

Lindholm, K.J. (1987) *Directory of bilingual immersion programs: Two way bilingual education for language minority and majority students.* Los Angeles, CA: University of California. Center for Language Education and Research.

Lindholm, K.J. (1988a) *The Edison Elementary School Bilingual Immersion Program. Student progress after one year of implementation* (Technical Report Series TR9). Los Angeles, CA: University of California. Center for Language Education and Research.

Lindholm, K.J. (1988b) *Evaluation of an 'exemplary' bilingual immersion program.* Los Angeles, CA: University of California. Center for Language Education and Research.

Lindholm, K.J. (1991) Theoretical assumptions and empirical evidence for academic achievement in two languages. *Hispanic Journal of Behavioral Science, 13,* 3–7.

Lindholm, K.J. (1994) Promoting positive cross-cultural attitudes and perceived competence in culturally and linguistically diverse classrooms. In R.A. DeVillar, C.J. Faltis and J.P. Cummins (eds) *Cultural diversity in schools: From rhetoric to practice* (pp. 189–206). Albany, NY: State University of New York Press.

Lindholm, K.J. (1999) *Dual language programs.* Presentation at the Annual Meeting of the New York Association for Bilingual Education, Rye, NY.

Lindholm, K.J. and Aclan, Z. (1991) Bilingual proficiency as a bridge to academic achievement: Results from bilingual/ immersion programs. *Journal of Education, 173* (2), 99–113.

Lindholm, K.J. and Aclan, Z. (1993) *Relationship among psychosocial factors and academic achievement in bilingual Hispanic and Anglo Students.* Paper presented at the Annual Meeting of the American Educational Research Association.

Lindholm-Leary, K. (2000) *Biliteracy for a global society: An idea book on dual language instruction.* Washington, DC: National Clearinghouse for Bilingual Education.

Loeb, M. (1999) *Directory of two-way bilingual immersion programs in the U.S., 1998–1999 Supplement.* Santa Cruz, CA and Washington, DC: National Center for Research on Cultural Diversity and Second Language Learning.

Mahrer, C. and Christian, D. (1993) *A review of findings from two-way bilingual education evaluation reports.* Washington, DC: National Center for Research on Cultural Diversity and Second Language Learning.

Marquez-Lopez, T. (1998) *Parental views on participation, dual language education, and bilingualism.* Unpublished Dissertation. New York, NY: Teachers College, Columbia University.

Martinez, J. and Moore-O'Brien, J.A. (1993) Developing biliteracy in a two-way immersion program. In J.V. Tinajero and A.F. Ada (eds) *The power of two languages: Literacy and biliteracy for Spanish-speaking students* (pp. 276–293). New York, NY: Macmillan/McGraw-Hill.

McCollum, P. (1994) Language use in two-way bilingual education programs. *Intercultural Development Research Association Newsletter, 21,* 9–11.

Mercado, C.I. and Moll, L.C. (1997) The study of funds of knowledge: Collaborative research in Latino homes. *CENTRO Journal of the Center for Puerto Rican Studies, IX* (9), 26–42.

Morrison, S.H. (1995) A Spanish-English dual language program in New York City. *Annals of the American Academy of Political & Social Science, 508,* 160–169.

Nieto, S. (1995) *Affirming diversity.* White Plains, NY: Longman.

Olmedo, I.M. (1997) Voices of our past: Using oral history to explore funds of knowledge within a Puerto Rican family. *AEQ, 28,* 550–573.

Pérez, B. and Torres-Guzmán, M.E. (1996) *Learning in two worlds: An integrated Spanish/English biliteracy approach* (2nd edn). White Plains, NY: Longman.

Pérez, B. and Torres-Guzmán, M.E. (in press). *Literacy in two-way bilingual education programs.*

Ramirez, J.D., Yuen, S.D. and Ramey, D.R. (1991) *Executive summary, Final report: Longitudinal study of structured English immersion strategy, early-exit and late-exit transitional bilingual education programs for language minority children,* (U.S. Department of Education Contract No. 300–87–0156). San Mateo, CA: Aguire International.

Rubio, O. (1995) Yo soy voluntaria: volunteering in a dual language school. *Urban Education, 29,* 396–409.

Slavin, R.E. (1990) *Cooperative learning: Theory, research, and practice.* Englewood Cliffs, NJ: Prentice-Hall.

Thomas, W. P. and Collier, V. (1997) *School effectiveness for language minority students. NCBE*

Resource Collection Series, 9. Washington, DC: National Clearinghouse for Bilingual Education.

Torres-Guzmán, M.E. (1990) Response to 'If not here, where? If not now, when?' In E. Gordon (ed.) *A study of minority student achievement in* *Montgomery County public schools*. New York, NY: Gordon and Associates.

Valdes, G. (1997) Dual language Immersion Programs: A cautionary note concerning the education of language minority students. *Harvard Education Review, 67* (3), 391–429.

## Questions

1.  How are two languages used in a Dual Language program? What language/linguistic philosophy, policies, provision and practices are important, and for what reasons?
2.  What sociocultural and (non-language) pedagogical features are there in Dual Language programs? Do these differ from mainstream schooling?
3.  Torres-Guzmán says that most bilingual education programs that are designated 'dual language' are two-way. What is a two-way dual language program? What are the advantages and disadvantages of two-way dual language programs?
4.  What criticisms are made of Dual Language schools? What claims are made for their effectiveness? What criticisms and claims seem supported by research, and which of these are educational and what are political?

## Activities

1.  Identify a two-way dual language program (or similar) in your vicinity. Interview a language minority and a language majority child who are receiving dual language instruction in mixed groups. Find out how each feels when the medium of instruction is not their mother tongue. Are there differences between the language majority child and the language minority child? Record their answers. Then write an essay summarizing the differences.
2.  Make a list of the 'dual language programs' that your local educational authority supports. Then contact by telephone at least ten of the schools in the list and ascertain what features, of those identified by Torres-Guzmán, the school supports. Prepare a report for your classmates.
3.  Ask five educators in one school what 'bilingual' means to them. Then ask them how the term 'bilingual' is used in their school. Record their answers on an answer sheet with three columns: one for their definition, one for the school's definition, one for your definition based on reading. Record on top of the answer sheet the characteristics of the school in question (example: size, public or private, urban or suburban, large language minority population or large language majority population, socioeconomic profile of the school).

    Different groups might interview educators in schools that have different characteristics. Ideally this includes a Dual Language school. Share the groups' answers. Make a chart with the class results.
4.  Observe a classroom with a linguistically heterogeneous group. This may be a two-way dual language program or another program with second language classes. Give a sociolinguistic profile of the classroom. Then record how languages are used (a) by the children in the classroom (b) by the teacher (c) by other staff in the school (d) parents when visiting the school (e.g. to fetch their children) (e) on wall displays and (f) by students in playground.

Share with the teacher the instances and variety that you have recorded. Ask for her understanding and interpretation of what was going on, and her evaluation of how effective is students' language development. Write an essay to describe and evaluate this conversation.

5. For one whole day, observe a bilingual student who is proficient in two languages. Note their language use at home, in the classroom, and outside the school and home. Place your observations on a record sheet designed by you or the class. Then write an essay summarizing the differences in language use in different domains.

6. Interview a monolingual teacher about the bilingual teachers in their school. Record her personal beliefs, ideas and characteristics. Find out how she feels about the employment of bilingual teachers and whether preferential treatment should be given in their employment, their value with language minority children and, in general, their teaching competences and their training. Then ask her about what she needs to know in her school about bilingualism, bilingual education, the language and culture of ethnolinguistic minorities. Tape and transcribe the interview.

7. Visit a dual language classroom. Survey the resource material available in the minority language. On a recording sheet, write the title, the amount of each title available, the subject, where published and in which language. What language dominates in terms of available resource material? Is there any material that is bilingual, that is, written in both the majority and the minority language? Observe the class for a day. Who uses the material in the minority language and how is it used? Who uses the bilingual material and how is it used? Record your answers.

## Further Reading

Baker, C. (2006) *Foundations of Bilingual Education and Bilingualism* (4th edn). Clevedon: Multilingual Matters (chapters 11, 12, 13).

Cloud, N., Genesee, F. and Hamayan, E.V. (2000) *Dual Language Instruction: A Handbook for Enriched Education*. Boston: Heinle and Heinle.

García, O. (2005) Lost in transculturation: The case of bilingual education in New York City. In M. Pütz, J. Fishman and JoAnne Neff-van Aertselaer (eds) *'Along the Routes to Power': Explorations of the Empowerment through Language*. Berlin/New York: Mouton de Gruyter.

Howard, E.R., Sugarman, J., Christian, D., Lindholm-Leary, K. and Rogers, D. (2005) *Guiding Principles for Dual Language Education*. Washington, DC: Center for Applied Linguistics. http://www.cal.org/twi/guidingprinciples.htm

Lindholm-Leary, K.J. (2001) *Dual Language Education*. Clevedon: Multilingual Matters.

Lindholm-Leary, K.J. (2005) Review of research and best practices on effective features of dual language education programs. http://www.lindholm-leary.com/resources/review_research.pdf

Lindholm-Leary, K.J. and Borsato, G. (2006) Academic achievement. In F. Genesee, K.J. Lindholm-Leary, W. Saunders and D. Christian (eds) *Educating English Learners: A Synthesis of Empirical Evidence*. New York: Cambridge University Press.

Valdés, G. (1997) Dual-language immersion programs: A cautionary note concerning the education of language-minority students. *Harvard Educational Review* 67: 391–429.

# Rethinking the Education of English Language Learners: Transitional Bilingual Education Programs

## Abelardo Villarreal

Campus principals can be bold and courageous people, but all of them must answer for the success or failure of students to reach high achievement standards. Having to answer for student success can be a rewarding and exhilarating experience that triggers the spirit for more of the same. Rationalizing student failure can be a demoralizing and belittling experience that can jeopardize a job and any hopes for upward mobility in the educational hierarchy.

School reform initiatives have become the hope for upgrading the achievement levels of all students. Of concern to many administrators are the English language learners who remain the most neglected and short-changed in the school reform movement with little significant increases, if any, on their achievement levels (Moss & Puma, 1995). The struggle to achieve equity-based excellence in education points to a need for rethinking the educational goals, strategies, and processes that presently shape educational programs. This article provides campus principals, in particular, insights about the impact of an inappropriate transitional bilingual education program for English language learners. It is an effort to demonstrate how negative attitudes, prejudices, biases, and misinformation about bilingual education programs lead to inappropriate practices and unfounded, unsubstantiated, and misinformed policies. In addition, it attempts to provide well-intentioned principals with ideas and strategies that can enhance the quality of their transitional bilingual education programs.

Genesee (1999) defines transitional bilingual education as 'the most common form of bilingual education for English language learners . . . [it] provides academic instruction in English

language learners' primary language as they learn English' (p. 13). Research and experience show that most transitional bilingual education programs are segregated and anemic. They operate in isolation, lack public and administrative support, languish in poorly designed models of instruction (August & Hakuta, 1997), and are staffed by personnel with preconceived notions on the innate and acquired abilities and aspirations of English language learners (Moss & Puma, 1995) and their families.

If recent population trends continue, the number of English language learners will increase to at least an additional one million students within the next decade (Council of Chief State School Officers, 1998). Although the educational level of English language learners has increased incrementally over the years (Moss & Puma, 1995), the overall results have been disastrous and have had a grave impact on this growing student population. This is evidenced by the fact that about 25% of English language learners repeat a grade by third grade (Moss & Puma, 1995).

There is a ray of hope, however. A small percentage of effective programs have provided some valuable insights about what works for English language learners (August & Hakuta, 1997). These successful programs have gone through the complete cycle of the change process – defining a quality program, acquiring buy in from staff, and providing an environment conducive to change – as shown by their institutionalization into the mainstream curriculum, while those struggling transitional bilingual education programs are stuck in the first step of the change process. All of these steps are key ingredients in a successful innovation.

During my 30 years of involvement in bilingual education as a parent, then as a teacher, curriculum developer, elementary school principal, secondary education director, university faculty and educational consultant, I visited numerous bilingual education programs and collected copious notes on what I observed. Also, over time, I have reviewed and analyzed numerous articles and research studies that support or oppose bilingual education. My recollections and conclusions are the major sources of information used to frame this article. There is a saying in Spanish that best characterizes the approach: '*Mas sabe el diablo por viejo que por diablo.*'

## Condition of Education for English Language Learners

Elementary English language learners ordinarily trail other students academically and are retained in higher percentages. Prospects, a national, longitudinal study mandated by the US Congress in 1995 (Moss & Puma, 1995), summarizes key findings as they relate to academic performance, instructional programs and practices, and competency of teaching personnel. Key findings include the following:

### Academic performance

- When compared to all third graders, 7% received a grade of unsatisfactory in reading compared to 16% of English language learners and 19% of English language learners in high-poverty schools. In mathematics, the gap is slightly higher ranging from 8% of all third graders receiving an unsatisfactory grade, to 18% of English language learners and 22% of English language learners in high-poverty schools.
- When teachers were asked about their perceptions relative to student ability and performance, they reported an even larger gap with perceptions of English language learners being lower.
- By third grade, 25% of English language learners compared to 15% of all other students have been retained in at least one grade.

### Instructional programs and practices

- Approximately 52% of English language learners receive content area instruction in a language other than English. Wherever a language other than English is used, 40% of the instruction in first grade classrooms is in English, while 50% of the instruction is in English in third grade classrooms. The percentage between the use of English and other language varies depending on high or low concentrations of English language learners. Traditionally, schools with high concentrations of English language learners tend to use the native language in higher proportions.
- Approximately one-third of first and third grade English language learners do not receive a special language program such as bilingual education or English as a second language (ESL).

### Staffing

- Many English language learners are in schools with no role models with the same ethnic background. This is an example of 'a mismatch between the diverse population of students and the relatively homogeneous population of teachers [that] makes it difficult for all students to have role models in school with whom they can readily identify' (Latham *et al.*, 1999: 23).
- An alarming percentage of teachers of English language learners do not have the credentials or training to teach atypical students with diverse needs. For example, approximately one-third of first grade English language learners and one-fifth of third grade English language learners receive instruction by a teacher credentialed in bilingual education.
- Henke *et al.* (1997) reported that although minority students comprised 32% in 1993–94, only 13% of teachers are minority teachers.

Since the early 1970s, pioneers of bilingual education, Dr José A. Cárdenas and Dr Blandina Cárdenas, have pinpointed areas of incompatibilities between school practices and the educational needs of minority children. In the midst of those tumultuous times involving litigation after litigation that sought an answer to a problem of national scope, Cárdenas and Cárdenas conceptualized the Theory of Incompatibilities, a framework for schools to use in understanding the factors contributing to the dismal failure of Hispanic children, the problems plaguing the education establishment, and the adequate instructional responses. Cárdenas and Cárdenas (1977) identified five areas of incompatibilities.

1. Poverty: Schools must adapt the program that 'fails to take into account these unique early development patterns and assumes (and requires) the same developmental level normally found in middle-class children' (p. 23).
2. Culture: Minority children bring a culture that schools sometimes fail to acknowledge and integrate into the curriculum.
3. Language: A student's first language must be considered in adjusting the curriculum and delivering instruction.
4. Mobility: English language learners are highly mobile; curriculum is designed for stable populations.
5. Societal Perceptions: Negative perceptions about these students create an environment of neglect and low levels of expectation.

More than 25 years later the research on effective bilingual education programs is providing evidence to support the 'theory of incompatibilities'.

## Framework for Classifying Transitional Bilingual Education Programs

Many states require school districts to implement, at a minimum, transitional bilingual education programs for English language learners at the elementary grades and ESL at the middle and high school grades. For example, the majority of elementary schools in Texas have strategically chosen transitional bilingual education programs over developmental bilingual education programs. It is the most politically expedient approach to take, less threatening and closest to maintaining the status quo, minimally disrupting the standard way of doing things.

A vast majority of schools choose transitional bilingual education programs simply because of their temporary nature and a philosophy that places the learning of English and through English as the ultimate and only goal of the program. Furthermore, many schools place the mainstream program as the only instructional program that will ultimately provide the English language learners with the minimal education that they need in order to survive and function in our political and economic system. Many of these programs operate

in a cloud of covert prejudices and biases against these students' abilities and their families' beliefs about the need for an education.

Since their inception, transitional bilingual education programs have been doomed to failure. There is, however, 'superficial' understanding of the need to teach in the native language (sometimes required by legislation and state mandates) and an assumption that English language learners learn content only in English. Many of these transitional bilingual education programs are based on the premise that English language learners reach the school doors with a language and a culture that interfere with the schools' learning opportunities. Then, there are administrators who firmly believe in the principles of good bilingual education instruction but succumb to the pressure of preparing students as soon as possible for the state's standardized achievement measure that is administered in English.

In all cases, principals find themselves in difficult predicaments, often times mandating instruction that favors the use of English and limiting the use of Spanish or any other language to only a few minutes. Contrary to what some bilingual education critics say, transitional bilingual education programs are overwhelmingly taught in English. Many lack a spirited and determined leadership necessary to make education work for English language learners.

Although limited in addressing the potential which language minority students bring to school, transitional bilingual education programs can have a positive impact on the academic achievement of English language learners. Philosophically, its major limitations stem from political expediency and a degree of public xenophobia that have corrupted efforts to provide a quality educational program for these students. English language learners already bring proficiency in a language other than English, a language that could be developed formally side-by-side with English, creating bilingual citizens with minimal effort. This student asset is ignored.

Furthermore, it is politically expedient to minimize the demands that a bilingual program will have on the existing teacher preparation programs, on existing teaching staff and administrators, and on the cost of education. If the academic performance of English language learners was the measure of instructional effectiveness of transitional bilingual education programs, one would have to conclude that this program type has been a dismal failure. There is, however, evidence that transitional bilingual education programs, when implemented correctly, can have a positive impact on the academic achievement of English language learners.

A close examination of existing transitional bilingual education programs in Texas reveals that two contextual conditions are primarily responsible for the success or demise of the program. These two conditions, called 'dimensions', embody the attributes of successful transitional bilingual programs in varying degrees. These dimensions are (1) support of the program at all levels and (2) knowledge base of bilingual education as evidenced through curriculum and instructional activities. Knowledge base refers to research-based knowledge in first- and second-language learning, bilingual education practices, and ESL methodologies. It ranges from the presence of a strong knowledge base in some key individuals in the school district to operational evidence of research-based practices at all levels of the school hierarchy. Support refers to moral, physical, and fiscal support for bilingual education and ESL methods. It is evidenced by educators' commitment to make education work for English language learners and by full fiscal support for competent staff and a quality curriculum. Figure 1 describes four classifications based on the degree to which transitional bilingual education programs show evidence of these two dimensions. The first prototype illustrated in Quadrant I represents those programs that have all the major attributes of a successful program. Quadrant II is the prototype that is perhaps most in use by many schools. It is referred to as an 'acquiescent' bilingual program because it adheres closely to the law. Quadrant III includes programs in schools with high concentrations of English language learners, which lack knowledge and sophistication, and which are under-funded both at the district and school levels. The last quadrant includes those programs in school districts that overtly oppose any special programs for English language learners.

The quadrants illustrate the unique characteristics of four categories of transitional bilingual education programs. Quadrant I represents programs that are responsible and produce high academic achievement results in English language learners. Quadrant II represents those with little support but that strive to comply with minimum requirements of the law. Quadrant III are those that provide a high degree of moral support but lack the knowledge, sophistication, and competent staff to implement a quality instructional program. Quadrant IV lacks moral support and shows little empathy with a concern for a quality educational program for English language learners. Programs in Quadrants II, III, and IV are referred to in this article as the struggling programs – programs responsible for the overall poor academic performance of English language learners.

## Successful Transitional Bilingual Education Programs: Quadrant I

Quadrant I transitional bilingual education programs 'talk the walk' (articulate what needs to be done) and 'walk the talk' (do what should be done). These programs evolve in academic environments that are determined to succeed and have no excuses for anything less than success. A major limitation is their philosophy to phase out the use and teaching of the native language once proficiency in English has been obtained. This philosophy negates what the English language learners bring – another language and another culture that are not part of the mainstream. Instead of seeing the language and culture as national assets that should be preserved and capitalized on, they are abandoned as soon as the child exits the bilingual education program.

A successful model of a transitional bilingual education program is based on the most recent knowledge of the linguistic, cognitive, and social development of language-minority children. Even though it is based on the most current knowledge about what works for English language learners, any model of instruction will require a more extensive evaluation that allows for applying findings to new situations with varying levels of similarities and differences. Successful transitional bilingual education schools have been able to neutralize or circumvent the effects of contextual issues (poverty, violence) within families and communities on the quality of education and achievement outcomes of English language learners.

Figure 2 is a checklist that elaborates on the attributes of Quadrant I transitional bilingual education programs. It is provided to help strug-

| Quadrant I – Committed, Unenlightened TBE Program | Quadrant II – Model TBE Program |
|---|---|
| • Low student outcomes and limited school engagement.<br>• Supportive and caring campus environment; low resources.<br>• An instructional plan that meets minimum requirements; integrated with mainstream curriculum.<br>• Good relations with community/parents; family involvement is limited to working to help the school.<br>• Lacks knowledge sophistication at all levels. | • Positive student outcomes and school engagement.<br>• Family/supportive campus environment.<br>• Pedagogically sound curriculum and instructional practices.<br>• Community/family involvement seen as imperative and encouraged. |
| Quadrant III – Recalcitrant TBE Program | Quadrant IV – Acquiescent TBE Program |
| • Low student outcomes and isolated from the mainstream campus.<br>• Hostile and stereotypical campus environment; low student expectations.<br>• Regular mainstream curriculum with some adaptations provided through teacher aides who can speak the language.<br>• Parents/community perceived as a liability; minimal parental involvement activities. | • Low student outcomes and limited school engagement.<br>• Supportive campus environment to comply with minimum requirements.<br>• Pedagogically sound instructional plan, but poor implementation and poor integration with mainstream curriculum.<br>• Limited community/family involvement encouraged. |

**Figure 1** Framework for classifying Transitional Bilingual Education (TBE) programs

gling programs establish improvement goals. It is also the backdrop for descriptions of schools with struggling transitional bilingual programs.

**Figure 2** Checklist of attributes of successful transitional bilingual education programs

*Conducive Environment*
• Values and celebrates student linguistic and cultural diversity (Lein *et al.*, 1997; Ogbu and Matute-Bianchi, 1986).
• Values all students, communicates high expectations (Lien *et al.*, 1997; Villarreal & Solis, 1998).
• Integrates instructional program and all students in the overall school operation (Berman *et al.*, 1995; McLoed, 1996; Tikunoff *et al.*, 1991).

*Spirited and Determined Leadership*
• Supports educational equity and excellence for all students (Carter & Chatfield, 1986; Lucas *et al.*, 1990).
• Imparts a sense of urgency for maintaining

high academic standards for all students (Lien *et al.*, 1997).
• Nurtures and sustains a family environment that is inclusive of parents, students, and teachers (McLoed, 1996).
• Expects and exerts pressure to excel (Goldenberg & Sullivan, 1994).

*Dedicated and Knowledgeable Staff*
• All staff members 'walk the talk' and team up to excel in the bilingual education program.
• Teachers consistently receive training and are provided technical assistance when the need arises.
• Teachers receive training that is aligned with the instructional plan prepared for English language learners (Milk *et al.*, 1992).
• Teachers are equipped with strategies and techniques consistent with phonetic and meaning-based approaches.
• Recruitment procedures are strict and seek the best-qualified staff for the bilingual education staff (Maroney, 1998).

- Teachers demonstrate a commitment to make education work for English language learners.
- Teachers receive training and know how to assess areas of student needs and plan instruction accordingly.

*Partnering with Community and Families*
- Relationships with the community and families go beyond just helping at school; they are characterized by a strong desire to get parents involved in the educational process (Robledo Montecel *et al.*, 1993).
- Community and families are perceived as assets that should be capitalized on and integrated into the school resources in a manner that values and seeks their contributions (Moll *et al.*, 1992).
- Families play a key role in promoting the cognitive and academic development of their children, and their contributions should be coordinated and integrated into the learning environment (Montemayor, 1997).
- Schools care for the welfare of families by providing opportunities to access various social services available in the community.
- Schools and families join forces to advocate children's rights (Robledo Montecel *et al.*, 1993).

*Accessible Learning Environment*
- Schools use a diversity of teaching approaches to ensure that all children have access to learning in the most efficient and effective manner (Lucas *et al.*, 1990).
- The learning environment is modified in a number of ways to accommodate the varying needs of English language learners (Berman *et al.*, 1995).
- Classroom teachers use family and community's 'funds of knowledge' to base and enrich instruction (Moll *et al.*, 1992).

*Program and Curriculum Alignment*
- Schools have a clear understanding of levels of language and content instruction and use these levels for instructional planning to facilitate transition and efficient progress (Berman *et al.*, 1995).
- Teachers from different grade levels produce and implement a seamless curriculum that flows uninterrupted (McLoed, 1996).

- Goals and objectives for the bilingual program flow from the mainstream curriculum; learning standards are not lowered.
- Schools support students exiting from the bilingual program and transitioning to the mainstream curriculum and address obstacles that could lead to failure in the mainstream program.

*Capitalizing on the Student Language and Cultural Resources*
- Schools celebrate and value a diversity of languages and cultures as community assets and valuable to the national interest (Lucas & Katz, 1994).
- Schools acknowledge the power of the first language in learning English faster and more effectively (Moll & Diaz, 1985).

*Inclusive and Comprehensive Curriculum*
- The curriculum is balanced to ensure that its literacy program develops basic and higher order thinking skills (McLoed, 1996).
- Teaching approaches are eclectic, customizing instruction with phonetic and meaning-based approaches (Adams & Bruck, 1995; Purcell-Gates, 1996).
- Schools ensure that reading comprehension and writing skills are developed in the strongest language and provide opportunities to demonstrate their transfer in English (Wong-Fillmore *et al.*, 1985).
- Instruction of skills and concepts addressed in the state-mandated test or standardized tests receive special attention through explicit skill instructional activities.
- Time is allocated specifically for explicit basic and higher order thinking skill instruction; time schedules vary accordingly (Escamilla, 1994).
- Teachers provide opportunities for student-initiated and student-directed learning activities.
- Teachers relate instruction to practical and meaningful student experiences (Pease-Alvarez *et al.*, 1991).
- English language learners have access to grade-level content; curriculum is not watered down (McLoed, 1996),

*Instructional Practices and Strategies*
- Teachers use periodic, systematic, and multiple student assessment measures to

inform the instructional decision-making process (Valdez-Pierce & O'Malley, 1992).

- Assessment is conducted in the student's native language and English when appropriate (McCollum, 1999).
- Student assessment results are discussed and used collaboratively with other teachers to plan and coordinate instruction (McCollum, 1999).
- Successful classrooms use cooperative and collaborative approaches to learning (Calderon *et al.*, 1996).
- Teachers build in redundancy in critical skills areas (Saunders *et al.*, 1998).
- Ample opportunities are provided for English language learners to hear adults who are native language speakers both at the social and academic levels (Calderon *et al.*, 1996; Gersten, 1996).
- Students are provided opportunities for interaction with English-speaking peers (McLoed, 1996).
- Questioning strategies require students to clarify and expand on understanding of text (Gersten, 1996). Teachers develop students' metacognitive skills and provide opportunities for students to show competence in selecting and using metacognitive skills (Dianda & Flaherty, 1995). Teachers check that instruction is comprehensible and modify instruction accordingly.

*Equity-Based Education Excellence*
- English language learners are integrated in both academic and social contexts with native English-speaking students (McLoed, 1996).
- The instructional program for English language learners maintains the high academic standards required for all students.
- TBE programs are an integral part of the mainstream curriculum.
- TBE programs have the facilities and resources available to do what they must do.

## Quadrant II, III, and IV Programs: The Struggling Program

Three profiles of transitional bilingual education programs (Quadrants II, III, IV) not only fail to address the attributes of effective educational programs, but also are flawed conceptually and operationally. Their flaws are consistent with the degree to which each prototype shares the following characteristics and myths:

1. Struggling programs usually share the philosophy that learning through English is crucial and perhaps the only and best way to teach English language learners.
2. All believe that using the native language may have some value but ignore that learning in the students' native language can lead to greater facility in learning English.
3. All maintain that achievement in students' native language must be verified in English before it is acknowledged.
4. There is blind faith on the appropriateness of the mainstream curriculum in English to meet the diverse needs of students.
5. There is a strong sentiment that students who speak a language other than English must strive to conform. The onus of responsibility for education is on the family and student.

Struggling programs differ among themselves; however, on their commitment to make education work for English language learners, their belief on the abilities of English language learners to succeed, and their ability to use theory and make it operational through practice.

The following scenario represents the attitudes of a counselor in Quadrant II and Quadrant IV schools as he indirectly attempts to influence and guide the parent to deny student enrollment in bilingual education.

### Scenario A

Mr Comesalsa is an elementary counselor who is responsible for the identification and placement of students who are eligible for special services because of their limited proficiency in English. He is responsible for following up with parents who indicate in the home survey that they speak Spanish at home most of the time.

'Good morning. Are you Victoria's parents?' asks Mr Comesalsa. 'You state in this form that your family speaks Spanish at home all the time. Because of that we will have to test Victoria. Do you know what will happen if we test Victoria and she is found to need special instruction because she does not speak English well?'

'No' answers the mother.

'Well, she will be placed in a bilingual

education classroom that is located in one of the portables. She will be learning Spanish.'

'Spanish! I thought she was coming to school to leam English. I can teach her Spanish at home. In fact, Victoria and my other kids speak English all the time at home. Let me correct that form', answers the mother. Quadrant II school districts (the acquiescent group) have the knowledge necessary and have made the commitment to at least comply with minimum state and federal guidelines. They 'talk the walk' but fail miserably in 'walking the talk'. These schools are, however, guided by an urgency to exit students from the program as soon as possible. Consequently, one will witness the phenomenon that students at the lower grades are doing exceptionally well but show a decline and a widening of the educational gap between English language learners and majority students.

The second scenario represents the conceptual shallowness of a Quadrant III transitional bilingual education program that is implemented in a context of support for English language learners' success academically.

### Scenario B

Mr Puro Corazon is a principal at an elementary school which has 65 students who have been identified as English language learners. During his first staff meeting with the faculty of La Esperanza Elementary School, he reviews the requirements of a bilingual education program.

'This year, our enrollment of English language learners has increased by about 20 students. We will have three bilingual education classes. In this school we must do whatever is needed to succeed with our English language learners', comments the principal.

'What happens in these bilingual education classes? I hear that they teach only Spanish. Is this correct?' remarks one of the new teachers in the campus.

'In our bilingual education classes, teachers are instructed to use as much English as possible. We value the students' language and culture. However, these students must develop their English as soon as possible. We stress the development of English', comments the principal.

'I took a course at the university in bilingual education methods and what was impressed on us was that state guidelines require the use of Spanish most of the time to ensure that concepts are learned. We were also told that state guidelines were just minimums and sometimes were in conflict with what research tells us needs to happen. Are we not following state guidelines?' reacts the new teacher.

'We are in compliance with state law and regulations. Keep this in mind, we do what we think we must do. Does that answer your question?' responds the principal.

Quadrant III schools have the 'heart in the right place' and are willing to do whatever is needed to improve the education of English language learners. In this paradigm, they are the committed, unenlightened schools. However, these schools are limited by a lack of knowledge and apathy toward upgrading their knowledge base. It is not uncommon to see such schools staffed with people whose whole career has been spent in that campus. There is a feeling of despair with the inability of many students to achieve, but learning takes place in a loving and caring environment. Students usually stay in school, but lack the necessary life skills to compete with other students in the real world, both academically and in their preparation for the workplace.

The third scenario represents the negative attitudes of a teacher in trying to influence a beginning teacher in a Quadrant IV school.

### Scenario C

Ms Maniorca is a second grade teacher who has been at this school for almost 25 years. She is well known in the community as a strict disciplinarian and one who retains at least 25% of her class every year. This community is approximately 75% Latino and 25% Anglo students. She regularly complains because the school has banned the use of lower first and high first grade classrooms. Consequently, she feels her students are not quite ready for second grade.

'It is that time of the year again. I have to decide who will be promoted and who will be retained. Somehow I will have to prove to this school that most of my students come with a number of deficiencies and need more than one year in first grade to begin to work close to where my regular students are', comments Ms Maniorca to Ms Ojald, a beginning teacher.

'What do you mean when you say "regular students"?' asks the beginning teacher.

'My regular students are those who already speak English and come from families where they care for their children. Many of my students come from families that speak only Spanish. This already puts them behind my regular students.

Their parents are not high school graduates, some of them have only four or five years of schooling. They really don't care; why should I?' answers the frustrated teacher.

'So, what is our responsibility to these students?' asks the beginning teacher.

'Take care of them until they reach the seventh grade. By then, they will be ready to drop out. There is no hope.'

Schools in Quadrant IV are referred to as recalcitrant schools. These schools refuse covertly to comply with the minimum requirements established by state and federal guidelines. They operate in environments where negative and stereotypical preconceived ideas exist about the abilities and aspirations of English language learners. Not only are their staff indifferent, but they also are hostile and are convinced that these students will eventually leave school.

## Challenges for Program Improvement

Struggling schools demonstrate school practices that are less than or diametrically opposed to what we know about successful transitional bilingual education programs. I use the major attribute categories in the checklist of the model program to describe the contrasting practices observed in the three prototypes of struggling programs. These practices provide a snapshot of what is happening in struggling schools. Furthermore, I provide some insights on key challenges for a struggling school principal. The list of challenges is not exhaustive but includes the most critical challenges. If addressed adequately (*con ánimo y corazón*), principals will definitely see an improvement in the program.

### Dimension 1: Program support and commitment

*A conducive and supportive climate*

A key finding is that community and school beliefs about the ability of English language learners to succeed academically and an ethos of high expectations for students are prerequisites to creating a sense of purpose and a shared commitment to *sí se puede*.

**Challenge: Make TBE an integral part of the mainstream curriculum**. It is not uncommon to find the bilingual education program operating in isolation with few, if any, links to the mainstream curriculum. It is also not rare to find schools garnering resources to upgrade the main-stream curriculum with few, if any, allocated for the bilingual education program curriculum. Had it not been for federal resources such as Title VII, the Bilingual Education Act, and additional funds provided for bilingual education by states, the bilingual program would probably be suffering from total neglect. In fact, curriculum content (grade level skills, concepts, and knowledge) should be basically the same for English language learners and other students. The delivery occurs in the students' native language or by using ESL techniques. Some schools begin by including bilingual education teachers in the campus committee designed to align the mainstream curriculum to the state-mandated test or academic standards. When the time comes to align materials to the locally approved academic standards, bilingual teachers form their own committee to select the appropriate materials to deliver the instruction. This alleviates the fears that bilingual education does not prepare students as well as the mainstream curriculum. The principal's responsibility is to communicate to teachers, parents, and the community that bilingual education is tantamount to the local mainstream curriculum and is not a remediation program. Students who progress academically through a bilingual education curriculum will be just as prepared as any other student in the district. In fact, the student in the bilingual education classroom will have also developed some proficiency in reading and writing in the native language.

**Challenge: Improve the school climate.** The climate that surrounds the instruction of English language learners must be positive, encouraging, and inviting for teachers, students, and their families. A sense of optimism and commitment must prevail. Administrators and teachers can communicate high expectations to students, including English language learners, and can show particular manifestations of high expectations. Some schools do this by creating banners that convey high expectations in both English and the native language. One school had a banner that read: 'Only apathy will stop us from reaching the highest star *Sólo la indiferencia nos puede parar de lograr la meta más alta.*' This banner was on the school marquee and would be placed at the entrance of each wing. Furthermore, teachers were asked to discuss with students what this meant each morning. Teachers and students collaboratively would identify their goal for that day. Families received training

*Practices that collectively created a less than conducive school climate*

| Quadrant II Acquiescent TBE Program | Quadrant III Committed, Unenlightened TBE Program | Quadrant IV Recalcitrant TBE Program |
|---|---|---|
| • Minimizes the importance of learning in the native language.<br>• Stresses the importance of teaching in English most of the time.<br>• Establishes responsibility to take advantage of learning opportunities for students.<br>• Maintains a remediation program until students are ready to exit bilingual education. | • Feels an urgency and cares for students' welfare.<br>• Articulates a high level of commitment to make education work for English language learners.<br>• Establishes programs with little direction or vision. | • Ignores and many times demeans the language and culture of English language learners.<br>• Provides 'sink or swim' approach to learning English and concepts.<br>• Has preconceived negative misconceptions of English language learners' abilities and aspirations.<br>• Isolates English language learners and provides basically remedial attention. |

from the school on ways to set and communicate high expectations for students. Whenever the school failed to reach its goal, the focus was not on finding an excuse but on how to adjust the instruction. In a study, Successful Texas Schoolwide Programs, the authors outline their findings around seven themes. One theme, 'No Excuses', describes how in spite of numerous obstacles and difficult odds, teachers and administrators are able to do what they feel is needed in order for students to be successful. A task for the principal is to get teachers, administrators, families, and communities together to develop a vision that is inclusive of all students. Nonnegotiable at these meetings are the following ideas: strive high; every student has the potential; no excuses; *Sí se puede*.

A diversity of languages and cultures in the school was validated through various cultural celebrations and the integration of English language learners in as many classes as possible. For example, at the first staff meeting of the year, the principal made it a point to talk about the different languages and cultures represented at the campus. Part of the principal's message was to use this campus asset and capitalize on it by discussing in teacher meetings and classes about the benefits of diversity. Students were provided an option to learn another language. In this particular case, a paraprofessional who was a teacher in Mexico but did not have the credentials in the United States was hired to teach Spanish. Each class had at least 45 minutes a week of Spanish language instruction.

### Spirited and Determined Leadership

A key finding is that leadership at both the administrative and classroom levels determines the level of commitment to make bilingual education programs a success that is manifested in increased academic achievement, low dropout rates, high graduation rates, and low retention rates.

**Challenge: Establish and nurture human relationships among educators, teachers and administrators, educators and students, and educators and families.** Goldenberg and Sullivan (1994) describe leadership as the 'cohesion that makes the other elements and components' of a program work together to create positive change (p. 12). Principals are charged with the task of establishing and nurturing relationships that collectively can have an impact on the quality of transitional bilingual education programs in a school. The issue of relationships cannot be underestimated as potent factors in creating a conducive environment.

In 1992, the Institute for Education and Transformation at Claremont Graduate School issued a report of research involving four culturally diverse schools that demonstrates the power that human relationships have on keeping and engaging students in school. Sergiovanni (1994) summarizes these findings around seven themes, each stressing the importance of caring

*Practices that collectively demonstrate weak campus leadership*

| Quadrant II Acquiescent TBE Program | Quadrant III Committed, Unenlightened TBE Program | Quadrant IV Recalcitrant TBE Program |
|---|---|---|
| • Provides limited support when resources are specifically available to address English language learner needs.<br>• Exerts pressure to excel with certain students.<br>• Feels responsibility to do only what the law requires.<br>• Allows for the minimal use of the student's language in the instruction. | • Shows poor leadership but 'talks the walk' effectively.<br>• Maintains and protects the status quo.<br>• Confuses management with leadership.<br>• Is an advocate of the rights of ALL children.<br>• Chides away from innovation and experimentation.<br>• Allows bilingual education teachers to do what they feel they need to do. | • Provides minimal support to enrich the curriculum for English language learners.<br>• Is indifferent and does little to address the school's ineffectiveness when working with English language learners. |

relationships based on mutual respect and trust. Furthermore, each theme relates some of the problems that emerge when such relationships are nonexistent or weak. Lessons learned from the study include the following:

1. Student depression and hopelessness are the by-products of poor relationships between educators and students. Schools must emphasize the importance of creating a partnership relationship with students and families based on a desire and commitment to make education work for students.
2. Students are conscious of race, culture, and class issues and seek to know and understand each other's culture. Schools must address these issues as part of the curriculum and consider them in the planning and delivery of instruction.
3. Students seek adult guidance from teachers and parents and desire to talk about values and beliefs. The myth that poor families have radically different values is debunked by this study.
4. Schools usually do not view these critical human relationships with much seriousness. Principals should revisit their campuses and study the relationships that prevail relative to the implementation of a transitional bilingual education program. If any of the answers to the following questions is no, it is critical that some form of intervention occurs. The questions are:

   – Do all teachers feel a responsibility for the academic achievement of English language learners?
   – Have you created a 'community of mind' as reflected on a shared vision and expectations of English language learners?
   – Does your faculty consider community people and families of students as assets that must be tapped to form partnerships with school people to design and deliver the best education possible for all students?

Other challenges to the principal include: (1) create an impetus and a vision of success without boundaries; (2) nurture exemplary educational environments that promote academic success and a safe, orderly, and caring environment; (3) leverage funding to garner necessary resources; (4) establish and consistently nurture a 'sense of family', and (5) provide opportunities for staff, students, and the community to celebrate their successes.

*A dedicated and knowledgeable staff*

A key finding is that teachers need support in various ways: exposure to new research findings, crafting an instructional model that meets the needs of English language learners, training and technical assistance on teaching skills critical to the instructional model, opportunities for collaborative planning, and a system of mentoring and coaching.

*Practices common to struggling Transitional Bilingual Education programs*

| Quadrant II Acquiescent TBE Program | Quadrant III Committed, Unenlightened TBE Program | Quadrant IV Recalcitrant TBE Program |
|---|---|---|
| • Helps teachers to implement an instructional plan developed externally.<br>• Training is focused in the development of English proficiency as soon as possible.<br>• Training, for the most part, is not connected directly to the instructional plan; it is haphazard and unfocused. | • Training on effective bilingual education methods and techniques is available and adequate.<br>• Districts and schools rely on external consultants for new knowledge about bilingual education programs.<br>• Capacity to design and implement a quality bilingual education program is not present in the district. | • Very limited efforts are made to train teachers and administrators on the linguistic and cultural needs of students.<br>• Recruitment of teachers who can communicate and work with English language learners is not a priority. |
| • Training for bilingual teachers is not a school district priority.<br>• Some bilingual teachers are not proficient in students' native language; many just barely communicate in that language.<br>• Some bilingual education classes are staffed with a monolingual English-speaking teacher with a paraprofessional who speaks the students' native language. | • Bilingual teachers possess adequate proficiency in the students' native language.<br>• District personnel fail to make the connection between bilingual education theory and practice. | • Training is not differentiated to address the needs of English language learners.<br>• At most, paraprofessionals receive training on ESL techniques. |
| • Knowledge about bilingual education is centralized with the director and supervisors of the bilingual education program.<br>• Knowledge about bilingual education is not dispersed among administrators and other key stakeholders. | | |

**Challenge: Provide opportunities for collaborative planning and designing of curriculum plan and lessons.** Sergiovanni (1994) describes the context in which a request for collaborative planning occurs as an 'ambivalence between the value of individualism and the need for community accounts for our discomfort whenever someone suggests that teaching practice become more collective' (p. 49). The fact that successful schools for English language learners require some degree of collective and collaborative planning presents a challenge for principals. Experience has shown that, although learning communities exist in most schools, the benefits of communities that were formed with some trepidation are minimal. Principals must face this challenge by allowing time for groups of teachers to define the role of the committee and the committee members and to establish rules that support partnerships.

Principals must set the example, provide ample opportunities for communities to form, celebrate successes of communities, provide support to fledgling ones, and guard the concept constantly.

**Challenge: Provide staff development opportunities to learn effective teaching strategies.** High expectations is a key training area – perhaps one of the hardest areas to address through professional development activities. August and Hakuta (1997) affirm this by acknowledging that 'one important way to raise teacher expectations is to raise student achievement by helping teachers acquire skills and knowledge needed to be more successful with students, rather than exhorting teachers to raise their expectations' (p. 185). The need to provide professional development opportunities that are closely associated with the instructional design or model cannot be overemphasized. The topics include specific learning and metacognitive strategies, cooperative learning, and thematic units in the native language and English.

Most of the literature on effective bilingual programs documents teaching practices (Berman *et al.*, 1995; Collier, 1995; García, 1988; Solis, 1998) that have been observed in classrooms where English language learners succeed academically. For example, Collier (1995) identifies three major themes: (1) highly interactive classrooms, (2) problem-solving activities, and (3) inquiry and discovery learning activities. Zehler (1994) augments this list to include a predictable environment, active participation in meaningful and challenging tasks, and providing support for understanding.

**Challenge: Recruit competent bilingual education teachers.** Recruiting bilingual education teachers who have their heart in the right place and are well informed on the most recent research on effective instructional practice is at the core of the problem. Principals in successful schools 'kept their ear to the ground' and always identified teachers who demonstrated the will and the competency to implement quality bilingual education programs.

Cárdenas and Cárdenas (1977) make recommendations about staffing a bilingual education program. Staff must be informed and acknowledge the unique characteristics of language-minority students. Second, staff differentiation is an alternative to adequately staffing

a bilingual program. Third, the program must embark on a massive retraining of teachers that includes 'regular' teachers. Last, there should be a program for lateral and upward mobility of bilingual education staff.

**Challenge: Provide guidance to new bilingual teachers; protect them from the influence of other teachers who overtly or covertly are sabotaging the bilingual education program.** New bilingual teachers are vulnerable individuals who learn quickly to accede to the whims of indecisive administrators and an apathetic faculty. Many new bilingual teachers are placed in 'no-win' situations and are overwhelmed by a feeling of 'loneliness in the wilderness'. In successful schools, principals provide opportunities for subdominant groups like new bilingual teachers to have 'access to decision making, creating internal advocacy groups, building diversity into organizational information and incentive systems, and strengthening career opportunities' (Bolman & Deal, 1997). New bilingual teachers are acknowledged for their atypical skills and commitment to equity-based educational excellence for English language learners.

### Partnering with community and families

A key finding is that strong parental and community involvement programs create a synergy between the school and the home that translates to greater student engagement and more meaningful participation in the educational process.

**Challenge: Map the assets represented in the community and in families and integrate them into the instructional plan.** Kretzmann and McKnight (1993) acknowledge the power that an asset-based partnership between the school and families can have on student academic success. This asset-based approach focuses on strengths of the family and embraces the 'we' concept where schools and families share an attitude of mutual resolve to seeking solutions that affect the quality of education. A caring and responsive school is the best guarantee of a community's future. The partnership that ensues provides a firm foundation for educational renewal and community regeneration. This partnership shares a vision and develops a blueprint for making that vision a reality. This strategy begins with the acknowledgment of strengths, the assets that are present, and not with what is absent or with what is problem-

*Practices common to struggling schools*

| Quadrant II Acquiescent TBE Program | Quadrant III Committed, Unenlightened TBE Program | Quadrant IV Recalcitrant TBE Program |
|---|---|---|
| • Minimal parental involvement that provides learning activities for parents to work more effectively with their children.<br>• Some literacy classes that are minimally related to preparing parents to teach their children. | • Parent involvement is usually strong; parent centers are the rule.<br>• School provides information to parents on social services. | • Parents are dissuaded from getting too involved in school activities.<br>• School perceives parents of English language learners as possessing values that are radically different. |
| • Provide enough parent activities to meet the requirements of the state or federal program.<br>• Parents are perceived as ill-prepared to meet their obligations as parents of school-age children. | • Although parents are involved in the political arena of the school, they usually have blind faith in teachers and administrators to teach their children.<br>• Parental involvement activities include supporting teachers in the classroom by volunteering their services. | • Parents are asked to come to school when problems arise with their children.<br>• School does not value the input of parents of English language learners.<br>• Schools have double standards in working with parents of English language learners. |

atic. Families and schools are not deficit-driven; they are strength and asset-driven.

## Dimension 2: Pedagogically sound curriculum and instructional program accessible learning environment

A key finding is that English language learners bring to school a diversity of assets and needs that require customized learning environments and approaches. No two schools and classrooms will have an identical approach to serving the needs of their student population.

**Challenge: Organize instruction in innovative ways; build flexibility in the bilingual education classroom.** There is no single way to specifically address the profile of a bilingual education classroom. No classroom is exactly the same; modifications and adjustments must be made to ensure that the instructional approach responds to the contextual conditions (Berman *et al.*, 1995) and is aligned with the characteristics and needs of English language learners. The challenge of creating the most appropriate instructional model rests with the school and community. Furthermore, schools with effective

transitional bilingual education programs create small organizational arrangements (Villarreal & Solís, 1998) e.g. families and academic teams to build cohesion and unity of purpose, to augment communication among teachers and to create a system of support. Principals must acknowledge, embrace, and promote diversity, and encourage innovation in instructional design.

**Challenge: Provide a challenging, intellectually enriching curriculum.** Bilingual education programs have been mislabeled as remedial programs since their inception. They were created to address a deficit-driven program of instruction for English language learners. It is not uncommon for parents to deny the enrollment of their children in bilingual education because of the stigma of remediation attached. The students' language and culture should be valued and seen as an asset and a strength to build upon and not as a deficit that must be obliterated. The instructional program for English language learners should be the same as the mainstream curriculum. The major difference lies in the language used for the delivery of instruction. The delivery will either be made

*Practices that collectively describe an unresponsive learning environment*

| Quadrant II Acquiescent TBE Program | Quadrant III Committed, Unenlightened TBE Program | Quadrant IV Recalcitrant TBE Program |
| --- | --- | --- |
| • Teachers primarily design their own bilingual education program.<br>• Teachers base their use of English or native language on readings that they make of what the principal wants. | • District develops one bilingual education program design that is used for all English language learners.<br>• Little modifications are made to the regular program. | • English language learners are consistently placed on 'sink or swim' situations.<br>• The onus of responsibility for learning is placed on the student.<br>• Most of the instruction for English language learners occurs in English.<br>• English language learners are consistently placed in remediation classes. |

in the students' native language or in sheltered instruction in English. The curriculum should be intellectually challenging, interactive, and meaningful. In addition, successful classrooms are print-rich. Books are available in the students' native language and English. Administrators, teachers, and community members should promote reading by allocating times for everyone including cafeteria workers, janitors, and office clerks to spend time reading.

*Program and curriculum alignment*

A key finding is that curriculum and instructional alignment between primary and elementary school, elementary school and middle school, middle school and high school, and high school and university is critical for the smooth transition of English language learners from one level to the next. Fragmentation of curriculum and philosophical differences creates an ethos of confusion and disconnectedness.

**Challenge: Align curriculum both horizontally and vertically.** Curriculum fragmentation is perhaps one of the most irresponsible school practices that contributes to the educational chaos in this country. Study after study reveals that scaffolding instruction in a manner that is incrementally more difficult is a more responsible approach. Teachers across grade levels must have opportunities to discuss the chain of skills and content that form the school's curriculum. Elementary teachers must have opportunities to align their curriculum by communicating with middle school teachers. Likewise, middle school

teachers must communicate with high school teachers.

Bilingual and nonbilingual teachers at each grade level should meet to plan their grade level instruction collaboratively thus ensuring alignment horizontally. This alignment is realized not only through planning but is extended to include team teaching, pairing of classes, and regrouping students (McLoed, 1996). In other words, English language learners should have the same opportunities as their English-speaking counterparts to take advantage of the curriculum.

*Capitalizing on student language and cultural resources*

A key finding is that the use of the native language for instruction and the integration of the culture into the curriculum form the foundation for concept development and the acquisition and learning of English.

**Challenge: Establish a program that capitalizes on the linguistic strengths of students and families in the community.** Campuses with effective bilingual education programs celebrate linguistic and cultural diversity in different ways. Banners and other important public displays at the school are written in two languages, at a minimum. Cultural celebrations, especially associated with the cultures represented in the school, are conducted and integrated into the school's curriculum. Teachers use cross-cultural interactions where students and teachers learn from each other's differences. Instruction is based on the structured use of at least two

*Practices that collectively describe a fragmented curricula*

| Quadrant II Acquiescent TBE Program | Quadrant III Committed, Unenlightened TBE Program | Quadrant IV Recalcitrant TBE Program |
|---|---|---|
| • Bilingual education teachers plan unilaterally without any coordination with regular teachers.<br>• There are no clear guidelines for the transitions from one language level to another or from one grade to the next.<br>• Exit level transitions are usually abrupt with no plan to smooth the impact of the change. | • Coordination between bilingual teachers on the same grade and between grades is minimal.<br>• All English language learners are given the same curriculum; little attempts are made to work with language levels.<br>• English language learners are provided ample opportunities to remain in the program as long as they need it. | • Students receive the general curriculum with little adjustments made to address the special needs.<br>• Repeating grades is the response for English language learners not at grade level.<br>• Early dropout signs are commonly found in English language learners since the early grades. |

*Practices common to struggling schools in using the native language and culture*

| Quadrant II Acquiescent TBE Program | Quadrant III Committed, Unenlightened TBE Program | Quadrant IV Recalcitrant TBE Program |
|---|---|---|
| • Native language is used minimally during the class day.<br>• Culture is usually regulated to holiday celebrations and other 'surface culture' activities.<br>• English is used as the language of instruction as much as possible. | • Native language instruction is promoted and valued.<br>• An attempt is made to use student experiences in the curriculum.<br>• Cultural activities have a high priority and are included consistently.<br>• There is a surface understanding of the value of learning the native language in learning English. | • Native language and culture are denigrated and openly criticized.<br>• The students' culture and experiences are considered a liability and should not be discussed in school.<br>• English language learners will learn English faster when taught in English through an immersion strategy. |

languages. Initially, the use of a specific language is based on the relative proficiency of the student in the two languages. In a transitional bilingual education program, teachers stress the need to develop reading and writing proficiency in the first language as a prerequisite to successful learning of English. Children's books reflect the variety of cultures and the benefits of diversity, and they are written in the languages used for instruction.

*An inclusive and comprehensive curriculum*

A key finding is that a curriculum, which capitalizes on the giftedness of all children, integrates instruction of basic skills and higher order thinking skills through phonetic and meaning-based instructional approaches and strategies.

**Challenge: Ensure and deliver grade level content.** Successful schools challenge English language learners with grade level content. They are aware that content is the same as that expected in the mainstream curriculum; delivery is different. In the bilingual education classroom, delivery can occur in the native language or in both English and the native language. The education of English language learners is also guided by the same educational standards that have been adopted by the local district. The selection of textbooks and other supplementary materials must be carefully scrutinized to ensure

*Practices that collectively demonstrate an inadequate curriculum*

| Quadrant II Acquiescent TBE Program | Quadrant III Committed, Unenlightened TBE Program | Quadrant IV Recalcitrant TBE Program |
|---|---|---|
| • Most of the instruction is skills based with a strong emphasis on phonetic skill development.<br>• For the most part, teachers feel that English language learners have an even more difficult task because they need to relearn these skills in English. | • There is strong emphasis on the need to develop the basic phonetic skills before any of the higher order comprehension skills are addressed.<br>• Although teachers talk about skills transferring to the other language, evidence in classrooms shows teachers reteaching skills in English. | • Strong emphasis on the development of phonetic skills in English, sometimes extending through the fourth and fifth grades.<br>• English language learners are isolated from the mainstream program both intellectually and physically. |
| • English language learners are placed in groups with intensive instruction on basic skills; little effort is shown to include the higher order skills.<br>• English language learners are drilled in material they cannot comprehend; they also participate in state-mandated test practice.<br>• Little opportunities are provided for students to take control of their learning.<br>• Classes use cooperative strategies in isolated classrooms with little opportunity to learn with other students. | • The major reason for grouping students is to facilitate the instruction of particular skills where certain students need help.<br>• A large portion of the day is used for training English language learners on passing the state-mandated test.<br>• Students are rarely provided opportunities to take part in the decisions affecting what they will learn. | • Classes are already remediation classes and English language learners are tracked in remediation activities all through their years at the elementary.<br>• English language learners are, for the most part, exempt from the state-mandated test and rarely participate in any program designed to develop test-taking skills. |

that these materials challenge English language learners at their grade level. Particular problems exist at the secondary level where English language learners are often denied 'access to regular science and mathematics courses because of poor English skills' (McLoed, 1996, p. 12). Successful schools conclude that English language learners are intellectually capable to learn this content. Schools must find ways of delivering this content by teaching in the native language, using sheltered instruction and other ESL methods. Anything less than grade level content will retard their normal progress in school and block them from access to an equal educational opportunity.

*Instructional practices and strategies*

A key finding is that successful teachers of English language learner students know how and when to use an array of instructional strategies that foster first and second language acquisition and develop cognitive and metacognitive skills.

**Challenge: Promote instructional approaches that foster biliteracy development and the acquisition of content.** Biliteracy development requires teachers to have a deep understanding of the role of the first language in the development of the second language. Teachers involved in delivering content instruction should be trained in second language teaching methodology and be able to pace and modify instruction to make

*Practices that demonstrate a limited set of instructional strategies*

| Quadrant II Acquiescent TBE Program | Quadrant III Committed, Unenlightened TBE Program | Quadrant IV Recalcitrant TBE Program |
|---|---|---|
| • English language learners participate in some classes with English-speaking peers.<br>• Experiences to hear role models in English and in the native language are limited.<br>• The program for developing English language proficiency is rarely planned and connected to the students' proficiency level in the native language. | • Instruction in basic skills is redundant, making the instruction reach a level of frustration and boredom.<br>• Not enough opportunities are provided for students to hear adults speak the native language and English from native speakers of those languages.<br>• Most of the talking is done by the teacher who must not 'waste precious instructional time.' | • English language learners remain with basic skills all through their elementary years.<br>• English language learners are usually in classes with native English language speakers. Their neglect shuts down English language learners and they rapidly disengage.<br>• Limited attention is placed on the pace of quality of the English language instruction. |
| • Questioning strategies usually require an answer explicit in the reading material or experience.<br>• Student assessment is often done in English, in a language that the student does not understand.<br>• Student assessment results rarely drive the instruction.<br>• Bilingual teacher does the assessment and makes unilateral decisions with the results.<br>• Instructional strategies are selected for their popularity and not for what best suit the needs of the English language learners.<br>• There is a preoccupation with development of metacognitive skills, but little is done because of the overemphasis on basic skills.<br>• Questioning strategies are basic and rarely challenge the student to think beyond simple answers.<br>• An attempt is made to use students' experience or capitalize on assets of the community in the instruction. | • Questions usually require a 'yes' or 'no' answer or a fill in the blank using the same statement from the reading material.<br>• Assessment is in English and the native language; but assessment results are rarely used to design instruction.<br>• Strong emphasis is placed on passing the state-mandated test.<br>• The most popular instructional strategy is direct teaching. Many of the other strategies are considered too difficult for the English language learners.<br>• Metacognitive skills are perhaps the last thing in the minds of many of these teachers.<br>• Instruction is comprehensible in the sense that students are rarely challenged to tackle higher order comprehension skills. | • Assessment is usually in English.<br>• Assessment results are used not to plan instruction, but to retain students in the same grade.<br>• English language learners are usually being taught in isolated groups by a paraprofessional who rarely has the opportunity to plan instruction with the teacher. |

it comprehensible. Collaborative and cooperative learning strategies provide opportunities for English language learners to interact with other students in meaningful and constructive ways that promote the use of biliteracy skills and cultural understanding by creating a forum for students to learn and appreciate each other's cultural differences and similarities. Thematic units have been used effectively by some successful schools. A living skills curriculum reinforces the benefits of positive character traits, personally and academically.

Research indicates that there is no set of instructional strategies that were present in every successful school that has been studied; each used a variety of instructional strategies and collaboratively adjusted instructional strategies to achieve better academic results. They were, however, guided by a shared and dynamic vision of success that kept them seeking for more effective methods to deliver instruction.

## Framing the Change: A Principal's Major Task

Bolman and Deal (1997) identify four sides of leadership that must be adjusted when introducing or adjusting a school innovation. Adjusting transitional bilingual education programs to create an environment that supports the attributes of a successful instructional program for English language learners requires a reexamination of the four sides of leadership and how action on the part of the principal can set the tone for successful change. These four sides of leadership include (1) structural, (2) human resource, (3) political, and (4) symbolic. Bolman and Deal (1997) state: 'ideally, managers combine multiple frames into a comprehensive approach to leadership. Wise leaders understand their strengths, work to expand them and build teams that can provide leadership in all four modes' (p. 317).

Below is a list of activities that a principal in a struggling transitional bilingual education program can implement to place the program on the road to recovery.

1. **Structural Leadership** (Organization designs which promote maximum efficiency and success.)
   – Conceptually and physically integrate the bilingual education program to the mainstream curriculum.
   – Coordinate activities with grade level lead teachers to involve bilingual teachers in planning and implementing grade level instruction.
   – Redefine tasks and responsibilities to show how every staff member can share in the responsibility to increase the academic achievement of English language learners.
   – Develop policies and procedures that are consistent with equity-based excellence in education for ALL students, including English language learners.

2. **Human Resource Leadership** (Capitalizes on skills, attitudes, energy, and commitment to reach goals.)
   – Create a philosophy and a vision of equity-based excellence as the cornerstone of a renewed way of seeing English language learners and their potential for success.
   – Map existing interpersonal relationships that promote the vision; create relationships that form partnerships among teachers and personnel including the ones who were never involved in these matters.
   – Nurture these relationships, redirect those relationships that are counterproductive, and celebrate relationships and partnerships that promote the vision and create a sense of family among all staff.

3. **Political Leadership** (Organizations respond to the whims of political interests.)
   – Plan overall strategies to address the hostility and the indifference that exist in the campus (and in the community) as a viable response to the needs of English language learners.
   – Establish and nurture a critical mass of staff members who promote equity-based excellence for the English language learners.
   – Work with the 'opposition' by creating coalitions of individuals with differing views on tasks where they share views. Being able to work together builds a bond that allows for differences to be openly discussed and negotiated.

4. **Symbolic Leadership** (A perspective guided by meaning, belief, and personal commitment.)
   – Unite around the vision of the school

and discuss its meaning for all students, including English language learners. Come up with manifestations of this new definition at all levels of the school operation. For example, English language learners may also be gifted and talented. Therefore, the school should manage to adjust the existing gifted and talented program to be inclusive of students with other diverse needs.

- Develop stories about the successes in education at the campus. Create stories about reasons for celebrating. Talk about ways to create more stories that relate successes with students including the English language learners.

- Divide the school into 'houses', each named after a university campus. The school's primary reason for calling each 'house' after a university is to provide an alternative to affiliation with gangs or other dysfunctional groups in the community or in school.

The knowledge about what to do is easy once these major leadership challenges are addressed. Principals in struggling transitional bilingual education programs must communicate the need and commitment to improve the quality of the program at the campus. The task is not easy, yet it is not impossible. Research shows that campuses have taken a 180-degree turn and have changed from a low performing to an exemplary status where all staff are one family having a powerful, positive impact on the lives of children. *Buena suerte*!

## References

Adams, M. and Bruck, M. (1995) Resolving the 'great debate.' *American Educator*, 19 (2) 10–20.

August, D. and Hakuta, K. (1997) *Improving schooling for language-minority children: A research agenda*. Washington, DC: National Academy Press.

Berman, P., McLaughlin, B., McLoed, B., Minicucci, C., Nelson, B. and Woodworth, K. (1995) *School reform and student diversity: Case studies of exemplary practices for English language learners*. Berkeley, CA: National Center for Research on Cultural Diversity and Second Language Learning and BW Associates.

Bolman, L.G. and Deal, T.E. (1997) *Reframing organizations: Artistry, choice, and leadership*. San Francisco, CA: Jossey-Bass Publishers.

Calderón, M., Hertz-Lazarowitz, R. and Slavin, R. (1996) *Effects of bilingual cooperative integrated reading and composition on students transitioning from Spanish to English reading*. Washington, DC: U.S. Department of Education.

Cárdenas, J. and Cárdenas, B. (1977) *The theory of incompatibilities: A conceptual framework for responding to the educational needs of Hispanic Americans*. San Antonio, TX: Intercultural Development Research Association.

Carter, T. and Chatfield, M. (1986) Effective bilingual schools: Implications for policy and practice. *American Journal of Education*, 95, 200–232.

Collier, V.P. (1995) *Acquiring a second language for school. Direction in language education*, 1 (4). Washington, DC: National Clearinghouse for Bilingual Education.

Council of Chief State School Officers. (1998) *State education indicators with a focus on Title I*. Washington, DC.

Dianda, M. and Flaherty, J. (1995) *Effects of success for all on the reading achievement of first graders in California bilingual programs*. Los Alamitos, CA: Southwest Regional Educational Laboratory.

Escamilla, K. (1994) Descubriendo la lectura: An early intervention literacy program in Spanish. *Literacy teaching and learning*, 1 (l), 57–70.

García, E.E. (1987, 1988) *Effective schooling for language minority students. Focus: Occasional papers in bilingual education 1*. Washington, DC: National Clearinghouse for Bilingual Education.

Genesee, F. (1999) *Program alternatives for linguistically diverse students*. Washington, DC, and Santa Cruz, CA: Center for Research on Education, Diversity and Excellence.

Gersten, R. (1996) Literacy instruction for language-minority students: The transition years. *The Elementary School Journal*, 96 (3), 228–244.

Goldenberg, C. and Sullivan, J. (1994) *Making change happen in a language-minority school: A search for coherence. EPR # 13*. Washington, DC: Center for Applied Linguistics.

Henke, R.R., Choy, S.P., Chen, X., Geis, S., Alt, M.N. and Broughman, S.P. (1997) *America's teachers: Profile of a profession, 1993–94*. Washington, DC: U.S. Department of Education.

Institute for Education and Transformation. (1992) *Voice from the inside: A report on schooling from inside the classroom Part I: Naming the problem.* Claremont, CA: Claremont Graduate School.

Kretzmann, J.P. and McKnight, J.L. (1993) *Building communities from the inside out: A path toward finding and mobilizing a community's assets.* Chicago, IL: ACTA Publications.

Latham, A.S., Gitomer, D., and Ziomek, R. (1999) What the tests tell us about new teachers. *Educational Leadership*, 56 (8), 23–26.

Lein, L., Johnson, J.F. and Ragland, M. (1997) *Successful Texas school wide programs: Research study results.* Austin, TX: The Charles A. Dana Center at the University of Texas at Austin.

Lucas, T., Henze, R. and Donato, R. (1990) Promoting the success of Latino language-minority students: An exploratory study of six high schools. *Harvard Educational Review*, 60, 315–340.

Lucas, T. and Katz, A. (1994) Refraining the debate: The roles of native languages in English-only programs for language minority students. *TESOL Quarterly*, 28 (3), 537–561.

Maroney, O.H. (1998, January) Who is teaching the children? More trained bilingual teachers are needed for excellent education. *IDRA Newsletter*, p. 6. San Antonio, TX: Intercultural Development Research Association.

McCollum, P. (1999, January) Breathing new life into language assessment. *IDRA Newsletter*, p. 3. San Antonio, TX: Intercultural Development Research Association.

McLoed, B. (1996) *School reform and student diversity: Exemplary schooling for language minority students.* NCBE Resource Collection Series. Washington, DC: National Clearinghouse for Bilingual Education.

Milk, R., Mercado, C. and Sapiens, A. (1992) *Rethinking the education of teachers of language minority children: Developing reflective teacher for changing schools.* Occasional Papers in Bilingual Education, Number 6. Washington, DC: National Clearinghouse for Bilingual Education.

Moll, L.C., Amanti, C., Neff, D. and González, N. (1992) Funds of knowledge for teaching: Using a qualitative approach to connect homes and classrooms. *Theories Into Practice*, 31 (2), 132–141,

Moll, L. and Díaz, R. (1985) Ethnographic pedagogy: Promoting effective bilingual instruction. In E. García and R. Padilla (eds) *Linguistic and cultural influences on learning mathematics: The psychology of education and instruction.* Hillsdale, NJ: Erlbaum.

Montemayor, A.M. (1997, September) The nurturing of parent leadership. *IDRA Newsletter*, p. 13. San Antonio, TX: Intercultural Development Research Association.

Moss, M. and Puma, M. (1995) *Prospects: The congressionally mandated study of educational growth and opportunity: Language minority and English language learners.* Washington, DC: U.S. Department of Education.

Ogbu, J.U. and Matute-Bianchi, M.E. (1986) *Understanding socio-cultural factors: Knowledge, identity, and school adjustment. Beyond language: Social and cultural factors in schooling language-minority students.* Los Angeles, CA: Evaluation, Dissemination, and Assessment Center, California State University.

Pease-Alvarez, L., García, E.E. and Espinosa, P. (1991) Effective instruction for language-minority students: An early childhood case study. *Early Childhood Research Quarterly*, 6, 347–361.

Purcell-Gates, V. (1996) Process teaching with explicit explanation and feedback in a university-based clinic. In E. McIntyre and M. Pressley (eds) *Balanced instruction: Strategies and skills in whole language.* Norwood, MA: Christopher-Gordon.

Robledo Montecel, M., Gallagher, A., Montemayor, A.M., Villarreal, A., Adame-Reyna, N. and Supik, J.D. (1993) *Hispanic families as valued partners: An educator's guide.* San Antonio, TX: Intercultural Development Research Association.

Saunders, W., O'Brien, G., Lennon, D. and McLean, J. (1998) Making the transition to English literacy successful: Effective strategies for studying literature with transition students. In R. Gersten and R. Jiménez (eds) *Promoting learning for culturally and linguistically diverse students.* Belmont, CA: Wadsworth.

Sergiovanni, T.J. (1994) *Building Community in Schools.* San Francisco, CA: Jossey-Bass Publishers.

Solís, A. (1998, January) Showcasing exemplary instructional practices in bilingual and ESL classrooms. *IDRA Newsletter.* San Antonio, TX: Intercultural Development Research Association.

Tikunoff, W.J., Ward, B.A., van Broekhuizen,

L.D., Romero, M., Castaneda, L.V., Lucas, T. and Katz, A. (1991) *A descriptive study of significant features of exemplary special alternative instructional programs. Final Report & Vol. 2: Report for practitioners.* Los Alamitos, CA: Southwest Regional Educational Laboratory.

Valdez-Pierce, L. and O'Malley, J.M. (1992) *Performance and portfolio assessment for language-minority students.* NCBE Program Information Series. Washington, DC: National Clearinghouse for Bilingual Education.

Villarreal, A. and Solís, A. (1998, January) Effective implementation of bilingual programs: Reflections from the field. *IDRA Newsletter.* San Antonio, TX: Intercultural Development Research Association.

Wong-Fillmore, L., Ammon, P., McLaughlin, B. and Ammon, M. (1985) *Learning English through bilingual instruction.* Final Report. Berkeley, CA: University of California.

Zahler, A.M. (1994) *Working with English language learners: Strategies for elementary and middle school teachers.* NCBE Program Information Guide. Washington, DC: National Clearinghouse for Bilingual Education (19).

## Questions

1.  What is transitional in Transitional Bilingual Education? Is the transition more than language?

2.  What advantages and disadvantages may transitional bilingual education have over mainstreaming/submersion? What are the differences between transitional bilingual education and the two-way dual language bilingual education programs described by Torres-Guzmán?

3.  Villarreal provides a checklist of the attributes of successful transitional bilingual education programs. Provide examples of at least ten of these, for example, how each of these would be visible in schools and classrooms. Put these attributes into a ranked priority list, from the most to the least important.

4.  From your experiences, write three Scenarios (A, B, C) to match those of Villarreal. Then compare your three scenarios, showing why they are different from each other, and what they particularly portray.

5.  List the challenges that Villarreal considers. Provide a school or classroom example of each, and how each challenge could be successfully solved.

## Activities

1.  Observe one child who has left a transitional bilingual education classroom for a mainstream classroom in the last six months. Describe in detail the challenges the child faces and the mechanisms the child uses to learn and socialize in the mainstream classroom. Share the observations with your class.

    Different students might observe children with different characteristics – age, sex, language, ethnicity and national origin, race, history of the group. Share your observations. Make a chart with the class results.

2.  Interview a classroom teacher about students who have recently exited from transitional bilingual education classrooms. What are the challenges and successes these children experience? Would increased knowledge about bilingualism help the teacher with those children? What would she need to know/learn about bilingualism and bilingual education? Transcribe your interview. Share with others in the class. Then write a class essay that takes into consideration the different viewpoints of teachers interviewed.

    Different students might interview educators in schools that have different characteristics – urban/suburban, primary/secondary, collaborative leadership/authoritative leadership, high/low number of students who speak other languages, heterogeneous/homogenous non-dominant groups. Share your answers with the class. Make a chart with the class results.

3.  Draw a chart to show the different types of leadership discussed by Villarreal. Talk to a Principal or a Deputy Principal and see if the different types are (a) recognizable to that Principal (b) into which type or types she/he feels best fits (c) what activities that person feels would be most influential with bilingual children.

4.  For one whole day, visit a program where there is a large number of bilingual students. Observe varying language practices (or their absence) in at least one classroom. Observe practices in the administration's office and in other offices in the school (e.g. that of the psychologist, the speech therapist, coordinators, etc). Also observe practices in the lunchroom and in the playground. Record all your observations. Then write an essay of why you can or can't consider this bilingual program a transitional one. Refer to specific practices you observed or things that were directly told to you.

5.  Find a parent who has taken her child out of a bilingual education program in the United States and one who has insisted that her child be kept in a bilingual classroom. Interview both of them. Question them on their beliefs and motives. Tape and transcribe both interviews and share the results with the class.

6.  Ask the following two questions to at least 20 language minority adults and also 20 language majority adults. Tabulate the answers and arrive at percentages. On a poster board, make a bar graph or a pie chart with your results:
    a.  'Do you think public funds should to be used to teach heritage languages/ethnic languages in public schools? Why or why not?'
    b.  'Do you think public funds should to be used to teach foreign languages in public schools? Why or why not? If yes, which languages should be taught? To whom? For how long? How?'

## Further Reading

Baker, C. (2006) *Foundations of Bilingual Education and Bilingualism* (4th edn). Clevedon: Multilingual Matters (chapters 10, 13).

García, E. (2005) *Teaching and Learning in Two Languages. Bilingualism and Schooling in the United States.* New York: Teachers College Press.

Genesee, F., Lindholm-Leary, K.J., Saunders, W. and Christian, D. (2005) *Educating English Language Learners: A Synthesis of Empirical Evidence.* New York: Cambridge University Press.

Smyth, G. (2003) *Helping Bilingual Pupils to Access the Curriculum.* London: David Fulton.

Tse, L. (2001) *'Why Don't They Learn English?' Separating Fact from Fallacy in the U.S. Language Debate.* New York: Teachers College Press.

# Part 2: History, Policy and Politics of Bilingual Education

# Accessing Language Rights in Education: A Brief History of the U.S. Context

## Terrence G. Wiley

This chapter addresses the question of the extent to which language minorities in the United States have been able to access language rights in education. In dealing with this issue, it is necessary to distinguish between the *right to access* an education that allows for social, economic, and political participation, and the *right* to an education *mediated* in one's mother tongue(s). For language minority students, both rights are essential if they are to participate in the broader society and maintain continuity with their home/community language.

Many children in the United States and a majority of children around the world enter schools where the language of instruction is different from the language spoken in their homes. Given the prevalence of language diversity in the United States and around the world, the fragile condition of language rights in education is lamentable. A small but persistent group of scholars has begun to address the issue (see for example, Kontra *et al.*, 1999a, 1999b).

A fundamental question underlying any discussion of educational language rights is the need to probe the assumptions about language rights more broadly. In this regard, Macías (1979) distinguishes between two types of rights. The first is 'the right to freedom *from* discrimination on the basis of language' (p. 41). This in essence is a right to protection. The second is 'the right to use one's language in the activities of communal life' (p. 41). This is essentially the right to expression. Macías concludes that 'There is no right to choice of language ... except as it flows from these two rights above in combination with other rights, such as due process, equal enforcement of the laws, and so on' (pp. 41–42). However, in order for language rights to be asserted, the 'identifiable and legal standing of a class based on language' must be recognized (p. 42). This latter point is particularly significant for understanding language minority rights in the United States and other Western countries, because of their emphasis on locating rights in the individual rather than in the group (Macías, 1979; Wiley, 1996a). In international law, 'all of the existing rights ... are individual rights and freedoms, although their manifestations may involve more than one individual' (de Varenenes, 1999, p. 118). In the United States, the salience of language rights is largely derived from their association with other constitutional protections dealing with race, religion, and national origin.

Historically, rights and privileges have been distributed *selectively* based on the recognition of legal status. The significance of such status was dramatically illustrated in the 1994 California election in which Proposition 187 was designed to restrict health and educational rights of immigrants and their children who lacked the status of legal residents. The proposition was approved by a majority of those who voted; those targeted by 187 were unable to vote. In public debates over 187, the major arguments were between those who contended that rights to health and education should be restricted to *citizens* and *legal residents*. Opponents of 187 maintained that these entitlements were *human* rights and that children's human rights should not be surrendered merely because of the legal status of their parents. Subsequently, most provisions of 187 have been struck down in court, yet the controversy over immigrant rights and entitlements echoed around the country. A formal assault (Proposition 227) followed in 1998 on the right of language minority children to be educated bilingually and the right of their parents to make that choice for them.

For many in the United States, the idea that a child who speaks a minority language or vernacular dialect should have a *right* to instruction in his or her language is a peculiar idea – one that is weighed against the argument that the need for a common language is greater than any claims of language rights by minorities. However, the idea of language rights is not new. In 1953, a UNESCO resolution held that every child should have a right to attain literacy in his or her mother tongue. More recently, Skuttnab-Kangas (1995) has put forward her own proposal for a declaration of children's linguistic human rights based on the following three premises: '(1) Every child should have the right to identify positively with her original mother tongue(s) and have her identification accepted and respected by others. (2) Every child should have the right to learn the mother tongue(s) fully. (3) Every child should have the right to choose when she wants to use the mother tongue(s) in all official situations' (Skutnabb-Kangas, 1995, p. 45).

On its face, the first premise has been supported by most learning theorists and to some extent by U.S. courts in recent decades. The need for children to identify positively with their mother tongues(s) has provided part of the rationale for federal bilingual education programs that were implemented in the late 1960s. Nevertheless, gaining support for children's linguistic human rights and translating it into school policy is a major challenge. For instance, schools, policymakers, and pundits have generally not accepted as legitimate 'non-standard' varieties of language such as Ebonics, Appalachian English, and Hawai'i Creole English, despite the authority of linguistic evidence that deems them to be legitimate (Rickford, 1999; Wolfram *et al.*, 1999).

The second premise of the declaration implies that every child should have the right to become literate in his or her mother tongue. Creating educational policies for this part of the declaration is complicated by the fact that the majority of the world's estimated 6,000 to 7,000 languages are not used in schools and that many are not used as languages of literacy. In the U.S., even among the major languages taught, there has been a chronic undersupply of certified bilingual teachers for several decades.

The third premise extends the scope of language rights beyond the domain of education to 'all official situations'. It implies that the government should provide sufficient resources to accommodate language minorities. In the United States, the right to some accommodation has been made in cases dealing with educa-

tional, legal, economic and political access, but language rights remain on a very tenuous legal foundation (Piatt, 1992). Around the world, language rights frequently are ignored in the formulation of educational policies. Unfortunately, even if organizations such as the United Nations support language rights, member nations, including the United States do not act on them because resolutions are not binding (Skutnabb-Kangas, 1999).

## The Historical Context of Language Diversity in the United States

Prior to European conquest and colonization, North America had a rich array of indigenous languages. In that portion of the continent that was to become the United States, the linguistic dominance of English, or what Heath (1976) referred to as the 'language status achievement' of the language, had occurred long before the first U.S. Census in 1790. Until the mid-19th century, a majority of immigrants were from predominantly English-dominant areas. Into the early 20th century, native language instruction and bilingual education were not uncommon in areas where language minority groups comprised a major portion of the local population (Kloss, 1977/1998).

In international discussions of language diversity, a distinction is made between *indigenous* language minorities and *national* language minorities (Skutnabb-Kangas, 1999). National language minorities are the language minority in a country other than where they are currently residing. In the United States, much of the discussion about language diversity and schooling has centered on immigrant language minorities. From an historical perspective, immigration has been an important source of language diversity. However, other sources are also important (see Table 1). Among the three major groupings of historical language minorities are (1) *immigrants* (including refugees), (2) *enslaved peoples* who were brought to the United States against their will, and (3) *indigenous peoples*. Macías (1999) expands the notion of indigenous peoples to include (a) those who inhabited an area that later became part of the United States prior to its national expansion into the region they occupied, and (b) groups that have an historical or cultural bond to the Americas before European colonization. In 1790, it is estimated that 23,000 Spanish-speaking people inhabited areas that would later became part of the southwestern United

States (Leibowitz, 1971). For many, language shift to English resulted not from choice, but as a consequence of involuntary immigration and enslavement, or annexation and conquest.

Territorial expansion and forced incorporation notwithstanding, immigration was the major source of language diversity in the 19th and 20th centuries. Contrary to popular beliefs about immigration, the percentage of recent immigrants in the late 20th century, as a percentage of the total population, was *less* than it was during the early 20th century (Wiley, 1996b).

## Educational Language Policies and the Broader Societal Context

A number of scholars contend that educational language policies are best understood in their relationship to broader societal policies, dominant beliefs, and power relationships among groups. Leibowitz (1969, 1971, 1974, 1982), for example, concluded that language policies have been used as instruments of *social control* (see Tollefson, 1991, and 1995, for related discussions of language planning as an instrument of *discourse, state,* and *ideological power*). Leibowitz's thesis was developed by analyzing the impact of official English policies and restrictive language policies across political, economic, and educational domains. He argued:

> The significant point to be noted is that language designation in all three areas followed a marked, similar pattern so that it is reasonably clear that one was responding not to the problems specifically related to that area (i.e., educational issues or job requirements in the economic sphere) but to broader problems in the society to which language was but one response. (1974, p. 6)

Leibowitz concluded that

> as English became officially designated for specific purposes, for example, as the language of instruction, or for voting, it was almost always coupled with restrictions on the use of other languages in addition to discriminatory legislation and practices in other fields against the minorities who spoke the language, including private indignities . . . which made it clear that the issue was a broader one. (1974, p. 6)

Leibowitz (1971) also compared the restric-

tive impact of English-only policies imposed on German, Japanese, and Chinese immigrants as well as on Native Americans, Mexican Americans, and Puerto Rican Americans. He concluded that the motivations to impose official English language and to restrict native languages in schools corresponded to the general level of *hostility* of the dominant group toward various language minority groups.

A synopsis of the historical effects of educational policies and language policies on linguistic minority students is represented in Table 2, which specifies the initial mode of amalgamation and the subsequent policy management of each group. Although English was universally imposed, the experience of each group differed. Some groups were more restricted and segregated than others. Historically, only African Americans experienced the full gamut of inhumanities, including 'compulsory ignorance' laws prior to 1865 (Weinberg, 1995).

The belief that *all* children deserve the right to educational opportunity in publicly supported education – let alone an equal opportunity to learn – received broad support gradually. It was not a widely held notion at the founding of the nation. During the 19th century, the idea that children should have a right to publicly supported education gained favor. However, even as it did, the right to equal educational opportunity was selectively withheld from many children of color, many of whom were also language minorities (Spring, 1994; Weinberg, 1995, 1997). Adding the force of law, the Supreme Court, in *Plessy v. Ferguson*, affirmed the dogma of segregated, *separate but equal* education, which stood from 1896 to 1954. It was not until the landmark *Brown v. Board of Education* (1954) decision that the court reasoned 'it is doubtful that any child may reasonably be expected to succeed in life if he is denied the opportunity of an education' (cited from Leibowitz, 1982, p. 162). In the *Brown* decision, race had been the singular focus. Skuttnab-Kangas (1995) has recently made a similar case for linguistic access:

> If you want to have your fair share of the power and the resources (both material and non-material) of your native country, you have to be able to take part in the democratic processes in your country. You have to be able to negotiate, try to influence, to have a voice. The main instrument for doing that is language . . . In a democratic country,

**Table 1** Historical overview of policies and events affecting the educational treatment and language rights of language minorities

| Time period | Policy orientations and key events | Implications for educational language rights |
| --- | --- | --- |
| 1740–1845 | Compulsory ignorance laws imposed under colonial rule and retained in slave codes of southern states. | Enslaved African Americans were barred from becoming literate until 1865. In some states, Whites could also be fined or punished for teaching African Americans to read. |
| | Treaty of Paris in 1783; Louisiana Purchase in 1803; Florida and adjacent areas annexed (1820). | Peoples in the Northwest Territories, and, subsequently, those in the Mississippi and Missouri river valleys were incorporated under U.S. territorial and later state laws. |
| | In 1819 the Civilization Fund Act enacted to promote English education and practical skills among Native American peoples. | Mission schools were established among some Native American peoples with less than spectacular results in promoting English and Anglo values. |
| | A Cherokee writing system developed (in 1822) by Sequoia. | Cherokee schools succeeded in promoting Cherokee literacy and biliteracy in English. By 1852 Choctaws, Creeks and Seminoles also operated their own school. |
| | German Bilingual Schools thrive, even amidst the Know Nothing Movement (1840–1850s). | German language instruction flourished through private and sectarian efforts in the Midwest. In 1837, Pennsylvania passed a law allowing for public schooling in German. In 1840, Ohio passed a law allowing for German-English public schooling. |
| 1845–1905 | Texas annexed 1845, followed by Oregon, Washington and Idaho by 1846; Treaty of Guadalupe Hidalgo and Mexican Cession (1848); Gadsden Purchase(1853); Alaska purchased in 1867; Hawaii, 1898; and Puerto Rico, 1901. | Peoples residing in Mexican territory were conquered and brought under U.S. territorial or state authority; indigenous/resident populations were incorporated and were subject to U.S. territorial and later state laws. |
| | The 'treaty period' ended (1871). The first 'off reservation' English-only boarding school established (1889). | Native Americans lost autonomy and governance of their schools. Among the Cherokee a gradual decline in literacy resulted as the policy of compulsory Americanization and English-only instruction persisted into the 1930s. |
| | German immigration peaked in the 1880s. | School-related English-only laws aimed at German Catholics were passed (1889), and subsequently repealed, Illinois and Wisconsin. |
| | *Plessy v. Ferguson* (1896) | The Supreme Court upheld the doctrine of 'separate but equal' racial segregation. |

| Time period | Policy orientations and key events | Implications for educational language rights |
|---|---|---|
| 1905–1923 | Eastern and Southern European immigration increases (to WWI). Immigration restricted on the basis of national origin. | German instruction was gradually declining in the schools (public and private), but was nevertheless still prevalent until WWI. During WWI, German instruction was banned or dropped in most states. A majority of states passed laws officially designating English as the language of instruction and restricting the use of 'foreign' languages. |
| 1923–1950 | *Meyer v. Nebraska* (1923) *Farrington v. Tokushige* (1927) | In 1923, the Supreme Court overturned a 1919 Nebraska law banning instruction in German. Several similar cases were decided during the 1920s, including one in Hawaii dealing with private schooling in Japanese |
|  | Tribal Restoration (1930s) | Deculturation policies aimed at Native Americans were relaxed from the 1930s to the 1950s. |
|  | Guam added as a Territory (1945) Philippines granted independence. | Pacific Island peoples were incorporated. |
| 1950–1960 | Native American Termination Policies. *Brown v. Board of Education* (1954) | Renewed restrictions on Native Americans. Termination of legal segregation (reversal of *Plessy v. Ferguson*). |
| 1960–1980 | 1964 Civil Rights Act 1965 Immigration Act The 1968 Bilingual Education Act Tribal restoration (Phase II). | Civil rights and immigration reform provided legal protections from discrimination. The U.S. government broke new ground in allowing for expediency-oriented educational language policies. Restrictive policies toward Native Americans were again relaxed. |
|  | *Lau v. Nichols* (1974) *Serna v. Portales* (1974) *Rios v. Read* (1978) *U.S. v. Texas* (1981) | The Supreme Court affirmed that School Districts must accommodate language minority children. Additional federal cases prescribed bilingual education in local contexts. |
|  | *M. L. King Jr. Elementary vs. Ann Arbor School District* (1979) | A federal court ruled that the Ann Arbor School District must accommodate speakers of African American English |
|  | *Casteñeda v. Pickard* (1981) | Criteria for acceptable program remedies were established. |

| Time period | Policy orientations and key events | Implications for educational language rights |
|---|---|---|
| 1980–2000 | English Only Movement 1981 to present | There was a return to official designations of English as the official language coupled with restrictionism during a period of increased anti-immigrant sentiment. |
| | Reagan Administration (1980–88) backs away from enforcement of *Lau* Remedies. Native American Languages Preservation Act (1990). | The federal government de-emphasized bilingual education as a remedy. Tolerance of Native American languages was expressed by the Federal government, which was largely symbolic. |
| | California's Propositions 63 (1986); 187 (1991); 209 (1996), and 227 (1998); Arizona's proposition 203. | A series of initiatives were proposed/passed in California and other states to restrict immigrant rights in education; and to restrict bilingual education. |

*Sources*: Crawford, 1992, 1995; Hernández-Chávez, 1994; Kloss, 1977/1998; Leibowitz 1969, 1971; Lyons, 1995; Macías, 1999; Wiley, 1998a, 1998b, 1999a, 2000; and Wiley & Lukes, 1996

it should be the duty of the school system to give every child, regardless of linguistic background the same chance to participate in the democratic process. If this requires that {at least) some of children {i.e., the linguistic minority children) become bilingual or multilingual, then it should be the duty of the educational system to make them bilingual/multilingual. {p. 42)

### Implications of Policy Orientations for Language Minority Educational Rights

In assessing various policies toward language diversity and their implications for educational language rights, it is helpful to locate them in a language policy framework. Table 3 provides an overview of policy orientations of the federal government, states, and other agencies with the power to impose policies or practices that have the force of policy.

Table 3 builds from Kloss (1977/1998), who limited his analyses to formal policies imposed by law. However, in the United States, language behavior and language rights more commonly have been shaped by *implicit/covert* policies and by *informal* practices that can have the same, or even greater force than official policies (see Schiffman, 1996; Wiley, 1999a). Thus, it is useful to apply Table 3 to both formal and informal policies and practices. *Implicit policies* include those that may

not start out to be language policies but have the effect of policy. *Covert policies*, as the word implies, are more ominous. They are policies that seek to use language or literacy requirements as a means of barring someone from social, political, educational, or economic participation (Wiley, in press). Historical examples include literacy requirements for voting and English literacy requirements for entry to the United States that have been used as gate-keeping mechanisms to exclude immigrants on the basis of their race or ethnicity (Leibowitz, 1969).

*Promotion-oriented* policies require governmental support. Historically, among language minority communities, there has never been any controversy over the need to promote English. By the 1920s, English had been designated as the official language of schooling in nearly all states. As a result, language promotion resources have flowed primarily into English instruction. At the institutional level, many colleges and universities have long had foreign/second language requirements, but college-level entry requirements for proficiency in English have helped to drive most language-related curricular policies since the late 19th century (Wright, 1980).

Although advocates of restrictive English-Only policies frequently depict contemporary advocates of bilingual education as being against the promotion of English, there is no evidence to support this. Most advocates of bilingual

**Table 2** Historical comparison of selected U.S. linguistic minority groups' initial modes of incorporation and subsequent educational treatments

| Ethnolinguistic group | Initial mode of incorporation | English compelled | Compulsory ignorance laws | Legally segregated | Excluded from schools | Quotas in higher education |
|---|---|---|---|---|---|---|
| African Americans | Enslaved | Yes | Yes | Yes | Yes | Yes |
| American Indians | Conquered | Yes | No | Yes | Yes | Yes |
| Mexican Americans | Conquered | Yes | No | Yes | No | Yes |
| Puerto Rican | Conquered | Yes | No | No | No | No |
| *Pacific Peoples* | | | | | | |
| Filipinos | Conquered | Yes | No | No | No | No |
| Micronesians | Conquered | Yes | No | No | No | No |
| Polynesians | Conquered | Yes | No | No | No | No |
| *Asian Americans* | | | | | | |
| Japanese | Immigrant | Yes | No | Yes | No | No |
| Korean | Immigrant | Yes | No | Yes | No | No |
| Chinese | Immigrant | Yes | No | Yes | Yes | No |
| Hong Kong Chinese | Immigrant | Yes | No | No | No | No |
| Taiwanese Chinese | Immigrant | Yes | No | No | No | No |
| Asian Indians | Immigrant | Yes | No | No | No | No |
| Cambodians | Refugee | Yes | No | No | No | No |
| Laotians and Hmong | Refugee | Yes | No | No | No | No |
| Vietnamese | Refugee | Yes | No | No | No | No |

Adapted with permission from Weinberg (1997, p. 314)

**Table 3** Policy orientations with implications for educational language rights

| Governmental/state/agency policy orientation toward language rights | Policy characteristics | Implications for language minority educational rights |
|---|---|---|
| Promotion-oriented policies | The government/state/agency allocates resources to support the official use of minority languages. | Examples outside the U.S. include the promotion of community languages, e.g. Welsh in the UK. |
| Expediency-oriented laws* | A weaker version of promotion laws not intended to expand the use of minority language, but typically used only for short-term accommodations. | E.g. Title VII bilingual education programs to accommodate perceived English deficiencies of speakers of languages other than English. |
| Tolerance-oriented policies | Characterized by the noticeable absence of state *intervention* in the linguistic life of the language minority community. | E.g. language schools; private/religious schools in which heritage/community languages are maintained by private resources. |
| Restrictive-oriented policies | Legal prohibitions or curtailments on the use of minority languages; age requirements dictating when a child may study a minority/foreign language. | E.g. Federal restriction on Native American languages in boarding schools; WWI era restrictions on foreign language instruction; Proposition 227 and similar measures, such as Arizona's Proposition 203. |
| Null policies | The significant absence of policy recognizing minority languages or language varieties. | Failure to consider the implications of language differences in instruction mediated only in English. |
| Repression-oriented policies | Active efforts to eradicate minority languages. | E.g. outside the U.S., include equating the use/instruction in a minority language as a political crime (see Skutnabb-Kangas & Bucak, 1994). |
| This table draws from and expands Kloss' schema (1977/1998; see also Macías & Wiley, 1998). The 'Null' and 'Repression-oriented' categories did not appear in Kloss' schema. Kloss also limited these categories to formal governmental/state policies. The contention here is that this schema can also be applied to institutional agencies and institutional contexts as well as to implicit/covert policies/practices. | | |

*Expediency-oriented policies are a subcategory of promotion-oriented policies

education and of linguistic human rights support the notion of 'English Plus', that is, they support the promotion of English *and* another language (Combs, 1992). Federally supported transitional bilingual education falls under the subcategory *expediency-oriented laws* (a subcategory of *promotion-oriented* policies in Table 3). *Expediency-oriented accommodations* are used to bridge contact between a minority population and the government, such as when the government/state sees a reason to try to improve communication with speakers of minority languages in order to facilitate assimilation (Kloss, 1977/1998; Wiley, 1999a).

A *tolerance-orientated* policy prevailed toward speakers of European languages up to the World War I era. During the colonial period and the early history of the republic, education among European-origin peoples was supported through private and sectarian means. In a climate of relative tolerance, German Americans provided support for schooling taught either in German or bilingually in German and English (Toth, 1990; Wiley, 1998a). Some states with large German-origin populations for a time even allowed for public supported education in German and German/English (Ohio and Pennsylvania), but, for the most part, it was incumbent on local and private stakeholders to foster education in community languages. African-origin peoples had a markedly different experience. *Restrictive* literacy policies appeared in slave codes in the 1740s. Slaveholders saw literacy as a direct threat to their ability to control the enslaved. *Compulsory illiteracy* laws remained on the books until 1865 (Weinberg, 1995). Kontra *et al.* note:

> The state/government can *restrict* minority languages in three ways. It can (1)... restrict the age-groups and the range of school subjects for which minority-medium education is provided... (2) [restrict] the number of languages through which education is made available... [and/or] (3) reduce the number of people entitled to minority medium education by obfuscation of who the rightholders/beneficiaries are. (p. 10)

During World War I, speakers of German, who were the second most populous linguistic group at that time, suddenly found themselves stigmatized and forced to use English (Wiley, 1998a). During the 1920s and 1930s, Chinese and Japanese community-based schools operated, often meeting resistance from territorial authorities in Hawaii and state authorities in California.

The *null* policy category (in Table 3) indicates the significant absence of policy. When educational policies have prescribed a one-size-fits-all approach, they have often disadvantaged language minority students by failing to address their special needs, histories, and circumstances (see Quezada *et al.*, 1999/2000). Unless policy prescribes a special program of study of the language of instruction, language minorities are excluded, or at best, systematically disadvantaged in learning academic subjects.

School-based language requirements and standards can covertly be used as surrogates for more overtly racist policies. For example, in 1924, English Standard Schools were implemented in Hawaii. Placement was based on tests of standard English that were used to sort children into 'standard', 'nonstandard', and 'feebleminded' educational tracks. Without resorting to overt racially based segregation, a system of racially segregated schooling was established largely on the basis of language proficiency. In his analysis of historical and contemporary school and university policies and practices in Hawaii, Haas (1992) concluded that many promote institutional racism. Among the examples he identified were failing to offer instruction in languages commonly spoken in linguistically diverse communities even when the communities have requested them; misassigning students to educational tracks based on their performance on tests of standard English which have been normed on national, rather than local populations (e.g. although about half of Hawaii's population is comprised of native speakers of Hawaii Creole English [HCE/'pidgin'], the SAT continues to be used as an entry requirement for admission to the state-supported university system); insufficient use of immigrant languages to communicate with parents; inadequately trained staff responsible for the education of language minority students; and underidentifying and underserving language minority students due to the failure to recognize them as language minorities. Romaine (1994) concluded:

> Speakers of HCE have been discriminated against through education in a school system which originally was set up to keep out those who could not pass an English test. In this way it was hoped to restrict the admission of non-white children into the English Standard schools set up in 1924, which were attended mainly by Caucasian children. By institutionalizing what was essentially racial discrimination along linguistic lines, the schools managed to keep creole speakers in their place, maintaining distance between them and English speakers until after World War II. (p. 531; cf. Agbayani & Takeuchi, 1986; Benham & Heck, 1998; Kawamoto, 1993)

As in the case of speakers of other 'non-standard' varieties of language, the failure of educators in Hawaii to recognize (through *null* policy) the language minority status of HCE as a distinct language variety positions its speakers as merely 'substandard' articulators of English. Thus 'deficiency' is located in the students, but not in the educational system responsible for educating them.

## Court Decisions on Language Rights and Educational Access

This section examines important U.S. court cases focused on language and educational access.

*Meyer v. Nebraska, 262 U.S. 390 (1923).* Following the xenophobia of World War I, Nebraska and other states passed laws prohibiting foreign language instruction. In many states, children were not allowed to study a foreign language until Grade 6, in others, not until Grade 8. The intent was to make foreign languages inaccessible during those ages when children would have the best opportunity for learning or retaining them. By 1923, several appeals challenging these restrictions had been filed to the Supreme Court (Piatt, 1992). The decisive case was *Meyer v. Nebraska* (1923). Meyer, a parochial school teacher, was convicted and fined for breaking a Nebraska law prohibiting foreign language teaching. Meyer appealed to the Nebraska Supreme Court and lost. The Nebraska court reasoned that teaching German to children of immigrants was unfavorable to national safety and self-interest. In 1923, the Supreme Court overturned the Nebraska court, arguing that in peacetime, no threat to national security could justify the restriction on teachers of foreign languages nor the limitation imposed on the parents who wished their children to learn them. By a 7–2 vote, the Nebraska law was held to be an infringement of the Due Process Clause of the Fourteenth Amendment (Edwards, 1923; Murphy, 1992; Piatt, 1992; Wiley, 1998a).

Although the *Meyer* ruling determined that unduly restrictive educational language policies were unconstitutional, it established a weak precedent for educational rights. The court accepted the hegemonic view that all citizens of the United States should be required to speak a common tongue (Murphy, 1992) and affirmed the 'power of the state to compel attendance at some school and to make reasonable regulations for all schools, including a requirement that they shall give instructions in English' (cited in Norgren & Nanda, 1988, p. 188). The Supreme Court's decision affirmed the official status of English-language instruction. Even after *Meyer*, German-language instruction never recovered its pre-war levels (Wiley, 1998a).

*Farrington v. Tokushige 273 U.S. 284, 298 (1927).* In a related decision, *Farrington v. Tokushige*, the Supreme Court, based on Meyer, ruled that the attempt by the territorial governor of Hawaii to impose restrictions on private or community-based Japanese, Korean, and Chinese foreign language schools was unconstitutional. *Farrington* was not without significance, because a large number of such schools had been established in Hawaii (Leibowitz, 1971) and California (Bell, 1935/1974), and many thrived during the 1920s and 1930s, just as similar schools do today. These heritage languages schools provided supplemental instruction in native languages to the English-only instruction provided in public schools. During World War II, however, the right to Japanese instruction was prohibited in federal internment camps in which Japanese Americans were imprisoned (U.S. Senate, 1943/1974).

*Lau v. Nichols 414 U.S. 563, 565 (1974) and Related Cases.* The most significant legal case since *Meyer* with implications for language minority students' educational rights was *Lau v. Nichols* (1974). As historical background to the case, several facts are worth noting. The case was filed in San Francisco. California, like many other states, had a prior history of discriminating against racial and ethnolinguistic minorities. In California, discrimination on the basis of race, at one time, had a legal basis in state law. Anti-Chinese groups even succeeded in lobbying the U.S. government to pass the Chinese Exclusion Act of 1882, which restricted Chinese immigration for ten years. In addition, segregation of Asian-origin students was legal in California from the late 19th century to the mid-20th century. As late as 1943, the California Constitution had affirmed legal segregation of school children of Indian, Chinese, Japanese, or 'Mongolian' parentage. This provision was not overturned until 1947. In 1905, the San Francisco School Board passed a resolution calling for the segregation of Japanese and Chinese students, arguing that its intent was

> not only for the purpose of relieving the congestion at the present prevailing in our schools, but also for the higher end that

*our* children should not be placed in any position where their youthful impressions may be affected by association with pupils of the Mongolian race. (Resolution, 1905/1974; emphasis added)

As in many educational discrimination cases, litigation resulting in *Lau* was born out of the frustration of failed efforts on the part of parents and community activists to receive appropriate educational programs for language minority children. According to Li-Ching Wang, a community leader involved in the four-year litigation, the Chinese-American community held meetings with the San Francisco school administrators over a three-year period. They had 'conducted numerous studies that demonstrated the needs of non-English speaking children, proposed different approaches to solve the problem', and staged demonstrations in protest of district inaction (De Avila *et al.*, 1994, p. 13). As a last resort, Chinese American parents and community leaders filed a lawsuit in 1970, based on the following facts:

1. 2,856 Chinese speaking students in San Francisco Unified School District (SFUSD) needed special instruction in English.
2. 1,790 [Chinese speaking students] received no help or special instruction at all, not even the 40 minutes of ESL [provided to some students].
3. Of the remaining 1,066 Chinese speaking students who did receive some help, 623 received such help on a part-time basis and 433 on a full-time basis.
4. Only 260 of the 1,066 Chinese students receiving special instruction in English were taught by bilingual Chinese speaking teachers. (De Avila *et al.*, 1994, p. 14)

The lower courts rejected the arguments of the plaintiffs. In 1973, the Ninth Circuit Court of Appeals sided with the school district, concluding:

> *The discrimination suffered by these children* is not the result of laws passed by the state of California, presently or historically, but is the *result of deficiencies created by the children themselves* in failing to know and learn the English language. (cited in De Avila *et al.*, 1994, p. 16; emphases added)

Twenty years after the *Lau* decision, Edward

Steinman, the attorney who had represented Kinney Lau, lamented that the attitude which had led to the struggle for *Lau* 'cannot be changed by a court decision . . . This statement [above] says that the child is inherently sinful for having the audacity not to know English when he or she enters the classroom' (De Avila *et al.*, 1994, p. l7). What is even more remarkable is the similarity of the 1973 reasoning of the Ninth Circuit Court to the editorial remarks in the *San Francisco Chronicle*, printed 66 years earlier, in support of the segregation of Japanese children:

> The most prominent objection to the presence of Japanese in our public schools is their habit of sending young men to primary grades, where they sit side by side with very young [white] children, because in those grades only are the beginnings of English taught. That creates situations which often become painfully embarrassing. They are, in fact, unendurable.

> There is also objection to taking the time of the teachers to teach the English language to pupils, old or young, who do not understand it. It is a reasonable requirement that all pupils entering the schools shall be familiar with the language in which instruction is conducted. *We deny either the legal or moral obligation to teach any foreigner to read or speak the English language. And if we choose to do that for one nationality, this is our privilege.* (U.S. Senate, 1906/1974, p. 2972; emphasis added)

In delivering the 1974 opinion of the Supreme Court, Justice William O. Douglas focused on the connections between language and race, ethnicity, and national origin:

> The failure of the San Francisco school system to provide English language instruction to approximately 1,800 students of Chinese ancestry who do not speak English, or to provide them with other adequate instructional procedures, denies them a meaningful opportunity to participate in the public educational program and thus violates §601 of the Civil Rights Act of 1964, which bans discrimination based on 'the ground of race, color, or national origin', in 'any program or activity receiving financial assistance'. (*Lau et al. v. Nichols et al.*, 414 U.S. No. 72–6520; Reprinted in ARC, 1994, p. 6)

And, contradicting the entrenched notion that schools are not 'legally or morally obligated to teach English', Douglas concluded,

> Basic English skills are at the very core of what these public schools teach. Imposition of a requirement that, *before a child can effectively participate in the educational program, he must already have acquired those basic skills is to make a mockery of public education.* We know that those who do not understand English are certain to find their classroom experiences wholly incomprehensible and in no way meaningful. (*Lau et al. v. Nichols et al.,* 414 U.S. No. 72–6520; Reprinted in ARC, 1994, p. 8; emphasis added)

Contrary to a common misunderstanding, *Lau* did not mandate bilingual education. The plaintiffs had not requested a specific remedy, and Douglas left the prescription of possible remedies open, stating: 'Teaching English to the students of Chinese ancestry is one choice. Giving instructions to this group in Chinese is another' (cited in ARC, p. 7). Soon after, federal authorities took the next step with the so-called *Lau* Remedies (see Crawford, 1992). The Lau Remedies attempted to spell out appropriate expediency-oriented policies that could be implemented in schools. However, these were subsequently withdrawn under the Reagan administration (see Crawford, 1995). Nevertheless, using *transitional* bilingual education (see Table 4) as a remedy was prescribed in several district court cases. The first was *Serna v. Portales Municipal Schools* in 1974 (*Serna* was also affirmed by the l0th U.S. Circuit Court of Appeals). Other important district court cases prescribing the remedy of transitional bilingual education include *U.S. v. Texas* (1981) and *Rios v. Read* (1978; see Leibowitz, 1982). However, in neither *Lau* nor related cases such as *Serna* did the courts address the constitutional issue of equal protection under the 14th Amendment. Rather, rulings were based on legislative protections against discrimination under the 1964 Civil Rights Act (Piatt, 1992).

The issue of determining whether or not the school districts have complied with *Lau* was left to federal courts to resolve (Jiménez, 1992). The definitive case to date is *Casteñeda v. Pickard* (1981). As Jiménez notes, the significance of *Casteñeda* is that it laid out an analytical framework or three-part test by which 'appropriate actions' by school districts 'to overcome language barriers' could be assessed (p. 248). The criteria were that any prescribed remedy must (a) be based on sound educational theory; (b) have a reasonable plan for implementation, including the hiring of appropriate personnel; and (c) produce positive educational results.

***Martin Luther King Jr. Elementary School Children v. Ann Arbor School District Board (1979).*** Children who speak non-standard language varieties, such as Hawaii Creole English, Appalachian English, and Ebonics, have often been ignored in discussions of language minority educational rights. The most important legal case in this area is *Martin Luther King Jr. Elementary School Children v. Ann Arbor School District Board.* Initially, this was brought as a racial discrimination suit in which race, class, and language were linked. Smitherman (1981) an expert witness for the defense, after the trial noted:

> The fate of black children as victims of miseducation continues to be the bottom line in the case. King began with a claim against the institutional mismanagement of the children . . . It ended with a claim against the institutional mismanagement of the language of the children . . . Our argument and Judge Joiner's ruling was that it is the obligation of educational institutions to accept it as legitimate. (p. 20)

Although the judge's ruling affirmed the status of Ebonics/African American English, his strategy in limiting the case to the single issue of language demonstrates how language is used as a substitute for issues involving race and class (Wiley, 1999b). The judge in the King case avoided race and class by focusing on the issue of language deficiency.

Several misunderstandings have developed regarding this case. One is that the judge ordered Ebonics/Black English to be taught or *promoted* in place of standard English. To the contrary, he was only trying to *accommodate* the children's language differences. Another misperception is that this case had the same force as *Lau* (see Baugh, 1995; Schiffman, 1996). However, unlike *Lau*, which reached the Supreme Court, *Ann Arbor* was decided only at the federal district court-level. The school district, which lost the decision, chose not to appeal it; thus, its impact was only relevant in the Ann Arbor District

**Table 4** A typology of bilingual education

| Type of program | Typical child | Language of the classroom | Societal and educational aim | Language and/or literacy aim |
|---|---|---|---|---|
| *Weak Forms of Education for Promoting Bilingualism and/or Biliteracy* | | | | |
| SUBMERSION (a.k.a. Structured Immersion) | Language Minority | Majority Language | Assimilation | Monolingualism |
| SUBMERSION (+ Withdrawal ESL) | Language Minority | Majority Language | Assimilation | Monolingualism |
| SEGREGATIONIST | Language Minority | Minority Language (forced, no choice) | Apartheid | Monolingualism |
| TRANSITIONAL | Language Minority | From Minority to Majority Language | Assimilation | Relative Monolingualism |
| MAJORITY Lang. + Foreign Language | Language Minority | Majority Language with L2/FL Lessons | Limited enrichment | Limited Bilingualism |
| SEPARATIST | Language Minority | Minority Language (out of choice) | Detachment/autonomy | Limited Bilingualism |
| *Strong Forms of Education for Promoting Bilingualism and/or Biliteracy* | | | | |
| Immersion | Language Minority | Bilingual, Initial Emphasis on L2 | Pluralism and Enrichment | Bilingualism and Biliteracy |
| Maintenance/Heritage Language | Language Minority | Bilingual with Emphasis on L1 | Maintenance/Pluralism/Enrichment | Bilingualism and Biliteracy |
| Two-way/Dual Language | Mixed Language Minority and Majority | Minority and Majority Languages | Maintenance/Pluralism/Enrichment | Bilingualism and Biliteracy |
| Mainstream Bilingual | Language Majority | Two Majority Languages | Maintenance/Pluralism/Enrichment | Bilingualism and Biliteracy |

This table is adapted with permission from Baker (1996, p. 172). Notes: (1) L2 = Second Language; L1 = First Language: FL = Foreign Language. (2) See pp. 172–197 for elaboration

(Baugh, 1995). Nevertheless, the decision demonstrates the potential of *expediency* policies for removing the sole burden for acquiring standard English from students who do not enter school speaking it (Wiley, 1999b).

In 1996,the Oakland School Board decided to use Ebonics as a bridge to school English. Its decision was widely ridiculed by the press and popular media, and more viciously attacked by hate-oriented Internet websites. What the press and media failed to focus on was the fact that the overwhelming majority of language minority children, including speakers of Ebonics, are being educated in standard English by many teachers who equate their students' language differences with language deficiencies (see Ramírez *et al.*, 1999).

## Language Minority Educational Rights in Institutional and Programmatic Contexts

In order to evaluate access to educational language rights, it is useful to analyze the various types of program models prescribed by legislation, or otherwise available, and to consider their particular goals for language minority students vis-à-vis the dominant society and in terms of their aims for language and literacy development as well (see Table 4).

The political debate over bilingual education in the United States has focused more on the phrase 'bilingual education' rather than on programmatic substance. As Lyons (1990/1995) has noted, the intent of one of the initial sponsors of federal bilingual programs, Senator Yarbrough, was to address the needs of Spanish-speaking children. Initially, the proposal for bilingual education had strong bipartisan support, with some three-dozen bills being put forth. In a compromise move to expedite passage of the legislation, the designated target population was redefined as being 'children of limited English-speaking ability'. This shift in terminology away from 'Spanish-speakers' had the appearance of being more inclusive. However, it also positioned the target population as members of a 'remedial' group, defined by the lack of proficiency in English. Amendments to the Bilingual Education Act of 1978 relabeled the target population as being 'limited English proficient' to underscore the emphasis on reading, writing, comprehension and cognitive skills in English. Yet 'the new definition, arguably clearer and more comprehensive, reinforced the deficit approach to

educating language minority students' (Lyons, 1990/1995, p. 3).

Under the Bilingual Education Act and its reauthorized versions, the majority of programs offered under the 'bilingual' label have been short-term *transitional* programs and programs in English as a second language. In Table 4, these models fall under the 'weak' category because they fail to promote or maintain native languages. Also the societal and educational aims of these programs as well as their language/literacy aims promote 'assimilation' and 'monolingualism' (in English) respectively. Many so-called educational 'reform' measures, such as Proposition 227 ('English for the Children') and Arizona's Proposition 203, have sought to restrict even 'weak' *transitional* models of bilingual education.

## Conclusion

The history of access to educational language rights in minority languages, from the colonial period to the present, indicates a mixed bag of official and unofficial policies. As English achieved highest status, colonial and early national policies and practices toward minority languages ranged from relative tolerance or indifference toward education in European languages and bilingual education, to the suppression of African tongues accompanied by compulsory ignorance laws imposed on enslaved African Americans. Policy differences toward each group suggest the extent to which language policies represented efforts to exert social control over various language minority groups based on their relative status vis-à-vis the English-speaking majority. From the early national period to the mid-19th century, policies toward Native Americans encouraged the acquisition of English over maintenance native languages. However, after the Civil War, policies toward American Indians shifted to *coercive assimilation* of English, accompanied by restrictions on the maintenance of native languages until the 1930s. From the late 1880s to the 1920s, restrictive policies (peaking during World War I) were also adopted toward European languages, most notably toward German, with the effect of reduced maintenance and a de-emphasis on German education in the schools. In the 1920s, the Supreme Court struck down the most restrictive prohibitions on 'foreign' language instruction. Nevertheless, it affirmed the goal of a monolingual English speaking society and the imposition of English as the medium of instruction. In the 1960s, during a climate of heightened concern for civil rights, greater educational opportunity for all, and 'remediation', bilingual education – with assimilation into English mediated education as its goal – was adopted as an *expediency* measure to promote greater educational access. During the anti-bilingual education movement of the 1990s, even weak forms of publicly supported bilingual education were subject to attack. California's Proposition 227 and Arizona's Proposition 203 were designed to strictly limit access to bilingual education and similar measures were introduced in a number of other states.

From the perspective of educational language rights, the 21st century begins with echoes of early 20th century restrictionism (cf. Tatalovich, 1995). At present, support for the right of language minority children in the United States to maintain their languages remains protected in principle. Unfortunately, the prospects for attaining such a goal survive largely outside the domain of federal education policy through the efforts of charter school *two-way immersion* programs (see Table 4) and freelance community-based organizations and private efforts. Thus, the struggle for educational language rights and linguistic human rights in the United States continues.

## References

Agbayani, A. and Takeuchi, D. (1986) English standard schools; A policy analysis. In N. Tsuchida (ed.) *Issues in Asian and Pacific American education*, (pp. 30–45). Minneapolis, MN: Asian/Pacific American Learning Resource Center, University of Minnesota.

Art, Research & Curriculum Associates (ARC), *Revisiting the Lau Decision: 20 years after*. Symposium Proceedings (November 3–4, 1994) (pp. 6–12). San Francisco, CA: ARC.

Baker, C. (1996) *Foundations of bilingual education and bilingualism*, 2nd edn. Philadelphia, PA: Multilingual Matters.

Baugh, J. (1995) The law, linguistics and education: Educational reform for African American language minority students. *Linguistics and Education*, 7, 87–105.

Bell, R. (1935/1974) Japanese language schools in California. Public school education of second generation Japanese in California. Reprinted from S. Cohen (ed.) *Education in the United States: A documentary history, Vol. 2*, (pp. 2974–2976). New York: McGraw-Hill. In *Educational-Psychology*, Vol. 1 (pp. 20–23). Stanford University Publications.

Benham, M.K.P. and Heck, R.H. (1998) *Culture and education in Hawaii: The silencing of native voices*. Mahwah, NJ: Lawrence Erlbaum.

Combs, M.C. (1992) English Plus: Responding to English Only. In J. Crawford (ed.) *Language loyalties: A source book on the official English controversy* (pp. 216–224). Chicago: University of Chicago Press.

Crawford, J. (1992) The question of minority language rights. In J. Crawford (ed.) *Language loyalties: A source book on the official English controversy* (pp. 225–228). Chicago, IL: University of Chicago Press.

Crawford, J. (1995) *Bilingual education: History, politics, theory, and practice* (3rd edn). Los Angeles, CA: Bilingual Education Services.

de Avila, E.A., Steinman, E. and Wang, L.C. (1994) Historical overview. In Art, Research & Curriculum Associates (ARC), *Revisiting the Lau Decision: 20 years after*. Symposium Proceedings (November 3–4, 1994) (pp. 13–21). San Francisco, CA: ARC.

de Varennes, F. (1999) *Language: A right and a resource approach to linguistic human rights* (pp. 117–146). Budapest: Central European University Press.

Edwards, I.N. (December, 1923) The legal status of foreign languages in the schools. *Elementary School Journal*, 24, pp. 270–278.

Haas, M. (1992) *Institutional racism: The case of Hawaii*. Westport, CT: Praeger.

Heath, S.B. (1976) Colonial language status achievement: Mexico, Peru, and the United States. In A. Verdoodt and R. Kjolseth (eds) *Language and sociology*. Louvain: Peeters.

Hernández-Chávez, E. (1994) Language policy in the United States: A history of cultural genocide. In T. Skutnabb-Kangas and R. Phillipson (eds) *Linguistic human rights: Overcoming linguistic discrimination* (pp. 141–158). Berlin: Mouton de Gruyter.

Jiménez, M. (1992) The educational rights of language minority children. In J. Crawford (ed.) *Language loyalties: A source book on the official English controversy* (pp. 243–251). Chicago: University of Chicago Press.

Kawamoto, K.Y. (1993) Hegemony and language politics in Hawaii. *World Englishes*, 12, 193–207.

Kloss, H. (1977/1998) *The American bilingual tradition*. Center for Applied Linguistics and Delta Systems: Washington, DC and McHenry, IL. Original work published 1977.

Kontra, M., Phillipson, R., Skutnabb-Kangas, T. and Varády, T. (eds) (1999a) Conceptualizing and implementing linguistic human rights. In *Language: A right and a resource approaches to linguistic human rights* (pp. 1–21). Budapest: Central European University Press.

Kontra, M., Phillipson, R., Skutnabb-Kangas, T. and Varády, T. (eds) (l999b) *Language: A right and a resource approaches to linguistic human rights*. Budapest: Central European University Press.

*Lau et al. v. Nichols et al.* (U.S., 563–572, No. 72–6520) Reprinted in Art, Research & Curriculum Associates (ARC), *Revisiting the Lau Decision: 20 years after*. Symposium Proceedings (November 3–4, 1994) (pp. 6–12). San Francisco, CA: ARC.

Leibowitz, A.H. (1969) English literacy: Legal sanction for discrimination. *Notre Dame Lawyer*, 25 (1), 7–66.

Leibowitz, A.H. (1971) *Educational policy and political acceptance: The imposition of English as the language of instruction in American schools*. Eric Document Reproduction Service No. ED 047321.

Leibowitz, A.H. (1974, August) Language as a means of social control. Paper presented at the VIII World Congress of Sociology, University of Toronto, Toronto, Canada.

Leibowitz, A.H. (1982) *Federal recognition of the rights of minority language groups*. Rosslyn, VA: National Clearinghouse on Bilingual Education.

Lyons, J. (1990/1995) The past and future directions of federal bilingual-education policy. In O. García and C. Baker (eds) *Policy and practice in bilingual education: Extending the foundations* (pp. 1–15). Clevedon, UK: Multilingual Matters. Reprinted from *Annals of the American Academy of Political and Social Sciences* 508, 66–80, 1990.

Macías, R.F. (1979) Choice of language as a human right – Public policy implications in the United States. In R.V. Padilla (ed.) *Bilingual education and public policy in the United States* (pp. 39–75). Ypsilanti, MI: Eastern Michigan University.

Macías, R.F. (1999) Language policies and the sociolinguistics historiography of Spanish in the United States. In J.K. Peyton, P. Griffin and R. Fasold (eds) *Language in action* (pp. 52–83). Creskill, NJ: Hampton Press.

Macías, R.F. and Wiley, T.G. (1998) Introduction. In H. Kloss, *The American bilingual tradition* (pp. vii–xiv). Washington, DC and McHenry, IL: Center for Applied Linguistics and Delta Symposium System.

Murphy, P.L. (1992) *Meyer v. Nebraska*. In K.L. Hall (ed.) *The Oxford companion to the Supreme Court of the United States* (pp. 543–544). New York: Oxford University Press.

Norgren, J. and Nanda, S. (1988) *American cultural pluralism and the law*. New York: Praeger.

Piatt, B. (1992) The confusing state of minority language rights. In J. Crawford (ed.) *Language loyalties: A source book on the official English controversy* (pp. 229–234). Chicago: University of Chicago Press.

Quezada, M.S., Wiley, T.G. and Ramírez, J.D. (1999/2000) How the reform agenda short-changes English learners. *Educational Leadership*, 57(4), 57–61.

Ramírez, J.D., Wiley, T.G., DeKlerk, G. and Lee, E. (eds) (1999) *Ebonics in the urban debate*. Long Beach, CA: Center for Language Minority Education and Research (CLMER) California State University, Long Beach.

Romaine, S. (1994). Hawaii Creole English as a literacy language. *Language in Society*, 23(4), 527–554.

Resolution (1905/1974) Resolution of the San Francisco School Board. Reprinted in S. Cohen (ed.) *Education in the United States: A documentary history, Vol. 2*, (p. 2971). New York: McGraw-Hill.

Rickford, J.R. (1999) Using the vernacular to teach the standard. In J.D. Ramírez, T.G. Wiley, H. DeKlerk and E. Lee (eds) *Ebonics in the urban debate* (pp. 23–41). Long Beach, CA: Center for Language Minority Education and Research (CLMER) California State University, Long Beach.

Schiffman, H.F. (1996) *Linguistic culture and language policy*. London: Routledge.

Skutnabb-Kangas, T. and Bucak, S. (1994). In T. Skutnabb-Kangas and R. Phillipson (eds) *Linguistic human rights: Overcoming linguistic discrimination* (pp. 347–370). Berlin: Mouton de Gruyter.

Skutnabb-Kangas, T. (1995) Multilingualism and the education of minority children. In O. García and C. Baker (eds) *Policy and practice in bilingual education: Extending the foundations* (pp. 40–62). Clevedon, UK: Multilingual Matters.

Skutnabb-Kangas, T. (1999) Linguistic diversity, human rights, and the 'free' market. In M. Kontra, R. Phillipson and T. Varády (eds) *Language: A right and a resource approaches to linguistic human rights* (pp. 187–222). Budapest: Central European University Press.

Smitherman, G. (1981) Introduction. In G. Smith-erman (ed.) *Black English and the education of Black children and youth: Proceedings of the National Invitational Symposium on the King decision* (pp. 11–31). Detroit, MI: Center for Black Studies, Wayne State.

Spring, J. (1994) *Deculturation and the struggle for equality: A brief history of the education of dominated cultures in the United States.* New York: McGraw-Hill.

Tatalovich, R. (1995) *Nativism reborn? The official English language movement and the American states.* Lexington, KY: University of Kentucky Press.

Tollefson, J.W. (1991) *Planning language, planning inequality.* New York: Longman.

Tollefson, J.W. (1995) Introduction: Language policy, power, and inequality. In J. W. Tollefson (ed.) *Power and inequality in language education* (pp. 1–8). Cambridge: Cambridge University Press.

Toth, C.R. (1990) *German-English bilingual schools in America: The Cincinnati tradition in historical context.* New York: Lang.

U.S. Senate (1906/1974) The *San Francisco Chronicle* on segregation of Japanese school children. From editorial, November 6, 1906, as quoted in Senate document no. 147, 59th Cong., 2nd Sess. (1906), p. 30. Reprinted in S. Cohen (ed.) *Education in the United States: A documentary history, Vol. 2* (p. 2972). New York: McGraw-Hill.

U.S. Senate (1943/1974). Description of Education in the Internment Camps. From Miscellane-ous Documents, 1–142, 78th Cong. 1st Sess. Document No. 96. Segregation of loyal and disloyal Japanese (1943), p. 11. Reprinted in S. Cohen (ed.) *Education in the United States: A documentary history, Vol. 2* (p. 2977). New York: McGraw-Hill.

Weinberg, M. (1995). *A chance to learn: A history of race and education in the United States*, 2nd edn. Long Beach, CA: California State University, Long Beach University Press.

Weinberg, M. (1997). *Asian-American education: Historical background and current realities.* Mahwah, NJ: Lawrence Erlbaum.

Wiley, T.G. and Lukes, M. (1996) English-only and standard English ideologies in the United States. *TESOL Quarterly*, 30(3), 511–535.

Wiley, T.G. (1996a) Language planning and language policy. In S. McKay and N. Horn-berger (eds) *Sociolinguistics and language teaching* (pp. 103–147). Cambridge: Cambridge University Press.

Wiley, T.G. (1996b) *Literacy and language diversity in the United States. Language in education: Theory and practice.* McHenry, IL: Center for Applied Linguistics and Delta Systems.

Wiley, T.G. (1998a) The imposition of World War I Era English-Only policies and the fate of German in North America. In T. Ricento and B. Burnaby (eds) *Language and politics in the United States and Canada* (pp. 211–241). Mahwah, NJ: Lawrence Erlbaum.

Wiley, T.G. (1998b) What happens after English is declared the official language of the United States. In D.A. Kibbee (ed.) *Language legislation and linguistic rights* (pp. 179–194). Amsterdam: John Benjamins.

Wiley, T.G. (1999a) Comparative histori-cal analysis of U.S. Language Policy and Language Planning: Extending the founda-tions. In T. Huebner and K.A. Davis (eds) *Sociopolitical perspectives on language policy and planning in the USA* (pp. 17–37). Amsterdam: John Benjamins.

Wiley, T.G. (1999b) Ebonics: Background to the current policy context. In J.D. Ramírez, T.G. Wiley, G. DeKlerk and E. Lee (eds) *Ebonics in the urban debate* (pp. 8–19). Long Beach, CA: Center for Language Minority Education and Research (CLMER). California State Univer-sity, Long Beach.

Wiley, T.G. (in press). Language policy and English-Only. In E. Finegan and J.R. Rickford (eds) *Language in the USA: Perspectives for the 21st century* (Cambridge: Cambridge Univer-sity Press).

Wolfram, W., Adger, T.C. and Christian, D. (1999) *Dialects in schools and communities.* Mahwah, NJ: Lawrence Erlbaum Associates.

Wright, E. (1980) School English and public policy. *College English*, 42, 327–342.

## Questions

1.  From the history of languages in the United States in the 19th/20th centuries, write (in more detail than in the chapter) about one example of promotion-oriented policy, expediency-oriented laws, tolerance-oriented policies, restrictive-oriented policies, null policies and repression-oriented policies.
2.  The Bilingual Education Act of 1968 referred to 'limited English-speaking' students. By 1978, the term 'limited English-proficient' (LEP) was adopted. Explain what the difference is between the two. What other terms have you heard referring to students who are learning a second language? How would you evaluate these terms?
3.  Explain the case of *Lau v. Nichols* and the Supreme Court's decision of 1974. Refer to the legal basis for this judicial decision. Does *Lau v. Nichols* mandate bilingual education? Then discuss the Lau Remedies and their history, including the relationship of Title VI of the Civil Rights Act and the Office of Civil Rights (OCR) to bilingual education.
4.  Summarize at least two other U.S. court cases that focused on language rights and educational access.
5.  What is the contradiction between (a) opposing bilingual education for language minorities and (b) supporting foreign language instruction. Refer to some examples of this contradiction in United States federal or state policy.

## Activities

1.  Search through the index of a major US daily, such as *The Washington Post* or *The New York Times*. Look for articles on the following:
    a.  Passage of the First Bilingual Education Act, 1968
    b.  The *Lau vs. Nichols* decision, 1974
    c.  Proposition 227
    d.  No Child Left Behind, 2001
    Different groups might search different newspapers and compare the reporting both with regard to coverage and attitudes expressed. For example, New York might be compared to Los Angeles; an English language daily might be compared to a non-English language daily. On a particular day, compare the number of articles, the length of the articles, and whether the attitudes are positive or negative. Make a chart with your results.
2.  Find out the educational language policy in one of the following countries,
    a. Aotearoa/New Zealand
    b. Wales
    c. Hong Kong
    d. Singapore
    e. Malaysia
    f. India
    g. The Philippines
    h. South Africa
    i. Bolivia
    (One importance source for this information is Tolleson, J.W. and Tsui, A.B.M. (eds),

2004. *Medium of Instruction Policies. Which agenda? Whose agenda?* Mahwah, NJ: Lawrence Erlbaum Associates.)

Then prepare a class table with the languages that are used as medium of education, the language education policy itself, and a short quote from the policy.

3.   Prepare a script with a group in which each of you takes on the role of parents arguing for appropriate bilingual education programs for your children in front of educational authories.

Different groups can take on different sociocultural and sociolinguistic characteristics. Act out your scripts in front of the class.

4.   Create a wall display depicting the history of one school that has engaged bilingualism in its past. Show how policy, provision and practice have changed over time.

5.   Imagine that the opening speaker in a debate argued that language minorities should not be allowed to retain their heritage language because it would allow them to use that power for their own enhancement and would weaken the political and economic stability of the country. Prepare a reply and deliver it in front of your class.

## Further Reading

Crawford, J. (2004) *Educating English Learners: Language Diversity in the Classroom.* Los Angeles: Bilingual Education Services.

Del Valle, S. (2003) *Language Rights and the Law in the United States: Finding Our Voices.* Clevedon: Multilingual Matters.

Dicker, S.J. (2003) *Languages in America: A Pluralist View* (2nd edition). Clevedon: Multilingual Matters.

Hall, J.K. and Eggington, W.G. (eds) (2000) *The Sociopolitics of English Language Teaching.* Clevedon: Multilingual Matters.

May, S. (2001) *Language and Minority Rights: Ethnicity, Nationalism and the Politics of Language.* London: Longman.

Migual, G.S. (2004) *Contested Policy: The Rise and Fall of Federal Bilingual Education in the United States 1960–2001.* Denton, TX: University of North Texas Press.

Ovando, C.J. (2003) Bilingual education in the United States: Historical development and current issues. *Bilingual Research Journal*, 27,1, 1–24. http://brj.asu.edu/content/vol27_no1/documents/art1.pdf

Wiley, T.G. and Wright, W. (2004) Against the undertow: Language-minority education policy and politics in the 'age of accountability'. *Educational Policy*, 18,1, 142–168.

# Language Interactions in the Classroom: From Coercive to Collaborative Relations of Power

## J. Cummins

### Introduction

In June 1998, California voters reversed almost 25 years of educational policy in that state by passing Proposition 227 by a margin of 61 to 39%. Proposition 227 was aimed at eliminating the use of bilingual children's first language (L1) for instructional purposes except in very exceptional circumstances. The origins of this controversy go back 25 years to the 1974 ruling of the Supreme Court in the *Lau v. Nichols* case. According to the Court judgment, the civil rights of non-English-speaking students were violated when the school took no steps to help them acquire the language of instruction:

> ... there is no equality of treatment merely by providing students with the same facilities, textbooks, teachers, and curriculum; for students who do not understand English are effectively foreclosed from any meaningful education. Basic English skills are at the very core of what these public schools teach. Imposition of a requirement that, before a child can effectively participate in the educational program, he must already have acquired those basic skills is to make a mockery of public education. We know that those who do not understand English are certain to find their classroom experiences wholly incomprehensible and in no way meaningful. (cited in Crawford, 1992a: 253)

The Court did not mandate bilingual education; rather it mandated that schools take effective measures to overcome the educational disadvantages resulting from a home–school language mismatch. The Office of Civil Rights, however, interpreted the Supreme Court's decision as effectively mandating transitional bilingual education unless a school district could prove that another approach would be equally or more effective. The Office of Civil Rights' interpretation of the Supreme Court decision sparked outrage among media commentators and educators in school districts which, for the most part, were totally unprepared to offer any form of bilingual instruction. The controversy has raged unabated since that time.

The debate leading up to the Proposition 227 referendum in California crystallized all of the arguments that had been advanced for and against bilingual education in the previous quarter century. Both sides claimed 'equity' as their central guiding principle. Opponents of bilingual programs argued that limited English proficient students were being denied access to both English and academic advancement as a result of being instructed for part of the day through their L1. Exposure to English was being diluted and, as a result, it was not surprising that bilingual students continued to experience difficulty in academic aspects of English. Only maximum exposure to English (frequently termed 'time-on-task') could remedy children's linguistic difficulties in that language on entry to school. Early in 1998, former Speaker of the House, Newt Gingrich expressed the views of many conservative policy-makers: 'When we allow children to stay trapped in bilingual programs where they do not learn English, we are destroying their economic future' (Hornblower, 1998: 44). According to Hornblower, 'He and other Republicans call for a return to the traditional expectation that immigrants will quickly learn English as the price of admission to America' (p. 44).

Proponents of bilingual education argued that L1 instruction in the early grades was necessary to ensure that students understood academic content and experienced a successful start to their schooling. Reading and writing skills acquired initially through the L1 provided a foundation upon which strong English language development could be built. The research literature on bilingual development provided consistent evidence for transfer of academic skills and knowledge across languages. Thus, L1 proficiency could be promoted at no cost to children's academic development in English. Furthermore, the fact that teachers spoke the language of parents increased the likelihood of parental involvement and support for their children's learning. This, together with the reinforcement of children's sense of self as a result of the incorporation of their language and culture in the school program, contributed to long-term academic growth.

In the context of Proposition 227, bilingual advocates argued that bilingual education itself could not logically be regarded as a cause of continued high levels of academic failure among bilingual students since only 30% of limited English proficient students in California were in any form of bilingual education. Gándara (1999) points out that in 1996 'more than one-third of teachers in bilingual classrooms were not fully credentialed, and while little is actually known about these teachers, the likelihood is that many were relying heavily on one of the 29,000 bilingual paraprofessionals employed in California's schools' (1999: 2). Thus, even before Proposition 227, 70% of California's ELL students were either in an all-English program or not receiving any services at all. Advocates of bilingual education could thus logically argue that the academic difficulties of ELL students were more appropriately attributed to the *absence* of effective bilingual programs than to bilingual education in some absolute sense.

The educational arguments on both sides of the issue represent, to a considerable extent, a surface structure for more deeply rooted ideological divisions. Opponents of bilingual education frequently characterized the use of languages other than English in schools as 'unAmerican' and many also expressed concerns about the number of immigrants entering the United States and the consequent growth of cultural and linguistic diversity (Crawford, 1992b). To them, the institutionalization of bilingual education by federal and state governments constituted a 'death wish' (Bethell, 1979) that threatened to fragment the nation. This ideological opposition to bilingual education frequently resulted either in lukewarm implementation of bilingual education or outright attempts to sabotage the program (Wong Fillmore, 1992). Underlying the educational arguments of many bilingual education advocates was the conviction that a history of oppressive power relations was a significant contributing factor to bilingual students' underachievement. For many generations, bilingual students had been punished for any use of their L1 in the school context and were discriminated against in virtually all areas of education, from segregated schools to biased curriculum and assessment practices. Schools traditionally had communicated a sense of shame in regard to children's language and cultural background rather than a sense of affirmation and pride. Thus, some degree of genuine recognition or institutionalization of children's language and culture in the schools was a prerequisite to reversing this legacy of coercive power relations.

This orientation was linked to the perceived desirability of adopting a pluralist rather than an assimilationist social policy in which the value of different cultures and groups was recognized and their contributions to American society respected (Banks, 1996; Ovando & McLaren, 1999; Nieto, 1996). Implementation of multicultural education in schools was the logical expression of this pluralist orientation to social policy. In the case of bilingual students, promotion of pride in students' language and culture through bilingual programs was frequently regarded as an integral component of a broader philosophy of multicultural education (Nieto, 1999).

This chapter attempts to provide a framework for understanding how the interactions that bilingual students experience in schools create the conditions for academic success or failure. The initial sections focus on linguistic and cognitive aspects of students' development while the subsequent sections attempt to place students' linguistic and cognitive development into a broader sociopolitical context.

Among the relevant linguistic and cognitive issues are the nature of language proficiency, the effects of bilingualism on children's cognitive and educational development, and the relationship between students' first and second languages (L1 and L2). Research focused on these issues can answer questions such as how long it typically takes English language learning (ELL) students to catch up academically in English as compared to gaining fluency in conversational English. The research can also address questions about the relationship between bilingual students' L1 and L2 and the outcomes of different kinds of bilingual programs. However, linguistic and psychological research provides few answers to questions regarding why some culturally diverse groups tend to experience persistent long-term underachievement, nor does it give us clear directions regarding the kinds of educational interventions that will be effective in reversing this underachievement.

For answers to these issues we need to shift to a sociological and sociopolitical orientation. We need to ask questions such as: Why is it that underachievement tends to characterize social groups that have experienced long-term devaluation of their identities in the broader society much more than social groups that have immigrated to the host country more recently? How are patterns of discrimination in the wider society reflected (or challenged) in the school context? To what extent do structures that have been set up in the school, such as the content of the curriculum, assessment practices, and the language of instruction, contribute to perpetuating discrimination and underachievement among certain groups of students? How can subtle and more obvious manifestations of bias be challenged by educators and communities working together? To what extent can we see our classroom instruction as 'neutral' with respect to relations of status and power in the wider society? For example, what messages are being communicated to students when we set out to do our jobs by 'just teaching the curriculum' as compared to teaching the curriculum in such a way that bilingual/ELL students' cultural and linguistic identities are affirmed?

The chapter argues that students' identities are affirmed and academic achievement promoted when teachers express respect for the language and cultural knowledge that students bring to the classroom and when the instruction is focused on helping students generate new knowledge, create literature and art, and act on social realities that affect their lives. Only a brief overview of these issues is provided in this chapter. The goal is to sketch

a framework for understanding the causes of bilingual students' academic difficulties and the kinds of intervention that are implied by this causal analysis.

## Psycholinguistic Principles

### Conversational and academic proficiency

Research studies since the early 1980s have shown that immigrant students can quickly acquire considerable fluency in the dominant language of the society when they are exposed to it in the environment and at school. However, despite this rapid growth in conversational fluency, it generally takes a minimum of about five years (and frequently much longer) for them to catch up to native-speakers in academic aspects of the language (Collier, 1987; Cummins, 1981b; Hakuta *et al.*, 2000; Klesmer, 1994). Collier's (1987) research among middle-class immigrant students taught exclusively through English in the Fairfax County district suggested that a period of five to ten years was required for students to catch up. The Ramírez Report data illustrate the pattern (Ramírez, 1992): after four years of instruction, Grade 3 Spanish-speaking students in both structured immersion (English-only) and early-exit bilingual programs were still far from grade norms in English academic achievement. Grade 6 students in late-exit programs who had consistently received about 40% of their instruction through their primary language were beginning to approach grade norms. Further analysis of a subset of these data (from a late-exit program in New York City) showed that the rapidity with which bilingual students approached grade norms in English reading by Grade 6 was strongly related to their level of Spanish reading at Grade 3. The better developed their Spanish reading was at Grade 3, the more rapid progress they made in English reading between Grades 3 and 6 (Beykont, 1994).

Gándara (1999), in summarizing data from California, has noted the 'large discrepancy' between the developmental patterns for oral L2 skills (measured by tests) as compared to L2 reading and writing during the elementary school years:

> For example, while listening skills are at 80% of native proficiency by Level 3 (approximately 3rd grade), reading and writing skills remain below 50% of those expected

for native speakers. It is not until after Level 5 (or approximately 5th grade) that the different sets of skills begin to merge. This suggests that while a student may be able to speak and understand English at fairly high levels of proficiency within the first three years of school, academic skills in English reading and writing take longer for students to develop. (1999: 5)

Hakuta *et al.*'s analysis of data from two California school districts in the San Francisco Bay area showed that 'even in two California districts that are considered the most successful in teaching English to LEP [limited English proficient] students, oral proficiency [measured by formal tests] takes three to five years to develop, and academic English proficiency can take four to seven years' (2000: iii). They label the one-year time period of 'sheltered English immersion' that Proposition 227 gives ELL students to acquire English 'wildly unrealistic' (2000: 13).

Outside of North America, Shohamy (1999) reports ongoing research being conducted in Israel that shows a time period of seven to nine years for immigrant students to arrive at similar achievements as native speakers in Hebrew literacy and slightly less in mathematics.

There are two reasons why such major differences are found in the length of time required to attain peer-appropriate levels of conversational and academic skills. First, considerably less knowledge of language itself is usually required to function appropriately in interpersonal communicative situations than is required in academic situations. The social expectations of the learner and sensitivity to contextual and interpersonal cues (e.g. eye contact, facial expression, intonation etc.) greatly facilitate communication of meaning. These social cues are largely absent in most academic situations that depend on knowledge of the language itself for successful task completion. In comparison to interpersonal conversation, the language of text usually involves much more low frequency vocabulary, complex grammatical structures, and greater demands on memory, analysis, and other cognitive processes.

The second reason is that English L1 speakers are not standing still waiting for English language learners to catch up. A major goal of schooling for all children is to expand their ability to manipulate language in increasingly abstract academic situations. Every year English L1 students gain more sophisticated vocabulary and grammatical knowledge and increase their literacy skills. Thus, English language learners must catch up with a moving target. It is not surprising that this formidable task is seldom complete in one or two years.

By contrast, in the area of conversational skills, most native speakers have reached a plateau relatively early in schooling in the sense that a typical six-year-old can express herself as adequately as an older child on most topics she is likely to want to speak about and she can understand most of what is likely to be addressed to her. While some increase in conversational sophistication can be expected with increasing age, the differences are not particularly salient in comparison to differences in literacy-related skills; compare, for example, the differences in literacy between a twelve and a six-year-old student in comparison to differences in their conversational skills.

Several obvious implications of these data can be noted. First, educating bilingual/ELL students is the responsibility of the entire school staff and not just the responsibility of ESL or bilingual teachers. The numbers of ELL students in many districts, together with the time periods typically required for students to catch up, means that 'mainstream' classroom teachers must be prepared (in both senses of the term) to teach all the students in their classrooms.

A related implication is that school language policies should be developed in every school to address the needs of *all* students in the school, and in particular, those students who require support in English academic language learning (Corson, 1998a). This also implies that administrators in schools should be competent to provide leadership in addressing issues of underachievement in culturally and linguistically diverse contexts.

A third set of implications concerns assessment issues. District-, state-, or nation-wide assessment programs that assess ELL students who are still in the process of catching up academically in English are likely to give a very misleading impression both of students' academic potential and of the effectiveness of instruction. Students who have been learning English for about three years in a school context perform about one standard deviation (the equivalent of 15 IQ points) below grade norms in academic English skills (Cummins, 1981b). If the interpretation of test results fails to take account of these data, highly effective schools with large numbers of

ELL students will appear ineffective to parents and policy-makers. This perception is likely to reduce student and teacher morale. Similarly, assessment of bilingual students who are referred for special education assessment is likely to give distorted results if the assessment is conducted only in students' L2.

In short, the differences between conversational and academic proficiency and the length of time required to catch up academically have major consequences for a variety of curricular and assessment issues. In particular, these data suggest that we should be looking for interventions that will sustain bilingual students' long-term academic progress rather than expecting any short-term 'quick-fix' solution to students' academic underachievement in English.

### The positive effects of additive bilingualism

There are close to 150 empirical studies carried out during the past 30 or so years that have reported a positive association between additive bilingualism and students' linguistic, cognitive, or academic growth. The most consistent findings among these research studies are that bilinguals show more developed awareness of language (metalinguistic abilities) and that they have advantages in learning additional languages. The term 'additive bilingualism' refers to the form of bilingualism that results when students add a second language to their intellectual toolkit while continuing to develop conceptually and academically in their first language.

This pattern of findings suggests that the proficiency attained by bilingual students in their two languages may exert important influences on their academic and intellectual development. Specifically, I suggested in 1976 that there may be threshold levels of proficiency in both languages which students must attain in order to maximize the cognitive, academic, and linguistic stimulation they extract from social and academic interactions with their environment (Cummins, 1976, 1979a, 1981a). Continued development of both languages into literate domains (additive bilingualism) is a precondition for enhanced cognitive, linguistic, and academic growth. By contrast, when bilingual students develop low or minimal literacy in L1 and L2 as a result of inadequate instructional support (e.g. in submersion programs), their ability to understand increasingly complex instruction (in L2) and benefit from their schooling will decline. The causal factors here are instructional and sociopolitical, but

students' L1 and L2 academic proficiency acts as a mediating or intervening variable which influences the quality and quantity of their classroom participation, and hence academic growth.

Diaz has questioned the threshold hypothesis on the grounds that the effects of bilingualism on cognitive abilities in his data were stronger for children of relatively low L2 proficiency (non-balanced bilinguals) (Diaz, 1985; Diaz & Klinger, 1991). This suggests that the positive effects are related to the initial struggles and experiences of the beginning second-language learner. This interpretation does not appear to be incompatible with the threshold hypothesis since the major point of this hypothesis is that for positive effects to manifest themselves, children must be in the process of developing literacy in both languages. If beginning L2 learners do not continue to develop both their languages, any initial positive effects are likely to be counteracted by the negative consequences of subtractive bilingualism.

Recent studies continue to support the idea of threshold levels of bilingual proficiency that influence students' academic and possibly cognitive growth (Lasagabaster, 1998; Ricciardelli, 1992). However, the hypothesis remains speculative and is not essential to the policy-making process. The central and well-supported finding is that the continued development of bilingual students' two languages during elementary school entails the potential of positive academic, linguistic and cognitive consequences.

The linguistic and academic benefits of additive bilingualism for individual students provide an additional reason to support students in maintaining their L1 while they are acquiring English. Not only does maintenance of L1 help students to communicate with parents and grandparents in their families, and increase the collective linguistic competence of the entire society, it enhances the intellectual and academic resources of individual bilingual students. At an instructional level, we should be asking how we can build on this potential advantage in the classroom by focusing students' attention on language and helping them become more adept at manipulating language in abstract academic situations.

### Interdependence of first and second languages

The interdependence principle has been stated as follows (Cummins, 1981a):

To the extent that instruction in Lx is effective in promoting proficiency in Lx, transfer of this proficiency to Ly will occur provided there is adequate exposure to Ly (either in school or environment) and adequate motivation to learn Ly. (p. 29)

The term *common underlying proficiency (CUP)* has also been used to refer to the cognitive/academic proficiency that underlies academic performance in both languages.

Consider the following research data that support this principle:

- In virtually every bilingual program that has ever been evaluated, whether intended for linguistic majority or minority students, spending instructional time teaching through the minority language entails no academic costs for students' academic development in the majority language (Baker, 1996; Cummins & Corson, 1997).
- An impressive number of research studies have documented a moderately strong correlation between bilingual students' L1 and L2 literacy skills in situations where students have the opportunity to develop literacy in both languages. It is worth noting that these findings also apply to the relationships among very dissimilar languages in addition to languages that are more closely related, although the strength of relationship is often reduced (e.g. Arabic–French, Dutch–Turkish, Japanese–English, Chinese–English, Basque–Spanish) (Cummins, 1991c; Cummins *et al.*, 1984; Genesee, 1979; Sierra & Olaziregi, 1991; Verhoeven & Aarts, 1998; Wagner, 1998).

A comprehensive review of US research on cognitive reading processes among ELL students concluded that this research consistently supported the common underlying proficiency model:

... considerable evidence emerged to support the CUP model. United States ESL readers used knowledge of their native language as they read in English. This supports a prominent current view that native-language development can enhance ESL reading. (Fitzgerald, 1995: 181)

In short, the research data show clearly that within a bilingual program, instructional time can be focused on developing students' literacy skills in their primary language without adverse effects on the development of their literacy skills in English. Furthermore, the relationship between first and second language literacy skills suggests that effective development of primary language literacy skills can provide a conceptual foundation for long-term growth in English literacy skills. This does not imply, however, that transfer of literacy and academic language knowledge will happen automatically; there is usually also a need for formal instruction in the target language to realize the benefits of cross-linguistic transfer.

### Conclusion

This sketch of psycholinguistic data regarding bilingual academic development shows that a substantial research and theoretical basis for policy decisions regarding minority students' education does exist. In other words, policy-makers can predict with considerable confidence the probable effects of bilingual programs for majority and minority students implemented in very different sociopolitical contexts.

First, they can be confident that if the program is effective in continuing to develop students' academic skills in both languages, no cognitive confusion or handicap will result; in fact, students may benefit in subtle ways from access to two linguistic systems.

Second, they can predict that bilingual/ELL students will take considerably longer to develop grade-appropriate levels of L2 academic knowledge (e.g. literacy skills) in comparison to how long it takes to acquire peer-appropriate levels of L2 conversational skills, at least in situations where there is access to the L2 in the environment.

Third, they can be confident that for both majority and minority students, spending instructional time partly through the minority language will not result in lower levels of academic performance in the majority language, provided of course the instructional program is effective in developing academic skills in the minority language. This is because at deeper levels of conceptual and academic functioning, there is considerable overlap or interdependence across languages. Conceptual knowledge developed in one language helps to make input in the other language comprehensible.

These psycholinguistic principles by themselves provide a reliable basis for the prediction of program outcomes in situations that are not characterized by unequal power relations between dominant and subordinated groups (e.g. L2 immersion programs for students from dominant language backgrounds). However, they do not explain the considerable variation in academic achievement among culturally and linguistically diverse groups nor do they tell us why some groups have experienced persistent school failure over generations. The next section addresses these issues and elaborates a framework that combines a causal analysis of educational failure with an intervention framework for reversing this pattern of failure. The focus is on how unequal power relations are played out and can be challenged in the interactions between educators and students in the school context.

## A Framework for Reversing School Failure

The starting point for understanding why students choose to engage academically or, alternatively, withdraw from academic effort is to acknowledge that *human relationships are at the heart of schooling*. All of us intuitively know this from our own schooling experiences. If we felt that a teacher believed in us and cared for us then we put forth much more effort than if we felt that she or he did not like us or considered us not very capable. A major study carried out in southern California in the early 1990s documented this 'common-sense' phenomenon:

> Relationships dominated all participant discussions about issues of schooling in the US. No group inside the schools felt adequately respected, connected or affirmed. Students, over and over again, raised the issue of care. What they liked best about school was when people, particularly teachers, cared about them or did special things for them. Dominating their complaints were being ignored, not being cared for and receiving negative treatment. (Poplin & Weeres, 1992: 19)

Teachers in these schools reported that their best experiences were when they connected with students and were able to help them in some way. However, they also reported that they did not always understand students who were culturally different from themselves. They also felt isolated and unappreciated inside schools by

students, administrators, and parents as well as within the larger society.

What determines the kinds of relationships that educators establish with culturally diverse students? To answer this question we need to look at the relationships that exist between dominant and subordinated communities in the wider society and how these relationships (henceforth *macro-interactions*) influence both the structures that are set up in schools and the way educators define their roles within the school context.

When patterns of school success and failure among culturally diverse students are examined within an international perspective, it becomes evident that power and status relations between dominant and subordinated groups exert a major influence. Subordinated groups that fail academically have generally been discriminated against over many generations. They react to this discrimination along a continuum ranging from internalization of a sense of ambivalence or insecurity about their identities to rejection of, and active resistance to, dominant group values. At both extremes, alienation from schooling and mental withdrawal from academic effort have been a frequent consequence.[2] The international trends can be illustrated both with reference to the historical situation of minority francophone students in Canada and also in relation to John Ogbu's (1978, 1992) theoretical work.

### Minority francophone students in Canada

Numerous studies have shown that disproportionate numbers of minority francophones in comparison to anglophones are characterized by the related phenomena of low educational levels and low levels of functional literacy (e.g. Baril & Mori, 1991; Gérin-Lajoie, Labrie & Wilson, 1995; Wagner, 1991). Various estimates put the rate of functional illiteracy among minority francophones at approximately double that of the majority anglophone population.

Wagner (1991) has provided an insightful analysis of the factors that combine to create the phenomenon that he terms *analphabetisme de minorité*, translated here as 'subordinated group illiteracy'. He argues that illiteracy among subordinated groups is not just quantitatively different from illiteracy among the general population; there is also a crucial qualitative difference. Two distinct forms of subordinated group illiteracy can be distinguished that have no counterpart in the general population. He terms these two phenomena *illiteracy of oppression* and *illiteracy of resistance.* Both derive from the basic problems of access to appropriate schooling and contact between minority and majority languages. He describes these two forms of subordinated group illiteracy as follows:

> Illiteracy of resistance, although caused by oppression, is to some extent instituted by the minority group itself which, wishing to safeguard its language and culture, and fearing assimilation, turns in on itself and rejects the form of education imposed by the majority group. At the extreme, the minority group would prefer to remain illiterate rather than risk losing its language. The group will cultivate the spoken word and fall back on the oral tradition and other components of its culture. By contrast, illiteracy of oppression is a direct consequence of the process of integration/assimilation at work in the public school and in the entire society; it results in the slow destruction of identity and of the means of resistance in the minority community; thus, it is brought about by the oppressive action of the majority society. (1991: 44–45; my translation)

Wagner's account of minority francophones' response to oppressive societal institutions is consistent with descriptions of the identity choices made by other marginalized groups in similar situations. The 'slow destruction of identity' brought about by remaining trapped in oppressive school and social situations echoes accounts of the ambivalence and insecurity in relation to identity that marginalized groups often experience. However, the preservation of identity, albeit an oppositional identity, through resistance often results in equally poor achievement (Fordham, 1990; Willis, 1977).

In the case of minority francophones in Canada, issues of identity and power have intersected both in classroom instruction and in school organization for most of the 20th century (see Duquette & Riopel, 1998 and Heller, 1994, 1999, for detailed reviews). Specifically, francophone communities have experienced long-term devaluation of their cultural identity and languages both in the school and wider society. In Ontario, for example, Regulation 17 passed in 1912 eliminated for more than 50 years the possibility for francophones to be educated in their

own language. Ambivalence in regard to cultural identity still emerges in debates about the proportion of French that should be included in French language schools. Wagner, for example, points out that in a context of societal oppression, education is often devalued and this can persist even when the minority controls its own schools:

> It can happen that the minority group devalues its own schools or refuses to have them because the group is ashamed of itself and its culture as a result of internalizing the critical or scornful views of the majority group. The fiercest adversaries of the 'French school' in Saskatchewan are francophones themselves. (Wagner, 1991: 41) (my translation)

### Ogbu's (1978, 1992) theoretical framework

Another example that illustrates the influence of societal power relations on educational achievement is the case of Burakumin in Japan. Burakumin perform poorly in Japanese schools as a result of their low social status but perform well after immigration to the United States because educators are unaware of their low social status in their home country. Thus, educators tend to have the same high academic expectations of them as they do for other Japanese students (Ogbu, 1992). Ogbu distinguishes between voluntary or immigrant minorities, who tend to succeed academically, and involuntary minorities who tend to experience academic difficulties. The former have immigrated to the host country with the expectation of a better life and generally have a positive orientation to the host community and no ambivalence or insecurity in regard to their own identities. Involuntary minorities, by contrast, were originally brought into the society against their will, for example, through slavery, conquest, colonization, or forced labour, and were often denied the opportunity for true participation in or assimilation into the mainstream society. The four major groups that experience disproportionate academic failure in the United States (African Americans, Latinos/Latinas, Native Americans, and Hawaiian Americans) clearly match the profile of involuntary minorities. Similarly, in the Canadian context, First Nations (Native) and minority francophone students underachieve academically in ways that would be predicted from Ogbu's dichotomy.

```
┌──────────────────────────────────────────────────────────────┐
│        COERCIVE AND COLLABORATIVE RELATIONS OF POWER           │
│    MANIFESTED IN MACRO-INTERACTIONS BETWEEN SUBORDINATED       │
│       COMMUNITIES AND DOMINANT GROUP INSTITUTIONS              │
│                                                                │
│                    ↙              ↘                            │
│                                                                │
│     EDUCATOR ROLE DEFINITIONS ↔ EDUCATIONAL STRUCTURES         │
│                                                                │
│                    ↘              ↙                            │
│                                                                │
│               MICRO-INTERACTIONS BETWEEN                       │
│                 EDUCATORS AND STUDENTS                         │
│                       forming an                               │
│                  INTERPERSONAL SPACE                           │
│                      within which                              │
│                 knowledge is generated                         │
│                          and                                   │
│                identities are negotiated                       │
│                                                                │
│                        EITHER                                  │
│        REINFORCING COERCIVE RELATIONS OF POWER                 │
│                          OR                                    │
│        PROMOTING COLLABORATIVE RELATIONS OF POWER              │
└──────────────────────────────────────────────────────────────┘
```

**Figure 1** Coercive and collaborative relations of power manifested in macro- and micro-interactions

However, Ogbu's distinction is undoubtedly oversimplified. It fails to explain the underachievement of some immigrant minority groups in the Canadian context (e.g. Afro-Caribbean, Portuguese-speaking, and Spanish-speaking students). Similarly, it does not account for considerable within group variance in academic achievement nor the effect of variables such as socioeconomic status (Cummins, 1997; Gibson, 1997). It is also likely that refugee students constitute a separate category that cannot easily be subsumed within the *voluntary–involuntary* distinction (Vincent, 1996).

In spite of its inability to account for the complexities of dominant–subordinated group relationships, Ogbu's distinction represents a useful starting point in conceptualizing the causes of underachievement among subordinated group students. It highlights important patterns of how coercive power relations operating in the broader society find their way into the structures and operation of schooling. The distinction must be conceived in dynamic rather than static terms. The status of groups may change rapidly from one generation to another in ways that a rigid dichotomy cannot accommodate.

For these reasons, I prefer to discuss the issues in terms of coercive and collaborative relations of power that encompass the important distinction that Ogbu has made as well as the other categories of difference that define inter-group power relations (e.g. racism, sexism, homophobia, discrimination based on language and/or cultural differences, etc.). This orientation also facilitates examination of how power relations in the broader society get translated into educational failure within the schools, and most importantly, how this process can be resisted and reversed.

The two diagrams (Figures 1 and 2) outline an analysis of the causes of school failure and the intervention model that forms the basis for the current theoretical framework. The framework (Figure 1) proposes that relations of power in the wider society (macro-interactions), ranging from coercive to collaborative in varying degrees, influence both the ways in which educators define their roles and the types of structures that are established in the educational system. Role definitions refer to the mindset of expectations, assumptions, and goals that educators bring to the task of educating culturally diverse students.

Coercive relations of power refer to the exercise of power by a dominant individual, group, or country to the detriment of a subordinated individual, group, or country. For example, in the past, dominant group institutions (e.g. schools) have required that subordinated groups deny their cultural identity and give up their languages as a necessary condition for success in the 'mainstream' society. For educators to become partners in the transmission of knowledge, culturally diverse students were required to acquiesce in the subordination of their identities and to celebrate as 'truth' the perspectives of the dominant group (e.g. the 'truth' that Columbus 'discovered' America and brought 'civilization' to its indigenous peoples).

Collaborative relations of power, by contrast, reflect the sense of the term 'power' that refers to 'being enabled', or 'empowered' to achieve more. Within collaborative relations of power, 'power' is not a fixed quantity but is generated through interaction with others. The more empowered one individual or group becomes, the more is generated for others to share, as is the case when two people love each other or when we really connect with children we are teaching. Within this context, the term *empowerment* can be defined as *the collaborative creation of power*. Students whose schooling experiences reflect collaborative relations of power participate confidently in instruction as a result of the fact that their sense of identity is being affirmed and extended in their interactions with educators. They also know that their voices will be heard and respected within the classroom. Schooling amplifies rather than silences their power of *self*-expression.

Educational structures refer to the organization of schooling in a broad sense that includes policies, programs, curriculum, and assessment. While these structures will generally reflect the values and priorities of dominant groups in society, they are not by any means fixed or static. As with most other aspects of the way societies are organized and resources distributed, educational structures are contested by individuals and groups.

Educational structures, together with educator role definitions, determine the micro-interactions between educators, students, and communities.

These micro-interactions form an interpersonal space within which the acquisition of knowledge and formation of identity is negotiated. Power is created and shared within this interpersonal space where minds and identities meet. As such, these micro-interactions constitute the most immediate determinant of student academic success or failure.

Micro-interactions between educators, students and communities are never neutral; in varying degrees, they either reinforce coercive relations of power or promote collaborative relations of power. In the former case, they contribute to the disempowerment of culturally diverse students and communities; in the latter case, the micro-interactions constitute a process of empowerment that enables educators, students and communities to challenge the operation of coercive power structures. The relationships sketched in Figure 1 are elaborated in Figure 2. The term *Exclusionary/Assimilationist* refers to the general orientation to education characteristic of most countries prior to the 1960s and still characteristic of many today. The goal of education was either to exclude certain groups from the mainstream of society or assimilate them completely. The term *Transformative/Intercultural* refers to the orientation required to challenge the operation of coercive relations of power in the school and wider society. This form of pedagogy entails interactions between educators and students that foster the collaborative creation of power; in other words, *empowerment*. Although *exclusionary* and *assimilationist* may appear to be opposites insofar as 'exclusionary' focuses on segregation of subordinated groups from the mainstream of schools and society while 'assimilationist' focuses on total integration into the society, in reality they are frequently two sides of the same coin: both orientations aspire to make subordinated groups invisible and inaudible. Minority groups constructed as 'racially different' have historically been subjected to exclusionary rather than assimilationist policies for the simple reason that 'disappearance' could not readily be achieved through assimilation. In addition, if assimilationist policies were applied to 'racial' minorities, it would imply inter-marriage across 'races' within the same 'melting pot'. This mixing of 'races' would implode the myths of racial superiority that have characterized most dominant groups in societies around the world.

It is easy to recognize the Exclusionary/Assimilationist patterns outlined in Figure 2

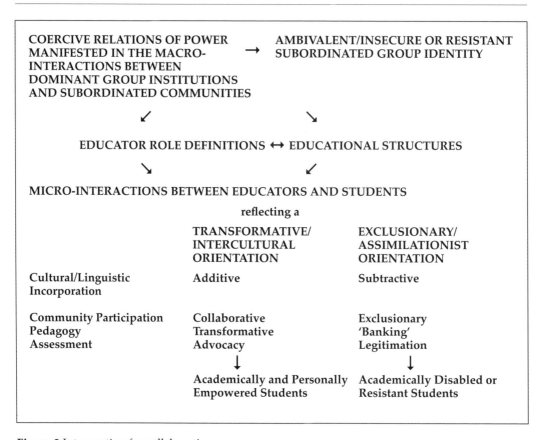

**Figure 2** Intervention for collaborative empowerment

as characteristic of historical realities in many countries. The extent to which they still characterize educator–student interactions is a matter for debate and school-by-school analysis.[3]

By contrast, *Transformative/Intercultural* orientations are based on principles of racial and cultural equality and a commitment to educate students for full participation within a democratic society. This implies providing opportunities for students to develop a form of critical literacy where they become capable not only of decoding the words, but also reading between the lines in order to understand how power is exercised through various forms of discourse (advertisements, political rhetoric, textbooks, etc.). The focus is on understanding not only what is said but also whose perspectives are represented and whose have been excluded.

The macro-interactions between dominant and subordinated groups in the wider society give rise to particular forms of educational structures that are designed to reflect the priorities of the society. Since dominant groups, almost by definition, determine the priorities of the society, education has historically tended to reproduce the relations of power in the broader society.

Examples of educational structures that reflect coercive relations of power are:

- submersion programs for bilingual students that actively suppress their L1 and cultural identity;
- exclusion of culturally diverse parents from participation in their children's schooling;
- tracking or streaming practices that place subordinated group students disproportionately in lower-level tracks;
- use of biased standardized tests for both achievement monitoring and special education placement;

- teacher education programs that prepare teachers for a mythical monolingual monocultural white middle-class student population;
- curriculum content that reflects the perspectives and experiences of dominant groups and excludes those of subordinated groups.

These educational structures constitute a frame that sets limits on the kinds of interactions that are likely to occur between educators and students. They *constrict* rather than expand the interactional space.

Societal macro-interactions also influence the ways in which educators define their roles in relation to culturally diverse students and communities; in other words, they influence the mindset of assumptions, expectations and goals that educators bring to the task of educating students. The framework presented in Figures 1 and 2 argues that culturally diverse students are empowered or disabled as a direct result of their interactions with educators in the schools. These interactions are mediated by the implicit or explicit role definitions that educators assume in relation to four organizational aspects of schooling:

- The extent to which students' language and cultural background are affirmed and promoted within the school; this includes the extent to which literacy instruction in school affirms, builds on, and extends the vernacular literacy practices that many culturally diverse students engage in outside the context of school (see, for example, Hardman, 1998; Heath, 1983; Lotherington *et al.*, 1998; Martin-Jones & Bhatt, 1998; Vasquez *et al.*, 1994).
- The extent to which culturally diverse communities are encouraged to participate as partners in their children's education and to contribute the 'funds of knowledge' that exist in their communities to this educational partnership (Moll *et al.*, 1992; Schecter & Bayley, 1998).
- The extent to which instruction promotes intrinsic motivation on the part of students to use language actively in order to generate their own knowledge, create literature and art, and act on social realities that affect their lives. The alternative is what Freire (1983) termed a *banking education* where

the teacher defines her role as depositing information and skills in students' memory banks.

- The extent to which professionals involved in assessment become advocates for students by focusing primarily on the ways in which students' academic difficulty is a function of interactions within the school context rather than legitimizing the location of the 'problem' within students.

These four dimensions namely, language/culture incorporation, community participation, pedagogy, and assessment represent sets of educational structures that will affect, but can also be influenced by, educators' role definitions.

It is important to note that students (and communities) do not passively accept dominant group attributions of their inferiority. Frequently, they actively resist the operation of the societal power structure as it is manifested in educational settings. An example is the three-day school boycott called by the Latino/Latina community in Santa Barbara when the school board voted to end the city's 25-year-old bilingual program in January 1998. Four hundred families set up their own alternative bilingual academy in a community centre (Hornblower, 1998).

For some students, resistance can contribute to academic development (Zanger, 1994); students work hard to succeed in order to repudiate their teachers' low expectations. However, more typically, resistance takes the form of mentally withdrawing from a coercive educational relationship. Unfortunately, this withdrawal usually entails severe costs with respect to academic success and upward mobility (Fordham, 1990; Willis, 1977). Students find affirmation on the streets rather than in the classroom. Armando Vallejo, director of the Casa de la Raza in Santa Barbara which housed the alternative academy set up by the parents who boycotted the school expressed his view that abolishing bilingual classes amounts to cultural genocide: 'Kids sit in the back of the classroom for a couple of years without understanding, and they get disillusioned. That's when they join gangs' (cited in Hornblower, 1998).

In summary, a central principle of the present framework is that the negotiation of identity in the interactions between educators and students is central to students' academic success or failure. Our interactions with students are constantly sketching a triangular set of images:

- an image of our own identities as educators;
- an image of the identity options we highlight for our students; consider, for example, the contrasting messages conveyed to students in classrooms focused on collaborative critical inquiry (*transformative education*) compared to classrooms focused on passive internalization of information (Freire's *banking education*);
- an image of the society we hope our students will help form.

In other words, an image of the society that students will graduate into and the kind of contributions they can make to that society is embedded implicitly in the interactions between educators and students. These interactions reflect the way educators have defined their role with respect to the purposes of education in general and culturally diverse students and communities in particular. Are we preparing students to accept the societal status quo (and, in many cases, their own inferior status therein) or are we preparing them to participate actively and critically in the democratic process in pursuit of the ideals of social justice and equity which are enshrined in the constitutions of most democratic countries?

This perspective clearly implies that in situations where coercive relations of power between dominant and subordinated groups predominate, the creation of interpersonal spaces where students' identities are validated will entail a direct challenge by educators (and students) to the societal power structure. For example, to acknowledge that culturally diverse students' religion, culture and language are valid forms of *self*-expression, and to encourage their development, is to challenge the prevailing attitudes in the wider society and the coercive structures that reflect these attitudes.[4]

In summary, empowerment derives from the process of negotiating identities in the classroom. Interactions between educators and culturally diverse students are never neutral with respect to societal power relations. In varying degrees, they either reinforce or challenge coercive relations of power in the wider society. Historically, subordinated group students have been disempowered educationally in the same way their communities have been disempowered in the wider society. In the same way as the attribution of inherent inferiority legitimated the

brutalities of slavery, the slaughter of indigenous peoples, and the exploitation of colonized populations in countries around the world, definitions of subordinated group students as 'genetically inferior' (e.g. Dunn, 1987; Jensen, 1969), 'culturally deprived', or simply suffering cognitive confusion as a result of bilingualism have been used to explain their poor academic performance and justify their continued educational exclusion. It follows from this analysis that subordinated group students will succeed academically to the extent that the patterns of interaction in the school challenge and reverse those that have prevailed in the society at large.

## Relationship Between the Intervention Framework and Psycholinguistic Principles

The analysis of power relations operating in educator–student interactions within the school context is intended to address a different, although complementary, set of questions than the analysis of psycholinguistic issues. Understanding how power relations operate in the process of identity negotiation between educators and students points to some of the causes of underachievement among subordinated group students and provides general directions for reversing this process. The intervention framework provides a lens through which the learning process can be observed and assessed. It allows us to look at the deep structure of learning. What matters is not whether a program is called 'bilingual', 'ESL' 'structured immersion' or 'mainstream', much more significant is what is being transacted in the interactions between educators and students. Some 'bilingual' programs make little attempt to develop students' L1 literacy skills or to promote students' pride in their cultural and linguistic heritage. By contrast, some predominantly English-medium programs may operate largely on the *Transformative/Intercultural* end of the continua in Figure 2. One example is the International High School at La Guardia Community College in New York City (DeFazio, 1997) in which students' pride and competence in their first language is strongly promoted despite the fact that instruction is predominantly through English.

It is doubtless much easier to promote students' bilingualism, involve parents (who may speak little or no English), and build on students' background experience, in the context of a genuine bilingual program than in a monolingual program. A shared language between teachers, students, and parents clearly facilitates communication. However, use of students' L1 for instructional purposes is no panacea. To be truly effective bilingual education should encompass a transformative/intercultural orientation to instruction that challenges the operation of coercive relations of power.

Essentially, the psycholinguistic principles are links in the causal chain that relate societal power relations to student outcomes. If it were the case that knowledge of two languages resulted in cognitive confusion and linguistic retardation (as some still appear to believe – for example, Dunn, 1987; Schlesinger, 1991), then any positive impact of bilingual education on students' sense of cultural identity would have to be weighed against the potentially negative cognitive consequences of bilingualism. Similarly, if less instructional time through English exerted adverse effects on the development of students' English academic skills (as most opponents of bilingual education claim), then bilingual education would indeed be a risky educational strategy.

The research data (noted above), however, are unequivocal in demonstrating that additive forms of bilingualism are associated with positive linguistic and academic consequences. They also show clearly that literacy in two or more languages can be promoted by the school at absolutely no cost to students' academic development in English. Thus, the psycholinguistic research findings, and the theoretical principles that account for these findings, open up significant possibilities both for enriching the personal and academic lives of bilingual students and for challenging coercive relations of power in the wider society. Educators who encourage students to develop their L1 literacy skills are not only promoting learning in the narrow sense, they are also challenging the coercive discourse in the wider society which proclaims that 'bilingualism shuts doors' and 'monolingual education opens doors to the larger world' (Schlesinger, 1991: 109). The psycholinguistic research illuminates these views (and the discourse surrounding Proposition 227 in California) not only as factually wrong but as forms of racism designed to return the educational system to the exclusionary/assimilationist orientations characteristic of the pre-Civil Rights era in the United States.

Similarly, the distinction between conversational and academic language proficiency together with the time periods required to attain grade expectations in English academic tasks, refutes the assumption that most bilingual/ELL students can catch up within a year of starting to learn English (as Proposition 227 claims). Again, the psycholinguistic data lay bare the coercive sociopolitical agenda that is at work in the claims of groups such as *US English*.

In summary, although they were elaborated at different times and addressed to different questions, the psycholinguistic and sociopolitical theoretical constructs intersect in fundamental ways. Both sets of constructs are essential components of the theoretical framework, as Figure 1 suggests. The psycholinguistic constructs are focused more on *knowledge generation* (i.e. learning) while the sociopolitical constructs focus on *identity negotiation* and its rootedness in societal power relations. The point of the framework is that one dimension cannot be adequately considered without the other. They are two sides of the same coin.

## Cognitive and Contextual Demands

The framework outlined in Figure 3 is designed to identify the extent to which students are able to cope successfully with the cognitive and linguistic demands made on them by the social and educational environment in which they are obliged to function in school. These demands are conceptualized within a framework made up of the intersection of two continua, one relating to the range of contextual support available for expressing or receiving meaning and the other relating to the amount of information that must be processed simultaneously or in close succession by the student in order to carry out the activity. While cognitive demands and contextual support are distinguished in the framework, it is not being suggested that these dimensions are independent of each other. In fact, as Frederickson and Cline (1990) point out, increasing contextual support will tend to lessen the cognitive demands – in other words, make tasks easier.

### Situating the framework

Before describing the framework, it is important to place it in an appropriate context of interpretation and to define some of the terms associated with it. In the first place, the framework, and the associated conversational/academic language proficiency distinction, focuses only on the sociocultural context of schooling. Thus, we are talking about the nature of language proficiency that is required to

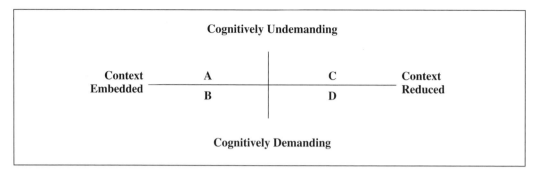

**Figure 3** Range of contextual support and degree of cognitive involvement in language tasks and activities

function effectively in this particular context. The framework was not intended to have relevance outside of this context.

Related to this is the fact that language proficiency and cognitive functioning can be conceptualized only in relation to particular contexts of use. Just as sociocultural or Vygotskian approaches to literacy emphasize that 'literacy is always socially and culturally situated' (Pérez, 1998a: 4) and cannot be regarded as content-free or context-free, language proficiency and cognitive functioning are similarly embedded in particular contexts of use or *discourses* which are defined by Pérez as the ways in which 'communicative systems are organized within social practices' (1998b: 23). Thus, the social practice of schooling entails certain 'rules of the game' with respect to how communication and language use is typically organized within that context. In short, in the present context the construct of *academic language proficiency* refers not to any absolute notion of expertise in using language but to the degree to which an individual has access to and expertise in understanding and using the specific kind of language that is employed in educational contexts and is required to complete academic tasks. Drawing on the categories distinguished by Chapelle (1998), *academic language proficiency* can be defined as the language knowledge together with the associated knowledge of the world and metacognitive strategies necessary to function effectively in the discourse domain of the school.

This perspective is consistent with an interactionist perspective on language ability 'as the capacity for language use' (Bachman & Cohen, 1998: 18). Current theoretical approaches to the construct of language proficiency have shifted

from viewing proficiency as a trait that individuals possess in varying degrees to seeing it as inseparable from the contexts in which it will be manifested. Thus, Bachman and Palmer (1996) use the term 'ability-task' to refer to the unity of ability and task (context) characteristics. Chapelle (1998: 44) similarly notes that a construct such as 'vocabulary size' 'cannot be defined in an absolute sense but instead is a meaningful construct only with reference to a particular context'. Thus, in the context of schooling, discussions of greater or lesser degrees of language proficiency or 'adequacy' of an individual's proficiency refer only to the extent to which the individual's language proficiency (CALP) is functional within the context of typical academic tasks and activities. As noted above and elaborated below, the characteristics of instruction (context) will determine the functionality or 'adequacy' of an individual's proficiency in the language of instruction as much as the degree of proficiency in any absolute sense.

In this regard, it is helpful to introduce the notion of *register* which will be elaborated further in subsequent sections. Register is defined in the *Concise Oxford Dictionary of Linguistics* (Matthews, 1997: 314) as 'a set of features of speech or writing characteristic of a particular type of linguistic activity or a particular group when engaging in it. ... journalese is a register different from that in which sermons are delivered, or in which smutty stories are told'. Registers are the linguistic realizations of particular discourse contexts and conventions. Academic language proficiency thus refers to the extent to which an individual has access to and command of the oral and written academic registers of schooling.

In summary, as students progress through the

grades, the academic tasks they are required to complete and the linguistic contexts in which they must function become more complex with respect to the registers employed in these contexts. Not only is there an ever-increasing vocabulary and concept load involving words that are rarely encountered in everyday out-of-school contexts but syntactic features (e.g. passive rather than active voice constructions) and discourse conventions (e.g. using cohesive devices effectively in writing) also become increasingly distant from conversational uses of language in non-academic contexts. The framework outlined in Figure 3 presents an analytic scheme for mapping in a general way how the construct of language proficiency can be conceptualized in terms of the intersections of cognitive (or information-processing) demand and contextual support in academic situations.

### Description of the framework

The extremes of the context-embedded/context-reduced continuum are distinguished by the fact that in context-embedded communication the participants can actively negotiate meaning (e.g. by providing feedback that the message has not been understood) and the language is supported by a wide range of meaningful interpersonal and situational cues. Context-reduced communication, on the other hand, relies primarily (or, at the extreme of the continuum, exclusively) on linguistic cues to meaning, and thus successful interpretation of the message depends heavily on knowledge of the language itself. In general, as outlined in the previous section, context-embedded communication is more typical of the everyday world outside the classroom, whereas many of the linguistic demands of the classroom (e.g. manipulating text) reflect communicative activities that are close to the context-reduced end of the continuum.

The upper parts of the vertical continuum consist of communicative tasks and activities in which the linguistic tools have become largely automatized and thus require little active cognitive involvement for appropriate performance. At the lower end of the continuum are tasks and activities in which the linguistic tools have not become automatized and thus require active cognitive involvement. Persuading another individual that your point of view is correct, and writing an essay, are examples of Quadrant B and D skills respectively. Casual conversation

is a typical Quadrant A activity while examples of Quadrant C are copying notes from the blackboard, filling in worksheets, or other forms of drill and practice activities.

The framework elaborates on the conversational/academic distinction by highlighting important underlying dimensions of conversational and academic communication. Thus, conversational abilities (Quadrant A) often develop relatively quickly among immigrant second language learners because these forms of communication are supported by interpersonal and contextual cues and make relatively few cognitive demands on the individual. Mastery of the academic functions of language (academic registers or Quadrant D), on the other hand, is a more formidable task because such uses require high levels of cognitive involvement and are only minimally supported by contextual or interpersonal cues. Under conditions of high cognitive demand, it is necessary for students to stretch their linguistic resources to the limit to function successfully. In short, the essential aspect of academic language proficiency is the ability to make complex meanings explicit in either oral or written modalities by means of *language* itself rather than by means of contextual or para-linguistic cues (e.g. gestures, intonation etc.).

As students progress through the grades, they are increasingly required to manipulate language in cognitively demanding and context-reduced situations that differ significantly from everyday conversational interactions. In writing, for example, as Bereiter and Scardamalia (1981) point out, students must learn to continue to produce language without the prompting that comes from a conversational partner and they must plan large units of discourse, and organize them coherently, rather than planning only what will be said next.

Evidence for the relevance and usefulness of the conversational/academic language distinction comes from observations made by Carolyn Vincent in an ethnographic study of a program serving second generation Salvadorean students in Washington DC:

> All of the children in this study began school in an English-speaking environment and within their first two or three years attained conversational ability in English that teachers would regard as native-like. This is largely deceptive. The children seem to have much greater English proficiency than they

actually do because their spoken English has no accent and they are able to converse on a few everyday, frequently discussed subjects. Academic language is frequently lacking. Teachers actually spend very little time talking with individual children and tend to interpret a small sample of speech as evidence of full English proficiency. However, as the children themselves look back on their language development they see how the language used in the classroom was difficult for them, and how long it took them to acquire English. (1996: 195)

In this respect, Vincent notes on the basis of her classroom observations: 'It is clear that student achievement is promoted by instructional practices such as cooperative learning, the use of manipulatives, and project-based lessons' (1996: 201). These are activities that place a significant emphasis on Quadrant B insofar as they tend to be cognitively demanding but contextually supported.

Pauline Gibbons has similarly expressed the difference between the everyday language of face-to-face interaction and the language of schooling in outlining the distinction between what she terms *playground language* and *classroom language*:

This playground language includes the language which enables children to make friends, join in games and take part in a variety of day-to-day activities that develop and maintain social contacts. It usually occurs in face-to-face contact, and is thus highly dependent on the physical and visual context, and on gesture and body language. Fluency with this kind of language is an important part of language development; without it a child is isolated from the normal social life of the playground …

But playground language is very different from the language that teachers use in the classroom, and from the language that we expect children to learn to use. The language of the playground is not the language associated with learning in mathematics, or social studies, or science. The playground situation does not normally offer children the opportunity to use such language as: *if we increase the angle by five degrees, we could cut the circumference into equal parts.* Nor does it normally require the language

associated with the higher order thinking skills, such as hypothesizing, evaluating, inferring, generalizing, predicting or classifying. Yet these are the language functions which are related to learning and the development of cognition; they occur in all areas of the curriculum, and without them a child's potential in academic areas cannot be realized. (1991: 3)

Thus, the context-embedded / context-reduced distinction is not one between oral and written language. Within the framework, the dimensions of contextual embeddedness and cognitive demand are distinguished because some context-embedded activities are clearly just as cognitively demanding as context-reduced activities. For example, an intense intellectual discussion with one or two other people is likely to require at least as much cognitive processing as writing an essay on the same topic. Similarly, writing an e-mail message to a close friend is, in many respects, more context-embedded than giving a lecture to a large group of people.

It follows that cognitive academic language proficiency is not synonymous with *literacy*. It is manifested as much in oral interactions in academic contexts as in written interactions. For example, a classroom or small group discussion of the social consequences of industrial pollution will draw on participants' familiarity with features of academic registers (e.g. how to express cause–effect relationships linguistically) and will reveal the depth and richness of their understanding of words and concepts. In Aitchison's (1994) terms, the extent to which students have built extensive semantic networks will be evident in the way they use and relate words and concepts in such discussions. Thus, words are not just known or unknown; there is a continuum with respect to depth of vocabulary / concept knowledge (Paribakht & Wesche, 1997; Verhallen & Schoonen, 1998). One of the major functions of schooling is to deepen and broaden students' knowledge of words and their meanings and to develop what Norah McWilliam (1998) calls *semantic agility*. Oral classroom discussions do not involve reading and writing directly, but they do reflect the degree of students' access to and command of literate or academic registers of language. This is why CALP can be defined as *expertise in understanding and using literacy-related aspects of language.*

Skourtou has provided a particularly clear description of how the processing of experience through language transforms experience itself and forms the basis of literacy:

> It seems to me that the entire process of language development both starts and ends with experience. This implies that we start with a concrete experience, process it through language and arrive at a new experience. In such a manner, we develop the main features of literacy, namely the ability to reconstruct the world through symbols, thus creating new experiences. Creating experiences through language, using the logic of literacy, whether speaking or writing, means that once we are confronted with a real context, we are able to add our own contexts, our own images of the world. (1995: 27)

Highlighted here is the fact that *context* is both internal and external, representing two sides of the same experiential coin; furthermore, the development of literate modes of thought cannot be separated from these experiential contexts.

### Implications for pedagogy

A central implication of the framework in Figure 3 for instruction of second language learners is that language and content will be acquired most successfully when students are challenged cognitively but provided with the contextual and linguistic supports or scaffolds required for successful task completion. In other words, optimal instruction for linguistic, cognitive and academic growth will tend to move from Quadrant A, to B, and from Quadrant B to D. Quadrant C activities may be included from time to time for reinforcement or practice of particular points. This progression corresponds very closely to the stages that Gibbons (1995, 1998) observed in her research on classroom discourse in science teaching. She distinguished three stages:

- Small group work.
- Teacher guided reporting.
- Journal writing.

Thus, students initially participated in small-group learning experiences where the language used was clearly context-embedded. Gibbons notes that 'children's current understandings of a curriculum topic, and their use of familiar "everyday" language to express these understandings, should be seen as the basis for the development of the unfamiliar registers of school' (1998: 99).

The small-group exploration and discussion was followed by a teacher-guided reporting session, where each group described what they had done and offered explanations for what happened, while the teacher interacted with individuals from each group, clarifying, probing and recasting. Talking with the teacher about what had been learned, since this did not involve the use of the concrete materials, led to a mode shift towards more decontextualized language. When students reported back to the whole class the results of their 'hands-on' science explorations (e.g. with magnets), they were pushed to shift towards less context-embedded ways of expression than had been the case in their immediate small group discussion of the phenomena they observed. The teacher guided their reporting back and extended their linguistic resources by introducing more formal precise vocabulary to express the phenomena (e.g. introducing the term *repel* as equivalent to what the children described as *push away*). In responding to students' reporting back, the teacher will 'use new wordings and ways of meaning – a new register' (1995: 27) which is likely to be comprehensible to students because they have already gained some schematic knowledge about the topic. Through this interaction, students and teacher *co-construct* deeper understandings of the phenomena and students acquire the linguistic tools to express their observations in the more formal language of scientific discourse.

The reporting back phase provided a bridge into the writing, which was the final activity of the cycle and linguistically the most context reduced (1995: 11). Students wrote a response in their journals to the question 'What have you learned?' They described what they had learned as a personal and ongoing record of their learning rather than as a piece of formal writing. This third stage corresponds to Quadrant D in Figure 3. Gibbons suggests that the journals 'provide some evidence of second language 'uptake' in that they reflect wordings which occurred in the process of jointly negotiated learner–teacher interactions' (1998: 106). She also notes that there is a place for Quadrant C activities insofar as the teacher also spent some time rehearsing or practising the new words with students in order to consolidate their acquisition (personal communication, October, 1999).

Mackay (1992) has used the quadrants framework to document the consequences of requiring students to carry out tasks that are overly complex and insufficiently scaffolded for their linguistic level. He plotted the instructional task sequences in Grade 6 and Grade 7 classes taught in English to Inuktitut L1 students in the Canadian Eastern Arctic. The Grade 7 teachers initiated instruction with relatively complex tasks (Quadrant D) and then retreated to considerably less complex tasks (Quadrants B, C, and finally A, in that order) in response to evidence that the original task could not be performed adequately. The consequence of this 'task reduction' was that students were not being stimulated to advance academically or cognitively because they were carrying out only cognitively undemanding and context embedded tasks. In Mackay's words: 'By employing task-reduction, [teachers] unwittingly and unintentionally trap students into a learning environment which may permanently deprive them of the opportunity for developing the proficiency and skills they need to enjoy academic success' (1992: 162–163). By contrast, in the Grade 6 class, the instructional sequence of tasks was much more developmental, progressing from quadrants A to C to B and finally to D. In this way, students were enabled to carry out relatively complex tasks such as writing answers to questions about planets in their personal notebooks.

### Internal and external context

As noted above, contextual support involves both internal and external dimensions. Internal factors are *attributes of the individual* that make a task more familiar or easier in some respect (e.g. prior experience, motivation, cultural relevance, interests, etc.). External factors refer to *aspects of the input* that facilitate or impede comprehension; for example, language input that is spoken clearly and contains a considerable amount of syntactic and semantic redundancy is easier to understand than input that lacks these features.

Douglas has similarly distinguished between external and internal aspects of context but suggests that these categories can be collapsed into 'an internal view of context as a cognitive construct created by language users for the interpretation and production of language' (1998: 146). In other words, what matters is how participants in a communicative event construct the context which is never static or

'external' but rather 'a dynamic social-psychological accomplishment' (p. 144).

The distinction between internal and external context parallels Chapelle's (1998) distinction between learner factors and contextual factors in determining language performance. Learner factors refer to the individual's knowledge of the world, knowledge of language, and strategic competence which, following Bachman (1990a) is defined as 'the metacognitive strategies required for assessing contexts, setting goals, constructing plans, and controlling execution of those plans' (1998: 44). Chapelle draws on Halliday and Hasan (1989) in describing *context* in terms of three overlapping theoretical components: field, tenor, and mode. 'Field' refers to the locations, topics, and actions present in a particular language use context (i.e. what is taking place). 'Tenor' includes the participants and the relationships among them (who is taking part), and 'mode' includes the channels (spoken/written) and genres involved in particular forms of language use (what part language is playing). She points out that even with the detailed description of context that these constructs permit, there is still the issue of how specific the description of context needs to be for particular testing purposes (e.g. all academic reading in university contexts as compared to science reading or research articles in chemistry, etc.).

This point highlights the fact that the degree of detail with which context is specified within any particular theoretical framework depends on the purpose of that framework. Thus, in the context of Figure 3, the continuum between context-embedded and context-reduced language is sufficient to capture the major underlying dimension that is relevant to language use and academic tasks in school contexts. Clearly, in different contexts or for different purposes (e.g. investigating sociolinguistic parameters of language use), a greater degree of specificity might be desirable.[5]

## Clarifications of the Conversational/ Academic Distinction

The distinction between BICS and CALP has been misunderstood or misrepresented by a number of commentators. For example, the distinction was criticized on the grounds that a simple dichotomy does not account for many dimensions of language use and competence, for example, certain sociolinguistic aspects of language (e.g. Wald, 1984). However, the distinction was not proposed as an overall theory of language but as a conceptual distinction addressed to specific issues concerning the education of second language learners. As outlined above, the distinction entails important implications for policy and practice. The fact that the distinction does not attempt to address all aspects of sociolinguistics or discourse styles or any number of other linguistic issues is irrelevant. The usefulness of any theoretical construct should be assessed in relation to the issues that it attempts to address, not in relation to issues that it makes no claim to address. To suggest that the BICS/CALP distinction is invalid because it does not account for subtleties of socio-linguistic interaction or discourse styles is like saying: 'This apple is no good because it doesn't taste like an orange'.

Another point concerns the sequence of acquisition between BICS and CALP. August and Hakuta (1997), for example, suggest that the distinction specifies that BICS must precede CALP in development. This is not at all the case. The sequential nature of BICS/CALP acquisition was suggested as typical in the specific situation of immigrant children learning a second language. It was not suggested as an absolute order that applies in every, or even the majority of situations. Thus attainment of high levels of L2 CALP can precede attainment of fluent L2 BICS in certain situations (e.g. a scientist who can read a language for research purposes but who can't speak it).

Another misunderstanding is to interpret the distinction as dimensions of language that are autonomous or independent of their contexts of acquisition (e.g. Romaine, 1989: 240). To say that BICS and CALP are conceptually distinct is not the same as saying that they are separate or acquired in different ways. Developmentally they are not necessarily separate; all children acquire their initial conceptual foundation (knowledge of the world) largely through con-versational interactions in the home. Both BICS and CALP are shaped by their contexts of acquisition and use. Consistent with a Vygotskian perspective on cognitive and language development, BICS and CALP both develop within a matrix of social interaction. However, they follow different developmental patterns: pho-nological skills in our native language and our basic fluency reach a plateau in the first six or so years; in other words, the rate of subsequent development is very much reduced in comparison to previous development. This is not the case

for literacy-related knowledge such as range of vocabulary which continues to develop at least throughout our schooling and usually through-out our lifetimes.

It is also important to point out that cognitive skills are involved, to a greater or lesser extent, in most forms of social interaction. For example, cognitive skills are undoubtedly involved in one's ability to tell jokes effectively and if we work at it we might improve our joke-telling ability throughout our lifetimes. However, our joke-telling ability is largely unrelated to our academic performance. This intersection of the cognitive and social aspects of language proficiency, however, does not mean that they are identical or reducible one to the other. The implicit assumption that conversational fluency in English is a good indicator of 'English pro-ficiency' has resulted in countless bilingual children being 'diagnosed' as learning disabled or retarded. Their fluency and native-like phonology in English masks the fact that they are still a long way from grade norms in English academic knowledge. Despite their developmen-tal intersections, BICS and CALP are conceptually distinct and follow different patterns of develop-ment among both native-speakers and second language learners.

An additional misconception is that the distinction characterizes CALP (academic language) as a 'superior' form of language proficiency to BICS (conversational language). This interpretation was never intended and was explicitly repudiated (Cummins, 1983), although it is easy to see how the use of the term 'basic' in BICS might appear to devalue conversational language as compared to the apparent higher status of *cognitive academic* language proficiency. Clearly, various forms of conversational language performance are highly complex and sophisticated both linguis-tically and cognitively. However, these forms of language performance are not necessarily strongly related to the linguistic demands of schooling. As outlined above, access to very specific oral and written registers of language are required to continue to progress academically and a major goal of schooling for all students is to expand students' access to these academic registers of language. However, the greater relevance of academic language proficiency for success in school, as compared to conversational proficiency, does not mean that it is intrinsi-cally superior in any way. Nor does it mean that the language proficiency of non-literate or non-schooled communities is in any way inadequate within the contexts of its development and use. In fact, one of the major reasons why non-middle class bilingual and monolingual children have tended to experience difficulty in school is that many schools have failed to acknowledge and build on the wide variety of culturally specific literacy events (oral and written) that children experience in their homes (e.g. Delpit, 1998; Martin-Jones & Bhatt, 1998). These literacy events (e.g. oral story telling) represent powerful occasions for learning particularly when classroom instruction integrates them with the learning of reading and writing in school (see, for example, McCaleb, 1994).

While all aspects of children's cultural and linguistic experience in their homes should form the foundation upon which literacy instruction in school builds, it is important not to romanticize the literacy and linguistic accomplishments of particular communities. These accomplishments form the basis for future development but in our current technologically oriented societies, specific forms of literacy and numeracy are required for educational success and career advancement. Instruction in school, as well as active engagement with books (Krashen, 1993), extends students' basic knowledge of syntax, semantics, and phonology, and their community-based literacy practices, into new functional registers or genres of language. Access to and command of these academic registers are required for success in school and for advancement in many employment situations beyond school.

Some investigators have also claimed that by 'the mid 1980s the dichotomy between CALP and BICS was largely abandoned by Cummins, although it has not ceased to influence subsequent research on second language acquisition and bilingual education' (Devlin, 1997: 82). This is inaccurate. I have tended to use the terms conversational and academic proficiency in place of BICS and CALP because the acronyms were considered misleading by some commentators (e.g. Spolsky, 1984) and were being misinterpreted by others (e.g. Romaine, 1989). However, the acronyms continue to be widely used in the field and from my perspective are still appropriate to use. Hence they are used interchangeably with conversational and academic proficiency in the present volume.[6]

A final point of clarification concerns the relationship of language proficiency to social determinants of minority students' academic development (e.g. Troike, 1984). The conversational/academic language proficiency theoretical construct is psychoeducational in nature insofar as it focuses primarily on the cognitive and linguistic dimensions of proficiency in a language. The role of social factors in bilingual students' academic success or failure was acknowledged in early work but not elaborated in detail. In 1986, I proposed a framework within which the intersecting roles of sociopolitical and psychoeducational factors could be conceptualized (Cummins, 1986). Specifically, the framework highlighted the ways in which the interactions between educators and bilingual students reflected particular role definitions on the part of educators in relation to students' language and culture, community participation, pedagogy, and assessment. It hypothesized that many groups of students have been educationally disabled in school in much the same way that their communities have historically been disabled in the wider society, and it pointed to directions for reversing this process. The framework argues that educational interventions will be successful only to the extent that they constitute a challenge to the broader societal power structure (Cummins, 1986, 1996).

## Notes

1. In legal declarations submitted in the wake of the passage of Proposition 227 in California, Kenji Hakuta and Lily Wong Fillmore each reported data showing what level of English language proficiency might be expected after one year of intensive exposure. Wong Fillmore's (1998) study conducted with 239 limited English proficient students showed that more than 60% of them fell into Levels 1 and 2 of the Language Assessment Scales after one year of intensive exposure to English at school. These levels indicate minimal English proficiency on the five-point scale. Hakuta (1998) examined data from the Westminister School District in Orange County California which has operated an all-English rather than bilingual education program. His conclusions are reproduced below:

    37. Several things are noteworthy about Westminster's data, particularly the use of it to show that the district's all-English 'program is successful in

overcoming language barriers' (Westminster declaration; para. 13).

38. The average LEP (limited English proficient) student in Westminster gains slightly more than one (1.1) language level per year of instruction. This means that if a student begins school in first grade at language Level A (i.e. a non-English speaker unable to function in English at any level), she or he will require *nearly 3 years* to be at Level D, which IPT test developers (IPT 1 Oral, Grades K–6, English forms C and D) designate as 'limited English speaking', and an additional *2 years* to become a fluent English speaker. Even on the face of it, Westminster's data appear to support the proposition that achieving English fluency requires approximately 5 years: A non-English speaker entering 1st grade will become 'limited English proficient' in late 3rd/early 4th grade and will not become a fluent English speaker until around the end of 5th grade (Hakuta, 1998).

In short, the presuppositions of Proposition 227 regarding the amount of time required to learn English for academic purposes are without empirical foundation.

2. The systematic devaluation of student identities within the school has been documented in contexts around the world that are characterized by coercive relations of power in the wider society. For example, Antti Jalava vividly describes the 'internal suicide' that he committed as a result of the rejection of his Finnish identity that he experienced in Swedish schools:

> When the idea had eaten itself deeply enough in to my soul that it was despicable to be a Finn, I began to feel ashamed of my origins ... To survive, I had to change my stripes. Thus: to hell with Finland and the Finns! ... A Swede was what I had to become, and that meant I could not continue to be a Finn. Everything I had held dear and self-evident had to be destroyed ... My mother tongue was worthless – this I realized at last; on the contrary it made me the butt of abuse and ridicule. So down with the Finnish language! I spat on myself, gradually committed internal suicide. (1988: 164)

Gloria Morgan, a Caribbean-origin educator in Britain, similarly highlights the ambivalence that bicultural pupils often develop in relation to both their cultural backgrounds:

> I suggest that children of African-Caribbean heritage in Britain are caught up between two cultures, one of which they see devalued and the other with which they do not fully identify but which is seen as superior by society. Just coping with being black and watching and listening as society devalues us can be stressful and contribute to low self-esteem, poor motivation, depression and even anti-social behaviour. (1996: 39)

3. Despite Canada's official policy of *multiculturalism*, exclusionary practices that devalue students' identities are still extremely common in schools. This is illustrated in a case study of one ten-year-old African Canadian male student (James, 1994). Although Darren was a leader on the playground and in recreational activities, in the classroom he was seen by his teacher as 'emotionally flat'. He participated minimally in class activities and justified this on the grounds that they were boring. James describes the instructional context as follows:

> Every teacher in Darren's school is white, as is the principal, the secretary, the lunchroom supervisors, and even the man who puts on the 'Scholastic Book Fair' presentations ... The curricular materials to be found in Darren's classroom are textbooks that have been used since the 1960s and 70s. One of these, a reading comprehension book, presents 'Canadian history' as a collision of white Europeans with 'primitive native tribes' who do such things as 'dance ceremoniously' ... If the images of blacks that Darren constantly encounters in classes are ones that present them as low achievers, 'primitive', and 'slum dwellers', and there are no discussions about these images, then this will operate to silence Darren. His experience is not acknowledged or validated; he is invisible; and moreover, he is powerless in challenging the teacher. No wonder then that Darren, like many other black students ... , finds his classes 'boring'

and refuses to ask questions which would help him with classroom tasks'. (1994: 26–27)

It seems clear from this and many other accounts of black students' educational experiences (e.g. Dei, 1996) that issues related to the social construction of identity within schools play a significant role in the extent to which African Canadian students continue to engage academically. Considerable Canadian data suggest that African Canadian students and their parents perceive education as extremely important but are frustrated in their educational aspirations by the systemic racism underneath the facade of multiculturalism in Canadian schools (Brathwaite & James, 1996).

4.  The perspective presented here is consistent with other recent accounts of the centrality of identity issues in language learning, social adjustment, and academic achievement (e.g. Kanno, in press; Igoa, 1995, 1999; McKay & Wong, 1996; Peirce, 1995; Tse, 1999). In 1996, I attempted to express the reciprocal nature of identity negotiation and its academic implications by suggesting that 'if teachers are not learning much from their students, it is probable that their students are not learning much from them' (1996: 4). Cristina Igoa expresses the same idea more poetically: 'Uprooted children need a safe place to make mistakes; a warm and friendly environment with no fear of ridicule or shame to speak or be silent. The nest is a place where every child's culture is valued; a place that makes it safe for the child to break out of a shell. . . . If we listen to immigrant children, they will teach us how to reach them' (1999: 6, 12).

Sheila Shannon (1995) has also documented the necessity for bilingual classrooms to become 'sites of resistance' (counter-hegemonic) if they are to be truly successful in promoting bilingualism. Teachers must recognize how the power of English as the high status language in the school and society undermines children's desire to speak Spanish and identify with their home culture. They must also take active steps to challenge and resist the unequal language status in bilingual classrooms by conveying an enthusiasm for Spanish and ensuring equity in materials and attention to each language. In Shannon's account of one bilingual classroom, we see how issues of power and identity are virtually inseparable from issues of language learning and academic achievement.

5.  Pauline Gibbons (personal communication, October 1999) has raised the issue of whether the notion of context-reduced is compatible with the dynamic notion of context associated with neo-Vygotskian theory. She suggests that less situationally embedded is a preferable term. Clearly, terms have different connotations which will change over time but the essential meaning is very similar, as the discussion of related theoretical constructs suggests.

6.  On a lighter note than some of the other misinterpretations of the acronums, Dr Tom Scovel shared with me the response of a student to an examination question in a Second Language Acquisition class that went as follows:

Bilingual Education is a controversial topic, largely due to politics, BICS, an organization that does not believe in bilingual education, feels that children can pick up language very easily but don't necessarily have to attend bilingual education classes.

## References

Aitchison, J. (1994) *Words in the Mind. An Introduction to the Mental Lexicon* (2nd edn). Oxford: Blackwell.

August, D. and Hakuta, K. (eds) (1997) *Improving Schooling for Language-Minority Children: A Research Agenda*. National Research Council, Institute of Medicine, National Academy Press.

Bachman, L.F. (1990a) *Fundamental Considerations in Language Testing*. Oxford: Oxford University Press.

Bachman, L.F. and Cohen, A.D. (1998) Language testing–SLA interfaces: An update. In L.F. Bachman and A.D. Cohen (eds) *Interfaces Between Second Language Acquisition and Language Testing Research* (pp. 1–31). Cambridge: Cambridge University Press.

Bachman, L.F. and Palmer, A.S. (1996) *Language Testing in Practice*. Oxford: Oxford University Press.

Baker, C. (1996) *Foundations of Bilingual Education and Bilingualism*. Clevedon: Multilingual Matters.

Banks, J.A. (1996) The canon debate, knowledge

construction, and multicultural education. In J.A. Banks (ed.) *Multicultural Education, Transformative Knowledge and Action: Historical and Contemporary Perspectives* (pp. 3–29). New York: Teachers College Press.

Baril, A. and Mori, G.A. (1991) Educational attainment of linguistic groups in Canada. *Canadian Social Trends* (Spring), 17–18.

Bereiter, C. and Scardamalia, M. (1981) From conversation to composition: The role of instruction in a developmental process. In R. Glaser (ed.) *Advances in Instructional Psychology*. Vol. 2. Hillsdale, NJ: Erlbaum.

Bethell, T. (1979, February) Against bilingual education. *Harper's Magazine*.

Beykont, Z.F. (1994) Academic progress of a nondominant group: A longitudinal study of Puerto Ricans in New York City's late-exit bilingual programs. Doctoral dissertation presented to the Graduate School of Education, Harvard University.

Brathwaite, K.S. and James, C.E. (1996) *Educating African Canadians*. Toronto: James Lorimer and Company.

Chapelle, C.A. (1998) Construct definition and validity inquiry in SLA research. In L.F. Bachman and A.D. Cohen (eds) *Interfaces Between Second Language Acquisition and Language Testing Research* (pp. 32–70). Cambridge: Cambridge University Press.

Collier, V.P. (1987) Age and rate of acquisition of second language for academic purposes. *TESOL Quarterly* 21, 617–641.

Corson, D. (1998a) *Language Policy in Schools*. Mawah, NJ: Lawrence Erlbaum Associates.

Crawford, J. (1992a) *Language Loyalties: A Source Book on the Official English Controversy*. Chicago: University of Chicago Press.

Crawford, J. (1992b) *Hold Your Tongue: Bilingualsm and the Politics of 'English Only'*. New York: Addison Wesley.

Cummins, J. (1976) The influence of bilingualism on cognitive growth: A synthesis of research findings and explanatory hypotheses. *Working Papers on Bilingualism* 9, 1–43.

Cummins, J. (1979a) Linguistic interdependence and the educational development of bilingual children. *Review of Educational Research* 49, 222–251.

Cummins, J. (1981a) The role of primary language development in promoting educational success for language minority students. In California State Department of Education (ed.) *Schooling and Language Minority Students: A Theoretical*

*Framework* (pp. 3–49). Los Angeles: Evaluation, Dissemination and Assessment Center California State University.

Cummins, J. (1981b) Age on arrival and immigrant second language learning in Canada: A reassessment. *Applied Linguistics* 1, 132–149.

Cummins, J. (1983) Language proficiency and academic achievement. In J.W. Oller Jr. (ed.) *Issues in Language Testing Research* (pp. 108–129). Rowley, MA: Newbury House.

Cummins, J. (1986) Empowering minority students: A framework for intervention. *Harvard Education Review* 15, 18–36.

Cummins, J. (1991c) Interdependence of first- and second-language proficiency in bilingual children. In E. Bialystok (ed.) *Language Processing in Bilingual Children* (pp. 70–89). Cambridge: Cambridge University Press.

Cummins, J. (1996) *Negotiating Identities: Education for Empowerment in a Diverse Society*. Los Angeles: California Association for Bilingual Education.

Cummins, J. (1997) Minority status and schooling in Canada. *Anthropology and Education Quarterly* 28 (3), 411–430.

Cummins, J. and Corson, D. (eds) (1997) *Bilingual Education. Vol. 5. Encyclopedia of Language and Education*. Dordrecht, The Netherlands: Kluwer Academic Publishers.

Cummins, J., Swain, M., Nakajima, K., Handscombe, J., Green, D. and Tran, C. (1984) Linguistic interdependence among Japanese and Vietnamese immigrant students. In C. Rivera (ed.) *Communicate Competence Approaches to Language Proficiency Assessment: Research and Application* (pp. 60–81). Clevedon: Multilingual Matters.

DeFazio, A.J. (1997) Language awareness at The International High School. In L. Van Lier and D. Corson (eds) *Knowledge about Language. Vol. 6. Encyclopedia of Language and Education* (pp. 99–107). Dordrecht, The Netherlands: Kluwer Academic Publishers, Inc.

Dei, G.S. (1996) *Anti-Racism Education: Theory and Practice*. Halifax: Fernwood Publishers.

Delpit, L. (1998) Ebonics and culturally responsive instruction. In T. Perry and L. Delpit (eds) *The Real Ebonics Debate* (pp. 17–26). Milwaukee, WI: Rethinking Schools.

Devlin, B. (1997) Links between first and second language instruction in Northern Territory bilingual programs: Evolving policies, theories and practice. In P. McKay, A. Davies,

B. Devlin, J. Clayton, R. Oliver and S. Zammit (eds) *The Bilingual Interface Project Report* (pp. 75–90). Canberra City: Commonwealth of Australia.

Diaz, R.M. (1985) Bilingual cognitive development: Addressing three gaps in current research. *Child Development* 56, 1376–1388.

Diaz, R.M. and Klinger, C. (1991) Towards an explanatory model of the interaction between bilingualism and cognitive development. In E. Bialystok (ed.) *Language Processing in Bilingual Children* (pp. 167–192). Cambridge: Cambridge University Press.

Douglas, D. (1998) Testing methods in context-based second language research. In L.F. Bachman and A.D. Cohen (eds) *Interfaces Between Second Language Acquisition and Language Testing Research* (pp. 141–155). Cambridge: Cambridge University Press.

Dunn, L. (1987) *Bilingual Hispanic Children on the US Mainland: A Review of Research on Their Cognitive, Linguistic, and Scholastic Development*. Circle Pines, MN: American Guidance Service.

Duquette, G. and Riopel, P. (eds) (1998) *L'education en Milieu Minoritaire et la Formation des Maîtres en Acadie et dans les Communautés Francophones du Canada*. Sudbury: Presses de l'Université Laurentienne.

Fitzgerald, J. (1995) English-as-a-second-language learners' cognitive reading processes: A review of research in the United States. *Review of Educational Research* 65, 145–190.

Fordham, S. (1990) Racelessness as a factor in Black students' school success: Pragmatic strategy or pyrrhic victory? In N.M. Hidalgo, C.L. McDowell and E.V. Siddle (eds) *Facing Racism in Education* (pp. 232–262). Cambridge, MA: Harvard Educational Review.

Frederickson, N. and Cline, T. (1990) *Curriculum Related Assessment with Bilingual Children: A Set of Working Papers*. London: University College London.

Freire, P. (1983) Banking education. In H. Giroux and D. Purpel (eds) *The Hidden Curriculum and Moral Education: Deception or Discovery?* Berkeley, CA: McCutcheon Publishing Corporation.

Gándara, P. (1999) *Review of Research on Instruction of Limited English Proficient Students: A Report to the California Legislature*. Santa Barbara, CA: University of California, Linguistic Minority Research Institute.

Genesee, F. (1979) Acquisition of reading skills in immersion programs. *Foreign Language Annals* 12, 71–77.

Gérin-Lajoie, D., Labrie, N. and Wilson, D. (1995) *Etude Interpretative des Resultats Obtenues par les Elèves Franco-Ontariens et Franco-Ontariennes en Lecture et en Ecriture aux Tests de Niveaux Provincial et National*. Toronto: Centre de recherches en education franco-ontarienne, OISE.

Gibbons, P. (1991) *Learning to Learn in a Second Language*. Newtown, Australia: Primary English Teaching Association.

Gibbons, P. (1995) *Learning a new register in a second language: The role of teacher/student talk* (Working Paper No. 1). University of Technology, Sydney.

Gibbons, P. (1998) Classroom talk and the learning of new registers in a second language. *Language and Education* 12 (2), 99–118.

Gibson, M.A. (1997) Complicating the immigrant/involuntary minority typology. *Anthropology and Education Quarterly* 28 (3), 431–454.

Hakuta, K. (1998) Supplemental declaration of Kenji Hakuta. Legal declaration in Appeal of Proposition 227. Available at http://ourworld.compuserve.com/homepages/jwcrawford

Hakuta, K., Butler, Y.G. and Witt, D. (2000) *How Long Does It Take English Learners to Attain Proficiency?* Santa Barbara, CA: University of California Linguistic Minority Research Institute.

Halliday, M.A.K. and Hasan, R. (1989) *Language, Context and Text: Aspects of Language in a Social Semiotic Perspective*. Oxford: Oxford University Press.

Hardman, J. (1998) Literacy and bilingualism in a Cambodian community in the USA. In A.Y. Durgunolu and L. Verhoeven (eds) *Literacy Development in a Multilingual Context: Cross-Cultural Perspectives* (pp. 51–81). Mahwah, NJ: Lawrence Erlbaum Associates.

Heath, S.B. (1983) *Ways with Words*. Cambridge: Cambridge University Press.

Heller, M. (1994) *Crosswords: Language, Education and Ethnicity in French Ontario*. Berlin: Mouton de Gruyter.

Heller, M. (1999) *Linguistic Minorities and Modernity: A Sociolinguistic Ethnography*. London: Longman.

Hornblower, M. (1998) No habla Español. *TIME* (January 26), 44.

Igoa, C. (1995) *The Inner World of the Immigrant Child*. New York: St. Martin's Press.

Igoa, C. (1999) Language and psychological dimensions: The inner world of the immigrant child. Paper presented at the American Educational Research Association Conference, Montreal, Canada.

Jalava, A. (1988) Nobody could see that I was a Finn. In T. Skuttnabb-Kangas and J. Cummins (eds) *Minority Education: From Shame to Struggle* (pp. 161–166). Clevedon: Multilingual Matters.

James, C. (1994) 'I don't want to talk about it': Silencing students in today's classrooms. *Orbit* 25, 26–29.

Jensen, A.R. (1969) How much can we boost IQ and scholastic achievement? *Harvard Educational Review* 39, 1–123.

Kanno, Y. (in press) Bilingualism and identity: The stories of Japanese returnees. *International Journal of Bilingual Education and Bilingualism*.

Klesmer, H. (1994) Assessment and teacher perceptions of ESL student achievement. *English Quarterly* 26 (3), 8–11.

Krashen, S. (1993) *The Power of Reading*. Englewood, CO: Libraries Unlimited.

Lasagabaster, D. (1998) The threshold hypothesis applied to three languages in contact at school. *International Journal of Bilingual Education and Bilingualism* 1 (2), 119–133.

Lotherington, H., Ebert, S., Watanabe, T., Norng, S. and Ho-Dac, T. (1998) Biliteracy practices in suburban Melbourne. *Australian Language Matters* 6 (3), 3–4.

Mackay, R. (1992) Embarrassment in the classroom. In A. van Essen and E. Burkart (eds) *Homage to W.R. Lee: Essays in English as a Foreign or Second Language* (pp. 153–163). Berlin: Foris Publications.

Martin-Jones, M. and Bhatt, A. (1998) Literacies in the lives of young Gujerati speakers in Leicester. In A.Y. Durgunolu and L. Verhoeven (eds) *Literacy Development in a multilingual Context: Cross-Cultural Perspectives* (pp. 37–50). Mahwah, NJ: Lawrence Erlbaum Associates.

Matthews, P. (1997) *The Concise Oxford Dictionary of Linguistics*. Oxford: Oxford University Press.

McCaleb, S.P. (1994) *Building Communities of Learners: A Collaboration among Teachers, Students, Families and Community*. New York: St. Martin's Press.

McKay, S.L. and Wong, S.C. (1996) Multiple discourses, multiple identities: Investment and agency in second-language learning among Chinese adolescent immigrant students. *Harvard Educational Review* 66 (3), 577–608.

McWilliam, N. (1998) *What's in a Word? Vocabulary Development in Multilingual Classrooms*. Stoke on Trent: Trentham Books.

Moll, L.C., Amanti, C., Neff, D. and González, N. (1992) Funds of knowledge for teaching: Using a qualitative approach to connect homes and classrooms. *Theory into Practice* 31 (2), 132–141.

Morgan, G. (1996) An investigation into the achievement of African-Caribbean pupils. *Multicultural Teaching* 14 (2), 37–40.

Nieto, S. (1996) *Affirming Diversity: The Sociopolitical Context of Multicultural Education* (2nd edn). White Plains, NY: Longman.

Ogbu, J. (1978) *Minority Education and Caste*. New York: Academic Press.

Ogbu, J.U. (1992) Understanding cultural diversity and learning. *Educational Researcher* 21 (8), 5–14 and 24.

Ovando, C. and McLaren, P. (eds) (1999) *The Politics of Multiculturalism and Bilingual Education: Students and Teachers Caught in the Cross Fire*. Boston: McGraw Hill.

Paribakht, T.S. and Wesche, M. (1997) Vocabulary enhancement activities and reading for meaning in second language vocabulary acquisition. In J. Coady and T. Huckin (eds) *Second Language Vocabulary Acquisition: A Rationale for Pedagogy*. Cambridge: Cambridge University Press.

Peirce, B.N. (1995) Social identity, investment, and language learning. *TESOL Quarterly* 29 (1), 9–31.

Pérez, B. (1998a) Literacy, diversity, and programmatic responses. In B. Pérez (ed.) *Sociocultural Contexts of Language and Literacy* (pp. 3–20). Mahwah, NJ: Lawrence Erlbaum Associates.

Pérez, B. (1998b) Language, literacy, and biliteracy. In B. Pérez (ed.) *Sociocultural Contexts of Language and Literacy* (pp. 21–48). Mahwah, NJ: Lawrence Erlbaum Associates.

Poplin, M. and Weeres, J. (1992) *Voices from the Inside: A Report on Schooling from Inside the Classroom*. Claremont, CA: The Institute for Education in Transformation at the Claremont Graduate School.

Ramírez, J.D. (1992) Executive summary. *Bilingual Research Journal* 16, 1–62.

Ricciardelli, L.A. (1992) Bilingualism and cognitive development in relation to threshold theory. *Journal of Psycholinguistic Research* 21, 301–316.

Romaine, S. (1989) *Bilingualism*. Oxford: Oxford University Press.

Schecter, S.R. and Bayley, R. (1998) Concurrence and complementarity: Mexican-background parents' decisions about language and schooling. *Journal for a Just and Caring Education* 4 (1), 47–64.

Schlesinger, A.J. (1991) *The Disuniting of America*. New York: W. W. Norton.

Shannon, S. (1995) The hegemony of English: A case study of one bilingual classroom as a site of resistance. *Linguistics and Education* 7, 175–200.

Shohamy, E. (1999) Unity and diversity in language policy. Paper presented at the AILA conference, Tokyo, August.

Sierra, J. and Olaziregi, I. (1991) *EIFE 3. Influence of Factors on the Learning of Basque. Study of the Models A, B and D in Second Year Basic General Education*. Gasteiz: Central Publications Service of the Basque Country.

Skourtou, E. (1995) Some notes about the relationship between bilingualism and literacy concerning the teaching of Greek as a second language. *European Journal of Intercultural Studies* 6 (2), 24–30.

Spolsky, B. (1984) A note on the dangers of terminology innovation. In C. Rivera (ed.) *Language Proficiency and Academic Achievement* (pp. 41–43). Clevedon: Multilingual Matters.

Troike, R. (1984) SCALP: Social and cultural aspects of language proficiency. In C. Rivera (ed.) *Language Proficiency and Academic Achievement*. Clevedon: Multilingual Matters.

Tse, L. (1999) Finding a place to be: Ethnic identity exploration of Asian Americans. *Adolescence* 34 (133), 122–138.

Vásquez, O.A., Pease-Alvarez, L. and Shannon, S. M. (1994) *Pushing Boundaries: Language and Culture in a Mexicano Community*. New York: Cambridge University Press.

Verhallen, M. and Schoonen, R. (1998) Lexical knowledge in L1 and L2 of third and fifth graders. *Applied Linguistics* 19 (4), 452–470.

Verhoeven, L. and Aarts, R. (1998) Attaining functional literacy in the Netherlands. In A.Y. Durgunolu and L. Verhoeven (eds) *Literacy Development in a Multilingual Context: Cross-Cultural Perspectives* (pp. 111–134). Mahwah, NJ: Lawrence Erlbaum Associates.

Vincent, C. (1996) Singing to a star: The school meanings of second generation Salvadorean students. Doctoral dissertation, George Mason University, Fairfax, VA.

Wagner, D.A. (1998) Putting second language first: Language and literacy learning in Morocco. In L. Verhoeven and A.Y. Durgunoglu (eds) *Literacy Development in a Multilingual Context* (pp. 169–183). Mahway, NJ: Lawrence Erlbaum Associates.

Wagner, S. (1991) *Analphabetisme de Minorité et Alphabetisme d'Affirmation Nationale à Propos de l'Ontario Français. Vol. I: Synthèse Theoretique et Historique*. Toronto: Ministère de l'Education.

Wald, B. (1984) A sociolinguistic perspective on Cummins' current framework for relating language proficiency to academic achievement. In C. Rivera (ed.) *Language Proficiency and Academic Achievement* (pp. 55–70). Clevedon: Multilingual Matters.

Willis, P. (1977) *Learning to Labor: How Working Class Kids Get Working Class Jobs*. Lexington: D.C. Heath.

Wong Fillmore, L. (1992) Against our best interest: The attempt to sabotage bilingual education. In J. Crawford (ed.) *Language Loyalties: A Sourcebook on the Official English Controversy*. Chicago: University of Chicago Press.

Wong Fillmore, L. (1998) Supplemental declaration of Lily Wong Fillmore. Legal declaration in Appeal of Proposition 227. Available at: http://ourworld.compuserve.com/homepages/jwcrawford

Zanger, V.V. (1994) 'Not joined in': Intergroup relations and access to English literacy for Hispanic youth. In B.M. Ferdman, R.-M. Weber and A. Ramírez (eds) *Literacy Across Languages and Cultures* (pp. 171–198). Albany. SUNY Press.

## Questions

1. Construct a flow diagram/chart to show the movement of actions and decisions surrounding Proposition 227.
2. Write short notes in your own words to show an understanding of (a) conversational and academic proficiency (b) the thresholds hypothesis (c) interdependence of the first and second languages (d) coercive and collaborative relations of power (e) additive and subtractive contexts.

3. What kind of politics does Cummins' suggest for language minorities? What for Cummins is the ultimate nature of the debate: language, culture, identity, ideology, power, politics or control?
4. In your own words, explain what Figure 3 means and its implications for pedagogy. Give specific examples of pedagogical practices that correspond to Cummins' notion that second language learners need to be challenged cognitively and given contextual and linguistic supports or scaffolds.

## Activities

1. Interview five immigrant students who have learned the majority language of the society in which they live as a second language in school. Find out how long it took them to function academically in the second language, what challenges they faced in school, what helped them in their second language development, whether their first language was a hindrance or a help. Share your findings with the class.

   Different students might interview immigrant students with different migration histories, age, ethnicities, race, languages, language scripts, social class. Put your individual findings on a class chart.
2. Observe a classroom with language minority students. Focus on the 'collaborative creation of power' within the classroom. Are there any? If so, describe them. If not, describe their absence.
3. Interview five monolingual majority-language parents in your community. Find out their interest in bilingualism for their children. In particular, ask them which non-English language would they want their children to learn and why? Then ask them about their support for:

   a. schools that would develop their children's bilingualism
   b. schools that would maintain the mother tongue of language minority students and develop their bilingualism.

   Record their answers on an answer sheet. Then write an essay integrating your findings.

   Groups might interview parents with different characteristics; for example, white vs. non-white, professionals vs. non-professionals, older vs. younger, mothers vs. fathers. Share the findings with each other, compare and discuss similarities and differences.
4 . In the library, research the sociolinguistic situation of the different Latino groups in the United States and of the different Asian groups. Refer to their migration history, their socio-demographic characteristics, their geographic concentration, their language use and proficiency, and their prospects for language maintenance or language shift. (One importance source for this information is McKay, S.L. and Wong, S-L.C. (eds) (2000) *New Immigrants in the United States*. Cambridge: Cambridge University Press.)

## Further Reading

Baker, C. (2006) *Foundations of Bilingual Education and Bilingualism* (4th edn). Clevedon: Multilingual Matters (chapters 8, 18).

Baker, C. and Hornberger, N.H. (eds) (2001) *Introductory Reader to the Writings of Jim Cummins*. Clevedon: Multilingual Matters.

Cummins, J. (2006) Identity texts: The imaginative construction of self through multiliteracies pedagogy. In O. García, T. Skutnabb-Kangas and M. Torres-Guzmán (eds) *Imagining Multilingual Schools: Languages in Education*. Clevedon: Multilingual Matters.

Cummins, J. (2000) *Language, Power and Pedagogy: Bilingual Children in the Crossfire.* Clevedon: Multi-lingual Matters.
Stritikus, T.T. and García, E. (2003) The role of theory and policy in the educational treatment of language minority students: Competitive structures in California. *Education Policy Analysis Archives*, 11, 26, 1–25. http://epaa.asu.edu/epaa/v11n26/

# Linguistic Human Rights in Education?

## Tove Skutnabb-Kangas

One of the **basic linguistic human rights** of persons belonging to minorities is – or should be – to achieve high levels of bi- or multilingualism through education. Becoming at least bilingual is in most cases necessary for minorities to exercise other fundamental human rights, including the fulfillment of basic needs. But today the education of both majorities and minorities in most western countries (and also elsewhere) functions in conflict with most scientifically sound principles about how education leading to high levels of multilingualism should be organized. As has been shown, education participates in attempting and committing linguistic genocide in relation to minorities. In relation to linguistic majorities, with the exception of elites, education today in most cases deprives them of the possibility of gaining the benefits associated with really high levels of multilingualism.

Sometimes linguistic human rights in education are, falsely, in my opinion, posited as being in conflict with other human rights.[1] Admittedly situations of great linguistic diversity combined with meager financial resources are complex – but on the other hand there is ample evidence from Africa and Asia and from multilingual immigrant minority education of the fact that unnecessary either-or stances (which the false positioning is often based on) are in the long run both costly and misguided, and tend to perpetuate elite dominance.

If multilingualism is more positive than monolingualism for the patients/victims and for the society as a whole, how can educational language planning help in getting rid of monolingualism? How should education be organised, so as to make **everybody** bilingual or multilingual at a high level? What is important is to develop models which combine the positive

aspects of at least three experiences. Firstly, the positive strand in the education of minorities, namely strong forms of 'multilingual' education. Secondly, the positive aspects in the education of both minorities and majorities, involved in antiracist 'intercultural' education. These two have so far, curiously enough, often had competing goals (see, e.g. Lo Bianco, 1994). Thirdly, they should be combined with the positive aspects of elite education. Present monolingually oriented reductionist educational language choices seem rather to combine the negative sides of the first two and none of the positive ones of the last. Today's educational models, with few exceptions, do not support the diversity which is necessary for the planet to have a future.

After defining bilingualism as an educational goal, I first list some of the key fallacies which lead to lack of language rights in contemporary educational language planning for some main groups. Then I present educational models which do not lead to high levels of multilingualism (non-forms and weak forms of bilingual education). They will be related to literacy and the lack of Universal Primary Education (UPE), and it is claimed that use of the wrong medium of education (i.e. not using the mother tongue) is the main **pedagogical** reason for lack of success of 'literacy' campaigns in the world (political, economic, and many ideological reasons have been discussed earlier). This is followed by a presentation of strong models of multilingual education. Finally, on the basis of the strong models, I will draw conclusions about prerequisites (also bilingual teachers) and principles which are important to follow if high level multilingualism is the educational goal.

Since hundreds of books and thousands of articles have been written about the subject (I have myself contributed a fair number), I will not give many specific references here and will keep the presentation at a fairly general, programmatic level. There are many specialised bibliographies in the area; several volumes of readers, encyclopedias, web-sites, etc. – and the reader is asked to consult them.

## What Kind of 'Bilingualism' is the Goal in 'Bilingual Education' Programmes?

We have seen that formal education can play a decisive role in killing minority languages. But is the opposite also true? How important is formal education in maintaining a minority language, in supporting threatened languages, in reversing language shift, or in reclaiming a language? Opinions differ. What we can say, though, is that educational conditions, and changes in the educational system, have often made a community aware of the need for other changes. Some of them the communities may be able to make themselves – for instance, decolonise their own attitudes and reorganise community life so as to use the minority language more among themselves, including in the family – there are many examples of this all over the world. Often most of the changes needed are political and economic, and the minority community cannot effect these on their own. Schools cannot save a language on their own (see Fishman, 1989, 1991, 1995, 1996b, 1998) but schools can be an important change agent. When assessing the many factors which influence the successful reproduction of a minority group, one conclusion is that education is often easier to change than many still larger-scale macro-societal and political structures, even when a major struggle is needed for educational change. The medium of education is one, if not the most, decisive factor in the multilingualism and the school achievement of the children of dominated groups – and, again, easier to change than some of the other major factors (the parents' socioeconomic status or their level of formal education, or the child's gender, age or length of stay in the country in the case of immigrant minority children). One recent example of the influence of education is from Wales. Farrell *et al.* (1998) analyse census data (1981 and 1991) from anglicised areas of South East Wales and show that 'education has been an effective agency of Welsh language production' (1998: 494). There are 'net gains in the percentages of younger Welsh speakers' (p. 489), and it can be shown that these are connected to the presence of Welsh-medium education. Other examples will be provided below.

In the following sections I will classify educational models in general in relation to what is called bilingual education. The classic definition of bilingual education (Andersson & Boyer, 1978) requires that the educational system uses two languages as media of instruction, in subjects other than the languages themselves. I will follow Colin Baker's classification into weak and strong forms of bilingual education (e.g. 1993). I have also added a third category, non-forms of bilingual education. Neither weak forms nor non-forms succeed in making children high level bi- or multilingual, whereas strong forms **have** succeeded in this. Since the three categories are based on to what extent the models succeed in enabling children to become **high level bi- or multilinguals**, we have to define this goal first.

When I use the term 'bilingualism', this should generally be understood as 'bi- and multilingualism'. Bilingualism as a goal implies by definition that (at least) two languages are involved. When dominant language representatives use the concept, they seem mostly to confine their interest in bilingualism to one of the languages and one of the groups only: the learning of the majority/ dominant language by minority children. The mother tongues of the minority children are in most cases tolerated as parts of the curriculum **only** if the teaching of (or in) them leads to a better proficiency in the majority language – and often they are not tolerated at all (see, e.g. Baker & de Kanter, 1982).

As a result of this, it is the minorities themselves who have to put a strong emphasis on the learning of the mother tongue and demand mother tongue learning as a linguistic human right. But minorities do of course want their children to learn the majority languages fully too. We want our children to become bilingual[2] as a minimum, not monolingual or strongly dominant in **either** of the two languages.

One of the confusing facts has been that many state educational authorities (representing the majority group) also claim that **they** too want our children to become bilingual. But when this claim is analysed, it often transpires that majorities and minorities use different definitions of bilingualism when they speak of it as the educational goal. That is one of the reasons why it is imperative to define 'bilingual' every time the term is being used. There are literally hundreds of definitions (see, e.g. Baetens Beardsmore, 1982; Haugen, 1964, 1972; Hoffman, 1991; Romaine, 1995; Vildomec, 1963; Weinreich, 1967, for presentations and analyses). I organise them

**Table 1**  Definitions of bilingualism

| Criterion | Definition: A speaker is bilingual who |
|---|---|
| 1. origin | a.  has learned two languages in the family from native speakers from infancy;<br>b.  has used two languages in parallel as means of communication from infancy |
| 2. identification  – internal<br>– external | a.  identifies herself as bilingual / with two languages and / or two cultures (or parts of them);<br>b.  is identified by others as bilingual / as a native speaker of two languages |
| 3. competence | a.  has complete mastery of two languages;<br>b.  has native-Iike control of two languages;<br>c.  has equal mastery of two languages;<br>d.  can produce complete meaningful utterances in the other language;<br>e.  has at least some knowledge and control of the grammatical structure of the other language;<br>f.  has come into contact with another language |
| 4. function | a.  uses (or can use) two languages (in most situations) (in accordance with her own wishes and the demands of the community) |

*Source*: Skutnabb-Kangas, 1984a: 91

according to the same criteria which I use in the mother tongue definitions, and give a sample in Table 1. (See Skutnabb-Kangas 1975, 1984a for references on who has used the various definitions.)

When majority group educational authorities talk about bilingualism as a goal for the education of immigrant or indigenous minority children, they often seem to mean either a non-demanding competence definition (for instance 3d or 3e) or the most general function definition (uses two languages). We minorities would prefer to use a combination of 2, 3 and 4, a definition which makes sure that the speaker has the chance to learn and use **both** languages at a very high level and to identify positively with both. The definitions used by the majority authorities confirm the picture of linguicism, because there are low expectations and almost no demands made on the minority child's competence in her mother tongue. It is often left to the home to teach it, and it is sometimes declared that 'taxpayers' money' should not go into 'supporting private ethnicity', conveniently ignoring the fact that minorities are taxpayers too and that majority children's private ethnicity is supported through all taxpayers' money in schools. Minority taxpayers are required to support majority language and ethnicity in schools, both for majority children,

and for their own (minority) children, even when it is subtractive for them.

My own definition (Definition Box 1) is specifically designed to describe the needs of indigenous and immigrant and other minority children. The goal of minority education should in my view be to enable the children to become bilingual according to this definition.

The implications of this definition for the educational system are far-reaching, and should be compared with the implications of less demanding definitions (for more detail see Skutnabb-Kangas, 1984a).

'Second language' should also be defined for the purposes of the educational models presented below. Except when clearly indicated, I use 'L2' or second language' to mean the language which is the **second in the order of learning for the student** (as opposed to the first language or a third or fourth language).

For some Deaf students a Sign language might thus be their second language in **this** sense.

One of the other common ways of defining a second language is to define it as a language that the student can hear and use in the immediate environment outside the home, a language which is not the student's mother tongue. In this definition the second language is contrasted

**DEFINITION BOX 1** Definition of bilingualism as an education goal

A bilingual speaker is one who is able to function in two (or more) languages, either in 'monolingual' or multilingual communities, in accordance with the sociocultural demands made on an individual's communicative and cognitive competence by these communities and by the individual herself, at the same level as native speakers, and who is able to identify positively with both (or all) language groups (and cultures) or parts of them (Skutnabb-Kangas 1984a: 90).

with a foreign language, which one does not use daily in the environment.

In this sense a Sign language might never become a mother tongue or even a second language for a Deaf student who has hearing parents and who never lives in a signing community.

After these clarifications we move to educational models. When these are categorised in terms of whether they reach the goal of **high levels of bilingualism** or multilingualism, what is intended is preferably 'bilingualism' according to my own definition above, or at least something very close to it. In addition, at least one, possibly two, or even several other languages can be learned at a high level. I consider it a realistic and feasible goal. It has been shown that in the education of both national minorities and elites, the goal can be reached, without the costs necessarily being higher than those of present educational models which do not reach these goals.

## Key Fallacies in the Education of Dominated Communities

On the basis of his study of factors influencing English teaching worldwide, especially in colonial and post-colonial education, Robert Phillipson (1992; and an earlier version in Phillipson & Skutnabb-Kangas, 1986a) identified what he calls 'the five key tenets of ESL/EFL'. These are

- English is best taught monolingually;
- the ideal teacher of English is a native speaker;
- the earlier English is introduced, the better the results;

- the more English is taught, the better the results;
- if other languages are used much, standards of English will drop.

As we also showed (e.g. Skutnabb-Kangas & Phillipson, 1989a), these tenets have in fact guided much of indigenous and immigrant minority education all over the world. All five are scientifically false and can rather be (and have been) labelled as fallacies (for a detailed analysis, see Phillipson, 1992, Chapter 6). These are then

- the monolingual fallacy;
- the native speaker fallacy;
- the early start fallacy;
- the maximum exposure fallacy;
- the subtractive fallacy.

To these, we could add at least the segregation tenet/fallacy:

- if minorities are taught in their own groups or classes or schools, especially through the medium of their own languages, this prevents integration and leads to/is segregation, ghettoisation.

Many of the myths about monolingualism could also be formulated as tenets/fallacies. The 'monolingual' and 'native speaker' fallacies will be commented on below in the section about bilingual teachers.

The **'early start' fallacy** is obviously closely connected to the 'subtractive' fallacy. Several types of programme have shown that if teaching a foreign language as a subject or teaching through the medium of a foreign language is additive, it **can** start early. Early foreign language teaching in 'mainstream' programmes shows it. On the other hand, a large longitudinal Swedish study (Holmstrand, 1980, 1982) showed that the gains of starting a foreign language as a subject early were minimal. The strong models below, **immersion**, and **two-way programmes** (see the definitions below), also show that additive early start with a foreign medium is perfectly possible. We do not yet know enough about the long-term results of **double immersion** (using two foreign languages as partial media of education; see Artigal, 1995).

On the other hand, if the learning of another language is **subtractive** (as it is in all the non-forms and weak forms of bilingual education), the earlier it starts the worse.

The **'maximum exposure' tenet** (the label comes from Jim Cummins), is maybe the intuitively most understandable of the tenets: the more the child uses L2, the better she learns it. It has also been shown to be a complete fallacy. If the quality of the instruction in L2 is the same in two models, one with maximum exposure, the other with little exposure to a dominant language, and provided that minority children receive high quality mother tongue medium instruction in the model with little exposure to L2, then there have been two types of result.

Either there is no relationship between time-on-task and results in the dominant language, meaning both groups perform equally well in L2, despite the mother tongue medium group having had much less exposure.

Alternatively, there is a reverse relationship: the **less** time is used on instruction through the medium of the dominant language, the **better** the results, again provided that the time is instead used on both good mother tongue medium teaching and good subject teaching of L2, given by bilingual teachers. For instance the Ramirez study in the USA is fairly clear on this (see Ramirez, 1992; Dolson & Mayer, 1992; and Cummins, 1992 and references in them for a discussion of the methods and findings). Several of Jim Cummins' recent publications have given overviews of the research findings in relation to maximum exposure.

The **subtractive fallacy** is an old one. For instance, the Norwegian School Law of 1880 (which has been called the 'Magna Carta of Norwegianisation'), paragraph 3, says: 'Instruction in the school is in the Norwegian language. The Lappish or Finnish languages are used only as a means of helping to explain what is impossible to understand for the children'. Every paragraph after this contains detailed instructions on how to restrain the use of Sámi and Finnish.

> Even if the majority of the children in a group do not understand Norwegian, the teacher must always keep the above regulations in mind and remember that it is imperative that the Lappish and Finnish languages are not used more than absolutely necessary . . . When the teacher converses with the children to make them understand, use of the Lappish or Finnish language must be avoided as much as possible; it should be noted in par-

> ticular that whole sentences and continuous passages of the Norwegian text must not be translated into Lappish or Finnish unless it is has been shown that this cannot be avoided without harm to comprehension. (quoted in Lind Meløy, 1981: 122–123)

It is instructive to compare this with the policy offered to children in Africa and Asia almost 100 years later, in the pedagogical tradition which still dominates English teaching: 'The teaching of vocabulary should be mainly through demonstration in situations. When, however, a very brief explanation in the mother tongue is sufficient to ensure that the meaning is fully and accurately understood, such explanation may be given.' (Makerere Report, 1961: 13, a report of the Commonwealth conference on the teaching of English as a second language, probably the most influential document on policy and methods for teaching English in ex-colonial countries). For analysis of the monolingual approach in teaching English as a foreign/second language see Phillipson, 1992, Chapter 6.

After the passing of the Proposition 227 in California, minority children will be placed in English-medium instruction after the first school year. If teachers give even the little support in the two examples above, this may lead to trouble because teachers may be fined if they use other languages.

Californian school authorities might learn from the mistakes of the Norwegians. It was important for the central and local authorities in Norway to control in a more detailed manner whether the teachers really refrained from the use of Sámi and Finnish. According to Karl Aas, Superintendent for Schools, in a communication to the Department of Education in 1899, there were many people who thought that the time had come to forbid the use of Sámi and Finnish as auxiliary languages and 'in addition to the teachers, competent men like the business people and civil servants have here voiced that opinion'. Ron Unz, the engineer behind Proposition 227 in Califomia, is a business man . . .). In Norway, most of these 'competetent men' were ethnic Norwegians. One of the Heads of Department in the Ministry had suggested in 1877 that only 'Norwegian' teachers should be appointed because 'experience seems to have shown that teachers of pure or mixed Sámi or Finnish ancestry are not capable of advancing the Norwegianisation among their compatriots with the success hoped for' (ibid., 19, 21). The teachers and the staff in the boarding schools were to be 'nationally minded' (Eriksen & Niemi, 1981: 257). In 1931 the then Superintendent wrote that it was 'completely unnecessary for teachers in Finnmark to have any education in Sámi or Finnish' (Lind Meløy, 1981: 27). This seems to be the Californian present stance too.

To counteract the **segregation fallacy** two distinctions are helpful, those between **physical as opposed to psychological segregation/integration** and between **segregation as a goal or a means**. For many dominated groups at least initial physical segregation from dominant group members seems to be a necessity in order to enable later integration psychologically and competence-wise. If physical segregation ensures that the students have a better chance of acquiring the prerequisites for integrating themselves both psychologically and physically later, then the initial physical segregation is used as a positive means towards a later integrationist goal. Minority students are, of course, psychologically integrated in their own classrooms, with other children with whom they share a mother tongue. Here they have a better chance of being appreciated for who they are and what they know, rather than the system defining them as deficient or below the norm, as is often the case when they are physically 'integrated' in dominant group classes. Forced initial physical integration into a dominant language and dominant group classroom may prevent dominated group students from acquiring the competencies they need, in their own language and culture, in the dominant language and culture, and in terms of content matter (I have discussed this in several chapters in my 1984a and, especially, in 1986, a book which has been translated into several languages, English not being among them[3]).

The beliefs in a monolingual L2-teaching methodology, monolingual teachers, maximum exposure, and the either-or thinking which results in forbidding the minority language or restricting its use, have today developed from the earlier more crude forms to their present more sophisticated forms. These are at least equally effective in committing linguistic genocide as have been shown. It is extremely important to recognise that the ideology is still the same.

## References

Andersson, T. and Boyer, M. (1978) *Bilingual Schooling in the United States* (2nd edn). Austin, TX: National Education Laboratory Publishers.

Artigal, J.M. (1995) Multiways towards multilingualism: the Catalan immersion programme experience. In T. Skutnabb-Kangas (ed.) *Multilingualism for All* (pp. 169–181). Series European Studies on Multilingualism 4. Lisse: Swets and Zeitlinger.

Baetens Beardsmore, H. (1982) *Bilingualism. Basic Principles*. Clevedon, UK: Multilingual Matters.

Baker, C. (1993) *Foundations of Bilingual Education and Bilingualism*. Clevedon, UK/Philadelphia, PA: Multilingual Matters.

Baker, KA. and de Kanter, A.A. (1982) *Effectiveness of Bilingual Education: A Review of the Literature. Final Draft Report*. Washington, DC: Department of Education. Office of Planning, Budget, and Evaluation.

Cummins, J. (1992) Bilingual education and English immersion: The Ramirez Report in theoretical perspective. *Bilingual Research Journal* 16 (1 and 2), 91–104.

Dolson, D.P. and Mayer, J. (1992) Longitudinal study of three program models for language minority students: a critical examination of reported findings. *Bilingual Research Journal* 16 (1 and 2), 105–158.

Eriksen, K.E. and Niemi, E. (1981) *Den Finske Fare. Sikkerhetsproblemer og Minoritetspolitikk i Nord 1860–1940* [*The Finnish Danger. Security Problems and Minority Policy in the North 1860–1940*]. Oslo: Universitetsforlaget.

Farrell, S., Bellin, W. Higgs, G. and White, S. (1998) The distribution of younger Welsh speakers in anglicized areas of south east Wales. *Journal of Multilingual and Multicultural Development* 18 (6), 489–495.

Fishman, J.A. (1989) *Language and Ethnicity in Minority Sociolinguistic Perspective*. Clevedon, UK/Philadelphia, PA: Multilingual Matters.

Fishman, J.A. (1991) *Reversing Language Shift. Theoretical and Empirical Assistance to Threatened Languages*. Clevedon, UK: Multilingual Matters.

Fishman, J.A. (1995) Good conferences in a wicked world: on some worrisome problems in the study of language maintenance and language shift. In W. Fase, K. Jaspaert and S. Kroon (eds) *The State of Minority Languages. International Perspective on Survival and Decline* (pp. 311–317). European Studies on Multilingualism, 5. Lisse: Swets and Zeitlinger.

Fishman, J.A. (1996b) Maintaining languages: what works and what doesn't. In G Cantoni (ed.) *Stabilizing Indigenous Languages*. Flagstaff, AZ: Northern Arizona University, Center for Excellence in Education.

Fishman, J.A. (1998) Review of Tove Skutnabb-Kangas (ed.). Multilingualism for all. *Language in Society* 27 (3), 413–415.

Haugen, E. (1964) *Bilingualism in the Americas: A Bibliography and Research Guide*. Drawer: University of Alabama Press.

Haugen, E. (1972) *The Ecology of Language. Essays by Einar Haugen*. Introduced and selected by A.S. Dil. Language Science and National Development Series. Stanford, CA: Stanford University Press.

Hoffman, C. (1991) *An Introduction to Bilingualism*. London: Longman.

Holmstrand, L. (1980) *Effekterna på Kunskaper, Färdigheter och Attityder av Tidigt Påbörjad Undervisning i Engelska* [*The Effects on Knowledge, Skills and Attitudes of Early Teaching of English*]. Pedagogisk forskning i Uppsala 18. Uppsala: Pedagogiska Institutionen, Uppsala Universitet.

Holmstrand, L. (1982) *English in the Elementary School. Theoretical and Empirical Aspects of the Early Teaching of English as a Foreign Language*. Acta Universitatis Upsaliensis, Uppsala Studies in Education 18. Stockholm: Almqvist and Wiksell International.

Lind Meløy, L. (1981) *Internatliv i Finnmark. Skolepolitikk 1900–1940* [*Boarding School Life in Finnmark. School Policy 1900–1940*]. Oslo: Det Norske Samalget.

Lo Bianco, J. (1994) *Australian Experiences: Multiculturalism, Language Policy and National Ethos*. Canberra: The National Languages and Literacy Institute of Australia.

Makerere Report (1961) *Report on the Conference on the Teaching of English as a Second Language*. Entebbe: Commonwealth Education Liaison Committee.

Phillipson, R. (1992) *Linguistic Imperialism*. Oxford: Oxford University Press.

Phillipson, R. and Skutnabb-Kangas, T. (1986a) *Linguicism Rules in Education* (3 vols). Roskilde: Roskilde University Centre.

Ramirez, J.D. (1992) Executive summary. *Bilingual Research Journal* 16 (1 and 2), 1–62.

Romaine, S. (1995) *Bilingualism*. Oxford: Blackwell.

Skutnabb-Kangas, T. (1975) *Om Tvåspråkighet och Skolframgång* [*On Bilingualism and School Achievement*]. Forskningsrapport nr 20. Åbo: Svenska Litteratursällskapet i Finland, Nämnd för samhällsforskning.

Skutnabb-Kangas, T. (1984a) *Bilingualism or Not – The Education of Minorities*. Clevedon, UK: Multilingual Matters.

Skutnabb-Kangas, T. (1986) *Minoritet, Språch och Rasism* [*Minority, Language and Racism*]. Malmo: Liber.

Skutnabb-Kangas, T. and Phillipson, R. (1989a) *Wanted! Linguistic Human Rights*. ROLIG-papir 44. Roskilde: Roskilde University Centre.

Vildomec, V. (1963) *Multilingualism*. Leyden: A.W. Sythoff.

Weinreich, U. (1967) *Languages in Contact. Findings and Problems*. The Hague: Mouton and Co.

## Questions

1. Using examples of people you know, show how bilinguals differ in their origins of language, identities, language competences and language uses. Are there bilinguals you know who fall outside these definitions of bilingualism?

2. What are the fallacies in education that Skutnabb-Kangas discusses? Give an example of a school or classroom (known or imaginary) that exemplifies each fallacy.

3. 'Schools cannot save a language on their own . . . but schools can be an important change agent'. What does Skutnabb-Kangas mean by this statement? Discuss in a small group.

4. What does Skutnabb-Kangas mean by linguistic human rights in education? Why is it so difficult to achieve?

## Activities

1. Visit an all-day school or supplementary school in which an ethnic language is taught and which is controlled by the ethnic community. Then visit a public school in which

the same ethnic language is taught. Report on the differences found in school structure, teaching approach, use of the ethnic language, administrators, educators, students and community.

2.   Select a specific ethnolinguistic group. Through interviews with ethnic leaders and others, make a Resource List of places that teach the language. Telephone or visit these places and obtain information on when classes meet, age group, admission requirements, tuition, etc. Complete the Resource List with this information. Create an overall copy of the Resource List by pooling findings from the class. Make copies and disseminate the overall Resource Lists drawn up for different ethnolinguistic groups by your classmates.

3.   Interview a person who was bilingual as a child, but is less so, or not so, now. When, how and why did their balance of languages, language identity, language competences and language uses in different domains change?

4.   Ask two language minority persons, one a monolingual speaker of a minority language who is a non-professional, and the other a bilingual person who is a professional, to tell you about a specific instance in which they have experienced:
     a.  overt language discrimination
     b.  covert language discrimination
     Tape and transcribe their answers. Then compare them. Write an essay summarizing your findings.

5.   Write a play script that reflects the phrase 'language death'. There are many ways 'language death' could be creatively interpreted. Choose the best script in the class and perform the play for other students.

6.   Make a poster in which you portray a mosaic of different languages and their cultures. Display the posters. Select the best for permanent display.

## Further Reading

Baker, C. (2006) *Foundations of Bilingual Education and Bilingualism* (4th edn). Clevedon: Multilingual Matters (chapters 9, 10).

García, O., Skutnabb-Kangas, T. and Torres-Guzmán, M. (eds) (1996) *Imagining Multilingual Schools: Languages in Education*. New York: Teachers College Press.

Krashen, S. (1999) *Condemned Without a Trial: Bogus Arguments Against Bilingual Education*. Portsmouth, NH: Heinemann.

Skutnabb-Kangas, T. (2000) *Linguistic Genocide in Education – Or Worldwide Diversity and Human Rights?* Mahwah, NJ: Erlbaum.

Skutnabb-Kangas, T. and Phillipson, R. (eds) (1994) *Linguistic Human Rights: Overcoming Linguistic Discrimination*. Berlin: Mouton de Gruyter.

# Hard Sell: Why Is Bilingual Education So Unpopular with the American Public?

## James Crawford

Bilingual education has been controversial in the United States since the 1970s. Nevertheless, over the next two decades, it continued to enjoy support from the liberal wing of the Democratic Party and from ethnic politicians, such as the Congressional Hispanic Caucus. When Congress reauthorized the sixth – and final – version of the Bilingual Education Act in 1994, it endorsed a cherished goal of the program's advocates. The stated purpose of the law was no longer simply to foster English language acquisition and academic achievement for limited-English-proficient (LEP) children. For the first time, it would also seek to develop, 'to the extent possible, [their] native language skills' (IASA, Title VII, 1994). Sidestepping a contentious issue that had dominated the 1988 reauthorization of Title VII, legislators eliminated the practice of 'earmarking' funds on the basis of language of instruction. In competing for federal grants, school districts would have the flexibility to choose between various pedagogical models, both bilingual and English-only. Soon the Clinton Administration became active in promoting approaches designed to cultivate bilingualism, including 'two-way' bilingual instruction for English-speaking and language-minority students. The U.S. Secretary of Education declared: 'It is high time we begin to treat language skills as the asset they are, particularly in this global economy' (Riley, 2000).

Many advocates for bilingual education in the 1990s believed the program was entering a new era of public acceptance, as well as marketability to Anglo-American parents. Support from policymakers seemed assured. Then the bottom dropped out. In 1998, California voters overwhelmingly approved Proposition 227, an initiative to dismantle most bilingual instruction in the public schools. Similar measures soon passed by larger margins in Arizona and Mas-sachusetts but failed in Colorado (see Table 1). Although only three states have taken this drastic step so far, together they enroll 43 percent of the nation's English language learners (ELLs).

Meanwhile, the Bush Administration proposed and Congress adopted the No Child Left Behind Act (2002), repealing the Bilingual Education Act and expunging all references to bilingualism as a pedagogical goal. In the name of 'flexibility', the new law turns most federal funding for English-learner programs into block grants administered by the states. Yet, in the name of 'accountability', it features provisions such as mandatory, high-stakes testing in English that are likely to discourage states and districts from supporting native-language instruction.

Because of these policy reversals, the continued availability – perhaps even the survival – of bilingual education for language-minority students in the United States is suddenly in doubt. How did this come to pass?

The short answer is that, in recent years, public opinion has become increasingly hostile. Substantial numbers of Americans who were once supportive of bilingual education, at least in its transitional forms, have moved into the English-only camp. Among politicians and journalists, who both reflect and influence public attitudes, similar trends are evident. Understanding the basis of this shift is key to understanding the present and future prospects of bilingual education.

Obviously, it is important to consider the opinion polls in this area. But such surveys have been generally crude in approach and inconsistent in results. For a more nuanced analysis, it is helpful to study the public debates over bilingual education, especially in the context of electoral campaigns. While attention has been paid to the rhetoric of English-only proponents, arguments

**Table 1** Anti-bilingual education initiatives and enrollments of English language learners, by state, 1998–2002

| Year | Legislation | State | Yes vote | ELLs (2001) |
|------|-------------|-------|----------|-------------|
| 1998 | Proposition 227 | California | 61% | 1,511,646 |
| 2000 | Proposition 203 | Arizona | 63% | 135,248 |
| 2002 | Question 2 | Massachusetts | 68% | 44,747 |
| 2002 | Amendment 31 | Colorado | 44% | 59,018 |

*Sources*: California Secretary of State; Arizona Secretary of State; Massachusetts Elections Division; Colorado Elections Division; National Clearinghouse for English Language Acquisition

supporting bilingual education have rarely been subjected to analysis.

This paper will seek to remedy that omission, exploring the ways in which the issue has been framed by the program's advocates as well as its critics, and the relative success or failure of these approaches. It will begin with a brief overview of voter attitudes toward bilingual education before campaign arguments have been heard. It will consider opposing hypotheses about sources of opposition to the program. It will analyze the various paradigms that have been used to explain bilingual education and evaluate the strategies that have been used to resist English-only campaigns. It will conclude with some recommendations on improving advocacy for language-minority students.

## First Impressions

In the fall of 1997, bilingual educators in California awoke to an unpleasant surprise. An initial opinion survey, conducted eight months before election day, indicated overwhelming support for Proposition 227. Asked whether they would support a measure to 'require all public school instruction to be conducted in English and for students not fluent in English to be placed in a short-term English immersion program', 80 percent of registered voters said yes. That figure included 84 percent of Latinos, 80 percent of moderates, 73 percent of Democrats, and 66 percent of liberals (Los Angeles Times Poll, 1997).

The survey did not mention that if the ballot initiative were adopted, schools would have to dismantle successful bilingual programs; children would 'normally' receive just 180 school days of English instruction before being reassigned to regular classrooms; parents' right to choose native-language instruction would be

severely limited; teachers could be sued personally for alleged violations of the English-only rule; and no repeal or amendment of the law would be possible through the normal legislative process (English Language in Public Schools, 1998).[1] As debate proceeded and voters began to learn about such provisions, support for Proposition 227 declined. Nevertheless, it is clear that the initial poll struck a responsive chord with the term 'English immersion', which connotes an intensive English program tailored to the needs of children learning English.

These results are consistent with other surveys that present the educational options as a zero-sum game. For example, a recent poll commissioned by Public Agenda asked: 'Should public schools teach new immigrants English as quickly as possible even if this means they fall behind, or teach them other subjects in their native language even if this means it takes them longer to learn English?' Among public school parents overall, 67 percent favored teaching English as quickly as possible; among immigrant parents, 73 percent expressed this view (Farkas and Johnson, 1998) found 63 percent support for English immersion versus 33 percent support for bilingual education; the responses were roughly equivalent across ethnic groups. In these and other surveys, language-minority parents have been, if anything, more likely than other respondents to favor an emphasis on English instruction over native-language instruction.

Yet such surveys elicit questionable information about what Americans firmly and truly believe, because they spread false assumptions; many are likely to bias responses against bilingual education. In fact, there is no need to hold children back in English while they learn school subjects in their native language, or to hold them back academically while they acquire

English. Quite the contrary. A generation of research and practice has shown that developing academic skills and knowledge in students' vernacular supports their acquisition of English (see, e.g. Ramírez et al., 1991). At first impression, laypersons tend to find such conclusions counterintuitive, a bit like the advice to 'go West to get East'. But when opinion surveys explain the principles involved – for example, how time spent learning to read in the first language is not wasted learning time because literacy skills transfer to a second language – respondents are generally supportive of bilingual approaches (for a review of this research, see Krashen, 1999).

For most Americans, however, explanations of how bilingual education works are seldom available. Few voters have any direct contact with programs for English learners; they rely on information that is second-hand, superficial, and often erroneous. Media accounts tend to perpetuate stereotypes and misconceptions (McQuillan & Tse, 1996; Crawford, 1998). So do policymakers like Rod Paige, the Bush Administration's secretary of education, who told a journalist: 'The idea of bilingual education is not necessarily a good thing. The goal must be toward English fluency' (Hargrove, 2001).

Advocacy groups have also helped to shape attitudes – at least of the negative variety. While opponents have spent millions on campaigns to discredit bilingual education, supporters of the program have rarely engaged in public relations work. Professional groups like the National Association for Bilingual Education have never made it a priority, even following the crushing defeats for their field in California, Arizona, and Massachusetts. For the most part, they have allowed biased media accounts and unfair criticism by opponents to go unanswered.

Over time, this imbalance has taken a toll. Before the advent of the English-only movement twenty years ago, Americans were generally supportive of native languages in the classroom. In the Houston Metropolitan Area Survey (1983), for example, 68 percent of respondents agreed that schools should be required to offer bilingual education. A national poll conducted that same year found a 67 percent favorability rating for bilingual education among non-Hispanic Americans who had an opinion about it, and 82 percent believed that 'too little' was being spent on such programs (Huddy & Sears, 1990). But as ideological attacks mounted, attitudes changed significantly. Comparing polls from the late 1990s with those from the previous decade, Krashen (2002) found 'a shift of about one-third of the public from mild support (those who would allow one or two years of bilingual education . . .) to the all-English position, with only about 33 percent of the public remaining solid supporters of bilingual education'.

## Racism or Ignorance?

This trend mirrors the level of support for English-only initiatives in the three states where they have passed. But favoring immersion is one thing; banning native-language instruction is quite another. What was it that motivated voters to approve these extreme measures? Two contending explanations have emerged: (1) prejudice against Latinos and other linguistic minorities, and (2) misunderstanding of bilingual education.

Representing the first view, a leader of the organized No on 227 campaign attributes the outcome to 'a reservoir of anger, distrust, and even hate focused on bilingual education, bilingual educators, and immigrants – particularly Spanish-speaking immigrants' (Olsen (1998, p. 4). California's disproportionately white, English-speaking electorate was expressing 'the sense of Spanish ruining this country, the sense of our nation in threat. The sense that upholding English as the language of this nation is a stance of protecting a way of life – this outweighed every argument we could wage to try to defeat 227. This is what we were up against and still are' (p. 8). Olsen concludes that most voters' minds were closed to considering the case for bilingual education: 'It's not just that they don't understand it – they don't like it' (p. 9).

An opposing hypothesis (advanced by myself and others) is that, while ethnocentrism undoubtedly inspires some opposition to bilingual education, ignorance about the subject is a more important factor. According to Krashen (1999), opinion surveys 'suggest . . . that support for Proposition 227 was to a large extent because people felt they were voting "for English"' (p. 95). Indeed, when likely 'yes' voters were asked to explain their motives, 73 percent endorsed the statement: 'If you live in America, you need to speak English' (Los Angeles Times Poll, 1998a). Respondents seemed to view bilingual education as a diversion from, rather than a means toward, that end. If one accepts this as a factual premise, replacing the program with a more effective way to teach English seems not merely reasonable, but beneficial to language-minority students – precisely the argument advanced by sponsors of the initiative.

Of course, some might argue that the English-only supporters in the survey did not sincerely care about the needs of these children, that they were merely unwilling to acknowledge the racism that motivated their votes. In rejecting the Ignorance Hypothesis for the unpopularity of bilingual education, Macedo (2000) asserts:

> This is tantamount to saying that racists do not hate people of color; they are just ignorant.... [O]ne has to realize that *ignorance is never innocent* and is always shaped by a particular ideological predisposition. On another level, the explanation that racist acts or the attack on bilingual education are due to ignorance does not make the victims of these acts feel any better about their victimization. (emphasis added)

Obviously, without entering the minds of the voters, such allegations are difficult to prove. Individuals' motivations are rarely pure or simple, whatever their politics. Feelings about racial and ethnic identity influence the way we perceive the world. There is no question that anti-immigrant biases can and do make some Americans 'uneducable' about the evidence favoring bilingual education. It does not logically follow, however, that all – or even most – skeptics are in this category.

The most thorough study of this issue (Huddy & Sears, 1990) concluded that 'symbolic racism' was a significant predictor of opposition. Nevertheless, such attitudes – including 'resistance to special favors for minorities, anti-Hispanic sentiment, nationalism [directed against immigrants], a general desire for lower levels of government spending, and a resistance to foreign-language instruction' – together accounted for only '25.9 percent of the variance in opposition to bilingual education' (p. 130).

What proponents of the Racism Hypothesis are really saying is that support for bilingual education is sacrosanct – an issue on which good and honest people can never disagree. They suggest that anyone who questions the program's value must have a sinister agenda. Yet those who implicitly advance this claim have offered no evidence on its behalf, other than their own moral outrage. Nor have they accounted for contradictory data, such as the

substantial number of Americans who simultaneously support civil rights and oppose native-language instruction, in the erroneous belief that it segregates immigrant children, fails to teach them English, and limits their opportunities. Latinos (37 percent), Asian Americans (57 percent), Democrats (47 percent), moderates (59 percent), and liberals (36 percent) were well represented among the Californians who voted in favor of Proposition 227. In the same exit poll, only 13 percent of 'no' voters cited 'Bilingual education works' as their reason for opposing the initiative (Los Angeles Times Poll, 1998b). By refusing to discuss the issue of pedagogical effectiveness – or to defend bilingual education in any way – the No on 227 campaign failed to educate many voters who might have been convinced to support the program on its merits (Crawford, 2000). Given those circumstances, it would seem difficult to distinguish the racists from the well meaning but misinformed.

This question has rarely been debated among advocates for bilingual education. Perhaps it should be. Assumptions about negative public attitudes – whether they are based primarily on racism or primarily on ignorance – have played a major role in shaping political strategies for opposing English-only initiatives. Except in one case, those strategies have been unsuccessful. Advocates need to understand why in order to learn from their mistakes.

That said, it should be noted that neither hypothesis is a very sharp instrument for analyzing the ideological obstacles to be overcome. For example, neither can explain the historic slippage of support for bilingual education. There is no reason to believe that Americans are any more hostile toward immigrants and Spanish speakers in 2003 than they were in 1983, the year the English-only movement was launched. If anything, nativism is on the decline. Both Republicans and Democrats are beginning to recognize Latinos as an important voting bloc, and are courting them as never before. Numerous politicians, including the president of the United States, have made a point of learning some Spanish and speaking it in public. It is undeniable that many Anglo-Americans still object to governmental uses of languages other than English. But their visceral reactions are becoming less common now that linguistic diversity is becoming more so.

There is also no evidence that voters know any

less today about methods of teaching English learners than they did in the past. Ignorance about these matters has been constant and pervasive. Huddy and Sears (1990), analyzing data gathered twenty years ago, found that 68 percent of Anglo respondents were unable to provide a 'substantially accurate' description of bilingual education and that 55 percent reported giving little or no thought to the issue.

It is unlikely, of course, that many Americans who have no direct stake in programs for English learners will spontaneously see a need to become knowledgeable in this area. But that does not mean advocates should stop combating misconceptions, especially among journalists, politicians, and other opinion leaders. Ways of thinking about bilingual education can be changed – as, indeed, they have been changed through the relentless propagandizing of opponents in recent years. Educating the voters is not merely a question of curing their ignorance of the facts. Macedo (2000) is correct to stress the importance of the ideological context in which the facts are arranged. The framing of an issue normally determines its political fortunes. For advocates seeking to intervene effectively, the challenge is to determine what the ideological context is and how it functions, rather than relying on moral assumptions to formulate strategy.

## Framing Bilingual Education

Ruíz's (1984) 'orientations in language planning' can be usefully applied to describe rationales for bilingual education:

- *Language as problem* treats limited English proficiency as a handicap for children, as well as a liability for the country, that cries out for remedial attention. Educators need to address the language mismatch between home and school so these students can join mainstream classrooms, earn their diplomas, and become self-supporting. This largely describes the orientation of legislators who drafted the original Bilingual Education Act (1968) and similar state legislation, which emphasized the transition to English as rapidly as possible.
- *Language as right* focuses on equal educational opportunity for minority children whose needs have often been neglected. Viewed through this lens, bilingual education becomes a way to overcome

language barriers that obstruct students' access to the curriculum and keep them from succeeding academically. This was the orientation of language minority parents who sued school districts in cases like *Lau v. Nichols* (1974) demanding an end to the practice of 'sink or swim' instruction.
- *Language as resource* stresses the value of conserving cultural capital – bilingualism in particular – both for individuals and for society. Bilingual education offers a way to develop skills in the heritage language as well as in English and, conversely, to introduce children to the dominant culture without destroying their home culture. This orientation has been associated with the English Plus response to the English-only campaign that emerged in the mid-1980s, but it was largely shared by educators who launched the 'bilingual movement' in the mid-1960s (see Crawford, 2000b).

These distinct approaches might also be described, respectively, as the Remedial Paradigm, the Equal Opportunity Paradigm, and the Multiculturalist Paradigm. Each is more or less consistent as a logical framework and each builds on political values, such as promoting social welfare and productivity, ensuring fair play, and fostering ethnic tolerance. Despite the differences in emphasis, the contradictions among these paradigms are not always obvious. In explaining bilingual education, some advocates (myself included) have incorporated elements of all three. Where the differences become salient is in the public discourse, as policy alternatives are thrashed out. To illustrate this phenomenon, a bit of history is helpful.

## Paradigm Drift

Although the Equal Opportunity Paradigm played a limited role in deliberations that led to the Bilingual Education Act (1968), it became prominent by the mid-1970s. This was due partly to the prevailing political winds, which favored attention to minority rights, and partly to policy developments at the federal level such as *Lau v. Nichols* (1974). One of the few language cases ever to reach the U.S. Supreme Court, this decision had a huge impact on the way Americans thought about bilingual education. Simply put, the court's ruling made schools – not parents or children – responsible for coping with limited English proficiency. Neglecting the issue, as schools had typically done, would henceforth be considered a violation of LEP students' right to an equal education. The court declined to require bilingual instruction, but the Ford and Carter administrations soon did so where school districts had failed to meet their obligations. Using a set of informal guidelines known as the Lau Remedies, officials aggressively enforced the new mandate. Meanwhile, in the Equal Educational Opportunities Act (1974), Congress made the *Lau* decision an explicit part of federal law. Additional lawsuits by Latino parents followed, resulting in further mandates for bilingual education.

Members of the public knew little about the legal technicalities or the pedagogical research in this area. But in principle, the Equal Opportunity Paradigm was not difficult to grasp. It meant opening up the curriculum as a matter of social justice to children who had long been excluded. Bilingual education appeared to be the most promising way to accomplish this goal, according to the federal government and states such as Massachusetts, which also made the program mandatory. Few Americans at the time were inclined to second-guess this conclusion.

On the other hand, it would be a mistake to overestimate the strength of such convictions. When asked what to do about the problem of 'families who come from other countries [with] children who cannot speak English', 82 percent of a national sample said these students should 'be required to learn English in special classes before they are enrolled in the public schools' (Gallup Poll, 1980). Clearly, the Remedial Paradigm remained alive and well. Anglo-Americans who understood bilingual education as a transition to English were likely to support it – unlike those who understood it as a program designed to maintain other languages (Huddy & Sears, 1990). While the Multiculturalist Paradigm was popular with educators and ethnic activists, among the public it was more likely to inspire opposition than acceptance.

By the late 1970s some grumbling was audible. Members of Congress were concerned by a national study that found English learners were not doing especially well in federally funded bilingual programs (Danoff *et al.*, 1978). Some were alarmed that 86 percent of these programs cited the development of students' Spanish skills as one of their goals. Noel Epstein (1977), a *Washington Post* editor, complained in an influential monograph that bilingual educators' goal was to promote 'affirmative ethnicity' – using public funds to preserve minority cultures – rather than a quick transition to the mainstream. The allusion to affirmative action, which was also coming under attack (e.g. in *Bakke v. Regents of University of California*, 1978), was hardly accidental. Reflecting the new impatience with 'special favors' for minorities, Congress banned federal funding for language maintenance programs in 1978. Substantial support for developmental bilingual education would not be restored until the 1990s.

Nevertheless, there was no direct assault on the Equal Opportunity Paradigm – only on the Multiculturalist Paradigm. Support for using bilingual programs to teach English and equip minority students to succeed remained strong. It was the idea of maintaining other languages that drew political fire, first, because it contradicted the idea of a quick transition to English, and second, because it implied a takeover of the program by ethnic militants with a different agenda. Determined opponents of bilingual education, such as Senator S.I. Hayakawa of California, began to argue that the program had nothing to do with civil rights. The real impact, he charged, was to maintain Spanish language enclaves, discourage immigrants from assimilating, and encourage Quebec-style separatism (Hayakawa, 1982). Language as problem, indeed. After leaving Congress in 1983, Hayakawa cofounded an organization called U.S. English to popularize this line of argument and to lobby for English as the nation's official language.

Meanwhile, the Lau Remedies had become a target of criticism. School districts resented the bilingual mandate, and nearly every education interest group opposed a Carter Administration plan to make it a permanent regulation. Soon after, Ronald Reagan was elected on a promise to limit 'big government'. Civil rights regulations in this area were withdrawn and enforcement virtually ceased. Throughout the 1980s federal courts grew increasingly conservative and unsympathetic to petitions for bilingual education. Reagan Administration officials stressed 'local flexibility' rather than local obligations to provide effective programs. They leaked an internal review of the research literature claiming there was no conclusive evidence for the effectiveness of bilingual instruction as compared with all-English approaches (Baker & de Kanter, 1981). Few educational researchers – and none with expertise in language acquisition – endorsed this conclusion. Nevertheless, Reagan's secretary of education William Bennett (1985) cited the report in declaring the Bilingual Education Act 'a failed path'. He argued that 'a sense of cultural pride cannot come at the price of proficiency in English, our common language'. In a sadistic touch, Bennett accused bilingual educators of practicing language maintenance, knowing full well that – while many of them favored developmental approaches – his department was funding transitional programs only. Actually, this was part of a calculated strategy. Bennett sought to pin the Multiculturalist label on bilingual education, hoping to overshadow its Equal Opportunity rationale.

The program's defenders counterattacked by accusing the Education Department of lowering expectations for language-minority students – in effect, for espousing the Remedial Paradigm. James J. Lyons (1985), lobbyist for the National Association for Bilingual Education, charged that Bennett's single-minded focus on the language problem had 'redefined the meaning of equal educational opportunity. . . . [N]o one with an ounce of sense would say that a child who has mastered English but who has not learned mathematics, history, geography, civics, and the other subjects taught in school was educated or prepared for life in this society' (p. 14).

### 'English Plus'

The Spanish-American League Against Discrimination (SALAD), a Miami-based group of Cuban American educators, issued a manifesto that echoed this theme. But it went further, explicitly embracing the Multiculturalist Paradigm:

> Secretary Bennett fears that 'we have lost sight of the goal of learning *English* as key to equal educational opportunity.' We fear that Secretary Bennett has lost sight of the fact that English is *a* key to equal educational opportunity, necessary but not sufficient. English by itself is not enough. NOT ENGLISH ONLY, ENGLISH *PLUS*! . . . English Plus math. Plus science. Plus social studies. Plus equal educational opportunities. English plus competence in the home language. . . .
>
> 'Our common forefathers speak to us through the ages in English.' My fore-

fathers did not speak English, nor did my *foremothers*. Neither did the ancestors of Native Americans, Puerto Ricans, Hispanics in the Southwest and California territories, the French in the Louisiana Territory, the Germans in the Midwest, or the Asians, Italians, Poles, Greeks, Arabs, or Afro-Americans throughout this nation. Linguistic chauvinism has no place in today's interdependent world. . . . To say that we make our country stronger because we make it 'U.S. English' is like saying that we make it stronger by making it 'U.S. White'. It is as insidious to base the strength or unity of the United States in one language as it is to base that strength or unity in one race. (Quoted in Feinberg, 2002, pp. 238–239; emphases in original)

For most opponents of the English-only movement, English Plus soon became the chief rallying cry and policy alternative (Combs, 1992). While championing the civil rights of language minorities, it put greater stress on the benefits of multilingual skills (EPIC, 1987). This tendency is summed up in popular slogans like 'Two languages are better than one' and 'Bilingualism is beautiful'. Allies in Congress sponsored an English Plus Resolution (1995) citing the national interest in developing language resources that would enhance U.S. trade, diplomacy, culture, social welfare, and human relations. Such high-minded arguments – which are hard to fault in principle – appealed especially to language educators, ethnic advocacy groups, and persons who were already bilingual. The problem was that English Plus generated limited enthusiasm in other quarters. Perhaps that was because improving foreign language teaching hardly seemed an urgent matter for most Americans, who placed it on a par with, say, improving music or art instruction. Meanwhile, the broader multiculturalist campaign to celebrate 'difference' was beginning to provoke a backlash. To many, the meaning of English Plus was not immediately obvious (English plus *what*?), which created further suspicions (Combs, 1992).

Most problematic was the fact that English Plus tended to reinforce the ideological frame that Hayakawa and Bennett were trying to erect: that the priority of bilingual education was not to teach English but to maintain other languages. This described neither the aspirations of most language-minority parents nor the reality of most bilingual classrooms. It sounded credible, however, as educators talked less about civil rights and more about the wonders of speaking two languages. By the 1990s the Multiculturalist Paradigm had come to dominate their advocacy. The Stanford Working Group (Hakuta *et al.*, 1993), for example, successfully pressured Congress and the Clinton Administration to add heritage language development as a priority in awarding Title VII funds. (The expert panel's other recommendations for improving the education of English learners were couched primarily in terms of school reform and accountability.) Further encouragement came from a major federal study (Ramírez *et al.*, 1991), which confirmed that developmental bilingual education was a superior way to foster academic achievement in English and bilingualism, too. Truly 'the best of both worlds', as enthusiasts had sloganized in the 1970s. But now it was the world of language diversity that most excited the field. For many educators, the goal of bilingualism seemed to occupy a higher moral plane than the goal of success in the English mainstream. This viewpoint remains common. A recent bilingual education conference featured the following keynote addresses: 'Language Education Policy in a Multilingual Globalized World', 'Just About Everyone Can Become Bilingual', and 'Let's Cure Monolingualism and Save the World' (NYSABE, 2003).

Meanwhile, many researchers had tired of the polarized and simplistic debate over bilingual versus English-only instruction (e.g. August and Hakuta, 1997). Transitional programs, often fraught with weaknesses unrelated to language, had few enthusiasts. Yet there was increasing excitement about two-way bilingual education, or – to use the more sanitized term – 'dual immersion'.[2] Here was a perfect example of English Plus. Rather than a special program to help disadvantaged students overcome academic deficits, this would be an enrichment program designed to serve all students. The theory was that language-majority and language-minority children would both contribute valuable resources, learn each others' languages at no cost to academic achievement, and everyone would benefit. If enough English-speaking parents could be won over, the future of bilingual education would be secure. As it happened, two-way programs did grow significantly – more than tenfold – between 1987 and 2001 (Center for Applied Linguistics, 2002). Despite limited

evidence from controlled studies (see Krashen, forthcoming), their pedagogical promise has been widely hailed. Politically, however, things did not work out quite as planned.

## English-Only, Phase II

For U.S. English, bilingual education served as a convenient symbol for the menace of bilingualism: a source of 'language ghettos', divided loyalties, and illiteracy in English. In one magazine advertisement assailing the program, it used the headline: 'Last Year Our Government Spent Nearly $8 Billion Abusing Children'. Such scare tactics were effective in fundraising and advocacy for English-as-official-language legislation. But the rhetoric was so extreme and the nativism so transparent that U.S. English seldom played any serious role in policy debates. The group engaged in some minor skirmishes, but it never mounted a frontal assault on bilingual education. It concentrated instead on promoting English-only restrictions in government, from which native-language instruction was routinely exempted. If there was ever a paper tiger, U.S. English was it. More sophisticated predators, however, were lurking nearby.

The new opponents presented themselves as mainstream conservatives, not single-issue zealots. By posing as advocates for immigrant parents, they saw a way to reconstruct the Equal Opportunity Paradigm as a frame for attacking bilingual education. In a widely circulated *Reader's Digest* article, Linda Chávez (1995) told the stories of children allegedly victimized by a 'multibillion-dollar bureaucracy' – misassigned to bilingual classrooms, held there against their parents' will, and prevented from learning English. While Russian, Korean, and Chinese children were given 'intensive ESL classes', she charged, Hispanic students were forced to study mostly in their native language and held back academically. Her so-called Center for Equal Opportunity financed a lawsuit on behalf of Latino parents in New Mexico, claiming their children were being discriminated against by state policies mandating Spanish instruction. A federal judge later threw out the case (*Carbajal et al. v. Albuquerque Public Schools*, 1999), but it more than paid for itself in media exposure. The tables were turned: bilingual education was now portrayed as a civil rights violation.

This claim received wider circulation in 1996, when a group of Spanish-speaking parents pulled their children out of school for two weeks, claiming that the Los Angeles school district was refusing to teach their children English. At least, that was how the news media portrayed these events: as an epic tale of downtrodden immigrants rebelling against autocratic officials. The reality was more complicated. To remove their children from bilingual classrooms, all the parents would have needed to do was go to the school principal's office and sign a form. But the local activist who organized the boycott – and also provided child care on which the parents depended – urged them not to do so. This prolonged the conflict and generated negative headlines for bilingual education around the country (Crawford, 1998).

Enter Ron Unz, a software millionaire, aspiring politician, and 'movement conservative'. Immediately he recognized a target of opportunity. Here was a liberal do-gooder program, a relic of the 1960s welfare state, that was being rejected by its intended beneficiaries. No one appeared to support or understand bilingual education except those employed to run it and their academic supporters – in other words, people whose opinions could be dismissed as self-serving. Organizing public opposition would be simple in any case, because teaching students in Spanish when they needed to learn English seemed to defy common sense. The purported victims would make wonderful poster children – literally – while parents carrying picket signs would recall images of the Chicano civil rights movement; except that the shoe would be on the Right foot this time. The California legislature had been deadlocked over bilingual education for years by ethnic politics, but a ballot initiative would not face that problem. It would attract enormous media attention, both for the issue and for the sponsor himself. Unz was prepared to finance the campaign single-handedly. So he formed a political action committee, named it 'English for the Children', and laid out his case on the Internet:

Begun with the best of theoretical intentions some twenty or thirty years ago, bilingual education has proven itself a dismal practical failure, especially in California. Today, 25% of all California children in public schools – almost 1.4 million – are classified as not proficient in English. . . . We believe that the unity and prosperity of our society is gravely threatened by government efforts to prevent young immigrant children

from learning English. Our initiative will end bilingual education by ensuring that all California schoolchildren are taught English, unless there are special circumstances and their parents object. If it passes, today's immigrant children will be given the same opportunity to become educated, productive members of society that our own immigrant ancestors enjoyed. (English for the Children, 1997)

Bilingual education versus English acquisition, failure versus opportunity, preventing children from learning English versus ensuring their right to do so. The Equal Opportunity Paradigm could sound convincing even when turned inside out. To bolster his case, Unz seized on an obscure statistic. 'Under the current system, centered on bilingual education', he charged, 'only about 5 percent of these children each year are found to have gained proficiency in English. *Thus, our state's current system of language instruction has an annual failure rate of 95 percent*' (English for the Children, 1997; emphasis in original). In fact, less than a third of the state's English learners were in fully bilingual classrooms. Neither research nor experience supported a one-year standard for English acquisition, and – for the record – that year's 'redesignation rate' was 7 percent. But the news media seemed to fall in love with Unz's sound-bite and seldom applied any critical scrutiny. The '95 percent failure rate' became a mantra repeated in scores, if not hundreds, of press reports during the campaign (Crawford, 1998).

To burnish his 'pro-immigrant' image, Unz took pains to distance himself from U.S. English and other traditional English-only groups, with their anti-Latino baggage. Moreover, in drafting Proposition 227, he inserted a provision guaranteeing that 'all California school children have the right to be provided with an English language public education' (English Language in Public Schools, 1998, Sec. 320). Nativist fringe groups, which wanted to terminate public services to 'illegal aliens', predictably attacked the initiative. This boosted Unz's credibility with the news media and with moderate and liberal voters who were already skeptical of bilingual education. Most conservatives, meanwhile, needed no convincing to oppose the program. It's no wonder that Proposition 227 started out with 80 percent support in the polls.

## Survival Strategies

Faced with this juggernaut, bilingual education advocates sought advice from political professionals on how to respond to Unz's initiatives in California, Colorado, and Massachusetts (in Arizona they lacked the resources to do so). These consultants commissioned polling and focus groups to sample the views of likely voters, and they returned with the news that bilingual education was rather unpopular. In California, for example, 79 percent of respondents felt that schools 'spent too much time teaching students in non-English languages'; 69 percent thought that the state was 'spending $400 million a year on a failed program'; and 74 percent believed that English immersion 'would move students quickly into regular classrooms'. When counter-arguments to Proposition 227 were tested, the most promising were the threat of personal lawsuits against educators (61 percent said that might persuade them to vote 'no'); the arbitrary mainstreaming of English learners after one year (57 percent); and the folly of mixing students by age and grade (55 percent) (Citizens for an Educated America, [1997]).

Based on these surveys, the political consultants reached essentially the same conclusion in all three states: *If voters perceive this measure as a referendum on bilingual education, it will pass easily. A winning strategy would have to divert their attention to other issues – for example, to various extreme provisions of the initiative.* In other words, none of the familiar paradigms for explaining the program looked promising. The only hope would be to change the subject, rather than try to make the case for bilingual education. As one campaign consultant told an expert in the field who had been invited to debate Ron Unz:[3]

> I CANNOT win on the facts – at least not as you and my other friends in the bilingual community would articulate them. And as you know, Unz does not play fair. Therefore, my job is to create confusion and controversy rather than debate dueling test scores with Ron. Liberals spend too much time beating their chest in righteous defeat. . . . Winners make the laws! (Welchert, 2002; emphasis in original.)

Generally speaking, the official campaign groups opposing Unz followed this advice. In California, they went so far as to post it on their web site: '*DO NOT* get into a discussion defending bilingual education' (Citizens for an Educated America, 1998; emphasis in original). But the No on 227 campaign never found its voice, jumping from one diversionary tactic to another without arousing much voter interest. Arizona opponents of Proposition 203 focused primarily on the threat to 'parents' rights' – in a state where school choice is revered – but also got nowhere. (This approach never received a serious test, however, because the campaign was so disorganized, divided, and underfunded.) In Massachusetts, the No on Question 2 committee used as its main slogan 'Don't Sue Teachers', another poll-driven strategy that proved disastrous, allowing Unz to score his biggest landslide in a reputedly liberal state. Opponents of Colorado's Amendment 31, who called themselves English Plus, adopted a similar ploy of diverting attention from bilingual education to the initiative's unsavory features. They stressed the potential cost to taxpayers, the punitive provisions for educators, and the denial of parents' right to choose. But there the results were quite different, as Unz suffered his first defeat in what most considered a conservative state. The same day that he won by 36 percentage points in Massachusetts he was losing by 12 percentage points in Colorado (see Table 1).

What accounts for the disparity in outcomes? On the surface, it would seem that if the strategies were similar, the difference must have been in how they were executed or in what the English-only side did wrong. According to its leaders (Escamilla *et al.*, 2002), Colorado's No on 31 campaign was well organized and broad-based. It also benefited from a $3 million contribution from a local billionaire who had a child in two-way bilingual education. The money enabled opponents to mount an intensive advertising blitz against the initiative in a state where most voters are concentrated in a single media market. Their counterparts in Massachusetts worked hard, but were less successful on all of these counts. With limited resources behind it, the Don't Sue Teachers message never caught on. The campaign had limited impact beyond the ranks of progressive educators. Meanwhile, the English-only effort in Colorado relied heavily on two political mavericks, Rita Montero and Dick Lamm, who – along with Unz himself – alienated the state's Republican establishment. In Massachusetts, by contrast, the Republican candidate for governor made support for Question 2 a centerpiece of his winning campaign.

Another plausible explanation is that the libertarian, albeit conservative, culture of Colorado was simply inhospitable to a heavy-handed English-only mandate. That hypothesis is undercut, however, by the fact that Arizona, a neighboring state with similar traditions, overwhelmingly approved an Unz initiative in 2000. While parental choice and local control of schools are popular in both states, voters are generally more pragmatic than ideological. They tend to ask: 'Choice for what purpose?' Absent a convincing case for bilingual education, libertarian objections to either Amendment 31 or Proposition 203 would seem to have played a minor role in these elections.

One might also speculate that money proved decisive in Colorado. No doubt the $3 million contribution was extremely helpful – putting the English Plus campaign in the same league as candidates for governor and U.S. Senator. But opponents of Proposition 227 also raised a substantial sum, nearly $5 million, enabling them to run television commercials throughout California. Ultimately, the No campaigns in both states outspent the English-only side on advertising by about 20–1.

## How the 'Good Guys' Won

There was one other significant difference. In Colorado, Unz's opponents tried a new type of diversionary approach, which could be summarized as: *If you can't beat racism, then try to exploit it.* Their television commercials stressed the initiative's threat to Anglo children, charging that it would 'knowingly force children who can barely speak English into regular classrooms, creating chaos and disrupting learning' (*Rocky Mountain News*, 2002a). By implication, a vote to preserve bilingual education would be a vote to preserve segregation.

On the day after the election, the political consultants for English Plus, John Britz and Steve Welchert, laid out their strategy for a journalist (Mitchell, 2002). First, they had determined early on that bilingual education was too complicated to explain to skeptical voters. 'Nobody understands what it is', Britz said. 'We didn't'. Second, 'our polling show[ed] no sensitivity to the Latino culture in Colorado. . . . If this is about being Mexican, for Mexicans, about Mexicans, it's gone'. They concluded that, to win over a largely Anglo electorate, they had to appeal directly to Anglo self-interest:

An 'a-ha' moment came in September, Britz said. They were interviewing what they considered a typical suburban voter – female, Republican, a parent. The woman was adamant in her support of 31. Then Britz said her own children would be affected. That her child's teacher might be distracted by having to work with students who know little English. 'She turned', he said. 'She said, *"They're going to put them in my kid's class?"'* That moment led to what would become a key slogan for No on 31 – the controversial 'Chaos in the Classroom' theme hammered home in their TV ads. . . .

[T]he TV spots are dark, showing still pictures of sad-looking children while an announcer ominously lists the faults in Amendment 31. In one, the announcer states children who speak little English, largely Hispanic students, would disrupt the education of 'your children' – presumably the majority white families of Colorado. . . .

As for the merits of the campaign and the criticism it has drawn, the two say that's politics. Welchert recalls [an] early meeting with Hispanic leaders. 'Do you want to win?' he asked them, 'or do you want to be right?' (Mitchell, 2002; emphasis added)

This well circulated message was qualitatively different from any that Unz's opponents had used before. And it appears to have been effective. In an election in which Republicans swept most offices statewide, Amendment 31 was easily defeated, failing in 54 of 64 counties (CNN.com, 2002). While a majority of Latinos appear to have voted against the English-only measure – as they have generally done in other states[4] – they represented just 10 percent of Colorado's electorate, down from 14 percent in 2000 (Sailer, 2002). It was the white Anglos, including many conservatives who broke from their usual pattern of support for Unz, that made the difference. 'Chaos in the Classroom' is the most likely explanation.

Notwithstanding its success, questions remain about the strategy. Is there a price to be paid when English-only opponents exploit racism toward Latino children? Does their credibility suffer when they implicitly endorse the segregation of English language learners? How secure is bilingual education in the long term when its advocates make little attempt to defend it against criticism? Can this struggle be won by tricking the voters, without honestly addressing their concerns and correcting their misconceptions? Do the facts matter at all in this debate?

Escamilla *et al.* (2002) argue that 'the significance of this victory' in Colorado should outweigh any tactical compromises that were made:

> To date, we are the only state that has been able to mount a significant fight against Ron Unz and his one year English Immersion 'poison pill' for ELL children. . . . What does this mean? It means that for the first time, in years, our teachers, administrators, parents and children have something to celebrate instead of something to fear. It means that for even a short little while we can think that sometimes 'the good guys win'.

While declining to defend the message of the TV spots, the English Plus leaders insist that they had overcome Unz's lead in the polls even before the $3 million in advertisements began to air. Presumably, they could have won without them. Yet they fail to explain how their campaign otherwise differed from those that failed so badly in California, Arizona, and Massachusetts.

Pimentel (2002) offers a more forthright justification for how the 'good guys' won:

> Campaigns, unfortunately, are often not about who has the facts, but about who has the most effective message. . . . In Colorado, a big part of the message was, essentially, that Spanish-speaking children would be mainstreamed too soon. The implicit message: Your own kids will suffer because they will be in classes with kids who don't speak, read or write English well. Unz promptly accused the anti-initiative folks of scare tactics and race-baiting. (Which strikes me a lot like the pot calling the kettle black). But truth is a defense here. Kids in English immersion are more likely to be pushed into the mainstream before they're ready. It's why so many educators oppose efforts to dismantle bilingual ed. Yes, 'chaos in the classroom', as the commercials were tagged, probably wasn't intended to appeal to Colorado voters' sense of fairness. . . . A billionaire trumps a millionaire. Not fair? Probably. But neither have been English-

for-the-Children campaigns that relied on simplistic, coded and well-funded messages to elicit knee-jerk reactions.

This kind of reasoning, by Pimentel and others, seems like a rather slippery slope. There is a logical progression between the premises that:

- Strong opposition to bilingual education among the American public is based largely on bigotry.
- Bigots cannot be persuaded by rational arguments about what is best for English language learners.
- If the facts do not matter in this debate, defending bilingual education against erroneous charges is a waste of time.
- The English-only campaign is so unjust that any tactics that work in opposing it are legitimate – including tactics that exploit racism toward LEP children.

Certainly, there was some truth in the English Plus advertisements. Unz's initiatives require English learners to be mainstreamed after one year, before most of these children are ready. That arbitrary approach is likely to harm students' academic growth and place undue demands on mainstream teachers, which would mean less attention to the needs of other students. All children could suffer. It is a reasonable argument, which opponents had used before. What was new in the Colorado campaign was the implication that bilingual education should be preserved as a way to segregate minority children so they would not disrupt the education of English-speaking children. That goal, if not the means, would be endorsed by most nativists and denounced by most Latino parents. Such a cynical tactic seems to break faith with the core constituency of bilingual education, a risky proposition for a program with so few active supporters. It could also damage what credibility the field has left with journalists, politicians, and other opinion leaders. Indeed, the 'chaos' commercials were vilified in a Colorado newspaper that opposed the initiative (*Rocky Mountain News*, 2002a).

In appealing to Anglo voters, the English Plus consultants accurately gauged the weakness of the Multiculturalist Paradigm. But by making no argument about the benefits of bilingual education for English learners, they abandoned the Equal Opportunity Paradigm for (at best) the Remedial Paradigm, which conceives language-minority students as a 'problem' for the schools and for society (cf. Gallup, 1980). Moreover, by offering no defense of bilingual education on pedagogical grounds, they opened the door to restrictive legislation in the future. Governor Bill Owens, a Republican who opposed Amendment 31 because of its sue-the-educators provision, nevertheless endorsed the 'worthy goal' behind it: a mandate for English immersion (Sanko, 2002). A 'moderate' bill along those lines failed in the Colorado legislature in 2003, but is likely to be back next year.

## What Next?

In responding to English-only campaigns, advocates face some fundamental choices. First, should they continue to rely on diversionary tactics to mislead voters and outmaneuver opponents? Or should they work actively to explain the rationale for bilingual education and win public support on its merits? So far the former approach has worked once, thanks to an unprincipled message and a billionaire's donation. The latter remains largely untried. In the intellectual battle over bilingual education, the campaigns opposing Ron Unz surrendered without firing a shot. Lacking the resolve to defend their profession or the wherewithal to divert voters' attention, they suffered disastrous defeats in three states. Surely there is a lesson here.

Second, advocates need to decide how to organize themselves for maximum effect. Are professional organizations now supplying the needed leadership? Is their focus on legislative lobbying, to the exclusion of media work and community outreach, sufficient to improve the standing of bilingual education? Or would an activist approach make more sense, one that attempts to shape public opinion and mobilize grassroots support? At a time when traditional allies, including most Latino politicians, are keeping a low profile on the issue, do bilingual educators need to take more responsibility for their own fate? It should be noted that, as individuals, numerous members of the field are already devoting themselves to advocacy in various ways. Some are making headway, scoring occasional victories at the local level. The campaigns against Unz's initiatives demonstrated, however, that without sustained and coordinated efforts, the impact of such work is usually limited. Those who hope to prevent

further erosion of political support and further English-only restrictions need to regroup behind more effective approaches.

Finally, for advocates who recognize the urgency of the situation, there is the question of strategy. Should they rely primarily on the Multiculturalist Paradigm, seeking to win over the American public with arguments like 'bilingualism is beautiful'? Or should they revive the Equal Opportunity paradigm, which once generated passion in Latino communities and sympathy among many Anglos? Writing more than a decade ago, Huddy and Sears (1990) were accurate in predicting political adversity for bilingual education to the extent it 'is portrayed as cultural and linguistic maintenance'. Their article appeared just as the Multiculturalist Paradigm began to become dominant within the field and among some federal and state policymakers. During the 1990s, as public resistance increased, advocates became increasingly wedded to this approach – for example, showering attention on two-way programs that still enroll just 1–2 percent of the nation's LEP students. Simultaneously, they downplayed the role of bilingual education in fostering English acquisition and academic achievement in English. Yet those goals remain paramount not only with the American public, but also with language-minority communities. While many parents place value on bilingualism as well, opinion surveys leave no doubt that equal opportunity is their chief concern. The former should by no means be ignored. But the latter deserves a great deal more emphasis than it has recently received.

Times have changed, of course. There is no guarantee that a rationale for bilingual education that made sense to many Americans in 1973 or 1983 would be equally compelling in 2003. But the Equal Opportunity Paradigm offers some clear advantages. First, it would help to assuage public worries that the program has been diverted from its original purpose: to prepare English learners to succeed in an English-dominant society. Second, it would provide a context to clarify how bilingual education works, debunk pervasive myths, and address honest concerns about whether students are learning. Third, it would inspire renewed activism among language-minority parents and communities. Finally, it would appeal to all Americans' best instincts – in particular, their sense of fairness – and challenge them to do what is best for language-minority children.

## Notes

1. For a survey more detailed than the Los Angeles Times Poll – and yielding very different results – see Krashen *et al.* (1998).
2. Other labels include 'dual language' and 'two-way bilingual immersion'.
3. Stephen Krashen had been invited to represent English Plus, the group opposing Unz in Colorado, in a September 4, 2002, debate sponsored by the Denver School Board. Krashen withdrew after English Plus informed him that they were urging all supporters of the No on 31 campaign to stay 'on message' and that the message would not include any defense of bilingual education (S. Krashen, personal communication, April 25, 2003).
4. No exit poll sampled Latino voting on Amendment 31, although county results indicated substantial opposition (*Rocky Mountain News*, 2002b). In California, 63 percent of Latinos said they had opposed Proposition 227 (Los Angeles Times Poll, 1998b). An exit poll by the Gaston Institute at the University of Massachusetts, Boston, reported that 92 percent of Latinos in urban areas voted against that state's Question 2 (Hayward, 2002). No exit poll was conducted for Arizona's Proposition 203; voting patterns in heavily Latino precincts were mixed, ranging from strong opposition in Tucson to mild support in Phoenix.

## References

August, D. and Hakuta, K. (eds) (1997) *Improving schooling for language-minority students: A research agenda.* Washington, DC: National Academy Press.

Baker, K.A. and de Kanter, A.A. (1981) *Effectiveness of bilingual education: A review of the literature.* Washington, DC: U.S. Department of Education, Office of Planning, Budget, and Evaluation.

*Bakke v. Regents of University of California* (1978) 438 U.S. 265.

Bennett, W.J. (1985) In defense of our common language. Speech to the Association for a Better New York, September 26. Rpt. in J. Crawford (ed.), *Language loyalties: A source book on the official English controversy* (pp. 358–363). Chicago: University of Chicago Press, 1992.

Bilingual Education Act (1968) P.L. 90–247. January 2.

*Carbajal et al. v. Albuquerque Public Schools* (1999)

D. New. Mex. Case No. CIV 98–279 MV/DJS. May 11. [Online]. Available: http://ourworld. compuserve.com/homepages/JWCRAWFORD/carbajal.htm

Center for Applied Linguistics (2002) Two-way immersion programs: Features and statistics. [Online]. Available: http://www. cal.org/twi/directory/

Chávez, L. (1995) One nation, one common language. *Reader's Digest* (August): 87–91.

Citizens for an Educated America (1997) *California's Unz initiative on bilingual education: Summary of focus groups and statewide voter survey.*

Citizens for an Educated America (1998) *Sample letter-to-the-editor points.*

CNN.com (2002) Elections 2002 – County results: Colorado Amendment 31. [Online document:] http://www.cnn.com/ELECTION/2002/pages/states/CO/I/01/county.000.html

Combs, M.C. (1992) English Plus: Responding to English Only. In J. Crawford (ed.) *Language loyalties: A source book on the official English controversy,* (pp. 216–224). Chicago: University of Chicago Press

Crawford, J. (1998) The bilingual education story: Why can't the news media get it right? Presentation to the National Association of Hispanic Journalists, Miami, June 26. [Online]. Available: http://ourworld.compuserve.com/homepages/JWCRAWFORD/NAHJ.htm

Crawford, J. (2000a) The Proposition 227 campaign: A post mortem. In *At war with diversity: U.S. language policy in an age of anxiety* (pp. 104–137). Clevedon, UK: Multilingual Matters.

Crawford, J. (2000b) The political paradox of bilingual education. In *At war with diversity: U.S. language policy in an age of anxiety* (pp. 84–103). Clevedon, UK: Multilingual Matters.

Danoff, M.N. *et al.* (1978) *Evaluation of the impact of ESEA Title VII Spanish/English bilingual education programs. Vol. 3, Year two impact data, educational process, and in-depth analysis.* Palo Alto, CA: American Institutes for Research.

English for the Children (1997) Proposition 227: The 1998 California 'English for the Children' initiative. [Online document:] http://www. onenation.org/index.html

English Language in Public Schools (1998) Initiative statute (Proposition 227) [Online]. Available: http://Primary98.ss.ca.gov/VoterGuide/Propositions/227.htm

English Plus Information Clearinghouse (EPIC) (1987) Statement of purpose. Rpt. in J.

Crawford (ed.) *Language loyalties: A source book on the official English controversy* (pp. 151–153). Chicago: University of Chicago Press, 1992.

English Plus Resolution (1995) H. Con. Res. 83 (104th Cong., 1st Sess.), July 13.

Epstein, N. (1977) *Language, ethnicity, and the schools: Policy alternatives for bilingual-bicultural education.* Washington, DC: Institute for Educational Leadership.

Equal Educational Opportunities Act (1974) 20 U.S.C. §1701 et seq.

Escamilla, K. *et al.* (2002) Colorado's Amendment 31: An emic perspective. November 11. AZBLE Listserv. [Online document:] http://lists.asu.edu/cgi-bin/wa?A2=ind0211&L=azble&F=&S=&P=8957

Farkas, S. and Johnson, J. (1998) *A lot to be thankful for: What parents want children to learn about America.* New York: Public Agenda Foundation.

Feinberg, R.C. (2002) *Bilingual education: A reference handbook.* Santa Barbara, CA: ABC-CLIO.

Gallup Poll (1980) Education, September 5. In *Public opinion, 1980.* Wilmington, DE: Scholarly Resources, Inc, 1981.

Gallup Poll (1998) Bilingual education, June 6. In *Public opinion, 1998.* Wilmington, DE: Scholarly Resources, Inc, 1999.

Hakuta, K. *et al.* (1993) *Federal education programs for limited-English-proficient students: A blueprint for the second generation.* Stanford, CA: Stanford Working Group.

Hargrove, T. (2001) Many Hispanics in charter schools. *Rocky Mountain News,* November 2.

Hayakawa, S.I. (1982) Testimony on S. 2002. In U.S. Congress, Senate Committee on Labor and Human Resources, Subcommittee on Education, Arts, and Humanities, *Bilingual education amendments of 1981* (97th Cong., 2nd Sess.), April 23.

Hayward, E. (2002) Voters go for change in state bilingual ed. *Boston Herald,* November 6.

Houston Metropolitan Area Survey (1983) Houston, TX: Center for Public Policy, College of Social Sciences, University of Houston.

Huddy, L. and Sears, D.O. (1990) Qualified public support for bilingual education: Some policy implications. *Annals of the American Academy of Political and Social Science* 508 (March): 119–134.

Improving America's Schools Act (IASA) (1994) P.L. 103–382, Title VII. October 20.

Krashen, S.D. (1999) *Condemned without a trial: Bogus arguments against bilingual education.* Portsmouth, NH: Heinemann.

Krashen, S. (2002) Evidence suggesting that public opinion is becoming more negative: A discussion of the reasons, and what we can do about it. [Online]. Available: http://ourworld.compuserve.com/homepages/JWCRAWFORD/Krash11.htm

Krashen, S. (Forthcoming) Two-way bilingual education: What does the research really say?

Krashen, S., Crawford, J. and Kim, H. (1998) Bias in polls on bilingual education: A demonstration. [Online]. Available: http://ourworld.compuserve.com/homepages/JWCRAWFORD/USCpoll.htm

*Lau v. Nichols* (1974) 414 U.S. 563.

Los Angeles Times Poll (1997) *Study #400: California issues and politics.* October 15 [Online]. Available: http://www.latimes.com/extras/timespoll/stats/pdfs/400ss.pdf

Los Angeles Times Poll (1998a) *Study #410: California politics.* April 13 [Online]. Available: http://latimes.com/extras/timespoll/stats/pdfs/410ss/pdf

Los Angeles Times Poll (1998b) *Study #413: Exit poll, California primary election.* June 2. [Online]. Available: http://www.latimes.com/extras/timespoll/stats/pdfs/413ss.pdf

Lyons, J.J. (1985) Education secretary Bennett on bilingual education: Mixed up or malicious? *NABE News* 9 (1): 1, 14. Rpt. in J. Crawford (ed.) *Language loyalties: A source book on the official English controversy* (pp. 363–366). Chicago: University of Chicago Press, 1992.

Macedo, D. (2000) The colonialism of the English Only movement. *Educational Researcher* 29 (3). [Online]. Available: http://www.aera.net/pubs/er/arts/29–03/macedo03.htm

McQuillan, J. and Tse, L. (1996) Does research really matter? An analysis of media opinion on bilingual education, 1984–1994. *Bilingual Research Journal* 20 (1): 1–27.

Mitchell, N. (2002) Colorado hands English immersion backer his first loss. *Rocky Mountain News,* November 6. [Online]. Available: http://www.rockymountainnews.com/drmn/election/article/0,1299,DRMN_36_1526987,00.html

New York State Association for Bilingual Education (NYSABE) (2003) Conference program. [Online]. Available: http://www.nysabe.org/

No Child Left Behind Act (2002) P.L. 107–110, Title III. January 8.

Olsen, L. (1998) Reflections on the key role of two-way bilingual immersion programs in this Proposition 227 era. Keynote speech,

Two-Way Bilingual Immersion Conference, Santa Barbara, CA, June 28.

Pimentel, O.R. (2002) Bilingual-ed issue turns on money. *Arizona Republic*, November 16.

Ramírez, J.D., Yuen, S.D. and Ramey, D.R. (1991) *Final report: Longitudinal study of structured English immersion strategy, early-exit and late-exit transitional bilingual education programs for language-minority children*. San Mateo, CA: Aguirre International.

Riley, W. (2000) Excelencia para todos – Excellence for all: The progress of Hispanic education and the challenges of a new century. Speech delivered at Bell Multicultural High School, Washington, DC, March 15.

*Rocky Mountain News* (2002a) Editorial: The lies told about Amendment 31. October 22.

*Rocky Mountain News* (2002b) Hispanics on 31. November 7.

Ruíz, R. (1984) Orientations in language planning. *NABE Journal* 8 (2): 15–34.

Sailer, S. (2002) Analysis: Whites, not Latinos, win for GOP. United Press International. November 12. [Online]. Available: http://www.upi.com/view.cfm?StoryID = 20021111–033923–4196r

Sanko, J.J. (2002) Owens decries bilingual plan. *Rocky Mountain News*, October 2.

Welchert, S. (2002) RE: bounced back. Email message to S. Krashen, August 28. [Quoted with the author's permission.]

## Questions

1. List the reasons why Crawford believes that bilingual education is controversial and unpopular with major elements of the U.S. public. Which of these reasons do you think are based on evidence and which result more from prejudice?
2. What are the grounds given in this article for advocating bilingual education? Which of these grounds do you think are based on research, which on advocacy, and which are a mixture?
3. What are the beliefs of the English-Only movement according to Crawford? What is different about their two phases? What, in contrast, are the English Plus beliefs?
4. Trace the development of bilingual education policy in the United States from 1968 when the Bilingual Education Act was passed to the present.
5. Crawford argues that the Equal Opportunity Paradigm is the strongest platform to advocate bilingual education in the U.S. What is meant by an Equal Opportunity Paradigm? Why does Crawford believe this produces the strongest case?

## Activities

1. Using the WWW, research: Proposition 227 in California, Proposition 203 in Arizona, Question 2 in Massachusetts and Amendment 31 in Colorado. What were the main elements in each initiative? What did surveys and polls reveal about public opinion? What marketing and advocacy techniques were used? What role did Ron Unz play? What were the outcomes?
2. What is the distinction between language as a problem, right and a resource? Give examples of each orientation at both an individual person and societal level. Compare answers in a group and decide into which language orientation the leaders (e.g. politicians) of local community best fit.
3. Prepare a debate with people speaking for and against bilingual education. Present the debate to a wider audience, and ask the audience to vote at the end for or against bilingual education. Ensure that the debate includes definitions of bilingual education.

4.  Design a poster with one or a few slogans to market bilingualism in children. Commence with one of the following slogans or create your own:

    'Blessed with Bilingual Brains'.

    'Two Languages: Twice the Choice'.

    Add suitable images from the WWW, and create a WWW page or poster to display the slogan and images.

## Further Reading

Baker, C. (2006) *Foundations of Bilingual Education and Bilingualism* (4th edn). Clevedon: Multilingual Matters (chapters 9, 17, 18).

Crawford, J. (2000) *At War With Diversity.* Clevedon: Multilingual Matters.

Crawford, J. (2004) *Educating English Learners: Language Diversity in the Classroom.* Los Angeles: Bilingual Education Services.

Del Valle, S. (2003) *Language Rights and the Law in the United States: Finding Our Voices.* Clevedon: Multilingual Matters.

Dicker, S.J. (2003) *Languages in America: A Pluralist View* (2nd edition). Clevedon: Multilingual Matters.

Hall, J.K. and Eggington, W.G. (eds) (2000) *The Sociopolitics of English Language Teaching.* Clevedon: Multilingual Matters.

Miguel, G.S. (2004) *Contested Policy: The Rise and Fall of Federal Bilingual Education in the United States 1960–2001.* Denton, Texas: University of North Texas Press.

# Part 3: Languages and Literacies in Bilingual Education

# Processes of Immersion Education

## R. Johnstone

THIS CHAPTER:

- Addresses two aspects of the research specification:
  - What skills and teaching materials teachers require, and
  - How pupils respond to immersion teaching.
- Outlines a range of instructional strategies that are considered useful for immersion-teaching.
- Demonstrates that more recent research underlines the importance of 'analysis' as well as 'experience', the teaching of 'syntax' as well as 'meaning', and the development of a less 'teacher-directed' and more 'learner-centred' approach.
- Identifies differences in strategies that are appropriate for 'early' and 'late' immersion programmes and in strategies that appear to be used by 'successful' and 'less successful' immersion learners.
- Explains the reasons underlying immersion learners' spontaneous use of English (L1) in class.
- Reports on the extent to which immersion at present is considered to cater for learners with special needs, whether with disabilities, learning difficulties or gifted.
- Underlines the centrality of the parents' role in their children's immersion education.

## Processes of Teaching and Learning

### Instructional strategies

Insight into what an immersion teacher's job entails is conveyed in Snow's (1990b) review. She suggests that immersion teachers, as compared with 'regular' teachers, have particular demands made on them in respect of: preparation of lessons; children's vocabulary development; introducing children to another culture; and personal attributes, in particular patience and flexibility. They also require skills in dealing with parents, and as such have to be well-versed in the 'whys', the 'hows' and the 'whens' of immersion. In addition a range of instructional strategies are particularly important in immersion teaching, which include:

- use of body language
- predictability in instructional routine
- drawing on children's background knowledge to aid their comprehension
- extensive use of realia, visuals and manipulatives
- review of previous material
- building-up of redundancy
- indirect error correction
- variety of teaching methods and materials
- use of clarification and comprehension checks.

Met's (1991) report identified a number of competencies for immersion teaching which included being:

- well-versed in the elementary school curriculum
- aware of how to modify their immersion language input so as to match their learners' limited comprehension
- trained to use linguistic strategies such as elaborating or simplifying their output and to help their learners develop skills in the 'negotiation of meaning'.

### Process-product relations

*More than teacher-fluency is required*

Netten and Spain (1989) argue that when

immersion programmes were first introduced it had been assumed that their success could be attributed to 'use of the target language as the language of classroom instruction'. However, they claim that much more than use of the target language is needed and that particular attention must be paid to instructional processes: ' . . . it does not appear to have been foreseen that instructional differences in the classroom could have an effect on the level of competence attained in the second language' (Netten & Spain, 1989: 484). Their own prior research (e.g. Netten & Spain, 1983) in Newfoundland and Labrador had suggested that while average levels of performance (immersion French compared with regular English) may have been the same, the actual levels of achievement of individual learners may vary greatly. Their 1989 study found different processes in different classrooms, and this appeared to be bringing about different results. Productive classroom strategies seemed to consist of creating a rich language environment and widening the range of possibilities for communication. However, in some classes less verbal and more non-verbal attention seemed to be paid to lower achievers. This had the effect that they received fewer opportunities for using their immersion language in class, which in turn was likely to have a negative impact on the development of their immersion language and thereby their learning potential at primary school. The research team concluded that the conventional wisdom of immersion teaching needed re-appraisal. More than fluency in the immersion language was needed. In particular, the education of immersion teachers needed to focus on their acquisition of a deeper knowledge of classroom processes and development of a range of classroom communication skills.

### Teachers' different conceptions of what language is for

Another confirmation of the importance of teaching-learning processes in the immersion classroom comes from Laplante's (1996) qualitative study of two Grade 1 immersion teachers. This suggested that the pupils' learning was very much influenced by the concept of language and language proficiency that the teachers held, since this influenced their selection of particular classroom activities. One teacher clearly held a view of language as serving the transmission of knowledge. As such, she did not favour interventions from her pupils. These tended to be

ignored, refused or deflected. As a consequence the pupils' opportunities for output in their immersion language were limited. The other teacher however had a concept of language as a tool for exchanging and sharing experiences. There was more inter-subjectivity in the lessons. Her learners used the immersion language in order to share their experiences, to refine their ideas and to justify their views. This was serving to build up an extended language resource that would meet their self-initiated needs.

### 'Experiential' and 'analytic' teaching

Harley (1991) distinguishes between experiential and analytic teaching in immersion classrooms, building on a research review that she and others (e.g. Allen *et al.*, 1990) had previously undertaken. The two modes are set out in Figure 1 which draws on and adds to Harley's distinction.

Good practice would ensure that both modes were activated in order to avoid the dangers that arise if one of them is allowed to dominate the other.

In addition to the experiential-analytic dimension, Harley argues there are other dimensions that may be used in order to locate different approaches to immersion-teaching. The three dimensions comprise:

Dimension 1: Experiential. . . . . . . Analytic
　　　　　　　　(as illustrated above)
Dimension 2: Implicit . . . . . . . . . . Explicit
Dimension 3: Inter-lingual . . . . . . Cross-lingual.

Too much emphasis on **implicit** processes may produce learners who fail to meet the rigorous demands of accurate speaking and writing, whereas too much emphasis on **explicit** processes may lead to over-use of abstract terminology which may not be adequately understood.

### Use of L1 to establish cross-lingual meaning

In immersion teaching when first introduced it had been assumed that meanings would be communicated within the immersion language, i.e. **intra-lingually**. Harley argues however that a recent development in immersion classrooms has been the legitimisation and use of **cross-lingual** strategies including translation to and from the first language. Observations of immersion classrooms for some time had indicated that young learners spontaneously used their common first language with each other in order to make their own

| Experiential | Analytic |
|---|---|
| Message-oriented focus | More focus on the L2 code (e.g. grammar, vocabulary, sound-system) |
| Exposure to authentic L2-use in class | Clarifies form-function-meaning relationships |
| L2 is the vehicle for teaching and learning important subject matter-use in class | Provides regular feedback to help learners restructure their developing internal representations of the L2 code |
| Teacher tends to do much or most of the talking | Provides guidance on the use of L2-learning strategies |
| Assumes learners acquire the underlying L2 rule-system through 'use' and 'absorption' | Assumes that cognitive processing is needed, in addition to experiential acquisition |
| Dangers: Learners' L2 development may 'fossilise' (reach a plateau) and they may show a tendency for 'smurfing' using small number of high-coverage items (e.g. 'chose', 'aller', 'faire') rather than develop to express more precise meanings | Dangers: May over-emphasise accuracy; may pay too much attention to form rather than to form-function-meaning relationships |

**Figure 1** Experiential and analytic immersion teaching
Adapted from Harley, 1991

connections with the meaning of what their teacher was saying to them in the immersion language. She concludes: 'This study provides evidence that through analytic teaching that includes a cross-lingual element, it is possible to undo so-called fossilised errors' (Harley, 1991: 250).

### 'Semantic' and 'syntactic' processing

Kowal and Swain's (1997) account of immersion classrooms argues that teachers have generally enabled their learners to engage in **semantic processing**, e.g. to derive meaning from what the teacher says in the immersion language and to express themselves in that language, but that **syntactical processing** (implying some command of structure) has lagged behind. They claim that immersion learners approximate to native-speaker levels in the comprehension skills of listening and reading but not so in the productive skills of speaking or writing. This points to the importance of finding ways of integrating content and language teaching, rather than always treating them separately, and it implies introducing a 'focus on form' into the teaching of important subject-matter.

One possible way of improving learners' productive command of structure is through Swain's 'output hypothesis'. This assumes that simply providing opportunities for speaking in the immersion language does not result in the gradual acquisition of accurate output. Instead, tasks have to be designed that encourage learners not only to engage in extensive speaking but also to seek systematic and relevant feedback from their peers and teachers, thereby improving their syntactic processing skills.

### Dictogloss

A specific technique that proved helpful in the encouragement of syntactic processing was the 'Dictogloss'. This consists of reading a short dense text at normal speed to learners who take notes. They then work together in groups in order to reconstruct the text from their shared resources. The various group-versions are then analysed in whole-class sessions, with the learners discussing the strengths and weaknesses of their own versions. The elements that are likely to be jotted down as the text is being read are vocabulary (e.g. nouns, verbs and adjectives) and phrases. This means that in the reconstitution phase in groups the focus is likely to switch somewhat to structure and linking elements, thereby encouraging the learners to focus on syntactic and morphological form.

### Immersion teaching and learner-centredness

Halsall and Wall (1992) report a widespread move in western countries towards learner-centred approaches to education at school. They claim this was happening in Canada also, in the regular English-language programmes but they noted a perception that this was less the case in French immersion classes. There, it was thought the teacher tended to remain more in an instructional mode, in order to provide the L2 input that the learners needed but also because in the initial years of their immersion education learners would not possess the skills in their immersion language that they would need for full participation in a child-centred approach. A team of eight 'judges' was appointed, with backgrounds in education, psychology and speech pathology, to develop a 'child-centredness scale' consisting of several dimensions including: direction; physical organisation; active learning; subject integration; assessment/evaluation; choice; curricular flexibility; initiative; individualisation; language; and classroom management. The report provides only an initial indication since the study was small-scale, but it was established that the immersion classes were in fact more child-centred than the regular English-language ones. Because of the small size of the sample, the researchers advise caution, but nonetheless: 'the results clearly put to rest the belief that French immersion classes cannot be as child-centred as the child-centred regular program classes' (Halsall & Wall, 1992: 69). An excellent example of a learner-centred immersion approach with students at high school in Australia is given by Read (1999). The group received 5 hours per week of partial immersion in Indonesian for Indonesian and social education, amounting to 20% of their time. The teacher agreed certain procedures with the class on how they might cope with problems in comprehension:

- There would be no compulsion for them to speak Indonesian, though the teacher would not speak any English.
- They could work in pairs to check with each other that they had understood what the teacher was saying.
- They should keep asking questions until they felt confident they understood what the teacher was saying (Read, 1999: 4).

This generated a very different classroom approach, with students (particularly the boys) acting 'as self-appointed interpreters for the rest of the class' and with the lessons proceeding as a guessing game. 'The proportion of time on task

was very high; in fact, the most noticeable aspect of the immersion classroom was the learners' intense involvement and interest' (Read, 1999: 6).

## Pedagogy of 'late' immersion

### Bridging the L2 proficiency gap

Johnson and Swain (1994) argue that one of the differences between early and late immersion is that in late immersion the learners' first language is needed to a greater extent. Teachers of regular (non-immersion) programmes are expected to follow the regular curriculum at normal speed, and the same applies in immersion. However, with late immersion learners there is an 'L2 proficiency gap', which needs to be closed before learners are able to tackle cognitively demanding tasks. In order to close this gap, Johnson and Swain argue that the learners' first language is not only helpful but necessary. This applies not only in Canada (where much of Swain's research is located) but also in Hong Kong (Johnson). In Hong Kong it was concluded that only academically able and well-motivated learners are likely to benefit from late immersion, and that learners switching from a Chinese-medium to an English-medium education need an intensive bridging course which will take them towards the immersion language threshold level. Late-immersion teachers therefore need training in intensive teaching and in strategies for using the learners' first language in support of, rather than as a substitute for, the second language they are learning. Johnson and Swain report that late immersion in Hong Kong was not meeting the expectations of the community in relation to English proficiency, though it was achieving this in Canada.

### Key strategies for investigation by research

More generally they recommend that: 'the teaching strategies of experienced and effective late immersion teachers should be investigated to determine:

- How the problem of a massive L2 vocabulary deficit is being overcome.
- How time and opportunities are being created for students to develop speaking and writing skills, and by what means.
- What strategies are being used in maintaining the L2 as the comprehensible medium of instruction.

- What language support strategies assist students to maintain the L2 interaction with the teacher and with each other, and in extended writing.
- What strategies work best in preparing or adapting materials to match the L2 proficiency of students at the beginning of a late immersion programme.
- Whether there is a role for the L1 in late immersion classrooms, and if so, how the L1 is best used in support of the L2 and not as a substitute for it.' (Johnson & Swain, 1994: 225).

### Teaching vocabulary in immersion classes

Lapkin and Swain (1996) provide a detailed qualitative account of how one expert immersion teacher taught vocabulary. Previously their research had found that vocabulary instruction in immersion classes was mainly through incidental rather than formal learning, being associated with the study of texts in the reading part of French Language Arts. The main focus was on meaning, with less attention paid to words in relation to morphology, syntax, phonology, discourse or sociolinguistics. However, they claim that studies of the processes of effective instruction in bilingual or immersion settings from primary school to university (e.g. Wong Fillmore, 1985; Wesche, 1993) yield a different picture and that in effective immersion classrooms:

- teachers are consistent and natural in their use of the target language
- teachers communicate clearly their objectives and expectations
- lessons are 'routinised' or scripted so that new vocabulary and structures are signalled by characteristic patterns
- teachers provide multiple opportunities for learners to hear and digest new linguistic material through paraphrase, repetition and exemplification
- teachers often repeat learner utterances, so that new vocabulary items are reiterated in several appropriate grammatical and discourse contexts. (Lapkin & Swain, 1996: 246)

In their particular study the expert immersion teacher had a clear and systematic approach to the teaching of vocabulary. They were able to describe this as planned, systematic, written and oral, building on learners' prior knowledge,

direct and with focus on both meaning and form. By 'direct' they meant that the teacher exercised some control over the choice of vocabulary to be taught.

### Instructional materials and prior preparation

Met and Lorenz (1997) report that historically immersion teachers in the USA have found identification of instructional materials a major challenge. They claim that more recently materials have become more numerous but that obtaining appropriate materials is still an issue. There is greater variety available for French and Spanish immersion than for other languages because of Canadian French immersion and American-Spanish bilingual programmes.

Peters (1994) reports on the use of laser-discs in bilingual secondary education in Germany. The use of laser-discs gives random access to relevant subject material which is likely to improve learners' knowledge acquisition, presentation and repetition.

For readers of German Whittaker (1994) provides some excellent examples of how learners in years 5 and 6 at school in Germany were prepared for English-German bilingual instruction from Year 7. This reinforces the assumption that the success of late partial immersion is dependent on thorough prior preparation by means of an enhanced or intensified language programme.

### L1 and L2 immersion reading

Cashion and Eagan (1990) conducted a three-year longitudinal study of learners engaged in total French immersion. Although the learners had received formal instruction in French only, they began to read and write spontaneously in their first language (English) and used a range of strategies to enable them to achieve this.

Noonan *et al.* (1997) examined the effects of the order of languages in which learners were taught to read in early immersion classes. Two matched samples of Grade 3 French immersion learners were involved, with one being introduced to reading in French and the other to reading in English. The results showed no significant differences in English or French reading between the two groups by the end of Grade 3. The authors claim the study suggests that transfer of reading skills from one language to the other works in either direction.

The problem of Grade 1–3 children who drop

out of immersion and enter the 'regular' English language programme is discussed by Harley (1991). She states that questions have been raised about the incidence of reading problems among children who transfer out in the early grades. Referring to Morrison *et al.* (1986) she found that reading skills were a factor in 64% and 80% of cases respectively in two Ottawa education boards. However, according to Harley: 'There is no evidence that the reading problems of these children were caused by the fact that initial literacy skills were introduced in the second language. Had they been in the regular program, they might have had similar problems. And, in some cases the unavailability of remedial help appears to have contributed to parents' decisions to withdraw their child. The issue is one that requires more research, however. The relative merits of providing early reading instruction in immersion need to be examined, including the option of beginning reading instruction in English – an option which has in fact been adopted in one province (Manitoba) (Harley, 1991: 11).

Relatively little high-quality research appears to have been published on the roles of computers and multimedia in immersion classes. It is known that this is an area attracting much interest at the level of innovation and development, so it should not be long before high-quality research studies are adding to our knowledge of this potentially vital area. However, one such study already in existence is by Edwards *et al.* (2000) who evaluated the impact of bilingual multimedia storybook with pupils aged 6–10 in both Welsh-medium and English-medium schools. They found that it was not the computer alone which had a positive impact but also the discussions which it generated among the students and also with the teacher. They concluded that bilingual interactive software of this sort, backed by the discussions it generated, had particular benefits for the students' awareness of language.

### Strategies used by 'effective' and 'less effective' immersion learners

In an interim report of their six-year longitudinal study of the reading strategies used by early-immersion learners at Grades 3 and 4, Chamot and Beard El-Dinary (1999) found that many of these young learners were well able to describe their thinking and learning processes. This pointed to the early activation of a meta-

cognitive awareness. Their study, which drew on think-aloud interviews that were audio-taped and subsequently analysed, showed differences in strategy use between more successful and less successful immersion learners, which seemed to correspond to differences in strategy use already established in older learners. There were no differences in the total strategies used by the successful and less successful learners. However, the effective learners seemed to display a variety of strategies that they tried for a particular task whereas the less effective learners seemed to cling to ineffective strategies, possibly focusing too much on detail and relying more on phonetic decoding during reading. The more effective young learners made more use of background knowledge and inferencing in order to understand texts.

### Learners' use of English in French immersion classes

Evidence on immersion classroom processes in late primary is provided by Tarone and Swain (1995). They point to a tendency among immersion learners at that stage to use their first language (usually English) rather than the immersion language (French) in peer–peer interactions. Tarone and Swain argue that this phenomenon is predictable, given that the learners in question tend to have the class-teacher as their sole native-speaker model of the immersion language. This is helpful in developing language proficiency for purposes of academic learning but it leaves their more social peer–peer language relatively undeveloped. 'Learners have not learned the vernacular style they need for non-academic purposes. The result, we claim, is a sort of diglossia in which the L2 is used for institutional and academic purposes and the L1 vernacular is used for peer–peer social interactions' (Tarone & Swain, 1995: 173). Their use of English in class therefore is not necessarily an indication of antipathy towards French. Rather it implies that their lack of contact with native-speaker French peers means that they have not yet learnt how to use immersion French for interactions among their own age-group as a marker of their pre-adolescent or adolescent identity. This helps to explain their understandable recourse to young people's English (their first language) for this purpose.

Three pedagogical implications of the above phenomenon suggested themselves to the research team:

- it may be impossible in schools to teach a peer-group vernacular form of the immersion language, so immersion should aim to deal with the language of teaching and learning
- or, schools with immersion classes should do what they can to put their immersion learners in touch with learners who are native speakers of the language, e.g. through exchange visits (if they live at a distance from each other) or joint trips to places such as museums with built-in recreational time (if they live closer together)
- or, sociostylistic variation should be explicitly taught in immersion classrooms, in order to sensitise immersion learners to informal as well as more formal varieties of their immersion language.

The same theme is further developed by Swain and Lapkin's (2000) study of twenty-two pairs of Grade 8 French immersion students working on two tasks. They concluded (p. 26) that 'the L1 serves as a tool that helps students . . . to understand and make sense of the context and requirements of a task; to focus attention on language form, vocabulary use and overall organisation; and to establish the tone and nature of their collaboration'.

### Functional-analytic teaching of sociolinguistic variation

Lyster (1994) reports on a study of the teaching of sociolinguistic variation involving three teachers of Grade 8 French Immersion classes during French Language Arts over five weeks at 12 hours per week. Experimental and comparison classes were observed. The experimental classes performed significantly differently from comparison classes on sociolinguistic measures of written production, formal oral production and multiple choice. Functional-analytical teaching (emphasising accuracy and appropriateness) had improved the sociolinguistic competence of Grade 8 FI learners in at least two ways:

- by significantly increasing their ability in oral production to appropriately and accurately use *vous* in formal situations; and their ability in written production to appropriately use *vous* in formal letters, and, in the short run, to use polite closings in formal letters; and
- by significantly increasing their awareness

of socio-stylistic differences in the L2, including their ability to recognise contexts as being appropriate for specific utterances, and to recognise utterances s being appropriate for given contexts.

Of the teachers involved in the study, the one who proved most receptive to functional-analytic teaching tended to provide cognitively engaging feedback which pushed learners to be more precise in their choice of words, to produce more appropriate utterances, and to reflect on their performance through subsequent analysis and discussion. He also asked questions which built on learners' previous responses, thereby pushing learners to explain and further develop their knowledge of sociolinguistic features. In this way he succeeded in fostering an interplay between 'communication' and 'reflection on that communication' through 'discussions on language use' and 'group activities with an analytic focus'.

### Learners with disabilities or with learning difficulties

#### Inadequacy of current screening approaches

The problems of how best to respond to children with learning difficulties in immersion programmes are well set out by Wiss (1989). Referring to a long-standing concern as to whether immersion programmes are suitable for the full range of learners, Wiss argues that a properly scientific basis does not exist for screening children in advance. Wide-scale screening at present, she argues, 'could overidentify problems and possibly exclude many low socio-economic status or less bright children from entry. On the other hand, for various reasons, some children do not do well on immersion programmes and are switched out. The negative impact on children who might perceive a switch out of French immersion as a failure on their part greatly concerns parents and educators' (Wiss, 1989: 517).

Wiss also claims that many children experiencing difficulties in immersion would have the same difficulties in regular courses. 'Usually, these children have specific learning disabilities (LD) that include deficits in cognitive processing. Such deficits interfere with the acquisition and maintenance of fluid reading skills regardless of whether the learning environment is unilingual or bilingual. The children appear to develop adequate oral skills, with problems in the academic areas of reading and writing' (Wiss, 1989: 517).

### 'Children with specific disabilities' and 'children with problems in L2 learning'

She also argues however that there may be a sub-group who would have difficulties with immersion but not with the regular English programme. She draws a distinction between children with specific learning disabilities and children with problems in second-language learning, perhaps as a result of developmental immaturity. 'Developmental immaturity suggests that the maturational lag will diminish with time and that the child will have difficulties in early immersion only, and not in the unilingual program' (Wiss, 1989: 527). She argues that specific learning disabilities 'suggest underlying cognitive deficits that are intrinsic to the child, will be likely to be present throughout the child's life, and will create problems in either a unilingual or bilingual program' (Wiss, 1989: 527). 'For developmentally immature children, early immersion may not be ideal. For children with specific learning difficulties, a late immersion or core French environment may not be appropriate' (Wiss, 1989: 528). She specifically does not argue that learning disabled children should be counselled out of early immersion, but that 'children who may not benefit from early immersion be identified early and given alternatives for bilingual education' (Wiss, 1989: 528).

### Special educational needs of language minority students

An excellent general account of the special education needs of minority language students in respect of their first and second languages is provided by Cloud (1994) that includes sections on 'pre-referral', 'preventing erroneous referrals', 'using an ecological assessment approach within special education', 'distinguishing difference' from 'disability', 'cross-lingual assessment of disability', and 'diagnosing disabilities in students'. Similarly, Hamayan (1994) provides a general account of the language development of students with low levels of L1 and L2 literacy. Drawing on a range of research studies she concludes: 'The following classroom characteristics make for an environment that allows for literacy to emerge in a natural and efficient way:

- The classroom must be rich with meaningful environmental print.
- The construction of meaning must be the basis of all literacy activities.
- New literacy skills should be allowed to emerge naturally and in a low-anxiety environment.
- Literacy activities in the classroom must be motivating to children.
- Instruction about linguistic forms and structures should be embedded in meaningful functional language activities.
- Literacy instruction should be integrated with instruction of academic content.' (Hamayan, 1994: 298)

## Administration and Support

Relatively little research (most of it Canadian) appears to have been published in respect of administration and support for immersion education. In a review of the literature Dagenais (1990) found that the school principal had a central role in dealing with problems of administration and required to be sensitive to the complex political implications of immersion education. Lamarre's (1990) interviews with anglophone elementary school heads found they did not consider their lack of French to be a hindrance. However, they needed guidance in how to evaluate and support the French immersion staff in their schools and in how to evaluate the learners' achievements. Their concerns were: availability of resources, the integration of francophone teachers into what were mainly English-language schools and the transfer of immersion learners into the regular English language programme. A national survey of education boards administering French immersion (Canadian Education Association, 1992) found that key issues were: staffing, special services, programme design, teaching strategies, enrolment and in-service support. Safty's (1992b) study found that it could prove difficult to establish a positive school ethos if anglophone immersion teachers in the school did not perceive their principal as supporting them in their professional development needs, and concluded that bilingual administrators of schools with immersion classes were ideally to be preferred. Poyen and Rogers (1991) found that francophone immersion teachers tended to feel that the general attitude of the school was not entirely supportive of French immersion and concluded that positive leadership was necessary.

*A school Principal's view on establishing an appropriate ethos*

Writing as Principal of an immersion magnet school in the United States, Coffman (1992) attached high importance to the Principal's having at least a working knowledge of the immersion language. This enabled him to know what was going on in classrooms and at immersion staff meetings and to understand the learning and teaching processes. Being Principal of an immersion school was very hard work and often left him feeling frustrated and inadequate: 'What have I gotten myself into?' (Coffman, 1992: 156). This made it all the more important to be knowledgeable about the school's immersion goals and to be well versed in the theories of L1 and L2 acquisition and of immersion teaching. It was also important to attend to the social climate of the school, e.g. by ensuring that the immersion language appeared on all signs and displays, that telephones were answered with an L2 greeting and that at least a few L2 words were inserted into all correspondence with parents.

## Parental Involvement

Parents have a vital role to play, if immersion programmes are to be successful. This applies particularly to early total immersion, because here the parents have made a major investment, a declaration of faith in having their child educated through a language that is not the language of the home. In some cases this may be a language in which they they may have little or no fluency. Their contribution can take many forms but at the heart of it lie:

- establishing a role for the home in ensuring that their children's first language is not disadvantaged by their being educated at school through a second language
- offering moral support, encouragement and confidence to their children in their learning and use of their immersion language
- supporting the school, lobbying for resources and encouraging parents of potential immersion children.

The level of French will vary from one child to another in the same way as performance in mathematics, for example, will vary from child to child. Some students speak French making many mistakes while others might be taken for mother-tongue French speakers.

The language skills of French immersion students are consistently superior to those of core French students (who study French for 20 to 50 minutes per day). In general, immersion students' French oral and reading comprehension skills (receptive skills) will be almost on a par with those of native French speakers. Speaking and writing in the second language (productive skills) may not be as advanced as their comprehension (receptive) skills. We must remind ourselves that French for these children is, after all, their second language and that English is the predominant language in their environment.

To dwell too much and too critically on the quality of French spoken by immersion students is often a red herring because it ignores the fact that immersion students not only communicate effectively in French but also learn the skills of communication: selecting the right words with the right nuances, adapting communicative strategies to get the message across, cracking the right joke without making a cultural or linguistic gaffe, and establishing a positive environment by creating a friendly atmosphere with the native speaker.

It will take years of immersion schooling before your child will reach such a level of achievement and comfort in a second language. As an example, imagine yourself able to understand Chinese spoken by a native speaker at a normal speed and that you are able to communicate, in a normal way, albeit while making some mistakes with that person. Wouldn't that be wonderful?

French immersion teachers and parents should constantly seek out opportunities for the children to use their French with mother-tongue French speakers. The new technologies (Internet, video-conferencing, multimedia materials etc.) will help students to establish links with Francophone communities around the world. These opportunities for interaction should help students to improve their sociolinguistic skills.

**Figure 2** 'How good will my child's French be?'
*Source*: Obadia (1996)

In Scotland, Gaelic-medium primary education would not have come about if it had not had the strong support of parents who indeed have been a major driving force behind it, and a number of parents' associations for Gaelic-medium education have been formed. In Canada the Canadian Parents for French (CPF) is the national network of volunteers who promote and create opportunities for young Canadians to learn and use French, and has over 200 branches across the country. Although its support for French covers other forms of education including Core French (French as a subject), CPF has been particularly supportive of immersion. They have produced an impressive series of brochures, videos, pamphlets and even books that provide a wealth of high-quality information. One of their 1996 pamphlets for example is entitled: *French Immersion in Canada – Frequently asked questions.* The writer is André Obadia of Simon Fraser University, British Columbia, who is an international authority. His text (Obadia, 1996) provides authoritative responses to the following questions:

- Is French immersion for all children?
- How good will my child's French be?
- Is my child going to lose out in English or in subjects taught in French?
- How can I help at home?
- Should a child be transferred out of French immersion?
- Is there learning assistance in French immersion?
- Should I register my child in early immersion or in late immersion?

As an example, Figure 2 shows how he responds to parents in respect of the second question.

In addition, references are given for twenty-four research texts that parents might wish to follow up. The CPF book: *So you want your child to learn French!* (Fleming & Whitla, 1990, eds) is similarly written in an easily readable yet serious style and contains a wealth of relevant research-based information.

## References

Allen, P., Swain, M., Harley, B. and Cummins, J. (1990) Aspects of classroom treatment: Toward a more comprehensive view of second languge acquisition. In B. Harley, P. Allen, J. Cummins and M. Swain (eds) *The Development of Second Language Proficiency* (pp. 57–81). New York: Cambridge University Press.

Canadian Board of Education (1992) *French Immersion Today.* Toronto.

Cashion, M. and Eagen, R. (1990) Spontaneous reading and writing in English by learners in total French immersion. Summary of final report. *English Quarterly* 22, 30–44.

Chamot, A.U. and Beard El-Dinary, P. (1999) Children's learning strategies in language immersion classrooms. *Modern Language Journal* 83, 3, 319–338.

Cloud, N. (1994) Special education needs of second language students. In F. Genesee (ed.) *Educating Second Language Children. The Whole Child, the Whole Curriculum, the Whole Community* (pp. 243–277). Cambridge: Cambridge University Press.

Coffman, R. (1992) Immersion: A principal's perspective. In E.B. Berhhardt (ed.) *Life in Immersion Classes* (pp. 154–170). Clevedon: Multilingual Matters.

Dagenais, D. (1990) Principal's role in French immersion. *The Canadian School Executive* February 3–8.

Edwards, V. and Monaghan, F. (2000) Books, pictures and conversations: using bilingual multimedia storybooks to develop language awareness. *Language Awareness* 9, 3, 135–147.

Fleming, B. and Whitla, M. (eds) (1990) *So You Want Your Child to Learn French!* (2nd revised edn). Ontario: Canadian Parents for French (CPF).

Halsall, N.D. and Wall, C. (1992) Pedagogical practices in French immersion and regular English programs. *Canadian Modern Language Review* 49, 1, 60–73.

Hamayan, E.V. (1994) Language Development of Low-literacy Students. In F. Genesee (ed.) *Educating Second Language Children. The Whole Child, the Whole Curriculum, the Whole Community* (pp. 278–300). Cambridge: Cambridge University Press.

Harley, B. (1991) Instructional strategies and SLA in early French immersion. *Studies in Second Language Acquisition* 15, 245–249.

Johnson, K. and Swain, M. (1994) From core to content: Bridging the L2 proficiency gap in late immersion. *Language and Education* 8, 4, 211–229.

Kowal, M. and Swain, M. (1997) From semantic to syntactic processing: How can we promote it in the immersion classroom? In K. Johnson and M. Swain (eds) (1997) *Immersion Education: International Perspectives* (pp. 284–310). Cambridge: Cambridge University Press.

Lamarre, N. (1990) The experiences of anglophone elementary principals with French immersion programs in Alberta. Annual meeting of the Canadian Society for the Study of Education, Victoria, BC.

Lapkin, S. and Swain, M. (1996) Vocabulary teaching in a Grade 8 French immersion classroom: A descriptive case-study. *Canadian Modern Language Review* 53, 1, 242–256.

Laplante, B. (1996) Stratégies pédagogiques et représentation de la langue dans l'enseignement des sciences en immersion français. *Canadian Modern Language Review* 52, 3, 440–463.

Lyster, R. (1994) The effects of functional-analytic teaching on aspects of French immersion learners' sociolinguistic competence. *Applied Linguistics* 15, 263–287.

Met, M. and Lorenz, L. (1997) Lessons from US immersion programs: Two decades of experience. In K. Johnson and M. Swain (eds) *Immersion Education: International Perspectives* (pp. 243–265). Cambridge: Cambridge University Press.

Netten, J. and Spain, W. (1989) Learner–teacher interaction patterns in the French immersion classroom. *Canadian Modern Language Review* 45, 3, 485–501.

Noonen, B, Colleaux, J. and Yackulic, R.A. (1997) Two approaches to beginning reading in early French immersion. *Canadian Modern Language Review* 53, 4, 729–742.

Obadia, A.A. (1996) *French immersion in Canada. Frequently asked questions*. Ontario: Canadian Parents for French (CPF).

Peters, K. (1994) Using laserdiscs in bilingual schooling. *Der Fremdsprachliche Unterricht* 4, 94, 32–35.

Poyen, J. and Rogers, L. (1991) *Professional Development in French Education: An Investigation*. Calgary Board of Education and Faculty of Education, University of Calgary, Calgary, AB.

Read, J. (1999) Immersion Indonesian at Rowville Secondary College. *Babel* 34, 2, 4–9.

Safty, A. (1992b) French immersion: Bilingual education and unilingual administration. *Interchange* 23, 4, 389–405.

Snow, M.A. (1990b) Instructional methodology in immersion foreign language education. In C. Padilla, M. Amado, H. Halford and M.V. Concepción (eds) *Foreign Language Education: Issues and Strategies* (pp. 156–171). London: Sage Publications.

Swain, M. and Lapkin, S. (2000) Task-based second language learning: the uses of the first language. *Language Teaching Research* 4, 3, 251–274.

Tarone, E. and Swain, M. (1995) A sociolinguistic perspective on second language use in immersion classrooms. *Modern Language Journal* 79, 2, 166–178.

Wesche, M. (1993) French immersion graduates at university and beyond: What difference has it made? In J. Alatis (ed.) *Language, Communication and Meaning*. Georgetown University Roundtable on Languages and Linguistics. Washington, DC: Georgetown University Press.

Whittaker, M. (1994) Der bilinguale Vorbereitungsunterricht in der 5. And 6. Klasse – ein Praxisbericht. *Der fremdsprachliche Unterricht* 1, 94, 51–56.

Wiss, C. (1989) Early French immersion may not be suitable for every child. *Canadian Modern Language Review* 45, 3, 517–529.

Wong Fillmore, L. (1985) When does teacher talk work as input? In S.M. Gass and C.G. Malden (eds) *Input in Second Language Acquisition* (pp. 49–69). Cambridge: Cambridge University Press.

## Questions

1. Johnstone lists nine instructional strategies that are important in immersion education. Give a classroom example of each to show your understanding.

2. A distinction is made between experiential and analytic immersion teaching. What are the main differences? Write two short episodes from an imaginary classroom, with teacher–pupil dialogue, to illustrate the main differences.

3. What are the differences between intra-lingual and cross-lingual strategies in immersion classrooms? What is the impeptus for each kind of strategy? Why are cross-lingual strategies increasingly being used in immersion classrooms? How do these differ from the strict language use advocated in dual language classrooms in the United States?

4    What does the chapter say about the presence of students with learning difficulties and special needs in a bilingual school? What questions may be left unanswered by this section?

5.   In one page, create a bullet point list of the main points of this chapter, written for a WWW page for teachers in bilingual classrooms.

## Activities

1.   Research whether there are any immersion programs for the language majority in your area. If there are, make a Resource List with their location, requirements, tuition, size, languages, etc. If there's only one, describe it in detail. If there are no such schools, ask administrators in three schools how students learn languages other than the majority one and whether the program is successful. Then tell them about immersion programs, and ask them how they feel about them. Record their answers.

2.   Using the WWW, research cross-lingual strategies being used throughout the world. In particular, research the 'translanguaging' which is prevalent in Welsh bilingual classrooms. Watch the video available in the web. Report to the class.

3.   Using the WWW, research the approach known as Content and Language Integrated Learning (CLIL) that is being used throughout the European Union. Design a poster that clearly compares CLIL with immersion education as described by Johnstone.

4.   Interview at least five language majority parents about their interest in immersion bilingual education for their children. Share the results with your class and write an essay that clearly summarizes the view of language majority parents.

5.   Make a video of an effective immersion teacher. Identify the different instructional strategies the teacher uses in the video in a separate narrative section. Show to the class.

## Further Reading

Baker, C. (2006) *Foundations of Bilingual Education and Bilingualism* (4th edn). Clevedon: Multilingual Matters (chapters 13, 14).

Freeman, Y., Freeman, D.E. and Mercuri, S.P. (2004) *Dual Language Essentials for Teachers and Administrators*. Portsmouth, NH: Heinemann.

Hickey, T. (2001) Mixing beginners and native speakers in minority language immersion: Who is immersing whom? *Canadian Modern Language Review*, 57, 3, 443–474.

Johnson, R.K and Swain, M. (eds) (1997) *Immersion Education: International Perspectives*. Cambridge: Cambridge University Press.

# Multilingual Language Policies and the Continua of Biliteracy: An Ecological Approach

## Nancy H. Hornberger

## Introduction

Two scenes from the year 2000:

*18 July 2000, Johannesburg, South Africa*. In the course of my two-week visit at Rand Afrikaans University, I meet early this Tuesday morning (7:30 A.M.) with a group of young pre-service teachers enrolled in a one-year Diploma in Education program. The university has been bilingual from its founding, offering instruction in Afrikaans and English in a parallel dual medium format; in the post-apartheid period, rapidly expanding numbers of speakers of diverse African languages have enrolled.

About 20 students attend this English Language Pedagogy class where I have been invited to speak about bilingual education. Their teacher Judy is present, as is my host Elizabeth. At one point, I mention my dissertation research which documented 'classroom success but policy failure' for an experimental bilingual education program in Quechua speaking communities of Puno, Peru. The policy failure, I suggest, was at least partly due to some community members' resistance to the use of Quechua in school, which they had always regarded as a Spanish domain. Taking off from this, Judy asks what one can do about negative community attitudes which impede top-down language planning, citing the case of Black African parental demands for English-medium instruction in the face of South Africa's new multilingual language policy.

Later, when the discussion turns to the importance of the teacher's recogniz-ing and valuing students' languages and cultures even if they're not the teacher's own, Elizabeth takes the opportunity to demonstrate one such practice. Students are instructed to break into small groups to talk to each other about bilingual education for two–three minutes in their own languages. The result: four Nguni speakers (one Zulu, one Xhosa, two Swati), two Gujarati speaking women, three Afrikaans speakers, and one Portuguese speaker (who talks with me) form groups, while the rest of the class members chat to each other in small groups in English. The students clearly enjoy this activity and it generates lively whole class discussion.

*17 August 2000, La Paz, Bolivia*. On the first day of a three-day *Taller de reflexión y análisis sobre la enseñanza de castellano como segunda lengua* (Workshop of reflection and analysis on the teaching of Spanish as a second language), the Vice-Minister of Education welcomes workshop partici-pants, emphasizing to us that the key to the Bolivian Education Reform is Bilingual Intercultural Education, and the key to *that* is Spanish as a Second Language. In recent months, she tells us, questions have been raised about the Reform's attention to indigenous languages, and indigenous parents have begun to demand that their children be taught Spanish. Perhaps the Reform erred, she says, in emphasizing the indigenous languages to such a degree that bilingual education appeared to the public to be monolingual indigenous language education.

There are approximately 45 participants in the workshop: 15 technical experts from the Curricular Development Unit of the Ministry, a half-dozen representatives from PROEIB, the Andean regional graduate program in bilingual intercultural education at the University of San Simón in Cochabamba, Bolivia, another 8–9 Bolivian pedagogical experts, and about a dozen international specialists in bilingual and second language education (from Brasil, Chile, Ecuador, Mexico, Peru, Belgium, Germany, USA, and Sweden). Many of us had participated five years earlier in a similar workshop on the curriculum and materials for the teaching of the indigenous languages, principally the three largest languages Quechua, Aymara, and Guarani. The materials we reviewed then have been under implementation in the schools for a couple of years now.

Our charge this time is to review the Spanish as a Second Language curriculum and materials developed by the Curricular Development Unit and to make recommendations for improvement in design and implementation. Among the materials available for review are curricular guides, teaching modules for Spanish, bilingual modules for the content areas, cassette tapes and laminated posters, an 80-book class library, a literary anthology, and a series of six big books in Spanish, three of them based on traditional Quechua, Aymara, and Guarani folktales.

In the ensuing three days of intensive work across long hours (8 A.M. to 9 P.M.), discussions are remarkable for the honesty and integrity with which the Curricular Development Unit experts welcome critical scrutiny of their work. These experts worry about how best to teach Spanish to a school population which in many cases has little to no exposure to oral Spanish or to print media outside of the classroom; and so have opted for a richly communicative and literature-based curriculum design. Some of the second language experts are concerned that there is not enough explicit grammatical and lexical instruction and that the syllabus is not sufficiently incremental. Concerns from those who have seen the materials in use in

the field are of a different nature. They ask questions like: what are the implications for second language learning of teachers' frequent code-mixing in class, code-mixing prompted by the desire to communicate with the students in a language they understand?; by the same token, what are the implications for maintaining and strengthening the indigenous languages if one and the same teacher teaches in both the indigenous language and Spanish?

As these scenes readily show, the one language–one nation ideology of language policy and national identity is no longer the only available one worldwide (if it ever was). Multilingual language policies which recognize ethnic and linguistic pluralism as resources for nation-building are increasingly in evidence. These policies, many of which envision implementation through bilingual intercultural education, open up new worlds of possibility for oppressed indigenous and immigrant languages and their speakers, transforming former homogenizing and assimilationist policy discourse into discourses about diversity and emancipation. This paper points to two broad sets of challenges inherent in implementing these new ideologies, as they are evident in two nations which undertook these transformations in the early 1990s.

Post-apartheid South Africa's new Constitution of 1993 embraces language as a basic human right and multilingualism as a national resource, raising nine major African languages to national official status alongside English and Afrikaans;[1] this, along with the dismantling of the apartheid educational system, has led to the burgeoning of multilingual, multicultural student populations in classrooms, schools, and universities nationwide. The Bolivian National Education Reform of 1994 envisions a comprehensive transformation of Bolivia's educational system, including the introduction of all thirty of Bolivia's indigenous languages alongside Spanish as subjects and media of instruction in all Bolivian schools. Yet, to transform a standardizing education into a diversifying one and to construct a national identity that is multilingual and multicultural constitute ideological paradoxes which are a challenge to implement.

Recently, scholars are increasingly turning to the metaphor of ecology to think and talk about language planning, teaching, and learning in multilingual settings. In the first part of the paper, I explore salient themes of that metaphor – namely language evolution, language environment, and language endangerment – and argue that multilingual language policies are essentially about opening up ideological and implementational space in the environment for as many languages as possible, and in particular endangered languages, to evolve and flourish rather than dwindle and disappear. In the second half of the paper, I use my continua of biliteracy model as heuristic to consider two broad sets of challenges facing these multilingual language policies (as exemplified in the above scenes) and suggest that there is urgent need for language educators, language planners, and language users to fill those ideological and implementational spaces as richly and fully as possible, before they close in on us again.[2]

## Multilingual Language Policies, Ideology, and the Ecology of Language

The one nation–one language ideology, the idea that a nation-state should be unified by one common language, has held sway in recent Western history from the rise of the European and American nation-states in the 18th and 19th centuries on through the formation of independent African and Asian nation-states in mid-20th century and up to the present. Fishman wrote of the several score new members brought into the family of nations in the mid-20th century and of the nationistic and nationalistic ideologies underlying their choice of a national language: 'nationism – as distinguished from nationalism – is primarily concerned not with ethnic authenticity but with operational efficiency' (Fishman, 1969: 113). In either case, emphasis was on choosing *a* national language, *one* national language, whether it were a Language of Wider Communication serving nationistic goals or an indigenous language serving nationalistic ones.

Yet the one language–one nation equation is increasingly recognized as an ideological red herring (Woolard & Schieffelin, 1994: 60–61). For one thing, it is a relatively recent phenomenon when seen against the backdrop of human history. Referring not only to the Greek, Roman, Aztec, and Inca empires of ancient times but also to the more recent Austro-Hungarian and Ottoman empires, May writes in his recent book on the politics of language that 'empires were quite happy . . . to leave unmolested the plethora of cultures and languages subsumed within them – as long as taxes were paid' (May, 2001: 6).

Furthermore, in our day, twin pressures of globalization and ethnic fragmentation exert pressures on the one language–one nation ideology. May suggests that modern nation-states have had to reassess the limits of their sovereignty as a result of the rise of globalization and the 'burgeoning influence of multinational corporations and supranational political organisations', while at the same time minority groups increasingly exert their rights 'either to form their own nation-states . . . or for greater representation within existing nation-state structures' (May, 2001: 7). In like vein, Freeland notes that Latin American nations are particularly prone to two frequently mentioned effects of globalization from without and within: (1) the weakening of the state from the surge of transnational phenomena and (2) the weakening of the state from social and ethnic fragmentation (Freeland, 1996: 168). Certainly, African nations are similarly prone to these effects.

Gal suggests what might be considered a linguistic corollary to these pressures when she notes that global processes like colonization, the expansion of capitalism and transnational labor migration have replaced earlier processes of 'dispersion of populations and the peopling of the world', such that: 1) the characteristic form of language change in the modern era is the coming together of languages; and 2) the former 'relatively egalitarian linguistic diversity, based on small-scale languages whose speakers believe their own language to be superior, [has been changed] into stratified diversity: local languages are abandoned or subordinated to "world languages" in diglossic relations . . .' (Gal, 1989: 356). All of this points to two countervailing trends working together to break apart the one language–one nation ideology: the rise of English as a global language, hence infringing on national languages; and the reclaiming of endangered indigenous, immigrant, and ethnic languages at local and national levels, hence undermining the ascendancy of national languages.

### Ecology of language

As the one language–one nation ideology breaks apart, so too the language planning field increasingly seeks models and metaphors that reflect a multilingual rather than monolingual approach to language planning and policy. One such model is the continua of biliteracy (to be taken up below) and one such metaphor is the ecology of language; both are premised on a view of multilingualism as a resource. Ruiz (1984) like Fishman (1966a) before him, drew our attention to the potential of a language-as-resource ideology as an alternative to the dominant language-as-problem and language-as-right ideological orientations in language planning. Mühlhäusler argues that 'language planning until the 1980s was based on the premise that linguistic diversity is a problem' (Mühlhäusler, 1996: 311–312), but that it is now undergoing a conceptual shift toward recognizing linguistic diversity as an asset.

Einar Haugen is generally credited for introducing the ecology of language in his 1970 paper by that title (Haugen, 1972). Haugen himself points to an earlier, 1964 paper by Carl and Frances Voegelin, who suggested that 'in linguistic ecology, one begins not with a particular language but with a particular area, not with selective attention to a few languages but with comprehensive attention to all the languages in the area' (Voegelin & Voegelin, 1964: 2).[3] For his part, Haugen defines language ecology as 'the study of interactions between any given language and its environment', going on to define the environment of the language as including both psychological ('its interaction with other languages in the minds of bi- and multilingual speakers') and sociological ('its interaction with the society in which it functions as a medium of communication') aspects (Haugen, 1972: 325). He emphasizes the reciprocity between language and environment, noting that what is needed is not only a description of the social and psychological situation of each language, but also the effect of this situation on the language (Haugen, 1972: 334). Haugen argues for the heuristic value of earlier biological, instrumental and structural metaphors in understanding the life, purpose, and form of languages and goes on to invoke the tradition of research in human ecology as a metaphor for an approach which would comprise not just the science of language description, but also concern for language cultivation and preservation (Haugen, 1972: 326–329). He concludes with a comprehensive catalogue of ecological questions which Mühlhäusler later repeats (Haugen, 1972: 336–337; Mühlhäusler, 1996: 3–4).

For my purposes here, I am primarily interested in three themes of the ecology metaphor which are salient to me in writings on the ecology

of language; all of them are present in Haugen's original formulation. These are: that languages, like living species, evolve, grow, change, live, and die in relation to other languages and also in relation to their environment; for ease of reference, I will call these the *language evolution* and *language environment* themes. A third theme is the notion that some languages, like some species and environments, may be endangered and that the ecology movement is about not only studying and describing those potential losses, but also counteracting them; this I will call the *language endangerment* theme.[4]

In his 1996 book, *Linguistic Ecology*, Mühlhäusler advocates an ecological approach to languages which, like Haugen's approach, encompasses all three of these metaphorical themes. He argues that our focus must shift from consideration of 'given', countable languages to one on human communication in a holistic sense (Mühlhäusler, 1996: 8– 9) and proposes an approach which 'investigates the support system for a structural ecology of language rather than individual languages' (Mühlhäusler, 1996: 312–313); that is, he argues for consideration of *language evolution*. He 'sees the well-being of individual languages or communication networks as dependent on a range of language-external factors as well as the presence of other languages' (Mühlhäusler, 1996: 49) and claims that 'the focus of inquiry should be upon the functional relationship between the factors that affect the general interrelationship between languages rather than individual factors impacting on individual languages' (Mühlhäusler, 1996: 313); that is, he calls for a focus on *language environment*. Writing from a concern for the decline and loss of linguistic heterogeneity in the world, Mühlhäusler argues for applying ecological theory to the goal of language maintenance (Mühlhäusler, 1996: 311–324); that is, he writes from a concern for *language endangerment*, in the sense of both studying and counteracting language loss. He applauds the ecological metaphor for being action-oriented and prefers the partial and local explanations of an ecological approach to the complex yet ultimately mechanical explanations of a systems metaphor (Mühlhäusler, 1996: 2).

Others writing on an ecological approach to language planning elaborate on one or more of the metaphorical themes. Kaplan and Baldauf's work elaborates on the *language evolution* and *language environment* themes. They emphasize that language planning activity cannot be limited to one language in isolation from all the other languages in the environment (Kaplan & Baldauf, 1997: 271). Their model representing the various forces at work in a linguistic eco-system includes 'language modification constructs' (Kaplan & Baldauf, 1997: 289) or 'language change elements' (Kaplan & Baldauf, 1997: 296) such as language death, survival, change, revival, shift and spread, amalgamation, contact, pidgin and creole development, and literacy development, all processes of what I am here calling *language evolution*. With regard to *language environment*, the model also depicts agencies such as government and non-government organizations, education agencies, and communities of speakers, all of which have an impact on the multiple languages in the linguistic eco-system (Kaplan & Baldauf, 1997: 311). 'Language planning . . . is a question of trying to manage the language ecology of a particular language to support it within the vast cultural, educational, historical, demographic, political, social structure in which language policy formulation occurs every day' (Kaplan & Baldauf, 1997: 13); 'language planning activity must be perceived as implicating a wide range of languages and of modifications occurring simultaneously over the mix of languages in the environment – that is, implicating the total language eco-system' (Kaplan & Baldauf, 1997: 296).

Recent work by Phillipson & Skutnabb-Kangas (1996) and Ricento (2000) highlights the *language endangerment* theme of the ecology metaphor. Phillipson and Skutnabb-Kangas contrast two language policy options with regard to English worldwide: the diffusion of English paradigm characterized by a 'monolingual view of modernization and internationalization' and the ecology-of-language paradigm which involves 'building on linguistic diversity worldwide, promoting multilingualism and foreign language learning, and granting linguistic human rights to speakers of all languages' (Phillipson & Skutnabb-Kangas, 1996: 429). The juxtaposition of the linguistic imperialism of English over against multilingualism and linguistic human rights is clearly founded on a concern for the ongoing endangerment of many languages, displaced by one or a select few, and the need to counteract that endangerment and displacement. Mühlhäusler cites Pakir's (1991) term 'killer languages' in reference to the displacing effect of imperial English as well as

other languages such as Mandarin, Spanish, French, and Indonesian.

In parallel fashion, van Lier (2000) argues that an ecological approach to language learning emphasizes emergent language development; learning and cognition as explained not only in terms of processes inside the head, but also in terms of interaction with the environment; and learners' perceptual and social activity as, in a fundamental way, their learning. These three emphases can be understood as microlevel, sociocultural language learning parallels to the *language evolution, environment*, and *endangerment* themes in an ecological approach to language planning. Bringing sociocultural and sociolinguistic strands together in his ecological approach to literacy, Barton (1994: 29–32) provides a succinct and useful review of the use of the ecology metaphor in both psychological and social traditions in the social sciences.

Ricento argues that as the macro sociopolitical context of language planning has moved over the last several decades from decolonization through modernization and into the new world order, and as social science epistemologies have simultaneously moved from structuralism through critical theory and into postmodernism, so too the language planning field has moved from a focus on problem-solving through a concern for access and into an emphasis on linguistic human rights. In words that evoke the *language endangerment* and *language environment* themes outlined above, he suggests that the ecology-of-language paradigm may well be the conceptual framework for language planning in the future, precisely because of its emphasis on language rights and on connecting macro sociopolitical processes with microlevel patterns of language use (Ricento, 2000: 208–209).

In sum, an ecology of language metaphor captures a set of ideological underpinnings for a multilingual language policy, in which languages are understood to (1) live and evolve in an eco-system along with other languages (*language evolution*), (2) interact with their sociopolitical, economic, and cultural environments (*language environment*), and (3) become endangered if there is inadequate environmental support for them *vis-à-vis* other languages in the eco-system (*language endangerment*). All three of these ideological themes come into play in the following consideration of challenges facing the implementation of multilingual language policies in South Africa and Bolivia.

## Multilingual Language Policies and the Continua of Biliteracy: Implementation in Classroom and Community

The scenes from South Africa and Bolivia which opened this paper evoke broad sets of challenges at community and classroom levels. In the first instance, there are the challenges of confronting community attitudes favoring the language of power in the society, attitudes which are at odds with developmental evidence that children learn best from the starting point of their own language(s). There are also the challenges, at classroom level, of providing materials and interaction in multiple languages which are not necessarily spoken by all participants. In the continua of biliteracy model, the latter challenges relate to media and content of biliteracy, and the former to biliteracy development and contexts.

The *continua of biliteracy* is a comprehensive, ecological model I have proposed as a way to situate research, teaching, and language planning in multilingual settings. The continua of biliteracy model defines *biliteracy* as 'any and all instances in which communication occurs in two (or more) languages in or around writing' (Hornberger, 1990: 213) and describes it in terms of four nested sets of intersecting continua characterizing the contexts, media, content, and development of biliteracy (Hornberger, 1989a; Hornberger & Skilton-Sylvester, 2000). Specifically, it depicts the development of biliteracy along intersecting first language–second language, receptive-productive, and oral-written language skills continua; through the medium of two (or more) languages and literacies whose linguistic structures vary from similar to dissimilar, whose scripts range from convergent to divergent, and to which the developing biliterate individual's exposure varies from simultaneous to successive; in contexts that encompass micro to macro levels and are characterized by varying mixes along the monolingual-bilingual and oral-literate continua; and with content that ranges from majority to minority perspectives and experiences, literary to vernacular styles and genres, and decontextualized to contextualized language texts (see Figures 1 and 2).

The notion of continuum conveys that all points on a particular continuum are interrelated, and the model suggests that the more their learning contexts and contexts of use allow learners and users to draw from across the whole of each and every continuum, the greater are the chances for their full biliterate development and expression

(Hornberger, 1989a: 289). Implicit in that suggestion is a recognition that there has usually *not* been attention to all points. In educational policy and practice regarding biliteracy, there tends to be an implicit privileging of one end of the continua over the other such that one end of each continuum is associated with more power than the other, for example written development over oral development (Figure 3 depicts the traditional power weighting assigned to the different continua). There is a need to contest the traditional power weighting of the continua by paying attention to and granting agency and voice to actors and practices at what have traditionally been the less powerful ends of the continua (Hornberger & Skilton-Sylvester, 2000).

As noted earlier, the continua of biliteracy model, like the ecology of language metaphor, is premised on a view of multilingualism as a resource. Further, as the above overview reveals, the continua of biliteracy model also incorporates the language evolution, language environment, and language endangerment themes of the ecology of language metaphor. The very notion of bi (or multi)-literacy assumes that one language and literacy is developing in relation to one or more other languages and literacies (*language evolution*); the model situates biliteracy development (whether in the individual, classroom, community, or society) in relation to the contexts, media, and content in and through which it develops (i.e. *language environment*); and it provides a heuristic for addressing the unequal balance of power across languages and literacies (i.e. for both studying and counteracting *language endangerment*).

### Biliteracy development and contexts: Language and power in the community

Judy asked what one can do about negative community attitudes toward South Africa's multilingual language policy, referring specifically to Zulu, Xhosa or other Black African parental demands for English-medium instruction for their children. The Bolivian Vice-Minister of Education suggested that the National Education Reform might have erred in placing too much emphasis on indigenous language instruction at the outset, while neglecting instruction in Spanish as a second language. In both cases, the zeal of educators and policy makers for teaching children literacy on the foundation of a language they already speak appears to be at odds with a popular demand for the language of power.

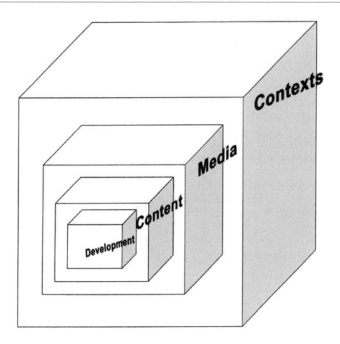

**Figure 1** Nested relationships among the continua of biliteracy

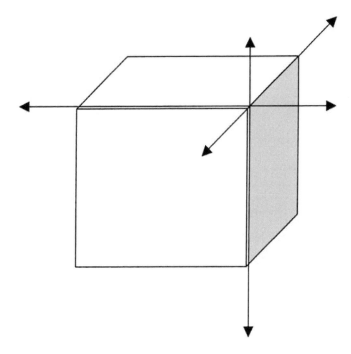

**Figure 2** Intersecting relationships among the continua of biliteracy

Traditionally <u>less</u> powerful <————>Traditionally <u>more</u> powerful

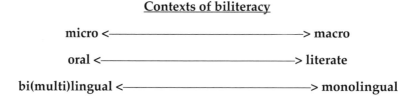

Contexts of biliteracy

micro <————————————————> macro

oral <————————————————> literate

bi(multi)lingual <————————————————> monolingual

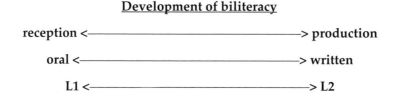

Development of biliteracy

reception <————————————————> production

oral <————————————————> written

L1 <————————————————> L2

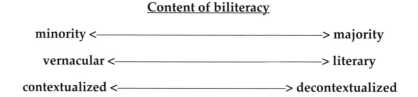

Content of biliteracy

minority <————————————————> majority

vernacular <————————————————> literary

contextualized <————————————————> decontextualized

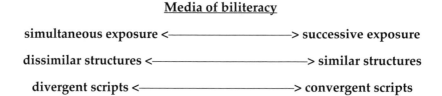

Media of biliteracy

simultaneous exposure <————————————> successive exposure

dissimilar structures <————————————> similar structures

divergent scripts <————————————> convergent scripts

**Figure 3** Power relations in the continua of biliteracy

The challenge of popular demand for the societal language of power is a very real one in contexts all over the world, one not to be lightly dismissed. In terms of the continua model, case after case shows that societal power relationships tend to favor the macro, literate, and monolingual ends of the context continua; and national policy and school curricula tend to focus primarily on second language, written, productive skills in biliterate development.

My dissertation study in Puno, Peru, in the 1980s had documented Quechua-speaking community members' resistance to the implementation of Quechua as a medium of instruction in the schools for ideological reasons largely having to do with Spanish being seen as the language of formal education and thereby of access to socioeconomic mobility and power (Hornberger, 1987, 1988a, 1988b). I concluded that unless the wider societal context could be geared toward valuing Quechua on a par with Spanish, 'policy failure' was inevitable; the schools, however well they might implement bilingual education, could not on their own counteract deep-seated ideologies favoring Spanish. Those same, enduring ideologies are the ones that the Bolivian Vice-Minister indexed in her opening comments at the Workshop, referring to Quechua and Aymara speaking communities of Bolivia some twenty years after my study in Peru; these ideologies still thrive throughout indigenous communities of the Andes.

Several South African scholars have recently documented or made reference to a similar set of ideologies in Black African communities of South Africa. There, English is the language of power, undergirded not only by the worldwide hegemony of English but also by the heritage of apartheid education which left in its wake a deep suspicion of mother tongue education. Banda explores the paradox whereby black and coloured parents increasingly demand English medium instruction even while academics and researchers agree that English medium instruction is largely responsible for 'the general lack of academic skills and intellectual growth among blacks at high school and tertiary levels' (Banda, 2000: 51); and he considers what would be needed to implement a truly additive bilingual policy. De Klerk undertook a survey and interview study in Grahamstown in the Eastern Cape Province, focusing on Xhosa-speaking parents' decisions to send their children to English-medium schools; among the reasons parents gave for

choosing an English school for their children were the need for a better education, the recognition that English is an international language and the hope that English would open the door to more job opportunities for their children (de Klerk, 2000: 204–205).

Interestingly, both Bolivia and South Africa have opened up implementational space for popular participation in establishing school language policies, South Africa via the School Governing Boards and Bolivia via the *Comités* which are part of the Popular Participation provisions of the Education Reform. The goal is to empower parents to make their own decisions about what languages will be medium and subject of instruction in their children's schools. Yet, it would appear that the implementational space for popular participation is of little avail in advancing a multilingual language policy if it is not accompanied by popular participation in the ideological space as well.

In a study carried out in six newly integrated schools in Durban in Kwazulu-Natal Province, Chick and McKay (in press) found a pervasive English-only discourse (along with a decline of standards discourse and a one-at-a-time discourse of classroom interaction) affecting classroom teaching. English-only discourse was evident for example in principals' and teachers' rejection of the use of Zulu in classes other than in Zulu lessons, a practice for which they cited as reasons that students need to improve their English, that students need English for economic advancement, and that the African National Congress itself uses English as a means of reconciling rival ethnic groups (at odds with the ANC's publicly stated position) (Chick, 2000). Yet, the same study also found evidence of counter discourses, namely a multicultural discourse and a collaborative, group work discourse. 'A number of teachers, primarily younger teachers, stated that they have discovered that the judicious use of Zulu in classrooms can be beneficial and are permitting the use of Zulu even when it runs counter to school policy' (Chick, 2000: 7); and one teacher in a former Indian elementary school had started doing more group work since attending an in-service workshop on Outcomes-Based Education, finding it advantageous in that quick progress can be made when 'brighter and more fluent learners can explain to others exactly what is required' (Chick, 2000: 12). Chick attributes the emergence of these new discourses among teachers to the ideological space which the new language policies opened up (Chick, 2000: 13).

Similarly, while Bloch and Alexander acknowledge that the languages of South Africa are situated along the macro-micro context continuum with English at the most macro (powerful) end and the indigenous African languages clustered at the most micro (powerless) end, and with Afrikaans somewhere along the middle, they go on to make clear that what is at stake with the new multilingual language policy is the 'gradual shift of power towards the languages of the majority of the people, who continue in linguistic terms to be treated as a social minority' (Bloch & Alexander, 2001: 5). They report on the work of their PRAESA[5] group at Battswood Primary School in Cape Town, where the 'intention is to develop, try out, and demonstrate workable strategies for teaching and learning, using additive bilingualism approaches'; they see themselves as working at the 'less powerful micro, oral, and multilingual ends [of the context continua] as [they] develop ways to challenge the power relations that exist at macro, literate, and monolingual English levels of the continua in the school and the wider society' (Bloch & Alexander, 2001: 10).

What then does the continua model tell us about what to do in cases such as those depicted in the opening vignettes? The work of Chick and McKay and of Bloch and Alexander is consistent with the argument from the continua model that what is needed is attention to oral, multilingual interaction at the micro level of context and to learners' first language, oral, and receptive language skills development (that is, to the traditionally less powerful ends of the continua of context and development). It is consistent as well with the 'classroom success' story that my dissertation told alongside the 'policy failure' account referred to above (Hornberger, 1987). That is, despite the ideological privileging of Spanish for school contexts, Quechua speaking children were seen then (and continue today) to clearly thrive from the greater participation in oral classroom interaction which receptive and productive use of their first language afforded them (Hornberger, 1988a, 1989b). In other words, what is needed is to find as many ways as possible to open up ideological spaces for multiple languages and literacies in classroom, community, and society. The continua model is a heuristic to assist in that ecological endeavor. We turn now to consideration of the media and content through which this

can be accomplished and the power imbalance among languages subverted.

### Media and content of biliteracy: Language and identity in the classroom

South African Professor Elizabeth encouraged her young pre-service teachers to speak and use their languages to discuss their own educational experiences and views in the classroom, thereby modeling a practice they might use with their own multilingual, multicultural students in the future. The Bolivian Curricular Development Unit experts sought to provide richly communicative and literature-based curriculum and materials for indigenous language speakers to learn Spanish, and raised questions about the implications of code-mixing practices in classroom interaction. In both cases, the negotiation of multiple languages, cultures, and identities among learners (and teachers) who bring different resources to the classroom, is at issue.

The challenge of negotiating across multiple languages, cultures, and identities is a very real one in classrooms all over the world, one not to be lightly dismissed. Yet, on the whole, educational policy and practice continues blithely to disregard the presence of multiple languages, cultures, and identities in today's classrooms. In terms of the continua model, case after case shows that majority, literary, decontextualised contents and similar, convergent, standard language varieties as successively acquired media of instruction, are the established and expected norms in educational systems everywhere.

Multilingual language policies offer a stunning contrast to these expectations, opening up a space where minority, vernacular, contextualised contents and identities can be introduced and a range of media – including dissimilar, divergent, nonstandard varieties as well as visual and other communicative modes – can be employed simultaneously in instruction. Andean teachers in a course I taught on bilingual intercultural education wrote narratives about some of their experiences along these lines. One teacher opened up a Mother's Day celebration to a child's recitation of a Quechua poem and another opened up her language class to the dramatization of a local story, using local materials and local music. In each case, the results were an impressive display of the learners' talents, accompanied by greater intercultural understanding of all those involved. These teachers made use of media and content that have historically been excluded from the school, and thereby subverted the power imbalance among the languages and literacies in the school environment (Hornberger, 2000: 191–192).

Pippa Stein writes along these lines in recounting experiences with two projects she has worked on with pre-service and in-service language teachers in Johannesburg, both of which encourage students' use of a range of representational resources in their meaning making, including the linguistic mode in its written and spoken forms, but also the visual, the gestural, the sonic, and the performative modes (paraphrasing Kress & van Leeuwen, 1996). A reflective practitioner, she is exploring 'ways of working as a teacher using certain pedagogies which re-evaluate the value of a resource in the classroom', specifically with the goal of ascribing equal value to resources brought by historically advantaged and historically disadvantaged students. Both the Performing the Literacy Archive Project and the Photographing Literacy Practices Project focus on literacy because 'issues of literacy are at the heart of educational success in schools', but in them the students 'explore meaning-making in multiple semiotic modes'. Drawing on her reflections and on written and video documentation of the students' work over the several years she has done these projects with language teachers, Stein shows how these pedagogies 'work with what students bring (their existing resources for representation) and acknowledge what [historically disadvantaged] students have lost'. As she puts it, it is 'the saying of the unsayable, that which has been silenced through loss, anger or dread, which enables students to re-articulate their relationships to their pasts. Through this process of articulation, a new energy is produced which takes people forward. I call this process of articulation and recovery re-sourcing resources' (Stein, in press).

The PRAESA group has been carrying out another effort at including practices at the traditionally less powerful ends of the content and media continua as resources in instruction in their work at Battswood Primary School with 30 Xhosa and 19 English/Afrikaans bilingual children, as they have progressed from their first days in Grade One up to the present, their third year of primary school. Bloch and Alexander report on this work in the following terms: 'Regarding the media of biliteracy, we encourage simultaneous exposure for the Xhosa and English speaking children to both languages with an emphasis on the children's first language . . . we are concentrating mainly on Xhosa and English, while at the same time not excluding Afrikaans. Our ongoing challenge, in terms of Xhosa language learning for the English/Afrikaans speakers is to try and inspire them enough, and teach the language in ways that motivate them to learn "against the odds" of any real incentives which promote Xhosa as either necessary or even desirable in the wider society' (Bloch & Alexander, 2001: 12). As regards the content of biliteracy, 'the teachers have had to move from the safety of the decontextualised content of a rigid phonics-based part-to-whole skills programme to face the real evidence of what their pupils actually know and can do, thereby drawing on contextualised, vernacular, minority (i.e. majority) knowledge' (Bloch & Alexander, 2001: 14–15).

To carry out these goals, they encourage oral, mother tongue and bilingual interaction; in grade one, the teachers sang many songs and did rhymes with the whole class, typing up the Xhosa rhymes and songs and putting them in plastic sleeves with an English one on one side and Xhosa on the other so that the children could serve as readers to each other. They use interactive writing and journal writing, with the English and Xhosa speaking teachers and PRAESA staff members writing back to the children in their respective languages, a strategy which has proved to provide powerful motivation for the children's use of both languages in their writing. The teachers read daily stories in both Xhosa and English, and have collected an adequate selection of Xhosa and English picture storybooks, which they encourage the children to read in bilingual pairs. The PRAESA group has begun to identify numerous strengths which such practices develop in the children, while simultaneously confronting the fact that most scholastic assessment tools do not measure the kinds of metalinguistic and interpretive skills which particularly stand out in these children.

What then does the continua model tell us about what to do in cases such as those depicted in the opening vignettes? The work of Stein and of Bloch and Alexander is consistent with the argument from the continua model that what is needed is attention to the diversity of standard and nonstandard language varieties, orthographies, and communicative modes and the range of contextualized, vernacular, minority knowledge resources that learners bring to the classroom (that is, to the traditionally less powerful ends of the continua of media and content). It is consistent as well with the on-the-ground experience of the Bolivian and South African educators who find that multilingual interaction in the classroom is inevitable and desirable if multilingual learners are to be encouraged to participate – in the classroom, in academic success, and, ultimately, in a truly democratic society. In other words, what is needed is to find as many ways as possible to open up implementational spaces for multiple languages, literacies, and identities in classroom, community, and society. The continua model is a heuristic to assist in that ecological endeavor.

## Conclusion

Bloch and Alexander express the hope that 'the window of opportunity will remain open for another few years and that the multiplication of such projects in different areas of South Africa involving all the different languages ... will shift the balance of power in favour of those for whom ostensibly the democratic transition was initiated' (Bloch & Alexander, 2001: 25). I share their optimism and their sense of urgency that we linguists and language educators must work hard alongside language planners and language users to fill the ideological and implementational spaces opened up by multilingual language policies; and as researchers to document these new discourses in action so as to keep those ecological policy spaces open into the future.

My sense of urgency about this is perhaps heightened because of recent accumulating events in my own country, where multilingual language policy spaces seem to be closing up at an accelerating rate and the one language–one nation ideology still holds tremendous sway. Analyzing the politics of official English in the 104th Congress of the United States, Joseph Lo Bianco writes of a U.S. discourse which he designates *unum* and which is all about opposing multilingual excess and national disunity, i.e. about homogenization and assimilationism. Also present, he found, was a discourse of *pluribus*, about diversity and emancipation, i.e. about language pluralism (Lo Bianco, 2001). Both discourses have arguably always been present in the United States, waxing and waning with the times, an ideological tension captured succinctly in the U.S. motto, *E pluribus unum* 'out of many one' from which Lo Bianco takes his designations.[6]

Though the United States traditionally has no national language policy, US language ideologies are evident in both national educational policy and state level language policies. In the latter half of the 20th century, there have been ecological policy spaces for multilingualism and the discourse of *pluribus* in, for example, the national Bilingual Education Act, now of more than 30 years standing, and in state language policies such as Hawaii's recognition of Hawaiian and English or New Mexico's of Spanish and English. Since 1980, however, when Hayakawa first introduced a proposed English Language Constitutional Amendment in Congress, the discourse of *unum* has been gaining ground as a growing number of states have passed English-only legislation.

Even more recently, the pace has picked up. At the state level, under the infamous Unz initiative, California and Arizona voters passed anti-bilingual education referenda in 1999 and 2000, respectively. In these states, multilingual language policies were thereby reversed (or severely curtailed) for ideological reasons before implementation could be fully realized, documented, and tested. In the debates surrounding passage of Proposition 227 in California, it became clear that (1) the public had very little understanding of what bilingual education really is; and (2) much of what passed for bilingual education in California was in fact not. The ideological discourse of *unum* prevailed over that of *pluribus*, with very little attention to the facts of institutional implementation.[7] At the national level, under the Bush administration, the Bilingual Education Act is undergoing threat of revision which would gut its potential to provide multilingual education for thousands of children who speak English as a second language. Instead, the emphasis is on 'moving them to English fluency' in a minimal number of years (National Association for Bilingual Education Action Alert, 23 April 2001; 3 May 2001). None of these trends bodes well for the pluralistic discourse of *pluribus* or a multilingual language ecology in the United States.

Happily, however, there is also a move afoot in recent years among U.S. linguists and language educators to help solidify, support, and promote longstanding grassroots minority language maintenance and revitalization efforts in the United States, under the rubric of 'heritage languages'.[8] The Heritage Language Initiative, which has among its priorities 'to help the U.S. education system recognize and develop the heritage language resources of the country' and 'to increase dialogue and promote collaboration among a broad range of stakeholders' (http://www.cal.org/heritage/), has thus far sponsored one national research conference in 1999 with plans for another in 2002 [see Wiley & Valdés (2000) for a selection of papers from the first conference]. In the intervening years, a working group of scholars was convened to draft a statement of research priorities now being circulated to researchers and policy-makers [available in Wiley & Valdés (2000) and at www. cal.org/heritage]; and a bi-national conversation on heritage/community languages between U.S. and Australian scholars took place in Melbourne (http://www.staff.vu.edu.au/languageconf/).

This Heritage Language Initiative, supported by both the Center for Applied Linguistics and the National Foreign Language Center, is at least in part about resolving the longstanding language policy paradox whereby we squander our ethnic language resources while lamenting our lack of foreign language resources. It further seeks to draw together and provide visibility and support for the myriad and ongoing bottom-up efforts at rescuing and developing U.S. indigenous and immigrant language resources [as documented in volumes such as Cantoni (1996); Henze & Davis (1999); Hornberger (1996); McCarty & Zepeda (1995, 1998) on U.S. indigenous languages; Fishman (1966b); Kloss (1977); Ferguson & Heath (1981); García & Fishman (1997); McKay & Wong (1988, 2000); Pérez (1998) on U.S. (indigenous and) immigrant languages; Fishman (1991, 2000); May (1999) on cases around the world including U.S. indigenous and immigrant languages].

The Heritage/Community Language effort is one which, I believe, takes an ecological, resource view of indigenous, immigrant, ethnic, and foreign languages as living and evolving in relation to each other and to their environment and as requiring support lest any one of them become further endangered. As linguists and language educators, we need to fill as many ecological spaces as possible, both ideological and implementational, with efforts like these and the Andean and South African efforts mentioned above if we are to keep the multilingual language policy option alive, not only in Bolivia, South Africa, the United States, and Australia, but in all corners of our multilingual world.

## Acknowledgments
This paper was originally presented as a plenary talk at the Third International Symposium on Bilingualism, held at the University of the West of England, in Bristol, UK, in April 2001. I am grateful to Stephen May and the members of the Organizing Committee for inviting me and providing the opportunity for me to pull these thoughts together; and I thank those present for their comments. I also thank Educational Linguistics Ph.D. student Mihyon Jeon for her thoughtful and detailed response and suggestions on an earlier version of the paper.

My gratitude goes to Professor Elizabeth Henning of Rand Afrikaans University for inviting and hosting me for a two-week visit in conjunction with the Qualitative Research in Education conference there. My thanks also go to Luis Enrique López, Director of PROEIB Andes (*Programa de Formación en Educación Intercultural Bilingüe para los Países Andinos,* Andean Graduate Program in Bilingual Intercultural Education) and to the Bolivian Ministry of Education for including me as participant in the La Paz *Taller* described in the Introduction.

## Notes
1. The nine languages are: Ndebele, Northern Sotho, Southern Sotho, Swati, Tsonga, Tswana, Venda, Xhosa, and Zulu.
2. In my usage here, 'language educators' includes linguists and researchers on language education, language teachers, language teacher educators, and others; 'language planners' includes both top-down and bottom-up, organizational and individual agents of language planning; and 'language users' includes learners, parents, community members, and others. In other words, I take an inclusive view of those who should be involved in the efforts described here.
3. Van Lier (2000) cites Trim (1959) as the first reference to ecology of language.
4. In recent and forthcoming volumes (Huss *et al.*, 2001; Liddicoat & Bryant, 2001; Maffi, 2001; Nettle & Romaine, 2000; Skutnabb-Kangas, 2000), scholars posit an ecology of language in not only a metaphorical sense but also a literal one, explicitly linking the maintenance of linguistic and cultural diversity with the protection and defense of biological and environmental diversity.

While I may share their views, that is not the focus of this paper.

5.	PRAESA is the Project for the Study of Alternative Education in South Africa, directed by Neville Alexander and based at the University of Cape Town. The team at Battswood Primary School includes one PRAESA staff member (Carole Bloch), assisted sometimes by a post-graduate student, a Xhosa speaking teacher, Ntombizanele Nkence, and a resident Battswood teacher, Erica Fellies (Bloch & Alexander, 2001: 11).

6.	Similarly, Cobarrubias identifies 'linguistic assimilation' and 'linguistic pluralism' as two typical language ideologies which have long co-existed in tension in the United States (Cobarrubias, 1983: 63).

7.	Similarly, May (2000), analyzing the Welsh case, writes that minority language policy must overcome both institutional and attitudinal difficulties in order to be successfully implemented at state level. That is, the minority language must be institutionalized in the public realm and it must gain attitudinal support from majority language speakers.

8.	While the term 'heritage language' has been in use, particularly in Canada, since the early 1970s, a brief search in the *Linguistics and Language Behavior Abstracts* covering 1973 to 2001 shows that the term has been gaining significant ground in the U.S. only in the last decade and in particular the last five years. Of 120 references, 100 date from 1991 or later; 68 of these from 1997 or later. While the majority of references are still to Canada's heritage languages, there is a growing number of references to U.S. indigenous (e.g. Hawaiian, Navajo, Oneida, Siouan) and immigrant (e.g. Chinese, Korean, Italian, Spanish, Yiddish) languages. Meanwhile, as Colin Baker has noted, the term sometimes carries a negative connotation of pointing to the (ancient, primitive) past rather than to a (modern, technological) future (Baker & Jones, 1998: 509); for perhaps this reason and others, the preferred term in Australia is 'community languages' (Clyne, 1991; Horvath & Vaughn, 1991).

## References

Baker, C. and Jones, S.P. (1998) *Encyclopedia of Bilingualism and Bilingual Education*. Clevedon, UK: Multilingual Matters.

Banda, F. (2000) The dilemma of the mother tongue: Prospects for bilingual education in South Africa. *Language, Culture and Curriculum, 13*(1), 51–66.

Barton, D. (1994) *Literacy: An Introduction to the Ecology of Written Language*. Oxford: Blackwell Publishers.

Bloch, C. and Alexander, N. (2001) A luta continua!: The relevance of the continua of biliteracy to South African multilingual schools. Paper presented at Third International Bilingualism Symposium, Bristol, UK, April.

Cantoni, G. (ed.) (1996) *Stabilizing Indigenous Languages*. Flagstaff: Northern Arizona University Center for Excellence in Education.

Chick, K. (2000) Constructing a multicultural national identity: South African classrooms as sites of struggle between competing discourses. Paper presented at Nessa Wolfson Colloquium, University of Pennsylvania, November.

Chick, K. and McKay, S. (in press) Positioning learners in post apartheid South African schools: A case study of selected multicultural Durban schools. *Linguistics in Education*.

Clyne, M. (1991) *Community Languages: The Australian Experience*. Melbourne: Cambridge University Press.

Cobarrubias, J. (1983) Ethical issues in status planning. In Juan Cobarrubias (ed.), *Progress in Language Planning* (pp. 41–86). Berlin: Mouton.

de Klerk, V. (2000) To be Xhosa or not to be Xhosa . . . that is the question. *Journal of Multilingual and Multicultural Development, 21*(3), 198–215.

Ferguson, C.A. and Heath, S.B. (eds) (1981) *Language in the USA*. New York: Cambridge University Press.

Fishman, J.A. (1966a) Planned reinforcement of language maintenance in the United States; Suggestions for the conservation of a neglected national resource. In Joshua A. Fishman (ed.), *Language Loyalty in the United States: The Maintenance and Perpetuation of Non-English Mother Tongues by American Ethnic and Religious Groups* (pp. 369–411). The Hague: Mouton.

Fishman, J.A. (ed.) (1966b) *Language Loyalty in the United States: The Maintenance and Perpetuation of Non-English Mother Tongues by American Ethnic and Religious Groups*. The Hague: Mouton.

Fishman, J.A. (1969) National languages and languages of wider communication in the developing nations. *Anthropological Linguistics, 11*(4), 111–135.

Fishman, J.A. (1991) *Reversing Language Shift: Theoretical and Empirical Foundations of Assistance to Threatened Languages.* Clevedon, UK: Multilingual Matters.

Fishman, J.A. (ed.) (2000) *Can Threatened Languages be Saved? 'Reversing Language Shift' Revisited.* Clevedon, UK: Multilingual Matters.

Freeland, J. (1996) The global, the national and the local: Forces in the development of education for indigenous peoples – the case of Peru. *Compare, 26*(2), 167–195.

Gal, S. (1989) Language and political economy. *Annual Review of Anthropology, 18,* 345–367.

García, O. and Fishman, J.A. (eds) (1997) *The Multilingual Apple: Languages in New York City.* Berlin: Mouton.

Haugen, E. (1972) *The Ecology of Language.* Stanford, California: Stanford University Press.

Henze, R. and Davis, K.A. (eds) (1999) Authenticity and identity: Lessons from indigenous language education. *Anthropology and Education Quarterly, 30*(1) (entire issue).

Hornberger, N.H. (1987) Bilingual education success, but policy failure. *Language in Society, 16*(2), 205–226.

Hornberger, N.H. (1988a) *Bilingual Education and Language Maintenance: A Southern Peruvian Quechua Case.* Berlin: Mouton.

Hornberger, N.H. (1988b) Language ideology in Quechua communities of Puno, Peru. *Anthropological Linguistics, 30*(2), 214–235.

Hornberger, N.H. (1989a) Continua of biliteracy. *Review of Educational Research, 59*(3), 271–296.

Hornberger, N.H. (1989b) Pupil participation and teacher techniques: Criteria for success in a Peruvian bilingual education program for Quechua children. *International Journal of the Sociology of Language, 77,* 35–53.

Hornberger, N.H. (1990) Creating successful learning contexts for bilingual literacy. *Teachers College Record, 92*(2), 212–229.

Hornberger, N.H. (ed.) (1996) *Indigenous Literacies in the Americas: Language Planning from the Bottom Up.* Berlin: Mouton.

Hornberger, N.H. (2000) Bilingual education policy and practice in the Andes: Ideological paradox and intercultural possibility. *Anthropology and Education Quarterly, 31*(2), 173–201.

Hornberger, N.H. and Skilton-Sylvester, E. (2000) Revisiting the continua of biliteracy: International and critical perspectives. *Language and Education: An International Journal, 14*(2), 96–122.

Horvath, B.M. and Vaughan, P. (1991) *Community Languages: A Handbook.* Clevedon, UK: Multilingual Matters.

Huss, L., Grima, A.C. and King, K. (eds) (2001) *Transcending Monolingualism: Linguistic Revitalisation in Education.* Lisse, The Netherlands: Swets & Zeitlinger.

Kaplan, R.B. and Baldauf, R.B. (1997) *Language Planning from Practice to Theory.* Clevedon, UK: Multilingual Matters.

Kaplan, R.B., Baldauf, Jr., R.B., Liddicoat, A.J., Bryant, P., Barbaux, M-T. and Pütz, M. (2000) Editorial. *Current Issues in Language Planning, 1*(1), 1–10.

Kloss, H. (1977) *The American Bilingual Tradition.* Rowley, MA: Newbury House.

Kress, G. and van Leeuwen, T. (1996) *Reading Images: The Grammar of Visual Design.* London: Routledge.

Liddicoat, A.J. and Bryant, P. (eds) (2001) Language planning and language ecology: A current issue in language planning. *Current Issues in Language Planning, 1*(3) (entire issue).

Lo Bianco, J. (2001) What is the problem? A study of official English. Paper presented at the annual meetings of the American Association for Applied Linguistics, St. Louis, MI.

Maffi, L. (2001) *On Biocultural Diversity: Linking Language, Knowledge, and the Environment.* Washington, DC: Smithsonian Institution Press.

May, S. (ed.) (1999) *Indigenous Community-based Education.* Clevedon, UK: Multilingual Matters.

May, S. (2000) Accommodating and resisting minority language policy: The case of Wales. *International Journal of Bilingual Education and Bilingualism, 3*(2), 101–128.

May, S. (2001) *Language and Minority Rights: Ethnicity, Nationalism and the Politics of Language.* Essex, UK: Pearson Education.

McCarty, T.L. and Zepeda, O. (eds) (1995) Indigenous language education and literacy. *Bilingual Research Journal, 19*(1) (entire issue).

McCarty, T.L. and Zepeda, O. (eds) (1998) Indigenous language use and change in the Americas. *International Journal of the Sociology of Language, 132* (entire issue).

McKay, S.L. and Wong, S.C. (eds) (2000) *New Immigrants in the United States: Readings for Second Language Educators.* New York: Cambridge University Press.

McKay, S.L. and Wong, S.C. (eds) (1988) *Language*

*Diversity: Problem or Resource?* New York: Newbury House.

Mühlhaüsler, P. (1996) *Linguistic Ecology: Language Change and Linguistic Imperialism in the Pacific Region.* London: Routledge.

Nettle, D. and Romaine, S. (2000) *Vanishing Voices: The Extinction of the World's Languages.* New York: Oxford University Press.

Pakir, A. (1991) Contribution to workshop on endangered languages, International Conference on Austronesian Linguistics, Hawaii (cited in Mühlhaüsler 1996).

Pérez, B. (ed.) (1998) *Sociocultural Contexts of Language and Literacy.* Mahwah, NJ: Lawrence Erlbaum.

Phillipson, R. and Skutnabb-Kangas, T. (1996) English only worldwide or language ecology? *TESOL Quarterly, 30*(3), 429–452.

Ricento, T. (2000) Historical and theoretical perspectives in language policy and planning. *Journal of Sociolinguistics, 4*(2), 196–213.

Ruiz, R. (1984) Orientations in language planning. *NABE Journal, 8*(2), 15–34.

Skutnabb-Kangas, T. (2000) *Linguistic Genocide in Education – or Worldwide Diversity and Human Rights?* Mahwah, NJ: Lawrence Erlbaum.

Stein, P. (in press) Re-sourcing resources: pedagogy, history and loss in a Johannesburg classroom. In M. Hawkins (ed.) *Social/Cultural Approaches to Language Learning, Teaching, and Teacher Education.* Clevedon, UK: Multilingual Matters.

Trim, J.L.M. (1959) Historical, descriptive and dynamic linguistics. *Language and Speech, 2,* 9–25.

van Lier, L. (2000) From input to affordance: Social-interactive learning from an ecological perspective. In J.P. Lantolf (ed.) *Sociocultural Theory and Second Language Learning* (pp. 245–259). Oxford: Oxford University Press.

Voegelin, C.F. and Voegelin, F.M. (1964) Languages of the world: Native America Fascicle One. *Anthropological Linguistics, 6*(6), 2–45.

Wiley, T. and Valdés, G. (eds) (2000) Heritage language instruction in the United States: A time for renewal. *Bilingual Research Journal, 24*(4) (entire issue).

Woolard, K.A. and Schieffelin, B.B. (1994) Language ideology. *Annual Review of Anthropology, 23,* 55–82.

## Questions

1. What is meant by 'ecology of language'? How does a language ecology have similarities and differences to the ecology of living and endangered species? What is the difference between language evolution, language environment and language endangerment?

2. From your own experience, provide examples of variety in (a) contexts of learning (b) development of biliteracy (c) content of biliteracy and (d) media of biliteracy. Such variety should ideally mirror both the sub dimensions in each of these four headings, *and* some of the variety possible within a sub dimension. For more detail see: N.H. Hornberger (ed.), 2004, *Continua of Biliteracy: An Ecological Framework for Educational Policy, Research and Practice in Multilingual Settings.* Clevedon: Multilingual Matters.

3. Hornberger regards the right-hand end of her 12 subdimensions as traditionally more powerful. On each of these sub dimensions, briefly say why one end of the dimension is more powerful. You may wish to read Hornberger and Skilton-Sylvester (2000) to help answer this question.
   Reference: Hornberger, N.H. and Skilton-Sylvester, E., 2003, Revisiting the Continua of Biliteracy: International and Critical Perspectives. In N.H. Hornberger (ed.) *Continua of Biliteracy: an Ecological Framework for Educational Policy, Research, and Practice in Multilingual Settings.* Clevedon: Multilingual Matters.

4. What contrasts and similarities does Hornberger find between the US and South Africa in language policy? What is implied in a language policy of (a) *unum* (b) *pluribus* (c) *E pluribus unum*?

## Activities

1. Discuss in small groups what are the top priorities in 'creating successful learning contexts for bilingual literacy'. Then observe a bilingual classroom where biliteracy is valued. What are the main strategies of that classroom? What literacy practices are observed and in which languages? What literacy materials and media are used and in which languages? Is there evidence of majority language literacy only, or biliteracy or multiliteracy? Report your findings to the class.

2. Make an inventory of all the media (including electronic texts and technology) used in the teaching of biliteracy in a bilingual classroom. Identify their language and language variety(ies) used, genres, country where published, richness and variety of content, richness of language, quality of printing, quality of illustrations, ethnic content, bicultural and/or multicultural content and gender content. Compare the list of media and texts to teach literacy in the majority language with that to teach literacy in the minority language. Compare the availability of media texts in English and other languages, their quality, their content, and the differences in their classroom use. Are there any bilingual texts? How are those used? Then observe at least one lesson in each language. How are the different media and texts used? How would you evaluate their use? Find examples that are ethnocentric.

3. Observe two literacy lessons in two languages in a specific classroom. Describe practices, including texts, questions, peer interaction, role of listening, reading, speaking and writing, and grouping (if applicable). What are the differences in literacy instructional strategies and literacy practices in both languages? Do children's experiences relate to their literacy acquisition? Is there any differentiated literacy instruction for students who are second language learners and students with disabilities?

4. Visit a school where biliteracy is important. Make a video-tape of a literacy lesson in English and one in the non-English language. Show it to the class and write an essay comparing both practices. If possible, different groups should visit schools for different ethnolinguistic groups, with differences in script, directionality, etc. Reflect on how the structure of language itself may affect literacy practices. How is meaning constructed in the two literacy classes?

5. Visit a classroom with a large number of language minority students. Describe their literacy practices, both in English and if available, in a non-English language. Then visit another classroom at the same grade level where there are few language minority students (possibly a private school). Describe their literacy practices. Contrast the difference between the two. If possible, make a video-tape to share with the class.

6. Brainstorm about ways in which the web might be used to support students' biliteracy practices. Develop a teaching unit for a particular grade level using the web.

## Further Reading

Baker, C. (2006) *Foundations of Bilingual Education and Bilingualism* (4th edn). Clevedon: Multilingual Matters (chapter 14).

Blackledge, A. (2000) *Literacy, Power and Social Justice*. Stoke on Trent: Trentham.

Hornberger, N.H. (ed.) (2003) *Continua of Biliteracy: An Ecological Framework for Educational Policy, Research, and Practice in Multilingual Settings*. Clevedon: Multilingual Matters.

Hornberger, N.H. (2004) The continua of biliteracy and the bilingual educator: Educational linguistics in practice. *International Journal of Bilingual Education and Bilingualism*, 7, 2&3, 155–171.

Martin-Jones, M. and Jones. K. (eds) (2000) *Multilingual Literacies. Reading and Writing Different Worlds.* Amsterdam: John Benjamins.

New London Group (1996) A pedagogy of multiliteracies: Designing social futures. *Harvard Educational Review* 66, 60–92.

Reyes, M. and Halcon, J. (eds) (2001) *The Best for Our Children: Critical Perspectives on Literacy for Latino Students.* New York: Teachers College Press.

# Writing in a Second Language Across the Curriculum

## Pauline Gibbons

### The Curriculum Cycle

Let's turn now to what these principles might look like in the classroom. Derewianka (1990) and others involved in the 'genre' movement in Australia have identified four stages (named the Curriculum Cycle) through which a particular text type can be made explicit to students. These four stages of the Curriculum Cycle have come to be known as *building up the field*, *modeling the text type*, *joint construction*, and *independent writing*. Each of these stages has a particular teaching purpose:

- *Stage 1: Building the Field*. In this stage the aim is to make sure that your students have enough background knowledge of the topic to be able to write about it. The focus here is primarily on the content or information of the text. At this stage, children are a long way from writing a text themselves, and activities will involve speaking, listening, reading, information gathering, note taking, and reading.
- *Stage 2: Modeling the Text Type*. In this stage the aim is for students to become familiar with the purpose, overall structure, and linguistic features of the type of text they are going to write. The focus here is therefore on the form and function of the particular text type that the students are going to write.
- *Stage 3: Joint Construction*. Here the teacher and students write a text together, so that students can see how the text is written. The focus here is on illustrating the process of writing a text, considering both the content and the language.
- *Stage 4: Independent Writing*. At this stage students write their own text.

It's important to recognize that this Curriculum Cycle may take several weeks or longer to go through and may be the overall framework for an entire topic. It is not a single lesson!

Here are some classroom activities that you might find useful for each of the stages. Not all activities will be appropriate for all ages, and they also are not all appropriate for use in the teaching of every text type. In addition, from your general teaching experience you can no doubt think of other language-focused activities and ways of developing the topic. However, the activities suggested here illustrate how this approach to writing integrates speaking, listening, reading, and writing, and integrates language with curriculum content.

As an example, let's imagine that you want to help children write a report – that is, a factual account of what something is (or was) like. First, you need to make a decision about what curriculum topic would require students to write a report. (In this case, let's say dinosaurs.) Always be sure to consider what you have already planned to teach (in any curriculum area). It's important that the Curriculum Cycle should be based on your regular curriculum – it shouldn't be seen as an 'add-on' to what you would normally be teaching.

### Stage 1: Building Knowledge of the Topic

The aim here is to build up background knowledge, and so the focus is primarily on the 'content' of the topic. Since the primary purpose of this stage is to collect information, some of the activities could be carried out by groups of students in their mother tongue, although they will need to use English to share the information with others. A useful form of classroom organization for a number of the activities discussed here is an **expert/home grouping**. This kind of organization involves note-taking, listening, speaking, and reading, and it provides a genuine need for authentic communication. While collaborative learning strategies are important for all children, they offer to ESL children a range of situations in which they are exposed to and learn to use subject-specific language.

Again, the expert/home grouping strategy for collaborative learning depends on groups of children holding different information from others in the class. You can vary how you do this, but as a general principle, different groups of students become 'expert' in a different aspect of the topic during a particular activity. In this example, groups of four to six could choose to carry out research on a particular dinosaur. Once they have become 'experts', the students regroup so that the home group contains one student from each of the 'expert' groups. The experts' job is to share what they have learned with the rest of the group.

Here are some ways to build up a shared knowledge of the topic. They are in no particular order but are simply examples of activities that you could use. As you can see, an important aspect of this stage is that it involves a lot of speaking, listening, and reading, and develops a range of research skills.

- Build up a **semantic web** of students' current knowledge of the topic, teaching new vocabulary as appropriate.
- Use **wallpapering** to collect ideas based on students' current knowledge.
- Gather a list of questions from the children of things they would like to find out about (e.g. *why did the dinosaurs disappear?*). For beginner ESL students, this also models the structure of question forms.
- Read about the topic with students using shared reading or big books. This could include both nonfiction and fiction texts. If you use both kinds, there is an opportunity to discuss with students the different purposes of each. With a narrative text you could also talk about what is fact and what is fiction, and ask children what facts (if any) they have learned about dinosaurs from the story.
- Use pictures to elicit or teach vocabulary. You could also get students to match labels to simple line drawings, introducing more technical vocabulary such as *horns, jaws, curved teeth, crest, spine, thumb claw, scaly skin, tail, plates, spikes.*
- Develop a **word wall/word bank** about the topic, where technical vocabulary can be displayed.

- Use **jigsaw listening** to extend the children's knowledge base. Each group could listen to audiotaped information about a different dinosaur, or a different theory about why they disappeared. They could make notes and later share the information with the rest of the class, either in groups or with the whole class.
- Use technological resources (the Internet is a wonderful resource for many topics) to access additional information. Here is a context where you could again use a home/expert grouping.
- Get the students to **interview** an expert in the field. They could write a letter inviting an expert into the classroom and prepare questions to ask.
- Use a **picture and sentence matching** game. Get younger or beginning ESL children to match pictures and sentences about dinosaurs (e.g. *Stegosaurus had a row of plates on its back* and *Diplodocus was the longest of all the dinosaurs*). You could turn this into a barrier game whereby Student A reads out a sentence – *It has a row of plates on its back* – and Student B points to the appropriate picture.
- Use **barrier games** such as Find the Difference to describe the appearance of dinosaurs, such as by finding the differences between Stegosaurus and Triceratops. (See Figure 1.)
- Use the topic to develop library skills by visiting the library and getting the students to suggest where they might find the specific information they are looking for.
- Watch a video and provide an **information grid** for pairs of children to complete as they watch. Or you could use two sets of questions, with one half of the class answering one set, in pairs, and the other half answering the other set, in pairs. Later, pairs from each half could form groups of four and share their information.
- Visit a museum and give different groups of children different questions to research. Children would later share information in the expert/home groups as mentioned earlier.
- As an ongoing activity during this stage, build up an **information grid** with the class that summarizes the information the students have gathered. This could be formed on a large sheet of paper and displayed on the wall. This is a 'working document', not an end in itself, so both

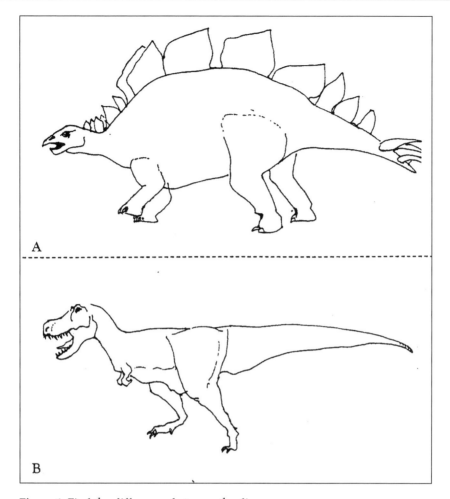

**Figure 1** Find the differences between the dinosaurs

you and the students can add to it as they discover more information. Encourage children to do this whenever they learn something new. Alternatively, children can also develop their own information grids, individually, in pairs, or in a group. In the following stages, these information summaries will be very important.

• Use the topic to practice or introduce grammar structures that are particularly meaningful to the topic. For example, although scientists know a great deal about dinosaurs, there is much that is still speculative. We don't know for sure why dinosaurs became extinct, nor why they grew so large. Very recent evidence suggests that they may have been warm-blooded. It is important for learners to be able to express these uncertainties, and this would be a meaningful context in which to introduce or remind students about how to use modality, the way in which speakers express degrees of likelihood or probability (e.g. *may be, perhaps, might, could be*), or degrees of usuality (e.g. *sometimes, often, frequently*). Ways of expressing probability could form a word bank (e.g. *might have been, may have been, possibly, probably, perhaps, it is possible that*) from which students can construct sentences:

*Perhaps dinosaurs disappeared because the climate changed.*
*Dinosaurs might have disappeared because the climate changed.*
*They probably communicated with their eyes and the sounds they made.*
*They may have been warm-blooded.*

## Stage 2: Modeling the Text

This stage aims to build up students' under-standings of the purpose, overall structure, and language features of the particular text type the class is focusing on. You should choose a text that is similar to the one you will use in the next stage (joint construction) and to the one that students will eventually write themselves. Model texts may be commercially produced, teacher-written, or texts written previously by other students. It is helpful to have this model text on an overhead or a large sheet of paper, so that you can talk about it as a class more easily. For our example, you would choose a short report about dinosaurs, or about a particular dinosaur.

During this stage, introduce some meta-language – language to talk about language – to the students as it is needed. Words like *connec-tives, organizational structure, text type, verbs,* and *tense* will make it easier for you to talk about the key features, and for the students to self-evaluate their own texts later. Contrary to much debate about the place of the teaching of 'grammar', research in Australia has shown that students do not have difficulty in understanding these concepts, and that providing a label helps make explicit key aspects of writing (Williams, 1999). The principle here, of course, is that these gram-matical terms are taught *in the context of language use.* Here are some steps to follow.

- Read and show the model report to the students, and discuss with them its purpose – to present factual information on a topic. (If students are already familiar with narratives, you could discuss with them the difference between the purposes of a narrative and of a report.)
- Draw attention to the organizational structure or 'shape' of the text, and the function of each stage (e.g. reports begin with a general statement, the purpose of which is to locate what is being talked about in the broader scheme of things, and the rest of the report consists of facts about various

aspects of the subject). Then focus on any grammatical structures and vocabulary that are important in the text. You may want to focus on modality, as discussed earlier, or on the verbs *be* and *have,* since these are very common in information reports. (Note, however, that here they will be used in the past tense since we are referring to things no longer in existence.) Alternatively, you might prefer to let the students themselves decide on these features, in which case you will need to provide careful guidance and questioning, and the students will probably need to examine several examples of the same text type.

- Students in pairs do a **text reconstruction** of part of the report, where they sequence jumbled sentences into a coherent text. Alternately, you could mix up the sentences from two reports so that students must first sort out which sentence belongs to which report, and then sequence them.
- Use a **dictogloss** to provide another model of the text type. The content of this should be taken from the current topic (e.g. you could choose a text that describes one of the dinosaurs the children are researching). In turn, this will also be a source of further information.
- Use the model text as a **cloze** exercise, making the 'gaps' according to the gram-matical features or vocabulary you are focusing on. Children will also enjoy using a **monster cloze** or a **vanishing cloze**.
- Use part of the model text as a **running dictation**.
- Once the students have a clear idea of the characteristics of a report (or whatever text type you are focusing on), remind them of these characteristics and, write them up as a chart that can be displayed on the wall.

## Stage 3: Joint Construction

At this stage, students are ready to think about writing, although they will not yet be writing alone. The teacher or students decide on the topic they will write about, but again it should be an example of the same text type, such as a report on one type of dinosaur. To ensure that students have sufficient background knowledge, encourage them to draw on the information grid the class developed in Stage 1.

It will help you to understand the teaching purpose of this stage if you return to Chapter

1 and the example of Nigel talking with his parents. There we saw how the story Nigel told was jointly constructed – while the *meanings* were initiated by Nigel, his parents helped with the *wording*. This is a natural process, and for most adults an intuitive one. The joint construction stage of writing mirrors the same process. The students give suggestions and contribute ideas while the teacher scribes, and together the teacher and students discuss how the writing can be improved. Throughout the process, the teacher and students constantly reread together what they have written, with the teacher asking questions like these:

*What do we need to start with?*
*Is that the best way to say it?*
*Can anyone think of a better word than that?*
*Is this all OK now? Can anyone see anything that needs fixing up?*

You should also remind students of the model texts they have looked at. For example, ask questions such as:

*Can you remember what the other reports were like?*
*What do you think we should talk about next?*

At this stage, teacher and students together discuss the overall structure of the text, suggest more appropriate vocabulary, consider alternative ways of wording an idea, and work on correcting grammatical mistakes, spelling, and punctuation. This is a time when there can be an explicit focus on grammar, but, unlike the traditional classroom, it occurs in functionally relevant ways – in the context of actual language use, and at the point of need.

In the following excerpt, which is taken from a joint construction of an explanation about how a telephone works, two students below talk about language. The excerpt shows evidence of quite sophisticated understandings about using reference words.

*We keep repeating 'the exchange', 'the exchange', 'the exchange'.*
*Let's put 'it' instead.*
*But they won't know what 'it' is!*
*Yes they will 'cause we've already said it.* (from Derewianka 1990: 59)

At the joint construction stage, then, the teacher

encourages students to focus on all aspects of writing. But this stage should also model the process of writing: as suggestions are made, the teacher will cross out, amend, and add words. Once this first draft is complete, the teacher or a student can rewrite it on a large sheet of paper, and it can remain in the classroom as an additional model text.

While the joint construction stage is teacher-guided, it should not be seen as teacher-dominated. The teacher does not simply write her 'own' text. Rather, her role is to take up the ideas of the students, leading the discussion of any linguistic aspects of the text that students are still learning to control. This is a very important part of the curriculum cycle because it illustrates to students both the *process* of composing text, and a *product* that is similar to what they will later write themselves.

## Stage 4: Independent Writing

This is the final stage of the cycle, when students write their own texts. They can do this writing individually or in pairs. For our example, they could choose a dinosaur to write about (but not the same one as used in Stages 2 and 3). By now there has been a considerable amount of scaffolding for the writing. Students have developed considerable background knowledge about the subject, are aware of the linguistic characteristics of the text type, and have jointly constructed a similar text. This preparation, or scaffolding, for writing will help ensure that they have the knowledge and skills to be able to write their own texts with confidence.

As students write, remind them about the process of writing: doing a first draft, self-editing, discussing the draft with friends and later with the teacher, and finally producing a 'published' text. The published texts can be displayed in the classroom or made into a class book. If you photocopy a few of the students' texts (with their permission), they will also serve as useful models and resources for other classes.

## References

Derewianka, B. (1990) *Exploring How Texts Work.* Portsmouth, NH: Heinemann.

Williams, G. (1990) Grammar as a semiotic tool in child literacy development. In C. Ward and W. Renandya (eds) *Language Teaching: New Insights for the Language Teacher Series 40.* Singapore: Regional Language Centre SEAMO.

## Questions

1.  Using you imagination, give an integrated illustration of a cycle that involves the four stages of: building the field; modeling the text type; joint construction; independent writing. The example should be capable of implementation in a local classroom.
2.  Gibbons suggests that 'building knowledge of a topic' is the foundational stage of learning to write in a second language. Does this imply a celebration of the student's heritage language and culture, or enculturation into the second language community?
3.  What is the role that Gibbons assigns to the students' mother tongue in the development of writing in a second language?

## Activities

1.  Collect an instance of a particular bilingual student's writing in the following genres: an autobiography, a personal letter, a poem, a fantasy story, and a narrative essay. Evaluate the students' writing across genres. Where is the student a most efficient writer, what strategies are used, and why? How does the student's bilingualism seem to affect these genres?
2.  Ask five language minority students who are bilingual to write a short story in their mother tongue about a fictional young character who lives in the old country. A week later, ask the same five students to write the same short story, this time using English. Compare stories. What are the differences in structure, lexicon and message? What could these differences be attributed to? How much of the other culture do you think can be transmitted through English? What consequences does this have for instruction?
3.  Tape and transcribe at least one half hour of literacy instruction from any of the following settings:
    a.  a second language class with a large number of students who are second language learners and speak the same first language as the teacher
    b.  a bilingual class where instruction is taking place in the students' second language
    c.  a two-way dual language program in which there are linguistically heterogeneous groups

    Analyze the language use during literacy instruction in the classroom. If two languages are used (by either students or teacher), say when, why and how. If they're separated (by either students or teacher), say when, why and how. Share the transcript with the teacher of the class. How does the actual use of language(s) differ from the teacher's perception of how the language is used?

    Whenever possible, different groups should tape different settings so that comparisons can be made.
4.  Observe a language minority child at home. What literacy practices can be observed at home by parents, siblings and her/himself and in which language are those conducted? Then observe the same child in her/his classroom. How do the literacy practices observed in school differ from those at home?
5.  How is it possible for an English-monolingual teacher in your locality to use the heritage language resources of her students in a linguistically heterogeneous class? Describe specific practices. What are the consequences of these practices for both language minority and language majority students?

6.  Create a short dual language book for children of a particular age. Get one parent and one teacher to give you feedback on a draft. Then get two parents and their children to use the book, and see if another draft is needed. Share the completed product with the rest of the class. Send the best two or three books to a publisher to see if they will publish or place as WWW pages on the internet.

## Further Reading

Brisk, M.E. and Harrington, M.M. (2000) *Literacy and Bilingualism. A Handbook for ALL Teachers.* Mahwah, NJ: Erlbaum.

Echevarria, J. and Graves, A. (1998) *Sheltered Content Instruction.* Boston: Allyn & Bacon.

Echevarria, J., Vogt, M. and Short, D. (2000) *Making Content Comprehensible for English Language Learners: The SIOP Model.* Boston, MA: Allyn and Bacon.

Hull, G. and Schultz, K. (eds) (2002) *School's Out! Bridging Out-of-School Literacies with Classroom Practice.* New York: Teachers College Press..

Pérez, B. (2004) *Becoming Biliterate. A Study of Two-Way Bilingual Immersion Education.* Mahwah, NJ: Lawrence Erlbaum.

Smyth, G. (2003) *Helping Bilingual Pupils to Access the Curriculum.* London: David Fulton.

# Scaffolding Instruction for English Language Learners: A Conceptual Framework

## Aída Walqui

The linguistic landscape of American schools is changing rapidly. In the decade between 1992 and 2002, the enrolment of English Language Learners grew by 84% while the total K-12 population grew by only 10%. ELLs are no longer exclusively new immigrants to the USA. In middle and high schools, 57% of them represent the second or third generation of immigrants to the USA (Batalova & Fix, 2005). Although these adolescents have been educated exclusively in US schools, they are still learning English, failing academically and dropping out of school in large numbers (Fry, 2003; Ruiz de Velasco & Fix, 2000).

There is an urgent need to turn around this situation. In this paper I present a pedagogy of rigour and hope. I maintain that it is possible for second language learners to develop deep disciplinary knowledge and engage in challenging academic activities if teachers know how to support them pedagogically to achieve their potential. While the focus of the paper is on secondary English Language Learners learning via the medium of English, the ideas presented here also apply to elementary schooling and to the teaching of academic courses in students' native languages.

Education never takes place in a vacuum but is deeply embedded in a sociocultural milieu. Thus learning is a matter not only of cognitive development but also of shared social practices. The cognitive and the social go hand in hand in classroom learning. The primary process by which learning takes place is *interaction*, more specifically, an engagement with other learners and teachers in joint activities that focus on matters of shared interest and that contain opportunities for learning.

The social nature of learning has consequences at several different levels. At the global level, English Language Learners' perceptions of how the majority society accepts or rejects the culture and language they bring to school are extremely important for their eventual success in school (Cummins, 1984; Skutnabb-Kangas, 1984; Verhoeven, 1990). In every programme for English Language Learners, students' culture and language need to be appreciated and validated through class practices. Such validation of students' identity can only occur at levels that are deep and genuine rather than superficial.

Learners need to experience the global and local contexts in which their academic life is embedded as consistent and positive. If they are, then learners can develop their academic identity, because they will be treated with respect and they will be valued and listened to as 'speakers in their own right' (Kramsch, 1996). In such a climate, learners can develop skills of language use and argumentation in the different subject matter areas. They will have the 'right to speak' (Peirce, 1995) in class, and they will participate actively in their own and each other's academic development. In accordance with Lave and Wenger's theory of situated learning, their participation may be 'peripheral' at first, but it is always 'legitimate' (Lave & Wenger, 1991). In other words, students who are learning the language and practices of the discipline – mathematics, for example – may at first feel hesitant to contribute, and they may not have full control of the register and discourse of the subject matter. They will, however, feel legitimate if they recognise that the expectation of teachers and other more capable peers is that they, too, will soon become full-fledged members of that community as they become more socialised into it. There are a number of ways in which teachers can assist students in developing language and subject matter knowledge from the interactive, sociocultural perspective sketched here. One such way, scaffolding, is particularly consonant with sociocultural theory (SCT) and is well suited to English Language Learners.

## Learning from a Sociocultural Perspective

SCT is based primarily on the work of Lev Vygotsky, a Russian psychologist, educator, philosopher and art critic, who lived from 1896 to 1934. The main tenets of Vygotsky's learning theory can be summarised as follows:

- Learning precedes development.
- Language is the main vehicle (tool) of thought.
- Mediation is central to learning.
- Social interaction is the basis of learning and development. Learning is a process of apprenticeship and internalisation in which skills and knowledge are transformed from the social into the cognitive plane.
- The Zone of Proximal Development (ZPD) is the primary activity space in which learning occurs.

Let's look at these main features in turn.

### Learning preceded development

Vygotsky takes issue with traditional psychology for assuming that development is a prerequisite of learning. Traditional psychology assumes that learning can only be successful after the learner shows that the relevant mental functions have already matured. From this standpoint, all else would be premature instruction and would therefore be useless. Instead, Vygotsky proposes that learning is only useful if it is ahead of development, that is, if it challenges learners to think and act in advance of their actual level of development.

### Language is the main vehicle of thought

Vygotsky does not claim that there is no thought before language. Rather, he claims that thought and language arise separately but that when language arrives on the scene, thinking and speech intermingle and merge, and in so doing transform one another so that

both become quite different as a result of their 'merger'. Language starts as social speech, as dialogue. In fact, Vygotsky, like his contemporary, the Russian linguist Bakhtin (1981), considers all language, spoken and written, as dialogical rather than monological. This means that the basic unit of language is conversational interaction, not sentence structure or grammatical pattern.

The internalisation of social speech, of dialogue, is mediated by private speech, as when a child speaks to herself to facilitate a difficult task. For example, she might be thinking to herself, 'Hmm. . .let's see . . .what if I . . .no, no, no, that wouldn't work, but what if I . . .' and so on, clearly using language that is social in origin. Whenever a task is very difficult, inner speech can be made overt in order to mediate between the task demands and the available resources. By talking to herself the child (or learner) attempts to marshal resources and control the task. Gradually, as speech is internalised, it changes shape, both syntactically and semantically, but even so it remains essentially social and dialogical.

### Mediation is central to learning

The difficult concept of mediation is generally regarded as the centrepiece of Vygotsky's theory of learning. In its most literal sense, mediation is the use of a tool to accomplish some action. To till the soil, the farmer uses a spade or a plough. The spade or plough mediates between the farmer and the soil, making the desired result – soil that is ready for sowing and planting – easier to accomplish. The child learns to use tools of various kinds: sticks, cups, spoons and so on. Many of those tools are culturally and historically produced. They are made available to the child in social interaction, thus adding another layer of mediation: activity mediated by tools is mediated by social interaction. When language comes along, it provides the most powerful mediation tool of all: mediation by signs, or semiotic mediation. Pointing is accompanied or replaced by linguistic reference, the immediate environment becomes describable and can be commented upon, expectations can be raised about future talk (e.g. when children learn to use phrases such as 'Guess what?'), past experiences can be recounted and relationships can be described. Thought can be socially shared and can break away from the bounds of the here-and-now.

## Social interaction and internalisation

The basis for all learning is social interaction. Vygotsky emphasises that social interaction precedes the development of knowledge and ability. Consciousness, the notions of self and identity, physical skills and mental abilities, all these have their origin in social interaction between the child and parent, and between the child, peers and others, including teachers. Vygotsky (1978: 88) points out that 'human learning presupposes a specific social nature and a process by which children grow into the intellectual life of those around them'. In addition, he asserts that 'every function in the child's cultural development appears twice, on two levels. First, on the social, and later on the psychological level; first, between people as an interpsychological category, and then inside the child, as an intrapsychological category' (Vygotsky, 1978: 128). An important consideration that Vygotsky stresses is that the social function and the corresponding mental function are not the same: the process of internalisation is a process of transformation, involving appropriation and reconstruction. Solitary work, either in tests or in classroom activities, is incompatible with Vygotsky's conception of pedagogy. As all knowledge and ability arises in social activity, all learning is co-constructed, and nothing is ever gained by taking the interactional dimension out of the equation. There is a role for individual work in SCT, but only in the context of collaborative work.

## The Zone of Proximal Development (ZPD)

The ZPD is the best known construct in SCT. The most straightforward and most often quoted definition of ZPD is the following:

> It is the distance between the actual developmental level as determined by independent problem solving and the level of potential development as determined through problem solving under adult guidance or in collaboration with more capable peers. (Vygotsky, 1978: 86)

While the concept of the ZPD is widely known, it is also frequently misunderstood. The common failure to see the connections between the concept and Vygotsky's theory as a whole means that the ZPD concept is difficult to differentiate from other instructional techniques that

systematically lead children, with the help of an adult, through a number of steps in the process of learning some set of skills. For Vygotsky, the context in which the interactions occur is of crucial importance (Tudge, 1990). The ZPD was developed as a research tool, as a means of establishing the developmental/learning potential of children, particularly children with learning disabilities (such as deaf or blind children) in the Institute of Defectology, which Vygotsky was then directing. He complained that traditional mental tests only tested the already achieved level of competence ('the past'), but that if children received appropriate assistance, their performance would be more predictive of what they might be able to achieve ('the future'). Thus he made mental testing a more collaborative, guided experience instead of the solitary, individual performance it had hitherto been. He conducted rigorous experimental studies that showed clear evidence that his ZPD-based testing was a better predictor of success than the traditional individual test. It is interesting to note that assessment and testing have, to this day, never managed to incorporate the collaborative features that Vygotsky introduced the better part of a century ago. Individual, solitary performance continues to be the norm in educational testing at all levels. Even though alternative assessments, in the form of portfolios or collaborative projects, are an accepted practice in many schools, they are not accorded significance in the debate about school performance rankings and accountability measures.

Vygotsky extended the concept of the ZPD to pedagogical activity, even though he did not work out a detailed theory of instruction using the ZPD as a guiding metaphor (Wells, 1999). This work was left to others, after Vygotsky's death. In the USA and other Western countries, Vygotsky's thinking, and the ideas flowing from the ZPD, did not begin to have an impact on education until the 1980s.

## Scaffolding

Creating contexts for linguistic and academic learning in the ZPD occurs in part through the scaffolding of social interaction. Scaffolding is closely related to the ZPD. In fact, it is only within the ZPD that scaffolding can occur. As we saw above, working in the ZPD means that the learner is assisted by others to be able to achieve more than he or she would be able to achieve alone. Scaffolding refers to the detailed circumstances of such work in the ZPD. According to David Wood, scaffolding is tutorial behaviour that is contingent, collaborative and interactive (Wood, 1988: 96). Behaviour is contingent when an action depends on (i.e. influences and is influenced by) other actions. It is collaborative when the end result, whether it is a conversation or the solution to a problem, is jointly achieved. And it is interactive when it includes the activity of two or more people who are mutually engaged.

### Scaffolding as structure and process

The original idea of scaffolding comes from the work of Jerome Bruner, who defines scaffolding as follows:

> a process of 'setting up' the situation to make the child's entry easy and successful and then gradually pulling back and handing the role to the child as he becomes skilled enough to manage it. (Bruner, 1983: 60)

Bruner's notion of scaffolding was developed in the 1970s in the context of an intensive investigation of six infants (ages 7–18 months) over a period of 10 months, as they and their mothers played games. The researchers focused particularly on the game of 'peekaboo', which was played frequently over the entire period. The game consists of an initial contact, the establishment of joint attention, disappearance, reappearance and re-establishment of contact. These are the obligatory features of the 'syntax' of the game, whereas other features, such as vocalisations to sustain the infant's interest, responses to the infant's attempts to uncover the mother's face, etc. are optional. These 'non-rule bound' parts of the game are an instance of the mother providing a 'scaffold' for the child (Bruner & Sherwood, 1975: 280).

The game becomes conventionalised, a ritual, but at the same time it allows for variations. Gradually there is a shift in agency, a 'takeover', with the child becoming self-directed and the roles of agent and recipient being reversed. Eventually the child can play the peekaboo game on her own, with a toy animal, or with other children or adults.

There are two distinct but related elements in this example. On the one hand we have the conventionalised, ritual structure that is more or less constant (though flexible), and on the other hand we have an interactional process that is jointly constructed from moment to moment. Just as

in the case of the scaffolding around a building, there is a facilitative structure of supports and boards (temporal and changeable, which the workers need to carry out their work), and there is the actual work that is being carried out.

In pedagogical contexts, scaffolding has come to refer to both aspects of the construction site: the supportive structure (which is relatively stable, though easy to assemble and reassemble) and the collaborative construction work that is carried out. Some educators are uneasy with the term scaffolding, because in normal usage it refers to a rigid structure, not the fluid dynamics of collaborative work that we associate with working in the ZPD (Gibbons, 2003). Indeed, if we think only of the support structure without focusing on the actual construction work, then such a reservation is justified. Most importantly, then, the dynamics between the scaffolding structure and the scaffolding process must be kept in mind. The process is enabled by the scaffolding structure, and a constant evaluation of the process indicates when parts of the scaffolding structure can be dismantled or shifted elsewhere. In education, scaffolding can be thought of as three related pedagogical 'scales'. First, there is the meaning of providing a support structure to enable certain activities and skills to develop. Second, there is the actual carrying out of particular activities in class. And, third, there is the assistance provided in moment-to-moment interaction. Schematically, this can be represented in the following way:

Scaffolding 1    Planned curriculum progression over time (e.g. a series of tasks over time, a project, a classroom ritual)

Scaffolding 2    The procedures used in a particular activity (an instantiation of Scaffolding 1)

Scaffolding 3    The collaborative process of interaction (the process of achieving Scaffolding 2)

We can see how the sequence here moves from macro to micro, from planned to improvised, and from structure to process (Gibbons, 2003; van Lier, 1996). As we all know, plans have a way of changing as they are being carried out. In particular, pedagogical action is always a blend of the planned and the improvised, the predicted and the unpredictable, routine and innovation.

So, even though the three scales suggest a

top-down structure, there is also bottom-up change that can affect and transform the scaffolding at the top. As scaffolding is premised upon the notion of handing over (by the teacher) and taking over (by the student), assistance provided should always be only 'just enough' and 'just in time'. As the students are able to do more and gradually come to be more in charge of their own learning, the upper-level (macro) scaffolds are changed, transformed, restructured or dismantled.

### Features of pedagogical scaffolding

All three scales of pedagogical scaffolding have six central features, according to van Lier (2004). As in any type of scaffolding, they are contingent, collaborative and interactive. However, in an educational setting, these features are further refined and features specific to schooling are added:

*Continuity*

Tasks are repeated, with variations and connected to one another (e.g. as part of projects).

*Contextual support*

Exploration is encouraged in a safe, supportive environment; access to means and goals is promoted in a variety of ways.

*Intersubjectivity*

Mutual engagement and rapport are established; there is encouragement and non-threatening participation in a shared community of practice.

*Contingency*

Task procedures are adjusted depending on actions of learners; contributions and utterances are oriented towards each other and may be coconstructed (or, see below, vertically constructed).

*Handover/takeover*

There is an increasing role for the learner as skills and confidence increase; the teacher watches carefully for the learner's readiness to take over increasing parts of the action.

*Flow*

Skills and challenges are in balance; participants are focused on the task and are 'in tune' with each other.

### Scaffolded interaction differentiated from IRF

Often the scaffolding process arises in a context of spoken interaction, when the utterance of one participant is completed or taken further by the utterance of another participant. Bruner has called this kind of collaborative talk 'ratchet-like' (cited in Cazden, 1992: 103). Scollon, in an investigation of mother–child discourse, has labelled it 'vertical construction', as the utterances are produced interactively and, once transcribed, are read down the page (Scollon, 1976).

In classroom settings, it is important to understand the difference between spoken interaction that scaffolds student learning and interaction that imposes a 'recitation script', as Tharp and Gallimore (1988) call it. Most teacher–student talk is of the scripted type (Wells, 1999) and is commonly known as Initiation-Response-Feedback (IRF). The two examples below demonstrate these two kinds of teacher–student spoken interactions that might occur in a classroom of English Language Learners. If we juxtapose the three utterances on the left (Gibbons, 2002) with three utterances from the longer extract on the right (Walqui, 2001), we can see superficial similarities (e.g. both sequences consist of a teacher question, student response and teacher follow-up), but also fundamental differences, as the glosses below the utterances indicate.

During IRF, as in the example above, the teacher wants students to demonstrate that they know a particular word, to practise pronouncing words or phrases, or to display knowledge of facts. In scaffolded talk, as illustrated, the teacher is intent on letting the students speak for themselves and encourages them to be precise and to present a clear argument. Such interactions scaffold students' discipline and language learning simultaneously.

### Beyond the expert–novice context

So far we have discussed the ZPD and scaffolding from the perspective of a more knowledgeable person (a teacher or parent) interacting with a less knowledgeable person (a student or child). However, in the work of several researchers (Donato, 1994; Gibbons, 2002; Mercer, 1995; Rogoff, 1995), the idea of scaffolding has been expanded to include not only an expert–novice relationship, but also a relationship of equal knowledge, such as in a group of learners working on a shared task. Such scaffolding can be called 'collective scaffolding' (Donato, 1994; Moll, 1990), and researchers

| Initiation-Response-Feedback | Scaffolded teacher–student talk |
|---|---|
| | **S**: It's like everybody should get the same rights and protection, no matter, like, race, religion. |
| | **T**: Yeah. Everybody. |
| | *The teacher acknowledges the student's response and waits.* |
| | **S**: No matter if they are a citizen or illegal, they should get the same protection. |
| **T**: What season comes after fall? | **T**: I agree with you, but why do you say that with confidence? |
| *The teacher knows the answer and is checking to see whether the student does.* | *The teacher is asking the student to justify or elaborate her thinking* |
| | **S**: Because it says that. |
| | **T**: Because it says that? |
| **S**: Winter. | *The teacher acknowledges the student's response and continues to* |
| **T**: Good girl. | *wait for justification or elaboration.* |
| *The teacher evaluates and approves the student's answer* | **S**: Also because it [the 14th Amendment] says it should not deny any person of the right to life, liberty and property without due process. |
| | *The student draws on evidence for her thinking.* |
| | **T**: Okay, not any <u>citizen</u>? |
| | *The teacher highlights a key aspect of the 14th Amendment.* |
| | **S**: Any <u>person</u>. |
| | *The student consolidates her understanding.* |
| | **T**: Okay, so is the 14th Amendment helpful to you? |
| | *The teacher connects the student's learning to her experience, as an immigrant.* |

have shown that students working in groups can produce results that none of them would have been capable of producing on their own. In such circumstances learners create zones of proximal development for each other and engage in mutual scaffolding. As an example, Gibbons (2002: 19) reports a small group's process of planning how to report a science experiment. One participant, Emily, is a fully bilingual speaker of Chinese and English and the others are English Language Learners. The following is a brief extract of the interaction, and we can see how it illustrates both the vertical construction and the collective scaffolding that we have described:

**Milad**: It stuck together because. . .
**Maroun**: And it stuck together because it was. . .
**Emily**: It was on a different side.
**Gina**: It was on a different side and the other one's and. . .
**Emily**: And the poles are different.
**Gina**: And the poles are different.
**Milad**: And em. . .when we put on the first side it stuck together. . .

At the end of this group activity, one of the learners, Gina, is chosen to report the group's findings to the whole class. Gibbons reports that Gina's performance was more fluent than it was likely to have been 'without the initial talk in a group' (Gibbons, 2002: 20). Gibbons also points out that the spoken language used in the group report begins 'to sound more like "written" language' (p. 20). The suggestion is that scaffolded interaction among peers connects conversational language to academic discourse, both written and spoken.

In addition to the two contexts of scaffolding discussed so far, the expert–novice context and the collective scaffolding context, van Lier (1996) suggests two further contexts in which students can work within their ZPD. They can work with someone who is at a lower level of understanding, and the need to teach the other person is an opportunity to verbalise, clarify and extend their own knowledge of the subject matter. Finally, they can draw on their own resources – the models remembered from their teachers and peers and other resources in their environment – to supplement the shortcomings of their own knowledge

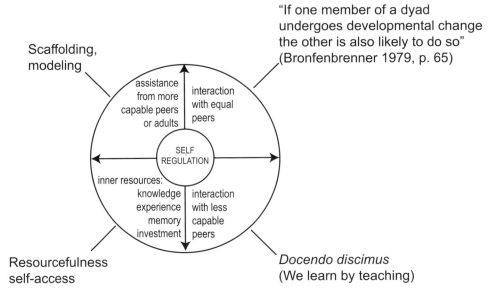

Figure 1 Expanded ZPD (van Lier, 2004)

and skills. Thus, the student has available at least the following four sources of scaffolding:

(1) being assisted by an expert, when the learner receives guidance, advice and modelling;
(2) collaborating with other learners, when learning is constructed together;
(3) assisting a lower-level learner, when both have opportunities to learn; and
(4) working alone, when internalised practices and strategies, inner speech, inner resources and experimentation are used.

In all four participation contexts, the learner has opportunities to learn, but of different kinds. When assisted by a more capable other, a learner can experience models of successful learning or participate in more complex social activities, as suggested in Vygotsky's original ZPD (see also Lave & Wenger, 1991). When working together with other learners, discovery and joint construction occur; when one learner discovers something new, the partner will experience this discovery too. When teaching a less accomplished peer, a learner needs to organise her thoughts and actions and achieve maximum clarity of expression. We learn by teaching, as the ancient saying goes. Finally, a learner can internalise teaching and learning strategies, rely on inner resources,

and experiment and try new angles, in a self-directed way. Figure 1 shows these four potential contexts of learning as aspects of an expanded ZPD.

## Scaffolding Instruction for English Language Learners in Secondary Schools

English Language Learners benefit from the same good teaching as all learners do, but they need even more of it as they are working to accomplish English learning and content-area learning simultaneously. A number of scaffolding approaches, both general and specific, are especially appropriate for these students engaged in 'double duty'.

### General approaches for scaffolding English Language Learners' learning

Careful teaching first prepares students, by focusing their attention on key processes and ideas, before engaging them in interactive tasks to practice using these processes and concepts. Cyclical curricula (i.e. curricula that are not based on a linear progression of items but, rather, on the cyclical reintroduction of concepts at higher levels of complexity and inter-relatedness) lead to a natural growth in the understanding of ideas and to self-correction of misunderstandings.

Frequently, however, a concern for immediate comprehension overtakes what we know about the best ways to promote learning. Howard Gardner (1989: 158–159), speaking of education in general, puts it as follows:

> First of all, when you are trying to present new materials, you cannot expect them to be grasped immediately. (If they are, in fact, the understanding had probably been present all along.) One must approach the issues in many different ways over a significant period of time if there is to be any hope of assimilation.

Teachers must explain how students learn – to students! Too often students are the last to know. For English Language Learners, this is especially damaging. They need to understand that their feelings of vagueness and frustration are valid. At the same time, teachers should carefully prepare learners by setting up tasks that will prepare them to be successful at what will be required of them. Tasks involving complex language are prime candidates for scaffolding. Without such support, English Language Learners might very well not succeed.

Because scaffolds are by definition temporary, as the teacher observes that students are capable of handling more on their own, she gradually hands over responsibility to them. This 'kid-watching', to use Yetta Goodman's apt expression (Goodman, 1978), implies that the teacher carefully monitors the learner's growing understanding and developing academic skills – providing scaffolds and challenges as the need arises.

Rather than simplifying the tasks or the language, teaching subject matter content to English Language Learners requires amplifying and enriching the linguistic and extralinguistic context, so that students do not get just one opportunity to come to terms with the concepts involved, but in fact may construct their understanding on the basis of multiple clues and perspectives encountered in a variety of class activities. As Gibbons (2003) puts it, the teacher provides message 'abundancy', also referred to as message 'redundancy'. The following vignette from a project-based unit on linguistics is a good example of message abundancy:

> The teacher is going over a class assignment in which his English learner students need to write a series of five letters to an acquaintance. Students first read the assignment to themselves. Then the teacher explains the task, providing students with several ways to understand an important word he has introduced:
>
> **T**: You can use your native language to write your letters, but there is a caveat . . . a stipulation . . .there is something you have to do. You need to summarize your ideas in a paragraph in English. (DeFazio, 2001) Message abundancy here is expressed by the written assignment, by the teacher's review of the assignment, by his providing a paraphrase of the particular vocabulary that may be very difficult for students to understand and (as is evident on the video recording of this event) by his verbal emphasis and body language as he elaborates.

### Types of instructional scaffolding to use with English Language Learners

Assisting English Language Learners' performance in English as a second language class or in subject matter classes taught in English can be done in many different ways. Six main types of instructional scaffolding are especially salient: modelling, bridging, contextualisation, building schema, re-presenting text and developing metacognition.

### Modelling

Students need to be given clear examples of what is requested of them for imitation. When introducing a new task or working format, it is indispensable that the learners be able to see or hear what a developing product looks like. From that point of view, walking students through an interaction or first doing it together as a class activity is a necessary step. As one 10th grade student noted:

> In my chemistry class I can always do well because the teacher first demonstrates an experiment, and then we try a similar one. Then he asks us to write down the procedure and the conclusions in groups of two or four. I can do it. I can even use the new words because I know what they mean. (Walqui, 2000: 94)

Teachers of English Language Learners should seriously consider keeping (photocopying)

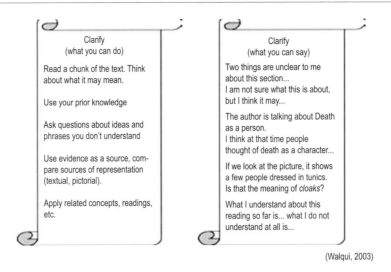

(Walqui, 2003)

**Figure 2**  Clarifying bookmark

examples of student work for demonstration purposes. Such examples may serve not only to set performance guidelines or standards, but also to encourage and stimulate students by the evidence of past students' progress in the accomplishment of similar tasks.

In addition to modelling tasks and activities and sharing examples of student work, it is important to model appropriate language use for the performance of specific academic functions, such as describing, comparing, summarising, evaluating and so on. The bookmark shown in Figure 2 (front and back), for example, can be used by students to support their ability to work with peers in discussing a text. The bookmark structures for students a way to practice the clarification of concepts and language as they interact in dyads. One side of the bookmark makes explicit to students what they should do as they clarify ideas or seek clarification for them. The other side provides students with some concrete examples of phrases they may use as they engage in clarification activities.

*Bridging*

Students will only be able to learn new concepts and language if these are firmly built on previous knowledge and understandings. Comprehension is widely understood to require 'the weaving of new information into existing mental structures' (Tharp & Gallimore, 1988: 108).

As students start realising that their everyday knowledge is not only valued in class but, in fact, desired, a sense of wellness is achieved that promotes further development. This does not always come easily.

A common bridging approach is to activate students' prior knowledge. Anticipatory guides are a way to do this so that students produce written as well as spoken language. At the beginning of a new topic the teacher may ask her class to collaborate to fill out a two-column anticipatory guide, with one column for what students know about a topic and the other for questions about the topic that they are interested in answering. If students are not used to this, if they are used to a teacher monologue or a recitation script, they may be surprised and confused at first. The teacher will almost be able to hear the words going through their minds: 'Listen, if we knew that, we wouldn't be in this class. You are teacher, you tell us'. As they progress, students learn that they do, in fact, know quite a bit and can predict or infer even more. Once the class as a whole has modelled for themselves how to complete such charts, pairs or small groups can easily fill them out for other topics as may be introduced.

When initially introducing two-column anticipatory guides, it may be wise to ignore students' nominations of erroneous information. As students are first learning to trust what a surprising amount they already know, it is probably

Read the following statements and first decide whether you agree with them or not. After reading the article, decide whether the text supports your opinions. If it does not, explain why not using your own words. Save questions that remain unanswered for the conclusion of this unit.

| | Opinion | | Finding | | Evidence: explain using your own words |
|---|---|---|---|---|---|
| | Agree | Disagree | Agree | Disagree | |
| 1. Religion was not important at all to people's lives during the Middle Ages | | | | | |
| 2. During the Middle Ages people of all classes went on pilgrimages – a kind of group tour – for religious purposes | | | | | |
| 3. Mediaeval women were free to do what they thought was best for them. Men respected their decisions. | | | | | |
| 4. There was corruption in the church during the Middle Ages. For example, pardons for sins were sold to people. | | | | | |
| 5. A mediaeval knight had to be chivalrous above all. That means he had to respect an honourable code of behaviour | | | | | |

**Figure 3** Extended anticipatory guide: Pilgrimages as representation of mediaeval life
*Source*: Walqui, 2003

the wrong time to point out mistakes. However, it becomes important to address misinformation and incorrect connections if it appears they will be stumbling blocks later on.

Extended anticipatory guides, such as the one in Figure 3, allow the teacher more control in focusing students on the most important aspects of an assignment while at the same time engaging their prior knowledge. In the example, the teacher prepares students for a unit on mediaeval pilgrimages by using statements that incorporate crucial terms – which she will clarify – and getting students to start thinking about the topic. Having read the relevant text, students will revisit their original impressions and explain why their original responses were supported by the text or not.

Another important aspect of bridging is establishing a personal link between the student and the subject matter, showing how new material is relevant to the student's life, as an individual, here and now. Other ways of bridging include asking students to share personal experiences related to the theme that will be introduced in the lesson or assigned reading. For example, as a way of preparing students to read Francisco Jimenez's short story, 'The Circuit', students are asked to think about the following questions, jot down their answers, and share them with a partner:

> Have you ever had to leave behind someone or something that you loved? What happened?
> How did the experience make you feel?

### Contextualising

Many educational researchers have pointed out differences between everyday language and academic language (e.g. Bernstein, 1971; Cummins & Swain, 1986; Heath, 1983). Because everyday language is embedded in rich context and is situation-dependent, learners can rely on nonlinguistic information to compensate for possible linguistic shortcomings. Academic language, on the other hand, is decontextualised and situation-independent; in order to comprehend such language the learner must rely on language alone (Cloran, 1999).

One of the greatest problems English Language Learners face in content-area classes is reading the textbooks. Not only is the language academic, but it is usually very dry and dense, with few or no relevant illustrations, and presented in a linear rather than cyclical way. Embedding this language in a sensory context by using manipulatives, pictures, a few minutes of a film (without sound) and other types of realia (authentic objects and sources of information) can make language accessible and engaging for students, as this eighth-grade English Language Learner indicates:

> I couldn't make any sense of what happened in the Middle Ages and the lives people led. I could understand 'castle' and imagined a beautiful castle in my dreams. When the teacher showed us a four-minute clip of

an old film, it all clicked, and I could make sense of all those other words – knights and vassals and all that. (Walqui, 2000: 94)

Teachers may also provide verbal contextualisations by creating analogies based on students' experiences. Effective teachers continually search for metaphors and analogies that bring complex ideas closer to the students' world experience.

### Schema building

Schema, or clusters of meaning that are interconnected, are how we organise knowledge and understanding. If building understanding is a matter of weaving new information into pre-existing structures of meaning, then it becomes indispensable for teachers to help English Language Learners see these connections, through a variety of activities.

In preparation for a reading assignment, for example, a teacher may ask students to preview the text, noting heads and subheads, illustrations and their captions, titles of charts, etc. In this way, students begin their reading with a general sense of the topic and its organisation, with their schema already activated and ready to accept new connections.

Similarly, in preparation for a mini-lecture, a teacher may present an advance organiser and walk students through the most important pieces of information that will be discussed. The use of this organiser will serve several purposes: it will promote schema building in anticipation of the topic being introduced, it will focus the learners' attention on important aspects of the information to come, and if it is in graphic form for note-taking purposes, it will alleviate students' anxiety by letting them know beforehand what information they should be able to understand.

Students in general, and English learners in particular, need to be able to process information from the top down – having a general knowledge of the broad picture before studying the details – as well as from the bottom up, using vocabulary, syntax, rhetorical devices, etc. (Carrell, 1984). Furthermore, by presenting in advance the skeleton of a lesson, we can lower the students' apprehension and help them tolerate ambiguity, which as Rubin (1975) has argued, is one of the most important features of the good language learner.

The compare/contrast matrix in Figure 4 illustrates how a teacher initially bridges to students' prior knowledge and interests in preparation for

| | Field work in California, now | Factory work in Leeds, 1835 |
|---|---|---|
| What is a typical day for a worker? | | |
| Working conditions (who works, schedule, benefits, breaks, etc.) | | |
| What improvements in working conditions do the workers want | | |

**Figure 4** Compare and contrast matrix
*Source*: Walqui, 2003

building their schema about the target content. The students live in the agricultural valley of Salinas in California, know a lot about fieldwork, and can readily complete the first column of the advance organiser. The teacher has prepared students to use the information they know, their schema about field work, to foster an understanding of new concepts, in this case, relating to the Industrial Revolution. As a follow-up to this activity, students will be reading a primary source that discusses the daily routines of factory workers in England during the first Industrial Revolution.

*Re-presenting text*

One way in which teachers invite students to begin the appropriation of new language is by engaging them in activities that require the transformation of linguistic constructions they found modelled in one genre into forms used in another genre. It has been argued (see, for example, Moffet, 1983) that there is a progression in the ability of language users to use different genres within academic discourses. In terms of language use, this continuum starts with asking students to say what is happening (as in drama or dialogue), then what has happened (narratives, reports), then what happens (generalisations in exposition) and, finally, what may happen (tautologic transformations, theorising). In this fashion, students can access content presented in more difficult genres by the act of transforming it into different genres, especially those that are more easily produced. Short stories or histori-

cal essays, for example, can be transformed into dramas or personal narratives.

This kind of language learning often engages students in the accomplishment of tasks that are interesting and meaningful for them, where the emphasis is placed on the communication that is being carried out rather than on its formal aspects, and where the resulting learning is powerful. For example, if students have read a journalistic article about the challenges for immigrants in the USA, they may not have understood a lot of new vocabulary yet understood the main issues or events described. In this case, the teacher wants students to revisit the text, but with a purpose other than attending to the new terminology. The task is for students to re-present the article as a play. The teacher presents small groups each with a scenario that corresponds to a section, or moment, in the text. Each group then collaborates to create a dialogue with as many characters in it as there are group members. To accomplish the task students have to go back to the text, reread it, and discuss the situation, issues and people involved to decide what those people, as characters in a dialogue, would say to each other. As the team collaborates on a dialogue, each person makes a personal copy of the script, with the least experienced students in the team assisted by their more capable peers. Groups proofread their scripts and rehearse their re-presentation. Depending on the number of groups/moments, one or two complete presentations of the 'play', or re-presentations of the article, are performed in front of class (the number of performances depends on how many groups/moments have been assigned). At the end of the session, students will not only have understood much better the human dilemmas inherent in the situations described in the article, but they will have used new language, written it, and even practised and performed it.

The opportunities for every student in class to do all this have been maximised, and all students will have engaged in instructional conversations as the teacher monitored activities throughout the class. The less proficient students are not excluded since, aided by their more proficient peers, they have essential tasks to perform, tasks that are just as demanding for them as the more complex tasks are for the more advanced English Language Learners. In other words, every student performs at the limit of his or her ability. In the following excerpt, four students collaborated on the first moment of the class re-presentation of their reading in language arts of Hamlet (incorporating as well their study of the US judicial system in social studies). Student 1 is a relatively new English Language Learner, so his role is the simple one of court clerk. At the same time, Student 1 has written and rehearsed with his group members the full script.

> **S1**: Good morning ladies and gentleman, I will ask you to stand up because your honor is about to enter this court.
> **S2**: You may be seated. We're here today to hear the testimony of the defense and prosecution. The prosecution will present the case of King Hamlet, who is accusing King Claudius and Queen Gertrude of the crown of betrayal. I now call on the prosecution to make your opening statements.
> **S3**: Dear jury. We come here to prosecute King Claudius, twisted and very unusual with no limits; an ambitious man. Someone who sacrificed his own brother, his own cousin and people around him, to get what he wants. Somebody who will not turn off any evil behavior to get what he wants. Somebody with no morality and now twisted in his eyes, kill, and kill with full awareness of his behavior. Somebody that made six people dead in his own kingdom and house, because of his twisted and very sick ambition. Somebody that took his brothers wife the day after his brothers funeral and spy and contribute to his own

cousin's death, and that of six other people. Now we gather here to bring him to justice.
> **S2**: I now call on the defense to make his opening statements.
> **S4**: Today I'll be defending my client King Claudius. I'll be defending him to show you people of the jury that every single charge against my client, King Claudius, is not worthy of hearing because King Hamlet is mentally ill. I'll also be showing you that the marriage between King Claudius and Queen Gertrude is pure and sincere and based in love. Today in this courtroom, I'm going to show you the innocence [of Claudius] and mentally illness of King Hamlet.
> **S2**: Prosecution, you may now begin to present your witness.
> **S3**: We call first to bring King Claudius to the stand. . .                      (Heisler, 2001)

Other types of text re-presentations include transforming a poem into a narrative, changing a third-person historical narrative into an eye-witness account, asking students to transform scientific texts into letters, producing cooperative posters of a story with a quote, etc.

### Developing metacognition

Metacognition has been defined as 'the ability to monitor one's current level of understanding and decide when it is not adequate' (Bransford *et al.*, 1999: 35). It refers to the ways in which students manage their thinking, and it includes at least the following four aspects:

(1) consciously applying learned strategies while engaging in activity;
(2) knowledge and awareness of strategic options a learner has and the ability to choose the most effective one for the particular activity at hand;
(3) monitoring, evaluating and adjusting performance during activity; and
(4) planning for future performance based on evaluation of past performance.

Successful subject matter classes for English Language Learners foster metacognition and, along with it, learner autonomy – through the explicit teaching of strategies, plans of attack that enable learners to successfully approach academic tasks. Metacognitive strategies are derived from studies of how experts carry out specific tasks. The development of Reciprocal

Teaching, for example, was based on Brown's research (1980) on how successful readers tackle complex text. In collaboration with Palincsar, then an elementary school teacher, they translated these findings into pedagogical strategies and taught children to deliberately follow the processing activities: read, summarise, ask questions, predict. Reciprocal teaching (Brown & Palincsar, 1985), think-alouds and self-assessment activities with rubrics are examples of such strategies. As with other kinds of interactions in the class, metacognitive strategies need to be modelled and practised as a whole class before students attempt them in pairs or small groups. As students begin their independent use of the strategies, the teacher continues to carefully monitor the implementation.

In the case of reciprocal teaching, for example, once students become comfortable with this strategy, the teacher will be able to see students successfully engaged in all steps of the process: pairs or groups of students independently reading a text, questioning each other, discussing questions that go well beyond recall and trying together to solve problems related to the understanding of the text. To get to this point, the teacher will have been very deliberate in introducing each step, having students practice each step and having students explain each step.

One technique in introducing learning routines is the simple use of posters: a poster that lists the steps of the routine being practised and another that is an ever-growing list of all the routines the class has mastered. With the first poster, numbered steps for students to refer to, the teacher can focus on monitoring student learning rather than answering procedural questions. With the other poster, a list of all the learning strategies students now have available to them, students have a visual reminder of what they can already do and even explain. What these posters also represent is a very convenient way to orient new students to class activities. The posters signify that any student is able to introduce a newcomer to the class to any activity, thus gaining confidence in his own abilities while helping out a fellow student (and the teacher).

## Conclusion

Scaffolding makes it possible to provide academically challenging instruction for English Language Learners in secondary schools. It supports the idea that the only good teaching is that which is ahead of development. A number of practical strategies and tasks can be used to provide rigorous, deep, challenging and responsible education to students who need to develop conceptually, academically and linguistically.

English Language Learners whose teachers invite them to engage in high-challenge academic tasks in English may initially complain. As they realise, however, that their teachers also provide them with high levels of support, and become increasingly aware of their progress and the tools needed to attain it, they will build up confidence in themselves and their own abilities.

Academic instruction for English Language Learners can break traditional moulds to provide a rich, stimulating, highly interactive curriculum for language minority students. It is not, however, easily done. Teachers need to be well versed in their subject matter to be able to provide students with as many scaffolds as are needed to assist their learning. They also need to become involved in professional growth and form partnerships to discuss, peer-coach and advance theoretical understandings of their practice. The very best classes for English Language Learners will not only improve students' performance, but will also create more successful, aware, self-assured and articulate teachers. Needless to say, for this to happen, districts and schools must support the growth of teacher expertise in teaching English Language Learners.

Finally, I would like to address a frequently asked question about pedagogical scaffolding for English Language Learners: what's new in scaffolding instruction for academic language development? Isn't it simply good teaching? It is true that many of the strategies involved have long been recognised as excellent pedagogy. What's different is that for our English learners we need to use them more extensively, continuously building scaffolds as the need arises, and we need to communicate their purpose and uses to students. While for the native speaker two tasks may be sufficient to understand and practice a concept, the English Language Learner may need four or five different tasks to achieve similar competence. It will take teachers of English Language Learners longer to teach their units, and they may not be able to teach as much in terms of detailed content. But as Ted Sizer (1991) has argued, in education less can be more. The way to get that 'more' is for the 'less' to be amplified, for 'message abundancy' (Gibbons, 2003) to surround, engage and support learners. In this way, English Language Learners in a secondary content class can reap just as much academic profit from the mainstream subject matter as their native-speaker counterparts. Material is redistributed, different elements are emphasised, but the increased depth of learning that results from a scaffolded approach more than compensates for whatever elements are left out. We may have 'covered' less, but in the end we will have 'uncovered' more.

## References

Bakhtin, M. (1981) *The Dialogical Imagination*. Austin: University of Texas Press.

Batalova, A. and Fix, M. (2005) *English Language Learner Adolescents: Demographics and Literacy Achievement*. Washington, DC: Center for Applied Linguistics.

Bernstein, B. (1971) *Class, Codes and Control. Volume 1: Theoretical Studies Towards a Sociology of Language*. London: Routledge.

Bransford, J., Brown, A. and Cocking, R. (eds) (1999) *How People Learn. Brain, Mind, Experience, and School*. Washington, DC: National Academy Press.

Brown, A. (1980) Metacognitive development and reading. In R.J. Spiro, B.C. Bruce and W.F. Brewer (eds) *Theoretical Issues in Reading Comprehension: Perspectives from Cognitive Psychology, Linguistics, Artificial Intelligence, and Education*. Hillsdale, NJ: Lawrence Erlbaum.

Brown, A. and Palincsar, A. (1985) Reciprocal teaching of comprehension strategies: A natural history of one program for enhancing learning. Technical Report No. 334. ERIC Document Reproduction Service. ED 257 046.

Bruner, J. (1983) *Child's Talk*. New York: Norton.

Bruner, J. and Sherwood, V. (1975) Peekaboo and the learning of rule structures. In J.S. Bruner, A. Jolly and K. Sylva (eds) *Play: Its Role in Development and Evolution* (pp. 277–285). Harmondsworth, England: Penguin Books.

Carrell, P.L. (1984) Schema theory and ESL reading: Classroom implications and applications. *Modern Language Journal* 68 (4), 332–343.

Cazden, C. (1992) *Whole Language Plus*. New York: Teacher's College Press.

Cloran, C. (1999) Contexts for learning. In F. Christie (ed.) *Pedagogy and the Shaping of Consciousness* (pp. 31–65). London: Continuum.

Cummins, J. (1984) *Bilingualism and Special Education: Issues in Assessment and Pedagogy*. Clevedon: Multilingual Matters.

Cummins, J. and Swain, M. (1986) *Bilingualism in Education: Aspects of Theory, Research, and Practice*. London: Longman.

DeFazio, A. (2001) *Linguistics Letters*. Long Island City, NY: International High School.

Donato, R. (1994) Collective scaffolding in second language learning. In J.P. Lantolf and G. Appel (eds) *Vygotskian Approaches to Second Language Research* (pp. 33–56). Norwood, NJ: Ablex.

Fry, R. (2003) Presentation to the Council of Chief State School Officers meeting on educating adolescent English learners. Miami, Florida.

Gardner, H. (1989) *To Open Minds: Chinese Clues to the Dilemma of Contemporary Education*. New York: Basic Books.

Gibbons, P. (2002) *Scaffolding Language, Scaffolding Learning*. Portsmouth, NH: Heinemann.

Gibbons, P. (2003) Scaffolding academic language across the curriculum. Presentation at American Association for Applied Linguistics, Arlington, VA, March 25, 2003.

Goodman, Y. (1978) Kid watching: An alternative to testing. *National Elementary School Principal* 57, 41–45.

Heath, S.B. (1983) *Ways with Words*. Cambridge: Cambridge University Press.

Heisler, D. (2001) *State v. Hamlet*. Long Island City, NY: International High School.

Kramsch, C. (1996) The cultural component of language teaching. Zeitschrift fur Interkulturellen Fremdsprachenunterricht. On WWW at http://www.spz.tu-darmstadt. de/projekt–ejuornal/jg–01–2/beitrag/kramsch2.htm

Lave, J. and Wenger, E. (1991) *Situated Learning: Legitimate Peripheral Participation*. Cambridge: Cambridge University Press.

Mercer, N. (1995) *The Guided Construction of Knowledge: Talk Between Teachers and Learners in the Classroom*. Clevedon: Multilingual Matters.

Moffet, J. (1983) *Teaching the Universe of Discourse*. Portsmouth, NH: Heinemann.

Moll, L.C. (ed.) (1990) *Vygotsky and Education: Instructional Implications and Applications of Sociohistorical Psychology*. Cambridge: Cambridge University Press.

Peirce, B.N. (1995) Social identity, investment, and language learning. *TESOL Quarterly* 29 (1), 9–31.

Rogoff, B. (1995) Observing sociocultural activity on three planes: Participatory, appropriation, guided participation, and apprenticeship. In J. Wertsch, P. del Rio and A. Alvarez (eds) *Sociocultural Studies of Mind* (pp. 139–164). New York: Cambridge University Press.

Rubin, J. (1975) What the 'good language learner' can teach us. *TESOL Quarterly* 9, 41–51.

Ruiz de Velasco, J. and Fix, M. (2000) *Overlooked*

*and Underserved: Immigrant Students in U.S. Secondary Schools*. Washington, DC: The Urban Institute.

Scollon, R. (1976) *Conversations with a One Year Old: A Case Study of the Developmental Foundation of Syntax*. Honolulu: University Press of Hawaii.

Sizer, T. (1991) No pain, no gain. *Educational Leadership* May, 32–34.

Skutnabb-Kangas, T. (1984) *Bilingualism or Not: The Education of Minorities*. Clevedon: Multilingual Matters.

Tharp, R.G. and Gallimore, R.G. (1988) *Rousing Minds to Life: Teaching, Learning, and Schooling in Social Context*. Cambridge: Cambridge University Press.

Tudge, J. (1990) Vygotsky, the zone of proximal development, and peer collaboration: Implications for classroom practice. In L. Moll (ed.) *Vygotsky and Education: Instructional Implications and Applications of Sociohistorical Psychology*. Cambridge: Cambridge University Press.

van Lier, L. (1996) *Interaction in the Language Curriculum: Awareness, Autonomy and Authenticity*. London: Longman.

van Lier, L. (2004) *The Ecology and Semiotics of Language Learning*. Dordrecht: Kluwer Academic.

Verhoeven, L. (1990) Language variation and learning to read. In P. Reitsma and L. Verhoeven (eds) *Acquisition of Reading in Dutch* (pp. 105–120). Dordrecht: Foris.

Vygotsky, L.S. (1978) *Mind in Society*. Cambridge, MA: Harvard University Press.

Walqui, A. (1991) *Sheltered Instruction: Doing it Right*. MS. San Diego, CA: San Diego County Office of Education.

Walqui, A. (2000) *Access and Engagement: Program Design and Instructional Approaches for Immigrant Students in Secondary School*. McHenry, IL: Delta Systems for the Center of Applied Linguistics.

Walqui, A. (2001) Accomplished teaching with English Learners: A conceptualization of teacher expertise. *Multilingual Educator* 1 (4), 51–55.

Walqui, A. (2002) Scaffolding the teaching of the 14th Amendment. In N. Koelsch (ed.) *Teaching Social Studies to Adolescent English Learners*. San Francisco: WestEd.

Walqui, A. (2003) *Teaching Reading to Adolescent English Learners*. San Francisco: WestEd.

Wells, G. (1999) *Dialogic Inquiry. Toward a Sociocultural Practice and Theory of Education*. Cambridge: Cambridge University Press.

Wood, D.J. (1988) *How Children Think and Learn*. Oxford: Blackwell.

## Questions

1. Explain the concept of scaffolding in pedagogical contexts and identify some of its features.
2. How is scaffolded interaction different from Initiation-Response-Feedback?
3. What is 'collective scaffolding' and how does group work and cooperative learning relate to this concept?
4. Identify and discuss the six main types of instructional scaffolding.

## Activities

1. Observe a classroom in which the teacher is using a second language to teach content and literacy in that language. Describe all scaffolding strategies used by the teacher. What support is available to her?
2. Reflect on your experiences with learning in a second or third language (either as a student or a teacher) and describe them briefly. Make ten statements about such experiences (making sure that you define yourself as a student or a teacher). Compile a list of the ten statements that best describes students' experiences with content learning in a second or third language. Then compile another list for teachers' experiences.
3. Make a video of a second language or subject matter class taught by an effective teacher of second language learners. Identify the scaffolding strategies that are used in the video in a separate narrative section. Show to the class.

4.  Researching on two teachers you know (this teacher might be you), portray how they differ in their strategies and 'contexts' for biliteracy. Break up the table into four sections and provide examples of how the following is accomplished:

    I. Motivation
    a.  Increasing membership in the classroom community
    b.  Being attentive to specific community, program, and classroom characteristics
    c.  Taking an interest in, and holding accountable each individual

    II. Purpose
    a.  Social purpose
    b.  Task-focused purposes

    III. Text
    a.  use of basal readers or authentic literature
    b.  exposure to other genres

    IV. Interaction
    a.  structure of peer interaction
    b.  structure of teacher–student interaction
    c.  strategies for interacting with text:
        1.  classroom-based or community-based activation of prior knowledge
        2.  signaling understanding of text
        3.  analyzing features of text
        4.  reasoning about text.

## Further Reading

Carrasquillo, A.L. and Rodriguez, V. (2001) *Language Minority Students in the Mainstream Classroom* (2nd edn). Clevedon: Multilingual Matters.

Curtain, H. and Dahlberg, C.A. (2004) *Languages and Children. Making the Match. New languages for young learners, grades K-8*. Boston: Pearson.

Edwards, V. (1998) *The Power of Babel: Teaching and Learning in Multilingual Classrooms*. Stoke-on-Trent (UK): Trentham.

Fu, D. (2003) *An Island of English. Teaching ESL in Chinatown*. Portsmouth, New Hampshire: Heinemann.

Peregoy, S.F. and Boyle, O. (2001) *Reading, Writing and Learning in ESL. A Resource Book for K-12 Teachers*. New York: Longman.

Valdés, G. (2001) *Learning and Not Learning English: Latino Students in American Schools*. New York: Teachers College Press.

# Home to School and School to Home: Syncretised Literacies in Linguistic Minority Communities

## Clare Kelly, Eve Gregory and Ann Williams

After school, Jorna goes to Arabic classes from 5–7 p.m., four days a week. The book she takes from school, her elder sister helps her read. Her sister shows her the Bengali alphabet and they like to do drawing and writing together, turning it into a book. She likes to watch cartoons and Hindi films – her older brother brings them. She plays with the playhouse and listens to stories, but she can't move around too much because other people complain.                  (Kelly, 1996)

Over the past three decades, a particular paradigm of successful involvement by families in children's literacy has prevailed. Official education reports have stressed the importance of regular story-reading by parents from early infancy and the absence of this practice has been used by teachers and governments alike to explain early reading difficulties. As early as 1975, the Bullock Report (7.2) informed parents that

> The best way to prepare the very young child for reading is to hold him on your lap and read aloud to him stories he likes, over and over again ... We believe that a priority need is ... to help parents recognise the value of sharing the experience of books with their children.

The maxim 'Babies need books' has changed little during later decades. It was reiterated in the Cox Report in the late 1980s (1989: 16: 8):

> We hope that parents will share books with their children from their earliest days, read

aloud to them and talk about the stories they have enjoyed together.

In the 1990s, the School Curriculum and Assessment Authority Report on desirable outcomes for children's learning in nurseries (SCAA, 1996: 7) asked parents to support learning opportunities at home through 'reading and sharing books'. The Government White Paper on the implementation of the National Literacy Strategy (DfEE, 1997: 32) stated: 'Children who are read to regularly, hear stories, learn nursery rhymes, look at books, visit libraries and so on are much more likely to learn to read easily'. Most recently, the same message has been repeated in the Homework Guidelines (DfEE, 1998: 9) which stated: 'For children in Key Stage 1 homework should very largely consist of regular reading with parents and carers, looking at books together'.

Significantly, it is not enjoyment with any kind of print that counts. Both the official curriculum and the academic world in which teachers are trained only sanction and reinforce 'good' literature whose titles are provided in the curriculum; it is on these titles that the success of seven- and eleven-year-olds will be tested. Home experiences such as those of Jorna above are, therefore, excluded from the school model of success and even considered to be detrimental to school learning.

The crucial question for educators, however, is whether book and story-reading experiences at home are, in themselves, essential for successful cognitive and early reading development to take place. Or are they important simply because they reproduce what counts in early literacy tuition in British schools? In other words, does the problem of low achievement lie in inadequate parental involvement or in inadequate recognition by schools of the different strengths that children like Jorna might bring with them from their homes and communities? The answer is important, since we know that a number of new immigrant parents have always been and will always be unable to adopt school-based practices (Gregory, 1996; Greenhaigh & Hughes, 1999).

## Background

Although numerous studies from the English-speaking world point to the advantages for young children of family involvement in their literacy development, their emphasis has always been firmly and almost exclusively upon *parents* working with children *in specific ways* and often using particular school-sanctioned materials. Current models of *parental involvement in reading* in the UK are generally based on the following assumptions:

> *Assumption One* The same home reading programmes are suitable whether all the school is from a monolingual or first-generation linguistic minority background. Parents should be capable of helping their children through storybook-reading whether or not they are able to read English.

Researchers in the UK have generally shown a reluctance to recognise cultural differences in the learning practices of minority group families. A number of factors might be responsible for this. Since the debate on linguistic and cognitive 'deficit' or 'difference' (Bernstein, 1971; Labov, 1972), researchers and teachers have been anxious to emphasise *similarities* rather than differences in language use in the homes of different social classes (Wells, 1985; Tizard & Hughes, 1984). A second reason may well stem from the strong British tradition of *child-centredness* in early years education which is focused on the child as *individual* rather than a member of a cultural or ethnic group. Finally, recent government policy in the UK stresses the need to promote a 'common culture' (Tate, 1995) which will iron out cultural differences between groups. This aim is practically reinforced by the English National Curriculum (1995) which fails to acknowledge the learning practices of different minority groups. 'Equality of opportunity', a promise which is made in the Education Act of 1988, is currently interpreted as 'the same' provision. In practice, this means that families not benefiting from the 'equal opportunity' provided are viewed in terms of linguistic, cognitive or cultural deficit. Such a narrow definition of culture ignores the multiple pathways to literacy shown by both adults and children from minority groups in Western societies (Baynham, 1995; Kale & Luke, 1997).

> *Assumption Two* Home reading programmes are for *parental* involvement not wider family or community participation.

Current home reading programmes assume *parental* participation rather than involvement by the wider family or community in young children's reading. However, the role of siblings in children's learning has been the subject of various research studies; some reveal how young children learn social and emotional skills (Dunn, 1989) and cognitive skills (Cicirelli, 1976) from older siblings. Others show how in non-Western societies older siblings are often culture brokers who may be as influential or more influential than parents in socialising young children (Whiting & Edwards, 1988; Rogoff, 1990). Recent studies are beginning to highlight the special role which may be played by older siblings in linguistic minority families where parents do not speak the new language (Tharp & Gallimore, 1988; Zukow, 1989; Perez *et al.*, 1994; McQuillan & Tse, 1995; Gregory, 1998) and to suggest that the ways in which children learn from older siblings in the home environment may have implications for school learning. The role played by grandparents in home literacy teaching may also be significant in closely-knit families (Padmore, 1994; Williams, 1997), likewise other family members, such as uncles, aunts and older 'cousins' or 'friends' in the widest sense. These studies problematise the notion that parents will be the exclusive caregivers and 'teachers' in families of all backgrounds.

## Literacy and the Family: A Wider Theoretical Framework

The aim of this paper is to question the above assumptions and to explode the myth that linguistic minority children's reading success depends upon experience with 'authorised' reading experiences at home. The theoretical framework informing this argument synthesises perspectives from the 'New Literacy Studies', cultural psychology and cultural anthropology. The New Literacy Studies support an ideological model of literacy which signals explicitly that literacy practices are aspects not only of culture but also of power structures (Street, 1995; Baynham, 1995). Viewed in this way, school-sanctioned literacy – or 'Literacy', as referred to by Street (1995: 14) – is just one of a multiplicity of literacies which take place in people's lives, in different domains, for a variety of purposes and in different languages. Within this model, children and adults draw upon a number of different 'mediators of literacy'; such a mediator is defined as 'a person who makes his or her skills available to others, on a formal or informal basis, for them to accomplish specific literacy purposes' (Baynham, 1995: 39). They may be teachers at out-of-school community language classes, clubs, drama activities etc.; or they may be 'guiding lights' – mediators of literacy who are especially inspiring as mentors or role models, such as grandparents (Padmore, 1994) or siblings (Gregory, 1998).

Cultural psychology offers a 'cultural mediational model of reading' (Cole, 1996: 273) which recognises as vital the actual roles that significant 'experts' play in giving 'guided participation' (Rogoff, 1990) or 'scaffolding' (Bruner, 1986) to the learning of the novice. This concept is exemplified in the work of Wagner 1994, whose comparative study on children in Morocco shows how those engaged in formal learning of the Qur'an revealed different skills and strategies from those whose literacy learning took place only within the official school.

However, an important argument of this paper is that young people are not trapped within existing home and community practices. The children whose voices we hear below reveal a complex heterogeneity of traditions whereby reading practices from different domains are blended, resulting in a form of reinterpretation that is both new and dynamic. Duranti and Ochs (1996) refer to this type of blending as *syncretic literacy*, which merges not simply linguistic codes or texts, but different activities. Their example is the activity of doing homework by Samoan Americans, and they provide a finely-tuned analysis of the way in which Samoan and American traditions, languages, teaching and child-rearing activities are blended. In this paper, we argue that *contrasting* home and school strategies and practices may provide children with an enlarged treasure trove, upon which they can draw in the official English school.

## The Study

The findings below are drawn largely from a large bank of data, collected over seven years, on home, school and community reading practices among past and present generations of teachers and pupils in schools in Spitalfields, east London. The question investigated is: how do young children in Spitalfields, many of whom are of linguistic minority backgrounds, set about learning to read in their homes, communities and classrooms? The scope of the question is wide and separate phases of the research have addressed different issues attempting to piece together a complex jigsaw of the role of reading in the lives of families who, in many cases, do not fit those required by 'official' school demands.

This paper draws upon Phases 2 and 4 of the research (1994–1996 and 1998–1999) funded by the Economic and Social Research Council (R000 22 1186 and R000 222487). Phase 2 examined the literacy histories and current practices in seven Bangladeshi British and six monolingual families whose five-year-old children attended two neighbouring schools. The question investigated was: what is the nature of reading practices taking place in the children's lives, and how far do children transfer reading strategies from home to school and vice versa? (Gregory, 1998; Gregory & Williams, 1998). Phase 4 addresses the role of siblings as mediators of literacy in two east London communities and in tracing the work and play activities around literacy of ten Bangladeshi British and a similar number of monolingual families. Examples from monolingual children from other areas of London whose family literacy practices are recognised as 'valid' within the current 'parental involvement' framework have also been collected and analysed for the purpose of this paper.

A combination of methods from ethnography (participant observation, interviews, life histories etc.) and ethnomethodology (conversation analysis) has been used during different phases of the work. Ethnography was important in its aim to produce a 'cultural grammar' or a set of rules which need to be known in order to become a competent member of the group. The researchers themselves were teachers and shared in many of the experiences of the participants, spending considerable time in homes and classrooms and accompanying the families on shopping or other visits. At the same time, their task was to remain 'strange' to the situation in order to make explicit what is already known to the group. Ethnographic fieldwork went through the following stages:

(1) prolonged and repetitive data collection during contextualised observations which disturbed the interactions of the participants as little as possible;
(2) formulating questions and multiple hypotheses until a pattern is formed from the data to provide an analytic framework;
(3) narrowing the focus to generate a limited number of hypotheses or 'typologies' which are then subjected to further investigation;
(4) producing trustworthy evidence through a full and explicit description of the social world in which events studied take place.

Ethnographic methods enabled us to give a detailed account of the literacy practices taking place in homes, communities and classrooms as well as examine patterns of difference and similarity between groups. However, they did not provide insight into the moment-by-moment construction of meaning between child and partner during reading sessions.

The vital aspect of an ethnomethodological approach was to show how child and adult (or older sibling) created 'cultural knowledge' in the home or classroom together, rather than viewing knowledge as preconstituted by cultural or social class background. The aim was to show how adult (or older sibling) and child 'situate' themselves in the reading 'lesson' and how they both participated in teaching and learning through interaction and negotiation. We are analysing the data using the method of multi-layering (Gregory, 1998). This approach enabled us to examine (1) the social context within which individual functioning is embedded (in-depth ethnographic analysis), (2) individual teaching strategies (codings) and (3) the role of the child in negotiating interactions (conversation analysis). A useful example of the value of combining qualitative and quantitative approaches has been found in Rogoff and Gauvain's (1986) pattern analysis used to examine instructional discourse in mother/child dyads.

## Recognising Differences: Contrasting Materials, Mediators and Purposes

Current views of what counts as partnership between home and school are illustrated in the following two examples of school-oriented (mainstream) and monolingual families where

school reading practices are adopted and reinforced. For children from such families, experiences with books can often begin from an early age. The following vignette of Ben (33 months) sharing a book with his mother, while his sister Alice (15 months) looks on, illustrates how this practice offers an opportunity for close interaction between child and adult, but also enables a particular set of behaviours and expectations around books to be modelled and reinforced.

| Mother | Ben |
|---|---|
| That's an easy one. Get a more difficult one. | |

*(Ben looks through his books. His mother suggests 'Party'? Ben chooses another first and his mother reads its title: 'The Zoo'? Ben finally settles for 'Party', reading its title out loud.)*

| | | |
|---|---|---|
| 02 | | Hallo Alice |
| 03 | No, Alice you can't have this book. Mummy and Ben are looking at this book. 'Susie and John are going to a party'. What's she doing, Ben? | |
| 05 | Yes! What colour is it? | That party . . . that party . . . That . . . is it that one? *(pointing to the present)* |
| 06 | | Green |
| 07 | Nooo! | |
| 08 | | Blue |
| 09 | Bl–ue! What's she got on her feet? | |
| 10 | | White socks |
| 11 | Are they on her feet? | |
| 12 | | No |
| 13 | Now what's she doing? | |
| 14 | | Putting her shoes on |

| Mother | Ben |
|---|---|
| 15 Now, what's the boy doing? | |
| 16 | Putting trousers on |
| 17 Are they short trousers or long trousers? | |
| 18 | Long trousers. |
| 19 Have a look. You can see his knees. | |
| 20 Are they short trousers or long trousers? | |
| 21 | Short |
| 22 Yes they are, aren't they. | |

Belinda does not read the story through but pauses to consider the detail of the illustrations, using the book as a focus for developing Ben's language. She poses questions and checks Ben's responses if they are inappropriate. The emphasis here is on accuracy and serves the same function as the early lexical labelling behaviour previously referred to. This pattern of question-response-retort is a behaviour that Ben will recognise when he starts school and it is one that he is already beginning to internalise:

| Mother | Ben |
|---|---|
| 23 | What's Ann doing? |
| 24 What is Ann doing? | |
| 25 | Opening her presents. |

Such questioning techniques are just one characteristic of a school-oriented approach to literacy learning that may be adopted within the home. The following example illustrates how Isabel (aged 10) spontaneously adopts 'teacherly' behaviour when playing a game with her brother Alex (aged 4). The children are at home; the focus of the interaction is once more a book, although this time it is one that provides games, stories and quizzes for pre-school children. They have spent approximately 15 minutes playing one game from the book. They have now chosen a page on rhymes:

| Isabel | Alex |
|---|---|
| 01 OK. Log and . . . ? | |
| 02 | dog! |
| 03 Goodboy! Wiz . . . Lizard and . . . ? | |
| 04 | wizard! |
| 05 I gave it away a bit there, didn't I? Carrot and . . . ? | |
| 06 | parrot |
| 07 Well done! Coat and . . . ? | |
| 08 | dote! |
| . . . | |
| 26 Can you think of any other rhymes? | Mmm . . . |
| 27 | Hamster . . . and . . . mmm. I can't think of any more rhymes . . . Ah! (*shouts*), Bear and pear! |
| 28 Well done! What about cat and bat? | And bird and heard? (*laughs*) Back- |
| 29 | wards and Harrods! |
| 30 No, no, no, no, no | Oh . . . |
| 32 | |
| . . . | |
| 45 What about? | (*interrupts*) Cape and pape, paper |
| 46 | |
| 48 | No |
| 49 Mmm . . . Late and plate | |
| 50 | Mmm . . . Fence and paint! No, no, no . . . Fence and pence, pencil . . . |
| 51 Yes, pence, a pence, like one p. In other words, a pence. | |
| 52 | Book and pook! |
| 53 Naw, book and look! | |

| 54 | Oh yeah. Door and poor. Yeah. Video and pedeo |
| 55 *(both children)* | . . . N-a-w . . . |

The activity continues until the children's father joins in and suggests they make joke rhymes.

| *Isabel* | *Alex* |
| 81 House and louse | |
| 82 | Now I'm gonna tell one. Cupboard and hubbard. Mother Hubbard! |
| 83 Yes! | |

This playful scene between siblings, which lasts for over forty minutes, reveals the wealth of cultural and linguistic knowledge the two children share. They have a shared experience of nursery rhymes, and places that are cultural icons; a common understanding of rhyming words, and a deep knowledge of English. The encounter reflects the same pattern of interaction that was evident between Belinda and Ben and reveals the subtlety of Isabel's teaching style. She provides ample praise and encouragement for her brother, offering examples when he loses confidence, allowing him to experiment freely, yet correcting him when he makes a mistake. She pauses to allow him sufficient time to respond and suggests generalising beyond the page to their wider knowledge of rhyming words. In the following example, and on several other occasions, she explains words she thinks Alex may not understand:

| *Isabel* | *Alex* |
| | Rabbit and habit! |
| That's a good one. Do you know what a habit is? | |
| | Well, it's sort of . . . How do you describe a habit? It's something, sort of, you do a lot of . . . |

It is clear that the two children are already familiar with a school-oriented approach to literacy as they participate in this playful encounter which provides a strong scaffold for Alex's learning. It is likely that when Alex and Ben start school shortly, they will recognise familiar patterns of interaction around books and stories and will be well placed to make a smooth transition into the world of the classroom. But what about children who do not have this shared understanding; whose experiences around literacy do not reflect those of the school and whose understanding of the nuances of English may still be developing?

## Community Classes: A Different Kind of Learning

For most of the Bangladeshi British children in our Spitalfields study, education continues long after mainstream school has finished, as the following conversation with six year old Ruhul demonstrates:

1  **R:**   There are eighty-three children
2  **AW:** Eighty-three children in your Arabic class! And when do you go to that?
3  **R:**   Seven o'clock to nine o'clock
4  **AW:** On?
5  **RA:** A night.
6  **AW:** Every night?
7  **R:**   Monday to Friday
8  **AW:** Monday to Friday! You go for two hours every night! Aren't you tired?
9  **R:**   I don't feel tired
10  **AW:** No? And who goes with you? Anybody from your class?
11  **R:**   I go by myself . . . And some people go from upstairs . . . juniors
12  **AW:** And are you the youngest then?
13  **R:**   Yes and I'm on the Qur'an
14  **AW:** You're on the Qur'an now.

Ruhul explains that he is reading the last primer before starting the Qur'an. He goes on to explain more about the structure of his classes.

22  **AW:** How many teachers are there for eighty-three children?
23  **RT:** There's two
24  **AW:** Only two? Who are they?
25  **R:**   One is the Qur'an . . . you know, all the Qur'an he can say it without looking
26  **AW:** He can.. What's his name?
27  **R:**   I don't know. And one is . . . he can . . . he knows all the meanings
28  **AW:** Does he. Does he tell you the meanings?

29 **R:**   Yes he does.
30 **AW:** So do you just read the Qur'an for two hours? Is that what you do?
31 **R:**   Yes but I don't sometimes, I talk sometimes
32 **AW:** You don't!
33 **R:**   I do

(Williams & Gregory, 1999: 159)

This conversation gives some idea of the demands made upon children who participate in very different home literacy practices. For these children, learning to read and write is a complex business involving several languages. The home dialect of the London Bangladeshis is Sylheti, an unwritten variety of Bengali and so parents feel that it is important that their children learn to read and write standard Bengali if they are to maintain their own culture. Finally, as practising Muslims, the children must read the Qur'an and therefore attend Qur'anic school and learn to read in Arabic. Already at age six, Ruhul realises that literacy is a serious business.

The class which Ruhul attended every day after school is typical of Qur'anic classes everywhere. The sessions are usually two hours long: few concessions are made to the young age of some of the children and even the smallest are expected to concentrate for long periods:

> In this particular class there are two male teachers, one of whom is working with the more advanced children who are tackling the complicated word structures of the Qur'an. The other group consists of younger children who are in a different part of the room with the second teacher, grappling with sounds and letters and oral verse. Everyone sits on the mat swaying to the sound of his/her own voice. Although on initial appraisal the noise level seems high, little of this is idle chatter. It is the expressed wish of the teachers that children read aloud, partly to assist their learning, but more importantly so that Allah can hear. Children are encouraged to develop a harmonious recitation in unison with the gentle rocking to and fro which accompanies the reading. They are told that Allah listens to his servants and is pleased if they take time to make their reading meaningful ... 'Now, repeat after me', the teacher requests, 'Kalimah Tayyabh, la ilaha ilallaho, mohammadan rasolallahe'. He tells them to look at

him as they repeat ... I leave the room on the third recitation of the prayer and notice that the children have not wavered: all remain seated on the floor as they have done for the last hour and a half. (Rashid, 1996)

Teaching methods are traditional: the teacher reads a phrase and the children repeat after him until they are word perfect and the process continues with the next phrase. The pattern of listen, practise and repeat is shown clearly in the following extract, also taken from Rashid (1995):

> The teacher stands in the centre and calls upon each child in turn to recite the passage which they have reached in their reading of the religious primer or the Qur'an.
>
> **Teacher:** Read this, Shuma
> **Shuma:** Alif, bah, tah, sayh (*the names of the graphic symbols on the page*)
> **Teacher:** What was that? Say it again
> **Shuma:** Alif, bah, tah, sayh, jim
> **Teacher:** Yes, that's it, now carry on
> **Shuma:** Jim – jim, hae, kae, d- (*hesitates*)
> **Teacher:** Dal – dal, remember it and repeat
> **Shuma:** Dal, zal, rae, zae, sin, shin, swad, dwad,
> **Teacher:** (*nods*) What's next? Thoy, zoy
> **Shuma:** Zoy, thoy ...
> **Teacher:** No, no, listen carefully. Thoy, zoy
> **Shuma:** (*repeats*)
> **Teacher:** Fine, Now say it again from the beginning ...

(field notes, N. Rashid, April, 1995)

The Bengali classes take place in a variety of locations. Some are held in teachers' houses, some in the children's homes and some in community centres as the one described by Rashid below.

> Situated behind Petticoat Lane Market, this Bengali school is funded through the voluntary sector. It comprises two mobile rooms, the walls bare except for a few information posters made by the children. The room I enter has several rows of desks at which children sit quietly – some writing, others practising words under their breath. At the beginning, the teacher sits in front of the room, then starts to walk around. The children who are mumbling are practising the previous day's work and as the teacher

passes around, the voice of the child he is listening to is momentarily amplified so that the teacher can correct if necessary before moving on to the next. Later the children read, some at a fast pace whilst others read with careful deliberation. When the teacher reaches the child I have come to observe, she reads confidently and eloquently and the few mistakes she makes are firmly corrected. Parts that are not understood are explained briefly in Sylheti . . . and the lesson continues in this way to the end. (Rashid, 1996)

Teaching in the Bengali classes is equally traditional: children work on one primer at a time, progressing gradually through the series. As the following conversation indicates, learning Bengali, even if it takes place in someone's front room with a friend's mum as the teacher, is also a serious undertaking.

1 **AW:** Tell me what you do then on Saturdays and Sundays
2 **R:** I don't come to school
3 **AW:** You don't come to school but what do you do?
4 **R:** I go to Bengali school then I come home
5 **AW:** What time do you go to Bengali school?
6 **R:** Eleven o'clock to one o'clock
7 **AW:** And what do you do there?
8 **R:** We read Bengali
9 **AW:** And how do you do . . . how do you learn that then?
10 **AW:** And do you just have one book or do you have a lot of books?
11 **R:** There's book two, book three, book four, book five . . . there's lots of books
12 **AW:** Lots of books and which book are you on?
13 **R:** Book one
14 **AW:** Book one. Is it hard?
15 **R:** Easy!
16 **AW:** What do you have to do? Do you have to write in the book?
17 **R:** You've got to read it. And sometimes they say, 'You've got to write it without looking'.
18 **AW:** Write it without looking and then what do you do?
19 **R:** Then if I'm right..she..they tell us
20 **AW:** And who is your teacher?

21 **R:** There's two, Meli's dad and Jahanara's dad
22 **AW:** Jahanara's dad! Is he the teacher?
23 **R:** Jahanara's dad, and Tania..do you know Tania in Class One?
24 **AW:** No
25 **R:** Her mum

(Gregory & Williams, 2000: 174–175)

Although Ruhul is only six years old, he spends two hours every day, in addition to his mainstream school, in such classes. In contrast with the monolingual group who engaged mostly in informal literacy practices outside school, the Bangladeshi British children spent on average thirteen hours per week receiving formal instruction in organised classes. Thus their home literacy differs from that of many monolingual children in many respects. First, it is conducted as group rather than individual or paired activities, and an individual's progress (towards the completion of the Qur'an for example) is often marked by the whole group sharing sweets or other treats. Second, the purpose of reading is quite different from that of monolingual English children: learning to read and write in Bengali is seen as entering a cultural world and acquiring a language which was fought over during the violent struggle for independence from Pakistan in 1971; learning to read the Qur'an is necessary for taking on the Islamic faith and therefore an adult and serious occupation. Finally, even the task of reading at home in English is quite different for Bangladeshi British children. In this community where some parents are literate in Bengali but not necessarily in English, home reading usually means children reading their school texts not with Mum or Dad nor even with Grandma or Grandpa, but with those members of the family who are already fully proficient in English, i.e. the older sisters and brothers.

## Reading between Siblings: A Syncretism of Literacies

It was this 'booksharing' with older siblings that provided some of the most interesting insights into the young Bangladeshi British children's acquisition of literacy. The combination of cultures and learning styles the bilingual children were exposed to in their daily lives resulted in a unique method of tackling the school reading books at home. When the reading sessions were analysed, it became clear that the children were blending strategies learned in both their mainstream English school and in their Bengali and Arabic classes. This resulted in what we have termed 'syncretic literacy' (Gregory, 1998) with the repetitions and fast-flowing pace characteristic of the Qur'anic reading, grafted onto strategies adopted from lessons in the English mainstream school such as echoing, 'chunking' of expressions and predicting. The transcriptions also revealed that the older siblings employed a series of intricate and finely tuned strategies to support the young readers as they struggled with the text. In the early stages when reading with a child who was just beginning to read, the supportive 'scaffolding' was almost total, with the older siblings providing almost every word for the beginning reader. As the younger child's proficiency increased however, the scaffolding was gradually removed until the child was able to read alone. We were able to identify the following stages in the scaffolding of the young children's reading:

*Listen and repeat:* the child repeats word by word after the older sibling

*Tandem reading:* the child echoes the sibling's reading, sometimes managing telegraphic speech

*Chained reading:* the sibling begins to read and the child continues, reading the next few words until s/he needs help again

*Almost alone:* the child initiates reading and reads until a word is unknown; the sibling corrects the error or supplies the word; the child repeats the word correctly and continues

*The recital:* the child recites the complete piece.

The following extracts illustrates Stage 1 *Listen and repeat.*

| | Child | Sibling |
|---|---|---|
| 1 | | The postman |
| 2 | The postman | |
| 3 | | It was Tum's birthday |
| 4 | was . . . birthday | |
| 5 | | Ram made |
| 6 | Ram made | |
| 7 | | him a birthday card |
| 8 | him a birthday card | |

Stage 3 *Chained reading* is illustrated by the following extract.

| | Child | Sibling |
|---|---|---|
| 34 | | Okhta (this one) |
| 35 | | It's |
| 36 | It's a whobber. Meg . . . | |
| 37 | | Mog |
| 38 | Mog catched a fish | |
| 39 | | caught |
| 40 | caught a fish | |
| . . . | | |
| 44 | They cook | |
| 45 | | cooked |
| 46 | cooked a fish | |
| 47 | | and |
| 48 | and Owl had a rest. Meg was looking | |
| 49 | | looked out |

(Gregory, 1998: 43–44)

In Stage 3 we see Akhlak and his sister practising 'chained reading': the sister starts and Akhlak continues reading the next few words until he needs help again; the sister then either corrects or provides the word. Akhlak repeats the correction and continues. These home reading sessions are characterised by a very high number of turns and a fast-flowing pace, strategies that we have already seen in practice in the Qur'anic classes. It is notable that in spite of the child's young age, the focus is on print rather than on any illustrations. Furthermore, the older sibling's insistence on accuracy from the outset indicates that this is not play but serious work in which the roles of learner and teacher are clearly defined and not negotiable. As we shall see below, the children of first-generation immigrants take their role of mediator of new cultures, languages and literacies very seriously, even in play.

## Combining Experiences from Home and School

| | |
|---|---|
| 1 | Good morning class |

2                              Good morning
                              Miss Wahida, good
                              morning everyone.

3        I want to do the
         register. So, Sayeeda.

4                              Good morning Miss
                              Wahida.

5        Good morning
         Sayeeda
         OK. We've done your
         reading today.
         Now we are going to
         do maths.
         OK.

The scene is a flat in Spitalfields. Wahida, a Bangladeshi British child aged eleven, is playing schools with her eight-year-old sister Sayeeda. The pattern of the school day is reflected in the children's play. Maths is followed by a spelling test and a 'lesson' on homophones before assembly, followed by science, geography and art. Wahida demonstrates on the blackboard while Sayeeda writes in an exercise book. The following extracts show how Wahida has adopted the social, linguistic and cognitive rules of the classroom and how skilfully she scaffolds the learning of her sister by syncretising the knowledge she has gained from attending two schools, one during the day and the other each evening.

38 **Wahida**:   Well done, Sayeeda. I'm going to give you a sticker later on. A headteacher's sticker. *(after clearing throat)* Now, we're going to do a spelling test. Are you ready, Sayeeda?

39 **Sayeeda**:   Yes Miss.

40 **Wahida**:   I'm going to give you at least 20 seconds for each of them, OK? The first one is tricycle, tricycle. Tricycle has three wheels, tricycle. The next one is commandment, Commandment, I COMMAND you to do as quickly as you can. Commandment. Next one is technology. Technology is a subject. Once you're grown up, Sayeeda, you're going to do hard technology. The next one is polydron . . .

The spelling test continues until Wahida demonstrates the correct spellings on the board as Sayeeda marks her own work. Then the focus moves to homophones:

41 **Wahida**:   Well done! Only two wrong. Now we're going to do homophones. Who knows what's a homophone is? No one? OK. I'll tell you one and then you're going to do some by yourselves. Like watch – one watch is your time, watch. And another watch is I'm watching you. OK? So Sayeeda, you wrote some in your book, haven't you? Can you tell me some please. Sayeeda, can you only give me three please.

42 **Sayeeda**:   Oh I have to give five.

43 **Wahida**:   No Sayeeda, we haven't got time. We've only another five minutes to assembly.

(Gregory & Williams, 2000: 200)

It is hard to imagine that when Wahida began school at five, she spoke very little English. Six years on, she is using the appropriate language of the classroom and the lexis of particular subjects. It is clear she has internalised the social, cognitive and linguistic rules of the classroom and has made them her own. She has taken on a register that accurately reflects that of her teacher as she confidently conducts the class through both the rituals of the day (the register, lunchtime, assembly) and the conventions of the classroom (lining up, writing the date, marking work).

Wahida demonstrates her knowledge of teaching strategies as she gives direct instruction, encourages participation, provides demonstrations, and structures the cognitive demands of different 'lessons', giving ample praise and encouragement to her pupil, who readily cooperates in this sophisticated game. In both the spelling lesson and the session on homophones, Wahida scaffolds Sayeeda's learning by contextualising words and providing examples of their meaning.

Wahida's emphasis on spelling and homophones accurately reflects the 'word level work' recommended for children of Sayeeda's age, as part of the Literacy Hour. It is possibly no coincidence that she chooses to concentrate on word level work rather than sentence level which demands a sound knowledge of English grammar or text level work which calls for greater interpretation of the meaning and underlying structure of texts.

Some of the procedures she employs reflect the approaches that she would have experienced in her community school, where teaching methods focus more on listening, repeating and practising than on interpretation.

Wahida is syncretising what she knows from the different literacies of both school contexts, in a way that is recognised by her sister. Wahida demonstrates how children who come to school with experiences of literacy that do not conform to the official view, can learn to integrate the literacy of the classroom with their previous experience in a way that is creative and sophisticated and enables them to be effective literacy learners.

## Towards a New Paradigm of Inclusive Education for Linguistic Minority Communities

If early experiences at home and in the community are to be recognised and extended, it would seem important that teachers have time to listen to parents and to find out about their children's literacy experiences out of school. The statement at the beginning of this paper is the record of a conference between the parent of a Year 1 child and a teacher as part of the Primary Language Record (CLPE, 1988). The teacher concerned was able to plan more appropriately for Jorna as a result of finding out about the content and style of her learning at home.

Our studies show that parents should not exclusively be seen as the principal mediators of children's literacy. For many children, particularly those who have English as an additional language, siblings play a very important role in modelling and supporting their younger brothers and sisters and giving them an understanding of what it means to be literate.

This research reveals the strong link between work and play and the gap between children's experiences at home and what officially counts as learning. Our work has shown the wealth of learning that is going on in homes that do not subscribe to mainstream practices and the success that can arise if these children's experiences are recognised and built upon.

## Acknowledgements

We would like to acknowledge Ali Asghar and Nasima Rashid who worked on the project as well as ESRC R 000 221186 Family Literacy History and Children's Learning Strategies at Home and at School and R 000 4287 Siblings as Mediators of Literacy in Two East London communities. We would also like to thank the Drury family for participating in the work.

## References

Baynham, M. (1995) *Literacy Practices: Investigating Literacy in Social Contexts.* London: Longman.

Bernstein, B. (1971) A socio-linguistic approach to socialisation with some reference to educability. In D. Hymes and J. Gumperz (eds) *Directions in Sociolinguistics.* New York: Rinehart and Winston.

Bruner, J. (1986) *Actual Minds, Possible Worlds.* Cambridge, MA: Harvard University Press.

Centre for Language in Primary Education (1988) The Primary Language Record. ILEA.

Cicirelli, V.G. (1976) Mother–child and sibling–sibling interactions on a problem solving task. *Child Development* 47, 588–96.

Cole, M. (1996) *Cultural Psychology: A Once and Future Discipline.* Harvard, MA: Harvard University Press.

DfEE (Department for Education and Employment) (1997) *The Implementation of the National Literacy Strategy.* London: DfEE.

DfEE (1998) *Homework: Guidelines for Primary and Secondary Schools.* London: DfEE.

Dunn, J. (1989) The family as an educational environment in the pre-school years. In C.W. Desforges (ed.) *Early Childhood Education* (*The British Journal of Educational Psychology*, Monograph Series No. 4) Edinburgh: Scottish Academic Press.

Duranti, A. and Ochs, E. (1996) Syncretic literacy in a Samoan American family. In L.B. Resnick *et al.* (eds) *Discourse, Tools and Reasoning.* Berlin: Springer.

Greenhaigh and Hughes (1999) Encouraging conversing: Trying to change what parents do when their children read with them. *Reading* 33 (3), 98–105.

Gregory, E. (1998) Siblings as mediators of literacy in linguistic minority communities. *Language and Education* 12 (1), 33–55.

Gregory, E. and Williams, A. (1998) Family literacy history and children's learning strategies at home and at school: Perspectives from ethnography and ethnomethodology. In G. Walford and A. Massey (eds) *Children Learning: Ethnographic Explorations.* Stamford: JAI Press.

Gregory, E. and Williams, A. (2000) *City Literacies: Learning to Read Across Generations and Cultures.* London: Routledge.

Gregory, E. (1996) *Making Sense of a New World: Learning to Read in a Second Language.* London: Sage.

Heath, S.B. (1983) *Ways with Words: Language, Life and Work in Communities and Classrooms.* Cambridge: Cambridge University Press.

Kale, J. and Luke, A. (1997) Learning through difference: Cultural practices in early childhood language socialisation. In E. Gregory (ed.) *One Child, Many Worlds: Early Learning in Multicultural Communities.* London: Fulton/TCP.

Kelly, C. (1996) A closer look at parent–teacher discussions. *The Primary Language Record and The California Learning Record in Use: Proceedings from the PLR/CLR International Seminar.* El Cajon, California: Centre for Learning.

Labov, W. (1972) *Sociolinguistic Patterns.* Philadelphia: University of Philadelphia.

McQuillan, J. and Tse, L. (1995) Child language brokering in linguistic minority communities. *Language and Education* 9 (3), 195–215.

Padmore, S. (1994) Guiding lights. In M. Hamilton *et al.* (eds) *Worlds of Literacy* (pp. 143–156). Clevedon: Multilingual Matters.

Perez, D. *et al.* (1994) Siblings providing one another with opportunities to learn. *Focus on Diversity* 5 (1), 1–5. California: Bilingual Research Group, University of Santa Cruz.

Rashid, N. (1995) Field-notes from ESRC Project R 000 22 1186: Family literacy history and children's learning strategies at home and at school.

Rashid, N. (1996) Field-notes from ESRC Project R 000 22 1186.

Rogoff, B. and Gauvain, B. (1986) A method for the analysis of patterns, illustrated with data on mother–child instructional interaction. In J. Valsiner (ed.) *The Individual Subject and Scientific Psychology.* NY: Plenum Press.

Rogoff, B. (1990) *Apprenticeship in Thinking: Cognitive Development in Social Contexts.* Oxford: Oxford University Press.

SCAA (1996) *Desirable Outcomes for Children's Learning on Entering Compulsory Education.* London: HMSO.

Street, B. (1995) *Social Literacies: Critical Approaches to Literacy in Development, Ethnography and Education.* London: Longman.

Tate, N. (1995) Summing up speech at the International conference on teaching English as an additional language (SCAA) London, April 1995.

Tharp, R. and Gallimore, R. (1988) *Rousing Minds to Life: Teaching, Learning and Schooling in Social Context.* Cambridge: Cambridge University Press.

The Bullock Report (1975) *A Language for Life.* Report of the Committee of Inquiry appointed by the Secretary of State for Education and Science. London: HMSO.

The Cox Report (1989) *English for Ages 5–16.* London: Central Office for Information.

Tizard, B. and Hughes, M. (1984) *Young Children Learning.* London: Fontana.

Wagner, D. (1994) *Literacy, Culture and Development: Becoming Literate in Morocco.* Cambridge and New York: Cambridge University Press.

Wells, C.G. (1985) Pre-school literacy related activities and success in school. In D.R. Olson, N. Torrance and A. Hildyard (eds) *Literacy, Language and Learning. The Nature and Consequences of Reading and Writing.* Cambridge: Cambridge University Press.

Whiting, B.B. and Edwards, C.P. (1988) *Children of Different Worlds: The Formation of Social Behaviour.* Cambridge, MA: Cambridge University Press.

Williams, A. (1997) Investigating literacy in London: Three generations of readers in an East End family. In E. Gregory (ed.) *One Child, Many Worlds: Early Learning in Multicultural Communities.* London: Fulton.

Williams, A. and Gregory, E. (1999) Home and school reading practices in two East End communities. In C. Leung and A. Tosi (eds) *Rethinking Language Education.* London: CILT.

Zukow, P.G. (1989) Siblings as effective socialising agents: Evidence from central Mexico. In P.G. Zukow (ed.) *Sibling Interactions Across Cultures: Theoretical and Methodological Issues.* New York: Springer Verlag.

## Questions

1.  What kind of relationships between families, the school and young students does this article discuss?

2.  What do the authors mean by literacies? How is this different from literacy, or reading or writing?

3.  What are the 'principles for inclusive education' for minority language families that

this article recommends? How does this differ from traditional programs of parental involvement in children's literacy?

4. What are some of the differences between the teaching of literacy in English in mainstream schools and the teaching of Bengali and Arabic in community classes (or heritage language classes) in complementary schools as described by the authors?

5. What do the authors mean by 'syncretic literacy'? How is this manifested in the book-sharing episode shared by the authors.

## Activities

1a. List all the activities below in the first column of a table. In a second column, indicate which of the activities you practice, by putting a plus or negative sign next to the activity. In a third column, briefly explain your practice or give an explanation why you don't do it. (If you're not teaching, reflect on your experience as a student).

I. Learning about parents and their communities
   a. home visits
   b. visits to community-based organizations, shops, places of worship, places of entertainment

II. Information sharing through:
   a. weekly newsletter
   b. personal notes
   c. telephone calls

III. Get parents to participate in classroom and in school by:
   a. invitation to observe: time, days
   b. invitation to special events involving their children
   c. have parents help make bulletin boards and decorations
   d. invitation to school functions

IV. Parental empowerment in curricular decisions:
   Having parents advise, plan and develop programs that they feel are needed.

2. Find two parents, one working class and one professional, if possible in each of these four groups:
   a. Asian
   b. Latino
   c. White Anglo
   d. African American or Black West Indian

Give them the list below and ask them to rate their participation as follows:
   Frequently = 3, Sometimes = 2, Never = 1

Total the scores for each individual. Compare your findings across ethnolinguistic groups and also across social class.

You may tabulate the responses from the entire class and make a poster with the findings.
   a. tutoring children at home
   b. helping children with homework
   c. helping children sell raffle tickets or candy
   d. attending class activities
   e. accompanying children on field trips

      f.   attending parent–teacher conferences / meetings

      g.  helping out with Parent–Teacher Organizations

      h.  co-learners, attending workshops on children and schooling

      i.   decision makers, members of advisory boards or committees

      j.   advocates for change, attending school board meetings

3. For your classroom (or one of your choosing), design either a weekly newsletter to parents or a parent's handbook. Focus on language and cultural cooperation between home and school. Remember to decide on languages and their varieties, as well as content.

4. What type of parent involvement in school exists in your community? Are there differing types of involvement (e.g. moral, emotional, social, financial, physical)? How interactive is such involvement? Does such involvement differ according to language group, social class, both, or neither? How does such involvement change with grade and age?

5. Besides the Anglo conception of 'parental involvement', there are other practices and philosophies prevalent in education that do not always reflect the experience of language minorities. Read the following statements to at least five language minority professionals who have achieved well academically. Ask them to reflect on their experience growing up in a minority family, and to indicate whether the practice happened:

    Always = 4, Frequently = 3, Seldom = 2, Never = 1.

Then ask them to share with you other family influences that they think might have contributed to their academic success.

    1.  My mother or father read to me before going to bed.

    2.  There were children's books available to me.

    3.  We went out to visit museums and other institutions.

    4.  We went to the library to take out books.

    5.  I had structured after-school activities and lessons.

    6.  I belonged to 'clubs'.

    7.  My mother or father helped me with my homework.

    8.  My mother or father studied with me before a test.

5. Use the list and scale above to interview five successful minority professionals, and five successful majority professionals. Are there differences in home literacy practices?

6. Make a video of (a) a classroom with a mostly white language majority population and (b) a classroom with a mostly working-class non-white language minority population. Then select a student from each classroom. Visit the student at home, observe and record the following: language use at home, literacy practices, other child rearing practices. If there are specific literacy events in the home, try to video-tape these. Contrast and compare both situations. Share the videos with the class.

7. Select a school in which there are a large number of recently arrived students. Find out what kinds of literacy (or literacies strategy) is in place for them. Find out if the community has a 'school' (e.g. a Saturday school) for teaching heritage language literacies. Make an oral report to the class.

8. Locate between three and six bilingual children. Observe them in school and if possible

in the home. What is the 'synchronism' between school and home? What are the similarities and differences in literacy practices at school, at home and in the child's community?

## Further Reading

Ada, A.F. (1997) Mother-tongue literacy as a bridge between home and school cultures. In J.V. Tinajero and A.F. Ada, (eds) *The Power of Two Languages: Literacy and Biliteracy for Spanish Speaking Students.* New York: Macmillan/McGraw-Hill.

Blackledge, A. (2000) *Literacy, Power and Social Justice.* Stoke on Trent: Trentham.

Brisk, M.E. (2000) *Literacy and Bilingualism. A Handbook for ALL teachers.* Mahwah, New Jersey: Lawrence Erlbaum.

Edwards, V. (1998) *The Power of Babel: Teaching and Learning in Multilingual Classrooms.* Stoke-on-Trent (UK): Trentham.

Gregory, E., Long, S. and Volk, D. (eds) (2004) *Many Pathways to Literacy: Young Children Learning with Siblings, Grandparents and Communities.* London: RoutledgeFalmer.

Kenner, C. (2004) *Becoming Literate: Young Children Learning Different Writing Systems.* Stoke on Trent (UK): Trentham.

Reyes, M. and Halcon, J. (eds) (2001) *The Best for Our Children: Critical Perspectives on Literacy for Latino Students.* New York: Teachers College Press.

# Part 4: Issues in Teaching, Learning and Assessment in Bilingual Education

# The Pedagogy of Peace: Language Awareness in the Neve Shalom/Wahat Al-Salam Elementary School

## G. Feuerverger

If you wish to promote peace, begin with the children.
— Mahatma Mohandas Gandhi

### Emancipatory Discourse: 'Border Crossing' and Peacemaking

One of the greatest challenges in Israeli society is to overcome the fear and enmity that have evolved through the years of war between Jews and Arabs. One of the Jewish parents very eloquently expressed her hope, shared by all those connected with the school: 'We want our children to learn in friendship and joy, not in conflict and sorrow'. In order to make friends with 'the other', as the residents of this village are doing, we must confront the 'other' in the deepest part of our souls, in the psychological no-man's-land where the 'foreigner' lurks – 'he is the hidden face of our identity, the space that wrecks our abode, the time in which understanding and affinity founder' (Kristeva, 1991, p. 1).

In this chapter, I examine how the participants acknowledge the 'foreigner' whose language, culture, values, and traditions are different and who competes for the same geopolitical space. The possibility of collaboration instead of competition and hostility is being opened; the hegemonic discourses and institutions are being challenged, and transformative intergroup and interpersonal dialogues are being created. What immediately caught my attention when I began my visits to the school was that what these individuals were in fact doing was imagining a new way of life, inventing a new educational story by creating a curriculum with narratives (both Jewish and Palestinian) of home and displacement, of borders and crossings. Above all, theirs is a quest for authenticity in search of a peaceful future for their children.

The words of bell hooks (1991, p. 9) speak to this situation: 'To imagine is to begin the process that transforms reality'. The Neve Shalom/Wahat Al-Salam elementary school thus becomes a site of cultural encounters and a network of negotiations and reconciliations. Behind the idea of the 'binational space' of the school lies the anguish of oppression and dispersion, the fear of terrorism and incarceration, the memory of genocide and the agony of annihilation – all caught in the dream of devising an open discourse that will incorporate the linguistic, social, and psychological needs of both peoples.

This complex discourse of cautious hope with its promise of a better world was both overwhelming and fascinating. It illuminated my research journey and my writing, as well as the sharing of my own narrative with those of my participants in this extraordinary village. Max Van Manen (1990) explains that 'we gather other people's experiences because they allow us to become more experienced ourselves'. Michael Connelly and Jean Clandinin (1990, 1995, 1999) support this view and claim that narrative refers to the process of making meaning of experience by telling stories of personal and social relevance. Indeed, by presenting sketches of the language experiences of some of the students, teachers, and parents connected with the school, I discuss how language awareness operates in the school curriculum to create an educational system that is based on the principle of egalitarian coexistence between two nations; that is, the Jews and the Palestinians.[1] In this way we will explore the concept of language awareness in relation to the educational goals and activities of this binational/bicultural/bilingual school within the larger context of Israeli society.

## Theoretical Considerations

Language awareness is defined as 'a person's sensitivity to, and conscious awareness of, the nature of language and its role in human life' (Donmall, 1985, p. 7). Language awareness can be divided into five interrelated categories: (1) affective (for example, attitude formation), (2) social (improvement of intergroup relations), (3) power (choice in language acquisition and use), (4) cognitive (intellectual improvement), and (5) performance (enhanced proficiency). In this chapter, I concentrate, for the most part, on the affective and social domains of language awareness as they are embedded within the formal and informal structures of the school and more generally within the broader social and cultural system of the village. We will examine how language awareness plays a major role in this school in its overriding commitment to fostering an emancipatory discourse of education based on conflict resolution and peacemaking.

This alternative discourse underscores the need for a radical reconceptualization of Jewish-Arab relations in education and in Israeli society in general, and as such contests the dominant-subordinate power structures in the wider society. Eric Hawkins (1984, p. 6) claims that by developing language awareness in the classroom, ' . . . we are seeking to arm our pupils against fear of the unknown which breeds prejudice and antagonism'. I also agree with Norman Fairclough (1993), who claims that both macro and micro power factors operate in a given discursive context, and Chris Jenks (1991), who claims that by contesting hegemonic practices and raising critical language awareness in classrooms, we are liberating ourselves as teachers and our students from a dangerous narrowness of vision. David Corson (1999, p. 160) emphasizes this notion: 'When teachers encourage students to reflect critically on the language practices used in the school itself; it is a clear statement that this is the way teachers would like the world of discourse to be outside the school. By looking at real acts of emancipatory discourse in the school's setting, rather than at vicarious examples, students become empowered by the activities.' Tony Adams and Witold Tulasiewicz (1993, 1994) agree that language awareness is crucial in a multicultural society as a means for effective communication enabling enhanced instrumental use of language, as an emancipatory vehicle for asserting one's identity without clashing with

that of others, and as a tool for understanding others by developing linguistic sensitivity.

These notions are congruent with the social philosophy put forward by the critical theorist Roy Bhaskar (1986, 1989) in his reflections on language, power, and human emancipation. Briefly, his argument is that emancipation occurs when we make the move from unwanted to wanted sources of determination by changing the relations between human action and structural context. He proposes a 'much more subtle and complex view of society in which human agents are neither passive products of social structures nor entirely their creators but are placed in an iterative and naturally reflexive feedback relationship to them. Society exists independently of our conceptions of it . . . yet it is dependent on our actions, human activity, for its reproduction. It is both real and transcendent . . . ' He fully accepts the hermeneutical and postmodernist position that the production of knowledge about society is a part of the entire process of social production, that it is a part of its own subject matter and may transform the subject matter (Davies, 1999, pp. 18–19). In terms of schooling, Bhaskar's philosophy can be translated into language policies that give the culturally disadvantaged the right to determine and shape their own curriculum based on equality and power sharing. His theoretical notions offer us the makings of pedagogy suffused with aesthetic sensibility and egalitarian conscience.

One example of a school that fosters such an ideology is a multilingual/multicultural primary school in Auckland, New Zealand, which encourages pluralism and empowerment for aboriginal children through a language policy across the curriculum. (For a more detailed discussion, see Cazden, 1989; May, 1994.) Such attempts at genuine bilingual/bicultural education are relatively few and far between. Neve Shalom/Wahat Al-Salam is also a maverick school in its dedication to language and cultural inclusiveness, but it operates on a much more difficult frontier – that of open conflict between its two linguistic/national groups. The school attempts to weave into its tapestry of academic subjects the threads of both Jewish and Arab/Palestinian perspectives in Israel in order to transcend the profound problems of marginality, belonging, and conflict. This school and this village invite us to traverse a mirror of turmoil between both peoples and to touch the soul of their struggle. The school's philosophy states unequivocally that maintaining personal, social, national, and linguistic identity is of utmost importance. Its mission is to create national identities informed by moral vision and social ethics in order to provide an understanding of what it means to become active and critical citizens in a diverse, pluralistic Israeli society against the backdrop of conflict.

Language educators and researchers agree that it is essential to develop appropriate pedagogies that respond to the diversity of the social contexts in which the learners are situated. (See, for example, Cummins, 1994, 1999; Corson, 1993, 1995; Delpit, 1992; Krashen & Biber, 1988; García, 1994; Goodman *et al.*, 1987; Spolsky, 1989; Trueba, 1989; Wong-Fillmore, 1991.) We must explore the need for rethinking and reshaping an understanding of language awareness as a social phenomenon fundamentally linked to learners' sense of identity and self-worth within their communities as well as to notions of national belonging. For Arab students in Israel (and, in fact, for all students who perceive themselves to be in a subordinate position in their societies), it is important that their values and culture be represented within the mainstream curriculum, and especially within the texts that they read and write. (See, for example, Abu-Rabia & Feuerverger, 1996; Mari, 1985; Shohamy, 1993; Spolsky and Shohamy, 2000.) The Neve Shalom/Wahat Al-Salam school distinguishes itself in the way in which the dominant versus subordinate status of Arab students is contested within the structures and discourses of the school. The critical awareness of the asymmetry between Hebrew, the dominant language, and Arabic, the principal minority and second official language in Israel, underscores all classroom activities. The attempt to redress this imbalance focuses on interior psychological transformations within the students and teachers as a way of changing their worldview in the school and in the village, and ultimately in mainstream society.

## Complexities of the Hebrew-Arabic Asymmetry

The words of the school co-director describe the importance of language equality:

> Language is the essential tool for communication and learning. At this school, and from the preschool onward, the children who live in this village hear both languages, Hebrew

and Arabic, and they begin to speak both in kindergarten. When they arrive in the first grade, their ears are already attuned to both languages. They learn to read and write both languages, side by side, literally and figuratively.

I was witness to a collaborative educational conversation that offered the possibility of relationships among student and teacher, student and student, and teacher and teacher that honored their differential social, historical, cultural, and religious narratives as well as the complexities of understanding and interpreting the languages that they inhabit and the limits that those languages place on them. According to Martin Heidegger, 'it is in language that we construct, and extend our realities' (as cited in Chambers, 1994, p. 133) but to Jacques Lacan the *reél* 'constitutes that space left unmarked by language or signs'. It is in these paradoxical notions that we may be able to address the issue of borders, exile, homeland, and the intersection among them. My work as ethnographer is ultimately to interpret what I observed in the school and what I heard in the conversations with my participants in their search for meaning within the complex layers of the sociopolitical discourse in Israel. What emerged clearly is that, fundamentally, the discourse is not merely about a majority group versus a minority group. Through the dialectic of interviewer and interviewee, I began to understand that it is a much more complicated issue than the usual hegemonic one, because what we have here is a minority within a regional minority.

For the Arab Israeli, Hebrew is perceived to be the language of the oppressor; nevertheless, Hebrew is demographically only a minor language in the Middle East, without much international importance. Therefore, the lines of power and language are negotiated very differently within the physical reality of Israel as compared to outside of Israel in the Middle East and elsewhere. Certainly, within Israel this sociolinguistic phenomenon disrupts and thwarts Palestinian identity formation and complicates the issue of production and consumption of Arab/Palestinian culture in a broader sense. If the Palestinian Israeli is able to reach across both linguistic and national borders through literary articulation in Hebrew as well as Arabic, however, he or she is neither at home nor in exile, but in a curious space of 'in between', which can paradoxically become a place of power. This border zone and the hybrid text that it creates gives voice to the border dweller (Potok, in Barkan & Shelton, 1998). The Palestinian Israeli who becomes literate and literary in Hebrew is more advanced than the Jewish Israeli who (as a general rule) has not mastered Arabic to any great extent and thereby loses a certain sense of superiority. Such situations are rarely of concern in mainstream Israeli society, but for those on the 'borders', such as the villagers at Neve Shalom/Wahat Al-Salam, it becomes a salient issue. Most of the Jewish villagers are not nearly as fluent or literate in Arabic as their Palestinian counterparts are in Hebrew. Suddenly the dominating majority and the dominated minority have changed positions. On my most recent sojourn to the village, for example, I witnessed the discomfort at a teachers' staff gathering when the suggestion was made that some of the meetings should be conducted in Arabic rather than Hebrew. The Jewish Israeli teachers suddenly felt threatened because only a few of them would have been able to handle this new sociolinguistic reality. They were well aware of the lack of equality in the situation but they countered that, given the realities of their ages and very busy lives, it would be practically impossible for them to catch up and become as fluent in Arabic as the Palestinian teachers were in Hebrew. They did acknowledge that they were, unfortunately, products of a school system that did not promote good learning of Arabic – or other minority languages for that matter.

One Palestinian teacher explained it to me as follows:

> The Jewish Hebrew speakers were really rather stunned by this sudden loss of status in the meeting. It must have been a bit of a shock for them, even though their hearts are in the right place and they want bilingualism for their children. But I guess they feel it's too hard for them to really learn Arabic in earnest at this time in their lives. I can't blame them. It would be hard for anyone to learn another language, if you don't have to. That's what it's all about: Arabic being the minority language and therefore not necessary for getting ahead in the mainstream society. That is one symbol of our (Palestinian) sense of inferiority. At least what is good about this village is that they want to change it in the next generation

with their children. But we [the Palestinian teachers] are saying: Let's change it now in our meetings; at least a bit. It is difficult but it is again a symbolic gesture. If we want to be role models, let's start with ourselves, no?

Schools need to be viewed in their historical, societal, and relational contexts. The construction of teaching and learning is, in fact, a relational act and therefore a discourse of empowerment needs to be created out of the historical, social, linguistic, and cultural realities that are the bedrock of the forms of knowledge and meaning that teachers and students bring to school. Reciprocity is important. Reclaiming voice is important. Retelling and comparing stories are important. These activities, however, are not enough in themselves, and therefore need to be positioned within a larger social and intellectual perspective. In this regard, the school at Neve Shalom/Wahat Al-Salam can be located within the Freirian framework of a moral and political project that links the production of meaning to the possibility for human agency, democratic community, language reform, and transformative social action (see Paulo Freire, 1970). In this school the use of both languages has become emblematic of egalitarianism and mutual understanding both in formal and informal school activities. This reflects Roger Simon's (1992) assertion of ' . . . a view of human agency reconstructed through forms of narrative that operate as part of a pedagogy of empowerment . . . centered within a social project aimed at the enhancement of human possibility'. This pedagogical approach reinforces Freire's (1970) claim that all critical educators are also learners – but where is the Neve Shalom/Wahat Al-Salam school situated within the larger educational system of Israel? The following section addresses this question.

## The Israeli Educational School System: A Brief Overview

In order to familiarize the reader with the complexities of the Israeli school system, I include here a brief sociohistoric overview. The modern Israeli educational system began about fifty years before statehood and shares many similarities with other national school systems in developed countries. Its uniqueness, however, derives from the specific project of Jewish revival over the past 150 years and its geopolitical situation in the Middle East, from the genocide of the Holocaust which intensified the need for Jewish statehood, and from the successive waves of immigration that have taken place from that time to today. It is outside the scope of this book to discuss in detail the daunting challenges facing the Israeli educational system in absorbing a population as multicultural, multilingual, socioeconomically diverse, and conflictual as exists in this tiny country. As a result of this national, religious, and linguistic pluralism, the educational system is divided into two main separate systems: Jewish and Arab (Mari, 1978; Iram & Schmida, 1998). In addition, even within the Jewish population there are deep divisions between religious and secular Jews as well as between Ashkenazim (Jews from Eastern and Central Europe) and Sephardim (Jews from the Mediterranean and Arab/Moslem countries) (Ben-Rafael & Sharot, 1991).

Within the mainstream (Jewish) population, the Israeli educational policy from the beginning has encouraged a 'melting pot' approach. The goal is for all citizens to become 'Israelis' as soon as possible, and acknowledge the primacy of Hebrew regardless of their home culture and language (Nakoma, 1983; Shohamy, 1993). Indeed, until very recently, the Israeli curriculum did not focus on the maintenance of the cultural heritage and language of immigrants arriving from all parts of the Diaspora. This was in keeping with the official national (Zionist) policy of the 'ingathering of the exiles' and the consolidation of the Jewish people in Israel as embodied in the constitutional Law of Return of 1950 (Eisenstadt, 1967; Elazar, 1985), according to which every Jewish immigrant is entitled to Israeli citizenship. In fact, the need and the will to absorb Jews from the various exiles of their dispersion – particularly as a result of the plight of the survivors of the Holocaust after World War II – was the *raison d'être* for the establishment of the state of Israel in 1948 (Iram & Schmida, 1998).

One of the overarching goals of the Israeli educational system in the early years of statehood was to eradicate the negative connotations of Diaspora Jewry – symbolic of the Nazi destruction of European Jews during World War II (Urofsky, 1976; Gordon, 1995). Hand in hand with this objective was the responsibility of integrating immigrant children into the social fabric and cultural norms of the new society – first and foremost through teaching the Hebrew language, which was and remains a metaphor for Jewish nationalism and cultural integration. The Jewish settlers of modern Palestine under the British Mandate began the process of immigration in the late nineteenth century and came mainly from European countries with Western cultures. The survivors of the Holocaust also came from Europe. The wave of immigration in the early 1950s of Jews from Arab/Moslem countries in the Middle East and North Africa (Iran, Iraq, Yemen, Morocco, Tunisia, and Algeria), however, created new social challenges. Many of these Sephardim or Oriental Jews had large families and were not formally educated; they were thus ill equipped to face the modern, urban, and industrially oriented society that Israel was aspiring to develop. Consequently, there emerged a socioeconomic gap between these Eastern Jews and their more Western counterparts, the Ashkenazim (Peres, 1976; Smooha, 1978) which became evident in the school system by the fact that the Oriental students lagged behind in terms of occupational and social standing.

In the mid-1960s when this problem of disadvantaged student populations became salient, a policy of social integration was instituted and was defined as the bringing together of all students into a common system, regardless of ethnic origin, socioeconomic level, intellectual talents, and areas of interest, which placed them in heterogeneous schools and integrated classrooms. In spite of awareness of the importance of this policy, its implementation in the school system lagged behind due to a plethora of political, demographic, and financial reasons. (For more details, see Iram & Schmida, 1998.) Basically, the language and cultural heritage of the Oriental groups was not valued in the school system; this created a deep schism in Jewish Israeli society. In the early 1970s the social tension and ethnic protest which had begun in the late 1950s was renewed. There have been various attempts by the Ministry of Education to improve this social, economic, and cultural situation through a special program instituted in the 1980s named the 'Education Welfare Program'. It was intended to intervene at all levels of education, including family and community as well as a neighborhood renovation project (as discussed in Iram & Schmida, 1998, chapter 9). More recent waves of immigration in the late 1980s and 1990s from Ethiopia and the former Soviet Union have added to the complexity of the social fabric of Israeli society and as a result, a greater awareness of the need for a pluralistic, multicultural policy in the Israeli school system has emerged, with more emphasis on the diversity of cultures and traditions in Israeli schools. This relatively new multicultural policy addresses, at least in theory, the three major dilemmas in Israeli society: the division between Oriental and Western Jewry, the division between religious and nonreligious Jewry, and the division between Israeli Arabs and Jews (Masemann & Iram, 1987). Our focus here is on the third issue.

As discussed earlier, this particular Israeli hegemony is rather unusual and difficult to resolve because of the traumatic psychohistorical burden of genocide that lies behind it. In terms of Jewish collective psychology, one can understand the original 'melting pot' policy that was initiated in the early days of statehood. Shoshana Keiny (1999, p. 513) explains this national ideology within the context of the modern notion of human rights: 'Israel is both a young country, struggling with her existence, as well as an old traditional culture, carrying wounded memories of torture and genocide, a rather complex case to deal with in respect to the modern concept of human rights first declared by the UN at the end of World War II.' Within the educational system, it is noteworthy that Israel's national ideology has varied over time, moving from universalist, civil values to somewhat more particularist, ethnic (Jewish) values (Resnik, 1999). Indeed, the division between the Jewish religious and non-religious populations is not only unresolved but rather is intensifying as the religious groups gain increased political power.

The Israeli Arabs are left out of the picture altogether. Where do they fit in the overall construct of Israeli national identity and ideology? In spite of such complex social-psychological conundra, the state must focus more fully on comprehensive reforms given the increased violence in the West Bank and vicissitudes of the Israeli-Arab peace process. As Yaacov Iram and Miriyam Schmida point out (1998, pp. 93–94), 'an impressive change in learning standards at Arab high schools occurred in the middle of the 1970s . . . nevertheless a wide discrepancy still existed between the achievement levels of Arab and Jewish students, based on ethnic and religious factors . . . Although Arab schools are maintained in reasonable physical conditions, the gap between them and Jewish schools has grown larger in other areas. Many services that naturally exist in Jewish schools cannot be found in Arab schools.' They write that 'psychological counseling, and lessons in music, art, or sports

are lacking in the majority of Arab schools' and that 'one of the basic problems of Arab education from the beginning was the lack of teachers with adequate training. In the last twenty years there has been a considerable improvement in the educational level of Arab teachers . . . Another aspect of criticism is related to the quality of training given to Arab students in teachers' seminaries' (p. 95). Fortunately, in recent years more opportunities are beginning to open up for Arab teachers as a result of collaborative efforts with well-established teacher training institutes around the country.

Finally, the asymmetry of the Jewish and Arab school curricula is still prevalent. Iram and Schmida (1998, p. 99) claim that 'the critique of the Arab curricula began in the 1950s. It was asked why students in Arab schools were learning the Bible and not the Koran, and why the teaching of Arabic, Arab literature, and history did not receive proper attention. A comparison between history teaching objectives in Jewish and Arab high schools reveals that while Jewish schools stress national contents, the Arab curriculum overlooks them. Values of Arab-Jewish coexistence, together with Jewish majority status, are planted in the Arab student by repeatedly stressing the role that Arabs and Jews shared during history and the common fate of both peoples. However, values of coexistence are not passed down to Jewish students. Moreover, an Arab student is expected to know the importance of the State of Israel to the Jewish people, not to both Jews and Arabs' (p. 94). There have been some salient changes in the curriculum in the early 1970s, mainly the mention of the Arab nation as a central objective, but it remained ambiguous and did not relate to the Palestinian people. In the past few years, far more profound reforms began to take shape in light of the peace process, but there is still a long way to go in order to undo the asymmetry that exists.

## The Language of Peace: A Reflective Look at the Teachers and Learners in the Village School

What is hopeful about the Neve Shalom/Wahat Al-Salam model is the radical psychological shift in the village in its attempt to reconstruct ideology for the next generation. There is an existential recognition of the need for a reconceptualization of society – which is open to restructuring and therefore unsettling, but creates the basis for an alternative space.

For example, in the summer of 1999 one of the villagers offered an intensive Arabic course for the Hebrew-speaking teachers; it was attended by almost all of them. These are not easy moments for the participants, even those with the best of intentions. I tried to locate myself in this compelling human landscape in order to be able to pay respect to the efforts of these individuals pushing against all odds. I entered a space of personal, social, and moral reflection, of anxious and hopeful narratives, of social and political polemic, and of ambiguity. There was a story to tell about the choices being created by the teachers and I wanted to be worthy of the task of teller. Sara Lawrence-Lightfoot (1997, p. 9) suggests that the researcher as portraitist can search for what is good and healthy; she believes that there are 'myriad ways in which goodness can be expressed' and the researcher must try 'to identify and document the actors' perspectives'. I was interested in observing what was indeed going on in the classrooms of the village school that were expressions of 'goodness' within a context of language awareness and peacemaking. Were the children in fact crossing linguistic, literary, historical, and national borders, and in what ways? As ethnographer (and portraitist, in Lawrence-Lightfoot's terms), I stood 'on the edge of the scene – a boundary sitter – scanning the action, systematically gathering the details of behavior, expression, and talk, remaining open and receptive to all stimuli' (1997, p. 87).

Effective schools should be sites of linguistic, political, and cultural negotiation which encourage teachers to situate and scrutinize the borders of their own ideological discourses. 'Borders elicit a recognition of those epistemological, political, cultural, and social margins that define 'the places that are safe and unsafe, [that] distinguish *us* from *them*"(Anzaldua, 1987, p. 3, as cited in Giroux, 1991). 'Teachers need to be reflective practitioners who first examine themselves – their knowledge base, their attitudes, beliefs, values, and practices – and then develop approaches to teaching and learning which challenge and empower' (Jackson, p. 41, in Larkin & Sleeter, 1995). Teachers also need to become cognizant of what I call the 'unconscious myths' that have shaped the mental and physical landscape of their lives and which now motivate them in the planning of curriculum and in their choice of interpersonal classroom strategies. The Neve Shalom/Wahat Al-Salam school experience certainly affirms Henry Giroux's claim (1991,

p. 516) that teachers become 'border crossers' by being able to listen critically to the voices of their students. How are these shared narratives being played out in the village school? One of the main questions I asked was, 'How do teachers and students in this school negotiate knowledge of Arab and Jewish values through their language inter-action; for example, in history, geography, current events, and literature classes?'

In order to explore the discourses of peace and conflict resolution within curriculum development, pedagogical strategies, and interpersonal communication at Neve Shalom/Wahat Al-Salam, we now turn to excerpts of in-depth interviews I conducted with students and teachers both formally and informally as well as reflections of my classroom observations in the school. These data were tape-recorded and later transcribed. The methodological tools of field-note gathering and journaling were always central to this inquiry and were used on a daily basis.

I begin with a Palestinian teacher in the school, who explained how language awareness has offered a new pedagogical and social paradigm for the Jewish and Arab children:

> In this school Arabic and Hebrew both hold prominent positions and the children are fully aware of that in all classroom activities. Because each class has an Arab and a Jewish teacher, the children are exposed to two points of view. For example, I teach actualia (current events) with a Jewish teacher and we are able to discuss difficult, controversial issues immediately with our pupils. Language is such a key point here. Let's face it, learning the history of Israel in Hebrew is totally different from learning it in Arabic! Learning its history in both languages is the beginning of a whole new future. This is radical stuff! The Israeli War of Independence has a totally different connotation in Arabic and that awareness that we teachers can offer them opens new doors for these young people.

He is in effect agreeing with many researchers who claim that language is the essential means by which teachers shape their experiences and explain the world to themselves and also to their students. This participant went on to explain how he struggled to become not only fluent in Hebrew but also to excel in Hebrew literature at the Hebrew University In Jerusalem.

This was quite unusual for an Arab in the early 1970s and still is even today. I asked him about his motivation to pursue this course of study. He replied:

> To become a student in Hebrew literature meant I could conquer my insecurities about being an Arab minority person in Israel. It gave me a sense of confidence that changed my life and eventually brought me to this place in order that I can help other Arab students to overcome their inferiority feelings. It's all about language, identity, and power. Using both languages is a symbol of coexistence and the possibility of friendship, and gives me a sense of equality with Jewish Israelis.

This same teacher discussed at length his frustration about living in the 'space between borders', where he had no sense of belonging either to his Israeli self or to his Palestinian self. He, like Palestinian Israeli author Anton Shammas, who writes in Hebrew instead of Arabic, is 'in the space of exile at home . . . exile from a homeland that no longer exists except in nostalgia and ideological space' (Shammas, 1991). 'By writing in Hebrew, the language of his conquerors', Rena Potok (1998, p. 298) observes, 'the Arab Shammas can realize Derrida's ideal of speaking the other's language without renouncing one's own'. These words embody those of Maxine Greene (1973): 'For a man who no longer has a homeland, writing becomes a place to live'. Smadar Lavie (1992) suggests that 'these are individuals who must continually remap their border zones so that they can maintain their exilic home in the claimed homeland of the Jews' (quoted in Potok, 1998, p. 305).

The theme of cultural dislocation and fractured identity underlies the ambivalence that so many Palestinian Israelis experience in their everyday lives and is evident in the asymmetry of status between Hebrew and Arabic in Israel. Therefore, the original attempt at Neve Shalom/Wahat Al-Salam to teach both Hebrew and Arabic in the school curriculum in the early 1980s was more than just an interesting pedagogical idea; it was and still is in essence a powerfully subversive act. This community decision mirrors the tremendous force and agency of those Palestinian Israeli authors who write about their own lived experience in new literary forms and specifically in Hebrew, thus creating alternative norms

and value systems. The pedagogy in the school at Neve Shalom/Wahat Al-Salam can thus be regarded as a political act of resistance as well as an act of self-empowerment and carries within it the kind of critical language awareness that liberates.

Palestinian author Shammas, on a visit to the village in 1992, used these eloquent words to describe its pedagogy and educational commitment to peace in the village newsletter: 'It is always risky to be lured by metaphors, especially in the Middle East, but those who live in this "Oasis of Peace" have managed to achieve the impossible: by refusing to be lured, they have concretized a metaphor. We, who are still wandering in the desert, envy them.' He speaks of his feelings in terms of language awareness: ' At the age of eighteen I chose what I had no choice but to choose: namely, to regard Hebrew as my step-mother tongue. Sometimes I feel that this was an act of cultural trespass, and that the day may come when I shall have to account for it' (quoted in Shipler, 1986, p. 455).

Another Palestinian teacher in the school discussed the surprise that his father showed when he first came to visit his son in this village and met some of the children in the school:

> My father grew up in a little Arab village in the north of the country and was at first uncertain about why I should teach in a school where Jewish and Arab kids were together. He just wasn't sure how this would work. Then, on the first afternoon that he was here a little nine-year-old girl came up to him and spoke to him in Arabic. They had a lovely conversation and afterwards I told him this young student of mine was Jewish. He had assumed she was an Arab because her Arabic was so fluent. When he heard she was Jewish, his eyes filled with tears and he said he thought he would never see this. He was amazed at how all the children were getting along, jumping back and forth into Hebrew and Arabic. They were friends, and that was a revelation to him. That is the beauty of this place.

As participant-observer in this school, I came to recognize that knowing the existence of the 'foreigner', as Julia Kristeva puts it, is a central aspect of language awareness. I believe this can be defined as a sensitivity and a conscious understanding of the myriad languages and cultures in our world and of their roles for humanity. I began to understand more fully the dialectical relationship between language and thought in practical educational settings (see, for example, Bakhtin, 1981; Dewey, 1938; Vygotsky, 1962). As discussed earlier, I have been involved in multilingual education both personally and professionally as far back as I remember, and I believe that the bilingual (and multilingual) classroom must be a space where dialogue is seen as a necessary way to relate authentically to one another through collaboration, reflection, and expression (Kaiser & Short, 1998).

A Jewish teacher in the school confided in me:

> I never had the opportunity as a child to learn Arabic the way the Jewish children do here. And only now do I truly realize how it changes everything to simply be able to speak to one another in both languages. It really changes things; it's very symbolic. And the children are unconsciously very aware of this, I think. I will give you a concrete example. A new child came into my class from [a nearby Jewish village] and she did not know Arabic and stayed away from the Arab children. As time went on, she of course began to interact with the Arab children and began to learn Arabic. It was wonderful to see how her attitude changed in such a positive way. The very same is true for the Arab children who come to this school and begin to learn Hebrew and become friends with the Jewish kids.

A grade-six boy from a Jewish village stated why he enjoyed learning both languages at the school:

> I feel very different now that I can speak and read and write Arabic. I didn't have much to do with Arab kids before coming to this school and I was afraid of them because of all the terrorist things. But now I'm making friends with them and I can read stories about their lives and their heroes and their culture and it makes me understand them more and feel closer to them.

This kind of thoughtful teaching and learning is a transformative process which appreciates the complexities of bilingual, bicultural, and binational education within a landscape of conflict and war. It embodies Freire's (1970, p. 75) revolutionary perspective of social liberation in his assertion: 'There is no true word that is not at the same time a praxis (action-reflection). Thus to speak of a true word is to transform the world'. Indeed, I had the opportunity to observe the dynamics of meaning making through language and cultural awareness, which was grounded in reflective practice. This is what shapes the pedagogical landscape of Neve Shalom/Wahat Al-Salam. Knowing that one must learn to coexist with 'the other' is already a form of action, and naming the challenge is a way of overcoming it. The signature discourses of conflict resolution in each classroom underscore the school's fundamental commitment to peacemaking.

In the weeks that I spent in the school during my first sojourn, one bulletin board was dedicated to a project about the city of Jerusalem from the different religious and cultural perspectives. Linguistically, the symbols of peace were evident in the textual material that accompanied the various drawings. The Al-Aqsa Mosque was described in Arabic; the Western Wall had a text in Hebrew explaining its significance; and the Church of the Holy Sepulchre was discussed in Arabic. In the center of the wall display was a large story narrating the long and tumultuous history of Jerusalem in both languages. It seemed to me, as an observer, that the use of both languages in the story was a salient symbol of peace and it clearly explained that each child is taught to understand his or her culture and also learn about the culture of the others. The drawings, with their individual language texts, indicate that the goal is coexistence, respect, and friendship, but not assimilation. Religion is taught separately, but there are also joint discussions. What is essential, I was told, is that no one is appropriating anyone else's history or religion or culture. When possible, however, shared narrative accounts are created.

During my many classroom visits, I watched a constant effort at moral negotiation and dialogue for curriculum development within the differential sociohistoric and geopolitical narratives of that particular moment in history. Meron Benvenisti (1995) quoted the famous Israeli author A.B. Yehoshua to indicate the difficulties therein: 'History is potent, it has direction, and it has meaning' (p. 154). The tension arising from these issues was authentically and sensitively dealt with in classrooms, in the staff room, and on the playground.

One Hebrew literature teacher discusses the difficulties in creating curriculum that honors the perspectives of both peoples in its textual material:

> When the children learn Hebrew and Arabic it is crucial that they are exposed to narrative texts that open their eyes to the realities of the conflicts between their cultural groups. They need accurate, authentic accounts in their language classes as well as all across the curriculum. In fact, each teacher teaches his or her subjects in his or her own language. The children are exposed to both languages right from the beginning of their schooling. For each subject matter, time is set aside for vocabulary and grammar. It is a great challenge for the Hebrew- and Arabic-speaking teachers to provide pedagogy and materials that are linguistically and conceptually appropriate in meaningful contexts. We have had very tough moments of discord and loud debate in this work, because we do not sweep things under the carpet, and therefore we touch very painful and often unresolvable issues. But we go on, knowing that it is better to acknowledge the problems than to avoid them. And I think in the end only that kind of honesty makes learning possible.

I observed a great deal of peer tutoring between older and younger students, with both Arab and Jewish students helping each other with subject matter on the common ground of each other's language and culture. I was impressed by the power created in their collaborative learning and sharing of knowledge; this is encouraged by the school's emphasis on acknowledging the children as experts in their own literacy development. There are various writing activities: writing on personal subjects (for example, journal writing) as well as general class writing, and small-group cooperative writing ventures that are often presented to the class as a whole.

This kind of pedagogy creates a place where identities are constructed and is based on the belief that language learning takes place within a setting of authentic learning contexts that comes directly from the experiences of the children. For example, I recall the activities in a grade-one class where the children, guided by their teacher,

a vivacious young Arab woman from a nearby village, were crafting themes revolving around war and loss and a hope for peace and normalcy. Hebrew and Arabic were being used simultaneously and students' discussions reflected the actual experiences of their everyday lives. The students' 'ownership' of the curriculum was evident in this class, as it was in all the classes I visited. This approach is in keeping with Michael Byram's (1993) proposal for a model of language teaching for cultural awareness that combines both experiential and reflective learning, allowing for a greater degree of abstraction and critical analysis. (See also Feuerverger, 1994; Gumperz, 1977; Heath, 1983; Michaels, 1981; Nieto, 1992; Tabachnick & Yehoshua to Zeichner, 1993.)

What I continually witnessed in the classrooms was the contextualization and integration of language activities through the encouragement of real dialogue, inclusion, and fairness, and the sharing of stories as a means for better understanding 'otherness' and 'difference'. The asymmetry of the position of Hebrew and Arabic in Israeli society remains a huge issue. Below is a short interchange between myself and a Palestinian teacher of an upper elementary grade. She discussed how the school attempts to respond to this problematic reality with various innovative pedagogical approaches. She also shared with me her personal story of how she learned Hebrew in a [regular Arab] school when she was a young girl, which was so different from what goes on at Neve Shalom/Wahat Al-Salam:

Q: Can you tell me how you learned Hebrew and what it means to you?

A: I mean I know Hebrew. I had to learn it in order to succeed. But I hated what it represents to me as a Palestinian. Hebrew was powerful, and Arabic had no power. And the way the Ministry of Education designs the curriculum for learning Hebrew is ridiculous for Arabs. It's all about the Jewish identity and Hebrew Bible and literature. That is no way for an Arab child to want to learn Hebrew.

Q: And you had no place in it. I mean, there was no talk about Arab literature or history?

A: No.

Q: Not about your identity?

A: No, not at all. Now it is changing with the peace process. There is a lot more material about Arabic and Palestinian issues in the Hebrew classes in Israel. But then I needed it for university and so I learned it in spite of how bad I felt about Hebrew.

**Q:** It's good to know it's changing.

**A:** It is, but slowly. And still Arabic is seen as a foreign language rather than a second language. Those are two very different things.

**Q:** And it's not compulsory; it's not compulsory, huh?

**A:** Finally, many [Jewish] schools are changing that into a compulsory course. But they still don't see it as equal.

**Q:** I think it's a very important distinction that you just made. Because it's very different, learning a language as a second language as opposed to a foreign language. And what about on the other side, in Arab schools?

**A:** In the Arab schools, they start to learn Hebrew from the fourth grade.

**Q:** Of course the Arab kids need it more; it's not the same thing.

**A:** Yes, they really can't survive without it.

**Q:** But they must learn it with, as you say, with ambivalence, because, as you say, if they're learning that language in school without using symbols from their own culture in the texts, it's a problem.

**A:** Right. I see how the staff here at Neve Shalom/Wahat Al-Salam uses books from the beginning that teach Hebrew but are sensitive to the Arabs' needs. The kids accept each other and each other's language and culture. The schools in other parts of Israel need to do this very much.

**Q:** It makes complete sense.

**A:** Yeah, the child feels a sense of belonging . . .

Another Palestinian teacher shared some information regarding an increased awareness about the teaching of Arabic in the school, a new ad hoc pedagogical strategy using the Hebrew alphabet in order to overcome the barrier to Arabic conversational skills. (Conversational Arabic is completely different from literary Arabic, and as such poses enormous problems for Hebrew speakers, whose first language does not include such a complicated dichotomy.)

**Q:** [Could you] give me a sense of what you've been doing the last few months? [Describe h]ow things are changing or interesting things happening in the school, especially in terms of language, of course, that's my major interest . . .

**A:** You know, change takes a lot of time, so you understand that not everything that we want can be done in only one year, but at least we can start. So during the summer, we usually open a lot of questions about the educational system here, then we'll have decisions.

**Q:** With the parents do you mean, or with the teachers?

**A:** With the whole staff.

**Q:** With all the staff, yeah.

**A:** The big change that has happened is for the Arabic language. We now know how difficult it is to really make it as dominant as the Hebrew language. So, this year, the Jewish kids are learning more how to communicate the slang language, the daily language, much more than to read and write in Arabic. In the past, usually, they knew more to read and write than to speak, but we want them to communicate [colloquially].

**Q:** Yes, conversational.

**A:** They can't communicate in the literature of the language; they need the spoken language. So there are some books and some exercises that we can give them in Hebrew because they know to read Hebrew. From the second grade onward, we can give them these exercises in Hebrew letters, Hebrew letters instead of Arabic letters so they can read easily but they can learn how to speak, how to communicate. So we say that instead of taking up such [a] huge [amount of] time sitting and learning the [Arabic] letters and how to read (which is much more complicated than Hebrew) we want them to speak; and we know that they do not speak enough. There's less emphasis and there are some hours where they can still learn how to read and write but most of the hour, they do speak, and are finally learning to communicate and which kind of words to use daily at school, in the street, and so on.

**Q:** I see.

**A:** Hopefully that will help; and, of course, a lot of music with songs because the kids really like songs, so if I want them to know those words, I can put them in songs so they can really remember them.

**Q:** That sounds really wonderful.

**A:** You know, the Hebrew language, for the Palestinian Arab children, is not a problem. They feel that they need it and they can have it.

**Q:** That's true.
**A:** So this [approach] is for teaching the Arabic language to the Jewish children.

## The Sociolinguistic Background

The teachers whom I interviewed suggest that the intersection among education, language, and society cannot be ignored. Teaching and learning are dialogic in nature. Freire talks about dialogic action as an awareness of oneself as 'knower', an attitude which he named *conscientizacao*. This critical consciousness is informed by his philosophy of language and inspired by his respect for humanity. The villagers at Neve Shalom/Wahat Al-Salam embody Freire's focus on the discursive power of language, which brings them to the heart of Freire's pedagogy of knowing: that 'naming the world becomes a model for changing the world' (Freire & Macedo, 1987, p. xv). They are practicing an emancipatory theory of bilingual literacy by developing an alternative educational discourse and reclaiming authorship of their own national identities.

Indeed, Freire (1987) suggests that 'schools should never impose absolute certainties on students. They should stimulate the certainty of never being too certain – a method vital to critical pedagogy. Educators should also stimulate the possibilities of expression, the possibilities of subjectivity. They should challenge students to "discourse about the world"' (p. 57). My participants also reinforce Giroux's (1987) assertion that '... the pedagogical should be made more political and the political more pedagogical. In other words, there is a dire need to develop pedagogical practices, in the first instance, that bring teachers, parents, and students together around new and more emancipatory visions of community ... that the present is always a time of possibility' (p. 6). This chapter investigates how this Jewish-Arab elementary school distinguishes itself in the way in which emancipatory theory is used and encourages the subordinate status of Arab students to be liberated within the structures and discourses of the school. In order to reflect on these issues more deeply, the next section presents a discussion on second language learning in the wider Israeli society based on recent scholarly work in this area. From the macrosociolinguistic context of Israel we then will return to the microsociolinguistic one of Neve Shalom/Wahat Al-Salam in order

to see how it represents a radical departure from the hegemonic approach.

## Language Awareness and Second Language Learning in Israel

Learning a second language is a social phenomenon and is therefore influenced by social practice and context. Lev Vygotsky (1962, 1978) argued that learning begins in social interaction and continues on an individual basis, 'first between people ... and then inside the child' (1978, p. 57). Learning becomes socially meaningful, however, within particular social contexts: 'through culture humans share learned systems for defining meaning' (Erickson, 1986, pp. 32–33). The society in which the learner lives may either be supportive or nonsupportive to the second language learning process (Cummins & Danesi, 1990). Indeed, personal knowledge of the world has an overarching influence on how the written word is perceived by students. 'Reading does not consist merely of decoding the written word of language; rather it is preceded by and intertwined with knowledge of the world. Language and reality are dynamically interconnected. The understanding attained by critical reading of a text implies perceiving the relationship between text and context' (Freire & Macedo, 1987). Therefore, the discussion in this chapter is contextualized within a framework of socialization in two different cultural and linguistic 'worlds'.

Just as students' educational experiences inform their learning, so do their personal life experiences. What is exciting about Neve Shalom/Wahat Al-Salam is that these two separate worlds intersect in an unprecedented way and create an alternative interactional process. In this special case, language awareness is closely tied to a method of negotiating identities and inventing a new place to 'be'. It might be helpful to provide a context for this discussion by sharing findings from a research study carried out by a colleague from Haifa University, one component of which focused on the issues of Arab students learning Hebrew as a second language within the Israeli school system (Abu-Rabia & Feuerverger, 1996). The findings indicate that, in the Israeli-Arab social context, the learning of the second language (for example, Hebrew, by Arab students) is impaired to some degree due to the almost exclusive Jewish content of the texts. The Israeli-Palestinian conflict, which affects all aspects of society in Israel, is a major contributor to this problem; therefore, under these delicate circumstances it is imperative not to impose Jewish cultural content, but rather have Arabic content in the learning of Hebrew, the dominant language. The issue is a complex one. As many of my participants told me, the fact that Hebrew represents the 'oppressor' for Arabs in the Israeli context results in their consciously or subconsciously developing negative or ambivalent attitudes toward learning the language.

Furthermore, the Arab community comprises 17 percent of the total population of Israel. The members of the Arab minority learn the language of the majority group and spend more hours learning the Hebrew language and Jewish culture than they spend learning their own Arabic culture and language (Abu Saad, 1991; Al-Haj, 1995). Suffice to say that the learning of Hebrew as a second language is a very problematic activity for Arab Israelis on both a personal and institutional level. Embedded within this intergroup conflict is the competition between the learning of Arabic and Hebrew within the school system (for details about difficulties within the Arab educational system in Israel see Abu Saad, 1991). As the interviews indicate, the Palestinians, in the midst of their deep cultural ambivalence, are well aware that in order to succeed in Israeli society, their Hebrew language skills must be excellent. This second language success, however, interacts on a psychological level with a sense of betrayal toward their Arab national identity. The Arabs in Israel feel threatened by learning the Hebrew language and consequently show their motivation toward the Hebrew language only as an instrumental one, rather than one of identification with it, which is an integrative orientation (see, for example, Gardner *et al.*, 1979, a classic work on this topic). These observations corroborate the research work on various Arab minority educational situations in Israel which clearly indicates this sense of cultural ambivalence and feelings of deprivation on the part of students (as discussed in Al-Haj, 1987, 1995; Falah, 1989; Mari, 1985). Indeed, in most cases Arab and Jewish students are schooled separately; this makes the learning of Hebrew seem even more forced.

When minority students feel mistreated by the dominant group they often tend to reject second language learning and show loyalty to their own language and culture (Cummins, 1984; Cummins & Danesi, 1990). In this case, the pervasive tension between Arabs and Jews invades the school environment and hinders second language learning,

thus exacerbating the Arab students' negative feelings as a deprived and discriminated-against minority group (Abu Saad, 1991). Furthermore, these findings are congruent with Jim Cummins (1994), who focuses on 'the relations of power' in schools and suggests that the traditional teacher-centered transmission model can hinder the potential for critical thinking on the part of both teachers and students. He stresses that students from socially dominated communities are most at risk. Corson (1993) describes this learning problem in terms of cultural mismatch and misunderstanding. 'The conceptual world of a culture includes many classificatory systems and most of them are expressed or supported in the language of the culture. When the classificatory systems of two cultures come into contact, there is often a mismatch' (p. 49). He states that teachers need to be able to make the content of their lessons relevant to minority group children by 'interweaving the known experiences of the children themselves with the content of the curriculum' but he also argues that the most important challenge is in 'establishing a context for learning that is genuinely congruent with the culture of . . . minority children' (p. 51).

I concur with Cummins and Corson that schooling is mediated through discourse in some form or another, and therefore priority in establishing congruency depends on the appropriateness of the discourse. Corson goes on to cite John Gumperz (1977), who explains that through their interactions with others, individuals develop 'co-occurrence expectations' and 'contextualization expectations' as part of their communicative competence and that these expectations are often culturally specific. These concepts are very relevant to my interviews as I discuss with my participants the cultural content and cultural values of specific texts used in the second language learning classrooms of the Neve Shalom/Wahat Al-Salam elementary school – the only school in Israel where bilingualism, biculturalism, and binationalism are at the core of all learning and teaching. It is not surprising, then, that Neve Shalom/Wahat Al-Salam stands as a potential role model for change.

## The New Language Center in Neve Shalom/Wahat Al-Salam: Implications for Language Pedagogy

A greater awareness and imagination on the part of policy makers and educators are crucial in order to respond to the needs of minority language children struggling to balance their lives in more than one cultural world. Furthermore, in a social context in which there is overt intergroup conflict, a second language curriculum which reflects the cultural content of the learners could provide a very effective strategy to create feelings of self-esteem and equality and to narrow the psychological distance between the minority and majority groups, thus enhancing academic achievement. A critical language awareness is therefore required in order to encourage students, teachers, and policymakers to approach the social imbalance in the dominant-subordinate educational paradigm which Corson terms as 'a site of human struggle' (1993, p. 191). Accordingly, second language educational reform must include a restructuring of language curriculum that will take into account the motivational orientations of students in relation to their group status within differential sociopolitical contexts; for example, social settings where intergroup conflict exists, as opposed to more neutral settings where a problematic historical legacy is not part of the cultural and national ethos.

We as teacher-educators and researchers need to further explore these issues with a view to the construction and reconstruction of the meaning of language teaching and learning within a landscape of social change and transformation. A concrete example of this ideological stance is embodied in the recently created Language Center at the Neve Shalom/Wahat Al-Salam elementary school. At the end of the 1997–1998 school year, the co-director of the school wrote a short description of the status of the school at that moment, and then discussed the new Language Center as an innovative response to the asymmetry between Hebrew and Arabic as well as a supplement to the English language classes. An excerpt from his report follows.

> As a Hebrew-Arabic educational framework, the Neve Shalom/Wahat Al-Salam school must still work in a society in which one of the languages – Hebrew – is dominant. Even here the Arab children find it easier than the Jews to acquire the second language. One of the school's objectives is to find innovative ways to strengthen language skills in general and to raise the level and use of Arabic among the Jews in particular. Professor Elite Olshtein [is] from the Hebrew University's Research Institute for Innovation in Education. Professor Olshtein created the idea of a language learning center used for Hebrew-English language training in a few other schools in Israel. Professor Olshstein sent Judy Yaron to work with the Neve Shalom/Wahat Al-Salam teaching staff, which invested a great deal of energy in creating the first trilingual, language center including Hebrew, English, and Arabic. Opened in December 1996, sessions in the Language Center have become an integral part of the school curriculum.

> The center is a large room, comfortable and attractively designed, in which pupils independently choose language learning tasks that are well defined and explained so that students can work with a minimum of guidance. The center supplements the regular language courses by providing an enjoyable, unpressured learning atmosphere, which raises the pupils' motivation to take initiative in language learning. The room is furnished to provide 'corners' for audiovisual equipment, games, reading, computers, drama, worksheet activities, [and so on). The children look forward to sessions in the Language Center and this is in itself a sign of success. The center serves the school's broader goal of developing teaching techniques and materials that can be utilized by other schools. In this regard, the Language Center enjoys two particular advantages over other projects in the school. First, similar projects can be developed in conventional schools that do not necessarily have a Jewish-Arab enrollment. Second, the cooperation with the Center for Innovation in Education ensures that the experience accumulated in this project will in fact be used to enrich other schools in the country. The center has already become a place of pilgrimage for teachers and academics from Israel and abroad.

In one of several more excerpts from interviews with participants, one of the teachers in the school said:

> And now we have the Language Center – which is beautiful and has made a big difference and the kids love it. It really gives Arabic an equal status and shows the children that it needs to be learned

just like Hebrew and, of course, English – which everybody wants to learn because of its international importance. And I do think other schools in Israel will start to use the model of the Language Center. It could revolutionize the attitude toward Arabic in the society from what is in effect taught as a 'foreign language' to a 'second language'.

Another teacher who teaches Arabic and English explained it this way:

It is great to see the children really enjoying learning Arabic and Hebrew in a very 'hands-on' way. They feel like it's a real treat with all the lovely activity centers and the language games that they play. It's a very egalitarian atmosphere.

A grade six boy discusses his view:

I always look forward to the Language Center. I can feel like I'm a merchant in a store, or buying a dog in a pet shop, or going on a trip, and I have all sorts of conversations about these things with my friends in class. We make up skits and stories and then present them in class to everybody. We do it in Hebrew, in Arabic, and in English. It's a lot of fun and everybody gets involved.

The co-director continues in his report:

Only a few years ago our hopes were raised that a new era was about to open between Jews and Arabs in which problems would be solved by negotiation. Unfortunately, four years after the beginning of talks, peace still appears to be a distant dream. We are afraid of our past, of returning to the all too horrible and familiar periods of war. Yet our present offers little hope as the negotiations between Israel and Palestinians reach stalemate after stalemate and hostile and hateful acts continue to claim victims on both sides. This complex reality provides the seedbed for the Neve Shalom/Wahat Al-Salam Primary School, with its goal of educating a rising generation for peace and understanding between the two peoples. Ultimately, we feel sure that we will succeed. Despite the setbacks, dialogue is now accepted as the most appropriate

means to reach a solution to the national conflict in our area. Perhaps a reflection of this is found in the growing interest in our program from many different directions: the government, the academic community, the media, and Jewish [and] Arab families from a wide radius of the village. We can now point to other initiatives in the field that have been inspired and helped by our work and today we are more confident than ever that our educational model will become a growing influence in the field of Jewish-Arab education.

The school year ended with the tremendous news that our school has been accepted officially as an 'experimental school'. Hundreds of schools applied for this status and the Neve Shalom/Wahat Al-Salam Primary School was one of the only two primary schools to be accepted. When the school was finally recognized in 1993, we celebrated the fact that the Ministry of Education had given legitimacy to the existence of a Jewish-Arab bilingual school. The acceptance of our school as an experimental school means much more. It means that the Ministry is prepared to explore our methods to see what can be learned from them and what can be applied elsewhere in the country. This has been our dream from the outset. The extra funding that comes with this status (three to five years) will be primarily for curriculum development[.] By the end of the experimental period the school is expected to serve as a center that produces material and offers in-service teacher training in the field of bilingual Jewish-Arab education. Such recognition from the state is certainly a milestone in our development.

## Implications for Multilingual Education

One of the significant implications of the Language Center to the field of second language learning and multicultural education, in general, is that language curriculum becomes meaningful to students only when it is relevant to their personal lives and cultural backgrounds. In the case of many minority students in North America, many researchers claim, as Henry Trueba did, that 'the curriculum is not appealing to children because it escapes children's experience, and thus their interest and grasp of concepts' (1989, p. 143). Within the context of Jewish-Palestinian intergroup conflict, the need for establishing balance in the curriculum content is all the more urgent. The interviews with my participants certainly support this view. In this regard, teacher-educators and curriculum planners in Israel, for example, must provide an explicit framework of the expectations and needs of Arab students according to their minority / subordinate status. Michael Apple (1990) argues that the question for teacher educators and students is not *what* knowledge is most worthwhile in terms of curriculum, but *whose* (p. vii). For Arab students in Israel and, as mentioned earlier, for all students who perceive themselves to be in a subordinate position in their societies, it is important that their values and cultures be represented within the textual material of their second language curriculum, especially when that language represents the dominant group. It is therefore essential for language educators to listen to the students' own perspectives on the choice of texts and other materials as well as on teacher–student interaction, and even more generally, on the discourse of the second language classroom. We need to listen to the voices of the learners themselves concerning strategies for dealing with issues of reform in second language programs. The curriculum has the potential to either enable or handicap the student within the sociopolitical contexts that can encourage or hinder second language reading comprehension. These issues must be made more explicit at the teacher education level through the Ministry of Education in order for teacher-educators to gain a deeper understanding of how the dominant culture impacts on the realities of learning in the second language classroom.

## The Allure of English: A Language of Dominion

Concerning language awareness, it is interesting to note that the necessity to master English – the *lingua franca* or perhaps more appropriately, the *lingua dominatrix* – is perceived by all as essential. On this point there is no dissension between Jew and Palestinian anywhere in Israel. Its cultural imperialism is accepted by both sides, like it or not. Israelis are pragmatists; there is whole-hearted agreement in this vision: English is neither yours nor mine; it is what we all need to succeed. English transcends

the conflict, the cultural borders, the animosity. English is the world. English is freedom. English is power. English opens the door for all of us.

This is what one male Palestinian teacher says in regard to personal and professional reaction to the dominance of English in the world:

> If you don't know English, then you're not in the game. Today, for an Arab, it's very hard to keep up with what's happening in the world without English. For example, the works of Edward Said are in English. Only now are some being translated into Arabic. In the Arab world, they have books at universities and some are not updated; if they don't have the scientific books in English, then they don't have the latest books. English has the power; that's just the reality. We want to make sure we don't fall behind.

This female Jewish teacher explained it this way:

> Nobody will complain about learning English in schools anywhere in Israel. When it comes to English it's never enough. Without a good knowledge of English, we would become a country without any power in the world. Let's face it, Hebrew is certainly not very important; and even Arabic, which is spoken by many, many millions in the world, still doesn't have much international importance. Like I say, without English you might as well disappear. Who can change that? So everybody is interested in learning English.

Here is what a little eight-year-old Palestinian boy said:

> I know you want to practice your Hebrew and Arabic; but honestly, I want to talk with you in English because I want to learn it so bad. What does English mean to me? It means being able to travel when I get bigger.

A six-year-old Jewish child confided:

> English doesn't have any problems the way Arabic and Hebrew [do], which are always fighting with each other. I always feel excited about learning English.

A female Palestinian teacher describes below her childhood love affair with the English language, which continues to this day. She grew up in a town in the Galilee, a famous pilgrimage destination and therefore always full of tourists. As a young child she was fascinated by them and by the possibility of the different lifestyles that they embodied. Many of them spoke English, and she practiced using this language (which she was beginning to learn at school) whenever she could. English always represented for her a passport to freedom, opportunity, success, adventure, and joy.

> I would hang around the Church of the Annunciation and wait until the tour was over and then start to talk with the tourists. Maybe they humored me or maybe they thought it was exotic to be speaking with this little Arab girl in English.
>
> I first started learning it in school in grade four. I couldn't believe when I could start speaking in full sentences and they [the tourists] didn't mind. Also, I loved my English teacher in grade four. And the others also. Later in junior high school, I had a very bad teacher and I almost lost my English with that teacher.
>
> But in the last year of junior high, we had a wonderful, marvellous teacher and he had an American accent. That's where I got my accent. It's amazing how one teacher can make such a huge difference. He said, 'I will not let you go on until I see you progressing properly in English'.
>
> Arabic is my first language, so it didn't have adventure. Hebrew wasn't exciting because of what it meant for us Arabs in Israel. I wasn't attracted to it and tried to rebel against it by not learning it well. But I realized pretty early on that if I wanted to be accepted to university then what kind of bullshit am I doing – I needed Hebrew. And to communicate in the country where I live . . .
>
> But English was the dream! You know, it was like the dessert of life. It's the topping on the cake – you don't have to put it on top, but it makes everything so beautiful and sparkling. I know it sounds silly but you have to believe in love. So that's how the whole story began with English. I just love it.
>
> And so I would just say what I could to the pilgrims. It was such a good feeling and they always seemed so relaxed (maybe

because they were on holiday). If I didn't understand something, I would ask them. I would throw what I could in English. I encourage my own students to do that. Not to feel ashamed about what you know or the mistakes you make. I always say that language is like the sea. You throw into it what you can and you hold onto to what you have; you touch anything that will save you. It may be right, it may be wrong, but you're grasping onto it. Someone will correct you anyhow. But at least you're keeping the conversation afloat.
>
> Oh, I was crazy. I looked everything up in the dictionary. I just enjoyed looking at the words. Now I try to give my students that feeling.

Who can explain this *coup de foudre*, this falling in love with a language? I certainly understand it because it happened to me also, although in another context. I was able to relate to much of what this teacher shared with me. We grew up in very different places, yet we both recognized the learning of a second/foreign language for the magic carpet ride that it can be – given the right circumstances. To be seduced by a language is a profound experience. It can be as special as icing on a cake, or it can have the power to save your life. This is language awareness in its finest hour.

## References

Abu-Rabia, S. and Feuerverger, G. (1996) Towards understanding the second language learning of Arab students in Israel and Canada. *Canadian Modern Language Review* 52 (3), 359–385.

Adams, A. and Tulasewicz, W. (1994) Language awareness in an intercultural curriculum for schools. *Modern Languages: Entente Internationale. Education* 3 (xii). Cambridge University Press.

Al-Haj, M. (1995) *Education Empowerment and Control in the Case of Arabs in Israel.* Albany, NY: SUNY Press.

Anzaldua, G. (1987) *Borderlands/La Frontera: The New Mestiza.* San Francisco: San Francisco/ Aunt Lute.

Bakhtin, M. (1981) *The Dialogic Imagination.* Austin, TX: University of Texas Press.

Benevenisti, M. (1995) *Intimate Enemies: Jews and Arabs in a Shared Land.* Berkeley, CA: University of California Press.

Bhaskar, R. (1986) *Scientific Realism and Human Emancipation*. London: Verso.

Bhaskar, R. (1989) *Reclaiming Reality: A Critical Introduction to Contemporary Philosophy*. London: Verso.

Byram, M.S. (1993) Foreign language teaching and multicultural education. In A.S. King and M.J. Reiss (eds) *The Multicultural Dimension of the National Curriculum* (pp. 73–186). London: The Falmer Press.

Cazden, C. (1989) Richmond Road: A multi-lingual/multicultural primary school in Auckland, New Zealand. *Language and Education* 3, 143–166.

Chambers, I. (1994) *Migrancy, Culture, Identity*. New York: Routledge.

Clandinin, D.J. and Connelly, F.M. (1995) *Teachers' Professional Knowledge Landscapes*. New York: Teachers College Press, Columbia University.

Connelly, F.M. and Clandinin, D.J. (1990) Stories of experience and narrative inquiry. *Educational Researcher* 19 (5), 2–14.

Corson, D. (1993) *Language, Minority Education, and Gender: Linking Social Justice and Power*. Toronto, ON: OISE Press.

Corson, D. (1999) *Language Policy in Schools: A Resource for Teachers and Administrators*. Mahwah, NJ: Lawrence Erlbaum Associates.

Cummins, J. (1994) From coercive to collaborative relations of power in the teaching of literacy. In B.M. Ferdman, R.M. Weber and A.G. Ramirez (eds) *Literacy Across Languages and Cultures* (pp. 295–331). Albany, NY: SUNY Press.

Cummins, J. and Danesi, M. (1990) *Heritage Languages: The Development and Denial of Canada's Linguistic Resources*. Toronto, ON: Our Schools/Ourselves Educational Foundation.

Davies, C.A. (1999) *Reflexive Ethnography: A Guide to Researching Selves and Others*. London, New York: Routledge.

Delpit, L. (1992) The politics of teaching literate discourse. *Theory into Practice* 31, 285–295.

Dewey, J. (1938) *Experience and Education*. New York: Collier Books.

Donmall, B.S. (1985) Some implications of language awareness work for teacher training. In B.C. Donmall (ed.) *Language Awareness* (4th edn) (pp. 1–13). York, UK: National Congress on Languages in Education Assembly.

Eisenstadt, S.N. (1967) The absorption of immigrants, the amalgamation of exiles and the problems of transformation of Israeli society. In O. Kohen (ed.) *The Integration of Immigrants in Israel from Different Countries of Origin* (pp. 6-15). Jerusalem: Magnes Press.

Elazar, D.J. (1985) Israel's compound policy. In E. Krausz (ed.) *Politics and Society in Israel*. New Brunswick, NJ: Transaction Books.

Fairclough, N. (1993) *Discourse and Social Exchange*. Cambridge: Polity Press.

Feuerverger, G. A multicultural literacy intervention for minority language students. *Language and Education* 8 (3), 123–146.

Freire, P. (1970) *Pedagogy of the Oppressed*. New York: Seabury Press.

García, E.E. (1994) Language, culture, and curriculum. In L. Darling-Hammond (ed.) *Review of Research in Education* (pp. 51–98). New York: Teachers College Press.

Giroux, H.A. (1991) Democracy and the discourse of cultural difference: Towards a politics of border pedagogy. *British Journal of Sociology of Education* 12 (4), 501–519.

Goodman, K., Brooks-Smith, E., Meredith, R. and Goodman, Y.M. (1987) *Language and Thinking in School: A Whole-Language Curriculum*. New York: Richard C. Owen.

Gumperz, J. (1977) Sociocultural knowledge in conversational inference. In M. Saville-Troike (ed.) *Twenty-eighth Annual Roundtable Monograph Series in Language and Linguistics*. Washington, DC: Georgetown University Press.

Hawkins, E. (1984) *Awareness of Language*. Cambridge, MA: Cambridge University Press.

Heath, S.B. (1983) *Ways With Words: Language, Life, and Work in Communities and Classrooms*. Cambridge, MA: Cambridge University Press.

Iram, Y. and Schmida, M. (1998) *The Education System of Israel*. Westport, CT: Greenwood Press.

Jackson, S. (1995) Autobiography: Pivot points for engaging lives in multicultural contexts. In J. M. Larkin and C.E. Sleeter (eds) *Developing Multicultural Teacher Education Curricula* (pp. 31–44). New York: SUNY Press.

Kaiser, S. and Short, K. (1998) Exploring culture through children's connections. *Language Arts* 75 (3), 185–192.

Keiny, S. (1999) Reponse to 'Human rights in history and civic textbooks: The case of Israel'. *Curriculum Inquiry* 29 (4), 513–522.

Krashen, S. and Biber, D. (1988) *On Course: Bilingual Education's Success in California*.

Sacramento, CA: California Association of Bilingual Education.

Kristeva, J. (1991) *Strangers To Ourselves* (L.S. Roudiez, trans.). New York: Columbia University Press.

Lawrence-Lightfoot, S. and Hoffman Davis, J. (1997) *The Art and Science of Portraiture*. San Francisco: Jossey-Bass.

Mari, S. (1985) *The Arab Education in Israel*. New York: Syracuse University Press.

Masemann, V. and Iram, Y. (1987) The right to education for multicultural development: Canada and Israel. In N. Bernstein-Tarrow (ed.) *Human Rights and Education*. Oxford: Pergamon Press.

Michaels, S. (1981) Sharing time: Children's narrative styles and differential access to literacy. *Language in Society* 10, 423–442.

Nieto, S. (1992) *Affirming Diversity: The Sociopolitical Context of Multicultural Education*. White Plains, NY: Longman.

Potok, R.N. (1988) Borders, exiles, minor literatures: The case of Palestinian–Israeli writing. In E. Barkan and M.D. Shelton (eds) *Borders, Exiles, Diasporas* (pp. 291–310). Stanford, CA: Stanford University Press.

Resnik, J. (1999) Particularistic vs. universalistic content in the Israeli education system. *Curriculum Inquiry* 29, (4), 485–512.

Shipler, D.K. (1986) *Arab and Jew: Wounded Spirits in a Promised Land*. New York: Times Books.

Shohamy, E. (1993) A monolingual language policy in a diverse cultural society: The case of Israel. Paper presented at the International Conference on Education for Democracy in a Multicultural Society, Jerusalem.

Shohamy, E. and Spolsky, B. (2000) *New Perspectives and Issues in Educational Language Policy: A Festschrift for Bernard Dov Spolsky*. Philadelphia, PA: J. Benjamins.

Simon, R.I. (1992) *Teaching Against the Grain*. New York: Bergin and Garvey Press.

Smooha, S. (1978) *Israel: Pluralism and Conflict*. New York: Routledge and Kegan Paul.

Spolsky, B. (1989) *Conditions for Second Language Learning*. New York: Oxford University Press.

Tabachnik, B.R. and Zeichner, K.M. (1993) Preparing teachers for cultural diversity. In P. Gilroy and M. Smith (eds) *International Analyses of Teacher Education (JET Papers One)* (pp. 113–124). London: Carfax Publishing.

Trueba, H.T. (1989) *Raising Silent Voices: Educating the Linguistic Minorities for the Twenty-first Century*. Cambridge, MA: Newbury House.

Van Manen, M. (1990) *Researching Lived Experience: Human Science for an Action Sensitive Pedagogy*. London, ON: University of Western Ontario.

Vygotsky, L.S. (1962) *Thought and Language* (A. Kozulin, trans.). Cambridge, MA: MIT Press.

Wong-Fillmore, L. (1991) When learning a second language means losing the first. *Early Childhood Research Quarterly* 6, 323–346.

## Questions

1   What is language awareness? What kind of language awareness training is Feuerverger discussing in this chapter?

2   What are the language and cultural elements in the Neve Shalom/Wahat Al-Salam model? How do these connect with the hope for peace and improved relationships between Jews and Palestinians in Israel? What is the 'language of peace'?

3   What concerns are raised about the 'allure' of English? How is English seen to compare with Hebrew and Arabic?

4   Read one or more of Bekerman's articles listed in the Further Reading below (or the Tankersley article). How similar is Bekerman's research findings to that of Feuerverger? Do they share similar beliefs about the value of bilingual education for peace?

## Activities

1.   Select a language group in your locality (or a classroom you choose). By observation and interview, make a profile of students from that language group on the following:
     a.   the places where they shop (for food and clothing)

    b.  where they go for music and entertainment
    c.  religious places and religious services they attend
    d.  how they harmonize or not with other language groups
2.  Visit a local school with a varied ethnic enrollment, and ask teachers if they have any language awareness content in their classrooms. Also ask them about how 'peace' among children and among groups is addressed in the school. Write an account of your interviews.
3.  Create a colorful advertisement than links two key words: 'multilingualism' and 'peace'.
4.  Research on the WWW for references to 'peace' and ' bilingual education'. What sources and pages are predominant? What messages do such pages contain?
5.  Write your own personal narrative about your experience with minority languages, whether it's yours or that of others, as well as your experience learning a second language.

**Further Reading**

Bekerman, Z. (2003) Reshaping conflict through school ceremonial events in Israeli Palestinian-Jewish education. *Anthropology & Education Quarterly*, 34, 2, 205–224.
Bekerman, Z. (2005) Complex contexts and ideologies: Bilingual education in conflict-ridden areas. *Journal of Language, Identity, and Education*, 4, 1, 1–20.
Bekerman, Z. and Shhadi, N. (2003) Palestinian-Jewish bilingual education in Israel. Its influence on cultural identities and its impact on intergroup conflict. *Journal of Multilingual and Multicultural Development*, 24, 6, 473–484.
García, O. and Traugh, C. (2002) Using descriptive inquiry to transform the education of linguistically diverse US teachers and students. In Li Wei, J-M. Dewaele and A. Housen (eds) *Opportunities and Challenges of Bilingualism*. Berlin: Mouton de Gruyter.
Hélot, C. (2006) Imagining multilingual education in France: A language and cultural awareness project at primary level. In O. García, T. Skutnabb-Kangas and M. Torres-Guzmán (eds) *Imagining Multilingual Schools: Languages in Education*. Clevedon: Multilingual Matters.
Tankersley, D. (2001) Bombs or bilingual programmes? Dual language immersion, transformative education and community building in Macedonia. *International Journal of Bilingual Education and Bilingualism*, 4, 2, 107–124.

# Integrating Language and Content: How Three Biology Teachers Work with Non-English Speaking Students

Yu Ren Dong

## Introduction

In recent years, public schools in the United States have experienced a dramatic increase in the number of non-native English speaking students. According to a report from New York City Board of Education, there has been a more than 60% increase in the number of students who were limited English proficient (LEP), from 95,000 in 1988 to about 160,000 in 1999. Facing the rapidly increasing non-native English speaking student population in public schools across the nation in general, and in New York City in particular, all teachers are challenged by an urgent need for developing ways to make their instruction more effective and responsive to these English language learners' needs (ELL). Today's students with limited English proficiency struggle to keep up with their peers in mainstream classes. In middle and high schools, many of them spend two or three periods with English as a second language (ESL) teachers and the rest of their school day with subject matter area teachers who often have limited knowledge about their backgrounds and needs and lack strategies used to work with them effectively. The situation was often exacerbated with the increasing demands and graduation standards. Examining the 1998–1999 school year Regents Biology Exam results in New York City high schools, non-native English speaking students had only half of the average passing rate compared to their native English speaking peers (an average passing rate for the native English speaking students was 43.5%). Therefore, there is an urgent need for all teachers to be informed of the principles of second language acquisition and learning and trained to use ESL oriented methods and tech-

niques to include these students both physically and academically in their classroom instruction. This paper will examine specific ways how three biology teachers worked with non-native English speaking students in their sheltered ESL biology classes during the school year 1997–1998.

## Challenges for Non-native English Speaking High School Students to Learn Biology

Because of the curriculum set-up in high schools in New York City, biology is often the first course for non-native English speaking students to begin their science learning careers in high schools. The high school biology curriculum, which consists of students developing comprehensive vocabulary and literacy skills in reading, writing, and critical thinking and understanding of biology concepts, poses a tremendous challenge for all students, especially for non-native English speaking students. Students have to not only understand the concept behind specific biology terminology, but also are able to articulate their understanding in reading and writing. Researchers have voiced concerns about the sheer size of specialised vocabulary to be acquired by high school students in biology. According to this line of research (Anderson, 1990; Gibbs & Lawson, 1992; Leonard & Penick, 1993; Lumpe & Beck, 1996), a number of close to 10,000 words to be learned in a high school biology textbook makes it hard for native English speaking students, let alone for non-native English speaking students.

Often the high school biology textbook is written in a way oriented toward native English speaking students (Atwater, 1994; Hodson, 1993). The examples and the illustrations are based on the assumptions that readers grow up in this culture. As a result, teachers have to deal not only with students' lack of knowledge base, but also possible mismatches in interpretations of the issues and the knowledge base and learning and teaching styles that are different from that of the students' schooling back home in teaching of reading, writing, and critical thinking skills used in biology learning. For example, Gao (1998: 2) reported that 'students in China, learning is not only a means for knowing and understanding, but also for personal perfection, family honor, and social development'. Coming from Confucian traditions, Chinese people view teachers as 'models of good conduct and learning' (p. 4). As a result, a frequent use of questions, the technique that American teachers use to promote students' thinking and assess their learning, is often misconstrued by Chinese students. Students dare not and will not ask questions even though they might not understand what is going on in the lesson due to the respect for the teacher (Scarcella, 1992). Therefore, teaching linguistically and culturally diverse students is more involved in cross-cultural understanding and creating responsive teaching strategies in addressing these differences (Banks & Banks, 1997; Carrasquillo & Rodriguez, 1995).

## ESL Oriented Biology Instruction

Studies in second language acquisition have repeatedly shown that second language is best learned through content when students have a real purpose for learning and when language use is authentic, rich, and meaningful to students (Chamot & O'Malley, 1994; Enright & McCloskey, 1988; Swain & Carroll, 1987). Several studies (Adamson, 1990; Chamot & O'Malley, 1994; Enright & McCloskey, 1988) have found that non-native English speaking students will benefit more from learning the second language and academic content knowledge simultaneously rather than separately. One of the best ways of learning a new language is to learn it in the target language and in the real context of disciplinary specific language use, such as biology, social studies, maths, etc. Language learning in meaningful content stimulates motivation and provides real social purposes for speaking, listening, reading, writing and thinking. With a change of the student body in many public schools and where many ESL learners spend a great amount of time with their subject matter area teachers during the day, there is a need

for a change in pedagogy for all teachers to integrate language and content instruction and create rich and authentic contexts for language learning (Genesee, 1993). Therefore, content area teachers must join in the effort to educate ESL students with ESL/bilingual teachers by becoming knowledgeable about issues related to second language learning, learning specific ways of communicating with ESL learners, and providing language and content integrated instruction.

One way of making content area teachers' instruction accessible to ESL students is to modify their teaching to make it comprehensible for ESL students who might be at different levels of English proficiency. Conceptual knowledge of academic content is best learned through teachers providing comprehensible input (Krashen, 1985). The input can be made comprehensible by using more visual aids, audio aids, gestures, body movements, and facial expressions. Also, comprehension can be greatly enhanced if the teacher engages the students into active questioning, dialoguing, and writing through which the new knowledge becomes meaningful and internalized (Freeman & Freeman, 1998; Gersten, 1996; Snow *et al.*, 1989).

Research findings have demonstrated that many school-aged second language learners had had rich life experiences and prior education on the subject matter knowledge before coming to America. Identifying and making good use of the student's previous life and educational experiences can enhance both language learning and the academic content learning (Cummins, 1994; Freeman & Freeman, 1998). Second language learners' experiences and knowledge gained in their schooling back home can be transferred into the new learning situation with appropriate prodding and scaffolding. For example, even though the students may not know the English word for photosynthesis, they may have already had the concept established in their native language. So once the subject matter teacher identifies what students know and helps them to make the connection between what they are learning now and what they have already known, content specific concept learning speeds up because students only need to learn a new way of saying the old concept. Therefore, instead of focusing on what the second language learners do not know, the content teacher should seek what the students do know and build on an understanding of the new knowledge from there

(Chamot & O'Malley, 1994; Freeman & Freeman, 1998; Gonzalez & Schallert, 1999).

Despite an increasing discussion in the literature for responsive science instruction and integrated language and content instruction in dealing with non-native English speaking students (Bernhart *et al.*, 1996; Chamot & O'Malley, 1994; Krashen, 1985; Long & Porter, 1985; Pica & Doughty, 1985; Rupp, 1992), research on effective teaching methods and techniques in teaching biology concepts to ESL students is sparse (Lee & Fradd, 1996). No research has been done systematically to investigate how these principles are applied to actual teaching practice and what responsive and effective biology instruction looks like. Therefore, the purpose of this study was to compile responsive and effective teaching strategies through a year long observation of three biology teachers' instruction and a series of interviews with both the teachers and 18 students from these teachers' classes. The study was guided by the following questions:

(1) How do biology teachers make biology concepts comprehensible to culturally and linguistically diverse students?
(2) What are some of the effective teaching strategies and techniques that lead to student academic and language learning?

## Data Collection

### Two schools and biology curriculum

Located in Queens, a diverse borough of New York City, two New York City high schools chosen for the study had ESL student population composed of one-third of the total student body for one school and two-thirds for the other. Two Science Department Assistant Principals (AP) (Kelly and Sarah are pseudonyms) were both open to the new ideas and concerned about their ESL students' success in science. Collaborating with other science professionals, they had their teachers compile a detailed guideline for teaching biology to ESL students and bilingual glossaries in biology. They both strongly encouraged their faculty to implement these materials in their teaching. In addition, both of them assigned time for ESL Department chairs to come to do a workshop at one of their staff developmental meetings during the semester. Finally, the two invited the faculty to share teaching ideas and swap lesson plans and test designs to promote their professional growth and effective teaching.

The science departments in the two high schools adopted the New York State Regents Biology Variance curriculum at the time of the study. The curriculum used a thematic approach to content knowledge and focused on conceptual development and inquiry in learning biology. Both native and non-native English speaking students in these two high schools were placed in the Regents Biology Variance classes. In addition to their lab work and Regents exam, students in these classes were required to compile a biology portfolio that included four research and creative biology projects and to complete two in-class free response essays during the school year. This curriculum, according to both the science chairs and the teachers, though still very limited, was better than the previous curriculum in that it offered more chances and on-going process for students both native and non-native English speaking to succeed than relying on the Regents exam alone in the end.

### Teachers, school and students

After an initial contact and trial observations of eight biology teachers recommended by the science department chairs from four high schools, three biology teachers (their pseudonyms are Lisa, Sally and Mike) from two high schools were selected because of their successful experiences in teaching biology to ESL students. These three teachers' teaching experiences varied from two to six years. At the time, they were all teaching the ESL biology class, a sheltered biology class composed of all ESL students from various language, cultural, and literacy backgrounds and at different English proficiency levels. The three teachers, one male and two females, were in their late twenties and early thirties, two had already earned their master's degrees in general science and biology, and one was working on getting a master's degree at the time of the study. They all had the New York State teaching certification. However, only Sally had taken second language teaching and learning courses prior to the study.

Students from these three teachers' classes came from 15 countries and speaking 14 languages. Everyday, besides one period biology class, students attended two periods of ESL classes, one period of ESL global studies class, one period of a mainstream math class, one period gym, and other. Students varied in their knowledge of English and biology. Some had already learned biology for several years in their home countries before coming here; some had learned general science in their middle schools back home; others just started learning. Their English proficiency levels were also varied, ranging from level two, a beginning level to level six, an advanced level of English proficiency.

Between the 1997 and 1998 school year, I observed each of the three teachers once a week for a total of 24 weeks. Classroom observations were audio taped and then transcribed. Teaching materials, such as handouts and the textbooks, were gathered. Students' work, portfolios and tests were collected. Near the end of each term, I interviewed each teacher (each lasted for an hour) for their reflections on their teaching strategies and perceived ESL students' difficulties with biology learning. In addition, I also selected six students from each class for an interview (each lasted for half an hour) to gain insights into the students' learning of biology and their perspectives of their teachers' teaching.

## Results/Discussion

Results from the observations and the interviews revealed that the three biology teachers appeared to provide responsive and effective instruction to non-native English speaking students that were supported by research and welcomed by their students. Their successful teaching focused on the following areas:

- providing comprehensible input and integrating language and biology instruction;
- promoting language use and scientific thinking through group work;
- explicitly teaching learning skills;
- acknowledging cultural differences and using a modified classroom talk;
- appreciating diversity and using students' prior knowledge in biology instruction;
- enriching the curriculum and providing a rich language use environment.

### *Providing comprehensible input and integrating language and biology instruction*

Sally often said that teaching ESL students was different from teaching regular students in that you cannot take things for granted, assuming students would have known basic words. She often began her introduction of a new concept with what her students called 'a story'. For each

new vocabulary item that she was introducing, she would elicit from the students the words with a similar meaning and write them on the board next to the new word in the parenthesis. She wrote complete sentences on the board to facilitate students' understanding and their later study of their notes. Sally talked about her approach to providing comprehensible input at the interview during the interviews.

> You can see for example, the crayfish, for students who may never see crayfish or know crayfish. If a textbook never supplements the picture of crayfish, I, the teacher have to first to define a crayfish: What does it look like? What's the color? . . . So there are certain things that we take for granted, for example, we would say a blue jay and a sparrow, like common things that children would see on the curb when they grow up here. But for these children they may never see these things before since they are new to this country. So you really have to think backwards. If the child never saw the item, let alone the internal structure before, the first thing you have to introduce what it is and how it is and then you can teach biology.

In her efforts to make the content comprehensible and accessible to her students, Sally used modified or elaborated definitions of the new words, physical movements to create a mental picture of the meaning, and examples and analogies from students' daily life to provide the contexts for students' scientific knowledge building. The following is an example of these techniques at work:

**Teacher:**  Number ten is a large vacuole (wrote on the board). A vacuole stores the water and other substances for the cell. The vacuole in the animal cell is tiny because the animal can go and get water, right? But the trees cannot grow legs. So it has to absorb the water and holds the water in the cell and hold on to it (used gestures and physical movements).

**Student:**  Like camels, they hold up their water.

**Teacher:**  You got it. Same idea.

In this excerpt, Sally painted a clear mental picture of the word 'vacuole' by using simple language, physical movements, and a humorous comparison between an animal cell and a plant cell. After this, students were asked to draw both the animal cell and the plant cell and color them and explain them in writing in terms of the function and the structure of each organelle.

Facing the difficulty with biology concepts and vocabulary with all high school students in general, with non-native English speaking students in particular, Mike focused his teaching on stimulating students' curiosity of science and creating an understanding of biology concepts. He talked about his views on diverse students' abilities of learning science.

> I can get an idea by looking at those eyes. What's going on behind those eyes. Curiosity is usually a good indication of that. My opinion is if the kids are at least curious, that tells me that there is a function of ability in some language that they can think in that language ... I had kids who cannot speak English at all, but I can tell there is something going on, they just don't know what you are saying.

Mike's ESL biology class was characterised by stimulating and challenging questions and an effective use of visual aids to create a context for learning. An excitement about science came through his teaching when he began each lesson with a combination of visual aids and questions. Firmly believing in inquiry oriented science learning, Mike designed his lesson in such a way that abstract concepts were all transformed into concrete daily problems to solve. He would first pose open-ended questions based on daily life observations. These questions were invigorating and invited a wide range of reactions from the students which led his students to a meaningful and challenging learning process immediately. Students in his class did not passively learn the definition of the word, but the meaning behind it by asking questions and participating in doing, seeing, touching, listening, smelling, and talking about science. Mike talked about his approach to teaching biology to ESL students.

> When I teach the ESL classes, I am more in tuned to their language abilities. I would be more apt to ask questions, asking them about the words that they don't understand and take a little more time to go over the language ... Whatever the concept that I

teach I try to be as illustrative as possible with things that the students can do ... I know the word 'cell' is just a kind of an abstract idea. But if they look into the microscope and find all those boxes. Then I will say, what is it made of? They say little boxes. I say, yeah, that's what they are made of. OK, we call them cells ... Once you get the concept, then the vocabulary is easy because they can relate to something.

A class ritual was established. Mike would begin his lesson with a question or a problem along with his demonstration using manipulatives and realias for students to grapple with and to come up with their own questions that were the topic of the lesson on that day. Here is an example.

| | |
|---|---|
| **Teacher:** | Okay we have two beakers of water up here and one has a rock and one has some beans. OK, if I leave these things alone, say for one day, I come back and look at them tomorrow, how will they change? |
| **Student 1:** | The bean will grow. |
| **Teacher:** | Possibly the bean might grow some roots. |
| **Student 2:** | The rock might get weaker. |
| **Student 3:** | What happen to it? |
| **Teacher:** | The rock? So if this was in a river, right, rocks sitting on the bottom of the river. Would the rock be breaking up? |
| **Student 3:** | No. |
| **Teacher:** | That is because that water is moving, this water is not moving. What happens to beans when you leave it in water? |
| **Student 4:** | It gets soft. |
| **Teacher:** | It gets what? |
| **Student 4:** | Soft. |
| **Teacher:** | Did everybody hear that? Say it again. |
| **Student 4:** | The bean gets soft. |
| **Teacher:** | What about the rock? Will it get soft? |
| **Student 4:** | No. |
| **Teacher:** | Probably not. What question would we ask today? |
| **Student 5:** | What is the difference between the two? |
| **Student 6:** | How can water change living things? |
| **Teacher:** | That is very good. (Writes on the board the question: How can water change living things?) |

In the above episode, we see how Mike used the manipulative and open-ended questions to provoke students' thinking and to generate questions about the topic of the day, osmosis. Right after this demonstration, students were broken into groups of five to observe the change of the onion cell, comparing when it is soaked with water versus when it is soaked in the salt water. Students were asked to draw what they saw and describe the process. They were also encouraged to write down questions while comparing and contrasting. The class ended with Mike summarising the key points about osmosis and writing them on the board.

Compared to other teachers, Mike was most notable in providing a rich sensory engaging class. Throughout the school year, he used charts, manipulatives, overhead transparencies, pictures, posters, diagrams, etc. During my year long observations, for each lesson, he employed visual aids, ranging from three to ten, and did demonstrations and hands-on activities to create a rich context for students to comprehend the concept. According to him, teaching through multiple senses can not only make the abstract concept easier to visualise, but also keep the students' concentration and motivation high. Here are a few students' comments at interviews about Mike's teaching.

> His way of teaching is good because he gets everything understandable. I like biology.

> Everyday I look forward to his biology class because you don't know what kind of stuff he is going to bring. He uses a lot of visual aids and that makes learning much easier and fun.

> I really like his questions to make us think. We are all involved in class by his questions. We can find each other's ideas too.

> I prefer his questions. If he asks a question and you answer, then you know what you are learning. Also the group activities like we did yesterday are much better.

### Promoting language use and scientific thinking through group work

Believing in cooperative and experiential learning, Lisa regularly used group work and hands-on activities to help students with the understanding of the abstract concepts. These activities, using the idea of the Zone of Proximal Development, where the teacher supported, aided, and prodded for students' own exploration of meaning through oral interaction, fostered students' language acquisition and content knowledge development. Students' talking about the task also enhanced their language learning through authentic and meaningful communication with each other. The following is an episode taken from an activity where students learned how a sickle cell disease was inherited, a topic of genetics, by randomly choosing two beans from the mix of the red and white beans representing sickle and normal cell alleles repeatedly. Notice near the end Lisa made sure that not only students generated more conversations among themselves and had fun in doing the activity, but also comprehended an important concept: that is how and why the sickle cell alleles, represented by red beans decreased as the population reproduced itself from one generation to another.

**Student 1:** I got AA. (meaning two white beans)

**Student 2:** Yeah, I got SS. (meaning two red beans)

**Student 3:** Oh, cool, she got SS. What did you get?

**Student 4:** SS.

**Student 3:** Put them back.

**Student 1:** You screw up, you cannot put these beans back. These are with sickle diseases. They are dead already. What did you get? (the one did not close his eyes in picking)

**Student 3:** AA.

**Student 4:** All right, let's count them.

**Student 3:** (report to the teacher) We got 15 AAs, 2 SSs, and 4 ASs.

**Teacher:** Why are there always more white beans than red beans in this population?

**Student 3:** Because we have more white beans.

**Teacher:** Why do we have more white beans?

**Student 2:** Because white is dominant.

**Teacher:** Why is it dominant?

**Student 1:** Because they don't have disease and they are going to live longer.

**Teacher:** That's it, that's it. Does everybody hear that? If you have two SSs, the individuals are going to die and not to pass their genes on. So therefore, that number of SSs is going to decrease in the population.

In this group activity, Lisa intentionally withdrew herself first from the teacher's role and designed a task which students had to work with each other and converse in order to solve the problem. Pay attention to the group members' interaction; obviously the anxiety to speak in front of the whole class was reduced and they focused more on the task and the meaning rather than on the accurate form of language structure. They used more turns and everyone had a chance to speak. Also, they spoke in a dialogue fashion, revealing several functions of language use, such as asking questions, clarifying, commenting, joking, demanding, etc. This rich language use very often did not occur with the teacher and the student interaction; as shown in the above, once Lisa came to check for their understanding of the topic of the lesson, the students' responses returned back to typical classroom talks.

### Explicitly teaching learning skills

Lisa also believed that ESL students needed an explicit instruction on certain learning skills such as dictionary use and strategies for reading comprehension. She periodically brought in dictionaries and bilingual glossaries and required every student in her class to bring a bilingual dictionary to her biology class. Here is an example of Lisa's bringing students' attention to use dictionaries to find the meaning of the new words and effective ways of reading:

**Teacher:** What does accessory mean? Who has a dictionary? The question says: what are the accessory organs of the digestive system? What does accessory mean?

**Student:** A job.

**Teacher:** Who has a dictionary? What does accessory mean?

**Student 1:** (looked into the dictionary) Accessory means additional.

**Teacher:** Additional (wrote on the board 'additional' besides accessory). What about your bilingual dictionaries, what did it say about accessory? (Students called out the definitions in their native languages) OK, good. Once you find out the meaning of the word, put down the meaning on the side of accessory. Then continue reading. (paused and gave students time to take notes from their dictionaries) Any questions?

**Student 2:** Does it also mean main?

**Teacher:** There is a difference between accessory and main. Accessory means there are parts of the digestive system that are important but they are not the main part of the digestive system. So accessory means the top of the stomach (drew a stomach on the board). Are we all clear? Remember, you put stars next to these important parts so later on you can come back and review.

In this observation, Lisa was teaching her students not only the content but also the reading skills. She not only told but also modelled for her students how to approach a new word in the reading and how to highlight key concepts for reading comprehension and review. She paused to let her students take notes and follow through the procedure. Students all liked Lisa's way of teaching as they said the following at the interviews:

> [Lisa] explains things very clearly and patiently to make sure that everyone understands.

> When I was first placed in the ESL biology class, I thought it must be a dumb class. Now, I know these students in that class and they are smart. Our teacher made us talk and have fun in the biology class.

> [Lisa] really teaches us things we need for school. For example, she demands we have our bilingual dictionary and later buy an English-English dictionary. I learned new words from these dictionaries and my reading has improved.

### Acknowledging culturally varied ways of schooling and using a modified classroom talk

Recognising that some of his students were not used to participating in class discussions and tending to defer to the teacher as an authority in their schooling back home, Mike used varied strategies to constantly train his students to talk about science in class. Mike's lecture was loud and clear. He used wait time when he asked a question. He did not only call on those who raised their hands, but also those who kept silent once he sensed they were ready. For example, knowing that one of his Chinese students had been in his biology class for almost a year, but still did not speak a word in class, he tried to urge her to join in class discussion.

**Teacher:** So another reflex is blinking. Everybody blinks, you blink your eye. It is not voluntary. Reflexes are involuntary. How does blinking protect you? Do you know what protect means?

**Student 1:** To keep you from harm.

**Teacher:** OK, so how does that protect you? How are you doing this with your eye, opening and closing? How is that protection? Win Xiang?

**Win Xiang:** (didn't answer)

**Teacher:** Want to help her out? (pointed to her neighbour)

**Student 3:** Keeping it from [becoming] dry.

**Teacher:** Did you hear what she said? (asked Win Xiang again)

**Win Xiang:** (nodded her head but still didn't answer verbally).

**Teacher:** Did you hear what she said just now? Can you repeat what you said? (asked the whole class)

**Student 4:** Keeping it from [becoming] dry.

**Teacher:** Can you repeat what he just said? (walked to Win Xiang and asked her for the third time)

**Win Xiang:** Keeping it from dry weather [sic].

**Teacher:** Good. Can somebody repeat what Win Xiang said loud so that everyone can hear it?

**Student 5:** When your eyes are dry you blink to moisten it [sic].

**Teacher:** Guys, did you hear that now? It keeps it from drying and keeps dirt from getting into the eye, so it protects it.

Here we see an example of Mike using several turns to get a quiet Chinese student to participate in the class discussion. Two interesting elements in the teaching comes out. First, instead of leaving the quiet student alone, Mike held a high expectation for her. At the same time he elicited responses from other students first to set up a non-threatening environment to prompt her to speak up in the end. This incident turned out to be a turning point for this Chinese student. After that I noticed an obvious change in her that she participated frequently in class.

## Appreciating diversity and using students' prior knowledge in biology teaching

Having taken courses in multicultural education and second language learning and teaching in her master's programme, Sally was keenly aware of her students' language and cultural backgrounds and the struggle they went through in learning the new language and the new culture. This understanding led her to approach ESL students differently from the way that she approached her native English students as she remarked at the interview.

> There are so many cultures in my class. Even Pakistani children from different areas of Pakistan take different foods. And we have Bengali students and students from India, they are from one part of the world, but they are so different. And there are Chinese children and they are different all over, which makes it rich, but also at the same time it can make them feel left out if you don't talk about something related to them . . . I am trying to get them to feel comfortable no matter what their answer is, it's a good answer. We will work from there and we will use it as a base, maybe not the answer that I am looking for, maybe it's just the stepping stone. So they feel comfortable enough to take risks and I think that helps the learning process . . .

Observing Sally's class, one finds her bringing in students' prior knowledge and home cultural and educational experiences to the learning task whenever it was possible. Sally's class was never quiet, instead, students were active participants in class discussion, asking questions and responding to a problem. Students' questions and opinions were not ignored or dismissed but listened, validated, and appreciated by the teacher. In her class, even the newcomers were not left alone. They were arranged to sit with the students who spoke the same language so that they could translate the lesson to them in the first few weeks or they were assigned to sit close to the teacher so that she could give extra help and checking on their understanding constantly.

Sally believed that the challenge for her students in learning biology was to make sense of the concepts that they were learning through actively participating in the learning process. Sally wanted her lesson to build on what students already knew, the cultural and educational backgrounds that they brought with them through class discussion about science. Because of her efforts and a sincere and positive attitude, her students felt comfortable to ask a question, to respond to her questions, and to communicate for the real purpose of learning biology. In a lesson on female menstrual cycle, an active dialogue was initiated by the student and an interaction between the student and the teacher dealing with biology is shown in the following class observation excerpt.

**Student 1:** Miss, I have a question.
**Teacher:** Go ahead.
**Student 1:** When does the female cycle start?
**Teacher:** When does the female menstrual cycle start in an average girl? Remember the article I brought you in earlier. It could start as early as 8 or 9, or it could start at 13 or 14.
**Student 2:** Even 19.
**Teacher:** What made you say that?
**Student 2:** My mom said they can have babies in that age [19].
**Teacher:** Oh, that's true. The female menstrual cycle can begin as early as 8 years or as late as 19 years of age. It is individual. For every single girl it is different. One girl may start say 10 years of age, 11 years of age and yet her sister may start at 15. Every girl is a little different.

Here we see students take many linguistic risks by contributing to a meaningful discussion. Students' genuine questions about the topic and their perspectives gained from home were well accepted and validated. Building on that understanding, Sally elaborated and reinforced the key concept. Sally's sensitivity to students' cultural knowledge was also reflected on her flexibility in allowing her students to include their home cultural component in the projects and homework. For example, several of her students used their home country diets to make a food pyramid. Also, many students had interviews with doctors or nurses from their own countries for their science projects.

Students in Sally's class all liked her way of teaching biology, and many students noted that she was their best teacher among all teachers in that school. Here are a few excerpts from students' interview responses:

She is my best in this school. She once brought in a crayfish for us to look at.

That makes me remember. Yesterday she brought in a model of the cell membrane of a human's brain. It's exciting. Biology is my favorite subject.

[Sally] is funny and she is nice to foreign students.

[Sally] explains things very clearly so that everyone understands. Also, she answers all the questions that we ask.

I think the best way for a teacher to teach is like her. She is talking biology like giving us a story about biology. I am so interested in listening to her stories about biology and getting to ask or answer questions about them.

### Enriching the curriculum and providing a rich language use environment

Students taught from the Regents Biology Variance curriculum conducted four science projects related to the topics that they learned throughout the year. These four projects were a report on the visit to American Natural History Museum, monthly journal entries on their observations of a natural phenomenon or an experimental study with the plants and animals, reading report on a specific medical science development in the magazines and newspapers, and interview report on someone in the field of medical sciences. One student from Albania who had been in the US for half a year interviewed her father and wrote,

I interviewed an Albanian doctor specialised in cardiology. He has been working for 30 years at the medical field. I interviewed him because it was my desire to recognise his interesting career, which is dedicated to human service . . . At the end of this investigation I asked myself that do I want to enter this career? My early childhood dream has been to be a doctor. Raised in a family where my father is a doctor and looking to him and admiring him for what he was doing, I always wondering what else can I be better that being a doctor. Having this dream I have been working hard all these years to gain a strong background in school.

One student from Indonesia who had been in the US for three years wrote journal entries about her experiment with and observation of the two plants, one with sunlight and the other without any light. Here is an excerpt from her journal.

> April 29, 1998
>
> The plant [*Accent Carmine Impatiens*] in the shoe box is almost dying. The unborn baby flower is all dead. Some of the leaves are already fallen apart. I could see the difference now between the second plant [and this one]. The second plant [at the window] is still green. Most of its leaves are green and little turn black . . . I give them water. The second plant looks very nice and the leaves are wide like yesterday's leaves. The branches are growing taller. By now I could answer my own questions between the two plants that I experimented . . .

Another student from Bosnia and who had been in the US for only half a year wrote a letter to *The New York Times* editor to argue against cloning after reading articles on cloning in that newspaper.

> It's not an easy thing to have a clear idea about something like cloning that is new and seems to be interesting. By this entire picture that I gave, I think that supporting and approving the idea of 'cloning' destroys the saintly concept of the family is and a healthy family is more useful than 'cloning' is.

A third student from Bangladesh and living in the US for a year and half wrote about his reflection on the trip to American Museum of Natural History to see an exhibition on diversity and evolution.

> I have learned a lot about earliest humans and their activities. I also learned about our earliest ancestors and how were they like with us. I may never would have learned it if didn't go to the museum. Thanks once again to my science teacher to gave me an opportunity to do my project about our ancestors.

Although the above students' writing has errors, the idea shines through. It reveals that when students are challenged to learn in an authentic and meaningful way, they will make leaps in developing both language and academic

content knowledge. The reading and writing experiences that these students had extended their thinking and expressed their intelligence about biology in a relevant and a new way. By linking biology learning with reading and writing activities, teachers fostered students' both language and academic learning skills simultaneously.

Connected with the teaching topics, all three teachers often assigned their classes reading passages taken from popular science magazines and newspapers and writing assignments based on the reading. For example, in learning about environmental issues, students in Sally's class were assigned to read a poem about how our earth changed into only a ball a few feet in diameter, floating around us (see Figure 1).

The reading to writing questions were:

(1)  Do you agree with the author? Why or why not?
(2)  Is the Earth a special place? Why or why not?

One student wrote:

> Yes, I agree with the author because it is true. When the earth is small everybody will take care of it. When it's huge nobody can take care of it. They cannot see what's happening to the world, how we are destroying the earth, and how we are killing lots of living things for survive some people. I think the earth is special because it's very beauty and wonder. It has nature, animals, people and most special about it is that it's the only one. So as future generations we just want to say 'People should take care of this earth'. We should not only care for ourselves. We should also take care of animals, trees, etc.

As shown in the above, a reading activity here was used as a content specific activity and was introduced creatively and meaningfully to make connections with the textbook concepts. Unlike the discursive discourse used in the textbook writing, the poem was written using much personalised vocabulary and simple sentence structures. Thus, students who had difficulty with reading the textbook could easily read the poem for meaning. The poem was also used as a sound board for reflection that facilitates thinking. By

If the earth were only
A few feet in diameter, floating a
few feet above a field somewhere, people
would come from everywhere to marvel at it.
people would walk around it, marveling at its big
pools of water, its little pools and the water flowing
between the pools. People would marvel at the bumps
on it, and the holes in it, and they would marvel at the
very thin layer of gas surrounding it and the water suspend
ed in the gas. The people would marvel at all the creatures
walking around the surface of the ball, and at the creature in
the water. The people would declare it precious because it
was the only one, and they would protect it so that it would
not be hurt. The ball would be the greatest wonder known
and people would come to behold it, to be healed, to
gain knowledge, to know beauty and to wonder how it
it could be. People would love it, and defend it with
their lives, because they would somehow know
that their lives, their own roundness, could
be nothing without it. If the earth
were only a few feet in
diameter

**Figure 1** The Floating Earth – Author unknown (Winter, 1990)

doing extra reading like this students not only fully understood the concept, but also learned to express themselves in science.

## Conclusion

The findings of the study offer implications for teachers to work effectively with linguistically and culturally diverse students. The three teachers' approaches to these students and the learning tasks they designed, though varied, are still similar in principle in that they all strongly believed in the abilities of their ESL students. They all verbalised and demonstrated their belief that all students can learn. Those beliefs and expectations are conveyed through their daily teaching. As Lisa, Sally and Mike have shown, when there is a language barrier, when students lack background knowledge about a subject, and when the new concept is abstract, instead of demanding students to figure it out, they adapt their teaching to create the maximum opportunity for learning. With the rapid growth of non-native English speaking students in science classrooms, this kind of understanding, orientation, and effort becomes important.

In their creation of a positive and challenging biology learning environment, the three teachers used a range of strategies consistent with the literature of teaching diverse students in both second language teaching and science education (Banks & Banks, 1997; Carrasquillo & Rodriguez, 1995; Chamot & O'Malley, 1994; Enright & McCloskey, 1988; Freeman & Freeman, 1998; Gersten, 1996; Krashen, 1985; Swain & Carroll, 1987). In working with diverse students whose native language is not English, they are more attentive to their students' backgrounds and cultural differences (Freeman & Freeman, 1998; Scarcella, 1992). They all took on the role of both a language teacher and a science teacher (Richard-Amato & Snow, 1992; Genesee, 1993; Spurlin, 1995). In their classrooms, language and biology are not independent of each other but closely interwoven. The three teachers all tailored their instruction to ease students' difficulties with content knowledge by adjusting their input and using various ways to convey meaning (Enright & McCloskey, 1988; Krashen, 1985). When these teachers show that they do care and bring content knowledge to a level that students can comprehend, students do appreciate and learn.

Both the teachers and students in this study have articulated a need for more enrichment and elaboration of the content knowledge rather than simplification. Extra readings, more student and student interactions, and after school science projects as demonstrated here seem to be both promoting language development and providing the intellectual challenge. Two major linguistic and cognitive benefits of using these speaking, reading, and writing activities in biology learning are worth noting. One, the experiences that these students had, such as interviews with a scientist, a series of observations of a scientific problem, a reflection on a museum visit and on reading a scientific article, have enabled them to make the connection between science learning in school and in real life. Two, teachers' use of reading, writing, listening, and speaking activities, specially Lisa's group work, reduced speaking anxiety and enabled students to communicate science and use speaking to do scientific reasoning. These activities provide the students with ample opportunities and rich contexts for active language use and language and literacy skills development (Chamot & O'Malley, 1994; Freeman & Freeman, 1998; Snow *et al.*, 1989). All this shows that when working with linguistically and culturally diverse students, subject matter area teachers do have an important role to play to speed up these students' second language learning and their academic success.

The findings of this study points to the need in teacher education for more exposure and practice of responsive teaching to linguistically and culturally diverse students. In teacher training programmes, preservice teachers need not only to learn about established research theories, but also field tested methods and techniques for dealing with diverse learners. Surprisingly, among the three teachers, only Sally had taken courses in second language teaching and learning and multicultural education. It is essential for all teachers to have an understanding of multicultural and multilingual issues and training in teaching practices for dealing with linguistic and cultural differences before they go into the teaching field. As has been shown by this study, at the high school level, facing demanding subject matter standards, science teachers need more varied and detailed pedagogical knowledge in order to tailor their lessons to their students' needs. Knowledge about second language learners and modelling of effective teaching will benefit all teachers who are working with ESL students on a daily basis.

The effective strategies and techniques used by the three biology teachers offer us models for effective teaching practices. As our public schools in the 21st century are becoming more and more linguistically and culturally diverse, it becomes incumbent for all the teachers to become sensitive toward these diverse students' backgrounds and needs and modify their instruction so that second language students can succeed academically as they develop English proficiency.

## References

Adamson, H.D. (1990) ESL students' use of academic skills in content courses. *English for Specific Purposes* 9, 67–87.

Anderson, O.R. (1990) *The Teaching and Learning of Biology in the United States.* New York: Teachers College, Columbia University, Second IEA Science Study.

Atwater, M.M. (1994) Research on cultural diversity in the classroom. In D.L. Gabel (ed.) *Handbook of Research on Science Teaching and Learning* (A Project of the National Science Teachers Association) (pp. 558–576). New York: Macmillan.

Banks, J.A. and Banks, C.A.M. (1997) *Multicultural Education: Issues and Perspectives* (3rd edn). Boston, MA: Allyn and Bacon.

Bernhardt, E., Hirsh, G., Teemant, A. and Rodriguez-Munoz, M. (1996) Language diversity and science: Science for limited English proficient students. *The Science Teacher* 2, 25–27.

Carrasquillo, A.L. and Rodriguez, V. (1995) *Language Minority Students in the Mainstream Classroom.* Clevedon: Multilingual Matters.

Chamot, A.U. and O'Malley, J.M. (1994) *The CALLA Handbook: Implementing the Cognitive Academic Language Learning Approach.* Reading, MA: Addison-Wesley Publishing Company.

Cummins, J. (1994) The acquisition of English as a second language. In K. Spangenberg-Urbschat and R. Pritchard (eds) *Kids Come in all Languages: Reading Instruction for ESL Students* (pp. 36–62). Newark, DE: International Reading Association.

Enright, S. and McCloskey, M.L. (1988) *Integrating English: Developing English Language and Literacy in the Multicultural Classroom.* Reading, MA: Addison-Wesley Publishing Company.

Freeman, V. and Freeman, D.E. (1998) *ESL/EFL Teaching: Principles for Success.* Portsmouth, NH: Heinemann.

Gao, L. (1998) Cultural context of school science

teaching and learning in the People's Republic of China. *Science Education* 83, 1–13.

Genesee, F. (1993) All teachers are second language teachers. *The Canadian Modern Language Review* 50, 47–53.

Gersten, R. (1996) The double demands of teaching English language learners. *Educational Leadership* 53 (5), 18–22.

Gibbs, A. and Lawson, A.E. (1992) The nature of scientific thinking as reflected by the work of biologists and biology textbooks. *The American Biology Teacher* 54 (3), 137–151.

Gonzales, N. and Schallert, D.L. (1999) An integrative analysis of the cognitive development of bilingual and bicultural children and adults. In V. Gonzales (ed.) *Language and Cognitive Development in Second Language Learning*. Needham, MA: Allyn and Bacon.

Hodson, D. (1993) In search of a rationale for multicultural science education. *Science Education* 77, 685–711.

Krashen, S. (1985) *The Input-Hypothesis: Issues and Implications*. White Plains, NY: Longman.

Lee, O. and Fradd, S.H. (1996) Literacy skills in science learning among linguistically diverse students. *Science Education* 80, 651–671.

Leonard, W.H. and Penick, J.E. (1993) What's important in selecting a biology textbook? *The American Biology Teacher* 55 (1), 15–19.

Long, M.H. and Porter, P.A. (1985) Group work, interlanguage talk, and second language acquisition. *TESOL Quarterly* 19, 207–228.

Lumpe, A.T. and Beck, J. (1996) A profile of high school biology textbooks using scientific literacy recommendations. *The American Biology Teacher* 58 (2), 147–153.

Pica, T. and Doughty, C. (1985) Input and interaction in the communicative language classroom: A comparison of teacher-fronted and group activities. In S.M. Gass and C.G. Madden (eds) *Input and Second Language Acquisition* (pp. 115–132). Rowley, MA: Newbury House.

Richard-Amato, P.A. and Snow, M.A. (1992) *The Multicultural Classroom: Readings for Contents Teachers*. Reading, MA: Addison-Wesley Publishing Company.

Rupp, J.H. (1992) Discovery science and language development. In P.R. Amato and A. Snow (eds) *Multicultural Classroom: Readings for Content-Area Teachers* (pp. 316–329). Reading, MA: Addison-Wesley Publishing Company.

Scarcella, R. (1992) Providing culturally sensitive feedback. In P.R. Amato and A. Snow *Multicultural Classroom: Readings for Content-Area Teachers* (pp. 130–145). Reading, MA: Addison-Wesley Publishing Company.

Snow, M.A., Met, M. and Genesee, F. (1989) A conceptual framework for the integration of language and content in second/foreign language instruction. *TESOL Quarterly* 23, 201–217.

Spurlin, Q. (1995) Making science comprehensible for language minority students. *Journal of Science Teacher Education* 6, 71–78.

Swain, M. and Carroll, S. (1987) The immersion observation study. In B. Harley, P. Allen, J. Cummins and M. Swain (eds) *The Development of Bilingual Proficiency: Classroom Treatment* (pp. 190–341). Toronto, ON: OISE.

Winter, P. (1990) *Earth: Voices of a Planet*. Litchfield, CT: Earth Music Productions.

## Questions

1.  Yu Ren Dong suggests that one of the best ways to learn a new language is 'in the real context of disciplinary specific language use, such as biology, social studies, math etc..' What are the advantages and disadvantages of language minority students learning a majority language (e.g. English) through, for example, biology lessons in that majority language?

2.  What are the main strategies that the research suggests form 'successful teaching'? Particularly center your answer on language and cultural observations.

3.  Compare the three teachers in this article with one effective teacher you know and show the similarities and differences. Are all four teachers' techniques equally effective in language learning and in content learning?

## Activities

1. Observe a bilingual classroom where a science is being taught. First identify the bilingual classroom observed as to its type of bilingual education. Second, observe the use of language, and particularly note episodes (including phrases) when language minority students appear not to comprehend. Write a list of successful strategies that the teacher uses. Share these with the class.

2. Make an inventory of all the texts used in the teaching of science in a bilingual classroom. Identify their language and language variety(ies) used, genres, country where published, richness and variety of content, richness of language, quality of printing, quality of illustrations, ethnic content, bicultural and / or multicultural content and gender content. Compare the list of texts to teach science in the majority language with any written material used to teach science in the minority language. Then observe at least one lesson in each language. How are the texts used? How would you evaluate their use?

3. Develop a language-sensitive lesson in a content area. As the article suggests, consider the following: grade and language level, subject area, topic, core vocabulary, materials and human resources needed, skills, concepts, knowledge, thinking processes and attitudes engendered, extension activities and assessment.

4. Visit both an elementary school and a secondary school that have a large language minority population. Focus on one language minority student who has recently arrived and one who has been in the country for at least five years. Make a chart showing the courses / subjects each of the students take. Draw comparisons between the elementary and secondary curriculum, and between the curriculum of the recently arrived student and that of the student with longer residency.

5. Design a structure for an effective secondary school for language minority students in a community with which you're familiar. Make sure that you take the community's sociolinguistic profile into account. Then make a list of the features that the school would have. After preparing the list, prepare a speech to encourage prospective parents to send their children to this school. Set up a role playing situation in which you deliver this speech to the class (exactly as it would be given to prospective parents). Have the class evaluate its effectiveness.

6. Prepare a public oral presentation on the arguments for integration of language and content. Some in the class should take the position of opposing bilingual education, while others should role play being supporters of bilingualism as a goal. If your role is to oppose bilingualism, make sure you show how integration of language and content can be used to expedite the shift to the majority language. If your role is to support bilingualism and biliteracy, be specific about when this integration is dangerous and when it can be useful. Have a student panel evaluate who was most convincing.

## Further Reading

Baker, C. (2006) *Foundations of Bilingual Education and Bilingualism* (4th edn). Clevedon: Multilingual Matters (chapter 13).

Barwell, R. (2005) Ambiguity in the mathematics classroom. *Language and Education*, 19, 2, 118–126. (also other articles in that Issue on problems of language and science / mathematics content).

Carrasquillo, A.L. and Rodriquez, V. (2001) *Language Minority Students in the Mainstream Classroom* (2nd edn). Clevedon: Multilingual Matters.

Dong, Yu Ren (2004) *Teaching Language and Content to Linguistically and Culturally Diverse Students.* Greenwich, CT: Information Age Publishing

Ovando, C.J., Collier, V.P. and Combs, M.C. (2003) *Bilingual and ESL Classrooms: Teaching in Multicultural Contexts* (3rd edn). New York: McGraw Hill.

# Bilingual Classroom Studies and Community Analysis: Some Recent Trends

## Luis C. Moll

Most children attending bilingual education classes in the United States are working-class students. Although rarely addressed in the literature, this fact has major implications for the goals and nature of instruction in these classrooms. In comparison with the schooling of peers from higher-income families, instruction for working-class students, be it in bilingual or monolingual classrooms, can be characterized as rote, drill and practice, and intellectually limited, with an emphasis on low-level literacy and computational skills (see, e.g. Anyon, 1980, 1981; Goldenberg, 1984, 1990; Oakes, 1986; also see Goodlad, 1984). This reduction of the curriculum is not only in terms of content, but in terms of limited and constrained uses of literacy and mathematics, the primary instructional means.

This working-class 'identity' of bilingual education is also reflected in the types of questions and issues that guide bilingual education research. In general, the dominant issues in bilingual education are related to English language learning and assimilation of students into the mainstream, with scant attention paid to academic development or broader social and instructional dynamics. Typical questions include how to determine language dominance; how long the first language should be used in instruction; when to mainstream or transfer students to English-only instruction; and, of course, what sorts of language tests to use to evaluate the effectiveness of one program versus another.

García and Otheguy (1985, 1987), in their revealing research on private bilingual schools located within Cuban working-class (and other) communities in Dade County, FL, have pointed

out the myopia that seems to affect the field of bilingual education research. They report starting their study by trying to address some of the core bilingual education questions mentioned above (García & Otheguy, 1987: 85). They soon discovered that these questions were irrelevant or inapplicable to the schools they were studying. Indeed, their respondents could hardly make sense of their questions: 'These issues are not relevant at all to the people we interviewed. These community educators were only concerned about the best possible way of educating their own children. None of the [Cuban] schools focused solely on bilingualism or monolingualism as a goal. *In fact, there was remarkably little interest in language questions*' (p. 90, emphasis in original). Curricular issues common in bilingual education, such as remedial instruction, the categorization of children by language dominance, or the language of initial reading, were also dismissed by these educators as irrelevant if not nonsensical, and in some instances they had never even heard of them (pp. 90–92).

The primary concern in these schools, then, was not with the typical language issues associated with bilingual education, but with pedagogical issues and academic development, with providing a quality education for the children. Spanish and English fluency and literacy were simply expected and developed as unquestioned, valuable, obvious goals for Cuban children living and going to school in the United States. As the authors reported, in these schools, 'the use of both languages is considered the only natural – indeed the only conceivable – way of educating children' (1985: 13).

García and Otheguy (1987) concluded that

their initial research questions failed because they had uncritically accepted the status quo in bilingual public schools and the limited vision of what is important or what counts as education for these children. They wrote: 'We too had framed our original questions within what one might call the majority context, that is, the intellectual and pedagogical context within which most US-born, white, English-speaking educators frame their thinking about the education of linguistic minorities' (p. 92). This is a context that focuses on 'disadvantages', where explanations of these students' school performance usually assume they come from socially and intellectually limiting family environments, or that these students lack ability, or there is something wrong with their thinking or their values, especially in comparison with wealthier peers (Díaz *et al.*, 1986). This is also a context where the obsession with speaking English reigns supreme – as if the children were somehow incapable of learning that language well, or as if the parents and teachers were unaware of the importance of English in US society – and usually at the expense of other educational or academic matters. In short, to the extent that researchers and practitioners in bilingual education uncritically accept this limited vision of students, and the reductionist instruction that supports this vision, they help sustain beliefs and practices that severely constrain what bilingual teachers and students can accomplish.

## Some Recent Trends

In what follows, I present an example from a recent study in bilingual education that addresses broader social and academic issues than simply learning English, remedial instruction, or basic skills. This study takes what could be called a sociocultural approach to instruction (for additional examples, see Moll, 1990; Moll & Díaz, 1987; also see Cole, 1990; Newman *et al.*, 1989; Rosebery *et al.*, 1990; Tharp & Gallimore, 1988). This approach, influenced in great part by Vygotsky's (1978) and Luria's (1981) formulation of how social practices and the use of cultural artifacts mediate thinking, highlights how classrooms (or households) are always socially and culturally organized settings, artificial creations, whose specific practices mediate the intellectual work children accomplish. When classrooms are viewed in this way, a key focus of study becomes how (and why) children come to use essential

'cultural tools', such as reading, writing, mathematics, or certain modes of discourse, within the activities that constitute classroom life.

These studies, therefore, contribute to recent discussion in these pages and elsewhere on 'participatory' or 'apprenticeship' models of instruction that emphasize 'socializing' or 'enculturating' students into the important practices of, for example, a highly literate or scientific classroom community (see, e.g. Brown *et al.*, 1989; Palincsar, 1989; also see Farnham-Diggory, 1990; Goodman & Goodman, 1990; Heath & Mangiola, 1991; Hursch, 1989; Holt, 1990). As Resnick (1990) has recently explained in relation to literacy instruction:

> The shift in perspective from personal skill to cultural practice carries with it implications for a changed view of teaching and instruction If literacy is viewed as a bundle of skills, then education for literacy is most naturally seen as a matter of organizing effective lessons: that is, diagnosing skill strength and deficits, providing appropriate exercises in developmentally felicitous sequences, motivating students to engage in these exercises, giving clear explanation and direction. But if literacy is viewed as a set of cultural practices then education for literacy is more naturally seen as a process of socialization, of induction into a community of literacy practic*ers*. (p. 171, emphasis in original)

Creating the social and cultural conditions for this socialization into 'authentic' literacy practices, or into doing science and mathematics, is central to the studies cited above, and to the example presented below. Within this bilingual classroom, children are active learners using language and literacy, in either English or Spanish, as tools for inquiry, communication, and thinking. The role of the teacher, which is critical, is to enable and guide activities that involve students as thoughtful learners in socially and academically meaningful tasks. This emphasis on active research and learning leads to the realization that these children (and their families) contain ample resources, which we have termed *funds of knowledge*, that can form the bases for an education that far exceeds what working-class students usually receive.

Next I describe research that my colleagues and I are conducting in Latino (predominantly

Mexican) households and bilingual classrooms in Tucson, AZ (Moll & Greenberg, 1990;
Moll *et al.*, 1990). I first explain what we mean
by funds of knowledge and then present an
example of a teacher using this concept in the
teaching of literacy to bilingual students. This
study, I must emphasize, is only one of several
that is helping facilitate a critical redefinition of
bilingual education and its purposes (see, e.g.
McCarty, 1989). Each in its own way attempts
to create positive change in bilingual classrooms
by taking full advantage of the sociocultural
resources in the surrounding environment,
including the children's developing bilingualism
and knowledge, and in so doing, illustrates how
easily we educators have come to accept notions
of limitations and deficits in the education of
these children .

## A Funds-of-Knowledge Perspective

The guiding principle in our work is that the
students' community represents a resource of
enormous importance for educational change
and improvement. We have focused our analysis
on the sociocultural dynamics of the children's
households, especially on how these households
function as part of a wider, changing economy,
and how they obtain and distribute resources of
all types through the creation of strategic social
ties or networks (see, e.g. Vélez-Ibáñez, 1988;
Vélez-Ibáñez & Greenberg, 1989). For present
purposes, I will discuss only the breadth of the
knowledge that these social networks can facilitate for a household.

In contrast to many classrooms, households
never function alone or in isolation; they are
always connected to other households and institutions through diverse social networks. For
families with limited incomes, these networks
can be a matter of survival because they facilitate
different forms of economic assistance and labor
cooperation that help families avoid the expenses
involved in using secondary institutions, such as
plumbing companies or automobile repair shops.
These networks can also serve other important
functions, including finding jobs and providing
assistance with child care, releasing mothers, if
need be, to enter the labor market. In brief, these
networks form social contexts for the acquisition
of knowledge, skills, and information, as well as
cultural values and norms. Given their importance to a household's well-being, family members
invest considerable energy and resources in maintaining good social relations with others that make

up the networks. These relations are maintained
through participation in family rituals, such as
baptisms, *quinceañeras* (adolescent girls' 'debutante'
parties), and weddings, and through frequent, and
sometimes strategic, visits (Vélez-Ibáñez, 1988;
Vélez-Ibáñez & Greenberg, 1989).

From our perspective, the essential function
of these social networks is that they share
or exchange what we have termed *funds of
knowledge*: the essential cultural practices and
bodies of knowledge and information that
households use to survive, to get ahead, or to
thrive (see Greenberg, 1989). These funds of
knowledge are acquired primarily, but not exclusively, through work and participation in diverse
labor markets. With our sample, much of this
knowledge is related to the households' rural
origins and, of course, to current employment
or occupations in what is often an unstable and
highly segmented labor market (for examples,
see Moll & Greenberg, 1990; Vélez-Ibáñez &
Greenberg, 1989).

The knowledge and skills that such households
(and their networks) possess are truly impressive. To make the point, consider the information
presented in abbreviated form in Table 1. This
information was culled from our field notes and
interviews with a sample of 30 families. We have
visited families that know about different soils, cultivation of plants, seeding, and water distribution
and management. Others know animal husbandry,
veterinary medicine, ranch economy, and
mechanics. Many families know about carpentry,
masonry, electrical wiring, fencing, and building
codes. Some families employ folk remedies, herbal
cures, midwifery, and intricate first aid procedures.
And family members with more formal schooling
have knowledge about (and have worked in)
archaeology, biology, and mathematics.

We argue that these families and their funds of
knowledge represent a *potential* major social and
intellectual resource for the schools. Consider
that every classroom has approximately 30
students in it; these students represent 30 households *and* their networks with their respective
funds of knowledge. The key point is not only
that there are ample funds of knowledge among
these working-class households, but that this
knowledge is socially distributed. When needed,
such knowledge is available and accessible
through the establishment of relationships that
constitute social networks.

How can a teacher make use of these funds
of knowledge within the usual classroom condi-

**Table 1** A sample of household funds of knowledge

| Agriculture and mining | Economics | Household management | Material and scientific knowledge | Medicine | Religion |
|---|---|---|---|---|---|
| Ranging and Farming<br>  Horsemanship<br>  (cowboys)<br>  Animal<br>  husbandry<br>  Soil and<br>  irrigation<br>  systems<br>  Crop planting<br>  Hunting,<br>  Tracking,<br>  Dressing<br>Mining<br>  Timbering<br>  Minerals<br>  Blasting<br>  Equipment<br>  operation and<br>  maintenance | Business<br>  Market<br>  values<br>  Appraising<br>  Renting and<br>  selling<br>  Loans<br>  Labor laws<br>  Building<br>  codes<br>  Consumer<br>  knowledge<br>  Accounting<br>  Sales | Budgets<br>Childcare<br>Appliance<br>repairs | Construction<br>  Carpentry<br>  Roofing<br>  Masonry<br>  Painting<br>  Design and<br>  architecture<br>Repair<br>  Airplane<br>  Automobile<br>  Tractor<br>  House<br>  maintenance | Contemporary<br>medicine<br>  Drugs<br>  First aid<br>  procedures<br>  Anatomy<br>  Midwifery<br>Folk medicine<br>  Herbal<br>  knowledge<br>  Folk cures<br>  Folk vetinary<br>  cures | Catechism<br>Baptisms<br>Bible studies<br>Moral<br>knowledge<br>and ethics |

tions? We have been experimenting with various arrangements, including having teachers conduct household visits to document funds of knowledge (see Moll *et al.*, in press). Central to this work has been the development of after-school settings where we meet with teachers to analyze their classrooms, to discuss household observations, and to jointly develop innovations in the teaching of literacy, among other matters. These after-school settings represent social contexts for informing, assisting, and supporting the teachers' work: a setting, in our terms, for teachers and researchers to exchange funds of knowledge (for details, see Moll *et al.*, 1990).

Consider the work of a bilingual sixth grade teacher in our project, Ina A., and her development of what we have called the *construction module* (see Moll & Greenberg, 1990). She got the idea for the module (or thematic unit) from the work of other teachers and researchers in the after-school setting, who were experimenting with an instructional activity centered around the topics of construction and building. Construction, it turns out, is a topic of considerable interest to

the students and a prominent fund of knowledge among the households (see Table 1). Ina decided to implement this module in her classroom in an attempt to integrate home and school knowledge around an academic activity. Her efforts, summarized below, represent a good example of mobilizing funds of knowledge for instruction.

## Creating Strategic Social Networks for Teaching

After discussing with the students the idea of a module or theme study about construction, the teacher asked them to visit the library and start locating information, in either Spanish or English, on the topic. The students obtained materials, for example, on the history of dwellings and on different ways of building structures. Meanwhile, the teacher, through her own research in a community library and in the school district's media center, also located a series of books on construction and on different professions involved in construction, including books on architects and carpenters, and included them as part of the literate resources the class could use in developing the module. The students also built model houses or other structures as homework, using materials available in their homes, and wrote brief essays describing their research or explaining their construction (see Moll & Greenberg, 1990).

The teacher, however, did not stop there. She proposed to the class inviting parents or other community members who were experts on the topic to provide information that could expand the students' knowledge and work. The teacher reported that the children were surprised but intrigued by the idea of inviting their parents to the class as experts, especially given some of the parents' lack of formal schooling. The first two visitors were the father of one of the girls in the class, who worked for the school district, and a community member who worked in construction. The teacher was particularly interested in their describing their use of construction instruments and tools, and how they used mathematics in their work to estimate or measure the area or perimeter of a location, for example. The teacher described the visits as follows (from Moll & Greenberg, 1990):

> The first experience was a total success... We received two parents. The first one, Mr S., father of one of my students, works at [the school district] building portable classrooms. He built his own house, and he helped my student do her project. He explained to the students the basic details of construction. For example, he explained about the foundation of a house, the way they need to measure the columns, how to find the perimeter or area... After his visit, the children wrote what they learned about this topic. It was interesting to see how each one of them learned something different: e.g. the vocabulary of construction, names of tools, economic concerns, and the importance of knowing mathematics in construction. (p. 338)

Building on her initial success, the teacher invited others to make their expertise available to the class:

> The next parent was Mr T. He was not related to any of the students. He is part of the community and a construction worker. His visit was also very interesting. He was nervous and a little embarrassed, but after a while he seemed more relaxed. The children

asked him a great number of questions. They wanted to know how to make the mix to put together bricks... He explained the process and the children were able to see the need for understanding fractions in mathematics because he gave the quantities in fractions. They also wanted to know how to build arches. He explained building arches through a diagram on the board, and told the students that this was the work of engineers. (pp. 338–339)

What is important is that the teacher invited parents and others in the community to contribute *intellectually* to the development of lessons; in our terms, she started developing a social network to access funds of knowledge for academic purposes. In total, about 20 community people visited the classroom during the semester to contribute to lessons. The teacher used various sources of funds of knowledge, including the students' own knowledge and the results of their research, their parents and relatives, the parents of students in other classrooms, and the teacher's own social relationships, including other school staff, community members, and university personnel. These classroom visits were not trivial; parents and others came to share their knowledge, expertise, or experiences with the students and the teacher. This knowledge, in turn, became part of the students' work or a focus of study (Moll & Greenberg, 1990).

As the year progressed, these funds of knowledge became a regular feature of classroom instruction. The teacher also used homework assignments as a vehicle to tap the funds of knowledge of the students' homes and other locations, such as work sites. All of these activities, from the planning and interviewing to the preparation of a final product by the students, involved considerable reading and writing in both languages by the students. Literacy in English and Spanish occurred as a means of analysis and expression, not as isolated reading and writing exercises. To support the development of writing, and to enable individual assessments, the teacher organized peer-editing groups that focused on how to improve the writing to facilitate the clear expression of ideas, whether in English or Spanish. The teacher evaluated the students' progress by their ability to deal with new and more complex activities, and by their ability to read and produce more sophisticated writing to accomplish those activities.

Through the development of a social network for teaching, the teacher convinced herself that valuable knowledge existed beyond the classroom and that it could be mobilized for academic purposes. She also understood that teaching *through* the community, as represented by the people in the various social networks and their collective funds of knowledge, could become part of the classroom routine, that is, part of the 'core' curriculum. The teacher's role in these activities became that of a facilitator, mediating the students' interactions with text and with the social resources made available to develop their analysis, and monitoring their progress in reading and writing in two languages.

## Conclusion

A sociocultural approach to instruction presents new possibilities in bilingual education, where the emphasis is not solely on remediating students' English language limitations, but on utilizing available resources, including the children's or the parents' language and knowledge, in creating new, advanced instructional circumstances for the students' academic development. It is revealing, however, that our case study example, as well as other studies of this genre (e.g. Rosebery *et al.*, 1990), represent attempts at change that begin at the classroom level, with the teachers (and researchers) and the students actively shaping and giving intellectual direction to their work. These studies represent, therefore, positive examples, and perhaps a challenge to the instructional status quo, but certainly not systemic changes in bilingual education. It is, nonetheless, this focus on bringing broader research issues to bear on local circumstances that holds promise for change in bilingual education. As Goldenberg & Gallimore (1991) have remarked, 'The prospect of reforming schools depends on a better understanding of the interplay between research knowledge and local knowledge. The more we know about the dynamics of this interplay, the more likely it is that the research can have an effect on the nature and effectiveness of schools' (p. 2).

Our work, then, is an attempt at what could be called 'situated' change. We start with (or develop) the understanding that all classrooms are artificial creations, culturally mediated settings, in the Vygotskian sense, organized around beliefs and practices that control and regulate the intellectual life of the students. The role of the teachers within these systems is critical, as are their conceptions of what counts or is appropriate in the education of bilingual students, conceptions that are influenced by the larger school and societal context. We have found, as have others (e.g. Tharp & Gallimore, 1988), that although teachers may be quite willing to work for change, developing and implementing innovations is difficult and laborious work. Teachers, however, need not work alone; they can form study groups or other settings as special social and intellectual contexts to plan, support, and study change.

Within these settings teachers can collaborate with other colleagues, including researchers and parents, and receive assistance, as needed, in developing their thinking and their teaching. Creating and maintaining such supportive contexts with teachers seem to be indispensable aspects of obtaining positive change in education; that is, transformation in the conditions for teaching, and for thinking, is necessary if we are to obtain change in the students' classroom performance (see Richardson, 1990; Tharp & Gallimore, 1988, 1989).

The examples included herein illustrate that practical change can be socially arranged by using and developing the students', teachers', and communities' sociocultural resources, their funds of knowledge, in the service of that change. In doing so, researchers must redefine their roles, transform themselves from passive recorders or analysts of educational success or failure to collaborators in developing potential, exploring possibilities, and perhaps forging a vision of the children's future that will facilitate instead of constrain the education they experience in the present.

## Note

This study was funded by the Office of Bilingual Education and Minority Language Affairs (OBEMLA) of the US Department of Education, and formed part of the Innovative Approaches Research Project, directed by Charlene Rivera at Development Associates, Inc., in Washington, DC. The views expressed in this paper are those of the author and do not necessarily represent the views of OBEMLA.

# References

Anyon, J. (1980) Social class and the hidden curriculum of work. *Journal of Education* 162 (1), 67–92.

Anyon, J. (1981) Social class and school knowledge. *Curriculum Inquiry* 12 (1), 3–42.

Brown, J.S., Collins, A. and Duguid, P. (1989) Situated cognition and the culture of learning. *Educational Researcher* 18 (1), 32–42.

Cole, M. (1990) Cultural psychology: A once and future discipline? (CHIP Report No. 131). San Diego: University of California, Center for Human Information Processing.

Diaz, S., Moll, L.C. and Mehan, H. (1986) Sociocultural resources in instruction: A context-specifc approach. In California State Department of Education. *Beyond Language: Social and Cultural Factors in Schooling Language Minority Children* (pp. 187–230). Los Angeles: Evaluation, Dissemination and Assessment Center, California State University.

Farnham-Diggory, S. (1990) *Schooling.* Cambridge, MA: Harvard University Press.

García, O. and Otheguy, R. (1985) The masters of survival send their children to school: Bilingual education in the ethnic schools of Miami. *Bilingual Review/Revista Bilingue* 12 (1&2), 3–19.

García, O. and Otheguy, R. (1987) The bilingual educating of Cuban-American children in Dade County's ethnic schools. *Language and Education* 1 (2), 83–95.

Goldenberg, C. (1984) Roads to reading: Studies of Hispanic First Graders at risk for reading failure. Unpublished doctoral dissertation, University of California, Los Angles.

Goldenberg, C. (1990) Beginning literacy instruction for Spanish-speaking children. *Language Arts* 87 (2), 590–8.

Goldenberg, C. and Gallimore, R. (1991) Local knowledge, research knowledge and educational change: A case study of early Spanish reading improvement. *Educational Researcher* 20 (8), 2–14.

Goodlad, J. (1984) *A Place Called School.* New York: McGraw-Hill.

Goodman, Y. and Goodman, K. (1990) Vygotsky in a whole language perspective. In L.C. Moll (ed.) *Vygotsky and Education* (pp. 223–50). Cambridge: Cambridge University Press.

Greenberg, J.B. (1989) Funds of knowledge. Historical constitution, social distribution and transmission. Paper presented at the Annual Meeting of the Society for Applied Anthropology, Santa Fe.

Heath, S.B. and Mangiola, L. (1991) *Children of Promise: Literate Activity in Linguistically and Culturally Diverse Classrooms.* Washington, DC: National Education Association.

Hirsch, B. (1989) *Language of Thought.* New York: College Entrance Examination Board.

Holt, T. (1990) *Thinking Historically.* New York: College Entrance Examination Board.

Luria, A. (1981) *Language and Cognition.* New York: Wiley and Sons.

McCarty, T.L. (1989) School as community: The Rough Rock demonstration. *Harvard Educational Review* 59 (4), 484–503.

Moll, L.C. (ed.) (1990) *Vygotsky and Education.* Cambridge: Cambridge University Press.

Moll, L.C., Amanti, C. Neff, D. and Gonzalez, N. (in press) Funds of knowledge of teaching: A qualitative approach to connecting homes and classrooms. *Theory into Practice.*

Moll, L.C. and Díaz, S. (1987) Change as the goal of educational research. *Anthropology and Education Quarterly* 18, 300–11.

Moll, L.C. and Greenberg, J. (1990) Creating zones of possibilities: Combining social contexts for instruction. In L.C. Moll (ed.) *Vygotsky and Education* (pp. 319–48). Cambridge: Cambridge University Press.

Moll, L.C., Vélez-Ibáñez, C., Greenberg, J., Whitmore, K., Saavedra, E., Dworin, J. and Andrade, R. (1990) Community knowledge and classroom practice: Combining resources for literacy instruction (OBEMLA Contract No. 300-87-0131). Tucson, AZ: University of Arizona, College of Education and Bureau of Applied Research in Anthropology.

Newman, D., Griffin, P. and Cole, M. (1989) *The Construction Zone: Working for Cognitive Change in Schools.* Cambridge: Cambridge University Press.

Oakes, J. (1986) Tracking, inequality, and the rhetoric of school reform: Why schools don't change. *Journal of Education* 168, 61–80.

Palincsar, A.M. (1989) Less charted waters. *Educational Researcher* 18 (4), 5–7.

Resnick, L. (1990) Literacy in school and out. *Daedalus* 19 (2), 169–85.

Richardson, V. (1990) Significant and worthwhile change in teaching practice. *Educational Researcher* 19 (7), 10–18.

Rosebery, A.S., Warren, B. and Conant, F.R. (1990) Appropriating scientific discourse: Findings from language minority classrooms (Technical Report No 7353). Cambridge, MA: Bolt, Beranak and Newman.

Rosebery, A.S., Warren, B. Conant, F.R. and Barnes, J.H. (1990) Cheche Konnen: Collaborative scientific inquiry in language minority classrooms (OBEMLA Contract No. 300-87-0131). Cambridge, MA: Bolt, Beranak and Newman.

Tharp, R. and Gallimore, R. (1988) *Rousing Minds to Life: Teaching, Learning and Schooling in Social Context*. Cambridge: Cambridge University Press.

Tharp, R. and Gallimore, R. (1989) Rousing schools to life. *American Educator* 13 (2), 20–25, 46–52.

Vélez-Ibáñez, C.G. and Greenberg, J. (1989) Formation and transformation of funds of knowledge among US Mexican households in the context of the borderlands. Paper presented at the Annual Meeting of the American Anthropological Association, Washington, DC.

Vygotsky, L.S. (1979) *Mind in Society*. Cambridge, MA: Harvard University Press.

## Questions

1. How has instruction for working-class students usually been characterized? What does Moll mean by 'a sociocultural approach to instruction'? How does this relate to 'critical pedagogy?'
2. What are 'funds of knowledge'? Make a list of the social networks that exist in your community and the funds of knowledge that they transmit. How are such 'funds of knowledge' shared among households?
3. Contrast how households work with how classrooms work. Why are social networks very necessary in working-class families?
4. Why are 'funds of knowledge' important for teaching language minority children? Give some examples of how teachers might use 'funds of knowledge' in their classrooms?

## Activities

1. The guiding principle in Moll's work is 'that the students' community represents a resource of enormous importance for educational change and improvement'. Design a poster in which you list the resources in your community that are valuable to children and schools, and in particular to language minority students and schools interested in bilingualism.
2. Visit two families from ethnolinguistic minorities and list their social networks and their funds of knowledge. Make a chart for the class.
3. Imagine a school where parents and other community members contribute intellectually in the classroom. Compose a policy for the school that lists:
    a. the aims and goals of this activity
    b. the frequency and process of the contribution
    c. the type of topics that would be included.
4. Design a classroom unit based on the 'funds of knowledge' of your community. Involve community residents in the planning of the unit. Share it with the class.

## Further Reading

Carrasquillo, A.L. and Rodriguez, V. (2001) *Language Minority Students in the Mainstream Classroom* (2nd edn). Clevedon: Multilingual Matters.

Moll, L.C. (2001) The diversity of schooling: A cultural-historical approach. In M. Reyes and J. Halcón (eds) *The Best for Our Children: Critical Perspectives on Literacy for Latino Students*. New York: Teachers College Press.

Pérez, B. (ed.) (1998) *Sociocultural Contexts of Language and Literacy*. Mahwah, NJ: Lawrence Erlbaum.

Valdés, G. (1996) *Con Respeto. Bridging the Distances between Culturally Diverse Families and Schools.* New York: Teachers College Press.

Valdés, G. (1998) The world outside and inside school: Language and immigrant children. *Educational Researcher* 27 (6), 4–18.

Valdés, G. (2003) *Expanding Definitions of Giftedness: The Case of Young Interpreters from Immigrant Communities.* Mahwah, NJ: Lawrence Erlbaum.

# English Language Learners with Special Needs: Effective Instructional Strategies

## Alba Ortiz

Students fail in school for a variety of reasons. In some cases, their academic difficulties can be directly attributed to deficiencies in the teaching and learning environment. For example, students with limited English may fail because they do not have access to effective bilingual or English as a second language (ESL) instruction. Students from lower socioeconomic backgrounds may have difficulty if instruction presumes middle-class experiences. Other students may have learning difficulties stemming from linguistic or cultural differences. These difficulties may become more serious over time if instruction is not modified to address the students' specific needs. Unless these students receive appropriate intervention, they will continue to struggle, and the gap between their achievement and that of their peers will widen over time.

Still other students need specialized instruction because of specific learning disabilities. The overrepresentation of English language learners in special education classes (Yates & Ortiz, 1998) suggests that educators have difficulty distinguishing students who truly have learning disabilities from students who are failing for other reasons, such as limited English. Students learning English are disadvantaged by a scarcity of appropriate assessment instruments and a lack of personnel trained to conduct linguistically and culturally relevant educational assessments (Valdés & Figueroa, 1996). English language learners who need special education services are further disadvantaged by the shortage of special educators who are trained to address their language- and disability-related needs simultaneously.

Improving the academic performance of students who are from non-English backgrounds requires a focus on the prevention of failure and on early intervention for struggling learners. This article presents a framework for meeting the needs of these students in general education and suggests ways to operationalize prevention and early intervention to ensure that students meet their academic potential.

## Prevention of School Failure

Prevention of failure among English language learners involves two critical elements: the creation of educational environments that are conducive to their academic success and the use of instructional strategies known to be effective with these students (Ortiz, 1997; Ortiz & Wilkinson, 1991).

Preventing school failure begins with the creation of school climates that foster academic success and empower students (Cummins, 1989). Such environments reflect a philosophy that all students can learn and that educators are responsible for helping them learn. Positive school environments are characterized by strong administrative leadership; high expectations for student achievement; challenging, appropriate curricula and instruction; a safe and orderly environment; ongoing, systematic evaluation of student progress; and shared decision-making among ESL teachers, general education teachers, administrators, and parents. Several other factors are critical to the success of English language learners, including the following: (1) a shared knowledge base among educators about effective ways to work with students learning English, (2) recognition of the importance of the students' native language, (3) collaborative school and community relationships, (4) academically rich programs that integrate basic skill instruction with the teaching of higher order skills in both the native language and in English, and (5) effective instruction.

### A shared knowledge base

Teachers must share a common philosophy and knowledge base relative to the education of students learning English. They should be knowledgeable about all of the following areas: second language acquisition; the relationship of native language proficiency to the development of English; assessment of proficiency in the native language and English; sociocultural influences on learning; effective first and second language instruction; informal assessment strategies that can be used to monitor progress, particularly in language and literacy development; and effective strategies for working with culturally and linguistically diverse families and communities.

### Recognition of the students' native language

Language programs must have the support of principals, teachers, parents, and the community. School staff should understand that native language instruction provides the foundation for achieving high levels of English proficiency (Cummins, 1994; Krashen, 1991; Thomas & Collier, 1997). Language development should be the shared responsibility of all teachers, not only those in bilingual and ESL classes.

### Collaborative school–community relationships

Parents of students learning English must be viewed as capable advocates for their children and as valuable resources in school improvement efforts (Cummins, 1994). By being involved with the families and communities of English learners, educators come to understand the social, linguistic, and cultural contexts in which the children are being raised (Ortiz, 1997). Thus, educators learn to respect cultural differences in child-rearing practices and in how parents choose to be involved in their children's education (García & Dominguez, 1997).

### Academically rich programs

Students learning English must have opportunities to learn advanced skills in comprehension, reasoning, and composition and have access to curricula and instruction that integrate basic skill development with higher order thinking and problem solving (Ortiz & Wilkinson, 1991).

### Effective instruction

Students must have access to high-quality instruction designed to help them meet high expectations. Teachers should employ strategies known to be effective with English learners, such as drawing on their prior knowledge; providing opportunities to review previously learned concepts and teaching them to employ those concepts; organizing themes or strands that connect the curriculum across subject areas; and providing individual guidance, assistance, and support to fill gaps in background knowledge.

## Early Intervention for Struggling Learners

Most learning problems can be prevented if students are in positive school and classroom contexts that accommodate individual differences. However, even in the most positive environments, some students still experience difficulties. For these students, early intervention strategies must be implemented as soon as learning problems are noted. Early intervention means that 'supplementary instructional services are provided early in students' schooling, and that they are intense enough to bring at-risk students quickly to a level at which they can profit from high-quality classroom instruction' (Madden, Slavin, Karweit, Dolan, & Wasik, 1991, p. 594).

The intent of early intervention is to create general education support systems for struggling learners as a way to improve academic performance and to reduce inappropriate special education referrals. Examples of early intervention include clinical teaching, peer and expert consultation, teacher assistance teams, and alternative programs such as those that offer tutorial or remedial instruction in the context of general education.

### Clinical teaching

Clinical teaching is carefully sequenced. First, teachers teach skills, subjects, or concepts; then they reteach using different strategies or approaches for the benefit of students who fail to meet expected performance levels after initial instruction; finally, they use informal assessment strategies to identify the possible causes of failure (Ortiz, 1997; Ortiz & Wilkinson, 1991). Teachers conduct curriculum-based assessment to monitor student progress and use the data from these assessments to plan and modify instruction.

### Peer or expert consultation

Peers or experts work collaboratively with general education teachers to address students' learning problems and to implement recommendations for intervention (Fuchs, Fuchs, Bahr, Fernstrom, & Stecker, 1990). For example, teachers can share instructional resources, observe each other's classrooms, and offer suggestions for improving instruction or managing behavior. ESL teachers can help general education teachers by demonstrating strategies to integrate English learners in mainstream classrooms. In schools with positive climates, faculty function as a community and share the goal of helping students and each other, regardless of the labels students have been given or the programs or classrooms to which teachers and students are assigned.

### Teacher Assistance Teams (TATs)

TATs can help teachers resolve problems they routinely encounter in their classrooms (Chalfant & Pysh, 1981). These teams, comprised of four to six general education teachers and the teacher who requests assistance, design interventions to help struggling learners. Team members work to reach a consensus about the nature of a student's problem; determine priorities for intervention; help the classroom teacher to select strategies or approaches to solve the problem; assign responsibility for carrying out the recommendations; and establish a follow-up plan to monitor progress. The classroom teacher then implements the plan, and follow-up meetings are held to review progress toward resolution of the problem.

### Alternative programs and services

General education, not special education, should be primarily responsible for the education of students with special learning needs that cannot be attributed to disabilities, such as migrant students who may miss critical instruction over the course of the year or immigrant children who may arrive in U.S. schools with limited prior education. General education alternatives may include one-on-one tutoring, family and support groups, family counseling, and the range of services supported by federal Title I funds. Such support should be supplemental to and not a replacement for general education instruction.

## Referral to Special Education

When prevention and early intervention strategies fail to resolve learning difficulties, referral to special education is warranted. The responsibilities of special education referral committees are similar to those of TATs. The primary difference is that referral committees include a variety of specialists, such as principals, special education teachers, and assessment personnel. These specialists bring their expertise to bear on the problem, especially in areas related to assessment, diagnosis, and specialized instruction.

Decisions of the referral committee are formed by data gathered through the prevention, early intervention, and referral processes. The recommendation that a student receive a comprehensive individual assessment to determine whether special education services are needed indicates the following: (1) the child is in a positive school climate; (2) the teacher has used instructional strategies known to be effective for English learners; (3) neither clinical teaching nor interventions recommended by the TAT resolved the problem; and (4) other general education alternatives also proved unsuccessful. If students continue to struggle in spite of these efforts to individualize instruction and to accommodate their learning characteristics, they most likely have a learning disability (Ortiz, 1997).

## Conclusion

Early intervention for English learners who are having difficulty in school is first and foremost the responsibility of general education professionals. If school climates are not supportive and if instruction is not tailored to meet the needs of culturally and linguistically diverse students in general education, these students have little chance of succeeding. Interventions that focus solely on remediating students' learning and behavior problems will yield limited results.

The anticipated outcomes of problem-prevention strategies and early intervention include the following: a reduction in the number of students perceived to be at risk by general education teachers because of teachers' increased ability to accommodate the naturally occurring diversity of skills and characteristics of students in their classes, reduction in the number of students inappropriately referred to remedial or special education programs, reduction in the number of students inaccurately identified as having a disability, and improved student outcomes in both general and special education.

## References

Chalfant, J.C. and Psyh, M.V.D. (1981, November) Teacher assistance teams – A model for within-building problem solving. *Counterpoint*, 16–21.

Cummins, J. (1989) A theoretical framework for bilingual special education. *Exceptional Children*, 56, 111–19.

Cummins, J. (1994) Knowledge, power, and identity in teaching English as a second language. In F. Genesee (ed.) *Educating second language children: The whole child, the whole curriculum, the whole community* (pp. 103–25). Cambridge, England: Cambridge University Press.

Fuchs, D., Fuchs, L.S., Bahr, M.W., Fernstrom, P. and Stecker, P.M. (1990) Prereferral intervention: A prescriptive approach. *Exceptional Children*, 56, 493–513.

García, S.B. and Dominguez, L. (1997) Cultural contexts that influence learning and academic performance. In L.B. Silver (ed.) *Child and Adolescent Psychiatric Clinic of North America: Academic Difficulties* (pp. 621–55). Philadelphia: Saunders Co.

Krashen, S.D. (1991) *Bilingual education: A focus on current research* (FOCUS Occasional Papers in Bilingual Education No. 3). Washington, DC: National Clearinghouse for Bilingual Education. Available:www.ncela. gwu.edu/ncbepubs/focus/focus.3htm

Madden, N.A., Slavin, R.E., Karweit, N.L., Dolan, L. and Wasik, B.A. (1991) Success for all. *Phi Delta Kappan*, 72, 593–99.

Ortiz, A.A. (1997) Learning disabilities occurring concomitantly with linguistic differences. *Journal of Learning Disabilities*, 30, 321–32.

Ortiz, A.A. and Wilkinson, C.Y. (1991) Assessment and intervention model for the bilingual exceptional student (AIM for the BESt). *Teacher Education and Special Education*, 14, 35–42.

Thomas, W.P. and Collier, V. (1997) *School effectiveness for language minority students* (Resource Collection Series No. 9). Washington: National Clearinghouse for Bilingual Education.

Valdés, G. and Figueroa, R.A. (1996) *Bilingualism and testing: A special case of bias*. Norwood, NJ: Ablex.

Yates, J.R. and Ortiz, A. (1998) Issues of culture and diversity affecting educators with disabilities: A Change in demography is reshaping America. In R.J. Anderson, C.E. Keller and J.M. Karp (eds) *Enhancing diversity: Educators with disabilities in the education enterprise*. Washington: Gallaudet University Press.

## Questions

1. What reasons are there for language minority students failing in school? List the reasons in the article why English Language Learners in the United States may show an achievement gap and are overrepresented in special education classes. What reasons are due to schools and the school system? What intervention and referral measures need to be taken when students have special education needs?

2. What is the difference between prevention, intervention and referral? How are they linked? What part does assessment/diagnosis play in prevention, intervention and referral?

3. What is 'early intervention'? List examples of early intervention and give a description of each.

4. What are the measures that must be taken prior to placing a language minority child in special education?

5. In your community, what role does a student's native language play in prevention, intervention and referral? What is current practice, and what would be ideal practice?

## Activities

1. Visit a school with special education classes. Survey the classes for language minority representation. Find out if language minority students are overrepresented in those classes compared to the total population in the school. Make a graph of your results. Interview the teacher of each class. Find out whether any bilingual instruction and/or services are available to language minority students in special education. Record your answers.

2.  Imagine that the opening speaker in a debate argued that language minority students enter school needing compensatory education. All children on entry should be assessed for their deficiencies in the majority language (e.g. English), and should then be separated and given English language lessons until they matched English native speakers' competence. The speaker used the 2001 No Child Left Behind legislation to support their arguments. Compose a reply that opposes this speaker.
3.  Interview three language minority parents whose children have been referred to special education. Find out how their experiences with their children's school differ. Record the interview on an answer sheet. Different groups might select parents with different characteristics, such as language, ethnicity, race, social class, educational level, gender, settlement history.
4.  Observe two different educational settings for bilingual children with special needs – an inclusive classroom and a self-contained special education classroom. Take extensive notes of the teaching and the learning in both classrooms, as well as on the use of the child's mother tongue. What are the advantages and disadvantages of each setting?
5.  Visit special education classrooms for three types of language minority students: (1) those with physical handicaps, (2) those with learning disabilities, (3) those with emotional disabilities. What are the differences in instructional strategies used in each? When is the child's first language most used?

## Further Reading

Artiles, A.J. (2003) Special education's changing identity: Paradoxes and dilemmas in views of culture and space. *Harvard Educational Review, 73,* 2, 164–202.

Artiles, A.J. and Ortiz, A.A. (2002) English language learners with special education needs. In A.J. Artiles and A.A. Ortiz (eds) *English Language learners with Special Educational Needs.* Washington DC & McHenry, IL: Center for Applied Linguistics & Delta Systems Co.

Baca, L.M. and Cervantes H.T. (1998) *The Bilingual Special Education Interface* (3rd edn). Upper Saddle River, NJ: Prentice Hall.

Baker, C. (2006) *Foundations of Bilingual Education and Bilingualism* (4th edn). Clevedon: Multilingual Matters (chapter 15).

Frederickson, N. and Cline, T. (2002) *Special Educational Needs, Inclusion and Diversity: a Textbook.* Buckingham (UK): Open University Press.

Genesee, F., Paradis, J. and Crago, M.B. (2004) *Dual Language Development & Disorders: A Handbook on Bilingualism and Second Language Learning.* Baltimore: Paul H. Brookes.

Ortiz, A.A. and Yates, J.R. (2002) Considerations in the assessment of English language learners referred to special education. In A.J. Artiles and A.A. Ortiz (eds) *English Language Learners with Special Educational Needs.* Washington DC & McHenry, IL: Center for Applied Linguistics & Delta Systems Co.

# The No Child Left Behind Act and English Language Learners: Assessment and Accountability Issues

**Jamal Abedi**

The No Child Left Behind Act (NCLB; Public Law No. 107-110, 115 Stat. 1425, 2002), the most recent reauthorization of the Elementary and Secondary Act of 1965, holds states using federal funds accountable for student academic achievement. States are required to develop a set of high-quality, yearly student academic assessments that include, at a minimum, assessments in reading/language arts, mathematics, and science. Each year they must report student progress in terms of percentage of students scoring at the 'proficient' level or higher. This reporting is referred to as adequate yearly progress (AYP). A state's definition of AYP should also include high school graduation rates and an additional indicator for middle and elementary schools. Each state establishes a timeline for all students to reach the 'proficient' level or higher, which must be no more than 12 years after the start date of the 2001–2002 school year, provided that the first increase occurs within the first 2 years.

AYP will be reported for schools, school districts, and the state for all students. In addition, AYP must be reported for the following subgroup categories of students: (a) economically disadvantaged students, (b) students from major racial and ethnic groups,[1] (c) students with disabilities, and (d) students with limited English proficiency (LEP). Students in the LEP[2] subgroup provide a useful focus for discussing critical issues regarding AYP subgroup reports. Students in the other three subgroup categories share some of the issues pertinent to assessing LEP students, and many LEP students are also members of at least one other subgroup category.

Technical issues relating to the testing of LEP students merit discussion. However, a thorough discussion of issues related to the education and testing of LEP students is beyond the scope of this article. The focus on AYP reporting for LEP students at this juncture is important because, although issues concerning their assessment have received attention for many years, educational inequity issues have yet to be resolved. This is especially pertinent as this population continues to increase rapidly in size, with particularly high concentrations in a few states. According to the most recent educational statistics (i.e. those for the 2000–2001 school year), the total number of students labeled as LEP in the nation's public schools is more than 4.5 million (or 9.6% of total enrollment; National Center for Education Statistics [NCES], 2002). This article discusses six LEP assessment issues as they relate to AYP reporting:

1. *Inconsistency in LEP classification across and within states.* Different states and even different districts and schools within a state use different LEP classification criteria, thus causing inconsistencies in LEP classification/reclassification across different educational agencies. This directly affects the accuracy of AYP reporting for LEP students.

2. *Sparse LEP population.* The number of LEP students varies across the nation, and, in the case of a large number of states and districts, the number of LEP students is not enough for any meaningful analyses. This might skew some states' accountability and adversely affect state and federal policy decisions.

3. *Lack of LEP subgroup stability.* A student's LEP status is not stable over time, and a school's LEP population is a moving target. When a student's level of English proficiency has improved to a level considered 'proficient', that student is moved out of the LEP subgroup. Those who remain are low performing, and new students with even lower levels of language proficiency may also move into the subgroup. Therefore, even with the best resources, there is not much chance for improving the AYP indicator of the LEP subgroup over time.

4. *Measurement quality of AYP instruments for LEP students.* Students' yearly progress is measured by their performance on state-defined academic achievement tests, but studies have shown that academic achievement tests that are constructed and normed for native English speakers have lower reliability and validity for LEP populations (Abedi, Leon, & Mirocha, 2003). Therefore, results of these tests should not be interpreted for LEP students as they are for non-LEP students.

5. *LEP baseline scores.* Schools with high numbers of LEP students have lower baseline scores, which have year-to-year progress goals that are much more challenging and might be considered unrealistic, considering that their students may continue to struggle with the same academic disadvantages and limited school resources as before.

6. *LEP cutoff points.* Earlier legislation adopted a compensatory model in which students' higher scores in content areas with less language demand (such as math) could compensate for their scores in areas (such as reading) with higher language demands. NCLB, however, is based on a conjunctive model in which students should score at a 'proficient' level in all content areas required for AYP reporting. This makes the AYP requirement more difficult for schools with many LEP students.

While it is quite clear that the NCLB legislators' intention is to improve the performance of subgroups of students who have lagged behind for many years, it might unintentionally place undue test performance pressure on schools with large numbers of targeted students. This is especially unrealistic when schools may still struggle with the same limited school resources as before.

Test performance pressure may still be a reality in spite of any extra resources NCLB may provide to prevent achievement lag (as part of both Titles I and III). The situation might also create divisiveness between parents and even students. For example, students in poor-performing subgroups might be blamed for a school's poor performance rating. Parents of other students might make the AYP situation worse by moving their children to other schools. Teachers might blame students if the school receives sanctions. The following elaborates on these points.

## Inconsistency in LEP Classifications Across and Within States

To begin discussing LEP students' AYP, we need to define the LEP population. The NCLB defines LEP students as (a) being 3 to 21 years of age, (b) enrolled or preparing to enroll in elementary or secondary school, (c) either not born in the United States or speaking a language other than English, and (d) owing to difficulty in speaking, reading, writing, or understanding English, not meeting the state's proficient level of achievement to successfully achieve in English-only classrooms.

The operational definition of LEP varies considerably across schools, districts, and states. Among the many different criteria introduced by NCLB and states for classification of LEP, the most important are (a) being a nonnative speaker of English and (b) scoring low on English proficiency tests. In school districts in several states, the first criterion, being a nonnative English speaker, is based on information garnered from a home language survey. Unfortunately, the validity of this survey is threatened by parents' concerns over equity of opportunity for their children, citizenship issues, and parents' literacy level (Abedi, 2003).

Abedi *et al.* (1997) found significant discrepancies between student reporting and the school records of students speaking a language other than English at home. The school record of the number of students speaking a language other than English at home was significantly lower than what the students themselves reported. Another study (Abedi, 2003) showed a low level of relationship between language proficiency test scores and the LEP classification code. This study reported an average correlation of .223 between scores on the Language Assessment Scales and LEP classification codes across grades, explaining less than 5% of the common variance. The relationship between standardized achievement test (Stanford 9, Iowa Test of Basic Skills) results and LEP classification codes reported in this study was also weak. For example, analyses of data showed that the correlation coefficient between Stanford 9 math concepts and students' LEP code ranged from 0.045 ($n$ = 35,981) to 0.168 ($n$ = 25,336), with an average correlation of 0.122 (explaining 1.5% of the variance). The correlation between math computation and LEP code ranged from 0.028 ($n$ = 36,000) to 0.099 ($n$ = 25,342), with an average correlation of 0.069 (explaining less than 0.5% of the common variance between the two variables).

Another issue concerning the LEP subgroup is its heterogeneity. LEP students exhibit differences in level of performance, language proficiency, and family and cultural background characteristics. For example, the results of a study of fourth- and eighth-grade LEP and non-LEP students suggested that parent education is highly related to student performance (Abedi, Leon, & Mirocha, 2003). LEP students of parents with less than a high school education had a mean reading score of 25.23 ($n$ = 30,091, $SD$ = 14.10), as compared with a mean of 40.35 ($n$ = 1,649, $SD$ = 19.56) for LEP students of parents with a postgraduate education. It is interesting to note that mean reading scores for some LEP students with higher levels of parent education were higher than mean reading scores for non-LEP students with lower levels of parent education. For example, the mean reading score for LEP students whose parents had a postgraduate education ($M$= 40.35, $SD$ = 19.56, $n$ = 1,649) was higher than the mean for non-LEP students whose parents had less than a high school education ($M$ = 37.08, $SD$ = 17.84, $n$ = 16,806). A similar trend was seen for Grade 8 reading scores, as well as for math content areas (Abedi, Leon, & Mirocha, 2003).

Once again, these data suggest that students labeled as LEP differ substantially in many aspects, including family characteristics, cultural and language background, and level of English language proficiency. Thus, the LEP subgroup is not a well-defined, homogeneous group of students. However, the present discussion of the issues concerning AYP theory and practice for the LEP subgroup continues based on the existing classification of LEP students.

## Sparse LEP Population

A serious consideration in valid and reliable AYP reporting is subgroup size. If there are not enough students in a subgroup category to provide *statistically reliable* data, then schools, districts, or states will not be required to provide disaggregated reports for this subgroup category. Linn *et al.* (2002) explained the technical aspects of disaggregated reporting and the sample size necessary to compile statistically reliable reports on subgroup categories. They indicated that for statewide and large-district reporting, the number of students in these subgroup categories might not be an issue, since there are large enough numbers of students in each subgroup. However, they warned that small districts and individual schools might not be able to report statistically reliable data because of small numbers of students in each subgroup.

To illustrate this issue, Linn *et al.* (2002) included a table of standard errors of the differences between two independent sample percentages as a function of number of students. In this table, the standard error of differences in the percentages ranged from 7.1 (with 100 observations per group) to 22.4 (with 10 observations per group). These data suggest that the higher the number of students, the smaller the standard error of difference in percentages. Linn *et al.* acknowledged the trade-offs between disaggregated reporting and protecting against mistakenly identifying schools for improvement as a result of low statistical reliability. As a conclusion, they suggested a minimum group size of 25 students, which is large enough to provide reasonably statistically reliable results and detailed enough to permit subgroup reporting. However, in order to detect a moderate level of change (e.g. 5 to 6 percentage points), several hundred subjects would be needed (Hill & DePascale, 2003).

Different states have different numbers of LEP students with different backgrounds. The number of LEP students across the states in the 2000–2001 school year ranged from less than 1,000 in Vermont (1% of the total student population) to more than 1.5 million in California (25% of the total student population). In 31 of the 50 states, LEP students account for less than 5% of the state's total student population, and in 13 states LEP students account for less than 1% of the student population (NCES, 2002). Dividing the already small number of students in these states across district and student background variables reduces the total LEP enrollment in some districts to a level that might not be sufficient to perform any meaningful statistical analyses. On the other hand, the consequences of excluding LEP students from AYP reporting would be grave, because LEP students' test results might then be excluded from subgroup accountability determinations and from state and federal policy decisions.

Furthermore, since LEP student populations in different parts of the country are of different cultural and language backgrounds, excluding LEP students in smaller communities from AYP reporting may give more weight to the results obtained for LEP students in larger communities. For example, the majority of LEP students in the nation (more than 76%) have Spanish as their home language (NCES, 2002). The other 24% of LEP students come from varying language, economic, and cultural backgrounds that might produce different academic performance results. However, owing to smaller numbers and sometimes suburban locations, they might be excluded from AYP reporting, while the results for LEP students in larger communities might be overgeneralized.

## Lack of LEP Subgroup Stability

A major problem in AYP reporting for LEP students is the lack of stability of the LEP subgroup. This lack of stability is due to systematic rather than random fluctuation. The LEP subgroup is the least stable among the four subgroup categories targeted for reporting by NCLB. When an LEP student makes significant progress in math and reading (the main subject area focuses of NCLB), he or she will be reclassified as fluent English proficient (FEP) and will no longer be part of the LEP subgroup. Therefore, members of the LEP subgroup, by definition, will almost always be among the low-performing group of students and will hardly make substantial progress. In addition, new students who continually move into schools at lower levels of language proficiency will contribute to the situation of instability. Thus, schools with large numbers of LEP students will continue to remain in the 'in need of improvement' category.

In response to this risk caused by the revolving-door nature of LEP populations, several states have proposed plans that approach a 'once LEP, always LEP' classification policy for AYP reporting. These states will include 'exited' LEP students in the LEP subgroup by expanding exit criteria to include years in which the students' progress is monitored (Erpenbach et al., 2003). As a means of illustrating the effect of LEP subgroup instability on test scores, a cohort[3] of

about 14,000 LEP students was followed for a period of seven semesters, from Grade 9 (in fall 1996) to Grade 12 (in fall 1999). Students who were reclassified as non-LEP were compared with those who remained in the LEP category. For these comparisons, median percentile scores in reading and math were used. Table 1 presents the results.

As Table 1 shows, at the starting point (fall 1996), all students in the cohort had been classified as LEP. Median percentile scores for this group were 12 ($n$ = 13,989) in reading and 21 ($n$ = 14,151) in math. After each semester, some of these students who had made progress were reclassified as FEP. For example, in spring 1997, about 5% of the LEP students were classified as FEP. The median percentile scores of LEP students remained about the same in both reading ($Mdn$ = 12, $n$ = 13,255) and math ($Mdn$ = 20, $n$ = 13,402), but the FEP students showed substantially higher performance in reading ($Mdn$ = 21, $n$ = 659) than those who continued to be classified as LEP.

Major differences between the LEP and FEP students were also observed in the subsequent semesters. The median percentile score of LEP students in reading decreased from 12 in spring 1997 to 8 in fall 1997, and the median score of FEP students decreased from 21 to 15. In math, however, performance remained almost unchanged from spring 1997 to fall 1997 for both LEP (20 in spring 1997 and 21 in fall 1997) and FEP (32 in spring 1997 and 30 in fall 1997) students. In the subsequent semesters, while the performance of both LEP and FEP students remained the same with minor fluctuations, the gap between the performance of LEP and FEP students became substantial. For example, in the last semester (fall 1999), the median reading percentile score for LEP students was 7 ($n$ = 3,809), as compared with a median reading score of 18 ($n$ = 3,685) for FEP students. For math, the median percentile score for LEP students was 20 ($n$ = 3,885), as compared with a median of 31 ($n$ = 3,712) for FEP students. While, as the data suggest, both the LEP and FEP students performed well below their native English-speaking peers, the gap between LEP and FEP students remained high. These data once again suggest that language proficiency is inevitably a strong determiner of test performance, a fact reflected in the difference between the performance of LEP and non-LEP students on linguistically complex content area test items (e.g. see Abedi, Courtney, & Leon, 2003).

**Table 1** Grade 9 fall 1996 LEP cohort SAT 9 percentile rank medians

|  | Reading SAT 9 (*n*) | | Math SAT 9 (*n*) | |
|---|---|---|---|---|
|  | LEP | FEP | LEP | FEP |
| Grade 9, fall 1996 | 12 (13,989) | NA (0) | 21 (14,151) | NA (0) |
| Grade 9, spring 1997 | 12 (13,255) | 21 (659) | 20 (13,402) | 32 (674) |
| Grade 10, fall 1997 | 8 (8,300) | 15 (1,313) | 21 (8,456) | 30 (1,324) |
| Grade 10, spring 1998 | 8 (7,549) | 14 (1,987) | 19 (7,694) | 28 (2,009) |
| Grade 11, fall 1998 | 6 (5,435) | 13 (2,447) | 19 (5,523) | 26 (2,463) |
| Grade 11, spring 1999 | 7 (4,701) | 19 (3,217) | 20 (4,807) | 30 (3,242) |
| Grade 12, fall 1999 | 7 (3,809) | 18 (3,685) | 20 (3,885) | 31 (3,712) |

*Note:* NA = not applicable

## Measurement Quality of AYP Instruments: Impact of Language Complexity on LEP Assessment

A concern specific to LEP students is the impact of language factors on their assessments. Because of the confounding of test language comprehension with student demonstration of content knowledge, LEP students may show improvement in content knowledge (such as math) only when their level of academic English proficiency increases (Abedi & Lord, 2001). However, the LEP population is perpetually growing, and students are often assessed in content areas without proper time to develop sufficient English proficiency for valid testing. Thus, schools with larger numbers of LEP students are more likely to be cited as being 'in need of improvement' than schools with fewer or no LEP students.

As specified in the NCLB, state-defined achievement tests are used in measuring students' yearly progress. Most states use different kinds of standardized achievement tests. These tests might function well for measuring the academic progress of native English speakers; however, the language complexity of test items in content-based assessments makes the reliability and validity of these tests suspect for LEP students (Abedi, 2002). Solano-Flores and Trumbull (2003) found that language factors interact with test items. That is, items that are linguistically complex contribute largely to the measurement error variance observed for LEP students. In addition, as a result of the influence of students' language background on their assessment, these tests might underestimate LEP students' performance in content-based areas.

Since most standardized, content-based tests are conducted in English and field tested with mostly native English speakers, they might inadvertently function as English language proficiency tests. LEP students might have trouble demonstrating their content knowledge because they are unfamiliar with the complex linguistic structure of the questions, they might not recognize certain vocabulary forms, or they might mistakenly interpret an item literally (Duran, 1989; García, 1991). Also, they may not perform as well on tests because they read more slowly (Mestre, 1988). In addition, issues related to standardized achievement tests are more profound with norm-referenced tests than criterion-referenced tests. In the case of LEP students, many states still use norm-referenced tests for AYP reporting (Erpenbach *et al.*, 2003).

Research has demonstrated that language background affects students' performance, particularly in content-based assessments (Abedi & Lord, 2001; Abedi *et al.*, 2000; Solano-Flores & Trumbull, 2003). A student possessing content knowledge, such as in mathematics, science, or history, is not likely to demonstrate this knowledge effectively if she or he cannot interpret the vocabulary and linguistic structures of the test. Minor changes in the wording of content-related test items can raise student performance (Abedi & Lord, 2001; Abedi *et al.*, 1997; Cummins *et al.*, 1988; De Corte *et al.*, 1985; Hudson, 1983; Riley *et al.*, 1983). Accordingly, one approach to testing LEP students involves rewording test items to minimize construct irrelevant linguistic complexity.

Recent studies have used the linguistic modification approach as an alternative in the

**Table 2** Numbers of LEP and non-LEP students and effect size estimates

|  | Number of students | | Effect size | | |
|:---:|:---:|:---:|:---:|:---:|:---:|
| Grade | LEP | Non-LEP | Reading | Math calculation | Math analytical |
| 3 | 996 | 13,054 | 0.18 | 0.07 | 0.15 |
| 6 | 726 | 12,628 | 0.24 | 0.09 | 0.18 |
| 8 | 692 | 11,792 | 0.22 | 0.09 | 0.15 |

assessment of LEP students. These studies compared student scores on NAEP original test items with tests containing parallel items in which the mathematics task and terminology were retained but noncontent vocabulary and linguistic structures were modified. The results of these studies consistently show higher performance for LEP students on linguistically modified test items (Abedi & Lord, 2001; Abedi *et al.*, 1997, 2000; Kiplinger *et al.*, 2000; Maihoff, 2002).

Some linguistic features slow down the reader, make misinterpretation more likely, and add to the reader's cognitive load, thus interfering with concurrent tasks. Indexes of language difficulty include word frequency/familiarity, word length, and sentence length. Other linguistic features that might cause difficulty for readers include passive voice constructions, comparative structures, prepositional phrases, sentence and discourse structure, subordinate clauses, conditional clauses, relative clauses, concrete versus abstract or impersonal presentations, and negation.

To illustrate the impact of language on content-based assessments, a brief discussion is provided of results from analyses of extant data (see Note 3) in which the performance of LEP and non-LEP students was compared on math analytical, math concepts, estimation, problem solving, and math computation involving varying degrees of language demand. Performance differences were estimated in terms of effect sizes (Cohen, 1988; Kirk, 1995, pp. 180–182). There were 996 LEP and 13,054 non-LEP students in the Grade 3 sample, 726 LEP and 12,628 non-LEP students in the Grade 6 sample, and 692 LEP and 11,792 non-LEP students in the Grade 8 sample. Table 2 shows effect sizes along with the numbers of students in Grades 3, 6, and 8 in reading, math calculation, and math analytical. As the data in Table 2 show, results were consistent across the three grade levels. For example, reading effect sizes were 0.18 in Grade 3, 0.24 in Grade 6, and

0.22 in Grade 8. The corresponding effect sizes were 0.07, 0.09, and 0.09 for math calculation and 0.15, 0.18, and 0.15 for math analytical.

For reading, the effect sizes across the grade levels ranged from 0.18 for Grade 3 to 0.24 for Grade 6. These effect sizes could be considered medium. For math analytical, the effect sizes ranged between 0.15 for Grades 3 and 8 to 0.18 for Grade 6; these effect sizes were substantially smaller than those for reading. For math calculation, the effect sizes ranged between 0.09 for Grades 6 and 8 to 0.07 for Grade 3. These effect sizes for math calculation were smaller than those for math analytical and much smaller than those for reading. The smaller the effect size, the smaller the performance gap between LEP and non-LEP students.

The results of these analyses suggest that the performance difference between LEP and non-LEP students was the largest in reading (the highest level of language demand) and the smallest in math calculation (the lowest level of language demand). Averaging over the three grades, effect sizes were 0.213 for reading, 0.160 for math analytical, and 0.083 for math calculation. The results of the analyses also show that the effect sizes were relatively smaller for lower grades (Grade 3) and became larger as the grade levels increased. This might also have been due to language factors, since there is greater language demand in higher grade assessments.

Results indicated as well that test items for LEP students, particularly those at the lower end of the English proficiency spectrum, suffer from lower reliability. To illustrate this point, the reliability of Stanford 9 achievement tests for LEP and non-LEP students was estimated by computing internal consistency (see Note 3). Table 3 presents results of internal consistency analyses for math, language, science, and social science items. Internal consistency (alpha) coefficients were computed separately for LEP, FEP, and native speakers (English only).

**Table 3** Grade 9 Stanford 9 subscale reliabilities and standard deviations

| Subscale (number of items) | English only (approximate $n = 180,000$) | | FEP (approximate $n = 38,000$) | | LEP (approximate $n = 53,000$) | |
|---|---|---|---|---|---|---|
| | α | SD | α | SD | α | SD |
| Math | | | | | | |
| Total (48) | 0.898 | 9.58 | 0.898 | 9.603 | 0.802 | 6.941 |
| Language | | | | | | |
| Mechanics (24) | 0.803 | 5.56 | 0.802 | 5.469 | 0.686 | 4.593 |
| Expression (24) | 0.823 | 5.78 | 0.804 | 5.522 | 0.680 | 4.732 |
| Average | 0.813 | 5.67 | 0.803 | 5.496 | 0.683 | 4.663 |
| Science | | | | | | |
| Total (40) | 0.805 | 6.52 | 0.778 | 6.104 | 0.597 | 4.694 |
| Social Science | | | | | | |
| Total (40) | 0.805 | 16.83 | 0.784 | 15.748 | 0.530 | 12.777 |

As the data in Table 3 show, alpha coefficients were highest for the English-only group, lower for the FEP students (who were nonnative English speakers reclassified as fluent), and lowest for the LEP students. The sizes of the alpha coefficients for English-only students were relatively stable across the content areas, ranging from a high of 0.898 for math to a low of 0.805 for science and social science. Among LEP students, however, alpha coefficients differed considerably across the content areas. In math, where language factors might not have much influence on performance, the coefficient for LEP students (0.802) was slightly lower than the coefficient for English-only students (0.898). In language, science, and social science, however, the alpha coefficient gap between English-only and LEP students was large. Averaging over language, science, and social science results, the alpha coefficient for English-only students was 0.808, as compared with an average coefficient of 0.603 for LEP students. Thus, language factors introduce another source of measurement error in LEP student test results that might not have much impact on native/fluent speakers of English (see also Abedi, 2002; Solano-Flores & Trumbull, 2003).

The results also showed that the correlation between standardized achievement test scores and other valid achievement indicators was significantly larger for the non-LEP than the LEP population. Structural models for LEP students demonstrated lower statistical fits. Factor loadings were generally lower for LEP students, and the correlations between the latent content-based variables were weaker for these students. Results suggested that language factors might cause such differences between LEP and non-LEP groups by creating a restricted range distribution of scores. Thus, language factors act as construct-irrelevant sources (Messick, 1994).

The data just summarized on the impact of language on the performance of LEP students and on LEP/non-LEP differences in psychometric characteristics of tests clearly suggest that assessment results are not directly comparable across the LEP and non-LEP groups. The data also show that, as a result of confounding of language and content, the performance of LEP students may be underestimated; thus, schools, districts, and states with larger numbers of LEP students must expend a substantially higher level of effort to satisfy the NCLB requirement of performance increases by the target date of no later than 2014.

## LEP Baseline Scores

Obviously, schools differ in terms of their resources, students' opportunity to learn, students' socioeconomic status, and education levels of students' parents. Some of these differences have been shown to correlate with students' performance on standardized achievement test scores (Abedi, Leon, & Mirocha, 2003). Schools are required to define a starting point or baseline for AYP based on scores from a state-defined achievement test administered during the 2001–2002 school year. Consequently, schools enter into the NCLB race at very different starting points. In general, schools with larger numbers of students in the LEP category will start with lower baseline scores. It is obvious that schools with lower baseline scores will have to spend more time and resources – significantly more than schools with higher baseline scores – in order to reach the level of proficiency by their target year (i.e. no later than 2014).

As an example, consider two schools with two different starting points. At School A, 78% of students are categorized as proficient or higher based on a 2001–2002 measure of academic achievement in reading/language arts and math. At School B, however, the starting point is 25%. At School A, annual performance needs to increase by less than 2% [$(100 - 78)/12 = 1.83\%$], while, in order for School B to satisfy the AYP requirement, it must have a yearly increase of more than 6%.

Thus, schools with LEP students have double duty. Not only must they excel in helping students learn more in content-based areas such as math, but they must also help them become more proficient in English so that they can better follow instructions and understand test questions. Schools not making adequate yearly progress will be deemed as 'in need of improvement' and might receive sanctions. For example, schools failing to make AYP for 4 consecutive years might be required to replace staff, fully implement a new curriculum, continue to offer public school choice, and provide supplemental services. The district will take these corrective actions even if a single subgroup of students fails to show sufficient progress. However, various economic, social, cultural, physical, and/or linguistic factors are impediments to academic progress as well as to the valid and reliable measurement of the progress of the targeted subgroups. For these students, making progress has always required extraordinary school resources, and measuring such progress often requires improved testing tools and/or procedures.

## Multiple Criteria and Cutoff Points in AYP

As mentioned, the NCLB is the most recent reauthorization of the Elementary and Secondary Education Act of 1965. The Council of Chief State School Officers (CCSSO; 2002) has elaborated on the accountability requirement differences between the 1994 reauthorization, known as the Improving America's Schools Act (IASA), and the 2001 reauthorization. Among the major differences are changes in the direction and emphasis of accountability. The IASA applies a *compensatory* model for accountability purposes. In this model, higher performance in one subject area will compensate for lower performance in another subject area. For example, higher performance in math may compensate for lower performance in reading/language arts. In contrast, NCLB applies a *conjunctive* model in which scores on all of the measures that are required for AYP must be above the criterion point or cut scores (CCSSO, 2002).

These two approaches may lead to different outcomes. As a means of illustrating this point, a comparison was made of compensatory and conjunctive models using data from a state with a large number of LEP students (see Note 3). This comparison involved the use of the cutoff point of the 36th percentile score established and used by the state. Based on the compensatory model, a student can be reclassified as non-LEP or be placed in the 'pass' category if a higher score in one area can compensate for a lower score in another. For example, if a student obtains percentile scores of 29 in reading and 43 in math, then the higher math score (7 percentile points higher) will help compensate for the lower reading score (7 percentile points lower). However, if the conjunctive model is used, this student will 'fail' since her reading score is below the cutoff point of the 36th percentile score, regardless of her math score. Table 4 presents the results of the analyses comparing the two models.

As the data in Table 4 suggest, the two models produce very different results. The conjunctive model is more conservative than the compensatory model in recognizing students' progress. For example, among Grade 4 students, 2,227 or 10% of LEP students were placed in the 'pass' category under the conjunctive model; in contrast, 20% of these students were placed in the 'pass' category based on the compensatory model. In Grades 7 and 11, smaller percentages of LEP students than in Grade 4 were placed in the 'pass' category based on both models. However, the difference between outcomes based on the two models was large. In Grade 7,

3.4% of LEP students were placed in the 'pass' category in the conjunctive model, as compared with 7.8% in the compensatory model. Similarly, in Grade 11, 3.3% of students were placed in the 'pass' category based on the conjunctive model, as compared with 13.1% based on the compensatory model. Among non-LEP students, the difference between the conjunctive and compensatory models was also larger (see Table 4).

Based on these data, it is quite clear that NCLB is more strict in terms of criteria to judge students' performance. The issues of compensatory versus conjunctive cutoff points are more pronounced for LEP students. As explained earlier, as a result of the impact of linguistic factors on assessment, LEP students have more difficulty with content areas high in language demand. For example, it has been demonstrated that LEP students have more difficulty in reading than in math. Even within the math content, they have more difficulty with items that are more linguistically demanding, such as problem solving. In general, there is a much larger gap between LEP and non-LEP students in reading than in math. Therefore, LEP students are more likely to stay in the 'fail' category for a substantial period of time owing to their low scores in reading.

### Other Factors Affecting AYP

The AYP measurement of LEP students is also affected by other factors, such as students' current capacity to understand instruction. As a result of English language barriers, LEP students may not benefit from teacher instruction at the same level as their non-LEP peers. Even when schools provide 'sheltered English' classes in content subjects, LEP students may not attain content mastery. Results of a recent study (Abedi *et al.*, 2004) involving more than 600 Grade 8 LEP and non-LEP students in math revealed that LEP students reported significantly less opportunity to learn than their non-LEP peers. Interestingly, in the observation phase of this study, the results showed that LEP students were less outwardly involved in classroom activities. They raised their hands less often than non-LEP students, and, when they did, teachers did not call on them as often as the non-LEP students. If LEP students require more time and practice to attain mastery in their language and content studies because of language and/or cultural factors, then their need for a higher level of opportunity to learn may directly affect their achievement measure

results and reflect poorly on schools that are actually performing well. More research needs to be done to explore the influence of other factors on the validity of AYP reporting for LEP students.

### Discussion

The disaggregated progress reports by subgroup mandated by the NCLB legislation will monitor the nation's goal of having 'no child left behind'. However, there are major issues in this disaggregated reporting among different subgroup categories (students who are economically disadvantaged, students from major racial and ethnic groups, students with disabilities, and LEP students). The NCLB requirement for subgroup reporting may give the impression that students in the subgroup categories start the achievement race at about the same level and can progress with other students at about the same rate. This might be an overly optimistic view of the situation of less advantaged learners. By focusing this discussion on the consequences for schools enrolling LEP students, we see how putting into practice the policy may produce invalid assessment and unreliable reporting while exacerbating the burdens of current educators. Following is a discussion of some challenges in AYP measurement and reporting for LEP students.

The results of research on the assessment of LEP students reported in this article and elsewhere suggest a strong confounding of language and performance. LEP students exhibit substantially lower performance than non-LEP students in subject areas high in language demand. The study findings suggest that the large performance gap between LEP and non-LEP may *not* be due mainly to lack of content knowledge. LEP students may possess the content knowledge but may not be at the level of English language proficiency necessary to understand the linguistic structure of assessment tools. The strong confounding of language factors and content-based knowledge makes assessment and accountability complex for LEP students and, very likely, students in other targeted subgroups.

Because of the strong effect of language factors on the instruction and assessment of LEP students, they lag far behind native English speakers. This leads to huge initial differences. That is, LEP students start with substantially lower *baseline* scores. More important, unless LEP students' English language proficiency is

**Table 4** Comparison of conjunctive and compensatory methods, 1999–2000

| | | Conjunctive method | | Compensatory method | | |
|---|---|---|---|---|---|---|
| | | Fail | Pass | Fail | Pass | Total |
| LEP students | | | | | | |
| Grade 4 | *n* | 20,003 | 2,227 | 17,784 | 4,446 | 22,230 |
| | % | 90.0 | 10.0 | 80.0 | 20.0 | 100.0 |
| Grade 7 | *n* | 10,455 | 363 | 9,979 | 839 | 10,818 |
| | % | 96.6 | 3.4 | 92.2 | 7.8 | 100.0 |
| Grade 11 | *n* | 3,527 | 119 | 3,170 | 476 | 3,646 |
| | % | 96.7 | 3.3 | 86.9 | 13.1 | 100.0 |
| Non-LEP students | | | | | | |
| Grade 4 | *n* | 14,642 | 14,602 | 10,787 | 18,457 | 29,244 |
| | % | 50.1 | 49.9 | 36.9 | 63.1 | 100.0 |
| Grade 7 | *n* | 18,457 | 12,167 | 14,885 | 15,739 | 30,624 |
| | % | 60.3 | 39.7 | 48.6 | 51.4 | 100.0 |
| Grade 11 | *n* | 12,998 | 8,271 | 9,732 | 11,537 | 21,269 |
| | % | 61.1 | 38.9 | 45.8 | 54.2 | 100.0 |

improved to the level of native English speakers – which is not an easy task – they will not be able to move at the same rate on the AYP progress line as do native English speakers.

It is clear that NCLB cannot have much of an effect on the initial performance differences between LEP and non-LEP students. A more sensible question here is whether or not NCLB can provide enough resources to schools with large numbers of LEP students to help them increase these students' language proficiency to a sufficient extent that they can progress with their native English speaker peers in both instruction and assessment.

Inconsistency in LEP classification across and within states makes AYP reporting for LEP students even more complex. If students are not correctly identified as LEP, how can their AYP be reliably reported at a subgroup level? Although NCLB attempts to resolve this issue by providing a definition for this group, its criteria for classifying LEP students may face the same problems as the existing classification system (Abedi, 2003; Zehler *et al.*, 1994).

Inconsistency in the classification of LEP students may lead to more heterogeneity in the LEP subgroup. With a more heterogene-

ous population, larger numbers of students are needed to provide the statistically reliable results required by NCLB. However, as elaborated here, the population of LEP students in many districts and states is sparse. In many states, there may not be enough students in a district or school to satisfy even the minimum number of 25 students suggested in the literature (Linn *et al.*, 2002). As indicated earlier, other researchers have argued that even 25 students may not be enough to provide statistically reliable results and have proposed a minimum group size of 100 students (Hill & DePascale, 2003). Considering the small number of LEP students in many districts and states, the small group size for LEP reporting would be another obstacle in regard to reliable AYP reporting.

The LEP subgroup suffers from yet another major problem related to AYP reporting: the lack of stability of this group. In many states and districts across the nation, LEP students' level of English proficiency is reevaluated regularly, and if they reach a proficient level of English proficiency, they move out of the LEP subgroup. While this helps the more English-proficient students receive more appropriate instruction and assessment, it results in the LEP subgroup continuing to be low performing. Thus, the students in this group will always be labeled as underachievers, and schools with large numbers of LEP students will be stuck in the 'need for improvement' category.

Some states with substantial numbers of LEP students have expressed concern over this issue. They have proposed ideas and negotiated with the federal government to ease the level of possible negative impact that this situation may have on school, district, and state accountability. For example, Indiana and Delaware will continue to include exited LEP students in the LEP subgroup for 2 years after they have been determined to be proficient in English. Georgia plans to include LEP students as long as they still receive services through the English for Speakers of Other Languages program, even if they have met exit criteria (Erpenbach *et al.*, 2003). In California, students redesignated as FEP will remain in the LEP category until they reach the proficient or above level on the California Standards Test in English-language arts for 3 consecutive years (California Department of Education, 2003); however, the question of whether this policy will provide a long-term solution to the problem of LEP subgroup instability or serve only as temporary relief remains unanswered.

Thus, measurement of the academic achievement of LEP students is much more complex than what the NCLB legislation conceives. A fair assessment of students in the four targeted subgroup categories requires much more serious consideration than is outlined in the law. Despite attempting to solve the age-old problem of heterogeneity among LEP students, the NCLB seems to perpetuate it, thereby leaving more room for children to be left behind.

On the other hand, I believe that the NCLB's attention to students in the four subgroup categories in general and to the LEP population in particular is a step in the right direction. It is promising, for example, to see that Title III of NCLB requires assessment of LEP students' English proficiency on an annual basis and is providing support to states to develop reliable and valid measures of students' proficiency. However, I believe that any decisions concerning assessment for all subgroups, particularly LEP students, must be informed by results of research and experience in the education community. I elaborate this point by discussing issues concerning states' development of English language proficiency measures. This may provide a good example of how recommendations provided in the NCLB might be implemented.

There are many existing tests for measuring students' level of English language proficiency. Some of these tests have been used frequently and over many years by different states and districts. In spite of the existence of such tests, states are developing new English language proficiency tests with funding through the NCLB's Enhanced Assessment Instruments. A reasonable explanation for this might be that states did not find that the existing tests provided reliable and valid measures of students' level of English language proficiency as required by NCLB. If this is the reason for the development of new tests, then the test developers should be aware of problems in the existing tests to avoid the same problems in the new tests.

For example, a careful review of some of the most commonly used language proficiency tests concluded that the tests differ considerably in types of tasks and specific item content and are based on different theoretical emphases prevalent at the time of their development (Zehler *et al.*, 1994). This suggests that, in the case of some of the existing tests, the English language proficiency domain was not operationally defined before the test development process. This and similar studies and reviews should inform the development process of new tests. For example, it is imperative that before any effort in developing an English language proficiency test, this domain be operationally defined. The definition should be based on current developments in the areas of psycholinguistics, developmental psychology, education, linguistics, and psychometrics. Content standards for English for speakers of other languages should also be considered (see Bailey & Butler, 2003).

Furthermore, in analyzing data from the administration of existing language proficiency tests, researchers have expressed concerns with the reliability and validity of these tests, the adequacy of the scoring directions, and the limited populations on which test norms are based. For example, analyses of several large data sets from different locations across the nation have shown validity problems in predicting LEP classification and lack of power in identifying different levels of English language proficiency among the LEP student population (Abedi, 2003;

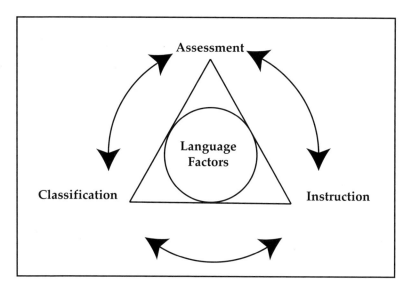

**Figure 1** Interactive school achievement model for LEP students

Abedi, Leon, & Mirocha, 2003). Those involved in the development of new English language proficiency tests should learn from such research and should conduct more analyses on the wealth of data that exist in this area. To be considered valid and reliable measures of English language proficiency, as outlined in the NCLB, new tests must first go through a rigorous validation process. Otherwise, there may not be a reasonable justification to spend the limited NCLB resources on English language proficiency test development.

As a final thought, assessment and accountability of LEP students cannot be pursued in isolation of other important factors. An effective education system for LEP students that may lead to a successful AYP outcome should include at least three interactive components (see Figure 1): (a) classification, (b) instruction, and (c) assessment. A problem in any one of these components may affect the other two. For example, a student misclassified as an LEP student may be assigned a different curriculum and thus receive inappropriate instruction. Alternately, inappropriate instruction may result in low performance, which may in turn result in misclassification. While each component has its unique role, they share common ground: the effect of language factors or barriers. For example, as explained earlier, unnecessary linguistic complexity of assess-

ment may threaten the validity and equitability of assessment among LEP students. Complex linguistic structure of instruction may negatively affect LEP students' ability to understand classroom instruction, and invalid assessment of students' level of English proficiency may result in misclassification. In a positive light, valid assessment may provide diagnostic information that can inform instruction and classification.

An effective way to help LEP students reach proficiency in the AYP model is to consider the broader picture using the interactive model just described. The following are a few critical needs.

1. *Improve current LEP classification and assessment.* There is a need to establish a common definition of English language proficiency and substantially improve the validity of LEP instruments. Among other things, validity of LEP assessment can be enhanced by avoiding cultural biases and reducing unnecessary linguistic complexity of assessments.

2. *Improve monitoring of progress.* Schools need effective and valid data collection methods that can be used to monitor LEP progress at every stage of a student's education. Weaknesses must be quickly addressed with appropriate instructional strategies.

3. *Improve teacher capacity.* LEP students need teachers who are well qualified in both language development and content, each of which plays a crucial role in LEP student achievement. The federal government can play a key role in this process by funding and encouraging programs that improve teacher capacity in this dual role. Teachers of LEP students should receive training in content delivery, language sheltering, and the teaching of academic language.
4. *Consider redesignated LEP students as part of the LEP subgroup that established the baseline score.* State plans allowing redesignated students to remain in the LEP subgroup for only a limited time are temporary fixes. While new LEP students are added to the subgroup, redesignated students should also be retained for AYP reporting. This 'semicohort' approach to tracking LEP students allows the progress of redesignated students to be counted toward subgroup AYP progress.

The academic progress of subgroups, especially LEP students, is much more complex than conceived by the NCLB. No facet of the challenge should be overlooked. We must continue to explore the many complex interrelationships among the factors that have the greatest influences on LEP achievement.

The purpose of this article has been to raise and discuss issues concerning accountability for LEP student achievement. It is hoped that policymakers will seriously consider these observations when making decisions on the assessment and accountability of LEP students. Based on the results of research presented here and elsewhere, policymakers, lawmakers, and decision makers are urged to take appropriate action to correct the inequities resulting from the NCLB in regard to the subgroups targeted by the legislation, particularly the LEP student subgroup. It is, however, encouraging that states, in collaboration with the federal government, are taking steps to remedy some of these issues. The hope is that these continued efforts will bring more fairness into the assessment of and accountability for LEP students.

## Notes

The work reported here was supported in part under a grant (R305B960002) from the U.S. Department of Education, Office of Educational Research and Improvement. The findings and opinions expressed do not reflect the positions or policies of the Office of Educational Research and Improvement or the U.S. Department of Education.

The author acknowledges valuable contribution of colleagues in preparation of this article. Joan Herman, Kathleen Leos, and Ron Dietel contributed to the article with their helpful comments and suggestions. Robert Linn contributed with his review of the article and helpful comments. Mary Courtney and Jenny Kao contributed substantially with comments and assistance in structuring and revising the article. Seth Leon provided valuable assistance with the data analyses. The author is also grateful to Eva Baker and Joan Herman for their support of this work.

1. The second subgroup category (students from major racial and ethnic groups) is not treated as a single aggregated group under NCLB. Rather, it consists of separate groups (e.g. African American/Black, Hispanic/Latino) as determined by states.
2. The author acknowledges the term 'English language learner' as an alternative to 'LEP'. Both refer to students who may be in need of English language instruction, a category that encompasses a wide range of learners, including students whose first language is not English, students who are just beginning to learn English, and students who are proficient in English but may need additional assistance in social or academic situations (LaCelle-Peterson & Rivera, 1994). 'English language learner' has been used as a more positive alternative to 'LEP', which some regard has having a negative connotation (August & Hakuta, 1998). However, in this article, the term LEP is used more often since it is more commonly used in research and practice.
3. Data were obtained from four different U.S. locations. One site was a large public urban school district in which Grades 3, 6, and 8 data were analyzed for the 1998–1999 school year. More than 89,000 students were enrolled in those grades during that school year, and about 14% were characterized as receiving bilingual services. Another site was a state with more than 1 million students enrolled in Grades 2, 7, and 9 during the 1997–1998 school year, of which

17% were LEP students. A third site was an urban school district with more than 22,000 students in Grades 10 and 11 during the 1997–1998 school year, of which 3.4% were LEP students. The fourth site was a state with more than 39,000 students enrolled in Grades 3, 6, and 8 during the 1997–1998 school year, of which 6.8% were LEP students. For further detail regarding these sites, see Abedi, Leon, and Mirocha (2003). In addition to the data sets just described, data from several filed studies conducted by Abedi and colleagues were used. For reports of these studies, visit the UCLA/CSE Web site at www.cse.ucla.edu.

## References

Abedi, J. (2002) Standardized achievement tests and English language learners: Psychometric issues. *Educational Assessment, 8*(3), 231–257.

Abedi, J. (2003) *The validity of the classification system for students with limited English proficiency: A criterion-related approach.* Manuscript submitted for publication.

Abedi, J., Courtney, M. and Leon, S. (2003) *Research-supported accommodation for English language learners in NAEP* (CSE Tech. Rep. No. 586). Los Angeles: University of California, National Center for Research on Evaluation, Standards, and Student Testing.

Abedi, J., Herman, J., Courtney, M., Leon, S. and Kao, J.C. (2004) *English language learners and math achievement: A study on classroom level opportunity to learn.* Los Angeles: University of California, National Center for Research on Evaluation, Standards, and Student Testing.

Abedi, J., Leon, S. and Mirocha, J. (2003) *Impact of students' language background on content-based assessment: Analyses of extant data* (CSE Tech. Rep. No. 603). Los Angeles: University of California, National Center for Research on Evaluation, Standards, and Student Testing.

Abedi, J. and Lord, C. (2001) The language factor in mathematics tests. *Applied Measurement in Education, 14,* 219–234.

Abedi, J., Lord, C., Hofstetter, C. and Baker, E. (2000) Impact of accommodation strategies on English language learners' test performance. *Educational Measurement: Issues and Practice, 19*(3), 16–26.

Abedi, J., Lord, C. and Plummer, J. (1997) *Language background as a variable in NAEP mathematics performance* (CSE Tech. Rep. No. 429). Los Angeles: University of California,

National Center for Research on Evaluation, Standards, and Student Testing.

August, D. and Hakuta, K. (eds) (1998) *Improving schooling for language-minority children: A research agenda.* Washington, DC: National Academy Press.

Bailey, A.L. and Butler, F.A. (2003) *An evidentiary framework for operationalizing academic language for broad application to K–12 education: A design document* (CSE Tech. Rep. No. 611). Los Angeles: University of California, National Center for Research on Evaluation, Standards, and Student Testing.

California Department of Education (2003) *2002 base adequate yearly progress report* [information guide]. Retrieved July 21, 2003, from http://www.cde.ca.gov/ayp/2002/aypinfog.pdf

Cohen, J. (1988) *Statistical power analysis for the behavioral sciences* (2nd edn). Hillsdale, NJ: Erlbaum.

Council of Chief State School Officers. (2002) *Making valid and reliable decisions in determining adequate yearly progress.* Washington, DC: Author.

Cummins, D.D., Kintsch, W., Reusser, K. and Weimer, R. (1988) The role of understanding in solving word problems. *Cognitive Psychology, 20,* 405–438.

De Corte, E., Verschaffel, L. and DeWin, L. (1985) Influence of rewording verbal problems on children's problem representations and solutions. *Journal of Educational Psychology, 77,* 460–470.

Duran, R.P. (1989) Assessment and instruction of at-risk Hispanic students. *Exceptional Children, 56,* 154–158.

Erpenbach, W.J., Forte-Fast, E. and Potts, A. (2003) *Statewide educational accountability under NCLB.* Washington, DC: Council of Chief State School Officers.

García, G.E. (1991) Factors influencing the English reading test performance of Spanish-speaking Hispanic children. *Reading Research Quarterly, 26,* 371–391.

Hill, R.K. and DePascale, C.A. (2003) Reliability of no child left behind accountability designs. *Educational Measurement: Issues and Practice, 22*(3), 12–20.

Hudson, T. (1983) Correspondences and numerical differences between disjoint sets. *Child Development, 54,* 84–90.

Kiplinger, V.L., Haug, C.A. and Abedi, J. (2000, April) *Measuring math – not reading – on a math assessment: A language accommodations study of*

*English language learners and other special populations.* Paper presented at the annual meeting of the American Educational Research Association, New Orleans, LA.

Kirk, R.E. (1995) *Experimental design: Procedures for the behavioral sciences* (3rd edn). Boston: Brooks/Cole.

LaCelle-Peterson, M.W. and Rivera, C. (1994) Is it real for all kids? A framework for equitable assessment policies for English language learners. *Harvard Educational Review, 64,* 55–75.

Linn, R.L., Baker, E.L. and Herman, J.L. (2002) *Minimum group size for measuring adequate yearly progress: The CRESST line.* Los Angeles: University of California, Center for the Study of Evaluation/National Center for Research on Evaluation, Standards, and Student Testing.

Maihoff, N.A. (2002, June) *Using Delaware data in making decisions regarding the education of LEP students.* Paper presented at the Council of Chief State School Officers 32nd Annual National Conference on Large-Scale Assessment, Palm Desert, CA.

Messick, S. (1994) The interplay of evidence and consequences in the validation of performance assessments. *Educational Researcher, 23,* 13–23.

Mestre, J.P. (1988) The role of language comprehension in mathematics and problem solving. In R.R. Cocking and J.P. Mestre (eds) *Linguistic and cultural influences on learning mathematics* (pp. 200–220). Hillsdale, NJ: Erlbaum.

National Center for Education Statistics (2002) *Public school student, staff, and graduate counts by state: School year 2000–01* (NCES Publication 2002–348). Washington, DC: Author.

Riley, M.S., Greeno, J.G. and Heller, J.I. (1983) Development of children's problem-solving ability in arithmetic. In H.P. Ginsburg (ed.) *The development of mathematical thinking* (pp. 153–196). New York: Academic Press.

Solano-Flores, G. and Trumbull, E. (2003) Examining language in context: The need for new research and practice paradigms in the testing of English-language learners. *Educational Researcher, 32,* 3–13.

Zehler, A.M., Hopstock, P.J., Fleischman, H.L. and Greniuk, C. (1994) *An examination of assessment of limited English proficient students.* Arlington, VA: Development Associates, Special Issues Analysis Center.

## Questions

1. From this article and from searching on the WWW, what are the main features of No Child Left Behind (2001) that affect bilingual students?

2. Under No Child Left Behind (2001), who is accountable to whom (include parents, students, teachers, schools, administrators, politicians, county, state and federal interests in your answer)? Portray this in a diagram or in words with reference to language minority children.

3. Specifically, what does this article indicate are the major *issues* in assessment for students with Limited English Proficiency? What are the dangers for such students? What kind of 'best practice solutions' might be offered.

4. What is a 'Limited English Proficient' student? Why is defining both 'Limited English' and 'proficient' a problem in assessment for accountability? How valid are assessments given such limitations in definition?

## Activities

1. Research the kinds of tests that are used to assess children's English language performance under No Child Left Behind (2001). Compare at least three tests to show that there are different implicit ideas of 'English language skills'.

2. In a local school of your choice, observe and interview to locate the testing arrangements under No Child Left Behind (2001). How fairly are language minority children treated by such assessment? Graph the scores of children in that school for at least one

grade, comparing first and second language English speaking children. What conclusions may be drawn?

3.  Using three to six students, profile their English language proficiency and use across as many contexts (domains) as possible: (e.g. classroom, shop, home, friends in the playground, with friends outside school, watching TV, reading outside school). How does their proficiency on an English test contrast with their use of English in a variety of domains?

4.  Bilingual teachers sometimes express the following feelings:
    a.  isolation
    b.  sense of inadequacy in language mastery
    c.  powerlessness
    d.  uncertainty regarding cultural identity
    e.  need to integrate theory and experience

    If you're a teacher now, reflect on your teaching experience and whether you've experienced these feelings. Write an essay in which you state what your feelings are for each of the above, and give specific instances that have brought on those feelings. If you're not teaching now, interview a teacher and relate her experience.

## Further Reading

Abedi, J., Hofstetter, C.H. and Lord, C. (2004) Assessment accommodations for English language learners: Implications for policy-based empirical research. *Review of Educational Research*, 74,1,1–28.

Baker, C. (2006) *Foundations of Bilingual Education and Bilingualism* (4th edn). Clevedon: Multilingual Matters (chapters 9, 15).

Figueroa, R.A. (2002) Toward a new model of assessment. In A.J. Artiles and A.A. Ortiz (eds), *English Language Learners with Special Educational Needs*. Washington DC and McHenry, IL: Center for Applied Linguistics & Delta Systems Co.

García, S.B. (2002) Parent–professional collaboration in culturally sensitive assessment. In A.J. Artiles and A.A. Ortiz (eds), *English Language learners with Special Educational Needs*. Washington DC and McHenry, IL: Center for Applied Linguistics & Delta Systems Co.

Torres-Guzmá, M.E., Abbate, J., Brisk, M.E. and Minaya-Rowe, L. (2002) Defining and documenting success for bilingual learners: A collective case study. *Bilingual Research Journal*, 26,1, 1–10. http:// brj.asu.edu/content/vol26_no1/html/art3.htm